HARVARD STUDIES IN BUSINESS HISTORY

1. JOHN JACOB ASTOR, BUSINESS MAN
BY KENNETH WIGGINS PORTER

2. JAY COOKE, PRIVATE BANKER
BY HENRIETTA M. LARSON

3. THE JACKSONS AND THE LEES: TWO GENERATIONS OF MASSACHUSETTS MERCHANTS, 1765–1844
BY KENNETH WIGGINS PORTER

4. THE MASSACHUSETTS–FIRST NATIONAL BANK OF BOSTON, 1784–1934
BY N. S. B. GRAS

5. THE HISTORY OF AN ADVERTISING AGENCY: N. W. AYER & SON AT WORK, 1869–1939
BY RALPH M. HOWER

6. MARKETING LIFE INSURANCE: ITS HISTORY IN AMERICA
BY J. OWEN STALSON

7. HISTORY OF MACY'S OF NEW YORK, 1858–1919: CHAPTERS IN THE EVOLUTION OF THE DEPARTMENT STORE
BY RALPH M. HOWER

8. THE WHITESMITHS OF TAUNTON: A HISTORY OF REED & BARTON, 1824–1943
BY GEORGE SWEET GIBB

9. DEVELOPMENT OF TWO BANK GROUPS IN THE CENTRAL NORTHWEST: A STUDY IN BANK POLICY AND ORGANIZATION
BY CHARLES STERLING POPPLE

10. THE HOUSE OF HANCOCK: BUSINESS IN BOSTON, 1724–1775
BY W. T. BAXTER

11. TIMING A CENTURY: HISTORY OF THE WALTHAM WATCH COMPANY
BY C. W. MOORE

12. GUIDE TO BUSINESS HISTORY: MATERIALS FOR THE STUDY OF AMERICAN BUSINESS HISTORY AND SUGGESTIONS FOR THEIR USE
BY HENRIETTA M. LARSON

13. PEPPERELL'S PROGRESS: HISTORY OF A COTTON TEXTILE COMPANY, 1844–1945
BY EVELYN H. KNOWLTON

HARVARD STUDIES IN BUSINESS HISTORY
XIII

EDITED BY N. S. B. GRAS
STRAUS PROFESSOR OF BUSINESS HISTORY
AND HENRIETTA M. LARSON
ASSOCIATE PROFESSOR OF BUSINESS HISTORY
GRADUATE SCHOOL OF BUSINESS ADMINISTRATION
GEORGE F. BAKER FOUNDATION
HARVARD UNIVERSITY

LONDON: GEOFFREY CUMBERLEGE
OXFORD UNIVERSITY PRESS

WILLIAM DWIGHT
First Treasurer

PEPPERELL'S PROGRESS

HISTORY OF A COTTON TEXTILE COMPANY

1844–1945

By

EVELYN H. KNOWLTON

Formerly Research Assistant in Business History
Graduate School of Business Administration
George F. Baker Foundation
Harvard University

HARVARD UNIVERSITY PRESS

CAMBRIDGE · MASSACHUSETTS

1948

PRINTED AND BOUND BY
THE COLONIAL PRESS INC.
CLINTON, MASSACHUSETTS, U.S.A.

To
MY HUSBAND

CONTENTS

PART II

MATURITY, 1870–1924

PART III

REJUVENATION, 1924–1945

ILLUSTRATIONS

TABLES

CHARTS

EDITORS' INTRODUCTION

THIS BOOK is a record of business success, undramatic and prolonged success. For nearly a century, dividends, wages, salaries, and taxes were regularly paid. But, then, success stories have not been popular in an age that has battened on the prosperity of its immediate ancestors. Over against the view that New England textile mills are inefficient and have made no improvements in the last fifty years, this book makes strange reading.

Here we have a history of the way in which business methods have been worked out. In the competitive system that is industrial capitalism success arises out of low-cost production. In this book we see how processes were carried out efficiently and economically from the traditional points of view. Competitive wages were paid and competitive prices charged. This book is an historical exposition in the field of classical economy: it rarely touches the fringes of social economy. In other words, men are men and not objects of charity.

Although the objective of the Pepperell Manufacturing Company was profit—through service to the public—still the company gave rise to direct social gains in attracting men and women away from the uneconomic and unsanitary rural "idyllic" homes to town houses that were a degree brighter and cleaner. In setting up a new village in the South, it exemplified this process very vividly and for the record. Of course, the influence of the industrial company was in part non-social, specifically, in so far as it would not permit the workers from the hills to keep their livestock in their homes.

In studying business techniques at work over a century, Mrs. Knowlton has dealt with procurement of supplies and private finance as well as the traditional production and marketing. The first-named is rarely dealt with, for business men are assumed always to sell, rarely to buy. This failure to deal with both ends of the distribution stream is one explanation of the failure to attain reality in business history. Also, the inability to secure information about the financing of a business commonly leaves a blind spot in our vision and appraisal.

In unfolding the business technique, the author gives us the materials for a decision as to what have been the over-all factors in Pepperell's history. She does not bring in the Sun, nor Venus, much less the Moon, all of which have been held to be factors in business. She emphasizes policy and operations. The first set of policy decisions involved location in Biddeford, Maine, where there were water power, ease of transportation, a supply of labor, proximity to Boston and New York markets, and location in a State that had neither high tax burden nor excessive restrictions. Once these decisions had been made, able executives had to be chosen; and then came the wise decision to let these executives have a free hand and to back them up as long as they were successful in their operations. The executives, over three generations of them, have given their best attention to procurement, production, sales, and finance, not to one or two or three of these but to all at once and always. True, for a period, the sales could best be handled by agents, but these agents were tied to the company by bonds of self-interest. Indeed, it is to a combination of eternal vigilance and strategic shifting of method that much of the success is to be ascribed.

Let us note this point that, while the economic historian would say that the Pepperell Manufacturing Company was successful because of water power, cheap transportation, labor supply, and market, the business historian goes beyond these, regarding them as passive, inert matters in themselves. It was the policy-formulation and the operation, the administration and the management, that were really fundamental, for these transcended the passive factors and made choices between them, as is well exemplified by the decision to buy one mill in the South and to set up a new one in the same region.

If we have to explain anything that is not on the surface, it is how the Boston group of investors was wise enough to devise and continue the policies and operations. Probably few persons would ascribe this business acumen to Boston itself, even to the Boston of a century ago. We cannot escape the inference, however, that the unbroken success of Pepperell was due, as Mrs. Knowlton says, to the inheritance of the good business practices and balanced attitudes from mercantile capitalists, the sedentary merchants who had predominated in Europe and America during the period about 1300–1830. If petty capitalists, growing into the stature of industrial capitalists, had founded and operated Pepperell, they would probably have gone into bankruptcy or been saved by State Street investment bankers. As it was, the executives of Pepperell were able to provide fixed capital and, above all, working capital, when needed, from local institutions or from friends and relatives.

Mrs. Knowlton abundantly illustrates the strategic part played by the second line of management, such as mill agents, superintendents, and foremen who managed and planned for the mills as if the mills were their own property. Even in the recent period, when scientific management was introduced into the mills, Pepperell's executives have retained the loyalty of this group of men. To many companies in America much of this loyalty, especially of foremen, has been recently lost. Perhaps this recent loss has been due in part to the dominance of top executives who have administered by remote control and organized and reorganized business without knowing the business itself—top executives who have given orders to men who have known the orders were wrong.

There are some things that Mrs. Knowlton does not deal with nor emphasize. After accounting for the rise of the textile industry, she gives but little prolonged attention to Pepperell's relations with the rest of the industry. The broad economic history of the country or the region she does not present, for she has little patience with padding. Economic historians have written of foreign commerce, the financial hegemony of New York, and the industry of New England. Here is a little bit of the reality of the industry of New England. If personal scandal interests Mrs. Knowlton, we have no way of knowing it. She passes over local comedy and tragedy, which might be regarded as at least interesting, even though not important. Big forces, such as the drives of sex, the love of freedom, and the doctrine of universal economic salvation are not dragged into the story. General business performance, as indicated by the secular trend in prices and profits and by the business cycle, long and short, get but scant attention, I regret to say. Always, the assumption of the author is that the reader is sufficiently matured in the field of business history to follow through a carefully documented story of a single business experience. And, then, Mrs. Knowlton has made no effort to help the reader over the bumps of experience by bridges of rhetoric.

We must judge this work as a history in essence, scientific history, the historian's type of history, one in which facts are wrung directly from original records and set forth objectively. Let the popularizer and the philosopher of history enter and prove his own fundamental inferiority. Mrs. Knowlton has been to Mecca: she has studied the records including the accounts.

Not only has Mrs. Knowlton used the original records of the Pepperell Manufacturing Company but she has interviewed older officers and key men in the business today. She has read widely. She has had the advantage of years of experience as grader and research assistant in the Graduate School of Business Administration at Harvard University. Though a woman, she was allowed informally to take the course in Business History there. The Pepperell research and composition occupied three years of full-time work.

Mr. Russell H. Leonard, president-treasurer of the Pepperell Manufacturing Company, has desired a factual history. How far this history was to be for the use of officials and how far for the education of the public is not clear. Students will be grateful to Mr. Leonard, however, for insisting on a serious study of business history. In our world of torn opinions and confused allegiances, real information as to private business is an essential anchorage for anyone seeking non-emotional guidance.

This study was undertaken after a survey of the available records had been made. The Company provided the records and the financial support for research, writing, editorial revision, and publication. It gave unstintingly its criticism of the work as finished, but in no way attempted to restrict the statements of fact, generalization, or opinion. The Harvard School of Business provided every accommodation for research and writing. The Business Historical Society has loaned its facilities for editorial revision and for the distribution of copies to those interested in the field who are also its members.

N. S. B. GRAS
June, 1947 H. M. LARSON

AUTHOR'S PREFACE

IN THE WRITING of this history of the Pepperell Manufacturing Company, advantages have been mixed with disadvantages. Fortunately, the former have greatly outweighed the latter. I have had access to quantities of important manuscript records near at hand, a situation which many research students do not enjoy. In Baker Library of the Graduate School of Business Administration of Harvard University, the Pepperell Manufacturing Company has deposited the bulk of its early records. But the very quantity of the records has forced a policy of selection and elimination, which I have adopted reluctantly. As is usually true, funds and time have been limited; I did, however, take a year longer than was originally planned for the study. On a few aspects of the Pepperell history, material was scanty, in particular on selling by an outside commission house during the first two periods of operation. The records for the third period now in Baker Library are not adequate; additional information had to be sought in the company's offices and plants. Since there was not time to explore fully the great volume of material for the third period, I have had to depend upon summary figures, conversations, and published articles.

Throughout the entire period of work Mr. Allyn B. McIntire, vice-president in charge of advertising of the Pepperell Manufacturing Company, has coöperated fully. He is the one through whom contacts with other members of the company have been made. In the Boston office Mr. Russell H. Leonard, Mr. William Amory, Mr. Amory Coolidge, Mr. Paul E. Crocker, Mr. Brackett Parsons, and Miss Dorothy M. Hobson have aided in many ways—providing material for their respective departments as well as talking over general problems. I am indebted also to Mr. Francis Boyd, Pepperell's legal counsel for a critical appraisal of the manuscript. Mr. Donald B. Tansill and

Mr. Morton P. Schapp, both of the selling office in New York, have provided assistance personally as well as permission to apply to their subordinates for aid in the accumulation of information. Men who formerly had ties with Pepperell have also aided; among these were Mr. Philip Y. DeNormandie, former treasurer of the Pepperell Manufacturing Company and partner in the selling house, Bliss, Fabyan & Co., and Mr. S. Robert Glassford and Mr. Robert Vanderbilt, who rose from the ranks to executive positions in the selling house.

Many others in the company also have contributed. In particular, during my visits to the various plants, I received the full coöperation of the agents, their assistants, and employees. All were willing to provide whatever I requested—whether old records or personal reminiscences of the mills. In my effort to present a history of these mills since their beginnings, I have been greatly aided by talks with many people in Biddeford, Maine, Lindale, Georgia, and Opelika, Alabama. Without their generous sharing of experiences I could not have become familiar with many aspects of the company's operations.

In securing illustrations for this book, Mr. McIntire has again been of great help, especially in providing those for the third period. Members of families connected with the company in the past have been generous: Mrs. Granville Clark made available a photograph of a crayon drawing of her grandfather, William Dwight; Mrs. Harold J. Staples supplied a photograph of her grandfather, William P. Haines; Mr. Cornelius N. Bliss, Jr., gave me a photograph of his father; and Mrs. P. H. Lombard loaned a photograph of her father, George F. Fabyan. Miss Helen Ballou has skilfully reconstructed the mills in Biddeford in 1850 from descriptions of the property and later isometric drawings. Mr. Richmond Fletcher Bingham has drawn diagrams and done the lettering on certain pictures.

The faculty and staff of the Graduate School of Business Administration have unstintingly assisted my efforts. The greatest debt of all I owe to Professor Gras, who has stimulated and guided me constantly during the years of research and writing. Not only has he been patient and generous of his time, but he also has made many valuable suggestions. Professor Melvin T.

Copeland read an early version of my first chapter on selling and suggested points of interest for later chapters. In the Business History Department, Associate Professor Henrietta M. Larson has remained ever ready to provide aid—in suggesting sources of published information and in giving counsel. The instructors, Mr. George S. Gibb and Mr. Thomas R. Navin, Jr., both engaged in writing histories of textile machinery companies, have also been helpful. Miss Josepha M. Perry for a year assisted in research and later read my chapters for general clarity. Several others have helped for shorter periods, both in research and in typing. For the final editing I am indebted to Mrs. Elsie Hight Bishop and Miss Hilma B. Holton. For the compilation of the index I am also indebted to Mrs. Bishop.

Finally I have been fortunate in the full coöperation of my husband, Dr. Harry Edward Knowlton, who has encouraged and criticized my work. He has acquiesced in the division of my time between this study and my family. Altogether my blessings have been incomparably greater than my troubles.

EVELYN H. KNOWLTON

Cambridge, Massachusetts
June 9, 1947

Part I

EARLY YEARS, 1844–1870

CHAPTER I

YANKEES ORGANIZE THE PEPPERELL MANUFACTURING COMPANY

Introduction to Pepperell

In 1850, in the small and inconspicuous town of Biddeford in southern Maine, a few Yankees organized a textile enterprise that was to have a remarkable record. This was the Pepperell Manufacturing Company. From its very foundation this company has flourished, while many others, started at about the same time, have withered on the vine. To us the great challenge is to determine why this company grew in strength through the years when others faded or were absorbed by rivals. In the history of Pepperell we are not confronted with just another Yankee yarn but are face to face with a century of effort and enterprise that has continuously served investing capitalists, employees, customers, and community. And in this story of growth we see not public guidance but private initiative, not charity doles but earned profits and wages.

About the time that Pepperell was started, it is true, conditions were favorable for the cotton textile industry. In those days it was the custom for men, women, and children to dress in costumes which required yards and yards of goods, of which a large proportion undoubtedly was cotton. The country as a whole was experiencing an expanding economy. There was still a frontier for those who could not find opportunities in the more thickly settled States in the East. There was also an expansion in purchasing power throughout the country following the upturn in business, beginning in 1843, and the discovery of gold in California in 1849. In the decade before the Civil War, with the exception of a short time in 1857 and 1858, there was therefore an expanding market for cotton cloth.[1]

It happened also that there were certain changes in business organization which were favorable to the formation of such a manufacturing concern as Pepperell. The old system of mercantile capitalism was giving way to the new system of industrial capitalism. Under mercantile capitalism the business man (often called the sedentary merchant) sat in his counting-house and managed his far-flung enterprises in trade, transportation, and banking. He handled the manufactured goods but rarely made them himself. Indeed, goods were at that time manufactured in small workshops and sold to the merchant for disposal at home or abroad. These merchants were well trained in business methods and particularly in the taking of risks. When the new system of specializing in one function, such as manufacturing or commercial banking or transportation, in other words industrial capitalism, entered the scene, many sedentary merchants chose one of these functions. Lucky the company that attracted the sedentary merchant, for he brought with him administrative skill and capital. Pepperell was to benefit from the participation in its affairs of these sedentary merchants or those who had absorbed the traditions of mercantile capitalism in Boston.

As the new system of industrial capitalism came to New England with its factories, railroads, steamship lines, and commercial banks, there was a second group that stood ready to profit from the new economic order and to assist in its growth. This was the group of petty capitalists, descendants of those who had arrived in New England in the *Mayflower* and in later ships reached its rocky shores. These petty capitalists had mechanical skill and managerial ability. They could manage a farm, a mill, or a store, or indeed all three at one time. The factory under industrial capitalism offered these petty capitalists a whole sheaf of alternatives. They could set up factories of their own; they could become mill agents; they could become foremen or skilled artisans inside someone else's factory. One might almost think that they had been waiting for Pepperell to come into their midst and offer them additional opportunities.

Such were some of the advantages that a new company such

as Pepperell enjoyed at that time. On the other hand, there were problems that constantly called for solution, and Pepperell's experience was no exception to the rule. Its history has been divided into three periods. During the first the chief problem was financing, during the second it was producing, and during the third it was selling. Throughout all of them the purchasing of raw materials, particularly cotton, was a continuing problem. Before embarking upon a study of these fundamentals, however, we must give some attention to the ancestry and organization of Pepperell, to which we now turn.

PEPPERELL'S ANCESTRY

As a man is influenced by his ancestors, the type of society, and the particular region into which he is born, so is it with a business enterprise. With these factors in mind we shall trace the various steps in the industrial development near the falls of the Saco River in southern Maine where Pepperell was born. A study of Pepperell's predecessors or ancestors uncovers the fact that, as in the case of many companies, these steps were many and were taken not in one grand spurt of energy but over several decades.

In the towns of Saco and Biddeford, separated only by the width of the Saco River, a long period of economic development had occurred even before 1850. Ever since the settlement of this area in the first decades of the seventeenth century, there had been small mills near the waterfalls, as there were in other localities throughout New England. They served a small but prosperous community by grinding corn, making cider, and sawing lumber. At this particular location there were many sites for such mills, since the river as it neared the ocean divided into two branches separated by several islands. On the western branch of the river the water rolled over a series of ledges, whereas on the eastern branch the water dropped precipitously about forty feet, forming Cataract Falls. Near these falls was a mill of which, at one time, Sir William Pepperell had been part owner. In fact, in the first half of the eighteenth century Sir William Pepperell had been a large owner of land on the eastern bank of the Saco River. In his honor, when the

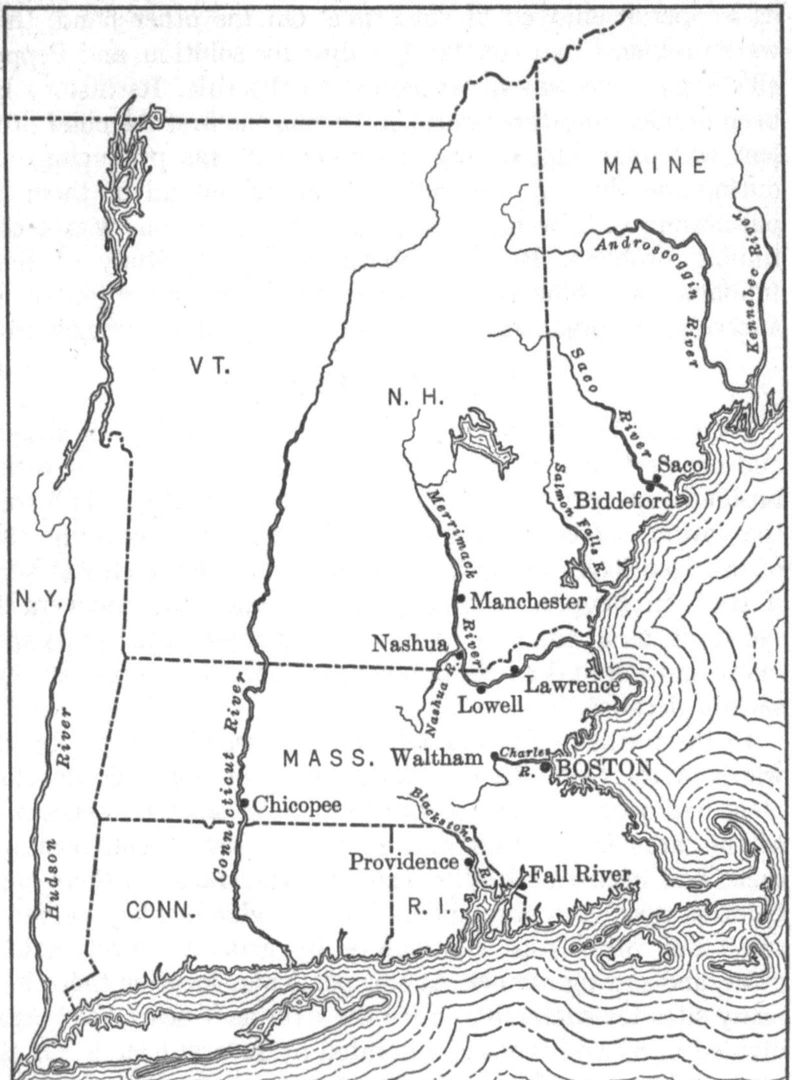

CHART I

TEXTILE-MANUFACTURING CENTERS IN NEW ENGLAND, IN 1850

settlement was divided three years after his death, the town on the east bank was named Pepperellboro. Later it resumed its earlier name of Saco. Ever since 1718 the settlement on the west bank has been known as Biddeford—later to become the location of the Pepperell Manufacturing Company.[2]

Since the surname of Sir William Pepperell was adopted by the company with which we are concerned, it is of interest to glance briefly at the history of one branch of this family in America. Sir William's father, also named William, came to the colonies from England in his youth, after a period as apprentice to a captain of a fishing vessel. He settled for a number of years on the Isle of Shoals, a fishing center off the coast of New Hampshire. There he prospered and after a time moved to the mainland, where he continued to succeed, developing the various activities which were characteristic of many successful colonial merchants. He had a store, dealt in lumber and fish, and built ships, sending them on voyages to the southern colonies, the West Indies, the Mediterranean, and England.[3]

Young William participated in these activities with his father. He invested some of his profits in land along the Saco River, entered into the business and social life of Boston, and married a member of one of the leading families of that city. After the death of his father in 1734, William Pepperell was recognized as one of the wealthiest men in New England. For many years he took part also in the political and military affairs of the colonies. He became famous for his leadership at the siege of Louisburg, for which he was given a baronetcy, apparently the first to an American colonist. For a year he was the social lion of London.[4]

In his family affairs, however, this William Pepperell was less fortunate. His only son, Andrew, died when young, unmarried. His daughter, Elizabeth, married Nathaniel Sparhawk. In 1759 Sir William bequeathed to their son, William Pepperell Sparhawk, the bulk of his fortune on the condition that the grandson would drop his last name, which later he agreed to do. Unfortunately for this branch of the Pepperell family in America, the second Sir William Pepperell was a Tory and fled to England at the beginning of the Revolution.

CHART II

Large Companies in Saco and Biddeford, Maine, 1811–1945

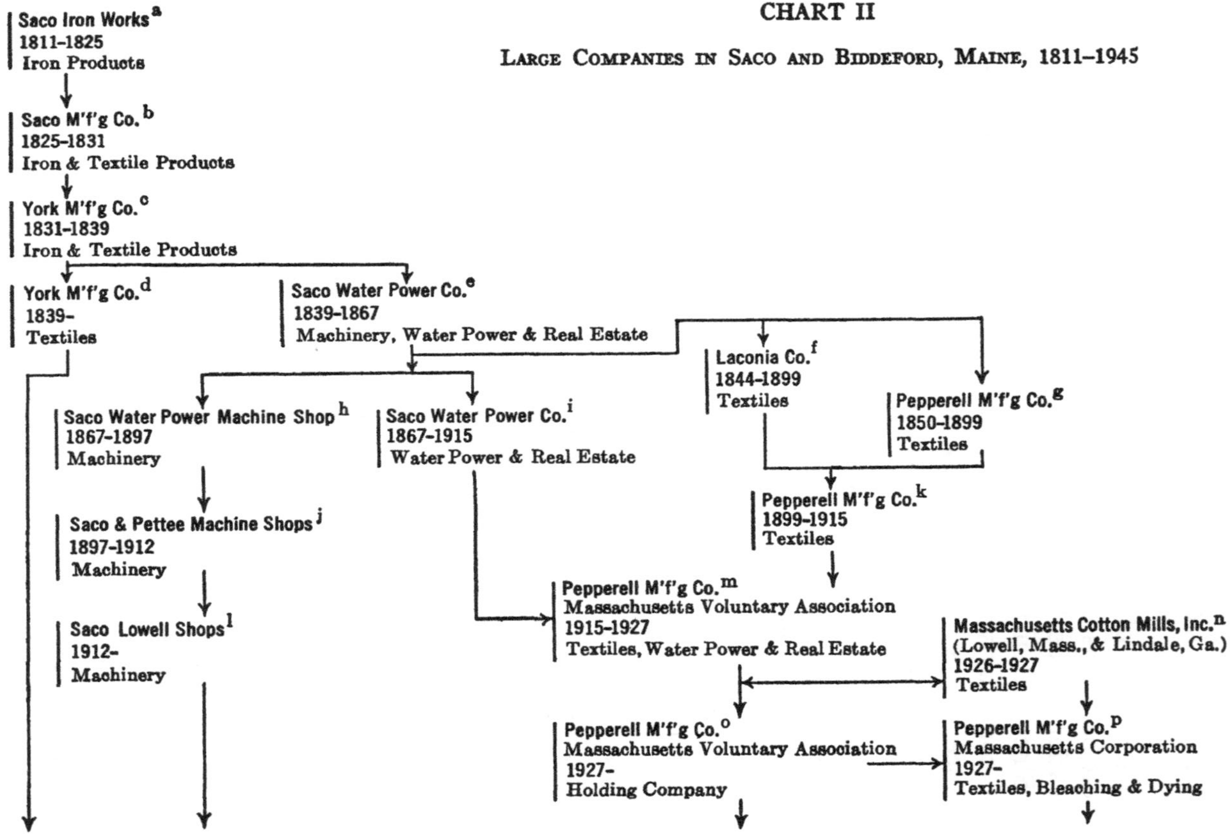

Transfer of Property and Changes in Functions of Large Companies in Saco and Biddeford, Maine, 1811–1945

[a] Saco Iron Works started in 1811 by Col. Thomas Cutts and Josiah Calef to make nails, spikes, and hoops on property on Factory Island in Saco.

[b] Saco Manufacturing Co., incorporated and organized in 1825, bought property of Saco Iron Works and continued iron works and started manufacture of cotton textiles in Saco.

[c] York Manufacturing Co., incorporated and organized in 1831, bought property of Saco Manufacturing Co., whose new mill had been destroyed by fire. It continued the manufacture of iron products and cotton textiles in Saco.

[d] York Manufacturing Co. transferred both property and manufacture of iron works to Saco Water Power Co. in order that the latter might develop necessary functions for industrial development in Saco and Biddeford. York continued cotton textiles in Saco. In the 1920's and 1930's, control obtained by outside power interests. In 1946, York merged with mills in Lewiston.

[e] Saco Water Power Co. was incorporated in 1837 and organized in 1839 to build textile machinery, make textiles, and develop waterpower and real estate. It secured part of its property from the York Manufacturing Co. and bought more in Biddeford. Never made textiles.

[f] Laconia Co., incorporated in 1841 and organized in 1844, was promoted by the Saco Water Power Co., which sold some of its property to the new company. Made textiles.

[g] Pepperell Manufacturing Company, incorporated in 1844 and organized in 1850, was promoted by the Saco Water Power Co., which sold some of its property to the new company. Made textiles.

[h] Saco Water Power Machine Shop incorporated and organized in 1867 to continue manufacture of textile machinery in Biddeford. It secured some of the buildings of the Saco Water Power Co.

[i] Saco Water Power Co. continued as a waterpower and real estate company, owned by Pepperell and Laconia jointly.

[j] Saco and Pettee Machine Shops incorporated and organized in 1897 to merge the Saco Water Power Machine Shop and the Pettee Machine Works. Shops continued for the manufacture of machinery in Biddeford and Newton.

[k] Pepperell Manufacturing Company secured a new charter in 1899, for consolidating Pepperell and Laconia. It continued the manufacture of textiles in Biddeford.

[l] Saco-Lowell Shops incorporated and organized in 1912 to merge the Saco and Pettee Machine Shops and the Lowell Machine Shop, which in 1905 had secured control of the Kitson Shop also of Lowell. From 1928 to 1932 manufacturing gradually moved from Lowell and Newton to Biddeford.

[m] Pepperell Manufacturing Company, Massachusetts voluntary association, in 1915 secured property of the Pepperell Manufacturing Company, a Maine corporation. In 1915, the Saco Water Power Co. ceased as an entity and became the land and waterpower department of Pepperell.

[n] Massachusetts Cotton Mills, Inc. incorporated and organized in 1926 to which the former property of the Massachusetts Cotton Mills in Lowell and Lindale was transferred. Its stock was transferred to the Pepperell Manufacturing Company.

[o] Pepperell Manufacturing Company, Massachusetts voluntary association, in 1927 became merely a holding company.

[p] Pepperell Manufacturing Company, Massachusetts corporation, in 1927 changed its name from the former one of Massachusetts Cotton Mills, Inc. To it within a few years all the property in Maine, Massachusetts, Georgia, and Alabama was transferred. This property included the former mills of the Pepperell Manufacturing Company, the Granite Mills in Fall River, and the Lewiston Bleachery & Dye Works.

Note: Dates on chart represent organization or change of functions.

Sources: Folsom, History of Saco and Biddeford, pp. 13, 15–16; MS. Saco Water Power Co., Laconia Co., Pepperell Manufacturing Company, Saco Water Power Machine Shop, Saco and Pettee Machine Shops, and Saco-Lowell Shops.

Although his estate was confiscated, his mother and grandmother were allowed a life interest in the property and continued to live in comfort in Maine.[5]

Other local people participated in the development of this section of southern Maine. One was the merchant and shipowner, Colonel Thomas Cutts, who bought much of the Pepperell land. In 1811 he formed a partnership with Josiah Calef of Boston for the purpose of manufacturing nails, spikes, and iron hoops. On Factory Island in Saco, they started the first of the new industries in Saco and Biddeford and provided the first opportunity for the investment of Boston capital in this locality.[6]

In the following four decades, as Chart II shows, several important steps were taken in the industrial development of Saco and Biddeford by men from Maine and Massachusetts. They organized the Saco Manufacturing Co., which bought the property of the Saco Iron Works and built a large mill for cotton goods on the western branch of the river. This mill was destroyed by fire, but on its foundations another company for making both cotton and iron products, the York Manufacturing Co., built its first mill, not of wood but of brick. This company was the third and last of the large ones to be located on the Saco side of the river.[7]

After a few years the promoters turned to the possibilities on the Biddeford side of the western branch of the Saco River. The York Manufacturing Co. sold some of its holdings of property to the Saco Water Power Co., which had been incorporated to perform many functions, among them the holding of real estate, the development of water power, the building of mills, and the manufacture of textile machinery. After this company had erected some of its buildings in Biddeford, it built machinery for York's fourth mill. Shortly thereafter it promoted a new cotton textile company, the Laconia Co. The Water Power Company's superintendent took part in the building of the Laconia mills and machinery and, at the same time, supervised the erection of a block of stores, a post office, a hotel, and a depot for the Portland, Saco, & Portsmouth Railroad Co.[8]

All these activities of the Saco Water Power Co. took money

—much more than the company had. In 1847 the stockholders applied to the Legislature of Maine for the right to increase the capital stock from $500,000 to $2,000,000. This was an important step in the development of Biddeford, a step which in fact led ultimately to the organization of the Pepperell Manufacturing Company. During the summer of 1847, stockholders pledged themselves to pay assessments on 1,067 shares of $500 each. This money was needed to finance the two new mills, which the directors planned to erect at once; an ambitious scheme—only one at a time had been erected for the other companies. But at this time optimism was in the air. The stockholders of the Saco Water Power Co. hoped not to be obliged to sell these mills, as they had had to do in the case of the property sold to Laconia. Earlier, on February 16, 1844, several of the local men had secured a charter for a new company, the Pepperell Manufacturing Company. In case the stockholders of the Saco Water Power Co. did not promise to provide adequate capital, the plan was for the promoters to appeal to them and others to subscribe to stock of the Pepperell Manufacturing Company. In this way, either through the old Water Power Company or the new Pepperell Manufacturing Company, they would raise capital for the development of manufacture in Biddeford.[9]

Troubles grew greater and greater from the fall of 1847 to the summer of 1850, when the Pepperell Manufacturing Company was at last actually organized. In September of 1847 the directors of the Saco Water Power Co. apparently disagreed about plans for the two new mills. Four of the nine resigned and were replaced by others. After this change the board voted, "That the Superintendent be instructed to proceed at once to lay out the whole proposed mill site in reference to the four mills, that can be placed upon it, and to cause the canal raceway, and all the underground work to be made in reference to the whole number of mills, and to cause two of the mills, and other necessary buildings to be erected, as soon as the same can be done."[10]

In the summer of 1848 another difficulty arose in the direction of activities in Biddeford. Jonathan Chapman, the treasurer of the Saco Water Power Co. and of the Laconia Co., died in the prime of life. For about two months, Samuel Batchelder acted as treasurer pro tempore. At the annual meeting in July the new treasurer selected was William Dwight, whose handsome appearance belied his business abilities. We are to meet him many times in these pages, and shall deal with him at length when he becomes a dominant figure in Pepperell's history. Although he may have agreed with the plans which his late brother-in-law, Chapman, had set up, there were inevitable adjustments in the operation of the two companies.*

Plans were made for having the machinery in the first mill completed and in running order by September 1, 1849. But during the winter of 1848–49, work did not proceed exactly as planned. Expenditures for these mills exhausted the capital provided by the stockholders and drew heavily upon the resources of the treasurer, who thereupon secured loans. In the summer of 1849 the stockholders of the Saco Water Power Co. were again requested to furnish more capital for completing the mills by subscribing to an additional thousand shares. They were told of the possibility of disposing of their mills to a new company if they did not do this. At this time, when business conditions were temporarily depressed, the stockholders were not enthusiastic over the prospects of investing more of their capital in Biddeford and subscribed to only 249 shares. The directors then decided to wait until spring, before going further in securing capital, when perhaps more stockholders would be willing to subscribe. The equipping of the mills with machinery was slowed down considerably.

In the spring of 1850 William Dwight gave up the idea that

* In the summer of 1848 Dwight and Wilder, members of a committee of the Saco Water Power Co. appointed to report on types of goods for the new mills, recommended heavy narrow sheetings for the first, and heavy drillings for the second, with the possibility of transfer of a portion of the machinery to the making of Canton flannels. They thus departed, in the case of one mill, from the twilled goods previously produced in Biddeford and Saco. They also departed from the customary arrangements for the manufacture of machinery: local shops had generally equipped local mills. For machinery for one mill the directors entered into negotiations with the Lowell Machine Shop; for the other the directors planned to have the local shop do the work.

the stockholders of the Saco Water Power Co., of which he was treasurer, would subscribe the necessary amount of capital in their own company and decided that it would be better to organize a new company, using the charter which had been obtained in 1844. But first he had to get the signatures of the majority of the incorporators to a notice calling for an organization meeting. This he accomplished, and late in March, 1850, a notice, which is given in Appendix 1, appeared in two Saco newspapers.

At this memorable meeting, held on April 9, 1850, in the counting room of the Saco Water Power Co. in Biddeford, the formalities of organization of the Pepperell Manufacturing Company were begun. Three of the original incorporators admitted associates from the stockholders of the Saco Water Power Co. They adopted the charter, accepted a set of bylaws, chose officers and directors, and voted concerning the subscription to stock and purchase of property. They elected as treasurer and director William Dwight, and, as clerk William P. Haines, another handsome man in the prime of life.

William Dwight's first major job as treasurer of the Pepperell Manufacturing Company was to get subscribers to two thousand shares of $500 each. To be sure, at the head of the subscription paper he showed that only $300 per share would be payable within twenty months. By the end of the time set, June 15, 1850, he had obtained subscriptions for only 427 shares. Undaunted, he then revised the terms of the sale of property from $600,000 to $500,000 and reduced the extent of the property, as he had been authorized to do by a vote of the directors of the Saco Water Power Co. He set up another subscription paper (given in Appendix 4), which was offered also to the stockholders of the Saco Water Power Co. By the last hour of the last day—July 10, 1850—it was not filled up, but somehow William Dwight had the courage to sign for the remaining 764 shares. He hoped that others could be reached who would take off his hands some of this huge block. Within ten days various people did take 238 shares (given also in Appendix 4), but he still held about a quarter of the stock, trusting that he could get still others to take some when they realized that Pepperell was an accomplished fact. Probably he knew that, if worst came to worst, he could turn to his family for funds since they would be unwilling to see a member crushed by a burden for which he was not wholly responsible.

With its capital stock thus subscribed for, on July 20, 1850, the details of organization of the Pepperell Manufacturing Company were completed and its first property acquired. This was the property which the directors and stockholders of the Saco Water Power Co. had agreed to transfer to the Pepperell Manufacturing Company. It contained, according to a vote of the directors of the promoting company, "certain parcels of real estate situated in Biddeford in the County of York and State of Maine, together with two mills, pickers, fixtures, and machinery therein, a counting house, cloth house, cotton house, boarding block, and other dwellings. . . ."[11] This property had cost the Saco Water Power Co. about $600,000, by May 15, 1850, and would cost nearly $200,000 more to complete as promised. For all this the new company paid only $500,000. Its stockholders thus benefited at the expense of those of the older company. Of course, for those who had invested the same proportion in the capital stock in both companies, the loss suffered by one company and the gain obtained by the other were offsetting factors. But unfortunately some were not able to invest in the new stock and resented the creation of the new company. Soon they were to see the new company become prosperous while the old company was not.

Thus Pepperell had come into actual existence only in the year 1850. Its creation had been successful, largely through the efforts of one determined man, William Dwight. The company was formed, not as a first choice, but as the alternative solution to plans which had miscarried. If all had gone well, the Saco Water Power Co. would have retained the mills and in time perhaps devoted its efforts entirely to producing cotton goods in place of making machinery, dealing in real estate, and providing water power which it actually developed.

PEPPERELL'S ORGANIZATION

The charter of the Pepperell Manufacturing Company (reproduced in Appendix 2) was a mixture of limitations, powers, and privileges. Apparently to appease the petty capitalists in Maine, the company was restricted more than the earlier companies in Saco and Biddeford had been. In addition to the usual restriction limiting the amount of real and personal estate in Maine to the full amount of the capital stock, there was also the restriction that no debt could exceed this investment in real and personal estate in Maine, nor exceed half the amount of the capital stock. If this restriction was broken, the incorporators and their successors (the stockholders) would become liable individually for the debts. Twice a year, the treasurer was to publish in a local newspaper "the amount of all the assessments, voted by the Company, and actually paid in, the net amount of the then existing capital stock, the amount of all debts due from said corporation, and also the amount of capital stock invested in real estate, buildings, machinery, and other fixtures." If the treasurer did not do this, or if he published false statements, he was subject to a fine of not more than $2,000 or to imprisonment of not more than a year.

In this charter the promoters and their successors were given the customary powers and privileges of manufacturing companies, as provided in the laws of the State. They were "authorized to carry on, at Saco Falls, in Saco and Biddeford, the manufacture of cotton, and such other materials as may be necessarily or conveniently connected therewith, and may erect and construct such machinery, mills, and other buildings as may be useful for that purpose." They were therefore more restricted in the variety of their operations than the parent, the Saco Water Power Co.

The charter of the Pepperell Manufacturing Company remained the same throughout the first twenty years of its operation with only one change. In 1856 the stockholders secured permission to increase the capital stock by $200,000, but the right was not used during our first period (1844–70).[12]

Another part of the company's framework was the set of bylaws, reproduced in Appendix 3, which were adopted at the meeting on April 9, 1850. They prescribed the methods of calling and holding meetings of the stockholders, the elections, duties, and privileges of the directors and officers, the payments for stock, and changes in the future. These bylaws, drawn up by William Dwight, did not cover adequately or specifically all the duties of the treasurer—for example, they did not mention his part in the purchase of cotton—but tended to follow a pattern of earlier bylaws, suitable for any corporation.

A few revisions in these bylaws took place in the following years. At the first annual meeting, July 25, 1850, the number of directors was reduced from nine to seven. At the next annual meeting it was voted to add a proposal previously made, "That no new mill or machinery therefore be built or contracted for until authorized by a vote of the stockholders at a meeting to be called for that purpose." [13] This provision was repealed, however, two years later. In 1858 the time of the annual meeting was changed. In 1866 the stockholders voted to make provision for a treasurer pro tempore in case the treasurer should be unable to perform his duties. These were the only alterations made in the original bylaws during the first twenty years of the company's operation.

Of the various groups which made up the company, the first, of course, comprised the stockholders, who grew in numbers from 117 on July 20, 1850, to 321 in 1870. We judge from such evidence as remains that the stockholders were content to play a minor rôle. They did not attend the annual and special stockholders' meetings in large numbers. At thirteen of the annual meetings the number present varied from 10 to 25. The attendance at the other eight meetings was not given, but judging from the activities of those present, we might conclude that the number was from three to six. During this first period, three special meetings were called; at two of these, three persons were present and, at one, only two. Such low attendance at both the annual and special meetings certainly indicated that few stockholders wished to exercise their right of control.

The stock of the Pepperell Manufacturing Company was rather closely held, with individuals and companies subscribing for blocks of varying size. Of the 98 different names on the subscription list at the close of business on July 10, 1850, and the 19 additional ones by July 20, 1850 (given in Appendix 4), William Dwight was the largest stockholder, although he was more than willing to sell from his block whenever anyone desired to purchase. In the fall of 1850 he transferred half of his remaining subscription to Pepperell's selling agent, Francis Skinner & Co. He agreed to sell as many shares from the agent's holdings as from his own to relieve both equally of the heavy financial obligation. On September 17, 1852, when stock certificates were issued, William Dwight had 262 shares and Francis Skinner & Co., 268 shares. One wonders whether Dwight was wealthy enough to pay over $75,000 in assessments. In 1852, to be sure, according to an account of the rich men of Massachusetts, he was credited with a fortune of $100,000, but some of his capital may have been invested in other undertakings. Francis Skinner, the senior partner in the selling house, was said to be worth $400,000. But the selling house probably could not easily pledge a large proportion of its capital in this one company.[14]

In addition to William Dwight, in July, 1850, there were 24 other stockholders who subscribed to 20 or more shares. They included merchants, trustees, and investors of funds and members of the new industrial capitalist group. Among the merchants engaged in trade with the Far East was Samuel Hooper, who took the largest number of shares, aside from Dwight, 80 in all. Among the trustees and investors was James B. Thornton of Scarboro, Maine, the only large local investor. Among the industrial capitalist group were Abbott Lawrence, a partner in the selling house of A. & A. Lawrence & Co.; the treasurers of two cotton textile companies, John Clark of the Great Falls Manufacturing Co. and Samuel Batchelder of the Portsmouth Steam Mills; and a selling house itself, Parker, Wilder & Co.[15]

Thus, on July 20, 1850, there were 25 stockholders who held altogether over two-thirds of the total number of shares. This concentration of holdings continued with only a slight lessening, at least for a score of years. According to the dividend records in 1860 slightly over half the shares were held by 29 stockholders, and in 1870 slightly less than half by 25. During the same period the number holding a few shares increased, as one would expect with the passing of one generation and the transferring of stock to another. Whereas in 1850 there were only 56 who held fewer than 10 shares, in 1860 there were 129 (of the total 194 stockholders), and in 1870 there were 268 (of the 321 stockholders). At the same time there was an increase in the number of women and trustees holding stock. Whereas in 1850 only 4 women and 5 trustees subscribed, in 1860 there were 27 women and 20 trustees, and ten years later, in 1870, 75 women and 46 trustees held stock as well as 5 educational institutions. Thus, within twenty years, Pepperell's stock had changed from one regarded as a speculative risk to one suitable for those desiring a regular income.

The second group of individuals important in the Pepperell Manufacturing Company was the board of directors. From the records of the directors' meetings we discover that the board met only occasionally, on the average five times a year. In eight years they met only three times annually, once to organize after the annual stockholders' meeting, and twice, in January and July, to declare the semiannual dividends. In the year 1866–67, however, they were called together eleven times to talk over problems involved in the acquisition by the two textile companies, Pepperell and Laconia, of the stock of the Saco Water Power Co.

Very few changes took place in the membership of Pepperell's board of directors during the first twenty years, as shown in Appendix 8. At the first annual meeting four directors were not reëlected, and the total number was reduced from nine to seven. After 1850 only five left the board, generally as a result of death or of retirement from business. The board then was relatively permanent. Also it was virtually self-perpetuating, since it nominated the candidates to fill the vacancies. Among the directors there was a diversity of background and of business interest. One of them, Samuel Batchelder, was considered an authority on manufacturing problems, since he had had many years of experience, first in his own small mill, then as agent of the Hamilton Manufacturing Co. and the York Manufacturing Co., and next as treasurer of the Portsmouth Steam Mills. Two directors, first Francis Skinner and then Josiah Bardwell, were members of Pepperell's selling house. Five were merchants, of whom at least four were engaged in foreign trade. One of them was also president of the

Massachusetts Bank and probably gave advice on financial matters.

More important than any other person in the company was William Dwight, director throughout this first period, treasurer for the first sixteen years, and president thereafter. Perhaps we may say that, if a company is the shadow of a great man, then this man was Dwight, at least in the earliest years. By inheritance and training, William Dwight was well suited for his position of treasurer. He came from a family which for several generations had been prominent in Springfield, Massachusetts. This family had adequate means to give its sons all the college and professional training which each thought necessary. William Dwight had been graduated from Harvard College in 1825 and had then studied law. In 1828 he entered the family mercantile business in the Connecticut valley. For a time he was a representative to the General Court of Massachusetts. By this time several members of William's family had left western Massachusetts. One of his uncles had established a bank in Geneva, New York, and another was a partner in a selling house in Boston. The family business, which had flourished for several decades, was thus breaking up, with several of the members becoming industrialists. William Dwight had the family characteristics of integrity, energy, and devotion to deserving causes. In particular he gave his attention to Pepperell, for which he had fought, rather than to the other two older companies in Biddeford, the Saco Water Power Co. and the Laconia Co. He was a strong supporter of the Union cause during the Civil War. In fact, a granddaughter relates a family story to the effect that he would pass by an acquaintance on the street whose sons had secured military substitutes. Personally he suffered heavily. Four of his six sons participated in the fighting—two were killed and two were impaired in health. These losses and his own illness following the war made him decide to resign his responsibilities in the two textile companies in Biddeford in the summer of 1866.[16] He continued on for a few years as treasurer of the Saco Water Power Co.*

* Two other officers are mentioned in the bylaws. One was the clerk of the corporation, who kept the records of meetings of the stockholders and the

Another important officer was William Pickering Haines, who had had education and professional training similar to Dwight's. For a time he practised law, and then for three years he was the real estate agent of the Saco Water Power Co. In 1850 he was appointed agent of the Pepperell mills in Biddeford; this position he held for the remainder of his life except for about four years, 1866 to 1871, when he served as treasurer. His place in Biddeford was filled temporarily by his son, Ferguson Haines.

During this period (1844–70) there were no drastic changes from the original situation. There was an addition to the authorized capital stock, which was not put into effect until after the end of this period. There were only a few minor changes in the bylaws. In the group of stockholders there was an increase in numbers of owners and of women and estates. The character of the stockholders remained the same—Yankees whose families had gained wealth in mercantile pursuits. In the board of directors only few changes took place as the result of the passing of the years. Among the officeholders, particularly the treasurers, the changes came as a result of illness and a wish to retire or return to a previous occupation. Throughout this period, then, the character of the Pepperell Manufacturing Company changed only slightly from the time of its organization.

* * *

In 1850 the Pepperell Manufacturing Company entered the ranks of large cotton textile companies of northern New England. To some extent Pepperell benefited from being the youngest of the large companies in Biddeford and Saco. Its first stockholders were secured from those who had invested earlier in the Saco Water Power Co., and thus it was not necessary to interest others in New England in the new company. Its

---

transfers of stock in the office in Biddeford; either the agent or an employee in the Biddeford office served as clerk. The other officer was the president, elected by the directors, who presided at meetings of both the directors and the stockholders. Up to 1870 this office was held by four men: first, John Clark, second, Samuel Hooper for two separate terms of office, third, J. J. Dixwell, and, finally, William Dwight.

directors were drawn from the group of stockholders. It secured as treasurer a man who had been for two years the treasurer of the Saco Water Power Co. and the Laconia Co. All these were advantages which promoters of a new company in a new place would have foregone. Pepperell apparently was forced to choose as its selling agent one who would buy a large block of stock. The result was, however, advantageous to the company, as we shall see later.

One cannot study the history of Pepperell without being impressed with the creative nature of the work that was involved. Organizing an industrial unit is a great social and business feat. We shall learn from the body of this book that the meeting of the challenges of operation was also an achievement of no mean note. But instead of going on with the story of Pepperell's development, we must stop to present the early history of the cotton textile industry in America. To be sure, there need be no apology for the treating of this subject, for it is of great importance in both economic and business history. Those who are already familiar with the story may skip to Chapter III.

CHAPTER II

THE COTTON TEXTILE INDUSTRY IN NEW ENGLAND, 1775-1850

IN NEW ENGLAND, during the seventy-five years before Pepperell's organization, the cotton textile industry was developing more rapidly than anywhere else in America. This region led in the spinning of yarn and the weaving of cloth, both through the use of water power. Of course this development in America did not come until after centuries of effort in the Old World. Cotton goods were introduced into Europe from Asia, where they had reached a high point of excellence. Into England about the end of the sixteenth century there came a trickle of imports of cottons from India, which in the following century increased to a steady stream. These cotton goods, however, had to struggle against the entrenched position of the indigenous woolen industry, which finally succeeded in bringing such pressure to bear that, at the beginning of the eighteenth century, the importation of both cotton and silk goods was prohibited. These goods kept on entering England, however, by the well-trodden routes of the smuggler.[1]

The unsatisfied demand for cotton goods in England provided a stimulus for inventors to apply their talents to the creation of machines which could produce these goods as cheaply as those brought in from India. As a result, far-reaching inventions were made in the eighteenth century, and England became the first country to produce cotton goods on a large scale with machinery driven by central power.

English merchants in turn exported these cotton goods to many countries throughout the world. In England's colonies in America these cottons competed with both homespuns and imported woolen goods. During the Revolution, however, the colonists had to depend wholly on their own products. Only then did they begin the encouragement of their domestic cotton textile industry, which led the way so conspicuously in the industrial development of America.

AMERICANS ENCOURAGE COTTON MANUFACTURE

After the first battles with British troops in 1775, Americans began to encourage the development of the cotton textile industry. Earlier they had been prevented by English regulations from manufacturing and adopting the improvements which the English had made, but they wished to be independent industrially as well as politically of their former mother country. In short, Americans were willing to aid individuals in order to get the industry established in this country.

During the Revolution, when trade with England was cut off, there was dire need for manufactured goods, including various textiles. The colonists felt the desirability of making the goods which previously they had imported. But there were many obstacles to such progress. The greatest was the lack of machinery and of men trained to run it. At first this seemed insurmountable, since in 1774 England had passed a law which prohibited the export of machinery and the emigration of mechanics and manufacturers.[2]

At this time cotton textiles in America were made by the primitive tools and machines that man had used from early times. The cotton as it came from the fields was picked over by hand to remove the seeds, leaves, stems, and other refuse—a slow process. Then the cotton was placed between a pair of cards—boards studded with wire teeth—which were used by hand to straighten the fibers and arrange them in parallel fashion so that they could be spun into yarn by the distaff or by the spinning wheel. Some of this yarn was wound on a beam which was then placed on the loom. From the beam many threads were run through harnesses to form the warp threads of the cloth. Some of the yarn was wound on a bobbin and placed in a shuttle, which was thrown over and under the warp threads to form the cloth. This shuttle yarn was called the weft or woof or filling. These steps were slow and costly, and it was no wonder that federal and State governments as well as societies offered inducements to stimulate the introduction of more efficient methods, such as the English had been developing.

Before 1790 the federal government had aided the cotton textile industry only slightly. In 1789 it had passed a tariff which was too low to protect domestic from foreign products. It was at this time that Alexander Hamilton became interested in the contribution of manufacturing to national wealth. In 1791 he presented a report to Congress which encouraged the diversification of business interests. Although at the time his report did not seem to be influential, later it formed the basis for arguments for high tariffs. At the time of the report, merchants in the principal ports in the North were almost wholly interested in foreign trade, which had recently opened up with various parts of the world. Elsewhere agriculture was still the chief interest, although in New England it was less profitable than in regions farther south.[3]

The various States also tried to stimulate interest in cotton manufacturing. Of particular note were the bounties granted by the General Court of Massachusetts for making models of carding, roving, and spinning machinery. This Court paid bounties to two Scotsmen and an Englishman, who were able, however, to construct only imperfect machinery. These machines were exhibited as State models and were available to all for copying. Copies were made at Beverly, East Greenwich, and Providence, but they proved unworkable. In Pennsylvania a similar bounty was paid for the construction of carding machines and spinning jennies, which also proved imperfect. A newspaper notice of this bounty had the fortunate effect, however, of inducing Samuel Slater to leave England and to come to America in 1789. As is well known, Slater became the outstanding figure in the early textile industry in America.[4]

In addition to individual attempts to introduce machinery into the United States, associations, similar to chambers of commerce today, were organized. As early as 1775 the United Company of Philadelphia was set up to aid domestic industry, but there is no evidence that it did anything for cotton textiles. In 1787 a Society for the Encouragement of the Useful Arts was also started in Philadelphia; this organization employed women to spin linen yarns by the old methods and engaged workmen to construct a carding machine and also jennies for spinning cotton. In 1789 the New York Society for the Encouragement of American Manufacturers was organized to manufacture linen and cotton cloths. While it was successful in using the old methods, it failed for a number of years in its effort to develop the new types of machinery for spinning cotton. It was here that Samuel Slater was employed for a short time in 1789, before he left for a more favorable opportunity in Providence.[5]

In New England, where success in evolving a new cotton textile industry actually began, it was not the popular clamor for a new industry but the initiative of Yankee merchants and the generally favorable background for manufacture that were effective. In New England agriculture on rocky hillsides and in narrow valleys was not so profitable as in other regions. Ambitious Yankees were turning to other occupations. Some harnessed the numerous small streams to provide power for mills to grind corn, to make cider, or to cut logs. Merchants in the principal cities were increasing their capital through foreign trade—part of which in time was available for investment in the new industry. Thus New England, with capital and men, was a favorable location for the new cotton textile industry.

SMALL SPINNING MILLS

It is probably no exaggeration to say that modern manufacture in America began in 1790 and in the cotton textile industry. It started in Providence, Rhode Island, where two Quaker merchants with capital and inefficient machinery turned to the above-mentioned Samuel Slater, formerly an apprentice in a cotton mill in England, where he had become familiar with machinery for spinning, carding, and roving, driven by water power.

In the summer of 1789 Samuel Slater, disguised as a farm lad, had left England for America. His years of training in a spinning mill had equipped him with many excellent ideas concerning machinery. He tried, first in New York, to correct machinery which had already been built, but soon despaired of success. Then he was willing to accept the offer of William Almy and Smith Brown, merchants in Providence, to start up a mill, with the prospect of becoming a partner. After deciding that their copies of the Massachusetts models were impossible to operate, they gave Slater freedom to build his own machinery, drawing upon his memory of Arkwright patterns in England. Slater actually built a frame with 24 spindles, two carding machines, a roving, and a drawing machine to be run by water power. In 1793 the partners moved the machinery from its location in an old fulling mill to a new cotton mill which they erected in Pawtucket. This building, called after a time the "Old Mill," has been kept as a memorial to the first successful attempt at cotton spinning in America.[6]

From the earnings of this mill Slater accumulated capital, so that in time he was able, with partners, to erect other mills. Other Englishmen came over here and followed his example; John Warburton, for instance, about 1795, put a cotton mill into operation in Connecticut. In 1803 John Slater came to Rhode Island. He brought to his brother, Samuel, knowledge of the mule for spinning, an invention of Samuel Crompton, which was not patented but was used after 1779 by many manufacturers in England to spin finer and softer yarns. Apparently knowledge of the mule had spread to New York by 1792, but we do not know how successful this earlier importation proved to be. At any rate, in spite of restrictive laws and long distance, the stream of information from England was kept flowing.[7]

Many of Slater's employees in time started cotton mills of their own. One of them was Benjamin Walcott, who in 1797 built mills at Cumberland, Rhode Island. In 1804 another, Charles Robbins, built a mill at New Ipswich, New Hampshire, apparently the first in that State. For some of these early mills machinery was acquired surreptitiously from England; for example, in 1804 John Lees secured for the mill at Byfield, Massachusetts,[8] both drawing and spinning frames and mules, concealed in casks labeled "Hardware."

For about fifteen years, when imports of cotton cloth were coming in regularly from England, progress in manufacture was slow. But the temporary cessation of imports in 1808 encouraged the building of many mills. It was estimated that in 1809 there were 37 mills, near Providence, in operation or in process of erection. By 1815 there were 140 in the same area which could produce yarns. Thus, in a few years the mills had multiplied many times.[9]

These mills had interesting characteristics which were different from those of the large companies which followed them. These characteristics, slightly modified, lingered on, however, in southern New England. Generally these mills were started with little capital. A merchant or an owner of an old mill site might furnish a little capital to a trained mechanic. The mills were small, with a few hundred spindles. They needed the services of comparatively few workers, who were often members of a few families. In 1810 it was estimated that a mill with 800 spindles required 40 persons—5 men and 35 women and children. Wages were low, given generally not in cash but in credit at the company store. In 1817 Slater paid his men from 75 cents to a dollar a day, the women on piecework about 75 cents a day, and the children as little as 50 cents a week. When Slater was acting as superintendent of two mills, he allowed himself a salary of $1.50 a day from each mill. All employees worked long hours—twelve a day on the average, six days a week.[10]

The great weakness of these mills was the fact that they produced yarns and not the finished cloth. To be sure, some of them were connected with workshops run by merchants where, on the old type of hand loom, yarns were woven into cloth. For 1809 it was reported that about a fourth of the yarn spun in Rhode Island was woven by 1,100 looms into bedtickings, stripes, ginghams, shirtings, sheetings, and counterpanes. The cost of weaving was high, particularly as compared with that in England, where power looms were used. During the War of 1812, William Gilmour introduced into southern New England a power loom, which, if it had been developed and manufactured for practical use before hard times fell on the textile industry again, might have saved many spinning mills from liquidation.[11]

The mills, after trade with England had been resumed in

1815, found that they could not compete with English manufacturers. Representatives of the cotton textile industry joined together in efforts to set up a protective tariff. In 1816 such a tariff was passed—a forerunner of many others—which to some extent protected American manufacturers from lower-cost English products. But the protection did not come in time to assist many of the small mills, which quickly passed out of operation and then perhaps were purchased by new petty capitalists who added power looms. Thus the heyday of the small spinning mills was brief. They, however, played an important rôle in the development of the industry: they trained men in the ways of factory production and they actually constructed machines, crude but promising.

LARGE INTEGRATED COMPANIES

During the War of 1812 a new type of enterprise was born: the large integrated company which performed all the processes for converting bales of cotton fiber into yards of cotton cloth. This new form of organization cut the cost of manufacture, particularly weaving. It enabled American companies to compete almost on equal terms with the most advanced concerns in England.

The new type of enterprise borrowed much from the old mercantile and the new industrial capitalism. From the former it took many terms, such as *treasurer* for the chief executive of the company, *agent* for the man in charge of operation of the mills, *superintendent* for the assistant to the agent or for the man in charge of construction and building of machinery, and *selling agent* for the man in charge of selling the finished goods. These terms persist today in this industry, although elsewhere, in other businesses, the *president* has become the chief executive, the *manager* has taken charge of production, and the *sales manager* has directed sales.

In a different way the integrated companies borrowed heavily from the early industrial capitalism in England and the United States, as we shall see in the case of the first successful company, the Boston Manufacturing Co. From England and from the early spinning mills in the United States these integrated companies obtained ideas about machinery and secured trained men. This borrowing gave these concerns tremendous initial advantages over the old companies, particularly over the first started by Almy, Brown, and Slater.

To a group of twelve Boston merchants, who in 1813 started the Boston Manufacturing Co. of Waltham, Massachusetts, traditionally belongs the credit for the introduction of the new type of enterprise—the large integrated company.

In particular the credit belongs to Francis Cabot Lowell, who applied his mathematical ability to designing machines for the company, and to Patrick Tracy Jackson, who contributed capital, a rich experience in foreign trade, and his full attention for a period of years as treasurer and agent. To the other ten men credit must be given for their willingness to subscribe to the capital stock—a recognized gamble.[12]

These merchants were willing to invest $100,000 at first and later $400,000, in the hope that the loom with which Lowell had been experimenting since his return from England in 1812 would prove successful. They invested their capital in land, buildings, and machinery at Waltham, on the Charles River. By the end of 1814 part of the first mill was almost ready to operate. It was equipped not only with Lowell's loom, but with carding and spinning machinery secured from the new machine shop at Waltham and older shops elsewhere in New England. The purchases of machinery included 300 throstle and 384 mule spindles. The mill also had good gearing, shafts, and waterwheels for running the machinery. In fact, the acquisition from many sources of all the necessary parts represents a noteworthy achievement on the part of the mill. Within a short time the promoters increased its capacity to 1,700 spindles.[13]

The Boston Manufacturing Co. drew skilled men from old centers. As its first superintendent (in charge of building and equipping the mills under the supervision of the agent), the directors chose a man from Amesbury, Massachusetts, Paul Moody, who had been employed for a time in a nail factory and was experienced in the construction and equipping of a cotton mill. Moody proved to be the man for the job: he was willing to search out old machinery and to introduce new when the old proved inefficient. Another Yankee was Ebenezer Hobbs, who, in 1819, was put in charge of erecting and running the bleachery. From England came Thomas Faulkner, whose passage the company paid. Apparently he contributed ideas about spinning.[14]

The new company in Waltham set up a labor policy which came to be typical of the so-called "Boston companies" and unlike the "Blackstone Valley mills" of southern New England. Instead of hiring whole families, the new company hired large numbers of single girls, generally between eighteen and twenty-five years of age. This policy was instigated by Francis Cabot Lowell, who, when traveling in England and Scotland, had seen the depressing spectacle of mills filled with young children, deformed and maltreated. For his new mills he determined to have adult workers, particularly girls, who had few opportunities for employment outside their homes and who would welcome the chance to earn a little money. He set up a system of boarding houses, with strict rules for their regulation, under the charge of reliable widows. Until about 1850 the girls, as well as the other workers in the mill, spent long hours at work, about thirteen and a quarter a day in both winter and summer. Wages for the girls were about $1.25 a week, from which 75 cents was subtracted for board.[15]

The Boston Manufacturing Co. started a practice of buying American cotton, a practice which the other large corporations were to follow. Some of this cotton was secured from merchants in the North and some from buyers who operated on a commission basis. The company used some short-staple upland cotton as well as the longer-staple grown on the coast of the Carolinas and in the Mississippi Valley.[16]

The company also started the practice of transferring to an outsider the responsibility for selling the finished goods. This method was to become customary for the large textile mills of northern New England for more than a century. An arrangement was made with B. C. Ward & Co. for selling the output. At first the Ward partnership sold the goods at auction, the customary method for imported goods. In 1819 it entered into a contract to become the sales agent for the company at a rate of commission of one per cent.[17]

From its start the Boston Manufacturing Co. fared so well that it increased its own capacity and encouraged the organization of other large textile companies. But the slow-flowing Charles River was not a promising stream for further expansion. The Boston promoters sought other sites on swifter streams in locations which generally had not been utilized by the spinning mills. The best-known of these places was Lowell, Massachusetts, located on the Merrimack River, where within seventeen years, from 1822 to 1839, nine cotton textile companies were to spring up. About the same time other new riparian companies were organized—on the Chicopee River, the Nashua River, the Saco River, as we have seen, and also on the upper Merrimack River. Outside New England there were only a few integrated companies. At Whitestown, New York, on the Unadilla River, and at Pittsburgh, Pennsylvania, on the tributaries of the Ohio River, companies started in the 1820's which gave promise of belonging to the group of large textile companies.[18]

All these mills more or less followed the pattern of the Boston Manufacturing Co.: they were integrated units rather than specialized units such as continued to prevail in England and died out in southern New England. Perhaps the Yankees saw that the American mills could not specialize at this time with any success—there was no wide market for their yarns at home or abroad. The specialized weaving mill would be under a severe handicap in America in so far as its supply of yarn would have to come from a distance. In particular, the first large undertaking at Waltham would have had to depend on a combination of land and water or on land transportation alone—slow, uncertain, and costly by wagons—to get yarns from the small mills around Providence. The promoters decided to combine all processes under one roof. The investors in the large companies were rewarded with large dividends, although perhaps not so large as they might have had for similar investments in several mills in England. They took part in passing tariff laws which ever since have protected the industry to some extent from foreign competition.

THE LARGER COMPANIES IN NEW ENGLAND DOMINATE IN 1850

As a result of the growth of integrated companies and of spinning mills, in 1850 there were in the United States over a thousand cotton textile companies. Although they varied considerably, together they comprised the most important manufacturing industry in the country, apart from the purely household industries.

The total number of cotton textile companies had grown tremendously in the first half of the nineteenth century. We have seen that in 1815 there were 140 spinning mills near Providence. In the following sixteen years the textile industry expanded in many States, with the result that the Friends of Domestic Industry could display statistics for 794 companies. In 1850, in twenty-three States and the District of Columbia, there were 1,094 companies in operation. The number of companies was not to grow much beyond this figure during the following century. The growth came rather in the size of undertakings.[19]

For the year 1850 we find considerable difference in size of companies. Only 41 have been discovered which had a capital of $250,000 or more, or had 25,000 spindles or more, all of them being in New England. Together these mills had $34,-000,000, or almost half the capital invested in cotton mills throughout the country. The remaining 1,053 companies had $40,000,000 capital, averaging about $40,000 apiece, but the figures as reported probably do not take full account of the capital in small mills. Of these small companies there were three which bore the Slater name, two in Massachusetts and one in Rhode Island. Thus, the small cotton mills actually survived, although overshadowed by the large corporations.[20]

During the first three and a half decades of the operation of large companies there had been years of difficulty in the industry, years when the companies could not maintain their unbroken records of dividends. For example, the oldest of them, the Boston Manufacturing Co., passed one semiannual dividend in each of four years and both in one year. From 1817 to 1826, when the company had the advantage of new products and few competitors, it made huge profits and paid tremendous dividends. The lowest annual dividend was $125 in 1818 and 1819 and the highest $300 in 1825, on stock whose par value was $1,000. This early record was probably extremely influential in interesting many other capitalists, petty and mercantile, to start other companies so that they too might reap huge dividends. For the years 1826 to 1850 Boston's dividends were less spectacular, with the lowest amount zero in 1842 and the highest $120 in 1828.[21]

In the large companies in the "Boston" group, stockholders were often the same. Using capital from other sources, at first they risked some in one venture and when that venture had proved profitable, they invested more in other companies. Since many of the stockholders were related by blood or marriage, they were interested in the prosperity of all the mills. They should have perceived that a rapid expansion without a similar growth in the market would make all the companies less profitable. Too many of them actually failed to realize this situation, although the statement was frequently made that the industry was overexpanded.[22]

This overexpansion was reflected in the prices received for cotton goods. In 1816 the price of Waltham sheetings was 30 cents a yard. Twenty-seven years later it had fallen to 6½ cents a yard, a drop of 78 per cent. To be sure, at the same time the price of raw cotton had fallen by almost the same percentage. The total cost of manufacturing, however, did not fall in the same proportion as raw cotton. Wages, which were second to cotton in contributing to the cost of manufacturing, probably rose during this period. In 1850 A. A. Lawrence said that women's wages had risen nearly threefold and men's doubled in the thirty-five years. He said that supplies were also higher. On the other hand, the improvement in machinery had tended to lower the cost of production.[23]

Much talked about were the labor policies of the large corporations. Of all the mills, those at Lowell were the most visited and the most praised or criticized. Among the noted visitors were Michel Chevalier, President Jackson, and Charles Dickens, all of whom described conditions in glowing terms.[24] Senator Clemens, however, took the opposite view and stated that "the Southern slave was better off than the Northern operatives." To this statement an operative objected; her reply, in which she described living conditions in Lowell, was published in the New York *Tribune*.[25]

About 1850 the era for the domination of Boston as the market for selling the products of the large textile companies of New England was ending, just as the center for the trade started to shift to New York. The years from 1815 to 1850 had formed a grand era for Boston where the merchants, who had known each other since childhood and who in many cases had married each other's sisters, had become the leading industrial capitalists. They could discuss the state of affairs in an informal manner on numerous occasions as well as more formally at their offices and at directors' meetings.

* * *

Even in these early years of bright promise the textile companies had not had unbroken success. They were adversely affected by the too rapid expansion of production in a limited market. They were disturbed by the fluctuations in business conditions during these years. In fact, a temporary recession in business in 1849–50 prevented the Saco Water Power Co. from securing further subscriptions for its own stock. Fortunately, the setback did not preclude a greater enthusiasm for the stock of the new company, the Pepperell Manufacturing Company.

When the Pepperell Manufacturing Company was organized in 1850, sixty years of manufacturing had occurred. The new undertakings were the first in the manufacturing development of the United States under the régime of industrial capitalism, and thus were valuable not only for themselves but also for their contribution to other industries.

CHAPTER III

PURCHASING COTTON FOR PEPPERELL

HAVING STOPPED to study the general development of the cotton textile industry in America, we may well return to our main theme. We recall that Pepperell was organized in 1850 and that the general prospects for business were good at that time.

After the erection of the mills and the installation of equipment, the job of Pepperell was to buy supplies, and, of course, this has remained a running problem to this very day. Of the many commodities needed, the outstanding one was raw cotton. Indeed the cost of this staple looms large in the total expense of the enterprise.

Pepperell, located in the northeastern part of the United States, obtained its cotton from the South, increasingly, as the years passed, from the newer cotton regions. The heavy demands, first of English and then of American manufacturers, had been pushing the cultivation back into the hinterland of New Orleans.[1] From that far-off port, as well as from Atlantic seaports, the executives of cotton textile companies had to secure their supplies. The raw cotton was of varying quality and its grade and market price changed with the seasons and with the years. A false judgment in purchasing could be costly. Indeed, the purchase of cotton created an inescapable speculative element that might well make any would-be manufacturer hesitate. Heavy risks had to be taken with the full knowledge that heavy losses might occur.

Obviously two possible types of persons were available to handle procurement—the old sedentary merchant and the new specialized trader. The latter had not yet won general acceptance within the cotton textile corporations, although orders for cotton were given to the specialist as well as to the merchant. This attitude toward the specialist can be explained on the ground that an executive was expected to carry on many activities including that of procurement. Thus it was natural to select a man from the mercantile capitalist group to be cotton buyer as well as treasurer. And none fitted this picture so well as the handsome William Dwight, who combined mercantile ability, financial acumen, business courage, and social acceptability.

COMPLEXITY OF COTTON BUYING

In purchasing cotton for the mills in Biddeford, William Dwight was handicapped greatly by lack of reliable data about cotton. To be sure he received regular trade information from the important centers, but the fact that the reports were colored by opinions and business interests made them unreliable. At this time there was no government service to furnish reliable, current information. Dwight, therefore, with the facts available had to judge the situation for himself and make his purchases accordingly.

During his first years in office Dwight received weekly prices-current from the leading cotton-marketing centers, such as New Orleans, Savannah, Mobile, Memphis, Charleston, and Apalachicola (Florida). Because mails were slow, the price sheets arrived some time after they had been published. Of most value were the annual numbers, issued in September at the beginning of the crop years, which summarized past as well as current conditions. In the 1860's Dwight received information from St. Louis as well as market reports of world conditions which were prepared by English interests. Many of these sheets have been kept and are part of the Pepperell manuscript collection.

In addition to this printed information, William Dwight obtained the individual views of many cotton buyers in the South. Some were written on blank pages of the prices-current; some were telegrams about purchases of cotton, but these messages were so uncertain that they were generally repeated in letters. Dwight drew upon other sources of information also. He subscribed, for example, to the *Manchester Guardian*, even then a leading English newspaper and significantly published in a textile center. Probably he corresponded with someone in England; at least, a letter to a cotton textile machinery manufacturer tells of his desire to do so.[2]

From all his sources of information, each year William Dwight had to make up his mind very definitely about how much he should pay for cotton, because this raw material incurred two-thirds of the cost of cotton manufacture and must be purchased economically. Apparently he discounted a bit the forecasts of a short crop frequently made by his southern correspondents. Once he stated tersely to a Southerner, "I think you are a short crop man and I am not." [3] Dwight also had to judge when the cotton would arrive at the markets. There was great variation in the time of arrival because of the weather, which also affected the quality and quantity of the crop. Furthermore he had to estimate the activity in the South of the numerous American purchasers of cotton. These were mainly of three types: southern commission merchants, also called factors; members of northern mercantile houses who were sent south; and representatives of northern mills. Dwight had to evaluate, too, the activities of foreigners who exported American cotton. In fact the English took much more than the Americans. For the year 1850–51, for example, over half of the crop was sent to English ports, a quarter to American, and the remaining quarter was divided about equally between French and various other ports. Both foreign and domestic buyers were influenced by world conditions. News from abroad, brought irregularly by ships, caused fluctuations in cotton prices in the South.[4]

The American purchasers, of less importance than the English, had to struggle to get their cotton at prices which would enable them to operate profitably. They were competing in a business in which the English were more experienced. Nevertheless William Dwight learned how to compete with the English and how to purchase with the least risk and the greatest profit.

SELECTION OF COTTON BUYERS

Throughout this period Pepperell purchased its cotton from merchants in the North, through commission merchants in the South, and through Dwight's own representatives who went south; but from time to time there were variations in the extent to which each type of buyer served the company. Temporarily the Civil War upset the established arrangements; it permanently weakened the commission merchant in the South and eliminated the system of mill representatives.

From 1850 through 1861 Dwight purchased cotton from the old and new marketing centers in the South. In order of importance to him they were Memphis, Mobile, Columbus (Georgia), Savannah, New Orleans, Apalachicola, Shreveport, and Galveston. In four of them, Columbus, Savannah, Apalachicola, and Galveston, he dealt only with southern commission merchants. In the others he favored purchasing through his own representative, although at times—for example, in Memphis from 1851 to 1854—he dealt with commission merchants, as Appendix 11 shows.

Dwight was fortunate in finding among those closely associated with him able men who were willing to go south and purchase cotton for Pepperell. Traveling in the South involved hazards, such as cholera and yellow fever, as well as dangers on ship and on railroad. At first Dwight continued the arrangements which he had made previously for Laconia with W. C. Hichborn, who purchased cotton in New Orleans for a number of northern mills; but in the fall of 1852 he gave up this arrangement. Then he started the practice of sending his own representative south. At first Josiah Bardwell, a clerk in his countinghouse, went alone. In the second year he was accompanied by William Dwight, Jr., and in the third year he was joined by Daniel Appleton Dwight, both of whom had served in their father's countinghouse in Boston. While William, Jr., did not continue in this work throughout the period, his younger brother Daniel did. The latter set up various partnerships for buying cotton. From 1855 to 1857 he was in partnership with Josiah Bardwell for buying cotton in Memphis and Mobile. At the same time he was a member of another company, first Dwight & Co. and then D. A. Dwight & Co. In 1857 he formed a partnership with George M. Gill of Memphis under the style of Dwight, Gill & Co. Through his other partnership he carried on business at Mobile and New Orleans; in the latter city he made arrangements for the Pepperell, Laconia, and York companies as well as for others in the North, to ship the cotton northward.

On their trips south, the representatives performed various functions. On Bardwell's first trip south during the winter of 1852–53 he did no purchasing but examined the work of the commission merchants. In Memphis, a new cotton center, he reported to William Dwight: "I would state that this [is] a hard place to buy cotton and the buyers have no correct idea about buying for the manufacturers, most of the cotton being bought and shipped to New Orleans and *there classed.* I am sure I had no idea of the loose manner of transacting business here."[5] It was at Memphis, nevertheless, that Pepperell secured more of its cotton than in any other center in the South. Starting in 1854 Pepperell's representative carried on the purchasing there. On his second annual trip Bardwell visited Savannah and reported that he thought Padelford, Fay & Co., large merchants, were not giving any preference to Dwight. He recommended a change to a smaller firm, Cohen & Fosdick, which advice Dwight followed. At Columbus, Bardwell differed with Hall & Deblois over the classing of strict middling cotton. Dwight, however, continued to deal with them.

During the years 1850–61 William Dwight purchased some of the cotton in the North. He did not do this regularly, but merely to fill in his supply from the South. In Boston he himself carried on this work of procurement. From 1850 to 1855 he bought cotton from 22 different suppliers, the majority of whom were merchants while the others were treasurers of cotton textile companies who wished to dispose of part of their inventory. From 1855 to 1859 he bought no cotton in Boston, but in 1860 he resumed buying there, securing cotton from seven firms. During the year 1860 he began to delegate this work in Boston to his son's firm, D. A. Dwight & Co.

In New York the treasurer and his personal representatives dealt not directly with the cotton merchants but through a brokerage house, usually Kinney, Eastons & Co. and its successor partnership, Eastons, Cahoone & Kinney. From 1852 to 1854 William Dwight made occasional trips to New York to keep in touch with the brokerage house, which secured cotton from 24 different merchants. In the fall of 1854 and thereafter he sent two of his sons and two men associated with them in business, except during the year 1860, when he himself again visited New York.

In the following years, 1862 to 1870, because of the Civil War, William Dwight had to rely largely on purchases in the North. His son's firm, D. A. Dwight & Co., carried on the buying in both Boston and New York, picking up cotton as it became available. When the blockade of southern ports was lifted, William Dwight resumed a few of his former connections in the South and made a few new ones. Daniel A. Dwight made a trip to the South in 1864 and bought cotton in New Orleans but he did not go again. He continued, rather, to carry on his buying in the North, and Pepperell's practice of having a representative visit the South was given up. Although for a time dealings continued directly with firms in the South, Pepperell was turning to the securing of cotton through buyers in the North.

DIRECTION OF COTTON BUYERS

In the first sixteen years of Pepperell's operations William Dwight gave buying instructions to the men and companies selected. For the next four years his successor, William P. Haines, probably continued this policy but the evidence, particularly his letters, for his term in office has been destroyed. We therefore refer largely to Dwight's term of office, when we find that he specified the quality, quantity, and price of the cotton which he wanted a buyer to get for him. He often changed the orders, as regards amounts and prices, when he felt that conditions warranted. In the first eleven years he devoted most attention to his principal markets, Memphis, Mobile, and Columbus. During the next nine years, 1862 to 1870, the treasurers concentrated their purchasing in the North—in New York and Boston. Since these two periods were so unlike we shall consider them separately.

In the purchase of cotton for Pepperell's mills in Biddeford, William Dwight had to keep in mind many points when giving his orders. Knowing the principal types of cotton goods to be produced, he had to decide which grades of cotton to select and where to buy them, since grades of cotton varied from place to place. On the whole, since the machinery in Biddeford was set up to take care of particular grades, Dwight could shift his requirements only slightly from one grade of cotton to another. In 1858–59, when all three mills were in operation, we find that he selected various grades of cotton in different centers, as shown in Table 1.

TABLE 1

COTTON RECEIVED AT THE MILLS, 1858–59

No. of Bales	Place of Purchase	Grade
1,395	New York	various grades
326	Columbus	middling fair to fair
364	Columbus	middling fair to fair
161	Apalachicola	middling fair
500	Mobile	middling fair
3,944	Columbus	strict mid. to mid. fair
2,202	Mobile	strict middling
2,189	Memphis	good middling
133	Apalachicola	good middling
300	Mobile	good middling

Source: Pepperell Manufacturing Company, MS, Agent's listing of cotton invoices, 1850–65.

If we leave out the New York cotton, which included many grades, we find that the rest varied from a low point of good middling to a high of middling fair to fair, with the average about strict middling. Also about 85 per cent of the total purchases came directly from the three centers of Columbus, Mobile, and Memphis. Although this year differed somewhat from the others in places of purchase, it does show operations in a fairly normal year as regards supply in the South.

To be sure of getting the qualities of cotton which he wished, Dwight gave orders for purchases early in the season. In most of the first eleven years, he secured seven-eighths of his supply before the first of March. In the year 1858–59 he had purchased all of it by the first of March, while by that month in the preceding year the percentage was lowest, about 46 per cent. Upset business conditions might explain that low figure. Dwight thus normally followed the practice of early purchases, which a contemporary said was of great importance to the successful operation of a cotton textile company.[6]

For most of his annual requirement of about 12,000 bales of cotton for Pepperell's three mills in Biddeford, William Dwight gave orders of various sizes to his buyers in the South. According to the invoices the orders to his own representatives were generally larger than those to the southern commission merchants. Whereas, for example, D. A. Dwight & Co. in Mobile filled out invoices for nearly 1,000 bales on the average, Padelford, Fay & Co. in Savannah filled out invoices for only 200 bales on the average.

An important factor in the orders which William Dwight gave to the buyers was the price to be paid for the cotton. He stated specifically, for example, "purchase 100 bales of mid fair at 8¾" [7] or "200 bales of strictly fair if fall to 8 cents." [8] Since his prices were often a fraction of a cent below the prevailing level, it appears that Dwight wanted the buyer to select cotton when prices sagged a bit. In December, 1851, he telegraphed W. C. Hichborn in New Orleans to suspend the filling of orders until the *Europa* arrived with news and then execute them deliberately.[9] Apparently Dwight thought that the news from abroad might be unfavorable (as it was) and therefore depress prices. In January, 1852, he wrote David Park & Co. that he hoped that the latter had bought cotton during the panic which followed the *Europa's* news.[10]

Variations in prices paid for cotton by Pepperell during the first eleven years are important. From invoices of cotton shipped we might compare the highest and lowest figures during the years, but this comparison would leave out the differences in quality and other charges which were part of the price of the cotton in the North. Perhaps the most significant figures to use are those for the average cost of cotton consumed by the mills at Biddeford, which varied from 10 to 14.7 cents a pound, as Appendix 12 shows. The average cost for a year, however, covered some purchases in the previous as well as the current year. These cost figures cannot, therefore, be compared strictly with average prices of upland cotton in New York, given in Appendix 13, which varied between 9½ and 13½ cents a pound. If we overlook differences in quality and time of purchase, we find that in four of the first eleven years, William Dwight's cotton cost more than the average price in New York. On the whole, however, Pepperell's cotton cost about a cent a pound less than in the New York market.

During the Civil War and the five years following, Pepperell's treasurers pursued different policies in their purchasing. During hostilities Dwight had to secure whatever cotton was available, no matter how poor the quality or how high the price. After the war Dwight, and then Haines, still had difficulty in getting cotton because its production in the southern States was handicapped by years of neglect as well as by ravages of war.

Although during the war Pepperell obtained some domestic cotton, a large part of its supply was foreign, including some from Turkey, Persia, India, China, and Japan. This cotton, of shorter staple, was quite different from the American. In the English market, Surat cotton (from India) was most unsatisfactory: the story is told of one mill operative who added his personal plea to his pastor's prayer for increased supplies of cotton, "O Lord, but not Surats." [11]

During the war years Pepperell's treasurer began the policy of purchasing cotton more frequently and in smaller lots, not only because of the difficulty in obtaining a supply but also because of the uncertain market for finished goods. In the great uncertainty of the fiscal year 1861–62 Pepperell purchased only 5 bales of cotton—and these were Surats. Indeed, in 1862, with little prospect of war orders for goods, William Dwight entered upon a most unusual procedure for Pepperell and sold some of the cotton which he had stored in Biddeford. By August 6, 1862, he had disposed of 1,250 bales, or about 600,000 pounds, at a profit of $125,000, or about 21 cents a pound on cotton which in 1861, according to the agent's records, had cost 12.7 cents a pound.[12] In the following years, however, Pepperell was one of the few fortunate companies which secured government business and kept their mills in operation most of the time. By the middle of 1864 cotton had become so scarce that Dwight was considering cotton pickings and cotton from old mattresses, but within the next few months cotton from the South became available in larger quantities, and in May, 1865, Dwight bought his last bale of foreign cotton.

While this crisis in supply was acute, D. A. Dwight & Co. bought cotton in New York and Boston. Since much of the cotton bought in New York was invoiced as Boston cotton, we cannot find out the exact proportions for each market. Altogether in these two cities, according to records kept by the agent, Pepperell secured 2,400 bales in the calendar year 1862, 9,900 in 1863, 7,300 in 1864, and 8,000 in 1865. The purchases continue to show smaller units and more frequent transactions. The number of invoices grew from 69 in 1863 to 183 in 1865, while the average size was decreasing from 123 bales in 1863 to 32 in 1865. These figures contrast with Pepperell's prewar average of 220 bales for each invoice. Even after the war the number of invoices was high—130 in 1869. The average size during the years 1866–69 was 70 bales.

Stocks of cotton in Pepperell's hands during these latter nine years also reflect a hand-to-mouth buying policy. At the end of the fiscal year, in June, they were typically about a quarter of the previous levels, as Appendix 12 shows. They averaged about 1,200 bales from 1862 through 1870 whereas from 1851 to 1861 they had been about 4,800. The lowest point of all was reached in 1865, when the stock on hand was only 593 bales—enough for about two weeks of full operation.

The average cost of cotton from 1863 to 1870 never touched the prewar figure of 12.7 cents a pound in 1860, as Appendix 12 shows. Pepperell's average cost reached 88.7 cents in 1865,

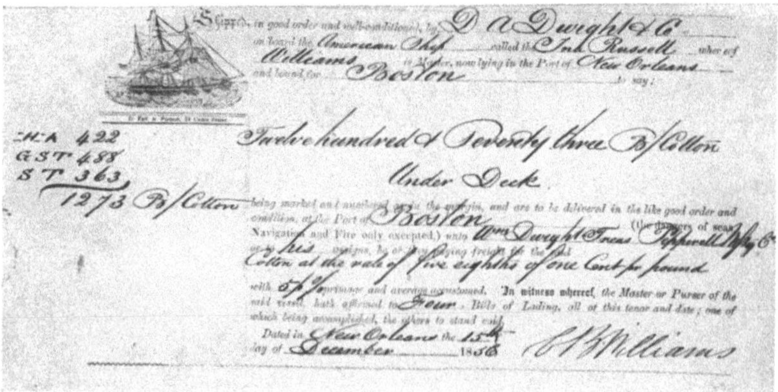

Shipped, in good order and well-conditioned, by D A Dwight & Co on board the American Ship called the Jno Russell whereof Williams is Master, now lying in the Port of New Orleans and bound for Boston to say:

H A 422
GST 488
ST 363
1273 B/Cotton

Twelve hundred & Seventy three B/Cotton

Under Deck

being marked and numbered as in the margin, and are to be delivered in the like good order and condition, at the Port of Boston (the dangers of seas, Navigation and Fire only excepted,) unto Wm Dwight Treas Pepperell Mfg Co or to his assigns, he or they paying freight for the said Cotton at the rate of five eighths of one Cent per pound with 5% primage and average accustomed. In witness whereof, the Master or Purser of the said vessel, hath affirmed to Four Bills of Lading, all of this tenor and date; one of which being accomplished, the others to stand void.

Dated in New Orleans the 15th day of December 1856

C H Williams

BILL OF LADING FOR COTTON, 1856

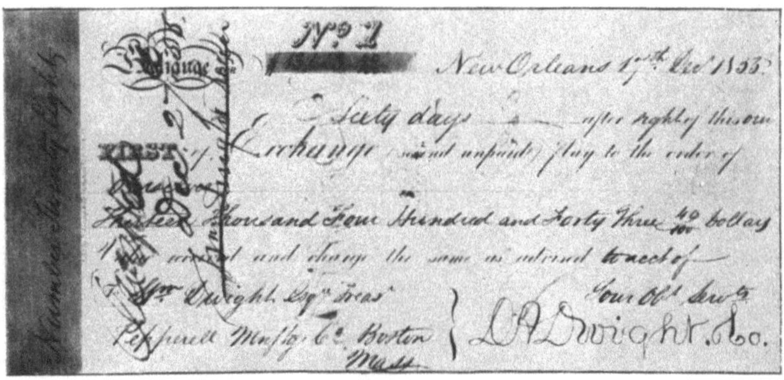

No 2

[redacted]

New Orleans 17th Dec 1855

Sixty days after sight of this our First of Exchange (second unpaid) pay to the order of

Thirteen Thousand Four Hundred and Forty Three 40/100 Dollars

and charge the same as advised to acct of

Wm Dwight Esq Treas
Pepperell Mfg Co Boston
Mass

Your Obt Servts
D A Dwight & Co.

COTTON ACCEPTANCE, 1855

declined to 23.2 cents in 1868, and ended this first period with 25.4 cents in 1870. Since the currency had changed with the issuing of greenbacks, these prices are not comparable with those in the 1850's. In 1867, for example, for cotton from Galveston the quoted price was raised 38½ per cent for payments made otherwise than in gold.[13]

OTHER DETAILS OF BUYING COTTON

After selecting the buyers and giving them instructions about the purchasing of cotton, the treasurer still had other details to handle before the cotton was ready for use in Biddeford. He determined and paid commissions to the various buyers, accepted their drafts, and arranged and paid for freight, drayage, storage, and insurance of the cotton. Although many of these charges had been determined by custom, to some extent the treasurer could alter them.

The most important expense was the reward to the buyers for their work. Dwight paid a percentage of the cost of cotton (before charges) in some cases. To some commission merchants and to his experienced representatives in the South he paid either 2 or 2½ per cent. To his apprentice representatives he paid expenses and salary and, when buying through a broker in New Orleans, he paid a lower commission, such as 1½ per cent to Dwight & Co. in 1855. To still other buyers in the South William Dwight paid definite amounts for each bale purchased, such as 50 cents a bale to D. Park & Co. and 75 cents to R. E. Orne of Memphis. In many cases, depending on the price of cotton, this latter arrangement came to less than the percentages would have amounted to. When Dwight's sons bought cotton in New York and Boston before and during the Civil War, they received one per cent of the cost of the cotton for their work. In addition, there might be a brokerage fee of 25 cents a bale.

Among the other charges which were incurred or arranged for in the South were storage, drayage, and wharfage of the cotton until the time of shipment north. In January of 1854, for example, N. H. Deblois, of Apalachicola, charged 20 cents a bale for storing one month, 10 cents a bale for drayage, and 6¼ cents a bale for wharfage.[14]

The merchants or representatives in the South sent drafts for payment for their work to Dwight, who wrote "Accepted" across the face and sent them back south. These acceptances then were discounted before their date of maturity, which was in some cases 30, 60, or 90 days after sight, although some were drawn on sight. The rate of discount varied with demand for credit, abroad as well as in northern cities. In September, 1852, for example, in New Orleans the discount rate, 60 days after sight, was ¾ to 1¼ per cent on New York and 1⅛ to 1¼ per cent on Boston. On London at the same time there was a 9¾ to 10¾ per cent premium.[15]

The southern buyers also completed some of the arrangements for shipping the cotton northward. From New Orleans, the principal port, they secured freight rates as low as ¼ of a cent a pound in some years and as high as 1¼ cents in others. Generally the rates were higher during the busier part of the season than at the beginning and end. While the annual statement of the *New Orleans Prices-Current of 1852* contained a table of freight rates to Liverpool, it did not have one for the northern ports of the United States. From bills of lading and letters, rates have been compiled for the year 1851–52 for four ports and are given in Appendix 14. Whereas freight rates from New Orleans to Liverpool varied from ¼ to 9/16 of an English penny a pound, rates from the same port to Boston varied from $1.25 a bale (or less than 1/3 of a cent per pound) in August to a high of ⅝ of a cent a pound in October, November, and May. Freight rates to Boston from Savannah were about ⅛ of a cent less than those from Mobile; from Apalachicola they were about the same as those from New Orleans.

From the time that the cotton was purchased for Pepperell, the treasurer had it insured against damage by fire and water and against other loss. At first he carried a policy with the American Insurance Co. which covered all the cotton for the following season from the time of purchase to arrival in Boston. He paid a premium of $2,500 for a coverage of $250,000. In 1854 he changed to another company, the Equitable Safety Insurance Co. It was in this year that the first large loss occurred. It came from loss and damage to cotton purchased in Shreveport during shipment down the Red River. Not until 1859 was final settlement arrived at, with the insurance company paying over two-thirds of the loss. As a result of this experience with careless handling of cotton and with the ensuing difficulty in collecting insurance, in 1856 William Dwight split his insurance between two companies, the American Insurance Co. and the Manufacturers' Insurance Co. In 1858 he gave up the former and added the Merchants' Insurance Co. In 1859 he insured also with the Boston Inland Mutual Insurance Co. to cover risks of shipment of cotton by steamer from Memphis to Cairo, Illinois, and thence by railroad to Biddeford—a new route for Pepperell's cotton.

Further insurance was taken out to guard against other risks, such as transportation from one port to another in the North. Dwight also took many policies to insure cotton during storage on wharves in Boston. These policies were written for specific lots of cotton. Although at first Dwight dealt with one company at a time for this service, later he dealt principally with two, the Manufacturers' and the Merchants', out of a total of nineteen companies. As one would expect, the rates for fire insurance varied according to the construction of the storehouses. In good brick buildings on Constitution Wharf the rate for one month was 6 cents per thousand dollars, while in wooden structures on Battery Wharf it was as high as 30 cents.

Among the other charges incurred in Boston was that of wharfage, which seems to have been standard at 4 cents a bale. Storage also was standard at 6 cents a bale a month. Dwight had to pay also for trucking cotton from one place to another. There was a charge for delivering the cotton from the wharves to the schooners which were to carry the cotton to Biddeford. This charge varied from 3 to 4 cents a bale in 1861. As soon as the cotton was placed on these schooners, William Dwight's personal responsibility was over, since thereafter he delegated the responsibility to the mill agent. The agent kept the accounts for transportation charges for cotton received from Boston and they became part of his general charge of manufacturing; all the other charges, from the price paid to the merchant to the loading of the cotton on schooners for Biddeford, were separate elements in the cost of manufacturing.

* * *

We have followed Pepperell's purchasing of cotton through two eventful decades. In part we have covered the relationship between two elements of the economy of the United States—the growing of cotton in the South and the manufacturing of cotton textiles in the North. Although these two regions disagreed and fought over the status of the Negro and the question of States' rights, those men who were doing business together showed a willingness to deal fairly with their associates in the other section before, during, and after the Civil War.

Each year the crop of cotton differed from that in the past. Buyers had to judge from limited information about the supply and shape their policies accordingly. Those who, like Pepperell's treasurer, followed a policy of purchasing their cotton early in the crop season had to form their judgments rapidly and buy quickly. The northern companies had to set levels for their buyers in the South which would make possible the purchase of large amounts of good-quality cotton at reasonable prices. Apparently Dwight did this well, since he secured his cotton economically.

During the first period of Pepperell's operation we seem to find an over-all success in the important task of buying raw cotton. This was, of course, only part of the work and constitutes only part of the story. Following in the order of logical effort comes the manufacture of the cloth, to which we now turn.

CHAPTER IV

OPERATING THE MILLS IN BIDDEFORD

IN THE FALL of 1850 William Dwight, the enterprising treasurer from Springfield, took up the job of organizing the mills in Biddeford. In several ways he followed the practices of large cotton textile companies in New England. For example, he appointed as agent of the mills a man from the petty capitalist class who, untrained in textiles, had demonstrated his managerial ability in other fields.* For knowledge of techniques this agent could rely on a group of overseers who had secured training in machine shops or other mills. For a supply of workers in the mills the agent could depend upon a few individuals trained elsewhere and upon many inexperienced Yankees, eager to work in the new industry.

The man whom Dwight appointed as agent for the Pepperell Manufacturing Company was William Pickering Haines. From past experience Dwight knew that he and Haines would work well together, although they differed in some respects: for example, Haines belonged to a different political party—the Democratic—in which he was active. Of Welsh descent, Haines was born in 1811 in a small town of southern New Hampshire. He attended Dartmouth College, from which he was graduated in 1831. Then he sought his fortune in Maine, which was experiencing a period of industrial development. He read law, first in South Berwick, and then in Saco with the governor of the State. In fact he became the latter's law partner until 1847, when he was elected senator in the Legislature of Maine and became real estate agent for the Saco Water Power Co. From 1850 until his death in 1879 he remained Pepperell's agent in

* In some respects, however, Dwight departed from the usual procedure. An outstanding example was the securing of machinery from several shops instead of solely from the local shop.

Biddeford, except for a few years, 1866 to 1871, when he served in Boston as treasurer of the two Biddeford textile companies. During these four years his son, Ferguson Haines, also a Dartmouth graduate and a partner in a wholesale hardware business in Portland, took his place as agent. But in 1871, when his father, in ill health, wished to return to his former duties in Biddeford, the son was willing to relinquish the office. Thus, for the twenty years of this first period and nine years of the next period, as we have divided the history of Pepperell's mills in Biddeford, we can say that the mills were under the Haines family's direction.[1]

PEPPERELL'S PROPERTY

For three years, from 1847 to 1850, two treasurers of the parental Saco Water Power Co., Jonathan Chapman and then William Dwight, had been directing the development of property for manufacturing cotton textiles in Biddeford. In 1847 Chapman had authorized Otis Holmes, the former agent of the Laconia Co. who had been transferred to the superintendency of the Saco Water Power Co., to build canals, erect buildings, and construct some of the machinery for the new mills. In 1848 Dwight continued the direction of Holmes' activities in Biddeford. By the summer of 1850 much of this work was finished and the remainder was nearing completion. By October, 1850, equipping of the mills had reached a stage where it was advisable for Pepperell to have its own agent for the mills. At that time Dwight turned over to William P. Haines the responsibility for Pepperell's property in Biddeford. During the following sixteen years Haines was in charge of this property. In 1854 he directed a major addition, a third mill and accompanying buildings. During the years Haines had trouble over the arrangement for water power from the falls in the Saco River. In 1866 this friction was eased somewhat by the purchase of the Saco Water Power Co. by two sister textile companies in Biddeford, Pepperell and Laconia.

Among the assets which the Pepperell Manufacturing Company purchased from the Saco Water Power Co. in July, 1850, were nine acres of land for four mills of 15,000 spindles, three

WILLIAM P. HAINES
First Mill Agent

OFFICES OF TEXTILE SALES AGENCIES IN BOSTON, 1860

PEPPERELL'S MILLS IN 1850

acres for boarding houses, and sundry buildings. In April, 1850, the Saco Water Power Co. had valued these twelve acres at $166,000. This seems a reasonable estimate when one considers that property for mill sites in Lowell was valued at the rate of $4.00 for each spindle in the proposed mill buildings. During the two following decades Pepperell did not add to its land in Biddeford—in fact, it did not utilize fully all that was in its original purchase.[2]

With the sale of the land went an arrangement for water power with which to run Pepperell's machinery. According to a vote of the stockholders of the Saco Water Power Co., Pepperell was "to lease for 999 years, with right to renewal, the Water Power, estimated at fifteen mill powers, for such price, and such annual rent reserved for said mill powers, and upon such other terms and conditions, as the Directors of the Saco Water Power Company may think fit to prescribe."[3] During the first years of the lease Pepperell paid rent at the rate of $300 a month, in 1854 at $400 a month, and finally from 1855 through 1866 at $500 a month.[4]

Inasmuch as it assisted the other Biddeford companies in acquiring property on the Saco River, Pepperell had other expenses in regard to water power. Although in 1847 the Saco Water Power Co. had acquired land to control the flow of the river over two dams between Biddeford and Saco and over two falls between Dayton and Buxton, in 1854 Dwight felt that still more land was needed to safeguard the water supply, particularly for Pepperell's mills, which were on the upper level while Laconia's were on both upper and lower levels of the canals. In his position as treasurer of the Laconia and Saco Water Power companies, he had difficulty in getting the approval of the boards of directors. Finally he triumphed, and the three companies secured the property farther up the Saco River as well as on its tributary, the Ossipee River.[5] But the controversy over water power was not ended. In 1860 the two textile companies began negotiations for securing the remaining property of the Saco Water Power Co. Not until November, 1866, was an agreement reached. Then, for $425,000 payable in notes dated January 1, 1867, Pepperell and Laconia purchased all the property of the Saco Water Power Co. In December, 1866, for $125,000 they sold to a new company the machine-shop property, while they kept the rest, holding it as a real-estate and water-power subsidiary.[6]

Before 1850, in order to bring the water into the Pepperell yard for the proposed mills, the Saco Water Power Co. had built an elaborate system of canals. The water came in at one level and dropped to a lower, flowing back through a tunnel directly below part of the channel of the incoming water. This work for the four mills Dwight estimated had cost $66,000. At the time Pepperell purchased the property, the mill work, including the necessary wheels and gearing to carry the water power into the mills, had also been completed for two mills at a cost of $43,600 for each mill.[7]

On the land in Biddeford which the Saco Water Power Co. sold to Pepperell, Dwight as treasurer of the former company had directed the erection of several brick buildings (see illustration opposite page 51). By April of 1850 he had built on the east side of the yard two mills, each 222 feet long, 75 feet wide, with six stories including attic and basement. In addition Dwight had erected a picker house which served both the mills, a combined cloth and cotton house on the north side, and a countinghouse on the south side. Outside the yard he built a long row of three-and-a-half-story boarding houses, with kitchens in the one-story ells.[8] His estimates for the cost of these buildings are shown in Table 2.

Only once during the next twenty years were there substantial additions to this first set of buildings. In February, 1854, Dwight submitted to the directors the plans for a third mill 332 feet long, of the same width and with the same number of stories as the first two mills. He planned also a repair shop and picker building, which brought the estimated cost of this new construction up to $125,000. This mill was to take the place of the two which had been proposed by the Saco Water Power Co. for the west side of the yard. In the following months construction of these buildings was begun. At about the same time, Dwight erected a carding building over the canal between the first two mills and a cotton house in the northwest corner of

TABLE 2

ESTIMATED COST OF BUILDINGS AND MACHINERY, UP TO APRIL, 1850

Mill No. 1	$73,600
Mill No. 2	70,000
Picker House	12,900
Cotton and Cloth House	25,000
Counting House	5,710
Boarding House Block	56,500
Total	$243,710

Source: Saco Water Power Co., MS, Report to the directors, April 25, 1850.

the yard. At last, in 1857, after almost a decade of discussion, lighting of the mills was changed from sperm oil to gas, with a resulting annual saving of about $1,000.[9]

During the remainder of this period the only change in the yard was the addition of stories to the carding building in 1868, making one long, continuous building on the east side of the yard which stretched out for 524 feet.[10] Thus by 1870 Pepperell owned three mills with their accompanying buildings in Biddeford; these, with alterations and additions, have been running ever since, a memorial to the excellence of planning and construction a century ago.

MACHINERY FOR THE MILLS

From 1848 to 1850 William Dwight as treasurer of the Saco Water Power Co. had attempted to get the best machinery available for the two new mills.* When in 1850 these mills became Pepperell's property, Dwight continued his efforts. As a result of the advice of the selling agent, Francis Skinner & Co., he made a major change in the machinery already in place in the first mill, while in the following years he made comparatively few changes in the first two mills and equipped the third mill with machinery. It should be emphasized that very rarely

* We should remember that Dwight was treasurer of the Saco Water Power Co., the Laconia Co., and the Pepperell Manufacturing Company.

do mills make major changes in existing machinery. In fact one can generalize that once a mill is equipped to produce a particular grade of goods with a particular combination of machines, the tendency is to continue to produce that grade, making alterations or additions to the machinery only when the providing of improved types seems urgently advisable.

From the summer of 1848 to July, 1850, William Dwight as treasurer of the Saco Water Power Co. had made plans for the equipping of the first two mills. For Mill No. 1 he ordered from the Lowell Machine Shop machinery for the manufacture of heavy narrow sheetings. For Mill No. 2 he arranged to have machinery for the manufacture of drills and jeans built by the local shop.[11] In both these mills the original layouts of the machinery were the same, with carding in the attic and fifth story, spinning in the fourth, dressing in the third, weaving in the second, and both weaving and spinning in the first, which was the basement. Of the machinery which is listed in Appendix 16 the most important was for the spinning and weaving. In each of the mills there were to be 117 throstle spinning frames of 128 spindles each and 456 looms. In the combined cloth and cotton house, the picker house, and the countinghouse, functions suggested by the names were carried on.

This machinery, run by water power, performed the same fundamental processes as today, although much more slowly and much less efficiently. The openers and pickers opened up the cotton and removed the seeds, leaves, and lice. The cards—two sets of them—continued the cleaning and started the straightening of the fibers. Between the two sets the lap winders functioned to form lap somewhat similar to cotton batting. The railway heads changed the fleece from the finisher cards into soft rolls of cotton, or slivers, and combined several slivers into one. Three sets of machines—the drawing frames, the speeders, and the extensors—combined, straightened out, drew out, and imparted a slight twist to the cotton. Then, either on filling or warp frames, the cotton was drawn out farther, spun, and wound on bobbins. The yarn on the warp bobbins was then rewound onto beams of several hundred parallel threads, sized or "dressed," and finally put on a larger beam of several thousand parallel threads. Then the beams were taken to the weaving room and put into place on the looms. Shuttles, with the filling bobbins enclosed, shot back and forth between the sets of warp threads to form the cloth.[12] These seem simple processes, but there was great difficulty in keeping machines running without interruption so that the cotton cloth could be produced cheaply.

For the machinery for Mill No. 1 Dwight as treasurer of the Saco Water Power Co. had promised to pay the Lowell Machine Shop $12,000 a month for ten months, starting on November 1, 1848, with the balance at the time of delivery, which was set as September 1, 1849. Actually the Lowell Machine Shop did not deliver all the machinery until April, 1850, at an estimated cost of $150,000. At the same time, Dwight put at $132,000 the cost of machinery for Mill No. 2, which was actually not ready for operations until the spring of 1851.[13] Equipping both mills had been delayed by the general business recession and by the difficulty of getting funds from subscribers to stock in 1849 and 1850.

In the fall of 1850 Dwight evidently became dissatisfied with the machinery in Mill No. 1. He was influenced by Francis Skinner, the senior partner of Pepperell's selling house, who wanted machinery for making shirtings instead of narrow sheetings. As a result, in the winter of 1850–51 Dwight sent the prospective superintendent of the Saco Water Power Co., S. J. Wethrell, abroad to inform himself about the best methods of making and operating textile machinery. Wethrell recommended mules for spinning the filling in Mill No. 1, rather than the throstle frames already in place. Dwight authorized him to buy one self-acting mule of Sharp & Roberts' pattern, the patent of which had expired, and Wethrell secured one from Hibbart, Platt, & Sons, of Oldham, England. Dwight planned that this mule would be used by the Saco Water Power Co. as a pattern in building others for Pepperell—in fact, 18 others of 576 spindles each. Apparently Wethrell's observations and a pattern were not a sufficient guide for building machinery in Biddeford. Dwight secured another mule from an American maker, Hawes, Marvel & Davol, of Phoenix, Rhode Island,

and at the same time arranged to have David Whitman, formerly connected with that Rhode Island shop but now in Lewiston, Maine, supervise the construction of similar mules. From this occasion came the hiring of Whitman as Pepperell's consulting engineer. After Whitman's death in 1858, A. D. Lockwood, also of Lewiston, took over his position.[14]

While Wethrell was abroad, he saw other machinery which he recommended for Pepperell's first mill. As a result, in 1851 Dwight ordered two slubbers and eight roving frames from Messrs. Higgins & Sons. Thus Pepperell profited by the change in England's policy about exporting machinery. To be sure, individual English shops, fearing that the machines would be used for patterns and that American machinery would eventually compete with English, were still loath to send machinery to America.[15]

With the receipt of the new machinery in 1851 and 1852, it was necessary to rearrange both the mills. Just where all the machinery was placed is not clear. Probably the mule frames for filling were placed in the third story of Mill No. 1, taking the place of the warpers and dressing frames. Eighteen of the throstle frames were moved into Mill No. 2 and at least seventeen were sold. Thus Mill No. 1 had not more than 10,496 throstle spindles and 11,520 mule spindles, and Mill No. 2 had 17,280 throstle spindles by the end of 1853.[16]

Other alterations took place in the second and third years of operation. Under the supervision of David Whitman the company altered the picker frames "after the similitude of Whiting's [*sic*] Picker Frame"[17] instead of purchasing new machines with a greater expenditure of money.

In the third mill building, erected in 1854, machinery was added in two stages, the first in 1855 and the second in 1856. The agent, William P. Haines, wrote to many machine companies asking for bids. Although he received many responses, he gave the contract for much of the machinery to the local Saco Water Power Co. at prices which the latter had cut to meet competition. Most important among the machines were the Saco shop's 512 narrow looms for shirtings and 156 wide looms for sheetings and 28 mules of 596 spindles each for the filling. In addition, Saco built drawing, fly, and dressing frames, slubbers, and railway boxes, which brought its total charges to nearly $200,000. Second in importance was the contribution of P. Whitin & Sons of Whitinsville, Massachusetts, which supplied cards, railway troughs, and 90 ring spinning frames of 128 spindles each, costing altogether almost $100,000. From the Lowell Machine Shop, Pepperell acquired castings, card grinders, frame dressers, warp spindles, engine lathes, fly frames, slubbers, and accompanying parts, which amounted to slightly more than $20,000. Walker & Hacking of Vulcan Works, Bury, England, supplied beater-scutchers and lap machines at a cost of over $7,500. In addition to these major shops there were a host of others which supplied parts for the machines. Prominent among these was the firm of E. D. & G. Draper, which furnished temples for the looms as well as shuttle guides and miscellaneous supplies.[18]

In all, the mere putting of a mill in operation involved many dealings with many people and many companies. Dwight and Haines shared the responsibility. Haines handled the business with the Saco Water Power Co. and with many suppliers of parts, while Dwight made contracts with the other machine shops.

By the end of 1856 Dwight and Haines had three mills in operation, which, according to the information available, had 67,696 spindles—39,296 in the first two mills and 28,400 in the third—as well as 912 looms in the first two mills and 668 in the third. After 1856 the treasurer and agent made few changes in machinery. One of these few was the order in 1862 for a cotton mixer and four openers from Richard Kitson of Lowell.[19]

The agent's semiannual ledger balances with the treasurer of Pepperell from the end of 1851 through the middle of 1865 give us measures of the value of the company's property in Biddeford. For the first twenty accounting periods Haines put the first two mills down at $269,105.74 each, apparently dividing in half the initial payment for the property in Biddeford and the expenditure for equipment during the rest of 1850. Actually, as we remember, this property was worth much more, about twice that amount. For the third mill, after it had been equipped, Haines put down the same amount regularly, about $560,000, although with slight variations before the end of 1862. At that time the miscellaneous fixed assets, comprising the accumulations spent for buildings, machinery, and furniture were allocated to the three mills. (The total fixed assets are given in Appendix 32.) It is interesting to note how little was spent during the years for furniture. In the countinghouse not a chair or desk was added after the middle of 1852.[20] This betrays the frugality of the Yankee in small matters linked with his liberality in large items.

Unfortunately, for the five years after the middle of 1865 such ledger balances are missing. We surmise that they were segregated in 1870, when a new management came in, and were never placed with the other records which accumulated in the attic over the counting room in Biddeford. But, since both Dwight and Haines desired to have excellent mills and machinery, we may assume the continuance of previous policies. This policy is summarized by these words written by Dwight to Haines during the crisis of 1857, "I often hear the expression that the best goods in the world are Pepperell's. But oh how I feel in these times the want of an abundant floating capital; but severe as the want is, I had rather suffer from it than from poor mills & machinery." [21]

YANKEE WORKERS

For workers to tend the machinery in the mills in Biddeford the agent drew upon small towns of northern New England and the French provinces of Canada as well as upon the older textile centers of this country and abroad. The majority, however, were Yankee girls who worked in the mills for a few years and then returned to their homes with savings. The others—men, women, boys, and girls—formed the nucleus of a permanent working class in Biddeford.

Times were propitious when the mill agent, William P. Haines, began to hire workers, since there were many operatives out of work in New England. During the winter of 1850–51 many were on strike, notably in Fall River, against a reduction in pay. Many in Lowell lacked employment because several mills were idle during the recession in business. In Biddeford times were also bad; the Laconia Company had cut its labor force and its wage rates. This meant that Haines had an opportunity to attract good workers at low wages—an opportunity which many companies missed when they started operations in boom times. Haines, then, did not need to send out a representative in a long black wagon to recruit girls, as many companies in Lowell had done earlier. The girls came freely to seek work in the new mills in Biddeford. Haines offered them the wages, hours, and conditions of work prevailing locally. He expected them to sign a contract book, agree to work the customary hours, and obey the company's regulations.[22]

We are fortunate indeed in having the contract book which Pepperell's first workers signed as they were hired from December 2, 1850, through October 18, 1854. It furnishes us with a wealth of information about hirings which we do not have for later years. We are lucky, too, in having a complete series of payroll books for this period as well as for the later periods of the mills in Biddeford. In addition we can draw upon miscellaneous summary books for further data. Together this information could be used for a much more comprehensive labor study than can be undertaken here.

Throughout the twenty years we find no evidence of an upward trend of employment in Pepperell's mills. This record was to be expected since, once the three mills had been equipped with machinery, little expansion in manufacturing capacity and in the working force could take place. On the average, during the payroll period of four weeks, there were about 400 workers in Mill No. 1, 450 in Mill No. 2, and 560 in Mill No. 3. Because of hirings, leavings, and absences these figures were about 20 per cent greater than the number of full-time workers needed. For hirings in the first four years we have compiled monthly figures, given in Appendix 20. In 1853, for example, when the first two mills were in operation, 866 people were hired—more than the average number at work in the mills. Using also the monthly figures for the number of employees in each mill, given in Appendix 21, we can say that there was a slight seasonal variation in the working force, with peak employment in the spring. This pattern agrees with the experience reported for mills in Lowell in 1845.[23]

Employment in the mills, then as now, varied with business conditions. In boom times the agent could expand the working force but slightly. He could, however, keep some of the workers a couple of hours later in the evening to increase production.[24] During difficult times the agent could cut the working force. In Mill No. 1, which produced shirtings for the domestic market, employment was steadiest throughout the twenty years. Following the panic in the fall of 1857 the agent cut this mill's labor force to 262 workers in one month and, in the slump before the conversion to government work in August, 1861, he reduced the number to 201. In Mill No. 2, which produced drills and jeans for the export and domestic markets, he cut the working force more seriously. In November, 1857, only 198 were on its payrolls. During the Civil War there were three periods of drastic cuts—to a mere handful of workers or to a shutdown. They occurred in August and September, 1861, March through August, 1862, and at the end of January and the beginning of February, 1863. Midway between the records of these two mills was that of the third, which produced shirtings and wide sheetings for the domestic market. The operation of Mill No. 3 was cut in November, 1857, not long after it had swung into full operation, when only 178 workers were left on the payroll. In the summer of 1861 only a few were at work in this mill. But, on the whole, we can say that employment in the Pepperell mills was quite steady, in fact steadier than in many of its contemporaries. One example of fluctuations was the Lyman Mills of Holyoke, which stopped for six months during the panic of 1857–58 and, after a period of operating at part capacity, closed down in July, 1862, for over three years. Estimates for the industry indicate not more than 30 per cent activity in January, 1858, and in the middle of 1862.[25] Pepperell's employees were then among the fortunate few at both times of difficulty.

The majority of the workers in the Pepperell mills were

women and girls. In the middle of 1852, for example, 66 per cent of those on the payroll in Mill No. 1 and 82 per cent of those in Mill No. 2 were females. The difference arose because of the nature of the spinning rooms for filling. In Mill No. 1 there were mule frames, which were tended by men and boys, while in Mill No. 2 there were throstle frames tended by women and girls. In the spring of 1869, near the end of this first period, we find women and girls still predominating: 68 per cent of the employees in Mill No. 1, 75 per cent in Mill No. 2, and 72 per cent in Mill No. 3. While the two mills with mule-spinning rooms, No. 1 and No. 3, had fewer women than the other mill, the differences were less marked than in 1852. These percentages were much higher than those for all textile companies in Maine in 1870, where 60 per cent of the working force was reported as female.[26]

Most of the workers in Pepperell's mills had had sufficient schooling to enable them to sign their names. In the contract book used from 1850 to 1854 we find only about 6 per cent who signed with a mark. This proportion was lower than that for signatures on the payrolls in 1852, which was about 11 per cent—the same as the average illiteracy for the State of Maine in 1850. The reason for this discrepancy between the contract book and the payrolls is not clear. We must therefore discount somewhat the increase which took place in the following years in failures to sign individually. By the spring of 1869, just before individual signatures were discontinued, we find that the percentage not signing personally was 37. This figure does not seem unreasonable when we consider that in 1870 in Biddeford 26 per cent of the people were foreign-born with an illiteracy of about 40 per cent.[27]

Another indication of the nature of the labor supply for Pepperell's mills was the workers' former places of residence, which we find for the first years in the contract book. In the first thirteen months of operation, December, 1850, through December, 1851, we find that 86 per cent of the workers were from Maine with over 20 per cent, about 300, from Biddeford alone. Of the other 14 per cent almost all came from New Hampshire and Massachusetts, with a sprinkling from elsewhere in the United States, particularly Rhode Island, and from Canada. In the following three years there were a few from Ireland, Scotland, and Germany. We cannot find out, however, the exact proportion of foreign-born, since many of the immigrants had lived in other places in the United States before coming to Biddeford.

Little indication of the workers' previous experience is given in the contract book. We might deduce that a few of those who came from mill cities had had textile experience. We find that in the first thirteen months 25 came from Fall River, 13 from Lowell, and 11 from New Bedford. In 1852 there were 34 from these three centers. In 1853 there was a falling off in numbers from these cities, and in 1854 there was an increase. The numbers seem to have fluctuated with the prospects of work in these centers. A letter from Haines to Dwight in July of 1851 reveals that many of those from Fall River had once been employed in the textile mills there. A mill agent charged that Haines had enticed away weavers; in denying this, Haines stated that he had an adequate supply of workers from northern New England. Shortly thereafter, however, he did seek experienced mule spinners in Fall River, according to an item in a bill book. Thus we know that at least a few of Pepperell's workers when first employed were experienced.

With these workers Pepperell seems to have had little difficulty about the length of the working day at a time when there was general agitation in New England over this matter. To be sure, at the beginning the agent had all employees sign a contract book agreeing to the customary working time, which averaged slightly more than twelve hours a day. This signing was to comply with the Maine ten-hour law, passed in 1848 and effective in 1849, which had the loophole that the restriction did not apply if there was a contract to the contrary in effect. Apparently prospective employees in Biddeford were glad of the opportunity for a job and did not protest signing, as some workers in Nashua did under New Hampshire's similar law. During the following years agitation in New England for the shortening of hours continued. In 1853, in order to discourage the passing of restrictive laws in Massachusetts, the Lowell corporations reduced their time to eleven hours a day. Shortly thereafter, in September, 1853, representatives of corporations in Maine and New Hampshire met and discussed the advisability of following Lowell's example. Apparently they recommended voluntary reduction to eleven hours—at least Haines reduced hours in Biddeford. Since the reduction was voluntary, the company could increase hours temporarily when greater production was desirable, as in 1858. After the Civil War there was unrest in Biddeford, as elsewhere, among the mule spinners. They demanded a ten-hour day, along with mule spinners in other mills, and during the period of protest they refused to work longer than ten hours. Their demands were unsuccessful, although for a time the mills in Fall River granted a ten-hour day.[28]

Evidently because of the need for capital for other purposes and because of the existence of adequate housing in Biddeford, Pepperell did not establish so paternalistic a system as that of the textile companies in Lowell. The company owned only one block of boarding houses accommodating about four hundred girls,[29] together with a few old houses on the land originally planned for further boarding blocks, rented to members of the supervisory group. It did not build a house for the agent: he was already living in his own home in Biddeford, on land given him by the Saco Water Power Co. Thus Biddeford was developing independently into a motley industrial city, housing the workers of the three mills and the machine shop, while its neighbor Saco continued as an attractive middle-class residential city.

In Pepperell's mills in Biddeford, judging from records of compensation, there was usually only one man earning a fairly comfortable salary—the agent. At first William P. Haines received $2,000 a year; then in 1853, $3,000; and in 1865, $5,000. At times he also received bonuses for his services: $500 in 1853, $2,000 in 1856, $5,000 in 1864, and finally $10,000 in 1866. What his son received as agent was not noted in the directors' minutes, as was his own salary. In 1866 the company, according to receipted bills, paid $2,000 a year to a superintendent, Reuben M. Hobbs, who was appointed to share the responsibility for operations. (Of his part in Biddeford we shall hear more in the following period.)

Next in rank to the agent, aside from the superintendent, were the overseers; they had charge of particular rooms in one mill or sometimes of the same type of rooms in two or three mills. According to the payroll books, Haines paid these men from $2.00 to $3.00 a day, depending upon their experience and responsibilities. These rates were slightly higher than at Lowell, where the Merrimack Manufacturing Co. paid $2.00 a day during this same period. In the following decade Pepperell did not increase the pay of these men; but by 1870 we find that Pepperell paid from $2.50 to $5.00 a day. The greater spread was caused by the promotion of a few of the older men and the introduction of a few young men at the lower end of the ladder. At this time Pepperell was paying more than the Merrimack Manufacturing Co., where the highest rate was $4.00 a day.[30]

In addition to the regular wages Pepperell gave semiannual bonuses to its overseers for holding to certain costs of production or for the performance of extra services. This practice began in 1852 and was kept up throughout the period. In February, 1852, Haines promised the overseers extra compensation if the costs in their departments did not exceed a certain amount per pound produced. As a result in July, 1852, he paid three overseers $75 apiece, two overseers $50 apiece, and another $30. Haines also provided an opportunity for the overseers to buy stock in the company by paying for it in installments. He paid their expenses for travel to other mills to inspect machinery. He sent one overseer abroad. It is understandable that the overseers remained loyal to Haines even when they were offered higher wages elsewhere.[31]

The assistants to these overseers, the second hands, were also able, ambitious, and coöperative. Haines paid them about half as much as the overseers. At the beginning they received $1.00 to $1.25 a day, and by 1870 they were getting from $1.58 to $2.00 a day, rates which were similar to those in Lowell.[32]

Wages for the majority of mill workers were low during these twenty years—very low when compared with the wages of today. On the other hand, such comparison is unfair because prices of the necessities of life were drastically lower a century ago, and, more significantly, the wants of the workers were fewer—fewer since there was not the multiplicity of goods and services which we have today with the intensive newspaper, magazine, and radio advertising to bring them to the worker's attention. It has been stated that a workingman's family of four could then live moderately in New York City with an income of $600 a year.[33]

For the two largest groups of workers, spinners on the throstle frames and the weavers, who generally were women and girls, wages improved during the two decades, as Appendix 23 shows. In 1852 the average weekly wage of the throstle spinner was $2.76 and that of the doffer was $3.23. Later when the two job classifications were combined the wages rose, particularly after the Civil War, to a high point of $4.80 a week in 1867, from which they soon declined and then rallied to $4.68 a week in 1870. The weavers experienced similar increases, starting at about the same level in 1852 and increasing to $5.60 a week in 1867.

There were comparatively few large groups of men in the mills. In the carding rooms there were small groups of homogeneous workers, and we have therefore selected from among these the pickers as typical of the unskilled men. As Appendix 23 shows, their weekly wage more than doubled during the two decades, starting with $4.04 in 1852 and reaching about $8.80 in the last four years of the period. In the weaving rooms there was a group of semi-skilled men, called today the loom fixers, who then were designated as section hands. In 1852 their wages were about double those of the female spinners and weavers, $6.63 a week on the average. But after the Civil War their wages did not rise so much as those of the unskilled help; they remained below $11 a week on the average.

During these first decades Pepperell attracted a working force to which, except for the supervisory group, it paid wages which were not adequate to support a family. The fact that many girls accumulated savings from their earnings seems to contradict this statement. We must consider, however, that the girls were equipped with clothing from home and spent little more than the charge for room and board. They therefore did not provide a test of self-sufficiency. They contributed to the establishment of a pattern of low wages, which in the following decades continued to be one of the characteristics of the industry. Then the Yankee girls were replaced by others who regarded their status of worker as permanent and who depended on their earnings to help support their families. It became the usual practice for more than one worker in a family to be employed by Pepperell.

VOLUME AND COST OF PRODUCTION

One of the important arrangements which the (mill) agent made was for the transportation of finished goods to the selling agent's offices in Boston and New York and of cotton and supplies to Biddeford. His main reliance for transportation of finished goods was by schooners which tied up at a wharf on Factory Island. Every two weeks he placed a load for Boston in either of two schooners, in one of which the company had a part interest. At times he shipped goods to Boston and New York by the railroad which ran nearby, but since railroad transportation was more expensive than shipping by water, he did this only when the selling agent needed goods in a hurry. Sometimes Haines sent goods to New York by schooner or propeller steamer from Portland. In 1859 Pepperell bought part interest in a schooner which plied between Saco and New York, carrying the finished goods to the sales agent's warehouse and bringing back the bales of cotton purchased in New York. Return loads from Boston consisted of cotton which had been stored there and miscellaneous mill supplies, such as oil for machinery and starch for dressing the warp beams. Coal for heating and for the gas plant usually came by barge to the Factory Island wharf.[34]

The agent left the routine running of the mills to the overseers, who were given almost complete authority to hire, train, fire, and make out the payroll for the workers in their rooms. The agent told the overseers about the changes which the treasurer and the selling agent proposed in the scheduling of the work. The overseers might make suggestions as to the best way of solving problems regarding changes, for example, how many looms could economically be changed from one type of goods to another. The overseers, in attempting to run their rooms as efficiently as possible, were handicapped in two ways: by the inefficiency of a constant stream of new workers; also by the nature of most of the machinery, since few machines had adjustments for automatic stopping when a thread broke. At the beginning there were self-actors only in drawing frames, mules, and warpers. As a result many operatives were required to watch the machines. Even for those machines having automatic devices, there were two girls for six drawing frames and a man and a boy for two mules of 576 spindles each. For the others, such as the throstle spinning frames, there were proportionately more workers. A girl tended only two or three spinning frames of 128 spindles each and not more than four narrow looms, while some took care of only two or three such looms.

Under the agent's supervision the overseers increased production, until, for the twelve months ending June 30, 1861, output reached a peak of almost 15,800,000 yards, as Appendix 25 shows. From 1852 through 1861 Mill No. 1 produced about 4,200,000 yards annually, on the average, mainly shirtings in four widths, 30, 33, 36 and 39 inches, with smaller amounts of jeans and flannels. During these ten years Mill No. 2 produced about 5,300,000 yards annually, on the average, concentrating on one width of drill and making shirtings, flannels, and jeans when the export market for drills was poor. For the four years when it was in production, 1857 through 1861, Mill No. 3 made about 4,300,000 yards a year on the average. But this figure in running yards does not take full account of the sheetings, which were 58, 77, 86, 96 and 105 inches wide. This mill also produced two widths of shirtings and one width of jeans. These ten years of production were much more nearly normal than the following nine years. To be sure, the mills were affected by the decline in the export business in 1854 and 1855 and by the depression which followed the panic of 1857.

The years 1862 through 1870, as Appendix 25 also shows,

brought more serious problems to the overseers than the previous decade. Production dropped to a low of less than 7,000,000 yards in 1862 and reached a high of slightly more than 14,000,000 yards in 1867. Also important were the shifts in types of goods. Heavier goods were introduced in all the mills: drills in Mills No. 1 and No. 3 and ducks in Mill No. 2. In addition new types of jeans and drills were added. These changes were made possible by the coöperation and ability of the overseers, who supervised the adjustments in machinery.

During the years 1851 through 1861 the overseers were successful in keeping the cost of the goods low—in fact, for the first eleven years they kept them to about 6.4 cents a yard on the average. In 1855 a low of 5.5 cents a yard was reached and in 1858 a high of 7.06. But some of the causes of the fluctuations, one of the principal of which was the price of cotton and the other the utilization of mill capacity, were outside their control. Yet the extremes for the first eleven years were not great, with a variation of not more than 15 per cent from the average cost of production, as shown in Appendix 36.

During the Civil War the total expense of manufacture rose rapidly, though less rapidly than the cost of cotton. For a few years the overseers attempted to fill government orders as quickly as possible in order not to suffer a loss from the rises in the price of cotton. In 1865, for example, we find that the expense of production was almost 600 per cent of that in 1860, but the cost of a pound of cotton was nearly 700 per cent of that of the same year. When cotton came in more abundantly from the South and prices fell rapidly, the overseers worked hard to get rid of the supply of cotton so that there would be no loss from a drop in the price of finished goods. By 1870 the cost of manufacturing was 190 per cent of 1860 and the cost of cotton was 200 per cent of 1860. Thus, at the end of the period, we find that the spread between total cost and cotton cost had narrowed, largely as a result of increases in wages.[35]

Although the agent left the management of the rooms to the overseers, there were still many areas for him to direct. One of them was the disposal of the cotton waste which accumulated during the picking, carding, and spinning of the cotton.

The agent arranged with the treasurer to sell the waste to manufacturers of paper, mattresses, and batting. This waste amounted to an appreciable part of operations. In the last six months of 1852, for example, salable waste was nearly 8 per cent of the cotton consumed and its sale brought in over $14,000.[36]

The treasurer considered the grades of cotton to be used for each type of goods. If a cheaper grade could be used, the economy might result in greater profits. In 1857, for example, Dwight suggested that cheaper grades might be used for goods which were to be bleached or dyed. He thought that some of the machinery, particularly that in Mill No. 3 for wide sheetings, might be segregated and put on different grades from the rest. At this time we find that only jeans and wide sheetings were bleached or dyed to any extent—the other goods were sold mainly in the brown.[37] Dwight thus proposed to the agent a change in operations, which undoubtedly led to greater profits in the following years.

Following directions emanating from the selling agent, Haines sent some of the goods to the various bleacheries and dye houses in New England. To the Boston Manufacturing Co. he sent shirtings and sheetings to be bleached, finished, papered, and put into cases. In 1864 Haines began sending a small portion of the wide sheetings as well as some jeans to the Lewiston Bleachery & Dye Works. To three other bleachery and dye works, the Danvers Bleaching Co., the Lowell Bleachery, and the Somerville Dyeing and Bleaching Co., all in Massachusetts, Haines sent drills, jeans, and flannels to be bleached, dyed, and finished. For many years the charges for this work remained the same, for example, all charged 2 cents a pound for bleaching and $\frac{1}{5}$ of a cent per yard for finishing the narrow goods. But during the Civil War charges rose: for example, the charge for dyeing drills and jeans increased from the previous figures of 7/8 of a cent to 1¼ cents per yard to 2 to 3 cents a yard.[38] Actually these charges were part of the sundry charges on sales, given in Appendix 35, and not part of the cost of manufacturing, although in a later period this method of reckoning was reversed.

Included in the other work which Haines supervised in Biddeford was the stamping of the goods sold in the brown. Some bore letters which denoted the types of goods, such as E's, O's, and R's, for shirtings, D's for drills, and J's for jeans. Other goods were stamped with names of fictitious mills, such as Irving, Dover, and Danvers, while others carried the names of places such as Berlin, Salisbury, Ballardvale, Woodfall, Rock River, Georgia, and Cumberland. Some of the goods bore stamps which denoted qualities, such as Beaver Skin, Lion Skin, Swansdown, and Moleskin for flannels and Lion and Dragon for drills.[39] All these marks were designed by the selling agent, who ordered them placed on various lots of goods. As we shall see later, one of the company's trade-marks, the Dragon, became well known abroad and finally became the company's house-mark.

There was another important area, which was later considered part of the cost of manufacturing, although the treasurer continued to make the arrangements—the insurance of the property in Biddeford against loss from fire. To be sure, the agent coöperated in enforcing regulations to safeguard the property. But the treasurer was the one to take out this insurance with many companies, particularly with the Boston Manufacturers' Mutual Fire Insurance Co., of which in 1850 Dwight had been one of the incorporating associates. He increased the coverage of the mills from about $100,000 in 1851 to over $1,000,000 in 1867. The charges were nine-tenths of one per cent of the coverage, and were included among the sundry charges on sales given in Appendix 35. Although the risk of fire was great, particularly in the picker house, Pepperell had only one small fire in its first picker building during the first twenty years. The fire damaged some cotton, estimated at less than $30, and made necessary some cleaning up and repairing at an expense of over $250.[40]

Although with the various coverages of insurance Dwight and Haines could rest easy about disastrous loss from fire and water, there was one risk against which they did not insure—injuries to the operatives while at work. Each time there was an illness or an accident to an operative, Haines paid whatever he thought necessary. At times he paid funeral expenses of those who died during their period of employment. Thus on an individual basis the company took care of accidents or sicknesses of the workers.[41]

Another charge which Haines paid was the taxes on the property in Biddeford, levied by city, county, and State, which were part of the general expenses of operation of the mills. In 1851 he paid almost $3,800. The addition of a third mill increased the taxes to over $8,000 in 1857 and over $10,000 in 1858. Thereafter the taxes increased slightly until the middle of the Civil War, when they mounted rapidly. By 1867 the taxes had reached a high of nearly $35,000.[42] These amounts did not include the special tax levied by the city of Biddeford, nor that levied by the federal government on sales during and after the war, which the treasurer included among the sundry charges.

The record of transactions involving the mills—the incoming of cotton and supplies, the expenses of running the mills, the production of goods, and the outgoing of the finished goods—was painstakingly kept by two clerks in the countinghouse in Biddeford under Haines' direction. The clerks did not, however, take care of the correspondence; Haines himself answered letters. For some of them he made letter-press copies but not for those which he wrote to the treasurer, those being of a confidential nature.

In setting up his system of accounts Haines had the experience of many other textile companies to guide him. Indeed, since the Boston Manufacturing Co. had been organized in 1814, there had been the tradition and the necessity of keeping accurate and detailed records and of reporting various figures to the directors and stockholders. Thus, long before 1850, the textile companies had worked out a system which they kept, with few changes, for about three-quarters of a century longer. Haines kept daybooks, cashbooks, bill books, lists of cotton invoices, payrolls, production records, mill expense figures, and a record of the disposal of cotton waste. These were primary books, which have been invaluable in the investigation of the company. Haines also compiled summary books. The most important of these comprised the semiannual statements which he submitted to the treasurer, who took from them various figures to be put into his own book of semiannual statements.

The team of Dwight, Haines, and the overseers broke down during the winter of 1865–66, when William Dwight became ill and his brother Thomas became treasurer pro tempore. When William Dwight resumed office in the summer of 1866 he asked to be relieved of his duties as soon as a successor could be found. Into his place as treasurer William P. Haines stepped, making his son Ferguson agent in Biddeford, to be assisted by a superintendent, Reuben M. Hobbs. Of the years 1866–70, we know little, since most of the evidence has been destroyed. From records of production and from difficulty with the mule spinners, we may gather that Ferguson Haines did not have his father's ability to get along with people and to encourage others to full achievement. In view of this fact, it was fortunate for the mills that in January, 1871, William P. Haines gave up the office of treasurer and returned to Biddeford as agent.

* * *

In the preceding pages we have followed the acquisition of land, buildings, and machinery and have seen the changes in the working force and in the planning of production and controlling of costs by the treasurer, agent, and overseers. For fifteen or sixteen years we have felt the impact of two strong men, William Dwight the treasurer, and William P. Haines the agent, who coöperated wholeheartedly. Just how outstanding Dwight and Haines were in their management of the business, we have no way of measuring. Any comparison with other companies has to be hedged with so many qualifications that the final statement seems of little value. No two textile enterprises were alike in buildings, machinery, and particular types of goods produced. We do know that Pepperell's mills came to be considered excellent by the trade and that its goods were in such strong demand that they could be sold at a profit.

CHAPTER V

AN AGENCY HANDLES PEPPERELL'S SALES

HAVING EXAMINED Pepperell's procurement of cotton and its manufacture into cloth, we are now ready to follow operations still further by a study of the distribution of the finished product. Following the customary method of large textile companies in New England, apparently originated by the Boston Manufacturing Co., the treasurer sought an independent organization to handle sales. William Dwight selected an agency from a group of sales organizations which in the preceding three decades had been growing in Boston. Some of these agencies had formerly carried on a mercantile business at their own profit or loss, but they had given up their several functions to specialize in one—the handling of goods for mills on a commission basis. Other sales agents had started in a small way as retailers, jobbers, or combining a number of functions, but had grasped the opportunity to become specialized sales agents. Dwight chose one of the latter, Francis Skinner & Co., a partnership which had already demonstrated its ability in many ways. Francis Skinner & Co. continued as Pepperell's distributing agency until 1870, when for a few months a successor partnership continued the selling. Then, in the autumn of that year Pepperell's management as well as its selling arrangements changed considerably, bringing to a close the first period of Pepperell's history.

Although Francis Skinner & Co. was not legally a part of Pepperell, it was in fact an intimate part of its business organization and must be treated as such. There are many persons in our own time who would like to see the major functions of business (such as production, marketing, and transportation) legally separated, so that large integrated companies would disappear. The relations of Pepperell and Skinner take on fresh interest when read in conjunction with any effort to return to the smaller and simpler units of a century ago.

ACTING BOLDLY

For many years Francis Skinner & Co. was among the leaders in the business life of Boston. Starting in a small way this selling house grew, particularly after the panic of 1837, when the senior partner, Francis Skinner, acquired a reputation for acting boldly when others hesitated. His reputation he increased by gaining the accounts of several promising textile companies in the 1840's and by being one of the first to have a partner in New York. He did not rest there, but until his death he sought to expand the business, adding the accounts of other new companies from time to time. These companies required capital, both permanent and working, which he was willing to advance in order to have their accounts. Thus he contributed to the prosperity of New England, not only by selling the woolen and cotton goods but by assisting in the expansion of manufacturing through the loaning of working capital.

Of the partners in the selling house Francis Skinner was the most important. He was born into the petty capitalist class of New England, which saw in the new specialization in business an opportunity for success with a small initial capital. Although he was the son of a successful doctor in a small community in Massachusetts, he had to assume responsibilities at an early age; his father died in 1810, leaving a widow with four children. The two older sons had already left home to work in country stores. The younger of them returned to help Francis run the family farm for a few years. Then they sold it. Perhaps Francis accompanied his brother Henry to Andover and sought employment in one of the small woolen mills there. In 1821, however, when twenty-four years old he was living in Boston. Probably in this year, he formed a partnership to handle domestic goods with James C. Dunn, under the style of Skinner & Dunn, despite the fact that he seems to have had little or no business experience. In 1825 or 1826 the partners separated, each finding a new partner. Skinner set up the house of Francis

Skinner & Co., whose title remained the same in the following decades, although partners changed from time to time.

Just when the partners turned to selling on a commission basis is uncertain; probably they added a few accounts to a combination of retail and wholesale business. Then, when sufficient accounts had been obtained, they dropped the earlier functions. This had occurred by 1831, according to a Boston directory of that year.[1] From the beginning of his business life in Boston Francis Skinner seems to have devoted all his energies and money to building up his firm. We should like to know more about his actions during the panic of 1837, but unfortunately we have been unable to discover definite contemporary evidence.*

* From directories we find that for many years Skinner boarded in Boston. In 1839 he married Elizabeth Cochrain of Northampton, Massachusetts, and established a residence on Beacon Hill, where in the following year his only son, Francis, was born. In the late 1850's the Skinners moved out to a "farm" in Newton, where they continued to live comfortably throughout the remainder of the elder Francis' life. The farm was, however, rather far from his office in Boston, which from 1837 to 1858 was on Milk Street and thereafter in a new building on Franklin Street.[2]

Concerning the background of the other partners in Francis Skinner & Co. we have only a few facts. We know that the first one, Phineas Fisk, had sold West Indies goods in Boston from 1818 to 1825. Apparently for five years he was willing to contribute capital and advice to his young partner, letting the latter's name appear alone in the partnership name. We surmise that Skinner's next two partners, William S. Lincoln and Henry K. Horton, who entered in 1831 and 1832, respectively, had gained their experience outside the city—at least previously they had not been listed as residents in Boston, and it is reported that they started as poor boys. By 1846 Skinner had added a third partner in Boston, Edmund F. Cutler, who had been serving as a clerk for three years. In 1857 Lincoln left and Josiah Bardwell took his place. Earlier, as we have seen, Bardwell had been Dwight's clerk and then his buying agent for cotton in the South. In 1865, upon Francis Skinner's death, his son, Francis, Jr., entered the house. Earlier, in 1862, he had been graduated from Harvard College and then gained experience in mills in Lewiston. In 1867 Horton died, but his place was not filled by another partner.[3]

There were other partners in New York, where a branch office had been established in 1846. The first was Henry A. Smythe, previously a commission merchant, who became a partner in 1846. He remained until 1857 or 1858; his place was taken by two others, William P. Brintnall and Lemuel Hayward. The latter stayed about two years, while the former continued throughout this

At this time there were few or no salesmen who scoured the country with trunks of textile samples from the commission houses. This was an era when the Boston business men expected the customers to go to them. In fact, a committee of commission merchants and jobbers reported in 1858 that they had "been bred to believe that the seller should keep his goods at home, and allow the purchaser to come to him." [6] This policy meant that the commission houses expected the distant jobbers to make trips to Boston once or twice a year, in the spring and fall, to see the goods and to place orders. As for the local jobbers, there could be more frequent visits with more frequent ordering of goods. To so radical a step as the setting up of branch offices in New York City, Boston business men were still objecting as late as 1858, twelve years after Francis Skinner & Co. had set up its New York office.[7]

As the years went by, Francis Skinner & Co. was able to offer more and more goods to the buyers. Whereas in 1832 this firm had handled the products of a few small mills (one cotton and five woolen), by 1850 it had acquired the accounts of a few large cotton textile companies—the James Steam Mill, the Naumkeag Steam Mill, and the Pepperell Manufacturing Company. Ten years later Skinner was selling, according to an advertisement, the cotton goods of the Pepperell, James, Bates, Porter, Franklin, Kennebec, Portland, Uncasville, Portsmouth, and Central mills and also the doeskins and cassimeres of the Burlington, Otter River, North Vassalboro, Wamsetta (not to be confused with Wamsutta), and other mills. By 1870 the house was handling the goods of additional large companies, including Laconia, Androscoggin, and Continental.[8]

In order to get many of these large accounts it was necessary

period. Evidently both had held junior positions in this or other firms. At any rate, Brintnall proved successful in getting customers in New York for Pepperell, as we shall see.[4]

In addition to these senior partners, there were a number of so-called junior partners, salesmen, and clerks. They were probably ambitious young men who saw a possibility of advancement to the status of partner. They shared none of the tremendous risks and little of the reward of the business. During these years it was customary to pay very small salaries to the routine workers. While several were promoted, others continued to work as employees for years.[5]

FRANCIS SKINNER & CO.

DOMESTIC GOODS COMMISSION MERCHANTS,

No. 69 Franklin Street, Boston,

AND

NO. 2 COLLEGE PLACE, ... NEW YORK,

HAVE FOR SALE

Fine Shirtings, Sheetings, and Jeans. Heavy Shirtings, Drills, and Flannels, from the Pepperell Mills.

Fine Brown and Bleached Shirtings, Sheetings, Jeans, and Canton Flannels, from the Naumkeag Steam Mills.

Fine Brown and Bleached Shirtings, Sheetings, and Sateen Jeans, from the James Steam Mills.

Fine Brown and Bleached Shirtings, Sheetings, Jeans, Canton Flannels, and a great variety of colored goods, from the Bates Mills.

Fine Bleached Sheetings and Shirtings, from the Porter Mills.

Bleached and Corset Jeans, from the Franklin Mills.

Light Sheetings and Shirting Stripes, Brown and Bleached Canton Flannels, from the Kennebec Manufacturing Company.

Shirting Stripes and Twilled Duck, from the Portland Manufacturing Company.

Shirting Stripes, from the Uncasville Manufacturing Company.

Fine Sheetings, from the Portsmouth Company.

Light Sheetings, from the Central Mills.

Also, Black and Fancy Doeskins and Cassimeres, in great variety, from the "Burlington," "Otter River," "North Vassalboro'," "Wamsetta," and other Mills.

ADVERTISEMENT OF FRANCIS SKINNER & CO., 1860

for the selling house or the partners to subscribe to stock or to advance funds for working capital. Except for Pepperell we know little about these financial arrangements until Francis Skinner's death in 1865. Then he left large blocks of stock (100 or more) in the Androscoggin, Bates, James, and Hyde Park companies and small blocks in Pepperell and Kennebec. When Henry K. Horton died two years later he held between 30 and 100 shares in the Androscoggin, Bates, James, Hyde Park, and Methuen companies. From the firm of Francis Skinner & Co., Horton's estate in 1869 received a large block of stock in the Franklin and Vassalboro companies and small amounts in Pepperell and Portsmouth.[9]

During the years when these textile companies were being organized, such subscriptions to stock by Francis Skinner & Co. and by the partners must have reduced tremendously their current personal income. But by the middle 1860's, however, the partners were benefiting from their earlier sacrifices. They were getting good dividends from the companies as well as large commissions on sales. From Pepperell alone in 1865 the selling house received more than $60,000 in commissions. If we multiply this several times to compute the commissions from all companies, it is evident that the agent received an enormous income for several years. Thus, at last the partners were repaid for the risks which they had taken earlier. By 1865 Francis Skinner was worth a million dollars, having multiplied many times the small capital which he had inherited from his father about half a century earlier.[10]

WORKING WITH PEPPERELL

The relations of Pepperell with its selling agent were much more complicated than appeared on the surface. Some of the terms of doing business together were stated in the contract between the company and the agent. Other terms can be pieced together from other bits of evidence. On the whole, the evidence is scanty chiefly since much business was transacted by word of mouth. Some material remains in the correspondence of the New York partner with Dwight and of various partners with Haines, but only for a few of the score of years. Other evidence can be secured from sales journals, which cover the distribution of the goods for most of this period.

On September 4, 1850, Pepperell's directors determined the initial terms of selling by Francis Skinner & Co. They approved a commission of one per cent on all sales and a reimbursement to the selling agent for all charges involved in selling, such as freight, storage, and insurance of the goods. These were customary payments to agents of large companies. In one way, however, Pepperell's arrangement was slightly different. Other selling houses had distributed part of their goods through sub-agents in New York, Philadelphia, and Baltimore, and the textile companies had allowed the sub-agents an additional 2 per cent. But Francis Skinner & Co. had a partner in New York, and Pepperell agreed to give 2 per cent additional on business done there, with the proviso that the total commissions to Skinner were not to average more than 1¾ per cent. To sub-agents in Philadelphia and Baltimore Pepperell allowed the customary 2 per cent additional. Also Pepperell granted ¼ per cent additional on colored goods, an extra commission which was usual at this time. (During the Civil War Pepperell changed the arrangement with sub-agents. To John S. Barry & Co. it allowed 5 per cent for commission and guarantee, and to Lewis, Wharton & Co. a commission of 2½ per cent.)[11]

Pepperell's first arrangement with Francis Skinner & Co. continued until the spring of 1853, when the commission to the agent was changed to 1½ per cent on all sales while that to the sub-agents remained the same, 2 per cent in addition. This change was not mentioned in the minutes of the directors at the time, in fact not until 1870, but it appears in the sales journal in 1853. It came as a result of the well-known and heated controversy which the outstanding cotton textile house, A. & A. Lawrence & Co., had stirred up among the treasurers of textile companies in the fall of 1851. Then the partners in the Lawrence firm announced that they were planning to open an office in New York and that they were raising the commission on all goods sold directly in Boston and New York to 1½ per cent, or, if the companies preferred, they would continue the previous one per cent for sales in Boston and add 2 per cent for those in New York. To stop such action the treasurers set up a committee, with William Sturgis as chairman. This committee reported at the beginning of 1852 that the Lawrence proposal would move the principal place of sale of dry goods from Boston to New York and that one per cent was ample for selling the goods in either city. The controversy raged until the spring of 1853, when a compromise was reached—1¼ on sales in Boston and New York, and not more than 3 per cent in all in Philadelphia and Baltimore. Although the Lawrences gave way slightly in the rate of commission, they gained their point about the importance of a New York office.[12] As a result of this and other moves, business in dry goods in Boston was to decline while New York was to become not only the center of imports but the "great emporium of trade." Boston's "commodious warehouses," railroads, and other facilities, provided for making it "the headquarters for the sale and distribution of manufactures" of New England, were no longer needed.[13]

It should be remembered that Pepperell took no part in this controversy and had no representative at any of the meetings to protest the Lawrences' proposals. Furthermore, the fact that the company had chosen a selling house with a New York partner indicates that it viewed the Lawrence move as a wise one, despite the possible adverse effects on Boston as a business center.

In the contract much was left unsaid about other financial arrangements between Pepperell and Francis Skinner & Co. Of great importance was the question as to how much stock the selling house was willing to subscribe. As mentioned already, the selling agent agreed to take half the stock left on Dwight's hands. On September 17, 1852, the day of issuing the first certificates, Francis Skinner & Co. had 268 shares. During the following years the holdings declined. The firm transferred title to some stock as collateral for long-term loans, 100 shares in 1853, and sold the remainder of its holdings, 162 shares, on Black Friday, October 13, 1857. In the 1860's the agent acquired stock which again it disposed of—sold and transferred as collateral. By the middle of 1870 the house of Skinner was again without stock. At the same time the partners individually held small blocks. Francis Skinner usually held ten shares, although on "Black Friday" he used them to get cash in order to prevent a weakening of his house. Thus, after the selling house had helped Pepperell by subscribing to stock at the beginning, it disposed of these holdings to tide itself over periods of distress.[14]

Nothing was said in the contract about the provision of working capital by the selling house. Apparently Dwight did not often need to call upon the agent for aid. In 1851 Francis Skinner & Co. did loan $75,000 to the company on a short-term basis. Later the agent aided in securing loans from Massachusetts savings banks, which were prevented by State regulations from loaning money directly to a company incorporated outside the State. It was necessary to resort to the artifice of loaning to William Dwight, Francis Skinner & Co., and Francis Skinner. During the Civil War the agent assisted the company to a great extent, when to get government business it was necessary to take certificates which matured in one year or notes which did not mature for three years. This government paper was usually held by the agent and explains the high balance due Pepperell from the agent, especially from June, 1863, through June, 1865, given in Appendix 32. In particular, the agent held United States government notes to the amount of $885,000 for about three years. During these war years the agent loaned to the company large sums as, for example, nearly $1,000,000 in short term loans in 1865. In the following years the agent continued to aid the company but not to such an extent as in the war years.[15]

For the major part of this period the sales agent did not take the responsibility for collecting the sales notes from Pepperell's customers, as some agents did for their clients. In fact, on the printed billheads sent out by Francis Skinner & Co. were the words, "Bought of Francis Skinner & Co., Note to order of the Treasurer of the Pepperell Manufacturing Co." [16] At times, however, Skinner did assist in collection, particularly after the panic of 1857 and during the depression which preceded the Civil War. During the War, when terms of sale grew shorter for many customers, the selling house took over the collection of the short-term paper, leaving to Dwight only the notes for longer periods, such as those written by Jordan Marsh Co. for four months. This division of duties continued throughout this period, with the selling house collecting the short-term paper and the treasurer the long-term notes, which were received from large customers for both the domestic and foreign markets.[17]

Although the sales agent's rôle was minor in finances, it was major in many aspects of production. Since many of the transactions between Dwight and Skinner were made orally, the full extent of this influence cannot be ascertained. We gather that Skinner suggested the types of goods which would be advisable for the mills to make. From early letters we find also that the agent suggested the number of looms to be put on each particular width of goods. Besides, the agent designed the various marks to be put on goods sold in the brown. Skinner & Co. did not seem to urge the practice of putting Pepperell's name on all domestic goods, but it did on the exports. In December, 1857, for example, Josiah Bardwell, then in the selling house, wrote that "the drills are going on a trading voyage up the 'Straits of Malacca' and I am anxious that the 'Dragon' should have a chance to make an impression where now only the 'Boott' are known." [18] The sales agent also directed the sending of goods to the bleacheries and the method of shipment, whether by boat or by rail.[19]

In the determination of Pepperell's general policies, the selling house also took a part, since it was represented on Pepperell's board of directors. From 1851 to his death in 1865 Francis Skinner was a director. Then, until the fall of 1870 Josiah Bardwell took his place. From 1851 to 1870 there is no evidence of any controversy over selling. Inasmuch as there were many difficult years when the other directors might well have questioned the sales agent's methods, this record seems remarkable.

Pepperell, then, in many ways was tied to the selling house of Francis Skinner & Co. Between them was a contract as well as other agreements. Pepperell paid commissions and charges while the sales agent helped in the determination of policies, subscribed to stock, assisted in getting loans and in collecting sales notes, planned changes in production, and directed the disposal of the goods. But the selling agent's chief job was always to find markets for Pepperell's goods, which is the subject to which we now turn.

GETTING CUSTOMERS FOR PEPPERELL

From 1850 to 1870 Francis Skinner & Co. and its successor partnership were successful in getting customers for Pepperell, not only dealers in the domestic market but also exporters to South America, the Near East, and particularly the Far East. Since these two types of customers operated quite differently, we shall consider them separately.

One reason why Francis Skinner & Co. proved so helpful to Pepperell was that it steered Pepperell along the line of specialties. In 1849, according to the *New England Union Mercantile Directory,* most of the 450 textile establishments in New England were producing plain heavy goods, such as narrow sheetings and print cloths. Comparatively few textile concerns were manufacturing specialties, such as shirtings, drills, and jeans made by Pepperell's first two mills. Just how far Francis Skinner & Co. may be said to have determined Pepperell's special products in the first instance is not clear, but at any rate it kept encouraging Pepperell to develop the specialty field. In 1854 it proved to be even more daring in selecting wide sheetings as a product for Pepperell's third mill. This was all the more notable in that only recently had New England mills attempted to produce wide goods. Although other companies later turned to the manufacturing of such products, Pepperell had been given a head start and was thereby well established in the market.

On the first of April, 1851, Francis Skinner & Co. sold the first bales of Pepperell's shirtings to jobbers in New York. The selling agent thus began a practice in the distribution of Pepperell's goods which continued with little change for nearly three-quarters of a century. In the domestic market Skinner distributed largely to wholesalers, or jobbers as they called themselves at that time. Some of these distributors still combined jobbing and importing of dry goods, since as yet even in Boston and New York, the leading centers for dry goods, specialization had not separated these functions. In addition, the agent sold to a few others, such as manufacturers of clothing and of industrial products.[20]

The tedious work of identifying, classifying, and locating customers and compiling sales for each from the daily postings in the sales journal for the first full year of selling for Pepperell —July, 1851, through June, 1852—has produced some definite information. We find that Francis Skinner & Co. reached 240 domestic customers. Of these the vast majority were located in New York and Boston, with 130 in the former and 51 in the latter city. In Philadelphia and Baltimore the sales agent distributed through 3 sub-agents as well as to 10 accounts directly from its offices. Elsewhere in the United States there was a scattering of outlets. In the North there were 12 customers, located in Portland, Worcester, Providence, Hartford, Albany, and Buffalo. In the South and West there were 15 customers, located in Charleston, New Orleans, Mobile, St. Louis, Louisville, and Cincinnati. In addition there were 19 customers whose location is not known, operating perhaps in all these or other cities but probably chiefly in the smaller ones, for which less information is available.

Francis Skinner & Co. sold most of Pepperell's goods to domestic customers in New York and Boston: in 1851–52, for example, 44 per cent of the total domestic sales were to customers in New York and 34 per cent to those in Boston. In Philadelphia and Baltimore the sub-agents distributed 3 per cent, while to customers there the agent sold 5 per cent directly. Elsewhere in the North the agent sold 2 per cent, and in the South and West 10 per cent, of the total domestic sales. Only 2 per cent cannot be located. Thus, New York ranked first in number of domestic customers and in dollar sales. Boston ranked second in both respects, but proportionally closer to New York in sales than in number of customers. The rest of the United States was of little importance.

Among these domestic customers in 1851–52 there were a few who took large amounts. In New York there were three firms that took goods worth over $10,000, but none of them continued to be important in later years. There was another customer, Bulkley & Claflin, who within the year became Claflin, Mellen & Co., and still later, in 1864, the well-known H. B. Claflin & Co. In 1851–52, the two partnerships purchased less than $1,200 worth of Pepperell's goods. This concern was to become Pepperell's most important customer for many decades. In Boston in 1851–52 the two companies which took more than $10,000 worth of goods were J. M. Beebe, Morgan & Co. and Jordan Marsh Co., both outstanding wholesaling houses.

It is interesting to note that Francis Skinner & Co.'s pattern for the distribution of Pepperell's goods in 1851–52 differed considerably from that of the competing house, A. & A. Lawrence & Co., which handled Laconia's goods. Since Laconia's records are not complete for the year 1851–52, we have compiled the sales (by customers) for the previous year. Of the domestic business the Lawrences distributed almost half, 42 per cent, through sub-agents in New York, Philadelphia, and Baltimore. In the remaining domestic distribution the Lawrences in Boston dealt with 213 customers—70 located in New York, 68 in Boston, 7 in Philadelphia, and 3 in Baltimore as well as 20 in other cities in the North and 8 in the South and West. Not identified were 37 domestic customers. Direct sales of domestic goods by the Lawrences were 24 per cent to buyers in New York, 20 per cent in Boston, 2 per cent in Philadelphia and Baltimore, 3 per cent elsewhere in the North, and one per cent elsewhere in the South and West, with 8 per cent not located. Thus, even in the sales of the Boston office, Boston was outranked by New York in number of customers and total sales made by the agent directly. The Lawrences relied more heavily on sub-agents than did Skinner for the distribution of goods. Although they had more customers in Boston than Skinner, Lawrence & Co. sold these customers proportionally less.[21]

When business was becoming dull and finished goods were accumulating, Francis Skinner & Co. resorted to an earlier method of disposing of goods—sale by auction. On August 25, 1857, such a sale was conducted by Wilmerdings & Mount, of New York City, in which they auctioned off to 23 customers over 350,000 yards of Pepperell's sheetings, which brought over $65,000 before charges. The auctioneers were given 4 per cent of sales for their commission and for guaranteeing the collection of customer's notes, in all almost $3,000. In addition Skinner paid the charges incurred for the catalogue and advertising. While this sale was planned before the failure of the Ohio Life & Trust Co., it was actually held the day after. Currently it was claimed that this failure hastened a series of events which brought on the panic of October 13, 1857. But fortunately for Pepperell, some of its goods had thus been disposed of before business reached the bottom. Sales by auction, however, were not favored except when deemed absolutely necessary, since the costs of distributing were higher, prices might be lower, and as a result the market in the following months might be depressed.

By the fiscal year 1859–60 Francis Skinner & Co. was selling Pepperell's goods in larger amounts to fewer domestic customers, estimated at about 200 in all, still concentrated in New York and Boston but with a greater scattering than earlier in the South and West. By that time the selling house was reaching customers in Chicago, Nashville, and Richmond, so that there were 25 customers in 9 cities in the South and West. This decrease in the number of customers from the 1851–52 figure may have come as a result of the panic of 1857; also by this time, Skinner could be more selective in customers for Pepperell's goods and was able to choose larger accounts than at the beginning. In New York the agent did a large business with Claflin, Mellen & Co., who took Pepperell's goods to the amount of $130,000. In Boston it sold $116,000 to J. M. Beebe & Co. and $56,000 to Jordan Marsh Co. It is amazing that Beebe bought almost as much as Claflin; evidently Boston jobbers could still compete for business with those in New York. In this year, 1859–60, one of the sub-agents in Philadelphia was important—D. S. Brown & Co., who sold over $33,000 of Pepperell's goods.

During the following years, when the pattern of sales was disturbed by the Civil War, Francis Skinner & Co. was fortunate in securing government contracts and other war business for Pepperell's mills. In 1861–62 Skinner obtained orders from the government for Pepperell duck which amounted to over $25,000 in value. The house also secured contracts for military supplies from others, such as Fox & Polhemus of New York, dealers in duck, and from several other companies, which in 1861–62 totaled almost as much as direct government contracts. In 1862–63 the agent received enormous orders from Fox & Polhemus, amounting to over $230,000, from other companies $60,000, but none directly from the government. In the third war year, 1863–64, Pepperell's agent sold still more goods for war purposes, over $600,000 worth. In addition to ducks it sold drills, jeans, and flannels. Three reasons for this success in getting business were the promise of early delivery, reasonable prices, and willingness to wait from one to three years for the maturing of certificates and notes which were given for these goods.

For the pattern of sales after the Civil War, we have little information—the last surviving sales journal of this period ends in 1867. From the journal we learn that the majority of customers in 1866–67, as well as the major part of the sales, were in New York and Boston. We also find that the sub-agents were more important than earlier. Two of them, which the selling house had acquired during the Civil War, handled large amounts: Lewis, Wharton & Co., of Philadelphia, sold over $80,000 worth and John S. Barry & Co., of Baltimore, over $420,000 worth. Skinner was reaching more jobbers in the South and West than formerly; indeed, it was selling to nine in St. Louis and eleven in Cincinnati.

Thus, we can conclude that the original pattern for selling to domestic customers changed somewhat between 1850 and 1870. Francis Skinner & Co., while continuing to concentrate in Boston and New York, turned over more and more of Pepperell's goods to sub-agents. Skinner sold to jobbers in a larger group of cities throughout the United States, but still gave much attention to the large houses in Boston and New York, which distributed not only to retailers but also to smaller jobbers in their regions.

During this first period, 1850–70, the selling agent planned to have part of Pepperell's production go abroad; in fact, the "perfect forty-yard" lengths of drills, produced in Mill No. 2 and stamped with a Dragon, were destined for export. But during these years there were disturbances, domestic and foreign, which prevented the development of a steady foreign market. There was the Crimean War from 1854 to 1856, the war involving China, Great Britain, and France from 1856 to 1858, and the internal war in China, the T'ai P'ing Rebellion, which lasted from 1848 through 1864. In 1858, when more treaty ports were opened in China, many more American goods were exported, among them Pepperell's Dragon drills. During our own Civil War, trade was cut off for about five years because American cottons were priced too high to be disposed of abroad.

In the first full year of selling, 1851–52, Francis Skinner & Co. sold goods for export to 15 merchants in Boston, 9 in New York, and one each in New Bedford and Philadelphia. During this year, as Appendix 31 shows, the foreign business amounted to $184,000 or 34 per cent of the total sales. This was a smaller percentage than for Laconia's goods in 1850–51, when A. & A. Lawrence distributed about 55 per cent in foreign markets. Almost $140,000 worth of Pepperell's goods for export were handled by Boston merchants and about $44,000 by those in New York. Of these merchants Dane, Dana & Co. of Boston were the largest purchasers, with over $65,000 worth. There were four other large purchasers, each of which took over $15,000 worth, one in New York, A. A. Low & Bros., and three in Boston, A. Hemingway, L. Nichols & Co., and Sampson & Tappan.

In the following years, as Appendix 31 shows, Pepperell's exports waxed and waned. In 1852–53 exports reached over $270,000 in value, from which they declined to a low of $10,000 in 1854–55. After this year exports increased again, reaching a high in 1860–61 of $580,000 in value. In the following year little went abroad, and in the next three years none. In 1865–66 the selling agent arranged for a smaller volume of exports, which was increased to $360,000 worth in the financial year 1866–67. For the last six months of 1867 the total was over

$130,000. Figures are not available for the remainder of this period.

Just how much cloth went to each foreign market we do not know. Many merchants in Boston and New York were doing business with houses in China; others were conducting trade with India. Some of them probably provided for stops on the west coast of America before proceeding to the Far East. Other merchants traded with the West Indies and still others with lands bordering on the Mediterranean.

In the records of Dane, Dana & Co., one of the Boston houses doing business with China, are found some of the details of the hazardous export business. We find, for example, that in 1852 this company arranged for the export of 300 bales of Pepperell's drills and 84 bales of Stark's and Suffolk's drills, the latter purchased at an eighth of a cent a yard less than Pepperell's. The company consigned the drills to a representative in Canton and Shanghai, "or in case of absence or accident" to another in Canton. Some of the drills, damaged in shipment, were sold at auction in Shanghai and the remainder were sold at the price of Pepperell's drills in Boston. Thus the merchants, even on the perfect goods, did not make money; in fact, they did not recover charges for shipping.[22] We find also that during the 1850's the merchants did not agree as to the advisability of exporting. In October, 1853, a merchant in New York wrote another in Boston, "As it regards drills, perhaps Griswold calculates upon the rule of contraries to make his operation a successful one." [23] On the whole N. L. & G. Griswold, one of Pepperell's customers, probably did not lose because of its bold policies, as the nickname "No Loss & Great Gain" indicated.

Nevertheless in this period the selling agent laid the foundation for an excellent foreign as well as domestic demand for Pepperell's goods. Since international affairs upset foreign trade, Francis Skinner & Co. could not build up the steady demand for Dragon drills which a later agent achieved. Fortunately for Pepperell, Skinner had other markets and other goods for Mill No. 2 to produce, thus enabling the company to maintain a good record of sales. Skinner increased gross sales from over $500,000 in 1851–52 to a prewar high point of almost $1,300,000 in 1860–61. While in the following year sales dropped to about half, they rose to new heights during the Civil War, to $4,000,000 in 1864–65. (After the Civil War, sales declined, with the estimate for the last year of this period, 1869–70, set at $1,500,000.) A large proportion of these rises came not by increases in volume but by higher prices, as we shall see in the following pages.

SETTING PRICES AND TERMS

For Pepperell's several types of goods Francis Skinner & Co. established prices, discounts, and lengths of credit. Although there was some variation in all three, depending on the particular customer, there were more significant differences by types of customer and over periods of time. The domestic varied from the foreign customer; the early years differed from those during and after the Civil War.

Since there are no early price lists available, a set of prices, using actual sales in January of each year for each type of goods, has been compiled. While there may be variations in prices within a year, there has been no attempt to follow them, since generally fluctuations were slight. In Appendix 30 the high and low prices charged for each type of goods, in the brown and when bleached and dyed, are recorded. From 1852 through 1861, variations were slight as compared with those in the following nine years. In 1852 Francis Skinner & Co. quoted prices of shirtings lower than in later years, perhaps to induce various jobbers to take Pepperell's goods. By 1854 it had increased prices to within a few per cent of the high point of 1860. For sheetings, introduced by the agent in March, 1856, we find that lower prices were not offered at the beginning; in fact, in January of the following year, prices of sheetings were higher than in the subsequent two years.

The pattern of prices was upset by the scarcity of cotton during the Civil War. From 1860 to 1865, prices of shirtings and sheetings increased about 400 per cent, while that for jeans rose almost 600 per cent. The price of duck in 1854, when Skinner had sold it before, had been 11½ cents a yard, but in 1865 the prices varied from 88 cents to $1.98 a yard. To be sure, the duck sold in 1854 weighed only 8 ounces per yard, while during the war it weighed 8, 10, and 12 ounces. When the price of cotton dropped after the war, the prices of finished goods did likewise. As one would expect, the drop was greatest during 1865 and 1866. By 1870, prices of Pepperell's goods were still lower, but wages had risen in many industries so that there was a good potential domestic market.

In the tabulations of prices per yard during January of each year there are some variations, which in the prewar years were generally less than a cent a yard for shirtings, drills, and jeans and from ½ to 2 cents for sheetings. This variation was tied in with discounts and with the size of the orders. On January 2, 1852, for example, according to the sales journal, Skinner sold shirtings to two customers at 6¼ cents a yard, with no discount, and to a third at 6½ cents, with a 4 per cent discount, which results in practically the same cost per yard. On the last day of January, 1852, Skinner sold the same type of shirtings to five customers, all at 6½ cents a yard, but with discounts varying from 2 to 7 per cent. The 7 per cent discount was given to Jordan Marsh Co., one of the large customers, as we have seen.

At the beginning Francis Skinner & Co. sold goods for the domestic market on credit of eight or nine months and by 1855 this firm had established the normal term as eight months. After the panic of 1857 the partners cut the terms of credit in many cases to cash or to four, six, and eight months. By 1859 six months had become the accepted length. Then to civilian customers during the Civil War the selling house gave terms of net 30, 60, 90, and 120 days, with 30 days the usual period. William Endicott, of Hovey, Williams & Co., reminisced later about this change as follows:[24]

> The advent of the Civil War led to a complete change in the whole credit system of the country. The fluctuating value of the depreciated currency made any credits quite hazardous, and when this became apparent in the early years of the War, sales were brought as nearly as possible to cash or a short-credit basis. This is largely the present usage, and the long credits have gone never to return.

During the war, as we have noted already, government business was on a basis of long-term paper—one to three years. After the war the selling agent continued 30 days as the usual period for credit to domestic customers. While we do not have Pepperell's sales journals from 1868 to 1870, we do have those for Laconia, for which Francis Skinner & Co. became the selling agent in 1864. Length of credit continued usually as 30 days, with occasional instances of longer credit.

To the export trade Pepperell at first extended credit for twelve months, sometimes with the additional charge of one or 2 per cent for interest for the period. Later, after the crash of 1857, it was customary to grant credit for a shorter period, eight or ten months. Interest was not charged, but discounts were given on the prevailing prices. When exports were resumed after the Civil War, the selling agency did not grant the old terms. Instead credit was granted for four or six months, with interest for the months after the first at 7 per cent. Also, it added a charge (hitherto not exacted) for boards and hoops on the bales. This implies that credit for either market, before an interest charge, was thirty days and that it was a seller's market for Pepperell's wares.

Although on the whole Francis Skinner & Co. was very fortunate in its choice of customers and sub-agents for Pepperell's goods, the firm had several who were caught in the panic of 1857 and in the depression of 1861. The resulting losses were not too great for Pepperell to bear, since each year it had been the practice to set aside 2 per cent of sales as a guarantee and insurance fund. Losses did reduce the accumulated funds considerably in 1857–58 and 1861–62 as Appendix 32 shows, but on the whole Pepperell's losses were less than the reserves set up. At the end of this period Pepperell did suffer a great loss, not directly from individual customers but from the selling house itself, as we shall see in the following section.

In this first period of operations, then, the pattern of prices and terms is complicated by the different treatment of domestic and foreign customers. The former type was accorded much shorter terms of credit than the latter. Both received about the same treatment as regards prices and discounts. The greatest change of all was the drastic reduction in length of credit to civilian customers during the Civil War—from dealing in months to days. Then thirty days became the usual period for credit; although this was to be modified in the following period, the dry goods trade did not go back to the former terms of six and eight months.

FAILURE OF THE SALES AGENT

The extraordinary period of success of Francis Skinner & Co. ended in 1865 with the conclusion of the Civil War and the death of Francis Skinner. Although the house continued for five more years, it was accumulating weaknesses in its structure, which led to its fall in 1870.

The death of Francis Skinner in 1865 dealt a tremendous blow to the selling house, since it was he who, although bold in enterprise, had kept the house sound during difficult times and had built it up to be one of the largest in the country. Some measure of its importance can be gathered from the size of Skinner's estate, which was valued at over $1,000,000. His share in the selling house was valued at $450,000. In the disposition of his property he continued to influence the partnership. To his widow and son he left personal property and set up trust funds of $100,000 each. He requested that the remainder of his estate be kept in the partnership or available to it for emergencies. He requested also that the selling house continue for five years, or a shorter time if the two trustees, Josiah Bardwell and Dwight Foster, so decided. He asked that the partners admit his son, Francis, Jr., into their number and that they admit no others. Thus, Francis Skinner provided for the continued life of his selling house by keeping his capital in it. He handicapped it, however, by the other two provisions, the entrance of his son and the exclusion of any new partner, at a time when the senior partners were reaching mature years.[25]

During the years 1865–70 the house was undermined on several sides. In 1867 death removed another partner, Henry K. Horton, whose will stipulated that his share in the house was to be withdrawn at the end of two years.[26] The three active partners, Brintnall in New York and Cutler and Bardwell in

Boston, then carried a heavy load. They continued part of the duties which before the Civil War Dwight had carried alone for the Pepperell Manufacturing Company—the collection of the sales notes and the securing of loans. But it was in 1869 that serious troubles began to accumulate for the selling house. In the fall of that year there was a gold panic and collapse in speculative stocks. Evidently the partners had participated to some extent in these speculations; at any rate, a later newspaper account mentioned the house's investments in southern railroad stock, which depreciated in value. At this time also there were several failures of dry goods jobbers, which added to the weaknesses of Skinner's position because the agent held their paper. A price war which was going on between two leading jobbing houses in New York weakened the market for dry goods. Furthermore Francis Skinner & Co. was paying out large sums of money to aid a sub-agent, John S. Barry & Co., and to no avail, since on January 3, 1870, the sub-agent failed. All these were contributing gusts which toppled over the already debilitated firm.[27]

By the end of January, 1870, Francis Skinner & Co. ceased to sell goods, transferring this function to Jordan, Bardwell & Co., a firm composed of Francis Skinner, Jr., Josiah Bardwell, and Eben D. Jordan of Jordan Marsh Co. During the spring and summer of 1870 all seemed to be going well, with Francis Skinner & Co. liquidating assets and collecting sales notes. In fact, in August, 1870, William P. Haines reported to Pepperell's directors that he had seen the schedules of property and watched the conversion of much of it without sacrifice. If the textile companies would continue the selling by the new partnership, he foresaw that Pepperell would be paid its balance.[28]

Suddenly on September 12, 1870, came the announcement of the failure of Francis Skinner & Co. with liabilities of $4,500,000. The directors and stockholders of many of the manufacturing companies for which the Skinner partnership had been acting seemed little disturbed by the effect on them; few of them attended their companies' annual meetings, which were held within the following ten days. Various committees, however, were appointed to investigate conditions. Finally the companies agreed to have a committee of the creditors handle the liquidation of the property of Francis Skinner & Co. Chief among the creditors was Pepperell with over $700,000 outstanding, and second was Laconia with almost $600,000. While banks, insurance companies, and individual creditors had been given collateral security of stocks or acceptances, the manufacturing companies had none. The last-named group lost largely because the sales agent had collected the sales notes, received payment, and then failed before turning over all the cash belonging to the manufacturing companies. Their losses were heavy—we are unable to ascertain how much, even for Pepperell. In 1878 the creditor companies agreed to relieve the surviving partners of their obligations. These partners had lost not only their share in the selling house but also their fortunes, except perhaps in so far as they had placed property in their wives' names or had set aside funds outside their control, such as the trust funds which Francis Skinner had set up for his son and widow.[29]

The failure of Francis Skinner & Co. was not unique during this period. To be sure, several selling houses were dissolved following the death of a partner, but several others had been forced to stop as the result of a panic. In 1857, for example, C. H. Mills & Co. failed, owing large amounts to textile companies.[30] This house was among those caught by the panic, which crippled its customers first and, despite all efforts to assist, carried it down too. In the case of Francis Skinner & Co. we find that during earlier difficult periods the firm had survived while helping its customers. One of the most outstanding examples was a loan of $385,000 to Claflin, Mellen & Co. as a mortgage on the new store on Worth Street in 1862. At the same time Skinner and other creditors agreed to take 70 cents on each dollar of Claflin's obligations. Later Claflin paid back the remaining 30 cents per dollar.[31] In 1869, however, Skinner's assistance to the Barry company was too much for the house to bear in its weakened condition.

Thus, in 1870 the selling house of Francis Skinner & Co. passed out of existence after a life of forty-five years. During these years the house, by subscribing to stock and selling goods, had played an important part in the birth of many companies. For these companies the house took an active interest in getting customers, even during the Civil War when few struggled to get war business. On the whole, although its failure brought losses upon many, the house had contributed to the industrial development of New England. Children and grandchildren of the original subscribers to stock in these manufacturing companies were to benefit from the enterprise and business sagacity of Francis Skinner.

* * *

In this chapter we have followed in some detail the operations of the selling agent of the Pepperell Manufacturing Company. We should not forget that the use of a selling agent reflected to some extent the old system of mercantile capitalism, in which merchants, staying close to their treasure chests and countinghouses, had appointed agents—subordinates—to carry on functions in distant places. The use of an independent partnership as a selling agent left Pepperell free to concentrate on the manufacturing function, after the manner of industrial capitalism, with its specialization and with its large-scale operations which were made possible by new machine techniques. At this time the selling houses, such as Francis Skinner & Co., offered certain services and advantages which the textile companies could not easily provide for themselves. They were aware of the need for financing through outside units, of which the selling agent might be one. Above all, they were conscious of their own shortcomings in the field of marketing, which was becoming highly intricate: they needed advice as to qualities and quantities of goods to produce.

Now it happened, and the circumstance was not unusual, that Francis Skinner, the senior partner in the house which Pepperell chose, had himself risen from the ranks of petty capitalists and not mercantile capitalists, though the spirit and methods of the latter were honored in his life and practice. Indeed, the late eighteenth and nineteenth centuries constituted a period during which these petty capitalists had an opportunity to rise to new heights. Long submerged as dependent factors in mercantile capitalism, they were experiencing opportunities for growth and independence. In fact, they were the human material out of which industrial capitalism was usually created. They often became the manufacturing agents, the operators of railroads and steamships, and the sellers of goods on commission, at wholesale and at retail.

Francis Skinner showed a creative capacity in the field of marketing. He was well equipped to build up his small store into a large specialized house. He became one of the notable industrial capitalists of New England and New York in the marketing field. There were many ways in which he demonstrated his affiliation with the new system of industrial capitalism. One of them was his increasing willingness to invest heavily for a long period in the companies for which he sold. In this respect he differed from many of his predecessors: they invested large sums in the new industries for a short time and then took their capital out to put it into still newer ventures. Skinner also was willing to assist his textile clients in securing working capital, which many of them lacked during their early years of operation. In performing this function the sales agent was rivaling the commercial bank.

Contrary to the Boston practice of staying at home and directing the efforts of agents elsewhere, Skinner exercised his independence of judgment by opening a New York office. He saw that business could be carried on more profitably by one of his partners on the spot than by a sub-agent who received the business of many agents. He also proved his ability by concentrating on jobbers near at hand, whose credit rating he could watch personally, rather than on those scattered over the country. Thus he was strong to weather storms, which blew occasionally over the country and toppled over the weaker firms. Also, although he did business with important exporters, he did not depend on them entirely for markets; he had alternative goods which could be sold to the domestic market. In addition, he thought of ways of making the cotton goods easy to sell. He adopted and maintained a policy of reliable quality: particularly was this true of goods which were exported, such as Pepperell drills stamped with the Dragon.

Skinner's prices and terms were fair. In good times he did not try to bargain too sharply with the buyers but kept prices at about the same levels. He granted the customary periods for credit but with greater certainty of payment than many agents experienced, since most of his customers were close at hand. He shortened the period of credit twice, after the panic of 1857 and during the Civil War, as others did. He seems to have resorted to sale by auction only once between 1850 and 1870, a practice which the regular customers probably did not like. They would have been glad, of course, to buy at lower prices, but in periods of poor business they would have had on hand a large stock of goods bought at higher prices. During the Civil War, Skinner secured government business for the various companies, partly because he made reasonable bids, partly because he knew he could fill the contracts in a short time with the coöperation of the mill agents, and partly because he knew the treasurers could find money with which to tide them over the long period before the government certificates and notes matured.

Skinner, however, could not live forever. For five years after his death in 1865 the partners, inferior in ability or experience, attempted to carry on the business but could not weather the storms of the late 1860's. Their failure in 1870 inflicted losses on the manufacturing companies, but, it is to be remembered, Skinner had assisted in building them up so that in the years to come they could cope with competition from new quarters—first in southern New England and then in the South.

CHAPTER VI

FIRM FINANCIAL FOUNDATION

IN THE PRECEDING chapters we have discussed the treasurer's rôle in the organization of the company, the buying of cotton, and the manufacture and sale of cloth. Although the treasurer played an important part in these operations, his chief function, after all, was the management of the financial affairs of the company.

Before considering this financial function, let us look back to see where treasurers originated. In the ancient world the first treasurers probably held the cash and valuables of temples and cities. In the Middle Ages there were treasurers in ecclesiastical organizations and in towns as well as in the national government. No business was big enough to employ a specialized treasurer much before the thirteenth century. In that century, and ever since, there has been a tendency for business organizations to grow to such proportions that a specialized treasurer has been required, regardless of the name applied to him. One of the early examples of a treasurer in business is found in the regulated companies or foreign trade associations which had a treasury built up primarily from the fees of the merchants who belonged to the association and who traded at their individual risk.

In the sixteenth century joint-stock trading and colonizing companies were created, which were administered by officials and directors. The Virginia Company of 1609 was primarily the "Treasurer and Company," [1] while the Hudson's Bay Company of 1670 was called the "Governor and Company." The charter of 1650 which incorporated Harvard College specified the "President and Fellows." Competition for primacy in business administration was at first between governor and treasurer and later between president and treasurer. In New England, banks and insurance companies emphasized the position of the president, while manufacturing concerns, at least around Boston, singled out the treasurer as the chief executive officer. To be sure, the practice soon developed to omit from the name of the company the title of the chief official, whether president or treasurer. Thus, "the Society for establishing useful Manufactures" was launched in 1791 in New Jersey without any reference to the chief official.

Of course, to the petty capitalist there had been no opportunity to specialize in finance and no need for a treasurer. To the mercantile capitalist finance, accounting, and control were all bound up together and held in the hands of the sedentary merchant. When industrial capitalism got under way, however, particularly when it attained the corporative form, there grew up an array of specialized officials, of whom the treasurer, particularly in New England manufacturing companies, assumed the leadership. In Pepperell to this day the treasurer has been all important, though in recent years the treasurer has also been the president. There could be little room for a chairman of the board, until the office of treasurer and president had been united.

Pepperell's first treasurer, as we have seen, was a man who was admirably suited to his task. William Dwight did an excellent job for the Pepperell Manufacturing Company, where he was the dominant figure from the beginning of the organization in 1850. Although he was also treasurer of the Saco Water Power Co. and the Laconia Co., for a number of years he did not have the wholehearted support of their directors and stockholders. As a result, he did not give so much of his attention to them as to Pepperell.

During the years in which he was treasurer of these companies Dwight did not devote himself exclusively to their management, but continued his activities as trustee of estates and investor of funds. These activities did not impair his effectiveness as treasurer but added to it, since from these connections he could get funds for the companies and information regarding impending changes in business conditions. Also from these activities he supplemented the income which he received as treasurer. He was thus not just a "salary man," a status which was looked down upon during this period, but a "merchant" who specialized in financial operations.

Quite different was the background and experience of the second treasurer, William P. Haines, as we have already seen. He did not have the experience and connections with business in Boston which were necessary in the trying years after the Civil War. He resigned in 1871 and let a more experienced man take over.

COUNTING ROOMS ON STATE STREET

Throughout his terms as treasurer William Dwight kept his counting rooms on State Street, an historic street of Boston which by the middle of the nineteenth century had become the heart of the financial district. At first Dwight had limited space at 61 State Street, in the City Bank Building, over the Granite Bank, where in 1848 he took over the rooms of his predecessor in the office of treasurer of the Saco Water Power Co. and the Laconia Co. In 1850 he signed a new lease for these rooms, agreeing to pay an annual rent of $300 as well as part of the taxes on the building. In the spring of 1855, after he had added the treasurership of the York Manufacturing Co., which he held for a brief time, he moved to the Globe Bank Building at 20 State Street to get more space. Here his annual rent was much higher. Pepperell's share, which may presumably have been a quarter of the total, was $275 annually, with the addition of taxes. By 1865 he was paying $500 a year for Pepperell's share, presumably then a third of the total. From 1866 to 1869 Dwight's successor, William P. Haines, continued in Dwight's counting rooms and then moved to Congress Street, from which in 1870 he moved again to the Sears Building on Washington Street. Although we know nothing about the adequacy of these last two offices, we may surmise that they were smaller than those at 20 State Street; Haines might not have thought so much space was necessary since he was carrying only part of Dwight's former duties.[2]

From various records we gather that these counting rooms

had the customary furnishings. At first Dwight kept the furniture of his predecessor in the Saco Water Power Co. and the Laconia Co., but in four or five years he added new desks and chairs as well as rugs. Two of the new pieces were a large piano desk and a cushioned armchair, for both of which he paid $46; doubtless these were for his own use. He bought a five-foot standing desk for a clerk to use when copying records or posting entries in daybooks, journals, or ledgers. In addition, he secured more chairs, some for his clerks and some for those who came to do business with him.

Dwight's compensation for his services as treasurer increased with the years. In 1851 he received $2,000 from Pepperell, $3,000 from Laconia, and $1,000 from Saco Water Power. In 1852 Pepperell increased its payment to $3,000 and in 1857 to $5,000. In 1856 Saco Water Power went up to $2,000, and in 1864 Laconia increased to $5,000. Thus, when he retired from the treasurership of the two textile companies in 1866 he was earning salaries which totaled $12,000 a year. Just what Haines received as treasurer we do not know, since it was not indicated in the minutes of the meetings of the directors. Presumably it was less than Dwight but more than the $5,000 a year which Haines had received as Pepperell's mill agent.

In the counting rooms, as was customary, Dwight and Haines employed only men or boys, even for the duties of sweeping and cleaning. In 1850 Dwight had two clerks, but as the work increased he added to the number. By 1855 he had three, and a year later four. At the time of his retirement from office he had only three clerks for the business of the three companies. Haines probably continued with the same number, although the evidence has been destroyed.[3]

At least one of these clerks remained for a long period, rising to a position of responsibility. This was Spencer W. Richardson, who served from 1852 to 1866. At the time of Dwight's retirement he turned to setting up a partnership with two of Dwight's sons for a brokerage business and later, separating from the Dwights, he became a member of Richardson, Hill & Co., which grew to be one of the largest brokerage houses in the country. For his services as clerk in Dwight's three companies his compensation had increased from $400 in 1852 to $3,000 in 1865. In addition, he received fees as clerk of the boards of directors. From Pepperell he received $100 a year to which, when he left in 1866, was added a bonus of $500.*

All the clerks carried out the details of the work assigned to them by the treasurer. They copied letters and various other records, made necessary mathematical computations, made out bills, and posted entries in the appropriate books. To us, a century later, these duties seem to have been tediously and uneconomically performed since a girl at a typewriter or a calculating machine could now do much more than two or three clerks did then.

A committee of the stockholders audited the records of the treasurer in the counting rooms in Boston. How much this committee did we do not know. We do know that in the 1850's each man received $10 annually for his services.[5] In 1863 the members of this committee were given authority to appoint other persons if they themselves were unable to act. It was not until 1870 that they were authorized by the stockholders "to employ an expert in case they were unable to attend to the duty in person." Since this authorization was to apply for the following fiscal year, which is beyond the first period of Pepperell's operations, we can say that no outside expert audited the company's books from 1850 through 1870.

The simplicity of the treasurer's counting rooms is shown by the low charges which were involved. The treasurer kept an account called "Incidental Expense Account of the Treasurer." Besides Pepperell's apportionment for the salaries of the treasurer and clerks and for the rent of the counting rooms, this account included only a few expenses, for such things as supplies, trips to Biddeford, advertising meetings of the stockholders, postage and telegraph charges, and subscriptions to

* Among the others in the countinghouse were a number who stayed only briefly; noteworthy among these were Josiah Bardwell, William Dwight, Jr., Daniel A. Dwight, and John C. Bancroft, Dwight's nephew and son of the historian, George Bancroft. These young men were paid little: in 1852, for example, Daniel A. Dwight earned $10 a month.[4]

Pepperell Manufacturing Company.

Certificate No. 55 Shares No. 353 to 614

Be it known, That William Dwight is Proprietor of Two hundred & Sixty Two Shares in the Corporate Property of the **Pepperell Manufacturing Company,** numbered Three hundred & Fifty Three to Six hundred & Fourteen inclusive subject to all assessments, regulations, and conditions of said Corporation, which Shares are transferable by assignment on the back hereof, recorded by the Clerk of said Corporation, and upon delivery of such assignment of this Certificate, a new Certificate or Certificates shall be issued, according to the interest of the parties.

In witness whereof, The Seal of the Corporation is hereunto affixed, this Seventeenth day of September Anno Domini one thousand eight hundred and fifty two.

J. Hooper PRESIDENT.

Attest, William Dwight TREASURER.

STOCK CERTIFICATE, 1852

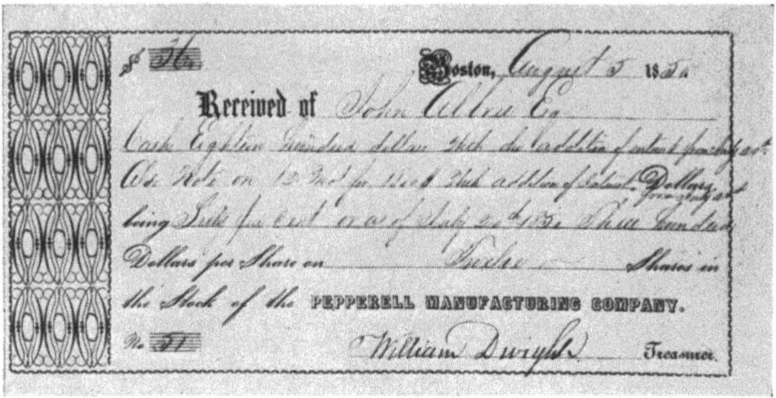

$ 36. Boston, August 5 1850.

Received of John Albree Esq.

Dollars

being

Dollars per Share on Twelve Shares in the Stock of the PEPPERELL MANUFACTURING COMPANY.

No. 51

William Dwight Treasurer.

ASSESSMENT RECEIPT, 1850

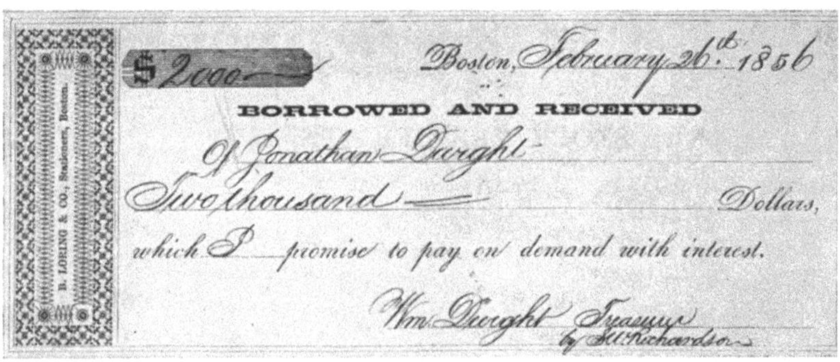

B. LORING & CO., Stationers, Boston.

$2000 Boston, February 26th 1856

BORROWED AND RECEIVED

Of Jonathan Dwight

Two thousand Dollars,

which I promise to pay on demand with interest.

Wm Dwight Treasurer
by H. Richardson

TREASURER'S DEMAND NOTE, 1856

newspapers and societies. Even when these charges were highest, in 1857–58, as shown in Appendix 35, they were only about $7,700 or .6 per cent of gross sales. Seven years later, in 1864–65, they were only $7,300, or about .2 per cent of gross sales. These seem small amounts and low percentages for the important work performed by the treasurer and his clerks.

Thus, unostentatiously, Dwight had set up his counting rooms in Boston. There he carried on the financial work for three or four companies with the assistance of a few clerks. There the directors met occasionally to approve Dwight's actions. For a time his successor, Haines, kept the offices on State Street and moved, twice within a year, to other less commodious offices.

OBTAINING SUBSCRIPTIONS TO STOCK

In the counting rooms in Boston, William Dwight drew up plans for securing payments by the subscribers to stock. He did not demand payment in full at once, but by installments. Although among his subscribers were members of some of the wealthiest families in New England, he knew that it would be difficult for them to get large lump sums. They would find it much easier to apply dividends received from other investments towards payments for stock over a long period of time.

For the subscribers to 2,000 shares of stock Dwight planned a system of conveniently timed payments for the first $300, the next $100, and the final $100 per share. Those who prepaid were given interest; those who lagged were charged interest. Originally Dwight arranged that the first assessment on the stock, $300 of the eventual $500, could be paid for in five installments by notes which matured in 4, 8, 12, 16, and 20 months. Some of the subscribers paid in full in the summer of 1850; others did not finish their payments until after the due date, March 20, 1852.[6] With most of this money Dwight met the obligation to pay for the property in Biddeford. He had reserved some for the further equipping of the mills.

Before this first $300 per share had been paid in, the directors recommended and the stockholders voted that the next $100 per share become payable. It was arranged that the stockholders could pay this in installments, two of $50 each, by giving notes payable three and six months after January 12, 1852. This capital was needed for equipping the mills and for current purposes. In July of 1852 the directors voted that, to subscribers who had paid their $400 per share, certificates of stock should be issued; this was done on September 17, 1852. At that time the stockholders, if they so desired, could transfer their holdings to others. Comparatively few availed themselves of this opportunity, since it was already becoming evident that the Pepperell venture was going to be a profitable one.

For a time Dwight had to be content with the subscription of $800,000 by the stockholders. He knew, however, that he would need more capital when all the proposed mills had been built. On March 14, 1856, he obtained from the Legislature of Maine authorization to increase the stock to $1,200,000.[7] It seemed reasonable that he would need $400,000 for erecting, equipping, and operating another mill. On June 9, 1856, the directors voted to call a special meeting of the stockholders to see about assessing themselves further. At this meeting, held June 19, 1856, the stockholders voted to assess only $200,000. Apparently this was all the directors recommended. At least, we can infer that there was no heated contest at this meeting, since only three local people attended. A few days later, the directors voted that $100 per share be paid on August 2, 1856. This concluded the contribution to capital by assessments of the stockholders during this period.

By the year 1857 the stockholders had completed their payments of $500 a share for the stock. But these payments did not even cover the investment in mills, machinery, and real estate in Biddeford. Dwight had therefore to seek other sources of funds with which to carry on the operations of the company. Thus did business history repeat itself: so much of the resources of the stockholders go into fixed capital that there is little or none left for working capital.

SECURING LOANS

William Dwight was able to supplement the permanent capital obtained from the stockholders by loans of three types—

long-term loans, notes payable on demand, and short-term loans. Since theoretically no sharp distinction can be drawn between the types, we have followed the classification of the treasurer. We see that long-term loans, or "permanent" loans as he called them, generally ran for at least one year, although some were for six months. In many cases they were renewed for additional periods. In several cases also, against the notation for long-term loans in his book of notes payable and receivable, were the words, "For 12 months or on call, 30 days' notice." Thus the three types were mixed, and only the treasurer's knowledge of the character of the lender could determine to which category a particular loan belonged.[8]

The sources for these loans were of five general types—savings banks, commercial banks, bankers and brokers, miscellaneous companies, and individuals and trustees with money to lend. All except the bankers and brokers made long-term loans, although in the case of Massachusetts savings banks, Dwight, as we have already seen, had to secure the money for Pepperell by the use of the names of Francis Skinner & Co., Francis Skinner, and himself. In the case of insurance companies he had to give the additional guarantee of Francis Skinner & Co. and himself. All five types of lenders made money available payable on demand. All except the miscellaneous corporations loaned on a short-term basis. Unfortunately we cannot get the total annual amount of each type of loan by each type of lender, since our source, notes payable, does not give complete information concerning the dates when the loans were repaid. We can, however, say that apparently Dwight relied heavily on those with whom he had business or family ties.

Long-term loans were the most desirable of the three types from the point of view of security, since they were written for definite periods of time and often renewed for additional periods. All evidence, however, points to their having borne the maximum legal rate of interest in Massachusetts, 6 per cent. Nevertheless large loans of this type were available. Unfortunately, because of the scarcity of capital, he could not rely upon this type to the exclusion of notes payable on demand. For 1857, from the book of notes payable and receivable, I have made an estimate of $200,000 outstanding of this type. During the Civil War all these loans were paid back, at a time when decreased operations required less working capital. In April of 1862, for example, Dwight paid two promissory notes owed to the Salem Savings Bank, drawn up first in 1859 for twelve months. The treasurer of the bank did not welcome this payment and wrote Dwight that he was sorry that the latter wished to pay his two notes. In the following years, 1863 through 1870, the treasurer secured few long-term loans. Evidently for a time Dwight sought other means to finance the long period before maturity of government paper.

William Dwight apparently was very wary about giving notes payable on demand. These loans, bearing an interest charge from 4 to 6 per cent, were safe enough in normal times but they were causes of trouble at times of crisis, when the lenders demanded immediate payment. Generally Dwight relied for this type of loan upon his business associates, friends, or members of his family, whose business affairs he knew well. He did secure money from commercial banks, which in 1857 demanded immediate payment. He obtained the necessary money by a means which we shall discuss in the following section. In 1862 Dwight was free of notes payable on demand, but in the following four years he again secured loans of this type. Apparently, his successor, Haines, did none of this type of borrowing.

Dwight relied to some extent on the third type of loan, the short-term loan, although again we cannot tell to what extent. These loans aided in financing the peak in cotton buying during the winter. In 1865 Dwight secured in all over $1,000,000 in loans of four and six months, and in addition Francis Skinner & Co. secured about the same amount. These figures are extreme, revealing the critical need for capital when funds had been tied up for some time in government paper. In the following years it appears that the selling house continued to assist in this type of loan, although in 1869–70 Haines secured short-term loans for slightly over $700,000. Interest on this type of loan, from evidence which remains, varied from 5 to 6 per cent.

A total picture of long-term loans, notes payable on demand,

and short-term loans outstanding can be secured from the figures for notes payable given among the liabilities in Appendix 32. We see that for the first four years they averaged about $300,000 and for the following nine, when the three mills were in operation, they averaged about $700,000, ranging widely from none in December, 1862, to a high of almost $1,900,000 two years later. Presumably in the following periods the notes payable declined with the resumption of civilian business.

The notes payable in this first period present graphically the ability, ingenuity, and wisdom of a treasurer in securing capital with which to carry on operations. It should also be noted that he preferred to get money from many sources so that no outsider was in a position to dictate the policies of the company.

SELLING COTTON

Twice William Dwight took an extraordinary step to obtain funds with which to carry on operations—he sold cotton already in storage in Biddeford. In September, 1857, Dwight asked Haines, the mill agent, to send him some bales of cotton "in the most expeditious & least noticeable way." Dwight shipped 800 bales of cotton to Liverpool in the latter half of 1857, for which he received 13.425 cents a pound on the average; this was above the average cost of cotton consumed in Biddeford during the preceding six months. This sale, which brought in cash of about $50,000, enabled Dwight to pay off notes payable on demand, which he was being pressed to pay. In 1862, when orders for cotton goods looked uncertain and many sales notes could not be collected, Dwight again sold bales of cotton from the supply in Biddeford, as we have seen in a previous chapter. During the summer of 1862 he sold 1,250 bales, which resulted in a profit of over $50,000. Dwight sold this cotton to buyers and treasurers of textile companies, twenty-one in all. Other companies in the United States probably were doing likewise at this time when prospects of manufacturing seemed doubtful and when the price of cotton was rising steadily. Of course the companies which obtained government business in the following months regretted parting with any cotton, since they had to buy at a still higher price. In the case of Pepperell, which had a large inventory on hand, the sale can be justified as a hedge against possible difficulties.[9]

DISCOUNTING SALES NOTES

William Dwight reduced the total needs of working capital by taking the sales notes received from the selling agent to banks and others to be discounted a few months before they were due. This means of shortening the time between the selling of goods and the receipt of payment customarily was resorted to during the period of long credits. Dwight took most of them to institutions in Boston. The Massachusetts Bank was the first discounter of Pepperell's notes and the largest from 1851 to 1862, when it stopped discounting regularly for Pepperell. This change can be explained partly on the grounds of notes for shorter periods and partly by the handling of most of the notes by the selling house. During the first eleven years of discounting, Dwight also took notes to the New England Bank and about twenty other banks, some of which discounted fairly regularly and some only occasionally. Most of these banks were in Boston, but there was a scattering elsewhere: in Springfield and New Bedford, Massachusetts, Manchester, New Hampshire, and Biddeford, Maine.[10]

In addition to discounting by the banks, called the "legitimate" way, since the maximum rate of legal interest could not be exceeded, Dwight found others who would discount Pepperell's sales notes. He had many dealings with bankers and brokers as well as with individuals with private capital, who discounted notes regularly or when it was especially profitable, as in 1856 and 1857.

The most dependable private discounter was Ebenezer Francis, who made a practice of this type of transaction. In the early 1850's he was credited with a fortune of $3,500,000 and was said to be the richest man in New England.[11] From 1853 through 1857 he took much of Pepperell's paper. After his death the trustees of his estate continued the practice, quite regularly in 1859 but less frequently thereafter. Dwight evidently could deal with Francis, a shrewd bargainer, who at one time was said to have let over $100,000 lie idle rather than take loans at a lower rate of interest than he wanted. There were a number of brokerage houses, about eight in Boston, which discounted Pepperell's sales notes. Among them was the house of Blake, Ward & Co. and its succeeding partnerships, Blake, Howe & Co. and Blake Bros. & Co., which discounted the notes quite regularly from 1853 through 1861. Another was Lee, Higginson & Co., which took the paper regularly from 1855 to 1862, except for a break in 1860.

From the balance sheets which Dwight made out each six months we can get the total amounts of notes receivable outstanding, as given in Appendix 32. There is much less fluctuation in the totals than one might expect in view of the changes in business conditions. At the end of 1857, for example, the treasurer had on hand $380,000 of these notes. This total was not reached again except in June of 1861, when it was $406,000. These highs were caused not by increased business but by the increase in undiscounted notes which the treasurer had on hand. The lows in the following periods, however, were brought about by a decline in business and the assignment of many claims to the suspense account. Typically the treasurer had on hand only about $150,000 of sales notes, about one-eighth of average annual sales from 1852 through 1865.

No accurate measure can be obtained throughout the first period of charges for discounting the sales notes. According to such scraps of information as we find and the comments of a commission stockbroker, Joseph G. Martin,[12] the banks' rates varied from 3 per cent to the maximum limit of 6 per cent. The rates of other discounters varied with business conditions, seasonal and cyclical. In the summer of 1852, for example, Ebenezer Francis discounted the paper at 5¼ per cent. In the spring of 1853 we find that Blake, Ward & Co. took Pepperell's notes with a 10 per cent discount. From the spring of 1853 to the summer of 1857, rates for Pepperell's paper varied between 6 and 12 per cent. The low was reached in June of 1855 and May of 1857. The high was reached in November and December of 1855, when rates in Boston were from 10 to 15 per cent.

Discount rates reached much higher figures during the panic in the fall of 1857, which reached a climax on October 13 and which declined slowly in the following two months of suspension of payments by Boston banks. Since cash vouchers are missing, we cannot follow in detail Pepperell's transactions at this time. According to a stockbroker, rates in Boston increased from 12 per cent in September to 36 per cent in October and November, from which point they dropped to 9 per cent in December. We have a record of an attempt by Josiah Bardwell to dispose of a note written by Claflin, Mellen & Co. in September. On the twenty-second Bardwell in New York wrote Dwight that he could not dispose of the note at any rate. On the following day he wrote again, describing the note as "too large and too short for these times," and saying, "Strong names can be had for 3 per cent a month." [13] Apparently he continued to try to dispose of the paper for the next few days, with no luck.

During most of the following three years, rates of discount were low, with paper not plentiful. Probably Dwight was able to have the banks take care of most of his needs. In the fall of 1860 we have records of rates of discounting by brokers. In the midst of tension over politics the rates rose rapidly, and in December reached 18 per cent. Blake Bros. & Co. discounted some of Pepperell's sales notes at this high rate. In 1861, business was stagnant and rates were low. On the first of August, Dwight took some notes for discounting to Lee, Higginson & Co. at 5½ per cent, and eight days later to Blake Bros. & Co. at 5 per cent. At the end of December, 1861, the banks suspended specie payments and did not resume them during the remainder of the period we are considering.

From 1862 to 1865, brokers took United States Certificates and Notes a few months after the date of maturity. How much they paid for them, we do not know. For the remainder of the first period we can learn nothing about the rate of discounting sales notes from Pepperell's records. From records of interest rates in Boston we find that there were fluctuations from 3 per cent in the summer of 1867 to 15 per cent in November of 1869.

During the 1860's Massachusetts at last modified her laws concerning interest. In 1865 the treasurer of the Commonwealth was authorized to borrow during the year at rates of interest approved by the governor. Shortly thereafter, the State legalized borrowing by the government or by individuals at rates not exceeding 7.3 per cent a year. In 1867 the State made it lawful to pay or receive discounts at any rate, provided that any rate higher than 6 per cent was recorded in writing, if the case was taken to the courts.[14]

Although we cannot find a complete record of discounts and rates of interest throughout this period, we can get a measure of the total interest on all types of loans and discounts of notes because the treasurer kept such an account, which is given in Appendix 35. We find considerable fluctuation in these figures, from $267 in 1863 to $114,000 in 1865. In the latter year, however, these charges were less than 3 per cent of gross sales, while in fairly normal years they were about 5 per cent. In 1857 they averaged about 7 per cent of gross sales.

With the reduction in the length of credit for sales in the last part of this period, the discounting of sales notes was no longer the problem that it had been earlier. But it had been one of the treasurer's duties for many years, helping as it did to lessen the total requirement of working capital.

DELAY IN PAYING BILLS

According to the custom of the times, William Dwight was not liable for the payment of many of the bills until a month to six months after they had been made out. This was true of drafts upon him by his cotton buyers in the South as well as by the mill agent in Biddeford. For various other supplies and services he was given a period of credit much longer than was to become customary in later decades. By postponing the meeting of bills he was able to shorten the period between payment for cotton and receipt of cash on notes for the sales of finished goods. This practice, then, reduced to some extent the total amount of working capital necessary for operations.

Most important of the bills Dwight had to pay were drafts for the purchase of cotton. Drafts from the South were usually payable a stated number of days after sight—30, 60, 70, 90, or 100 days. Dwight marked "Accepted" on the first copy of the draft which he received and sent it back to the South, where cash generally could be obtained by the drawer from the local banks.[15] Since purchasing was concentrated in about half the year, Dwight had seasonal need for funds; he secured these in the various ways we have discussed. During and after the Civil War buying cotton was not so seasonal as earlier, since much of the cotton was purchased in small lots throughout the year in the northern markets. But because the price of cotton rose to great heights during the war and did not drop to the prewar level in the following five years, the treasurer still had problems of finding capital with which to meet his obligations.

Next in importance were the drafts which the mill agent in Biddeford sent to the treasurer for acceptance. They ran from a few days to six months after sight. Dwight accepted them, and Haines took them to the Biddeford Bank for discounting. Generally Haines drew round amounts, such as $3,000 and $5,000 to meet the monthly payrolls. Just before the time of maturity of these notes, Dwight deposited funds in the Biddeford Bank to cover them.[16]

There were many other bills which the treasurer did not pay until several months after they had been rendered. Among them were bills for machinery, coal, oil, and bleaching. In 1853, for example, a bill of about $1,300 from the Lowell Bleachery ran for five months. Dwight kept a series of books with entries for the amounts which he was obligated to pay each month, for without such a system it would have been difficult for him to see in advance just what his monthly requirements would be.[17]

By all these methods—subscriptions to stock, loans, sale of cotton, discounting of sales notes, and use of periods of grace in the payment of bills—William Dwight sought to provide adequate capital for Pepperell's operation. Whether he did a better job than the treasurers of other companies we cannot tell until similar studies have been made. Whether he was peculiar in relying so heavily on his family and business associates for funds with which to operate the company we cannot tell, but we may surmise that he was fortunate in being able to do so and that Pepperell was among the fortunate companies in this period in having such a treasurer.

ESTABLISHING A SOUND FINANCIAL STRUCTURE

With funds secured from stockholders and by loans of various types, as well as with reserve funds and other surplus, William Dwight built up over the years the capital available to Pepperell. He invested these funds wisely in buildings and equipment and kept close watch over inventories and sales notes. He thus built a sound financial structure, which weathered the storm in 1870 and which continued to attract capable men to its management.

Dwight had a policy of setting up reserves against possible future emergencies and against known reductions in value. Previously we have mentioned his policy of setting aside each year 2 per cent of gross sales as an insurance and guarantee fund for sales. This provision was at a higher rate than experience demanded, as the building up of the fund, given in Appendix 32, shows. But until the war business with reduced risks was undertaken, Dwight continued the same rate of reserves. In 1864 he reduced the previous balance from over $180,000 to $20,000. We do not know what happened after civilian business had been resumed because the figures for December, 1865, through June, 1870, are missing.

By an apportionment from current profits each year, beginning in 1852, Dwight also built up a repair and reserve fund for buildings, which reached $1,000,000 in 1865. There seems to have been no rule for the additions; they depended upon the amount of profits. In 1858, as a most unusual procedure, he drew upon this reserve to maintain other balances and dividends. Unfortunately, after June, 1865, the series of figures for this fund is not available. This earmarking of part of the profits each year for taking care of depreciation of mills and machinery was judicious. In time, considerable amounts would have to be spent on renovation and repairs. But his policy of reserves meant that each year little was accumulated in the profit and loss balance. Dividends, therefore, had to come usually from current profits. Since on the whole these twenty years were prosperous ones, Dwight had no difficulty in maintaining this policy. But if the company had had several years of little or no profit, there is a question as to whether he could have continued his practices, with stockholders perhaps pressing for dividends and with below-par stock discouraging the loaning of funds.

Already we have discussed many items on the asset side of the balance sheet. Dwight was concerned over the levels of inventories of cotton and cloth. He followed the current practice of valuing inventories at actual cost. This procedure resulted in large fluctuations in profits as well as in assets when prices changed rapidly. The only moderating actions, usual during this period, which he might have followed would have been reductions in production or in purchase of cotton, of which we see only few examples in this period. On the whole, the treasurer and agent tried to produce as much as possible because markets were expanding.

William Dwight made Pepperell strong by building up its capital during years in which it was not easy to get money cheaply and safely. He did not waste this money, but spent it carefully for the things which he thought essential. Fortunately the company also made large profits and paid good dividends, as we shall see shortly.

REPORTS TO THE STOCKHOLDERS

At the annual meetings of the stockholders of the Pepperell Manufacturing Company in Biddeford, William Dwight and then William P. Haines usually had news of profitable operations to report. Few of the stockholders, however, bothered to attend these meetings; as long as they received dividends, they were willing to remain at home on annual meeting day.

How much the stockholders would have learned at these annual meetings, we do not know. According to the bylaws, the treasurer was "to render an account of his doings to the Stockholders at the annual meeting." All that was recorded in the minutes of these meetings was that the report of the treasurer was read to the gathering, and, on motion, it was voted that it be accepted. Probably the treasurer gave summary figures of assets and liabilities and of income, expenses, profits, and dividends. He might have shown the growing strength of the company as well as the yearly profits, which from 1853 through 1870 exceeded $100,000 a year, except in 1857. In fact, in three years, Dwight and Haines might have stated that profits exceeded $500,000, or more than 50 per cent of the capital stock. Certainly these were satisfying figures from which the directors declared generous dividends.

Without attending these meetings the stockholders knew that dividend days came twice a year, on the first of August and February. Some made special trips to Boston to collect their dividends personally at the treasurer's office, and some authorized others to collect the money. The first dividend, payable August 2, 1852, was $16 on each share for which $400 had been paid in. In each of the half-year periods through August, 1856, the stockholders were given the same amount. Then from February, 1857, through February, 1859, they received $20 a share, on which by that time they had paid $500. There was one exception to this regularity: in February, 1858, no dividend was declared, and this was the only passing of a semiannual dividend in the first twenty years. On the following seven dividend dates dividends were slightly larger, $25 a share twice and $30 a share five times.

Dividends fluctuated more during the latter part of the Civil War and the five years following. From 1863 through 1866 they were irregular in amount—pleasingly so to the stockholders. During these four years they received dividends totaling $1,025 a share, or an average of $256.25 a year. During the following four years they received smaller amounts, $385 a share, or an average of $96.25 a year. No wonder that the stockholders were content to let the treasurer and directors continue their policies while such dividends were the result. The stockholders in these first twenty years received a total of $1,834 a share, or, from 1852 through 1870, an average annual return of nearly 20 per cent on their investment.

This excellent dividend record was reflected in the prices at which the stock sold, given in Appendix 38. If a stockholder had wished to sell his shares, he could have made a profit at any

TABLE 3

DIVIDENDS, 1852–70[a]

Day Payable	Amount per Share	Day Payable	Amount per Share	Day Payable	Amount per Share
Aug. 2, 1852.....	$16	Feb. 1, 1859	$20	Feb. 1, 1865	$50
Feb. 1, 1853.....	16	Aug. 1, 1859	25	Aug. 1, 1865	50
Aug. 1, 1853.....	16	Feb. 1, 1860	25	Feb. 1, 1866	150
Feb. 1, 1854.....	16	Aug. 1, 1860	30	Aug. 1, 1866	75
Aug. 1, 1854.....	16	Feb. 1, 1861	30	Feb. 1, 1867	60
Feb. 1, 1855.....	16	Aug. 1, 1861	30	Aug. 1, 1867	50
Aug. 1, 1855.....	16	Feb. 1, 1862	30	Feb. 3, 1868	25
Feb. 1, 1856.....	16	July 18, 1862	30	Aug. 1, 1868	50
Aug. 1, 1856.....	16	Jan. 1, 1863	250	Feb. 1, 1869	50
Feb. 2, 1857.....	20	Feb. 2, 1863	100	Aug. 2, 1869	50
Aug. 3, 1857.....	20	Aug. 1, 1863	100	Feb. 1, 1870	50
Feb. 1858.....	(none)	Feb. 1, 1864	100	Aug. 22, 1870	50
Aug. 2, 1858.....	20	Aug. 1, 1864	150		

[a] Par Value $400 from 1852 to 1856 and $500 from 1857 to 1870.

Source: MS, PMC, Directors' records, July 17, 1852–Aug. 16, 1870.

time, except in 1857 and 1858, when the low points were $400 and $425, respectively. If he had wished to sell his shares shortly after the Civil War, he could have obtained $1,378 a share.

As far as we can discover, the stockholders of the Pepperell Manufacturing Company did not receive any printed reports from the treasurer during this period. Perhaps we should rejoice in this lack, since from the collection in Baker Library of annual reports of other companies, we learn that a printed report in this period usually indicated trouble.

In the case of the Pepperell Manufacturing Company during its first period of operations, after the months of difficulty in securing subscribers to stock until the summer of 1870, there was apparently not a single controversy among the stockholders to mar the tranquillity of operations. Of course there may have been some which were not reported. In September of 1870 there was certainly cause for strife because of the loss which the company suffered through the failure of the sales agent. Some directors may have felt that others were to blame. In the fall of 1870 many of the directors stepped out of office. At the annual meeting in September three were not reëlected—William Dwight, Samuel Hooper, and Josiah Bardwell. Later in the fall William Parsons and J. J. Dixwell resigned. This left only Thomas Wigglesworth and William P. Haines of the old board. Wigglesworth kept his position for many years. From August until the end of November, 1870, Haines was ill and his duties were carried on by two treasurers pro tempore.*

Just which day and month we should call the end of the first period in the history of Pepperell is not definitely set. Many occasions could be chosen: the change in the board of directors on September 6; the failure of the sales house, announced on September 12; the choice of another sales house on October 12; or the resignation of the treasurer on January 23, 1871. Since the change in the management of the company began at the annual meeting of the stockholders on September 6, 1870, and other changes occurred soon thereafter, let us call this date the end of one period and the beginning of the second.

REVIEW OF THE FIRST PERIOD, 1844–1870

In the first chapter we saw how William Dwight, with a charter granted in 1844, organized a company in 1850 to complete the plan for textile mills near the falls of the Saco River in Biddeford, Maine. The location was well chosen, with a stream to furnish water power as well as accommodation for ocean-going ships, in a community where textile enterprises had been carried on for several decades. Pepperell was fortunate, during a recession in business, in securing its property for manufacturing at a fraction of its actual cost from the Saco Water Power Co.

In the second chapter we turned aside to follow the previous history of the cotton textile industry in the United States. After a number of unsuccessful attempts to obtain machinery which

* In January of 1871 Haines gave up his duties in Boston. On January 21 the directors accepted his resignation as director; on January 23 they accepted it as treasurer.

could run by power, at last the Englishman, Samuel Slater, with the aid of Yankee merchants, set up machinery for spinning in southern New England. For a decade thereafter only a few spinning mills were established, but during the years of little or no trade with Europe many such mills sprang up on small streams throughout New England and the middle Atlantic States. Their owners carried on spinning and sold their yarn to others to make into cloth in their homes or in weaving sheds. In 1815, when trade was resumed with England, the cotton cloth thus produced could not compete in price with the English. Many of the small mills shut down.

Fortunately for American industry, during the War of 1812 a group of Yankee merchants started a large textile company in Waltham, Massachusetts, in which all operations in the production of cloth were carried on. These merchants were successful in their first attempt, and they and others set up additional large mills on the big rivers of New England. Aided by a protective tariff, they made these mills profitable. In these large companies the treasurer was the chief and only important officer. He delegated some responsibilities to a so-called agent, who ran the mills. He delegated other responsibilities to an outside company, called the sales agent, which sold the goods on commission. In Boston the treasurer himself carried on the financial functions and directed the purchase of cotton.

In the third chapter we followed the steps which Pepperell's treasurer took to get raw materials for the mills in Biddeford. We saw his dependence on those closely related to him, by blood or association, for the purchasing of more and more of the supply of cotton for the mills. During the Civil War, from necessity much more of the cotton than previously was secured in the North, in New York and Boston. In the years after the war the former pattern of cotton buying was not resumed, and cotton continued to be purchased in the North.

In the fourth chapter we examined the operation of the mills in Biddeford. The agent was a capable man, drawn from the petty capitalist class of New England, who coöperated with the treasurer in carrying out the latter's policies. The agent hired Yankees from northern New England as mill employees, who were willing to work for long hours at the prevailing rates of pay. Many of them were only temporary employees, working for a few years and then returning to their homes in the country. In Biddeford many of the unmarried girls lived in the company's boarding houses and others were accommodated in private houses in the town. The men employees occupied houses in the town, some of which were owned by the Saco Water Power Co. Perhaps as a result of these living arrangements, there were no sharp divisions between types of workers; all worked harmoniously together. Therefore, the mill agent was able to get their coöperation in producing an excellent quality of cotton goods at costs which enabled the company to compete successfully with others for a market.

In the fifth chapter we followed the selling of cotton goods by a selling agent on commission. We saw that Pepperell's agent, Francis Skinner & Co., was among the leaders in many respects. This partnership sought profitable markets for Pepperell's goods at home and abroad. Most of the domestic buyers were concentrated in the two cities, Boston and New York, where the Skinner agency had offices. The buyers for the export markets were also in these cities. They sent Pepperell's drills and jeans to many parts of the world, particularly to China and India. During the Civil War Francis Skinner & Co. got government business for Pepperell, so that its mills continued to operate profitably. In the following years the selling house kept the mills busy filling orders for both the domestic and export markets. Unfortunately for both Pepperell and the selling house, the latter developed weaknesses which led to its failure in 1870.

In the present chapter we have followed the activities of the treasurer of the company, particularly the financial transactions, which he carried on in his counting rooms in Boston. For sixteen years William Dwight acted as treasurer, not only of Pepperell, but also of Laconia and the Saco Water Power Co. For a few years he was also treasurer of the York Manufacturing Co.

We have noted that William Dwight secured capital for the company from individuals and institutions which were bound to him by family or business ties. Not receiving enough from these sources, he had to take the sales notes received from the sales agent to banks, bankers, brokers, and others to be discounted, as many other treasurers of the time did. Interest and discounts cut down profits, but not seriously. Dwight built up the capital structure so well that the company could survive the trying year of 1870.

William Dwight was able to report successful operations to the stockholders and to pay them substantial dividends without weakening the financial structure of the company. These stockholders, however, took little part in the affairs of the company. The directors, even, did little more than approve the treasurer's actions. Even in 1870, when the company lost much through the failure of its selling agent, the directors did not stir up a tempest but withdrew so that a new group and a new treasurer could direct the company.

Therefore, on a depressing note we end the chronicle of the first and successful period of Pepperell's long life. We know, however, that this depression was but temporary. Pepperell had been fortunate in its first group of men—William Dwight, the treasurer, who directed all activities and managed the financial affairs; William P. Haines, the mill agent, who ran the mills in Biddeford; and Francis Skinner, the senior partner of the selling house. The second group in office, from 1865 or 1866 to 1870, proved less capable; however, they were willing to step out and let others carry on the company, as we shall see in the following pages.

Part II

MATURITY, 1870–1924

CHAPTER VII

HORIZONTAL AND VERTICAL EXPANSION

WE HAVE NOW arrived at the middle years of Pepperell's career. Often this part of a company's existence is a time of danger, for the early impetus has passed and established policies and methods have been accepted as natural and proper if not inevitable. In addition, this middle period brought serious readjustments to the cotton textile industry as a whole and to the system of industrial capitalism of which the industry and Pepperell were a part. As if this synchronization of troubles was not enough, there was a steep decline in prices following the Civil War which did not reach its lowest point until the last years of the nineteenth century.

In a sense, the whole story of these 54 years should be told against the background of the industry, of industrial capitalism, and of changing business conditions as a whole. From the immediate standpoint of presenting Pepperell's own history there would be much to be said for weaving Pepperell into the closely woven fabric of the times. There are two difficulties in such a procedure, however, and they are decisive. First of all, a greatly extended treatment would be required, and, secondly, it is more important at this stage of business history to present the detailed story of individual companies. Some day these detailed stories of many units will constitute the basis of a well-authenticated business history of the United States. I shall therefore not write the general into the special but record the special so that the general may some day be richer and more revealing.*

* If the reader should have little interest in the details about expansion, he may find a summary on pages 147–150 of this chapter.

A NEW GROUP TAKES OVER THE MANAGEMENT

In the autumn of 1870 the crisis which occurred in the life of the Pepperell Manufacturing Company shook the local public's faith in several of the directors and officers but did not damage seriously the standing of the company. All but one of the former group of men stepped out and allowed a new group to take over, as shown in Appendix 9. These new men, of outstanding character and ability, again built up Pepperell to a high place in the industry.

Among those responsible for Pepperell's record in these years were the treasurers. Six of them during this period brought various backgrounds, experiences, and personalities into the company's life. We shall take a brief glance at each.

The first of these treasurers was John Adams Blanchard, who for many years had been a partner in a wholesale dry goods firm in Boston, first in Blanchard & Blodgett and then in Blanchard, Converse & Co. By 1856 he had retired from the latter and for ten years he carried on business alone as a merchant.[1] Blanchard had been one of Pepperell's stockholders for ten years before his election to the board of directors at the annual meeting in September, 1870. On the following day he was made treasurer pro tempore. Almost immediately he was confronted with difficult problems, since Francis Skinner & Co. failed a few days later. Blanchard carried on these duties until the end of November, when Haines was well enough to assume them again briefly. At that time Blanchard was elected president, a position which he held for four months. While still president he was elected treasurer, following Haines' resignation at the end of January, 1871. Blanchard continued as treasurer of Pepperell and also of Laconia from this time until his death on December 16, 1872. Although his period of service was short, he helped the company over a trying period. He demonstrated by his willingness to hold office that he thought matters could be straightened out without too much trouble.

The second treasurer, Edward Wainwright Codman, was also a Boston business man. For six years after his graduation

GEORGE DEXTER
Treasurer, 1877–1901

ROBERT McARTHUR
Mill Agent, 1887–1910

from Harvard College in 1854, he was a merchant on Central Wharf. In 1861 he entered his father's firm, Edward Codman & Co., dealers in wine, where he remained until 1868. Then for several years he evidently was in business alone.[2] Thus by inheritance and training Codman belonged to the old mercantile group of Boston, and he had had little acquaintance with the immediate problems of a treasurer of a cotton textile company. Elected to office in both Pepperell and Laconia at the end of 1872 or at the beginning of the following year, a most difficult time in the business world, he found himself beset with many complexities. Troubles arose in Laconia with which he could not cope. In August of 1877 he sent in his resignation to that company and, since it was customary for the same man to be treasurer of both Laconia and Pepperell, he also gave up his office in Pepperell in September.

In the selection of the third treasurer of this period Pepperell and Laconia were more fortunate. They secured one who, during a long period of office, put the companies into excellent shape. He was George Dexter, born in 1834, son of George Milton Dexter and Elizabeth Ann Amory Dexter. The father came from a professional family and the mother from a mercantile family. George Dexter, the son, was graduated from Harvard College in 1855 and evidently spent ten years thereafter in mercantile pursuits. According to one of his letters,[3] he passed nearly three years in Calcutta. Probably he was a clerk or junior member of an exporting house. By 1863 he was back again in America as a merchant in New York. Two years later, however, he was listed in a New York directory as a cotton buyer. In this business he continued for the next fourteen years, first with an office in New York and later with another in Boston. Thus he had excellent training in two fields which were important for Pepperell, exporting goods and buying cotton. By nature also, Dexter was equipped to be a successful treasurer. He made and kept friends by his frankness and honesty as well as by his generous nature. As we shall see later, this period demanded a treasurer who could coöperate with his fellow men. For twenty-four years he served Pepperell in this office and, for over twenty-one, Laconia also. For almost nine years more, until his death in July of 1910, he was one of Pepperell's directors.[4]

The next three treasurers were Harvard College graduates, an important factor in the business life of Boston. Unlike their predecessors, all three of them had had experience within the cotton textile business before they became Pepperell's treasurers.

Philip Yardley DeNormandie, who succeeded Dexter in 1901, had spent the first eight years after graduation from Harvard College learning the cotton business in the mills of New Bedford, where he gained experience in various departments. In 1899 he was made assistant treasurer of Pepperell and, two years later, treasurer. DeNormandie, an energetic, ambitious man, had no family fortune to supplement his salary as treasurer. In February of 1907, when he was offered a partnership in Bliss, Fabyan & Co., he resigned his position with Pepperell and took the other because it offered greater financial rewards.[5] He continued, however, for many years as one of Pepperell's directors or trustees.

The fifth treasurer of this period, William Amory, belonged to a family which had distinguished itself first as mercantile and then as industrial capitalists. His grandfather of the same name had been treasurer of the Amoskeag Manufacturing Co. from 1837 to 1876 and his father, Charles W. Amory, treasurer from 1898 to 1905. For fifteen years, after graduation from Harvard, Amory saw at first hand many of the difficulties of production and of cotton buying, first in the Amory Manufacturing Co. and later in the Amoskeag Manufacturing Co.[6] Amory served as Pepperell's treasurer for twelve years, resigning in 1919 to devote his time to his own business affairs. During his term of office the company changed from a corporation with a Maine charter to a voluntary association of Massachusetts, a change of which we shall learn more later. Amory has continued to be a trustee of the association as well as a director of the Massachusetts corporation which was set up in the third period.

The sixth treasurer, Walter Hinckley Bradley, also began his business career by starting at the bottom. For a year and a half after his graduation from Harvard, he worked in a cotton mill in New Bedford during the day and went to textile school in the evening. Then for a year he tried selling for a commission house in New York, but decided to return to mill work. After a short time in Lowell, Bradley was made superintendent of the Androscoggin Mills in Lewiston. There he stayed for three years until more responsible positions presented themselves: the general managership first of the French Broad Manufacturing Co. in North Carolina and then of several companies simultaneously in both the Carolinas. In 1915 he resigned these positions in order to become assistant treasurer of Pepperell.[7] For a time during the first World War Bradley served in the armed forces. In November of 1919 he was elected Pepperell's treasurer. Unfortunately he held this position during one of the most trying periods in the history of the cotton textile industry. After a war-time boom, which had led to the addition of plant capacity, the mills had to curtail production drastically. They took a severe cut in the prices of their inventories of cotton and cloth. In the fall of 1924 Bradley resigned. For a time thereafter, he held the office of vice-president, created for him.

In addition to the treasurers, there were other men who played a part in the management of the company—the directors and, after 1915, the trustees. Whereas in the 1870's merchants had been elected to the board of directors, in the following decades lawyers were added, as Appendix 9 shows. This was only natural, since after the Civil War many of the fortunes of the former business men of the old type continued to be held in trust for their widows and children by lawyers. The directors or trustees of the Pepperell Manufacturing Company, men of established position in Boston, had much in common. If we include the six treasurers as well as the twenty-one others, we find that five families provided each two members for Pepperell's boards. Sons, nephews, or cousins took the places left vacant by the death of relatives. There were other similarities in background; for instance, nineteen of the twenty-seven were graduates of Harvard College. Of course, we cannot help wondering how much Harvard's instruction helped to prepare them for their life's work.

There were also business ties not only with one another but with other groups in Boston. In 1905, for example, the seven directors were also on the boards of sixty other companies, trusts, and institutions which included insurance and banking interests. Among the connections of the directors were eighteen other textile companies.

These men had other ways of keeping in touch with developments outside Pepperell. There was the Arkwright Club of Boston, which was formed in 1880. Membership in it at the beginning was extended to about fifty chief executives of cotton textile companies. George Dexter was one of the first members and his successors also became members. One of the purposes of this club, which held monthly meetings, was to exchange information about the internal affairs of the various companies represented. For example, the members considered labor problems, which generally originated in Fall River, the hotbed of unrest ever since spinners and weavers of English birth or descent organized in the 1840's in order to better their conditions. The treasurers of the textile companies discussed changes in wage rates in Fall River and decided whether to follow by granting raises or by effecting cuts. They also discussed other business problems. If business was dull, they considered the advisability of limiting production for a time until stocks of goods had been reduced.[8]

During this period the Arkwright Club played an important part in legislation, both State and federal. Its members watched the legislatures of the New England States and brought influence to bear on measures which they considered detrimental to the industry in the North. In March, 1887, Dexter wrote a business friend that the impending passage of a ten-hour daily or sixty-hour weekly maximum working time in Maine would reduce production in that State about 8 per cent. In 1916 Walter H. Bradley opposed another proposed cut in maximum hours. Although the various mills in Maine contributed to a fund to fight it, this law did pass.

Over national legislation, particularly the tariff, members of the Arkwright Club were much concerned. Earlier we have noted the beginning of tariff protection for textiles. In 1861 and 1864, during the Civil War, a much higher duty for revenue purposes had been imposed on imports. This high rate remained substantially the same throughout this middle period, 1870 through 1924, although seven different tariffs were passed. In various letters George Dexter commented on the upsetting effect of the tariff on business, but we do not know how much Pepperell was affected directly by the rates. In one letter Dexter said that he was leaving for Washington to be there for tariff discussion. The Arkwright Club did not always act alone in trying to influence tariff legislation. In 1888, for example, the companies represented in its membership subscribed to the Protective League of New York, a national organization.[9]

The treasurers of textile companies joined another association in which men from the mills—agents and superintendents—also participated. In 1854 a group of men in the Connecticut Valley started an association which after the Civil War became the New England Cotton Manufacturers' Association, and later the National Association of Cotton Manufacturers. Pepperell's agents belonged to this association, and three of them, William P. Haines, Henry S. Howe, and Robert McArthur, were directors for a time. McArthur was also a vice-president of the association for three years and the president for two. During the first decades of its existence the principal concern was with technical developments, but in time, as the membership widened to include other interests, the fields covered became more varied. This is demonstrated by the types of committees in 1924—membership, exhibition, statistical, foreign trade, rates and transportation, industrial relations, technical, production costs, and tariff and taxation.

Although Pepperell's mill agents were not directors of their company, they played an important part in the making of company policies. We have discussed earlier the first agent of this period, William P. Haines. He was followed in office by Henry Saltonstall Howe. Like several of the treasurers, Howe was a graduate of Harvard College and started within the mills to work his way up to the top. After six years as mill agent for Pepperell and Laconia, 1880 through 1886, he left to become a member of the commission house, Lawrence & Co.[10]

The other two mill agents started much younger to work their way up. Robert McArthur, agent from 1887 through 1909, began to work in a textile mill as a child. He was promoted quickly and became overseer, superintendent, agent of a small mill, then of a larger one, and finally, at the age of forty-two, agent of the mills of both Pepperell and Laconia. From a letter written while he was in this last position, one gathers that he had the characteristic commonly attributed to those of Scotch ancestry: he was careful of the pennies as well as of the dollars entrusted to his management.[11]

The fourth agent, Ernest L. Morrill, was a native of Maine. He also started from the bottom, but had the advantage of a few more years of schooling than McArthur. At Laconia he was second hand, then overseer of spinning, and finally superintendent in 1906.[12] In 1910 he was made agent of the Pepperell Manufacturing Company, which then included the Laconia mills also, a position which he held throughout the remainder of this period.

In the group of men who directed Pepperell's affairs from 1870 to 1924 we thus find a considerable change from the preceding period. These men had different training as well as different business and social connections from those who had gone before. Because of, or in spite of, these forces they pursued a policy for Pepperell which proved sound for many years.

ENLARGEMENT OF THE PLANT IN BIDDEFORD

During this middle period of fifty-four years the treasurers and directors of the Pepperell Manufacturing Company authorized various changes in and additions to the buildings in Biddeford. They were concerned chiefly with structures of utility and safety, and as a result we find at the end of the period a crowded assemblage of plain brick buildings, of varying length, width, and height, in an arrangement not particularly pleasing to the eye.

As has already been pointed out, Pepperell's early buildings were erected at two different times. Before 1850 the Saco Water Power Co. had already constructed two mills, with a picker house on the east side of the yard, a cotton and cloth house on the north side, and a countinghouse on the south side. A few years later Pepperell built a third mill on the west side, built up the space between the first two mills, added another building on the north side, and constructed other necessary buildings in the yard, including machine shop, boiler house, coal shed, and smithy. In 1868 Pepperell added further stories to the building over the canal between the first two mills, thus starting a third era of building.

But Pepperell did not embark upon the proposed expansion of capacity until 1874. It needed the intervening years to recover from the loss incurred by the failure of Francis Skinner & Co. In 1874, however, the directors started a wave of building which did not subside for nine years. Under the direction of A. D. Lockwood, who continued to be the consulting engineer, they added to the first two mills, increasing their original capacity by about half. They constructed flat roofs for these additions instead of the steeply pitched ones of the first period. Although not so desirable aesthetically and architecturally, buildings with this type of roof were much better from the point of view of fire hazard and fire fighting. This style was followed in subsequent building. More storage space for cotton was needed. By the middle of 1879, four storehouses were acquired. Two were in the mill yard and two were outside—one near-by and the other about half a mile away, near the depot of the Boston & Maine Railroad. In the last two storehouses Pepperell owned a four-sevenths' and Laconia a three-sevenths' interest.

Much more building was planned for 1879, but the death of William P. Haines in July interrupted activities. However, within the next year or two the new agent, Henry S. Howe, directed the erection of more buildings. In addition to those already planned, further construction became necessary because of the destruction of the old cotton house by fire on December 3, 1880. This house was replaced by a new picker building. Two new cotton houses of moderate size were erected outside the yard but not far away from the mills. Near-by, across the street from Mill No. 3, Howe erected a building to contain a waste shop, a paint shop, and a harness shop.

Within the yard in the early 1880's the company built its fourth mill. It was much smaller than any of the others, only about two-thirds the size of Mills No. 1 and No. 2. This mill was located near the canal, between No. 1 Extension and the storehouse. At the same time the directors approved changes in Mill No. 3 which increased its productive capacity. The picker house on the north was joined to the mill, and at the south a small house was erected for a steam engine. At this time, also, the roofs of the first three mills were changed from a sharp pitch to flat tops.

These changes and additions comprised most of the construction for nearly thirty years. Since all types of construction expenses were grouped together, their exact cost cannot be ascertained from the records. Some measure of the activity within the financial year 1880–81 can be seen from the total expenditures for construction of nearly $300,000, given in Appendix 19.

During the following twenty-seven years, from 1882 to 1909, little was spent on buildings. This was a period when the mills of New England were affected by poor business conditions and by competition from new mills in the South. In 1890 the company obtained two plans for a fifth mill outside the yard. The carrying out of either plan was postponed for a time. Then two periods of depression with only a short interim of prosperity delayed action still further. In 1894 Dexter wrote McArthur, who had been mill agent since the beginning of 1887, that a partner in the selling house had returned from a trip south and recommended no increase in spindles for Pepperell but a maintenance of those already there "up to the mark." In accordance with this policy, Pepperell did not increase capacity appreciably for fifteen years. Within the yard some stories were added to existing buildings, and a connection between Mill No. 3 and its south picker building was built. Outside the yard the company acquired more storage space. In 1887 Pepperell bought out Laconia's interest in one storehouse. Two years

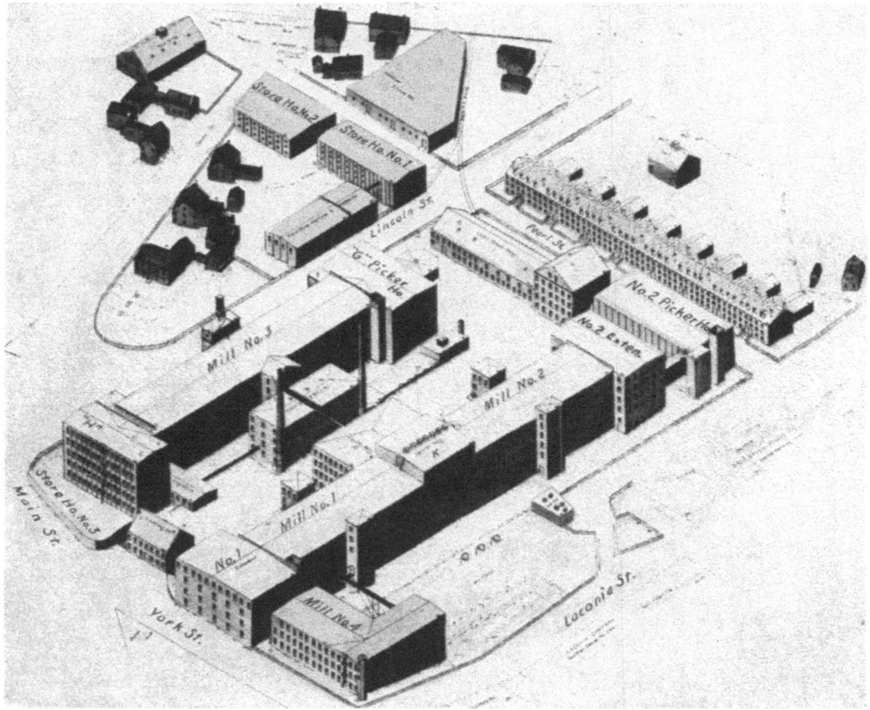

MILLS OF THE PEPPERELL MANUFACTURING
COMPANY, 1893

later an addition extended the building to a spur of the tracks of the Boston & Maine. On the other side of the tracks in 1899 Pepperell built another, and larger, storehouse. In this year, as we shall see later, Pepperell consolidated with Laconia and henceforth they were called the Pepperell and Laconia Divisions.

Not until his last year as agent of the Pepperell Division did McArthur have the responsibility of adding considerably to the plant. In 1909, as part of the fourth era of construction, he directed the erection of a new weave shed over the canal, near both Mill No. 1 and Mill No. 4 and covering about twice the area of Mill No. 1. McArthur resigned, however, before the plans for a large cotton house on the site of the old boarding-house block had been carried out. In the spring of 1910 his successor, Ernest L. Morrill, directed its construction. But this cotton house did not stand for long. On October 29, 1915, a fire broke out which did damage amounting to about $120,000 to the building and $325,000 to the raw cotton which it contained.[13] Since the building and its contents were covered by insurance, the company's loss was nominal. Within a short time, the storehouse was repaired.

No other construction of importance took place in the Pepperell Division during the remainder of this period. In 1922 and 1923 the trustees considered purchasing a southern mill. They gave up the idea, however, despairing of the possibility of acquiring a southern plant on favorable terms.

At the end of this period of fifty-four years, then, Pepperell had many more buildings than at the beginning. These additional buildings were planned with the assistance of experts. First A. D. Lockwood, who had been the consulting engineer for part of the earlier period, and then his firm of industrial engineers, Lockwood, Greene & Co., drew up plans for the mills. They planned an efficient utilization of space within each building as well as an economical arrangement of buildings. In the Pepperell yard, on the east and west sides, were two large masses of buildings. On the north were smaller buildings, while on the south, in the center, there was the original counting-house. Outside the yard were various storehouses for cotton and the finished goods as well as one building for miscellaneous work.

Any measure of the expansion of the Pepperell Manufacturing Company from 1870 to 1899 and of the Pepperell Division from 1899 to 1924 must be qualified in many ways. According to the treasurer's ledger balances, the physical plant about doubled in value during these fifty-four years. Since treasurers, however, were conservative in their statement of assets, these figures may not be accurate indicators. At any rate, the area covered by buildings doubled. There was about the same increase in the number of spindles, a common measure of activity in the industry, as shown in Appendix 17. It seems reasonable to conclude, then, that during the period the buildings about doubled in value, size, and capacity.

Between the years 1870 and 1924 construction was taking place in many other fields as well. In the cotton textile industry old companies were adding to their capacity while new ones, in the North as well as in the South, were erecting new buildings. In other industries, such as iron, steel, and automobile, construction of new plants was going forward rapidly. To facilitate the use of automobiles, new roads were being built throughout the United States. Residential and commercial construction was altering the character of the cities and towns all over the country. In fact, this was the period when the physical character of American life changed more radically than ever before.

CHANGES IN MACHINERY

Throughout this middle period of Pepperell's history the treasurers and directors had problems not only concerning plant expansion but also involving changes in machinery. They had to decide when to renovate the existing machinery, when to throw out the old and replace it with similar or with improved types, and when and how to rearrange their machinery so that the mills could operate more smoothly and efficiently. The treasurers and directors followed a general policy of purchasing machinery not at the peak of business prosperity but at times of poorer business.[14] Then they could command lower prices, more attention to details, and more prompt delivery of the machinery. This policy was made possible by a good liquid capital position, as we shall discover in a later chapter. We may note here, however, that such a policy is generally to be associated with financial industrial capitalism.

After the Civil War the treasurer and directors realized the necessity for many changes in equipment. They knew that most of the machinery was old, dating from the time of the original equipping of the mills. Although textile machinery has a reputation for lasting for many years, Pepperell's had been subjected to more than the usual wear and tear during the Civil War when the operatives were less skilled and repairs were more difficult to make than in normal times. In 1868 the directors voted to renovate the machinery in Mills No. 1 and No. 2 and estimated that the changes would take two or three years and cost about $200,000 for each mill.

This renovation, planned by A. D. Lockwood, was well under way in 1870 but it was not completed until late in the decade. Haines directed the work, which involved the examination of each machine, keeping the sound parts, readjusting or replacing worn parts, and replacing some machines entirely. As one would expect, renovation was needed most in machines where parts moved rapidly, as in the spinning frames. Haines made drastic changes in the spinning frames in Mills No. 1 and No. 2. From both he took out the old throstle spinning frames which had been installed originally and put in ring frames similar to those installed earlier in Mill No. 3. Ring spinning had the advantage of producing much more yarn than either throstles or mules, with, however, the use of much more power than the throstle.[15] In Mill No. 1 Haines took out the old mules also and replaced them with rings, so that both the warp and the filling were spun on the same types of frames. In Mill No. 2 he put in new mules in place of the old throstles to spin the yarns for twilled goods previously made in Mill No. 1. Although various machine shops in New England participated in this work, the neighboring Saco Water Power Machine Shop performed the largest part.

While these two mills were being renovated, similar work

was started on Mill No. 3. At the time of Haines' death, in July of 1879, part of the ring spinning and weaving equipment in that mill had been renewed. In the last six months of the year the superintendent, Reuben M. Hobbs, directed the work on the roving and the mule spinning.

By the middle of 1880 Pepperell's machinery was again in good working order in all three mills. Between 1869 and the middle of 1879 Haines had spent over $700,000 on this renovation; in 1879 and 1880 Hobbs and Pepperell's new agent, Henry S. Howe, spent another $50,000. Even so, the machinery was of the same design as that common in New England a score or more years earlier. Probably this retarded condition was characteristic of cotton mills at the time, since few major improvements had been introduced for many years. But within the next twenty years significant improvements came in three types of machinery—carding, ring spinning, and weaving.

First among the improvements which Pepperell adopted was a change in ring spinning. Ever since 1866, various men in New England had been experimenting with the object of making a lighter and faster spindle. By the beginning of 1880 Messrs. Fales & Jenks of Providence had an improved Rabbeth spindle for which there was a great demand. Howe tried out some of these spindles. They proved so satisfactory that he wrote asking for terms for 8,000 to be installed in the old frames in Mill No. 2. Since Fales & Jenks could not fill the order because of a rush of business, they turned it over to George Draper & Sons. In the fall of 1881 Howe gave the Drapers another order for 8,000 spindles for Mill No. 2. Thus, for a time the Drapers became important suppliers of parts for Pepperell's spinning frames, as they had been of temples for looms from the beginning.[16]

The Drapers continued to furnish spindles during the next few years although McMullen, superintendent of the Saco Water Power Machine Shop, developed his own modification of the Rabbeth spindle. In 1887, when Dexter and McArthur were planning a change in 16,000 spindles in Mill No. 3, they considered McMullen's new gravity spindle but felt that it was still inadequately tested. They ordered the Draper spindles although they gave McMullen the building of frames for the spindles. In 1889, for the warp spinning room of Mill No. 1, McArthur ordered 13,440 Draper spindles to be placed in Saco Water Power Shop's frames.

In 1891 McArthur began to give McMullen, of the local shop, orders not only for frames but for spindles as well. In that year he ordered 36 frames and 6,672 spindles for Mill No. 3. In 1894 he gave another order for 46 frames of 208 spindles each. This order was of great importance in that it marked the beginning of the replacing of all mules with ring frames. The treasurer planned to complete this change within a few years; actually the mules were not replaced by rings, however, until the first World War. This change from mules to rings increased not only the production per spindle but also the capacity of the rooms.

Few changes took place in the spinning rooms after 1912. During the first World War, as during the Civil War, the machinery received poorer treatment than usual. At its conclusion there was a need for renovation, but this was not undertaken within this middle period. In 1924 there were 136,672 spindles in the Pepperell Division—about twice the number in 1870. These spindles were quite different from the earlier ones in type and in speed of operation.

While Americans were experimenting with spindles, the English were making improvements in the system of carding. In 1885, after a visit to England, F. A. Leigh read a paper at a meeting of the New England Cotton Manufacturers' Association in which he told of the economies of production achieved by the English system, which used one carding machine with a revolving belt of cards, instead of following the American practice of using two machines with stationary cards. Although Pepperell had recently acquired some of the American-type improved Pettee cards, George Dexter was eager to try the English. Within a month after the meeting he ordered one from the English firm of Platt Bros. & Co. through Leigh, their distributing agent. In the following July, Dexter reported to his directors that he intended to replace the worn-out American cards with "English engines," provided that he continued to be as well satisfied with the latter as he was then; Pepperell actually did make this change in much of its carding equipment. By 1893, as Appendix 18 shows, there were more than 200 Platt carding engines in the three mills.

The English machine shops did not keep a monopoly of this business long. In 1891 McArthur gave an order to the Pettee Machine Works for 20 engines and three years later he ordered 45 more. By 1894 these American machines were significantly lower in price than the English, $550 as compared to $670 to $690. They also had the advantage of being serviced better.[17] No other significant change occurred in carding during the remainder of the period. These machines and others of the same type were in the mills as late as 1924.

About a decade after the improvements in spinning and carding, important changes in weaving took place. In 1895 George Otis Draper read a paper before a meeting of the New England Cotton Manufacturers' Association in which he told of all the changes which had recently been incorporated in the Draper loom, called generally the Northrup loom because of the part played by James H. Northrup in its development. This loom was so constructed that the filling thread was replenished automatically. Previously an operative had had to insert a new shuttle each time the thread was exhausted, about every five minutes. Another change was a warp-stop-motion which prevented the loom from continuing to run after a warp thread had broken. These changes the Drapers had incorporated into two-harness looms for plain weaving of narrow widths, but they had not as yet successfully applied them to more complicated weaving and to wider looms. In his paper Draper stressed the great labor saving which these looms made possible. Weavers could tend at least twice as many looms as previously, and thus the initial cost of the looms, although large, would be saved in a short time.

Pepperell was not among the first to order Northrup looms. Among the reasons for this delay was the fact that many of its looms used more than two harnesses and also that many were of extra width. The superintendent, furthermore, liked the old Colvin loom, of which there were over 2,000 in the mills in

1893, as Appendix 18 shows. In 1898 Dexter wrote McArthur that he thought it advisable to put $50,000 away each year into a new loom account. He estimated that the changes in looms would eventually amount to $700,000. About this time he investigated another stop-motion device. In 1901 McArthur gave Crompton & Knowles an order to apply a warp-stop-motion to some of the old looms which wove jeans.

In the spring of 1902 McArthur finally ordered from the Drapers 90 Northrup looms, 48 inches wide for plain weaves. Later in the year he ordered 318 more, 36 inches wide. A year later he became interested in wide looms and those with twill motion. He tried out both for a time, and within a few years he ordered some of each type. The replacing of the old-style loom with the improved Northrups had not been completed at the outbreak of the first World War. In fact, not until after peace had been declared did the last old-style loom disappear from the mills.

McArthur drove good bargains with the Drapers for machinery, especially in depression years. Perhaps the terms of purchase are best expressed in a letter from McArthur to the Draper Company in 1908, which in part is as follows:[18]

> The prices are on the basis of the last wide looms bought;—$285. for the 100″ loom; and from this, we are to be allowed $40. for each wide loom removed or $20. each for two narrow looms, in addition to the usual cash discount of $10. per loom. It is also our understanding that in the event of our continuing the use of some of our present wide looms, that we shall have the above allowance at such time as we may remove them provided at that time we have not been credited with the loom allowance on this purchase of new looms.
>
> About the extras, we are to have an allowance of 5% for all the equipment, including bobbins, shuttles, drop wires, temples, etc. etc. and it is agreeable to us that this allowance shall be considered as affecting the loom price [rather] than the items enumerated.

Thus Pepperell, during this period, made significant improvements in its machinery. We have discussed only the general renovation which took place from 1870 through 1880 and the important changes in spinning, carding, and weaving machinery thereafter. Many others occurred which cut the costs of production to a lesser extent but nevertheless significantly. There was, for example, the Barber knotter, of which Pepperell purchased six in 1901 for use in the spooling rooms. This small device, worn on a girl's hand, enabled her to tie together the ends of a broken thread and cut off the loose pieces very quickly.

Pepperell, with its adequate quick capital, was able to order machinery at advantageous times, get favorable terms, and pay for it within a short time. These are all factors of importance in any consideration of the question why Pepperell has maintained a record of success over such a long period.

PEPPERELL MERGES WITH LACONIA

In 1899 Pepperell used another means of enlarging, namely, by consolidating with its neighboring concern, the Laconia Co. Although some companies in other places had combined at an earlier date, consolidation was still not an easy thing to accomplish since stockholders of each company were likely to object to the terms given them.

There were many reasons for bringing about this particular merger. Since the beginning many of the stockholders and directors had been the same. The companies had always had the same treasurers; since 1864 they had had the same selling agents, and since 1872 the same mill agents. But each company had made its own record, and the stockholders of each were reluctant to consolidate on the terms which the directors drew up.

Laconia had been much less successful than Pepperell. From its organization in 1844 Laconia had had a checkered career. Its profits had fluctuated more violently with the ups and downs of business than those of Pepperell. In the first years of the Civil War Laconia had not had a share in government orders. During the last year or two of the war it had had the same selling agent as Pepperell, and had prospered. But in 1870, because it did not possess so large a reserve as Pepperell,

Laconia suffered more seriously from the failure of this selling agent. In 1871 the stockholders were forced to write down the old stock of 1,000 shares from a par of $1,000 to $400, and the issuing of 1,000 new shares at $400 par was authorized. In 1873 the issuing of 500 additional shares at $400 each was authorized. Each original holder of one share who had participated in the new issues as he was entitled to do had invested $1,600 in the company by 1873. He held two and a half shares, to be sure, but their total book value was only $1,000, which was the value of his one original share. These additional contributions in the early 1870's undoubtedly added to the stockholders' unwillingness to consolidate with Pepperell on the terms stated.

During the last three decades of the nineteenth century George Dexter, treasurer of both Pepperell and Laconia, tried to build up the position of Laconia, but he was handicapped by lack of adequate working capital. He obtained long-term loans from savings banks and individuals, as Dwight had done for both companies before the Civil War. Dexter tried to declare only small dividends so that he could accumulate a reserve. He did increase Laconia's earning capacity by adding new buildings and purchasing new machinery. The number of spindles was increased from 57,696 in 1870 to 93,000 in 1899, as Appendix 17 shows. Thus to some extent Laconia was in a much better position by 1899 than it had been before.

By various circumstances inherited from the past, Dexter was handicapped in making Laconia a profitable company year in and year out. Laconia had never had such a profitable line of goods as had Pepperell. During Laconia's first quarter-century, production was largely for export at a time when the export trade fluctuated violently with the various upsets in international affairs. During the period 1870 to 1899 Laconia was still in difficulties. One reason was the too great diversification of lines resulting from the practice of taking special orders for small amounts of goods. Laconia was also hampered by having a less able superintendent in charge, and he had to cope with the poorer help hired by the company. These and other factors, which we shall discuss later, hampered Dexter in his effort to develop Laconia to a point where it would be on a par with Pepperell.

Before 1899 two attempts had been made to merge the two companies, partly because of complications which arose over water power, and partly because of their interest in increasing productive capacity in Biddeford. In 1878 a committee from each company was appointed and met with the other to draw up plans which would be fair to both. (Report of Pepperell's committee is given in Appendix 5.) In substance, Pepperell was to have authority to increase its capital stock from $1,200,000 to $2,000,000. It was to purchase all Laconia's property for $1,000,000 and give Laconia's stockholders the right to purchase a new issue of 1,600 shares of Pepperell's stock at $700, a premium of 40 per cent above the par of $500, which closely represented the current opinion of the value of these shares. Laconia's stockholders were to be paid in cash for their shares. With this money they could invest in Pepperell or elsewhere. But at that time objection to the merger arose on both sides. The holders of about three hundred shares of Pepperell stock were against the consolidation. The directors therefore decided to postpone action for a time.

Again, in 1886, the directors attempted to bring about a consolidation. They planned to apply to the Legislature of Maine for an act to consolidate and for authorization to increase the capital stock to $2,550,000. Each of Pepperell's stockholders was to get 7½ shares of $100 par value in place of one old share of $500 par value. Each of Laconia's stockholders was to get three shares at $100 in place of one old share of $400 par value. The impelling motive at this time was to make possible an increase in the productive capacity of the Biddeford plants. Lengthy letters were sent out to the recalcitrant stockholders, samples of which are in Appendix 6. But a small group in each company continued to object to the consolidation. Finally, rather than stir up a dreadful public fight which might result in lawsuits, the directors again decided to drop the consolidation for a time.

Thirteen years later the third attempt to consolidate the two

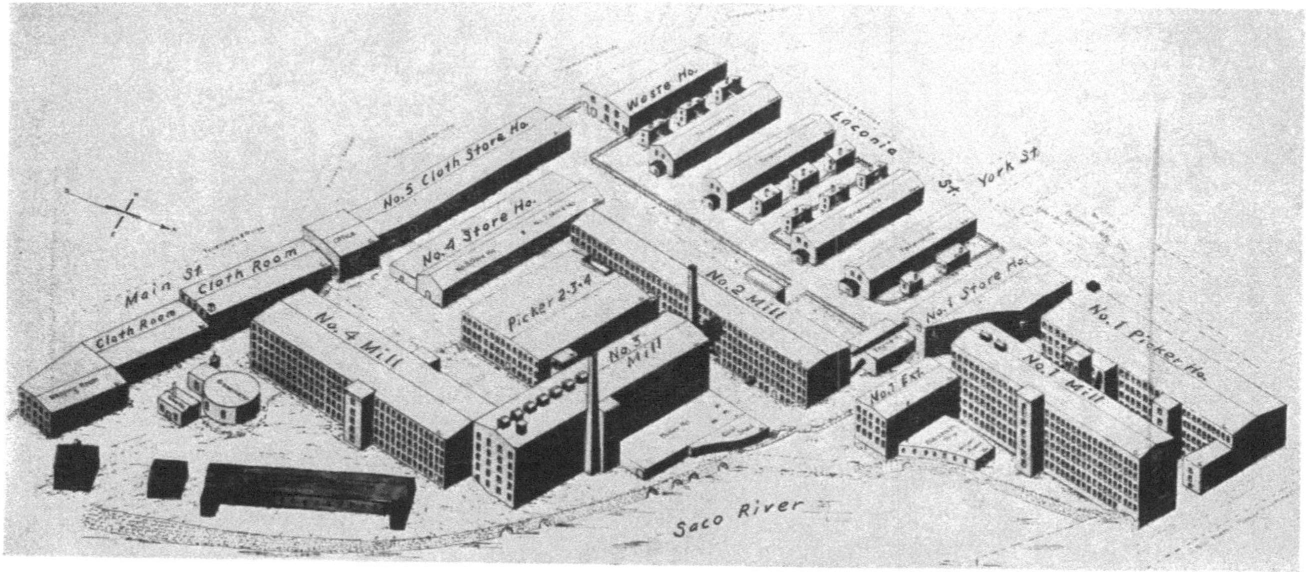

MILLS OF THE LACONIA COMPANY, 1893

companies was actually carried out. A circular letter, stating the reasons for and the terms of the consolidation, was sent to each stockholder together with a legal notice of the meeting to be held on May 10. (Copies of these documents are given in Appendix 7.) The terms of consolidation were similar to those offered in 1886. Pepperell stockholders were to get 7 shares of $100 par value for each $500 share held, and the Laconia stockholders were to get 3½ shares for each $400 share held. In addition, a cash dividend of $150 a share was to be declared for Pepperell stockholders and one of $50 a share for Laconia stockholders. By 1899 the curmudgeons of 1878 and 1886 had apparently died or disposed of their holdings. The stockholders met on May 10, and on the second ballot the vote for consolidation was unanimous. On the following day a notice of change of name for the new organization from the Consolidated Manufacturing Co., which had been temporarily adopted, to the Pepperell Manufacturing Company was filed with the Secretary of State in Maine. After the consolidation the two sets of mills were known as the Pepperell Division and the Laconia Division.*

Thus we have at last one, and only one, cotton textile manufacturing company in Biddeford, the Pepperell Manufacturing Company. Its total capital stock was $2,556,000, and the total number of spindles was 206,000. Although there had been a growth in the size of textile establishments throughout the country, there were at this time only a few larger than Pepperell; among them were Amoskeag of Manchester, Fall River Iron Works, Harmony Mills of Cohoes, New York, and Wamsutta of New Bedford.[19] Pepperell was included in the select group of large companies in an industry which was characterized by all sizes of enterprise.

* In the following years Pepperell added to the capacity of the Laconia Division. Following the erection of a weave shed and a cotton house for the Pepperell Division, the company constructed and equipped a weave shed for the Laconia Division on the site of its old boarding-house blocks, at an estimated cost of $700,000. As a result, Laconia's spindles increased from 93,000 in 1899 to 154,992 in 1914 and remained at that level throughout the rest of this period. By 1924 the total number of spindles in both divisions was 291,664, an increase of 40 per cent over the number in 1899.

NEW LAND AND WATER-POWER DEPARTMENT

In 1915 Pepperell officially assumed another responsibility, the operation of the Saco Water Power Co. as a real-estate and water-power department. In later years, however, Pepperell disposed of both these functions.

When the Saco Water Power Co. was organized in 1839, the directors had planned a variety of functions—operating mills, building machinery, developing water power, and owning various types of real estate. These were too many operations for one small company to carry on profitably. In 1850 Saco ceased to erect mills for its own operation on its own account—experience with the mills sold to Pepperell had been too disastrous. In 1867 the manufacture of machinery was given up; machine shops and foundry were sold to a group of men who organized the Saco Water Power Machine Shop. For forty-eight years after 1867 the Water Power Company continued to own real estate and provide water power, not independently but under the control of the two Biddeford textile companies.

From 1839 to 1867 the Saco Water Power Co.'s water-power development was important. As we have already noted, the company secured various holdings to improve the water-power situation for the Biddeford companies. After 1867 Pepperell and Laconia increased the supply of water to some extent in order to safeguard the mills from fire and to maintain enough power to run the mills during the summer and fall droughts. In many years operations were curtailed in the summer because water was low. But this was also a dull-market era, and a lay-off gave the operatives a desirable opportunity to visit their former homes in Canada.

After the Saco Water Power Co. had become the real-estate and water-power department of the Pepperell Manufacturing Company, Pepperell's management decided to turn over to others the responsibilities and potentialities of the Saco River. In 1918 the trustees voted to lease the property at Moose Road to the Cumberland County Power & Light Co. for a term of fifteen years. In 1930 Pepperell sold its steam power plant in Biddeford and its water-power properties on the Saco River to the same company for a considerable sum. After Pepperell had finished the electrification of its mills, it added to surplus nearly $1,000,000 left from this sale.[20] Thus the water-power potentialities, so intriguing in the first decades of the nineteenth century, were sold to a company which specialized in the development of power and which could devote some of its capital to the generation of power from the various falls of the Saco River.

Throughout the years the Saco Water Power Co. and then the Pepperell Manufacturing Company have played a minor rôle in the building and owning of real estate in Biddeford and Saco. For years the Water Power Company continued to own the property secured from the York Manufacturing Co. It sold lots and occasionally houses. In the early years it erected only a few buildings, such as a hotel, a block of stores, and a post office in the center of Biddeford. After 1867 the company erected a few more buildings—some in the 1880's and 1910's during periods of expansion of the mills. But in 1915, when Pepperell took over the real estate, the Water Power Company still had only a small number of housing properties—fourteen single dwellings, twenty-seven double, one three-family, and four four-family houses, and one for sixteen families. In addition, the company owned six stables. From 1918 to 1921 Pepperell purchased tenement houses for operatives, which it disposed of during the 1930's.[21]

For many years the Saco Water Power Co. had owned other property for commercial use, such as stores and wharves. From time to time these were improved, particularly the coal sheds and wharf facilities on Factory Island, which were used by various companies in Saco and Biddeford. After 1915, when they became Pepperell's property, these holdings were gradually disposed of, so that practically the only function of Pepperell in Biddeford was the manufacturing of cotton goods.[22]

PEPPERELL INVESTS IN A BLEACHERY

During this middle period of Pepperell's history again we find the company reaching out to add another function to its operation. Earlier we have seen that it had been content to have various bleacheries do the bleaching, dyeing, and finishing of such goods as were not sold in the brown. But in the early 1870's an opportunity came to take stock in a bleachery which had been started in Lewiston, Maine. The directors of Pepperell and Laconia thought it advisable to join with the various textile companies there rather than starting a bleachery of their own in Biddeford or continuing to send out their goods.

This bleachery, called the Lewiston Bleachery & Dye Works, had been leased in 1860 by the promoting company, the Franklin Co., to N. W. Farwell. When his lease expired in 1870, there was talk of changing this arrangement and getting in new capital. Two years later it was incorporated, with the interested companies taking stock. The Franklin Co. took 1,500 shares and the Androscoggin Mills, Bates Manufacturing Co., Laconia Co., and Pepperell Manufacturing Company each took 375 shares at $100 each.[23]

Investment in the Lewiston Bleachery & Dye Works proved profitable. Year after year Pepperell received dividends, which it set aside as a reserve and drew upon only occasionally. In 1878 the reserve was reduced by writing off the investment completely. Later the reserve was drawn upon at times of poor business or eliminated at times of change in capital structure. From 1872 through 1925 the dividends ranged from 70 per cent in 1892 to 5 per cent in 1914 and 1915. The average annual rate was 20 per cent. In addition, from 1913 on, the companies which owned stock received a bonus on business done for them, which ranged from 4 to 10 per cent annually with the average about 7 per cent.

But in the course of time troubles arose between the textile companies and the Franklin Co., which had been formed to promote the development of Lewiston. In 1909 the Franklin Co. sold out all its holdings of stock in the bleachery. Pepperell took 750 shares at $225 a share and sold half of this block to the Hill Manufacturing Co. Including the shares which had been Laconia's, it held altogether 1,125 shares, or three-eighths of the total. This fraction was not large enough to permit domination of the bleachery's policies.

While several companies were in control of the bleachery there was disagreement, as one would expect, over the work done for each company. In times of poor business, as in September, 1884, for example, Pepperell's treasurer would want an adjustment in the rates charged for the work. At other times the treasurer complained about the way the goods were handled. Any carelessness on the part of the bleachery hurt the reputation of the manufacturing company.

For years, judging by total charges for bleaching and dyeing as shown in Appendix 36, the volume of cotton goods sent to the bleachery remained about the same. The annual charges for the period from June 30, 1872, through June, 1898, varied from $49,000 to $87,000 with the average about $64,000, but there was little evidence of a rising trend. During the following period, when total charges included those for both sets of mills in Biddeford, this charge showed a decided upward trend. While that for the fiscal year 1900 was $149,000, that for 1924 was $820,000. This increase, almost 450 per cent, can be explained not on grounds of increased production by the mills, since actually production was almost 40 per cent less in the latter year, but by an increasing percentage of goods, bleached, dyed, and finished, and by an increase in rates.

By the end of this period Pepperell's trustees were faced with a serious problem. Whereas their investment in the bleachery had been profitable, they had little control over its work. More and more of Pepperell's goods were going there to be converted. Should Pepperell continue its policy or make a drastic change—to a new bleachery of its own or to ownership of the one in Lewiston? In other words, should the company integrate vertically? This problem was solved only in the third period, as we shall see later.

* * *

In this chapter we have seen many changes taking place in the span of the fifty-four years which I have called the middle period of Pepperell's history. We have noted that the company was successively managed by six men—as treasurers. The first three had had experience only outside the textile industry before they were elected Pepperell's treasurers, whereas the last three started within the industry. This change demonstrated that by the beginning of the twentieth century, even at the top level of management, specialized knowledge of the industry was needed.

An awareness of the industry as a whole is further evidenced by the fact that these men joined with other textile officials in the interests of protecting their companies. They sought to minimize foreign competition by working to keep a protective tariff. They also sought to prevent legislation in the various States which might result in reduction in the production of the mills. As members of the Arkwright Club they kept in touch with each other. Moreover, they learned at meetings of the New England Cotton Manufacturers' Association of technical developments in the industry. In these meetings the mill agents and superintendents also participated. Indeed, three of Pepperell's four mill agents in this period took an active part in this organization.

The treasurers, with the approval of the board of directors, planned the expansion of the mills in Biddeford. At the beginning of this period the treasurers started this program of expansion, which did not subside until 1883. During these years they added to the productive capacity of the mills, extending the storage space for cotton and finished goods in the following years. A second wave of building occurred in the period 1909–11, when the treasurer authorized the erection of a weave shed and a large cotton storehouse in the Pepperell Division and a weave shed in the Laconia Division.

At various times during this period the directors made changes in the machinery. The most outstanding, of course, was the improved equipment which they acquired for spinning, carding, and weaving. These new machines performed much more efficiently than the old. Some of them, such as the ring frames for filling, took up much less space than the mules which they replaced. As a result, much more machinery could be placed in the mills than had been the case previously.

Pepperell added to its productive capacity by consolidating with the Laconia Co. in 1899. In some respects we might regard this union as a mere change in form, since the two companies had been run by practically the same men since their beginnings. But there were dangerous possibilities in the separation of interest which might threaten the operations of both and which might hinder expansion. By this consolidation in 1899, which was the third attempt within twenty-one years, Pepperell almost doubled its capacity. At the end of another fifteen years, with the new buildings and machinery, Pepperell was about 40 per cent larger than at the turn of the century. After 1915 the plant in Biddeford was not expanded further.

Although the outstanding change was this horizontal expansion, to some extent Pepperell expanded vertically. It took over the management of the water power and real estate company which furnished power for the mills and some housing and other facilities for the operatives and various businesses in Biddeford and Saco. But this new venture was not too successful. At least, after the end of this period Pepperell got rid of both the water-power and real-estate property.

To some extent Pepperell really reached forward in its expansion. It invested in a bleachery in Lewiston, Maine, which converted its goods. Such integration was not unusual in the industry; in fact, many years earlier the Boston Manufacturing Co. and the Merrimack Manufacturing Co. had established their own bleacheries. But for many years the major part of Pepperell's goods did not need to be finished; they were sold in the brown to the consumers. Changes in custom in the United States, however, required that more and more of Pepperell's drills, jeans, shirtings, and sheetings be sent to the bleachery to be both bleached and dyed before being marketed.

During this period, then, Pepperell grew in many ways. But so did the industry. Many other established companies also expanded; many new ones, as, for example, those in Fall River and New Bedford, grew tremendously in these years. In other places, particularly in the South, many small mills were started. Although these changes are difficult to measure because of the inaccuracy and inadequacy of the figures reported to the government, we may say that the total number of establishments increased about 40 per cent in this period while total capacity increased about 400 per cent. There continued to be a predominance of small companies, as in 1850, and comparatively few large ones. In 1924 Pepperell belonged to a group of not more than fifty companies, which had at least 200,000 spindles and which probably had in place at least a third of the spindles in the United States. In many ways these large companies were the leaders in the industry, not only in the construction and equipping of mills but also in their operation.

CHAPTER VIII

MILL AGENTS CONTINUE ESTABLISHED PRACTICES

DURING THE MIDDLE PERIOD of Pepperell's history (1870–1924) the mill agents continued, with little change, the practices which had been established in the earlier period. They were not alone in this procedure. The officers of other large companies in the cotton textile industry saw little need for change in the methods which had worked so well earlier. Each company, however, did feel the pressure of greater competition within the industry. As we have seen, the officers tried to meet foreign competition by joining with others to seek protection through tariffs, and tried to meet domestic competition by seeking with increased capacity and improved machinery to get at least their share of the total business.

In this middle period Pepperell's four mill agents made few changes in policies in regard to the mills. This rigidity is to be expected when one considers the experiences of these men. The first was William P. Haines, who, of course, continued the policies which had proved successful during his earlier term of office, 1850–66. His successor, Henry S. Howe, who was mill agent from 1880 to the end of 1886, might have made changes, since he had a broader background than his successors; but unfortunately for Pepperell he left to become a partner in a selling house. As we have seen, Robert McArthur and Ernest L. Morrill, the two agents who followed them, did not have so broad a training as Haines and Howe; they were promoted from inferior mill positions. McArthur had gained his experience in other mills in New England, while Morrill had gained most of his in Biddeford. Although they had come from the working class, they did not advance greatly the relative position of the mass of workers under them. Perhaps we should not be surprised at this attitude in that period of industrial and financial capitalism.

Times were changing outside the walls of the mills, however. As we have noted in Chapter VII, there were shifts in the structure of business. Group action was taking the place of individual action. The executives of companies were banding together to fight for survival. The mill agents also joined in efforts of mutual aid. In the New England Cotton Manufacturers' Association at first they sought to share in the development of techniques in the industry and later to institute, with others connected with the industry, practices for the protection of the mills. The mill agents in several localities banded together to work out common action. Since Biddeford and Saco comprised a small industrial center, far removed geographically from the larger mill centers, the agents of Pepperell, Laconia, and York were invited by circumstances to work together informally.

Another sign of the changes in the times was the growing tendency for groups of operatives to band together for their own betterment. During the first part of this period there were small groups of skilled workers, such as mule spinners, loom-fixers, and weavers, who maintained organizations over long periods. During the second half, with the formation of national organizations of workers, the unskilled were drawn in. But, on the whole, during this period the workers were not immediately successful in achieving their aims. Some of them lost severely; the mule spinners, for example, hastened the destruction of their very occupation. But among the workers in general the ground work was laid for successful group action in later years.

The mill agents, driven on one side by the treasurers and directors in Boston and on the other by the operatives near-by, had no easy time in operating the mills economically. They tried various methods of keeping costs down, as we shall see in this chapter. These agents along with their assistants, the superintendents and overseers, demand our early attention.

At this point I can imagine that some readers will complain of the depths to which we are descending when entering into the actualities of operation. They might go along with us intellectually in considering the policy of top executives and emotionally in contemplating the work and lives of the other employees, but they want to stop short of the threshold of details of managers and management. Rightly or wrongly, it is this very attitude that I am trying to break down, for policy cannot be left in the upper reaches of the executives and labor cannot be understood without a study of superintendents and foremen. Indeed, the persistent neglect of the foreman group has come home to plague many a business unit and industry at the very time I am writing these pages.

A LOYAL AND CAPABLE SUPERVISORY FORCE

As in the first period, Pepperell was fortunate in having a loyal and capable supervisory force which paid constant attention to the operations of the mills and which helped to make the company profitable. On the whole, these men—agents, superintendents, and overseers—stayed with the company for long periods. They were skilled at their jobs and several of them, when the opportunity arose, were promoted to still more responsible positions in the company. Of course, there was another side to this long tenure—a man might outlive his period of greatest usefulness and might create problems which his successors would find it hard to solve. To some extent we may see traces of this weakness as we follow the careers of the men themselves.[1]

At the top of the mill hierarchy were the agents. We have already discussed some of their qualifications for their jobs in the preceding chapter. But we need to emphasize the encouragement that their success, particularly in the case of McArthur and Morrill, who started as poor boys with little education and who rose by their own efforts to positions of importance, gave to their subordinates, especially the superintendents and overseers. The mill agents were able to accumulate substantial fortunes since they received large salaries, only a portion of which was necessary for comfortable living in Biddeford. Their basic salary was generally $10,000, and they frequently received bonuses from the directors or trustees. The mill agents lived in comfortable houses—Haines in his own on Jefferson Street on land which the Saco Water Power Co.

had given him; Howe and McArthur in a company house overlooking the mills, at the corner of Adams and Jefferson Street; and Morrill in the old Cutts Mansion on Factory Island. For these houses the agents paid no rent.

The mill agent had the responsibility of running the mills. In the Pepperell countinghouse in Biddeford he saw to the general management of the Pepperell mills. Then, from 1872 on, when one man was agent of both Pepperell and Laconia, he had offices also in the Laconia countinghouse. This duality continued until 1911, when the offices merged and the office work was carried on wholly in Pepperell's countinghouse. For many years the agent wrote a daily letter to the treasurer about conditions in Biddeford and daily he received a letter from the treasurer about conditions in New England and the rest of the country. This exchange of letters kept the two men in close contact with each other, and trips to Boston by the agent or trips to Biddeford by the treasurer provided opportunities for discussion of policies concerning the mills. The reader can easily imagine how valuable such letters are for the purposes of the historian.

The agent also kept in touch with the selling house. A partner in the Boston office of the selling house gave instructions concerning the types of goods needed for filling orders and the places to which the goods should be shipped. The agent kept the selling house informed regarding shipments and goods on hand. The agent received other information about selling from the treasurer, who was in constant communication with the Boston office of the selling house.

The agent's correspondence with others reveals a host of details which he had to settle about machinery, about parts which small specialized companies made, and about supplies, such as starch. The agent did not write many of these letters with his own hand, but gave instructions to a clerk who actually wrote the letters which the agent in turn signed. After about 1903 these letters, according to records which remain, were written on a typewriter. Thus in many fields the mill agent kept up correspondence with the outside world. Not all details in the correspondence can be ascertained, since the major part of the extant records which remain are Pepperell's press copies of letters sent and originals of the letters between the agent and the treasurer. In other words, much incoming correspondence has disappeared.

At times there was an assistant agent. During McArthur's last three years as agent, Walter S. Mitchell, the former paymaster, took over part of the agent's routine duties. Later, in Morrill's time, Milton O. Dean, a former superintendent, served as assistant agent for about two years until in 1919 he accepted a position as agent of the Edwards Manufacturing Co. of Augusta, Maine. A little later, Howard A. Morrill, who had gained experience in the Whittier Mills of Georgia, was selected to help his father.

In the countinghouse at Biddeford the agent had the services of several clerks. One of them was designated as the paymaster, but he could also attend to other duties. At the beginning of this period there was one other clerk, but by 1924 there were about ten and in addition a purchasing agent.

At the time of the organization of the company the agent had carried all the responsibility for the direction of the mills, but in 1866, when William P. Haines became treasurer and his son, Ferguson Haines, was made agent, a superintendent was added to take over some of these duties. No clear division of duties seems to have been made then. A few of the duties concerned with the mills were retained by the agent, but many were given to the superintendent; among the former were the hiring and firing of overseers. This seems to us today a confused state of affairs, since the superintendent and not the agent had most of the dealings with the overseers. We wonder whether this confusion in the delegation of authority was peculiar to Pepperell. In time, of course, the superintendents had recognized activities in Biddeford, but we do not find them stated explicitly at the time of the creation of this job. We do find hints of them at the time of the search for a successor to the first superintendent, as we shall see shortly.

From 1866 to 1899, the latter being the year of consolidation with Laconia, Pepperell had had only two superintendents. In the following years to 1924 the Pepperell Division continued with the second superintendent, who was succeeded after a time by his son. Thus only three men held this important position for the mills in the old Pepperell yard by 1924. These three proved to be of extreme importance to the running of the mills and to the profitability of the company.

All three of these superintendents worked up from lower positions. Reuben M. Hobbs was employed by the Lewiston Mills, apparently in the office, when he applied for the newly created position of superintendent of Pepperell in 1866. For many years thereafter he remained in Biddeford as Pepperell's superintendent. In the latter part of 1879, after Haines' death, he carried on many of the mill agent's regular duties as well as the extra ones which were involved in the renovation of the mills. For this service the treasurer and directors were grateful and voted him a bonus of $1,000. They did not however make him agent, a position to which he aspired. In June of 1881 he surprised George Dexter, the treasurer, by writing that he had secured a good position elsewhere, in a cotton mill near Montreal.

To fill Hobbs' place George Dexter wrote Henry S. Howe that he wanted "a good manufacturer, to relieve you of care of the running of the mill." These two men talked over the possible candidates for the job. Two weeks later Howe wrote Dexter as follows about his candidate, George K. Gibbs:[2]

> I think I have got a first-rate man as Supt. I believe I spoke to you about him, Gibbs (agent) of the Springvale Mills—he once had charge of the weaving in Pepp. #3, and has had charge of the Springvale several years—about 43 years of age, a 6 footer, and as good man as Sprague or Boyd. Before going into the mill he learned the machinist trade and I feel will make *just* the man for us.

Later events bore out much of Howe's prediction. Gibbs adopted the Pepperell mills as his own and devoted his attention from early morn till late at night to their welfare. No detail was too minute for him to watch. At various times the treasurers and directors showed their appreciation by voting him bonuses and vacations. They did not fear that some other large company would entice Gibbs away since they recognized that he was not, according to Dexter's words, "stylish enough for an agent."

In 1911 the treasurer and directors demonstrated further their appreciation of Gibbs by selecting his son, E. Payson Gibbs, as his assistant and heir to the job. The son had worked previously in various places. He had been employed by Pepperell's machine shop, by the Kitson Machine Shop of Lowell, and then in at least two cotton textile companies—the Skenandoa Cotton Co., of Utica, New York, and the Langdon Manufacturing Co., of Stuyvesant Falls, New York. In the Langdon Co. young Gibbs had been superintendent.[3] He thus brought to Pepperell knowledge of operations elsewhere, particularly in regard to carding. He continued to assist his father until the latter's death in 1919. At that time he assumed the title of superintendent of the Pepperell Division, a position which he held throughout the remainder of this period.

Pepperell was thus very wise or fortunate in its selection of superintendents. They were loyal and devoted servants, giving a major part of their lives to the company, and no doubt they contributed greatly to Pepperell's success in this period.

Over the years the sister company in Biddeford, which in 1899 became the Laconia Division of the Pepperell Manufacturing Company, had not been so fortunate. Prior to 1899 Laconia had had two superintendents, James G. Garland from 1855 to 1872 and then James G. Brackett from 1872 to 1900. Both of these men had been concerned with the construction of the mills in Biddeford. The first turned from Laconia to set up a small company of his own, making special parts for looms, which is still in existence today in Saco,[4] while the second was content to remain as superintendent during the major part of his life. During the following years there were five superintendents for the Laconia Division. The first three had previously been employed in Biddeford; the last two came from other mills. The first of these five superintendents did not satisfy McArthur. In 1906 he was replaced by Ernest L. Morrill, who in turn in 1910 was promoted to McArthur's position. The third was Walter S. Mitchell, who previously had been McArthur's secretary and assistant. After four years he left to become the agent of another company. In his place Morrill put Milton O. Dean. In 1917 Dean accepted the position of superintendent elsewhere, but within a short time was induced to come back as assistant agent. The last superintendent was James Andrews, who was assisted by J. H. Herbert. Only one of Laconia's seven superintendents, then, found a lifetime challenge in Laconia. This was Brackett. The treasurer acknowledged that Brackett was an excellent mechanic and a fine man, but he was easy-going, did not give sufficient attention to details, and was not strong in discipline. Thus, for many years Laconia was not run so efficiently as Pepperell.

The compensation of these superintendents and assistants varied with their length of service and ability. Apparently the range of salary was from $2,000 to about $4,000. In addition, at times they received bonuses for extra services. One of them, George K. Gibbs, accumulated a considerable fortune, part of which was invested in Pepperell stock. At the time of his death in 1919, when the price of the stock was about $200, he held 830 shares.

The superintendents lived in comfortable houses: Hobbs and the two Gibbses in the old Tracy house, which Pepperell owned and which was located across the street from Mill No. 3. Since Laconia did not own a superintendent's house, special arrangements had to be made for each superintendent so that they too could live comfortably, free from payment of rent.

Not from any surviving records, but from conversations with those who themselves have been connected with the mills for a long period and whose families still earlier had such connections, I have found out just what the superintendent's duties were. We do gather a little insight from the phrase which I have quoted from Dexter's letter to Howe about the qualifications of a superintendent: "a good manufacturer, to relieve you of care of the running of the mill." The superintendent did that—he attended to the duties within the mills, while the various agents conducted business with the outside world.

According to the recollections of one overseer, it was the custom of the superintendent of the Pepperell Division to make one tour of inspection of all the rooms of the mills the first thing in the morning and another after lunch. He would see whether all the machinery was in operation; if not, he would question the overseer about the reason for its being stopped. He would glance at the overseer's records of the quantity of work which had been produced since the previous visit. If the weights of the cotton, yarn, or woven goods did not run uniformly according to the standards set, he would demand that a change be made. If a change was not possible in that room, then it would be made in the preceding room or rooms.

After the morning tour of inspection the superintendent at nine o'clock met the overseers of the carding, spinning, dressing, weaving, and cloth rooms in the Cloth Hall. There he would go over the cloth which had been rejected during the previous day. If there were oil spots on some, he would find out which overseer and which room were to blame. Frequently the overseer would receive harsh words about such troubles. If there were other defects, such as bolls or coarse threads in the weaving, he would demand an investigation into any of the processes which might be to blame for the preparation of the thread and the handling of it. By this daily discussion of difficulties, the superintendent kept a close control of operations.

Although the superintendent lacked the authority to dismiss an overseer who did not satisfy him, he could make life so unpleasant for the man that he might think he could do much better elsewhere. Nevertheless, the overseers on the whole stayed with the company for long periods.

The group of overseers or foremen was the third in importance in the mill's hierarchy. It included a number of men who might bear other designations, such as engineer and electrician. Each was the boss in his domain, although the big bosses, mill agent and superintendent, might interfere to some extent. During this period the number of men classed as overseers increased in spite of the tendency toward consolidation of jobs. One reason for this increase was the development of subordinate shops and of special technical jobs, which brought in a cotton inspector, a chief engineer, and a chief electrician as well as overseers of the waste house and of piping. Another reason was the addition of the Laconia Division in 1899. The consolidation of jobs in the following years resulted in only twenty-eight such subordinates in 1924 as compared to nineteen in 1871. We have not included the paymasters and the purchasing agent, who had offices in the countinghouse and who came under the direction of the agent.[5]

One wonders how well qualified for their jobs these overseers were. In the early years they were promoted from lower positions in the company, in other textile companies, or in machine shops—the only places in which to learn about the operations of machinery. But after 1876, when a textile school was started in Philadelphia, another source of trained men was available. Probably few in New England benefited from the three-year course there, but a larger number did take advantage of the textile schools which were set up about the turn of the century in the principal textile cities of Massachusetts—Lowell, New Bedford, Fall River, and Lawrence. About the same time, textile departments were started in several southern colleges. All evidence, however, points to the conclusion that Pepperell's overseers continued to be trained in mills or machine shops in this period rather than in the technical schools.

In a previous chapter we have discussed several of the early overseers, some of whom were still in the mills in 1871. Of the nineteen classed as belonging to the overseer group in 1871, seventeen had been employees of the Pepperell Manufacturing Company for at least eleven years and fourteen had been overseers for at least six years. One of the overseers, David Buck, hired in January of 1851, had been one of the first employees of the company. He had moved up from section hand to second hand and finally to an overseer of a weaving room. Most of the other overseers in 1871 and in the following years seem to have followed the same route within the company.

The duties of these overseers did not change much during this period. In the large departments they had general charge of the rooms, kept time records, hired and fired the help, and made out payrolls. In the smaller departments they had additional duties, such as making repairs on machines and looking over some of the goods rated as seconds. In the larger rooms they were assisted by second hands, who took over some of the duties, such as attending to the repairs.

The compensation of these overseers in general increased during this period. At any particular time, however, there was considerable variation in pay, depending on the degree of responsibility and experience of each man. In 1871 the overseers received from $2.25 to $5.00 a day, with the average slightly less than $2.90 a day. By 1893 the range was slightly higher, from $2.50 to $5.25 a day, with the average about $3.40. During the first World War wages soared: in 1919 they were getting from 50 cents to 90 cents an hour, with the average about 70 cents, for a fifty-four hour week. By 1924 their wages were still higher, from about 80 cents to $1.10 an hour. Only two men in the overseer group were paid on a weekly basis, the engineer and the electrician.

In addition to their regular compensation, William P. Haines had maintained a policy of giving bonuses to the overseers. But after his death in 1879, this policy seems to have been kept for only a few years and then dropped by the agents who followed him. Probably they did not realize, to the extent that Haines did, the contribution that these men made to the running of the mills. Not until the first World War do we hear again of the granting of bonuses, and even then this practice was not kept up for long.

Pepperell was served by a loyal and capable supervisory force. It differed considerably in many respects from the mass of the workers, as we shall see in the following pages.

FOREIGN OPERATIVES

The labor problems of this middle period were much more difficult than during the first period. Many of these problems were common to the cotton textile industry of the North. Before the Civil War the industry had found large groups of native workers, willing and eager to enter the mills and to work long hours for low wages. Some of these workers thought of their mill work as temporary and, after accumulating savings, went back to their own homes. In some localities the textile companies had finally to turn to others than Yankees—to foreigners or foreign-born from various lands, who also at first were willing to accept low wages and long hours. Workers gradually became more conscious of the few satisfactions which a lifetime of work in a textile mill brought them. They became imbued with the American desire for a higher standard of living for themselves and their children, and this desire became more evident in the period following the first World War.

During the years 1870 to 1924 the number of workers in Biddeford did not change in proportion to the expansion of the mills. In February of 1871, when William P. Haines again took over the running of the mills, there were approximately 1,500 operatives on Pepperell's payroll. Fifteen years later, when the capacity of the mills had increased nearly 40 per cent, there were 1,750 operatives, an increase of less than 20 per cent. By 1899, when the capacity was about 60 per cent greater than in 1871, the number of workers was about 2,000, or about 33 per cent above that of 1871. The number of workers in 1899 was at about the employment peak for this period. In the following years, although the capacity increased considerably, the number dropped significantly with the introduction of additional labor-saving machinery. In 1912 the Pepperell Division had again about 1,750 workers and in October, 1924, about 1,500. Thus the Pepperell Division ended the period with about the same number of workers that the Pepperell Manufacturing Company had had in 1871. Its production capacity meanwhile, as we have seen, had increased by over 90 per cent.

In 1899, through the consolidation with Laconia, about 1,600 other workers were added. In the following years the Laconia Division maintained about the same number of workers, while its capacity increased about 70 per cent.

Thus together the mills in Biddeford, which in 1871 had employed about 2,600 workers, ended this period, in the fall of 1924, with about 3,000. Although the totals for workers show comparatively little variation, changes of importance were taking place among the mass of the workers.

The workers in Biddeford came from various places. Some of them, like the majority in the first period, came from the small towns of New England. But these Yankees were dwindling into a minority in this period. In 1891, for example, Yankees comprised but 27 per cent of the total number employed in the Pepperell mills.[6] There are no data as to the percentages in the other years.

Workers from Canada came to predominate. There had been a few in the mills from the first; but after the Civil War, they came down on the railroad by the carload to Biddeford from the province of Quebec. By 1891 the percentage of French Canadians was 55, according to a letter written by the mill agent. By this time there were probably also children of early French Canadians who were working in the mills. The percentage of French Canadians by birth or descent probably increased in the following decades, since many French Canadians continued to arrive in Biddeford and in time their children and grandchildren sought employment in the mills.

In Biddeford this predominance of French Canadians was not challenged seriously by any other racial group, not even by the Irish. In cities in Massachusetts there were large numbers of the latter, but Biddeford was rather distant from the center of Irish immigration, Boston. In 1891 only 12 per cent of Pepperell's workers were Irish. Some of these were probably among those secured by the treasurer from recent arrivals in East Boston in the early 1880's. The number of Irish in Biddeford has continued to be relatively small.

From other parts of the British Empire came other employees. In a previous chapter we have mentioned the migration of a few English workers in the first years of Pepperell's operation; some migration continued throughout this middle period. By 1891 about 5 per cent of Pepperell's operatives were English.

For a time George Dexter made an effort to get Scottish women weavers into the mills. In the early 1880's he wrote to James Houston of Glasgow about selecting twenty women weavers who were to be sent over with their passage money prepaid by Pepperell. Other groups followed, men as well as women, some of whom were recommended by their friends in Biddeford. But these Scots proved an expensive experiment.

Some of them left before they had repaid Pepperell the amounts advanced, enticed away in several cases by other companies. On the whole, Dexter thought that the expense of obtaining them might be balanced by the pattern of conscientiousness and thrift which they set for the more easy-going French. In 1891 there were only nine Scots left in the mills.

As other national groups came to America from various parts of Europe and Asia, a few settled in Biddeford. By 1891 there were only ten foreigners outside the groups we have mentioned —three Swedes and seven Armenians. But later, others, Poles, Greeks, Albanians, and Turks, contributed to the melting pot of races in Biddeford.

Many problems arose in the hiring of people who spoke a tongue other than English. Since in the beginning the French Canadians thought of life in Biddeford as only temporary, they and their children did not attempt to master the English language. They continued to speak French. The children could not easily take advantage of the public schools. In time, French parochial schools were set up by the Catholic Church. Even today on the streets of Biddeford French is heard frequently.

When the French children did not go to school, it was natural for them to turn to work in the mills. Even after 1880, when a Maine law was passed that children under fifteen should attend school part of the year, some children continued to work in the mills of one company or another. The State inspector found that Pepperell had 46 children under fifteen in the mills in 1892 and 38 in 1893.[7] Over a score of years later, in 1915, there were still children in the mills, working with permits: the Pepperell Division had 59 between the ages of fourteen and sixteen while Laconia had 53.[8]

During this middle period the proportion of women and girls declined in the mills. By 1915, for example, they made up less than 50 per cent of the working force.[9] The decline can be attributed partly to the increase in improved automatic machinery and partly to the lower wages of foreign boys hired for jobs previously held by Yankee girls.

Little written evidence remains of the abilities of these various types of workers in the mills. Since the operatives were

CARDING MACHINES, BIDDEFORD, AFTER WORLD WAR I

RING SPINNING ROOM, BIDDEFORD, AFTER WORLD WAR I

hired by the overseers, there was no accumulation of such records in the countinghouse. We find no statistical records of hirings, firings, length of service, reasons for discharge, et cetera. We have only the recollections of several of the overseers that Pepperell had efficient workers. These overseers have said that the mixture of Yankees and French Canadians proved satisfactory. Both were industrious and coöperative, though there were, of course, a few exceptions. Mule spinners, for example, were always inclined to demand new privileges, as we shall see shortly.

The operatives, on the whole, improved their position throughout this period. They shared in the gradual reduction in hours of work. In 1887, by State law, the number of hours was cut from 66 to 60 for women and children under sixteen years old. Since women were indispensable in the mills, this law meant that the mills could not operate more than 60 hours. In 1910 the number of hours was similarly reduced to 58 and in 1916 to 54.[10]

The total pay of the operatives increased in spite of the reduction in number of hours worked. There were, however, many cuts and advances during this period. When business was poor, the operatives had to take cuts in rates of pay. Similarly, when business was good, they received an advance. Of course at the same time that the rates were reduced, there might also be a temporary reduction in the hours worked which is not disclosed in Table 4.

From this table of general changes in wage rates by the Pepperell Manufacturing Company, we conclude that in the 1880's and 1890's wage rates were cut, not at the beginning of depressed times but after a year or so of depression, and that rates were increased to approximately their former levels within a year or so. During the first World War, rates increased to nearly 300 per cent of their prewar level. After the war, rates were reduced in 1920 and 1922, but were raised again in 1922 and 1923. Thus by the end of the middle period, wage rates were still at the inflated heights of the war years. From Table 4 we see also that until 1913 Pepperell's workers were better off than the average worker in the cotton textile industry

TABLE 4

GENERAL CHANGES IN WAGE RATES OF THE PEPPERELL MANUFACTURING COMPANY AND AVERAGE HOURLY WAGES IN THE COTTON TEXTILE INDUSTRY OF THE UNITED STATES
1870–1924

Date[a]	Pepperell Mfg. Co. Advance %	Pepperell Mfg. Co. Cut %	Pepperell Mfg. Co. Index (1913 = 100)	U. S. Index of Hourly Wages, Cotton Textile Industry (1913 = 100)	Date	Pepperell Mfg. Co. Advance %	Pepperell Mfg. Co. Cut %	Pepperell Mfg. Co. Index (1913 = 100)	U. S. Index of Hourly Wages, Cotton Textile Industry (1913 = 100)
Dec. 1, 1873		10	([a])		Jan. 10, 1916	5		105	120.6
Apr. 1, 1880	10		83		Apr. 17, 1916	10		116	
Feb. 11, 1884		10	75		Oct. 30, 1916	7½		125	
Mar. 1, 1885	11		84		Jan. 1, 1917	10		138	143.0
Jan. 29, 1894		10	75	59.6	June 4, 1917	10		152	
June 3, 1895	10		83	59.1	Oct. 29, 1917	10		167	
Jan. 17, 1898		10	75	58.2	Apr. 1, 1918	10		187	179.9
Apr. 3, 1899	10		83	57.7	June 10, 1918	17		219	
Dec. 18, 1899	10		91		June 2, 1919	15		252	185.0
July 30, 1906	5		96	79.1	Dec. 1, 1919	12½		284	
Dec. 31, 1906	5		101		Dec. 20, 1920		22½	219	323.5
June 3, 1907	5		106	90.2	Feb. 13, 1922		20	175	222.4
Apr. 6, 1908		10	95	89.4	Sept. 11, 1922	25		219	
Mar. 11, 1912	5		100	98.8	Apr. 30, 1923	12½		246	255.0

[a] During the years in which William P. Haines was agent for the second time, 1871–79, apparently it was his general policy to make cuts and increases by departments. Only for Dec. 1, 1873, do I find evidences of cuts in all departments. Of the various groups in his time I find that the mule spinners and their back boys experienced very severe cuts. The mule spinners received the highest piece rate in May of 1872; during the following eight years they were cut eight times and raised four times. In June of 1880 their rate was less than half that of May, 1872. Their back boys' rates were changed less often and less severely; by February of 1879 these boys were earning a third less a day than in May of 1872. (MS. PMC, Payrolls, Mill No. 3, 1870–1880.)

Source: MS. PMC, Payrolls, 1870–86; Agent's general letter book, 1879–80, p. 220; 1883–85, pp. 171–172; Treasurer's letter books, 1884–87, p. 239; 1893–97, pp. 233, 587; 1897–1901, pp. 77, 89, 259, 459; 1904–07, pp. 552, 653, 851; 1914–17, pp. 729, 813; 1917–19, p. 395; 1920–21, p. 338; Assistant Treasurer's letter book, 1915–20, p. 126; Clarence Gove's little notebook for changes, 1894–1923; Stephen Jay Kennedy, *Profits and Losses in Textiles*, p. 251.

in the United States; at least they were if the year 1913 is used as the base. Wage rates in the industry, however, continued to rise in 1920, after Pepperell's had taken a cut. In 1923 the two indices were not far apart.

It is much more difficult to piece together the declines in Pepperell's wage rates which took place between 1870 and 1880 while William P. Haines was agent. Apparently he would cut the rates in one or two rooms at a time rather than throughout the mill. Since renovation was taking place in the mills, this practice was feasible. Perhaps the apparent cuts in rates were accompanied by greater productive activity, so that altogether the workers earned about the same amount. This field of investigation is very promising for other students—those who wish to make their contribution to the investigation of wage rates and of increased productivity resulting from improved machinery. Although Pepperell's records for this period include adequate series of payrolls and various records of improvements, an exhaustive study of them would prove very laborious. The results might, however, throw further light on our knowledge of the rewards of labor.

Another field for investigation is that of total weekly wages of the workers. This involves the laborious studies mentioned in the previous paragraph, as well as a knowledge of the groups which should be analyzed together. Without such a background, wages for many classes of workers are difficult to determine, since workers in the largest departments, such as the weaving and spinning, were paid partly on a time basis and partly on a piece-rate basis. Because of the differences among the workers, average weekly wage rates for all the workers mean little. We find for example that the weekly average on August 15, 1914, was $8.97 for 58 hours; on June 29, 1918, $18.53 for 54 hours; and on November 8, 1919, $21.17 for 54 hours.[11] These data reveal little more than the changes in general rates and the change in number of hours in the working week.

Another problem which might be studied further is the relative positions of various groups in the mills. We have found that the overseers received few cuts in rates and enjoyed many of the increases of their subordinates. But to what extent did the treasurer, the agent, and the superintendent consider that other groups should be treated separately? In the industry it is conceded that workers in the weaving rooms do receive more than those of similar skill in the ring-spinning and carding rooms. Perhaps this difference is an inheritance from the early years of organization of large companies. Then there was a supply of trained spinners but there were no trained weavers. Another group, which seems to have fared better than others at times, was the mule spinner. Although only a handful of them was needed to spin the filling compared to a hundred others in the ring-spinning rooms, why did the former consistently get much higher wages? In spite of the mule spinners' preferred position, the records which I have investigated for the 1870's show that these spinners and back boys received frequent and severe cuts in wages. How much did this practice of cutting wages contribute to the uneasiness of this group in the following decades?

Still another field for more complete investigation is worker welfare. We know that Pepperell had an eye for the welfare of the employees, at least to some extent. Any accident in the mills was taken care of by the company. A man or a woman who sustained an injury was attended by a local doctor, either at the mills or at his office near-by. When there were smallpox scares, the company arranged to have the operatives vaccinated in the mills at the company's expense. In 1901, at the time of such a scare, Gibbs remembered that similar vaccinations had taken place four times before—the last in 1886. But apparently not all the people in Biddeford were vaccinated, because in January and February of 1903 there was a serious epidemic of smallpox. About 160 persons had contracted the disease by the end of February. Later in this period, in 1919, Pepperell set up a nursing center in the former Laconia countinghouse.

The company also provided acceptable sanitary arrangements for the workers in the mills, according to the standards of the time. Many of the workers kept their outdoor clothing in small individual boxes which could be used as seats. Others could hang their clothing on the ends of the machines—a rather

AUTOMATIC LOOMS, BIDDEFORD, AFTER WORLD WAR I

poor arrangement. Today the workers have individual lockers for their clothing.

Some of the habits of the workers seem strange to us today. In the 1880's a State inspector told of the habit, among many of the workers, of using snuff.[12] Of course this involved no fire hazard comparable to the smoking of cigarettes, which represented a hazard of great importance inasmuch as cotton lint was flying around in practically every room. In time probably this habit was supplanted by chewing gum and by smoking in the rooms provided for the purpose.

The workers lived not far from the mills. A complete study from the records available cannot be undertaken at this time. Many of the unmarried people, girls and men, lived in the company boarding houses until these houses were taken down in 1909 and 1910. Some of the married ones lived in the company houses, such as the ten houses on Bradbury Street, often called the "Ten Commandments." Many others lived in their own houses or in rented quarters. A thorough study of housing in Biddeford would be an interesting project. One wonders how much the standards set for the company houses influenced the others. At one time a trustee reported that the company was planning to improve its houses and keep rents low, hoping that this would have a beneficial effect on housing in Biddeford.

Many of the French Canadians took trips back to their old homes in the summer time. In 1902, for example, the agent remarked that the workers were leaving for Canada the first of June, probably to engage in agricultural work in Quebec Province. They generally came back about the first of September. While they were gone, the agent frequently closed the mills for a time to give the others a vacation. These shutdowns were usually around the Fourth of July and Labor Day. The operatives had worked hard during the first months of the year and probably needed a change of scene, at least for a short time.

During this period we find few traces of labor unrest. Apparently the majority were content with their lot. They were earning cash wages which must have seemed high compared with the cash received on the farm. Many were probably saving a portion of their earnings to invest in a farm in Canada or in property in Biddeford. They were willing to continue to work long hours, as they had been accustomed to do on the farm.

But there was a small element among the workers which was not content. Probably this was smaller than in the larger mill centers in New England, particularly in Fall River, which had been a hotbed of labor unrest ever since the 1840's.[13] Some of the workers there, as well as a few in Biddeford, belonged to families which had been industrial workers for several generations. Among such workers were the mule spinners, frequently Englishmen. In this period we find that they struck several times to better their conditions. Usually these strikes were part of a movement throughout New England, sponsored by local organizations which often died out after the strike had been lost.

The first of these strikes in Biddeford occurred in June of 1881, a year after an epidemic of strikes. Not the mule spinners but their back boys went out, asking for higher wages. Without them the mills were forced to close for ten days. The company secured a few back boys from the outside and then, after nearly two weeks, the boys voted to return to work the following week. Neither a general wage increase nor an increase to the back boys was granted throughout the mill, but the agent agreed to raise a few weavers whose wages were below those prevailing elsewhere.

Twelve years later, in June of 1893, the second serious strike for Pepperell occurred. Then the mule spinners as well as the back boys struck for higher wages. McArthur, who was the agent, promised that he would investigate wages elsewhere and pay them at least as much as in similar mills, but not until after they returned to work. After two weeks the strikers returned. McArthur corresponded with several mills and visited others to determine rates for all types of workers. The results of his work were incorporated in a set of wage rates and duties of all the workers in the mills. Some rates he raised. The mule spinners' rates were increased by about a dollar a week, from \$11.42 to \$12.35 on the average. The back boys' weekly wages were raised considerably, from rates between \$1.20 and \$2.70

to $3.00 or $3.30. For other jobs in the mill, rates were increased somewhat so that the wages would be slightly higher than those in corresponding mills and so that the workers would stay in Biddeford rather than drift off to other centers.[14]

Pepperell's third strike occurred when the mule spinners went out in protest against the general reduction of wages which had been announced to take effect on January 17, 1898. This reduction took place almost universally in mills in New England, and similar strikes occurred throughout New England. At this time the treasurer made plans to get rid of all the mule frames eventually and to put in ring frames. This, however, did not take place immediately. The workers held out for seven weeks and then returned to work on the company's terms. In other mills they did likewise.

No other strike took place in the Pepperell mills until February, 1919, when one was called as part of a general campaign by the United Textile Workers of America for an eight-hour working day, as well as for union organization and the transfer of war bonuses to straight wages. Pepperell granted none of these demands, and after eleven weeks the strikers returned to work. In June, to be sure, Pepperell granted another wage increase, but what bearing the strike had had upon it I have not discovered.

At other times groups of workers expressed their dissatisfaction by walking out or threatening to do so—for example, when the number of hours was cut by law or when new machinery resulted in changes in rates for work. But either the agent or the superintendent was able to persuade them to remain at their jobs. According to the recollections of one of the overseers, George K. Gibbs was successful in such instances in convincing groups of workers to return to their machines.

How indicative this labor unrest was of the way the management handled the workers, it is hard to judge. Certainly there appear to have been fewer strikes in Biddeford than in many other mill centers in New England. On the whole, Pepperell had a coöperative body of workers. From time to time they were called upon to produce more and more with the improved machinery which was introduced. In the following pages we may see some of this increased productivity in our consideration of the mills' operation.

CONCENTRATION AND DIVERSIFICATION OF PRODUCTION

In an earlier chapter we have discussed the production of the Pepperell mills from 1850 to 1870. We found that production increased to an annual peak in 1860–61 of nearly sixteen million yards of goods, a height which the company did not reach again during the following decade. We discovered that in this early period Pepperell generally produced only a few lines of cottons—shirtings, sheetings, drills, and jeans—with occasional diversions to flannels and ducks. In the present section we shall carry further our examination of Pepperell's production.

During the first twenty-nine years of this period, 1870 to the spring of 1899, the usual orders came in from the treasurer and the selling house to the mill agents for more goods. To be sure, this period covers the years of general decline in prices and of business activity, 1866–97. During the first five years, 1870–71 through 1875–76, William P. Haines did not reach the height of production which he had achieved in 1860–61, as Appendix 27 shows. Besides general external factors working against prosperity, there were several internal factors such as changes in the directorate, in the treasurer, and in the selling house. The mills in Biddeford also needed renovation, as we have seen. After these early troubles had been straightened out, the mill agents—Haines, Howe, and McArthur—were able to produce an adequate volume of cotton goods. In 1895–96 McArthur reported a record production of thirty-four million yards with about 110,000 spindles. This production meant an increase of 127 per cent over that of 1860–61 and of 220 per cent over that of 1870–71. It meant a year's production of 300 yards per spindle, as compared to 230 yards per spindle in 1860–61.

Each of the three agents experienced one year when production was significantly below that of the preceding year. Both Haines and Howe had their lows during depression years, 1874–75 and 1884–85, when production was 13 and 5 per cent respectively below that of the preceding year. McArthur's poor year occurred not during the depression years of the 1890's, but later in the decade, in 1897–98, when the mills were closed for about ten weeks because of a strike. Production then was 6 per cent below that of the preceding year. But these cuts in production seem quite small when we consider the fluctuations in general business during the last part of the nineteenth century. They show how strong Pepperell's position was.

For a major part of these twenty-nine years before the consolidation with Laconia, the three agents were thus able to operate fairly close to full production. According to semiannual figures, however, they could not maintain the same rate of production throughout the year. Some of the workers, as we have noted, tended to take trips home in the summer. Also, the agents favored vacation periods about the first of July and September, when they closed the mills for a short time. As a result of this freedom in the summer, production in the last six months of the calendar year lagged somewhat below that in the first.

From 1899 to 1924 the agents, McArthur and Morrill, had capacity for producing many more yards each year. In 1899–1900 McArthur produced sixty-six million yards, with slightly over 200,000 spindles. Six years later he was able to report a banner year with the production of seventy-four million yards. This was almost the peak of production, but in 1915–16, Morrill reported seventy-five million yards. One wonders why the mills, after they had been expanded nearly 50 per cent, did not reach one hundred million yards a year, especially during the first World War. There may be several reasons, one of which was the reduction in hours of the work-week.

During this quarter-century, 1899–1924, there were many more years of significant cuts in production than in the preceding twenty-nine. In eight of them, four before and four after the first World War, production was at least 6 per cent lower than that of the preceding year. Generally these declines occurred with upsets in general business conditions. But many of these cuts were much more serious than in the preceding century. Had Pepperell reached a dangerous stage where it could not maintain its regularity of production in spite of unsettled conditions at home and abroad?

The types of goods which the mills produced, we conclude from the records, were principally the four lines set by the former selling house—shirtings, sheetings, drills, and jeans. There were, however, shifts within these four lines, as Appendix 26 shows; shirtings came to be of less importance. While the new selling house, J. S. & E. Wright & Co., suggested the addition of a few lines, these new types were not produced to the same extent as the first four. Sateens, the most important of the new lines, reached a peak of 20 per cent of total production in 1875–76 and declined relatively after that. Pepperell continued to produce substantially what it had produced in the first years of operation. Perhaps this willingness to keep on with the old was a sign of maturity. In the Laconia Division there was a different pattern of production. For years it produced a few large lines and many small special orders as the Laconia mills had been doing in the previous years.

During this middle period of Pepperell's history many other mills were turning to the types of goods which Pepperell had produced so profitably since its beginning. By 1912–13, according to Davison's *Textile Blue Book,* there were three hundred companies in the United States which were classified as producers of sheetings, shirtings, jeans, drills, and twills. Many of these producers were in the South and many were small. Moreover, the goods of the South generally did not bring such high prices for similar weaves and style—an inheritance, no doubt, from the first years of poor production after the Civil War. At the same time, Pepperell was one of the forty manufacturers of sateens listed in the United States—most of which at this time were in the North. It is no wonder, then, that in the face of increasing competition Pepperell did not produce a hundred million yards a year even though its machine capacity seems to have made that level possible.

From the records which remain I judge that the treasurers of the Pepperell Manufacturing Company continued to believe that quality should be maintained. In the first period, as we have seen, William Dwight had emphasized the quality of the goods, particularly of those for export. In George Dexter's correspondence with the mill agents occasional references to quality crop out. In 1880, for example, Dexter wrote to Howe, the new agent, as follows, "I would stick very close to the proper standard of quality and put all not up [to standard] into seconds . . . our name is too good to lose. Good goods, without regard to size of product—is my motto. Everything else hinges on that." [15]

We thus come to the conclusion that, in order to survive, Pepperell needed changes in its types of goods, by the end of this period. On the whole, the company had had glorious years of production in the nineteenth century, but production fluctuated more violently in the twentieth century. Pepperell had in Biddeford more machinery than could be operated to full extent. Its goods, many of which had been produced since the first years of operation, were made by numerous others in the North and South. In the following pages we shall see how Pepperell's costs compared with those of other textile companies.

CONTROL OF COSTS

Great efforts were made to keep the costs of manufacture down in this middle period. We have already seen that the company spent large sums on construction and machinery. The treasurer figured that costs would be less with such machinery, so that within a short time the machinery would pay for itself. Also, we have already seen that for a time the agent increased the number of workers on the payroll and then decreased the number. We have found that the agent changed wage rates of the operatives from time to time, thus varying the total cost of labor. Let us now consider the three major items of the cost of manufacture—cotton, factory payroll, and general expense.

Cotton always made up the greatest part of the cost of manufacture. Since the agent did not buy the cotton, we shall not be concerned here with its price or with the methods of its purchase. We shall take account of it only after it became the agent's responsibility. Some of the cotton was shipped to Biddeford by boat but much more came by railroad. To facilitate its handling, storage houses were built near a spur of the railroad tracks. There the cotton, as it was received, was stored away until needed.

Early in this middle period George Dexter established in Biddeford a control system for cotton, which persisted with little change throughout the period. In 1878 or 1879 he decided to have the cotton sampled and weighed at the time of arrival of the bales at the mills as a check on the quality and weights set down when purchased. These duties related more to his purchasing of cotton than to the agent's of handling the cotton. A man was trained for the job of classifying and weighing raw cotton at the company's expense. But he did not give satisfaction, and in 1881 was replaced by Robert A. Fairfield, formerly a clerk in the countinghouse. Fairfield continued as cotton classer and weigher throughout this period.

We find considerable variations in the amounts of cotton stored in Biddeford at the end of each accounting period. There is a series of figures for Pepperell from December, 1870, through December, 1898, and for the Pepperell Division in the following six-month periods through June, 1911. At that time the two accounting offices were combined, and henceforth one series of figures was kept for the two divisions. During the span from 1870 to 1911 we find that typically $500,000 worth of cotton was stored in December and only $300,000 in June. This is quite the opposite situation to that prevailing earlier, when we found that more cotton was stored in Biddeford in June than in December. Evidently it reflects the change to more rapid transportation of cotton from the South following the harvest.

Again, as in the Civil War and its postwar period, we find the pattern for cotton greatly altered by war. A series of figures gives the treasurer's balances with the mill agent for both divisions, the largest percentage of which was inventory of cotton; the typical figures for this balance in the three prewar years, December, 1911, through June, 1914, were $1,160,000 for December and $490,000 for June. For the following ten years the corresponding typical inventory figures were $4,180,000 and $2,750,000 respectively. War-time increases in the price of cotton and a change from the previous method of stating the value very conservatively—a change due to government regulations regarding the reporting of income for taxes—accounted for much of this tripling in value of cotton inventory.

According to the semiannual reckonings of the cost of manufacture, the cost of the cotton used grew gradually, and, as one would expect, it grew with the expansion of the mills. At times, however, there were periods when the cost of cotton was out of line with the trend of expansion because cotton prices fluctuated with business conditions. Since cotton prices rose rapidly during the first World War and did not return to the previous levels for more than a decade, the cost of cotton used in manufacturing mounted rapidly. But it was the treasurer, not the agent, who bore the responsibility for this cost, although the latter figured it into his total manufacturing expenses. Several times during the first World War, as we shall see in a later chapter, the treasurer added to the cost of the cotton used a large sum as a reserve against a later drop in the price of cotton.

Let us glance briefly at the records of the totals of other expenses of manufacture for similar periods—mill expense and general expense. Mill expense, as we have noted earlier, included only the pay of the employees—supervisory and operative—in the carding, spinning, dressing, and weaving rooms of the mills. This series of figures for December, 1870, through June, 1911, showed much less violent fluctuations than the series for cotton. This is as one would expect, even though changes in wage rates and in the schedule of hours upset the normal growth. From 1870 to 1899 the percentage of increase in mill expense was about the same as in the number of employees—33 per cent. Wage rates were apparently about the same at the two periods, although they had fluctuated in the interim. After the figures for the two divisions had been combined, the total mill expense, of course, increased considerably. During the first World War the workers shared in the inflation of wages and prices, as they had not done during the Civil War.

Similarly the general expense—salaries of the agent and the superintendent, wages of the workers outside the four major divisions of the mills, miscellaneous supplies, and various other expenses, such as taxes—showed little cyclical fluctuation but a gradual trend upward during the period December, 1870, through June, 1911. One part of this expense about which the treasurer and agent were concerned was taxes. Although it composed a minor part of the general expense, typically about 20 per cent, the agent, not unlike most taxpayers, always felt it should be lower. On each first of April the agent reported to the assessors of Biddeford the value of the company's property in the city. For land, buildings, and machinery he set a value based on the number of spindles. In 1880, for example, he set $12 for each of the 85,000 spindles. In addition, for that year he valued the cotton stored and in process at 12 cents a pound, the various supplies at a lump sum of $10,000, and the bales of cotton goods stored but not sold at $60 a bale.

Later in this period, in addition to the local taxes, came a federal income tax. This was not, however, added to the cost of manufacturing but paid directly from the profit and loss account. During and after the first World War this tax grew to a tremendous size—about $1,800,000 for the fiscal year 1919–20.

The total cost of manufacturing, composed of the three series —cotton, mill expense, and general expense—increased during this period of fifty-four years. On the whole the total manufacturing expense remained divided as earlier—66 per cent for cotton, 22 per cent for mill expense, and 12 per cent for general expense.

Although the major expense of manufacture was outside the agent's control, the agent was vitally interested in two other items. He set up a system of computing, for every four weeks, the labor cost in each part of each process per pound produced. Also, he figured the total mill and general expense per pound of cloth and per hank of yarn. The agent sometimes used these figures for one division to spur the others on to still greater effort.

Occasionally the treasurer commented in his letters about the expenses of the Biddeford mills as compared with others. We find many such comments in the middle 1890's when business was upset and competition with mills in the South was growing keener. As regards other mills in the North, Pepperell had some advantages and some disadvantages. Some of the advantages came from Pepperell's strong financial position—it could buy machinery when others did not have the funds. Other advantages came from natural or geographical considerations, as one would expect. In January of 1893 George Dexter remarked that freight rates for cotton from the South were the same to Biddeford and Saco as to Boston. On this item Pepperell was apparently in about the same position as the companies around Boston. Dexter said, however, that Pepperell's expenses were high for coal and taxes as compared with the mills in Fall River and New Bedford. But, on the other hand, mills in Maine were allowed to run more hours a week than those in Massachusetts. Perhaps, on the whole, Pepperell had a slight edge over mills in Massachusetts since labor was a much more important item than coal and taxes combined.

Compared with costs in the South, Dexter found that Pepperell's costs were much higher. In 1894 he reported to McArthur the differences in costs between the two sections as determined by Alford, of the selling house, in a trip to the South. Dexter wrote that the best southern mills had a labor cost of 25 per cent less than Pepperell's, a supply of excellent employees who were willing to work from 66 to 70 hours a week, good water power, and low taxes. He wrote also that he thought northerners should not underrate their competitors. He said, "The South can beat us in everything but one item—They are capitalized high. They have plenty of contented help and we have people who strive to ruin our business the moment we say lower wages. It's got to come to less wages here or more at the South & at the present there is no hope of the latter." [16] Dexter was therefore quite convinced that the northern mills could not compete with those in the South. He was content to let Pepperell and Laconia remain with no further expansion in Biddeford; however, he installed improved machinery where needed.

In fact, George Dexter was so convinced of the South's future that in 1896 he sent a petition to the Legislature of Maine for authority to increase the capital stock of Pepperell from $1,200,000 to $2,500,000 and of Laconia from $1,200,000 to $2,200,000, with the possibility of going "South if we find it costs too much to manufacture at the North." He mentioned two Massachusetts companies which were investing in the South, the Massachusetts Cotton Mills, of Lowell, and the Dwight Manufacturing Co., of Chicopee. But Dexter did not move South. The consolidation with Laconia which took place within three years absorbed much of his attention and time.

The following two treasurers, DeNormandie and Amory, as we have seen, held different views—at least, they increased the machinery of the combined mills by about 50 per cent. Business was good in much of the first decade of the twentieth century and excellent during a few years of the second. It is not, therefore, until the third decade that we hear again of the difficulties of operation and of the possibility of moving South.

Starting in December of 1922, the trustees explored the advisability of acquiring a plant in the South. They considered purchasing one which had been in operation for some time, but they did not purchase it. In fact, they were despondent about the possibility of acquiring a good southern plant in which to produce at costs comparable with those of companies in the South. In this depressed frame of mind they continued until the autumn of 1924, when they found a new treasurer, Russell H. Leonard.

* * *

In 1924 the Pepperell Manufacturing Company ended its middle period of existence. In Biddeford these years brought many changes. The mills had grown to more than double the size they had been in 1870. The two independent companies became one, at least legally, but the two divisions continued many of the practices of the separate companies. A more drastic change was necessary to make them into one economical operating whole. This change was to occur in the following period.

The supervisory force in Biddeford retained about the same character as in the earlier period. There were some changes, however, over the years. In place of men with college educations, the agents were men whose education had been less formally acquired. They retained most of the practices of earlier agents. One great change was the creation of an independent position for the superintendent. By 1881 George K. Gibbs had established the place for such a man—between the agent and the overseers—although the lines of control were not clearly drawn. The overseers continued to be recruited from the lower ranks within the company or within other textile companies and machine shops. They kept the duties of the earlier period—the hiring, firing, and supervising of the operatives in their departments.

The operatives changed in nationality, from predominantly Yankee to a mixture of French Canadian, Yankee, and Irish. They continued to be a coöperative group. They stayed with the mills, although they might take summer vacations. The few instances of friction which developed were generally over a change in compensation or in sympathy with others in the industry. The employees came to be paid better and better, but were still low in the scale of industrial workers.

With such a force—supervisory and operative—the mills were able for many years to increase their output far beyond the increase in machinery. But after a time the capacity outstripped the orders for goods and the mills did not operate to full capacity. Little by little, weaknesses crept in which needed to be corrected. Not until after the end of the second period, however, did a drastic change in the operation of the mills occur.

CHAPTER IX

PEPPERELL SELECTS ANOTHER SELLING HOUSE

IN THE AUTUMN of 1870, after the failure of the selling house for Pepperell's goods, the treasurer and directors of the Pepperell Manufacturing Company were faced with the problem of how their output should be handled in the future. Whereas there was no consideration of a change from the customary method of distribution through a commission selling house, there was a discussion as to which selling house to select. They chose one, established in Boston for decades, which recently had been expanding its operations. It was then J. S. & E. Wright & Co. which was in time to become Bliss, Fabyan & Co. With this house Pepperell began a connection in October, 1870, which continued throughout its middle period.

Some of my readers will wonder why I devote so much attention to the selling houses. The mere fact that we know so little about them would not justify the emphasis. The plain truth is that, though outside the legal framework of Pepperell, the selling house performed an *essential* function of the Pepperell business. In the third period (1924–45), indeed, this function was drawn into Pepperell's operations and all dependence upon a selling house was abolished.

NEW PILLARS IN AN OLD HOUSE

The new selling house for Pepperell's goods was conservative and strong. It was a combination of a father, John S. Wright, old and experienced in banking and selling; his two sons, Eben and John H. Wright, middle-aged, with less business experience; and two young men, not related by blood, who, after gaining experience in wholesaling, had recently been added. In 1874, after the death of John S. Wright, the two sons recognized the growing importance of the young partners by including their names in the firm name of Wright, Bliss & Fabyan. In 1882, after the Wrights' deaths, the firm name became Bliss, Fabyan & Co.—a style which it kept for several decades. These two men, Cornelius N. Bliss and George F. Fabyan, with other partners, outsiders and sons, built up the business over the years from a small one in 1870 to a large one during the first World War.

Ever since 1831 John S. Wright had been in the commission business in American goods, as Appendices 28 and 29 show, and he had acquired a fine reputation. A writer later said that he had the "finest sense of integrity and honorable dealing" and that he was "prompt and attentive to business, rarely absent from the counting room." [1] For many years he had been content to have a small selling house, but after the Civil War he and his sons saw the advantage of adding to the business. They took in Bliss and Fabyan as partners, as we have seen, and sent Bliss to set up an office in New York.

The most important of the partners in the selling house after the passing of John S. Wright was Cornelius N. Bliss. Not only did he build up the business in the New York office but he was active outside the business as well. He served on city and State committees in New York. For a time he was treasurer of the Republican National Committee and for a short period served as McKinley's Secretary of the Interior, but he refused other political opportunities which would take him too far and too long from his business. Both directly and indirectly, Pepperell benefited from these activities, particularly those which pertained to the protection of cotton goods from foreign competition.[2]

During the years when Cornelius N. Bliss was directing the sales in New York and adding luster to the firm, other partners in the firm were combining selling with the direction of textile companies as partners in Pepperell's former selling house had done. We find that Eben and John H. Wright and George F. Fabyan were in 1870 the treasurers of five textile companies altogether. Fourteen years later, three partners were treasurers of seven companies. This duality of function continued throughout the period. In 1924 two partners in Boston were the treasurers of six companies.[3] They, therefore, could not give full attention to selling problems. In fact, the Boston office became the headquarters for the management of mills and declined in importance in selling goods.*

Instead of having sub-agents in other cities, which had been the prevailing practice in the preceding period, the Wrights set up branch offices or selected representatives. This gave them more control over the selling than Skinner's previous method had attained. One of the early branch offices was in Philadelphia, but with the decline in importance of this city as a center, the selling house changed to a resident representative. About the turn of the century a branch office was opened in Chicago with one of George F. Fabyan's sons, George, in charge. This office was kept throughout the remainder of the period. Later still, representatives were secured in St. Louis and San Francisco.[6]

During this period J. S. & E. Wright & Co., and its successor

* Assisting the partners of the selling house were a number of other men. Among them were the junior partners, who bore less responsibility than the senior partners and consequently shared less in the profits of the company. There were also a number of salesmen, clerks of several kinds, and messenger boys. Many of this group started at the bottom rung. In time, if they showed ability and industry, they were promoted to more important positions. Some became salesmen in the home offices, and others became traveling salesmen. A few rose eventually near to the top of the ladder as junior partners. Such success had been achieved by 1919, for example, by S. Robert Glassford, who had started to work for the house in 1892.

During the fifty-four years of Pepperell's middle period, 1870 to 1924, the selling house maintained offices in Boston and New York. Several times the firm moved its Boston offices, which remained the keeper of the firm's records. In 1872 the Wrights' office on Franklin Street was burned out in the great Boston fire, which swept devastatingly through the commercial district almost as far as State Street. After being located in temporary quarters the office was established at 100 Summer Street, corner of Devonshire, remaining for nearly forty years in the heart of the dry goods commission and wholesaling district of Boston. Still later the firm returned to Franklin Street.[4] In New York during the same period the selling house had its most important office for selling; it moved twice, from Franklin Street to Thomas and then to a new building on Thomas Street, where for about sixty years it occupied the same offices in the center of the commission and wholesale business in cotton textiles.[5]

CORNELIUS N. BLISS
Senior Partner in the Selling House in New York

GEORGE F. FABYAN
Senior Partner in the Selling House in Boston

firms, thus continued to some extent the general pattern of operation which Francis Skinner & Co. had established earlier. In both companies some partners combined the rôle of treasurer of cotton textile concerns with that of a member of the selling house. Both houses maintained offices in the two most important cotton textile centers with sub-agents or branch offices and representatives elsewhere. But ties between the selling houses and their textile companies differed. As an illustration of this situation we shall consider in the following section the relations between Pepperell and its selling house.

LINKS BETWEEN PEPPERELL AND THE SELLING HOUSE

Many links similar to those between Pepperell and its former selling house, Francis Skinner & Co., were formed in this period between Pepperell and its new selling house, J. S. & E. Wright & Co. As formerly, there was a written contract between the two concerning the terms for handling the business, which were changed from time to time. Also, as formerly, the treasurers handled part of the selling job: earlier the treasurers had handled the discounting of the sales notes, but in this period they also attended to registration of trade-marks and to the advertising of goods. As formerly, there were other business links—partners in the selling house owned Pepperell stock and two of them, George F. Fabyan and then Philip Y. DeNormandie, were on Pepperell's board of directors or trustees. Also there were many personal ties between the men in the manufacturing company and the selling house. No exact measurement of the strength of all these links in the selling of goods can, however, be obtained from the records available.

In the fall of 1870 the treasurer and directors of the Pepperell Manufacturing Company had considered several firms before deciding on J. S. & E. Wright & Co. At a meeting on September 19, 1870, five directors expressed their unanimous choice of Gardner, Brewer & Co.; but a few weeks later on the first ballot six of the directors tied between George C. Richardson & Co. and J. S. & E. Wright & Co. On the second ballot the latter received the majority. Just why this change in attitude took place we do not know. All three of the selling houses were strong and well-established. We might surmise that one reason was that the first two had several large accounts, while the Wrights at that time had only small ones, as Appendix 29 shows. The directors, as had been the case twenty years earlier, may have wanted a house which would give first attention to Pepperell and felt that the other two houses would not have done so. Moreover, there may have been a personal reason since one of the directors, Lyman Nichols, was the father-in-law of John H. Wright.[7] At any rate, J. S. & E. Wright & Co. was chosen. Soon this selling house took several other large accounts from among those served up to about that time by Francis Skinner & Co.—Laconia, Bates, Androscoggin, Continental, and Franklin—but none of these was so large as Pepperell. In all, by 1873, as Appendix 29 shows, this selling house had the accounts of sixteen companies, nine more than in the middle of 1870. Most of these accounts were kept for long periods. A few of the companies were merged with others; a few passed out of existence; and a few made other arrangements about selling.

Pepperell's contract with J. S. & E. Wright & Co. on October 10, 1870, differed from the earlier one with Francis Skinner & Co. in several respects. The new rate was 1¼ per cent on all sales instead of the earlier 1½ per cent. The second important difference was that "Cash [was] to be collected and notes to be received on account of sales by J. S. & E. Wright & Co. as agents and passed over to the treasurer as soon as received." This was an acknowledgment of part of the change which had taken place previously in dealings with Francis Skinner & Co. That company during and after the Civil War had collected the sales notes and received cash for most of them. It had not, however, turned the cash over promptly enough to the textile companies. In 1870 the treasurer and directors were determined that such a condition should not recur.

In the contract in 1870 J. S. & E. Wright & Co. agreed "to endorse the notes of the corporation or sign as surety for the payment of such notes as the need of the corporation for money on occasion may require without additional charge." Such had been the practice earlier, but it had not been so explicitly stated in the contract.

Other terms were about the same as those made previously. Again the books of account pertaining to Pepperell's sales were to be kept separately from those of other companies. The sales agent was to render a weekly sketch of sales to the treasurer and a monthly account of sales in detail. Charges upon sales, other than the commission, were to be the actual amounts incurred for labor, truckage, postage, advertising, and freight. These terms on the whole were more favorable to Pepperell than the earlier arrangement.

For many years the terms with the subsequent partnerships remained the same. In fact, it was not until 1896 that any changes were made. At that time Bliss, Fabyan & Co. notified the treasurer that 1¼ per cent was not a sufficient commission, and as a result the directors voted to allow 1½ per cent. During the next twenty-five years the question of commissions came up only once. A committee was appointed by Pepperell's trustees in 1920 to investigate and report. As a result the existing rates were continued. Thus, with little change, the terms adopted in 1870 were continued for 54 years.

Pepperell needed services connected with sales other than those provided by the selling house. We know from extant letters that the treasurers themselves handled the matter of registration of trade-marks. By the end of 1881 George Dexter had arranged through the office of H. B. Claflin & Co. in Manchester, England, to register the Dragon drill there. Later he made arrangements for the registration of Laconia's Peacock drill and Beaver jean in England and for all of them in Germany, France, and Brazil. This all took place before trade-marks were registered in the United States under the new patent law of 1884. At the time of renewals about the end of the century, Dexter arranged to have the trade-marks registered in Shanghai and Japan by the China & Japan Trading Co. Later they were registered in other places, such as Chile and Cuba.

From the English office of H. B. Claflin & Co., George Dexter also obtained information about the violations of his trade-marks. In one case goods were found with a poorly marked Dragon. After an analysis of the starch, it was found that the goods in this case were Pepperell's drills, which, having been sea-damaged, had been "refolded, rebaled & probably restamped." Later the consul at Shanghai, the China & Japan Trading Co., and others assisted in suppressing fraudulent use of the trade-marks.

Toward the end of this period the treasurer felt the need for advertising the Pepperell name in the domestic market. Advertising circulars had been included with bales of goods for export, but no attempt had been made to reach domestic customers. In the spring of 1918 the treasurer, William Amory, considered various advertising possibilities. In the spring of 1920 the new treasurer, Walter H. Bradley, planned national advertising in magazines directed to the ultimate consumer, particularly the housewife, using a picture of Sir William Pepperell and a story of how the company got its name. Bradley turned to Perry Walton to prepare a booklet called *The Romance of Pepperell,* and to the Walton Advertising & Printing Co. for a program of advertising. But these efforts were handicapped because Pepperell did not have a distinctive product—its sheeting was similar to many others on the market. In 1922 Bradley hired a market analyst to survey the market for sheeting in ten States in the East and Middle West. From a series of interviews with retailers he found out that in many places Pepperell's Red Label sheeting was not well known. As a result Pepperell began building up demand for these sheets by distributing literature about the company and its products, with the aid of Franklin B. Shumway Co., an advertising agency in Boston.[8] The selling house coöperated in these plans, but the incentive came from Pepperell.

The new selling house was not so closely linked with Pepperell by ownership of stock as the former one had been. The firm itself acquired none, and the partners built up only small blocks. In August of 1871 the partners owned only 5 shares of the 2,000 outstanding. In 1880 they personally held 133, while probably influencing the owners of 41 more who were members of their immediate families or for whom they acted as trustees.

This made altogether only about 7 per cent of the total number of shares outstanding. In the following decades their proportional interest decreased. In 1890 it was only 3 per cent, in 1900 4 per cent, and in 1910 and 1920 about one per cent. Thus, as stockholders the partners in the selling house had little power. This contrasts sharply with the large number of shares which the house of Francis Skinner & Co., as well as its partners, held in the earlier period. Such a change was to be expected, however, since by 1870 Pepperell was well established and did not need to call upon the selling house for subscriptions to stock.

At the beginning of this period Pepperell's board of directors did not include a single member of the selling house. When a vacancy occurred in December of 1872, however, George F. Fabyan was elected and he continued to serve throughout the remainder of his life. After his death in 1907, Philip Y. DeNormandie, who had resigned his position as Pepperell's treasurer to become a member of Bliss, Fabyan & Co., was elected a director of Pepperell, and later a trustee; he held these positions for nearly a score of years. Thus, for long periods Pepperell had the services of important members of the selling house on its boards of directors and trustees. How much they contributed at the meetings of the boards cannot now be ascertained, since, according to the practice of the times, little except the actual voting on various measures was recorded. When George F. Fabyan died in 1907, we find in the directors' records an expression of appreciation of his part in Pepperell's success.

From the letters which Pepperell's treasurer wrote daily to the mill agent we gather that there were close ties between the treasurer and members of the selling house. Many of the treasurer's dealings seem to have been with one partner, Orlando H. Alford, of Boston. Dexter appears to have valued Alford's judgment highly, as we have already seen in one case concerning Pepperell's expansion.

From Pepperell's records we gather that, on the whole, Pepperell was fortunate in its arrangement with its selling house during this period. The links between the two were many—formal contract, participation in the selling function by the treasurer, stock ownership, directorship, and friendship. Not the least of these was the last, since it was perhaps the most important factor in bringing together members of the two concerns, the cotton textile company and the selling house.

THE SELLING HOUSE DEALS WITH MANY CUSTOMERS

In the middle period of Pepperell's history its selling house adhered to the policy of selling to important domestic customers located in the principal cities of the United States. It altered somewhat its dealings in export goods: instead of dealing only with American merchants, it distributed the goods to buyers of various nationalities. Since the evidence on distribution to customers is fragmentary, I have had to draw partial pictures for particular periods, trusting that they disclose somewhat the whole situation.

At the beginning of this period our detailed sales record consists of only a few daily sketches of sales in Boston and one journal of sales made by the New York office of J. S. & E. Wright & Co. for the period from October 31, 1870, through December 31, 1871. We cannot, therefore, get a full picture of distribution throughout the United States at that time. We can assume that the Boston office handled sales to wholesalers and others in Boston and elsewhere in New England and to a few customers scattered throughout the country. We find that the New York office seems to have devoted its attention to those in New York City, Philadelphia, and Baltimore, with only a scattering in the South and West. For this period of a year, two months, and a day, we find that there were nearly 300 different customers handled by the New York office, with about half of them in the three cities just mentioned. Since at that time the Boston office made about 60 per cent of the sales, it probably handled at least as many customers as the New York office.

After another quarter of a century, when we again have a series of sales records, ledgers for 1897 to 1913 and trial balances from 1906 to 1916, we find a somewhat different situation. From October, 1897, through December, 1900, according to a sales ledger, Bliss, Fabyan & Co. had about 800 customers for Pepperell's goods, which include those of both the Pepperell and Laconia Divisions. Although these figures are probably somewhat inflated by the inclusion of customers for a period of slightly more than three years, they do show roughly the number to whom Pepperell's goods were sold at the turn of the century. Probably this number was somewhat greater than that of Pepperell and Laconia in 1870 and 1871, when the new selling house took over the handling of the goods of the Biddeford companies. In the following years in the twentieth century the number of accounts grew. For the year 1916, according to the trial balances, there were about 1,300 customers. For the following years, until near the end of this second period, information is missing. For the year 1923–24 we can make an estimate from a sales journal of about 850 customers for the Pepperell Division alone. With customers added for the Laconia Division, the total number was probably about the same as in 1916.

A few of the total number of customers took a large share of the sales. Most outstanding for several decades was the firm of H. B. Claflin & Co., of New York, to whom Francis Skinner & Co. had also sold large amounts of Pepperell's goods. The Wrights and their successors continued to sell a large portion of Pepperell's goods to this company. Horace B. Claflin, the senior partner, built up his business in wholesaling, exporting, and importing, so that at the time of his death in 1885 his firm was said to be the largest of its kind in the world. Not only did Claflin build up sales in the New York office but he set up offices abroad. After his death, his son John became the head of the company, which continued to expand, adding retailing and manufacturing activities.[9]

In the records which we have available, we know of the purchases made by H. B. Claflin & Co. only from October 31, 1870, through December 31, 1871, and from 1897 to 1913. Although the records cover less than a half of the period involved, we can piece these sales together with other material to get a picture of the dealings with Pepperell's selling house. In the last two months of 1870 Claflin purchased $25,000 worth of Pepperell's goods. In the following year he purchased a much larger amount, $217,000 in all, or about 25 per cent of what was sold by the New York office and about 11 per cent of total sales by J. S. & E. Wright & Co. for Pepperell. Claflin evidently made a large portion of these purchases for distribution to smaller dealers in the United States. He bought shirtings, sheetings, jeans, and satinets, some in the brown, others bleached, and some dyed. For export, probably to his branch in Manchester, England, he bought drills in the brown. We cannot be sure about this, but all evidence in the records points to the fact that brown drills were treated separately. In November of 1870 he purchased 100 bales of drills, which cost over $7,000 and probably comprised about 28 per cent of his purchases from Pepperell in the last two months of that year. In 1871 he purchased 458 bales of brown drills, totaling almost $35,000, or about 16 per cent of his Pepperell purchases for that year.

For the following years, until 1897, we have no record of the amounts which H. B. Claflin & Co. bought from Pepperell through the sales agent. From the treasurer's letters we get an impression that relations with Claflin were good for domestic as well as for export business. George Dexter wrote quite frequently to Claflin's Manchester house about conditions in America and elsewhere, about registration of trade-marks, and about the violations of trade-marks which Claflin had unearthed. In letters to others Dexter gave information about the export business which Claflin handled and which went largely to India. In 1882 Dexter wrote Henry S. Howe, the mill agent, "I should think about 20 per cent of our drills are for India—but cannot be sure as the sales to Claflin are afterwards resold to exporters in Manchester." [10]

From the sales ledgers for 1897 to 1913 we can find the sales to H. B. Claflin Co., the newly incorporated successor to the old firm. After Pepperell's consolidation with Laconia in 1899, annual sales to Claflin averaged about $600,000. Claflin therefore took about 10 per cent of Pepperell's goods.

During a period of eight and a half years (January, 1906, to the middle of 1914), for which we have the monthly balances for goods purchased but not paid for by Claflin, we find that Claflin's balances were lowest in 1910 and highest in 1913. Figures for the latter year do not indicate good business but quite the contrary, since it was a period of depressed conditions throughout the country. Although we find that Claflin reduced his balances during the first half of 1914, we know that the firm was forced to close its doors on June 25, 1914. According to newspaper accounts, assets were $44,000,000 and liabilities $34,000,000, of which $4,000,000 was for merchandise. At that time John Claflin needed more capital to finance the vast empire of trade which he had built up; he did not wish to continue operations with short-term loans. In fact, his vast aggregation had to be split up. Within a few years three operating companies were formed. One of these was Claflin's, Inc., which took over the entire importing and jobbing business formerly conducted by H. B. Claflin Co. In the last year of Pepperell's middle period Claflin's, Inc., bought at the rate of less than $75,000 a year, while neither of the other two did any business with the sales agent.

This failure was of great importance to Bliss, Fabyan & Co. and to Pepperell, as we have shown, because for a number of years Claflin had taken 10 per cent of Pepperell's goods. It dramatically marked the end of one large national wholesaler who had reached out for other functions and probably called attention to the difficulties which other wholesalers were facing to survive in this period of change. In a way the collapse foreshadowed the liquidation of the selling house over a quarter-century later, since it was upon the foundation of business with large wholesalers that the success of Bliss, Fabyan & Co. had rested.

In 1870 we find that Field, Leiter & Co., predecessor of Marshall Field & Co., of Chicago, was among the most important of the domestic customers. In the last two months of 1870 and the year of 1871 this firm purchased over $63,000 worth of Pepperell's goods. From 1897 to 1913, according to the ledgers, Marshall Field & Co. purchased about $200,000 worth of goods annually. Still later, in 1923–24, the company purchased less heavily, in fact at a rate of less than $100,000 a year.

Throughout this period there were many other large wholesalers who bought Pepperell's goods through sales agents. Their business probably grew for a time and then shrank, although perhaps not so dramatically as that of Claflin. Others, who are studying the operations of selling houses, may find this an important field to investigate further.

We shall leave the history of these wholesalers' dealings with the sales agent by mentioning the names of a few of them. About the turn of the century there were a few large wholesalers doing business on a national or regional scale. In New York, besides H. B. Claflin & Co., there were three others, Sweetser, Pembrook & Co., Tefft, Weller & Co., and James H. Dunham & Co., who served vast territories. In Boston the two outstanding wholesalers were Farley, Harvey & Co. and Blodgett, Ordway & Webber, who served New England and to some extent the near West. In Chicago, besides Marshall Field & Co., the important wholesalers were three: Carson, Pirie, Scott & Co., John V. Farwell & Co., and James H. Walker & Co., who covered a large territory in the Northwest. In St. Louis there were four important wholesalers, Ely & Walker Dry Goods Co., Rice Stix Dry Goods Co., Hargadine, McKittrick Dry Goods Co., and Ferguson McKinney Dry Goods Co., who distributed to the South. About this time they made up the most important outlets for Pepperell's goods. Later some of these companies went out of the wholesale business—failed or turned to the retail field.[11]

In other large cities of the United States, as well as in the smaller ones, there were numerous wholesalers who distributed the goods locally. These cities included Philadelphia, Baltimore, Pittsburgh, Cleveland, Columbus, Indianapolis, Cincinnati, New Orleans, and San Francisco.

Another type of domestic customer was the domestic manufacturer of clothing and bed sheets and pillow cases. At the beginning of this period the most numerous were the shirtmakers. During the years, as customs changed and the tailor, dressmaker, and home sewer gave way to the mass production of garments, many other manufacturers of garments sprang up. From Pepperell's jeans several companies, among which were Wise Bros., Erlanger Bros., and W. H. Towles Manufacturing Co. of Baltimore, began to make long drawers for men. By the end of our middle period such garments were no longer worn to any extent; their place had been taken by knitted underwear.

The manufacture of sheets and pillow cases increased during this period. For many years some of Pepperell's sheetings were bought by Ernest Simons, of Port Chester, New York, who converted them into sheets and pillow cases. Among Simons' important customers, according to the treasurer's letters, was the Pullman Car Co. We can imagine that hotels and steamship companies demanded finished sheets and pillow cases at a time when American housewives were content to make them at home. By the end of this period, however, the housewives, particularly in the cities, who were much less self-sufficient than their country cousins, were interested in buying sheets rather than sheetings.

Still another type of domestic customer was the manufacturer who used the cotton goods in his own finished product. Such were the rubber-goods manufacturers to whom at the beginning of this period the sales agent sold small quantities of Pepperell's goods and, by the end of the period, large quantities. Such also was the manufacturer of abrasives, Baeder, Adamson & Co., of Philadelphia, a customer throughout this period. Sales to this type of user were growing, but many of the goods required were heavy and could be manufactured more cheaply in the South than in the North.

Few goods were sold to converters. After all, Pepperell's goods were suitable for bleaching and dyeing but not for fancy finishing, and Pepperell made arrangements for goods to be so converted on its own account at the Lewiston Bleachery & Dye Works.

During a few years of this period, as in the preceding one, government business was very important. During the first World War, Pepperell produced uniform cloth for the Army and Navy, sheetings for the medical department, and goods for the Red Cross, besides goods which were converted and sold by others to the government.[12]

On the whole, then, the buyers of cotton goods for domestic consumption presented a picture of complexity quite different from the simple one of the preceding period, when wholesalers were practically the only domestic purchasers. The manufacturers of clothing, of house furnishings, and of industrial fabrics were growing in number and importance and were insisting on purchasing directly from the sales agent and not through the wholesalers. Likewise retail units were demanding similar treatment. Thus the former basis of operation—sales to comparatively few outlets—was breaking down and resulting in higher costs to the selling house with the handling of more and more smaller customers. No longer could the sales agent rely on selling a major part of the mills' output in his main offices, over short periods in the spring and fall, with fill-in orders placed during other months.

Changes were also taking place in the nature of foreign customers. Already we have considered the place of Claflin in this field, but he ceased operations on a large scale before the disastrous effects of foreign competition were felt fully. In this period there was a change from the former routes around South America and Africa. As canals were built and railroads spanned continents, they were used to shorten the routes. In 1900, for example, George Dexter wrote that the shipments to Asia were made "via New York to England & thence via Suez Canal, or across the continent to San Francisco to Puget Sound, whichever route is at the time the cheapest." [13]

In another way the method of carrying on this export business was changed. No longer did the merchants rely on the slow and infrequent exchange of information by letters, but they kept in close touch with foreign markets by cable. Orders were cabled to New York and relayed to Biddeford, where goods were manufactured to fill them. Drills and jeans were in demand for export; flannels, wide sheetings, and osnaburgs were also exported. In fact, in times of poor business there was a tendency for Pepperell, like other firms, to manufacture more and more of these goods for the export trade. But Pepperell, because it had built up demand for its goods in previous years, could sell to better advantage than those who exported spasmodically.

A few of the large exporters of the early period were kept as customers by the sales agent for a number of years. Among them was A. A. Low & Co., who in the first half of 1871 took 665 bales of drills costing $44,000. Another was Russell & Co. But most of the old-time merchants of Boston and New York had disappeared by the end of the Civil War. Some had turned to concentrate on special functions in place of the many pursued earlier. Pepperell developed a group of specialized exporters, such as the China & Japan Trading Co., Ralli Bros., and the American Trading Co., who took large quantities for foreign markets.

For a few years about the middle of this period we have treasurers' letters and a memorandum which throw light on the importance of the export of Pepperell drills and Pepperell's place among American exporters. In 1895 George Dexter wrote that Pepperell exported more than 25,000 bales of drills a year to China and India. In 1904 Philip Y. DeNormandie wrote that he estimated that in 1899 Pepperell sent 30 per cent of all the American drills to China. According to a memorandum of figures which he kept, we see that exports to China during 1902 through 1907 were as shown in Table 5.

TABLE 5

DRILLS EXPORTED TO CHINA, 1902–07

Year	Pepperell's Drills Exported (Bales)	Pepperell's Exports as Percentage of American Total
1902	30,099	29
1903	17,820	18
1904	25,202	25
1905	27,160	13
1906	24,300	23
1907	5,850	49

Source: Letter from Philip Y. DeNormandie, Dec. 21, 1944.

Pepperell played an important part in the oriental market, but some foreign competition developed during this period. English competition was a possibility throughout, but it was not serious since English goods were different, typically much more heavily starched than the American. Of far greater importance was the competition by other foreign mills, particularly the Japanese. Of course, during the first World War, as during the Civil War, largely as a result of the rise in cost of cotton, the price of the finished goods increased. Chinese and Indians could not afford to buy American and European goods at the high prices. Thus, because of lower labor costs, Japanese goods were able to gain a foothold in those markets.

By the end of this period the possibilities for export were less favorable than earlier. Pepperell, in this field as well as in the domestic one, had lost much of the business of its old customers. Just how the selling house dealt with its customers throughout this period we shall discover in the following pages.

VARIATION IN TERMS TO CUSTOMERS

Terms of sale in this period differed considerably from those in the earlier period. Unfortunately there is little information about the terms of sale for Pepperell's goods, since few records remain. In fact, we get only a few glimpses of length of credit, price, and discount. In undertaking the selling of Pepperell's goods at the end of October, 1870, J. S. & E. Wright & Co. continued the practices of Francis Skinner & Co. To the vast majority of its customers credit terms of 30 days were granted; to a few credit was limited to 10 days; and to a few others extended to 60 days. To H. B. Claflin & Co. terms were "as usual," which we may interpret as meaning the 30 days that Skinner had granted in the preceding years. This pattern of credit was modified slightly in the following years. From 1897 to 1909, when the sales ledgers included notations on the period of credit, we find that in the vast majority of cases the period was 10 days. To a few it was 30 or 60 days. To only a handful—important wholesalers, including Claflin—was the period 4 months. During the following decade, terms were modified somewhat. In 1919 William Amory, then Pepperell's treasurer, stated that the great bulk of Pepperell's goods carried a discount of 2 per cent if paid for within 10 days and bills were payable 60 days from the shipment from the mill. Such, also, was the practice as recorded in the sales journal for 1923–24.

For other terms granted to the buyers, including prices and discounts, there is little information. Only at rare intervals can prices of the various types of goods be found. Prices were given in sales journals, price lists, and auction catalogues but not in sales ledgers and trial balances. For November of 1870 I have compiled a set of Pepperell's prices, which are as shown in Table 6.

TABLE 6

J. S. & E. WRIGHT & Co.

Prices for Pepperell's Goods on November 31, 1870

Type of Goods	Cents per Yard	Type of Goods	Cents per Yard
Drills, brown 30″......	11½	Sheetings, 7/4 brown 57″	22½
		" 9/4 " 77″	29
Jeans, brown 30″....	13½	" 10/4 " 86″	34
" bleached 28″....	13½	" 11/4 " 96″	39
" corset 28″....	13½	" 9/4 bleached	34
		" 10/4 "	39
Shirtings, N, brown 30″	9½	" 11/4 "	44
" O " 33″	10½		
" R " 36″	11½		
" E " 39″	12½		

A price list for the spring of 1873 shows that prices had advanced from one to 4 cents a yard over those of 1870. From an auction list for 1876 we find that prevailing prices had dropped considerably below those in 1870. Before the auction the price of 36-inch shirting in the brown, for example, was 8½ cents a yard and a satisfactory price at the auction was 7 cents. In 1902, according to the price list, the prices were still lower. The same type of shirting was 5½ cents a yard. But by 1908 prices had risen considerably. The shirting was 7¾ cents a yard. At the end of the period we again have prices for different types of goods from sales journals. In 1923–24 the shirting was 14½ cents a yard—a considerable increase over 1908 but presumably not so high as the postwar peak.

These prices were modified by discounts of two types—regular discounts for large purchasers and those which were added or subtracted as business conditions changed. The discount to a large purchaser generally was not more than 2½ per cent. We can give no measure of the extent of the other type of discount, since we have only a few instances. For 36-inch shirting in the brown we have a record of 7½ per cent in 1870; the same in 1873; 10 and 2½ per cent in 1902; 5 and 2½ per cent in 1908; and 10, 2½, 2½, and 2 per cent in 1923–24. From these few figures, about all we can conclude is that there seems to have been a greater tendency to grant larger discounts at the end rather than earlier in this period.

Sometimes, in order to clear out oversupplies of goods and to determine prices, the selling house arranged auction sales. We have records of such sales in May, 1876, October, 1882, August, 1883, November, 1893, and December, 1894.[14] After the last-mentioned date, the sales agent seems never again to have resorted to auctions for Pepperell's goods. Perhaps there was a tendency in the later depressions to use other means than auctions to get rid of goods and to determine prices.

Generally during this middle period, according to a member of the selling house, prices for Pepperell's goods were set and changed infrequently—perhaps twice a year when price lists were made up. If, however, there was to be a change upward, during the period of uncertainty the commission agent might supply the jobbers *on memorandum* until the proper price could be determined. During this interim the jobber was not billed, so that it was to his advantage to sell as many goods as possible. After the price had been determined, the jobber would be informed of what it was. This method of operating served to keep the goods constantly on the market and was advantageous to both mill and wholesaler.

Still another method was used by the selling house when conditions were improving. In order that wholesalers might not be embarrassed by a sharp increase, the house would notify them that the price at a certain time would be higher but first

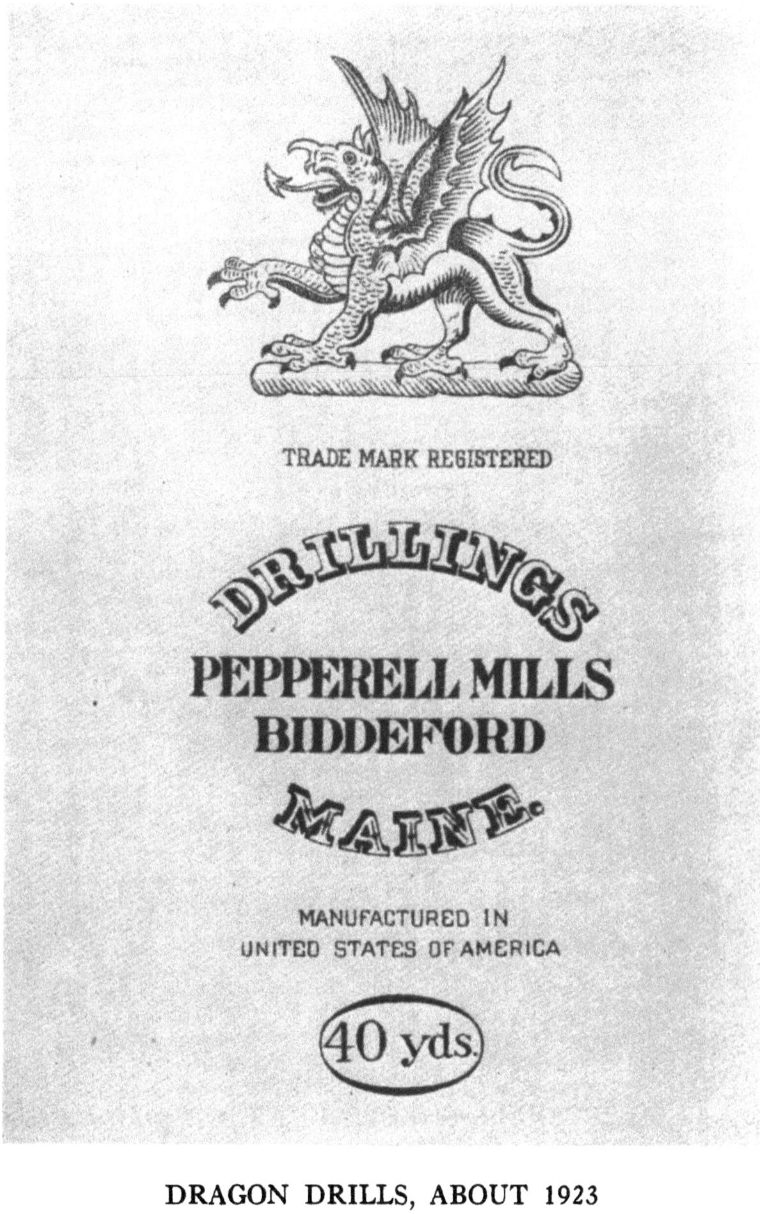

DRAGON DRILLS, ABOUT 1923

PEPPERELL SHEETING, ABOUT 1923

there would be an additional discount of 2½ per cent available for immediate orders. The wholesalers could then shift their prices to the retailers more slowly and avoid the risk of stopping sales.

The selling house thus resorted to various practices. Some of these practices were old, like the auction, whereas others, such as discount for payment within ten days, came into general practice in this period, when a better system of banking prevailed than had existed previously. But in this period insufficient attention was paid to merchandising. This and other weaknesses led to difficulty at the end of the period, as we shall see in the following section.

THE SELLING HOUSE NEEDS RENOVATION

For several years in the period 1870–1924 the selling house which Pepperell had chosen in 1870 continued to increase its sales of the company's goods. There were temporary drops in sales, to be sure, during depressed times, but on the whole these drops were not serious. There were also years of excellent business, but the best period was during the first World War, when sales boomed. These good years obscured somewhat the changes which were undermining the accustomed ways of selling cotton goods. There was a growing group of manufacturers of cotton garments, industrial users of cottons, and large retailers who did not want to buy goods through wholesalers. While the selling house was willing to sell to some of these buyers, it had not yet reached the point of consenting to sell to retailers. At the same time, hastening the breakdown of the former system, was the change in women's mode of living. These forces did not affect seriously the volume of sales by Pepperell's commission house until after the war. Fortunately for Pepperell, a group of stockholders took action before the company and the selling house were in a condition from which they could not be extricated.

Pepperell had a remarkable record of sales in this period (see Appendix 36). Sales rose from slightly over $1,800,000 in the fiscal year 1870–71 to $23,000,000 in 1919–20, an increase of over a thousand per cent in less than half a century. Both these figures were, however, affected by postwar inflations, particularly the latter figure. Before the war, in 1913–14, sales had reached the height of $6,700,000, an increase of about 270 per cent over sales at the beginning of this period.

This tremendous growth in sales did not mean that there were no temporary setbacks. In years of depressed business conditions sales were lower, but not disastrously so. Because of the methods of holding auctions to get rid of part of the surplus and of shipping part of the production abroad, Pepperell did not suffer a loss of more than 20 per cent of its previous sales in these poor years before the first World War. This was a remarkable record indeed, and one of which everyone involved could be proud.

Following the first World War, sales dropped as they had not done before. In 1920–21 and 1921–22 they were only slightly over $10,000,000, or less than 50 per cent of the previous high. In 1922–23 they bounced up to $15,300,000, but declined in the following year to $11,200,000. This last figure, to be sure, was much higher than for a decade earlier. On the grounds of dollar amounts of sales, Pepperell and Bliss, Fabyan & Co. did not need to be disturbed. Prices for their goods had risen to a greater extent than those for textile goods as a whole. Yardage of Pepperell's goods, however, had not risen during and immediately following the war; in fact, in 1920 it was slightly below the 1914 level and in 1924 it was 40 per cent below.

The commissions which the selling house received for its efforts fluctuated with sales. During the three decades in the nineteenth century, commissions from Pepperell increased from approximately $22,500 in 1870–71 to a high of nearly $33,000 in 1891–92. After the consolidation with Laconia in 1899, Bliss, Fabyan & Co.'s commissions increased much more rapidly, from about $72,000 in 1899–1900 to a high of $376,000 in 1919–20. Thereafter the commissions dropped, so that in the last year of this period they were $183,000.

Cause for concern over sales and commissions arose because of the increasing difficulty in getting large orders. In 1923 two members of the Bliss, Fabyan firm met in St. Louis and considered the problem; one of them wrote a report, but no account was taken of his opinion about necessary changes in selling. Apparently the senior partners were willing to continue the old methods which had proved successful for nearly a century. Contributing to the complications of the market situation for the selling house was the fact that it, unlike several others, did not have the accounts of southern mills which could compete on a lower cost basis.

After Russell H. Leonard had become treasurer of the Pepperell Manufacturing Company in the fall of 1924, many changes took place in the selling house. (See Appendices 28 and 29.) It was soon apparent that Bliss, Fabyan & Co. would lose the Pepperell account; by January, 1928, Pepperell had severed all connections. In order to give the younger partners of the selling house a chance, on July 1, 1927, the partnership was turned into a Massachusetts corporation, Bliss, Fabyan & Co., Inc. It acquired new accounts in the South through the organization of Alabama Mills Co. and through a merger with another house, Haywood, Mackay & Valentine, which had the accounts of several southern mills. Bliss, Fabyan & Co., Inc., had trouble with several of its old northern accounts. In the 1920's many of the Maine mills had come under Samuel Insull's control through his ownership of the New England Public Service Co. After his crash the mills in Lewiston and Saco, which had sold through Bliss, Fabyan & Co., Inc., were organized as the New England Industries, Inc., and in 1940 this group decided to set up its own selling organization. At the same time the Otis Co., of Massachusetts, decided to liquidate; this action involved the mills with which earlier it had consolidated, the Boston Duck Co. and Columbian Mills, all old accounts of the selling house. In 1940, therefore, only drastic action could have saved the selling house. The executives of Bliss, Fabyan & Co., Inc., decided to close the house rather than try to alter further their way of doing business. Thus ended the record of a selling house which had been in existence for 108 years.

* * *

CHAPTER X

THE TREASURER IN HIS COUNTINGHOUSE

IN THE MIDDLE period of Pepperell's existence the treasurer continued many of the practices of the earlier period. He kept, for example, a countinghouse in Boston. He moved its location twice, from Washington to Kilby Street and finally to Milk Street. These moves indicate to some extent the shift in the duties of the treasurer from financial matters to cotton buying. This shift reflected conditions of the times. With improved methods of communication and transportation, accompanied by the breakdown of the southern economy during the Civil War, cotton buying changed radically to reliance upon buyers in the North. At the same time there was an increase in capital available for investment, which relieved the pressure on the treasurers. Furthermore, changes in credit terms enabled the treasurers to turn their attention from the discounting of sales notes to other problems. But with a simplification of problems in many areas there were complexities in others, such as increased competition for markets. It was a wise treasurer who conserved his company's resources during the fluctuations in business conditions.

THE COUNTINGHOUSE

The treasurer in this period continued to be the chief executive of the Pepperell Manufacturing Company. In fact, except for short periods when successors were being trained, he was the only executive for this company. When necessity arose, services of experts for auditing, legal problems, transfer of shares, and advertising were secured. Until the first World War disrupted the normal pattern, expenses for the counting rooms remained low, but in the last decade of the period they climbed to new heights.

We have seen that the first treasurer of the Pepperell Manufacturing Company, William Dwight, maintained a countinghouse on State Street, the financial street of Boston during the nineteenth century. His successor, William P. Haines, kept his office on State Street for a few years, then moved not far away to Congress Street. By January of 1870, as we have seen, he had moved again to the Sears Building, across Washington Street from the old State House, on the edge of the wholesale dry goods and financial sections. Thus, to some extent Haines broke the intimate connection with the financial district and entered a different one.

This latter connection was maintained for the first twelve years of the middle period, since the treasurer continued to keep his countinghouse in the same location. But in 1882 George Dexter made a significant move: he set up his countinghouse in the Liberty Building on Kilby Street. This office was in the heart of the cotton buying and dry goods commission areas, a short distance away from the financial district. There the countinghouse remained for thirty years. In 1912, however, William Amory, then treasurer, moved it not far away to the Oliver Building at 141 Milk Street, still in the cotton-buying district, where it remained for the rest of this period.[1] We may infer that the changes in location indicate changes in the major interest and challenge of the treasurer, with a lag, to be sure, since leases ran for a number of years: from providing working capital, he turned to the problem of buying cotton on the best possible terms.

These countinghouses evidently remained as simple in furnishings as their predecessors had been. We lack details concerning them, except those given by the records of the petty cash expenditures for a number of years and by a letter which George Dexter wrote in 1882 about the heating arrangements for the new offices. At that time he wanted the steam pipes removed and the rooms heated by open fireplaces as they had been earlier. We know also that Dexter acquired a mahogany roll-top desk, which is today in the office of one of his successors. Thus we imagine that Pepperell's treasurer maintained the economical type of office which the old Boston merchants had set up and which for centuries merchants in other lands had kept.*

The directors and trustees, who held their meetings in the countinghouse, did not function as executives of the company. Generally when things were going well they met only three or four times a year. In years when there were problems, however, they met much oftener and assisted the treasurer in determining policies and in investigating conditions. In the first year of this period, 1870–71, they met very frequently—twenty-seven times in all. This was a year of trial when the company had to fight to maintain its financial standing after the loss inflicted by the failure of its selling agent. At times in the following years the directors met frequently—thirteen times in 1876–77, when there was trouble over the work of the treasurer, and fourteen times in 1898–99, when the details of the merger with Laconia had to be straightened out. In 1895 the president of the board of directors was recognized as carrying more responsibility than the others; he was voted a salary of $500 a year. But this was much less than the treasurer's, as we shall see shortly.

In the countinghouse throughout this period the treasurer continued to have the help of only a few clerks. In fact, until the first World War the treasurer kept a force of only three men or boys. Several of the clerks stayed for long periods—until they retired or died. During Dexter's term of office two of the three clerks had special duties, one connected with the

* For a number of years, as formerly, the treasurer of the Pepperell Manufacturing Company was also treasurer of the Laconia Co. and the Saco Water Power Co. In time these two companies were merged with Pepperell, as we have already seen, the treasurer's duties remaining the same. Only for a comparatively few of these fifty-four years was there an assistant treasurer. In 1899 Philip Y. DeNormandie was made assistant treasurer, but within three years Dexter resigned and DeNormandie took his place as treasurer. Thus the assistant's period of training was brief. In 1914 Walter H. Bradley was made assistant treasurer to William Amory. He served in this capacity longer than DeNormandie had, but his term was broken up twice: first by a six months' trip to the Far East for a group of financiers interested in the cotton industry, and second by about a year and a half's military service during the first World War. After his return to Pepperell in June of 1919, Bradley served for only a few months as assistant treasurer; in the fall he was made treasurer.

cotton-buying records and the other with finances. In fact, this financial assistant was made treasurer pro tempore during Dexter's absence of six months in 1898. But during the first World War the treasurer had difficulty in getting clerks; with trepidation, Amory hired one girl and then another. These girls succeeded. By the end of this period there were five clerks in the countinghouse: three men and two women. Thus, at last the treasurer had broken the tradition of the old-time countinghouse which was wholly masculine.

To this group in the countinghouse we must add others engaged in Pepperell's office work. First among these in point of time was the auditor. For a number of years in this second period the stockholders' committee on inspecting accounts had been authorized to employ an expert, in case none of the stockholders found it possible to attend to the duty in person. At the annual meeting of 1887 we find the name of such an expert mentioned for the first time. At that time Waldo L. Abbott was hired as auditor and continued in this capacity for thirty years. For the remaining years of this period Pepperell secured in his place the services of the accounting firm of Amos D. Albee Son & Co.

Other types of assistance were acquired during this period. Legal aid was secured from time to time when the need arose. Such aid was needed for plans for the consolidation with Laconia, finally consummated in 1899, and for the change from a Maine corporation to a Massachusetts voluntary association in 1915. Legal assistance was required at other times in minor matters, such as lawsuits and the registration of trade-marks. This assistance had not been needed in the earlier period, when the treasurers had been lawyers; in this middle period the treasurers were trained not in law but in commercial and industrial affairs.

In 1915 further assistance from outside the company was obtained which relieved the countinghouse in Biddeford, and to some extent the one in Boston, of much routine work. The Boston Safe Deposit & Trust Co. was made the transfer agent for stock at the time of the change from the Maine corporation to the Massachusetts voluntary association. In 1920, moreover, the treasurer turned to outside advertising agencies for assistance in bringing Pepperell's goods to the public notice and in analyzing the retail market.

For the expenditures of the countinghouse in this period we have fewer details than in the earlier period, since most of the cash vouchers and checks are missing. From the directors' and trustees' records we know that the salary of the treasurer was the principal expense for many years. The salary varied with the experience and responsibilities of the men. The first treasurer in this period, Blanchard, received an annual salary of $7,000 from Pepperell, but the amount from Laconia we do not know. (None of the treasurers received compensation for their duties with the Saco Water Power Co.) His successor, Codman, received $5,000 a year from each of the textile companies during his term of less than five years. The third, Dexter, started with $5,000 from Pepperell and $3,000 from Laconia in 1877 and received increases so that he was earning $10,000 with each in 1895;[2] in 1899, after the consolidation of the two companies, he took a lower amount, $16,000 in all. His successor, DeNormandie, started at a salary of $9,000 in 1901, which was increased three times to a final level of $15,000 in 1906. DeNormandie's successor, Amory, also started at $9,000 a year and was raised three times to a final level of $25,000 in 1918. The sixth and last treasurer of this period, Bradley, started at a salary of $15,000, which was continued during his five-year term of office.

The assistant treasurers received salaries much lower than those of their superiors. In that position DeNormandie received $5,000 a year, while Bradley started at the same amount with an increase of $500 a year for three years. These two men probably took into consideration when they accepted the positions that a promotion in this company or in other textile companies might result.

As to the compensation of the clerks we have meager information. From a notebook kept by one of them we glean a few facts. For many years those who came to the countinghouse as boys with no training, apparently to be employed as messenger boys, were started at less than $10 a week, in some cases even at $5.00 or $6.00 a week. In two instances they were raised finally to $50 a month. Several others with previous training who became valuable clerks were hired at a beginning salary of $125 a month and raised, at least in one case, to $300 a month within ten years. In 1917 the first girl in the counting-house was started at $16 a week. During the first World War the salaries of both men and women were increased greatly. The total payroll for clerks, which before 1917 had not exceeded $500 a month, at the end of 1922 was over $1,200 a month.

For the first four decades the treasurer's salary and Pepperell's half of the clerks' salaries comprised the greater part of Pepperell's incidental expense, as shown in Appendix 36. For almost thirty years of this second period, when Pepperell shared counting-room expenses with Laconia, incidental expenses rose from $10,000 to about $20,000. For fifteen years after the consolidation, when Pepperell bore the expenses alone, the total was about $32,000. During the war years and those following, the incidental expenses rose to dizzy heights, to a peak of $174,000 in 1923–24, an increase of 40 per cent over the prewar level. Included in these increasing totals were higher wages for the clerks, higher rent for the countinghouse, large amounts for supplies, and larger amounts for other services, notably for advertising.

The Treasurer Buys Cotton

In this middle period the treasurer of the Pepperell Manufacturing Company, like the treasurers of other large concerns, changed his method of buying cotton. Before the Civil War, as we have seen, William Dwight delegated much of the buying to his son and to a former employee, who went south during the season and finally established a firm in the South to do the buying. Dwight also bought cotton from merchants in the important southern centers, such as New Orleans, Savannah, Columbus, Apalachicola, and Galveston. But during the interruption of trade by hostilities other methods of operation had to be found. The treasurer continued to delegate much of the buying to his son's firm, which through the war purchased cotton in Boston and New York as quantities became available there from the various sources throughout the world. A disturbed state of affairs in cotton buying persisted after peace had been declared, since the growing of cotton as well as the marketing of it by southern merchants was greatly upset. Until 1870 the cotton crops increased slowly and not until 1880 did the crop exceed the bumper one of 1860.[3] Just when conditions really became normal we cannot say exactly, since the South did not really return to its prewar pattern.

For the early part of this period we find that the method of buying depended partly upon the treasurer in office. In the first year of this period, 1870–71, we find that the two successive treasurers, William P. Haines and John A. Blanchard, made many spot purchases of cotton in Boston obtaining almost 40 per cent of their annual total from buyers there. They also made heavy purchases of Mobile cotton, in all 27 per cent of the year's total. They bought also in nine other places: New York and eight centers in the South, including one new one, Selma, Alabama. But in no one of these places did they secure as much as 10 per cent.

In this year Blanchard was evidently carrying out Haines' policies, for in the next fiscal year, when Blanchard alone was treasurer, he purchased no cotton in the North. He secured cotton from six places in the South, the most important of which were, in order, Selma, Mobile, Memphis, and New Orleans. After Blanchard's death in the following year, Edward W. Codman took his place and apparently continued his predecessor's policies throughout the year.

Codman, during the rest of his term of office, followed Haines' rather than Blanchard's policies. At least in 1876–77, his last year in office, he made heavy spot purchases in Boston, although he secured additional cotton in both Mobile and Selma. Purchases in these three places amounted to 70 per cent of the total. In each of twelve other southern places he purchased less than 10 per cent.

In George Dexter's first full year of cotton buying, 1878–79, we find a mixture of the policies of Blanchard and Codman. Like the former, Dexter did not make heavy spot purchases in the North and, like the latter, he bought from many sources in the South. In this year Dexter secured cotton from nineteen places. From two in the South, Selma and Mobile, he secured over 50 per cent of the total. He obtained in New York only about 8 per cent of his requirements and in Boston very little. In 1880–81, Dexter modified his policies slightly. He still scattered his purchases over nineteen places, but secured no cotton in New York and only a little in Boston, purchasing most heavily in Selma, Atlanta, Galveston, and Mobile. We find also that he was securing cotton from many places not mentioned earlier, particularly in Texas.

Dexter's change in policy concerning cotton buying was significant for many reasons. Before he became treasurer of Pepperell, he had had his own company for cotton buying with offices in New York and Boston. He had traveled to New Orleans during the purchasing season. His knowledge of buying operations must, therefore, have been much greater than that of any of his predecessors. From his experience he must have realized fully that cotton growing was shifting, as it had been for years, to new lands farther west, and he was willing to purchase cotton from new places. Furthermore, his decisions were founded on the fact that better systems of communication and transportation were developing so that it was possible to ship cotton from the interior by rail or water throughout the year. From his own travels he knew that many of the old plantations which had been destroyed during the war were being supplanted by smaller holdings, the owners of which depended for credit on the small-town merchant. Earlier the large landowners had done business with the richer merchants in the principal cities.[4] Just how Dexter placed all his orders we do not know, inasmuch as records for these years give only the names of shippers in the South and of sellers of spot cotton in the North. Dexter may have bought some cotton from merchants in the South, some from merchants in the North to whom it had been shipped, and some from brokers in Boston who telegraphed orders to their southern shippers. The method of buying in the South declined, since it was difficult for treasurers in the North to deal with a large number of southern cotton buyers, with whom differences about cotton naturally arose. The treasurers of the cotton manufacturing companies in the North came to depend on the merchants and brokers in Boston and other cities. According to our records Pepperell by 1886 had adopted these two methods, at least in part. In a trade paper in 1886 it was said, "The representative of a corporation sits in his office in Boston or elsewhere, and has only to put a few packages of cotton outside of his door, thereby indicating that he is buying, to receive calls from a great number of persons anxious to provide him with material." [5]

In 1895 Dexter wrote to a southern buyer about the change in buying habits as follows:[6]

> I do not believe that with the present methods of doing business, which are every day drawing further away from what used to be cotton buying, that a Treasurer can, with any success, deal direct with a cotton buyer at the South, and stand any chance on advancing market, (that being the one we always buy on) of getting any cotton. The cotton buyers are now all operators & will offer as many bales as one wants to buy of any grade & any time of delivery.

He went on to say: "The Treasurer does not always get what he expects—but with the larger cotton houses he comes somewhere near it & secures cotton at times when he wants it. By the old order system he is now left out in the cold except at such times as no one else is buying." [7] In the following decades Dexter's successors in office continued his policies.

The first full picture of the relation of the cotton merchants and brokers in Boston to the southern offices is seen during Amory's term of office in the year 1911–12, for which we have Pepperell's cotton-purchasing sheets covering nearly 60,000 bales of cotton. We find in this year twelve companies selling cotton to Pepperell. Amory did the most business with Charles Storrow & Co., brokers, about 30 per cent of the total. Storrow secured cotton for Pepperell largely from one company in Alabama and a little from two others in Texas and Oklahoma. To Stephen M. Weld & Co., merchants, Amory gave the second largest amount of business, about 18 per cent of the total. Weld secured cotton from seven companies in Alabama and from one in Arkansas. The ten other merchants and brokers with whom Amory dealt secured cotton from these States as well as from Georgia, Mississippi, and Tennessee.

By 1923–24 we find that the treasurer, Walter H. Bradley, assisted by Amory Coolidge, was purchasing from seventeen merchants and brokers in Boston, relying heavily on Charles Storrow & Co. for about 40 per cent of Pepperell's requirements and on Stephen M. Weld & Co. for almost 24 per cent. In that year the cotton came not only from the usual centers in the South but also from Los Angeles, California.

Thus, for the major part of this middle period the treasurer of the Pepperell Manufacturing Company purchased cotton through either merchants or brokers with offices in Boston. In fact, for many years the treasurer had purchased all his cotton in this way. In 1920 Bradley wrote to a southern cotton buyer as follows: "Referring to your letter of July 21st, [I] would say it is the policy of this Company to purchase all cotton through either brokers or merchants with offices established in Boston." He went on to be specific, "For your information, would say that we purchase cotton from your district (southern Georgia) through Charles Storrow & Co., B. H. Dickson & Co. and one or two others." [8]

Many events made possible this change from the system used before the Civil War. We have already mentioned better communication facilities—the telegraph became more dependable and reached many more places. Also a system of railroads developed, so that it was possible to ship cotton from small towns either directly to the North or to ports in the South. We have noted that earlier there were difficulties in getting cotton to these ports, since the water in the rivers might not be at the right levels. In fact, during this period the system of railroads connecting with the North developed so rapidly that many of the old southern ports which were accustomed to handling a tremendous bulk of cotton swiftly declined in importance.

At the same time there was a development of exchanges for cotton, not only in New York but in the South as well. The principal southern one was in New Orleans, but many others were established throughout the cotton-growing section. In other places there were general commodity exchanges which also assisted in the buying and selling of cotton. Thus, there were many centers in which the cotton grower as well as the cotton buyer or merchant could get the latest information about the price of cotton, the size of the current crop, and forecasts about future conditions. This enabled them all to carry on business in a more intelligent fashion.[9]

In this period the New York and New Orleans exchanges carried on an extensive business in futures. During the Civil War, when cotton was difficult to get and the price was ever mounting, the buying of cotton for future delivery had become a popular practice. We cannot determine from our records whether Pepperell or its cotton agent at that time, D. A. Dwight & Co., had hedged purchases of cotton. With the establishment of the exchanges, however, dealings in futures developed to a much greater extent. They were used not only by those who wanted to hedge their contracts, but also by those who were interested primarily in speculating in cotton. This latter practice has aroused much criticism throughout the country and has concealed the beneficial activities of hedging.

The exchanges maintained strict rules for the conduct of business which members had to follow. Exchanges facilitated greatly the purchase of cotton by manufacturers. A company treasurer was able to give an order to a merchant or broker in Boston, who could telegraph immediately to one of his southern suppliers for cotton for future delivery. The supplier would find a seller among the farmers who had carried their cotton to secure a certain price. At the same time that the Boston broker bought cotton in the South he might hedge to protect himself from changes in price by selling futures on the New York Cotton Exchange.[10] Such was the practice to which Dexter was referring when, in 1895, he wrote to the southern buyer that methods of doing business were every day drawing farther away from what used to be cotton buying.

This system of hedging purchases by the merchant or broker in the North made the part played by the treasurer much simpler. During much of the crop season he could get the various grades of cotton in sufficient quantities. As in the earlier period the treasurer bought many grades. In 1870–71, for example, he bought from strict middling through to ordinary and even stained cottons, with the larger part classed as low middling, middling, and stained. By the end of this period the treasurer was, however, buying a larger proportion of the higher grades. In 1923–24, he ordered nearly 40 per cent of strict middling cotton with only a little "tinged" or "leafy."

For many years the course of cotton purchases was upward, as Appendix 15 shows. There were, of course, years of poorer business conditions, when the treasurer curtailed his purchases, perhaps with a larger stock on hand than usual. Causes for the increase in quantities were, as we have seen, expansion of capacity of the Pepperell mills during the nineteenth century, the consolidation with Laconia in 1899, and the further expansion of the mills in the following decade.

During the years for which we have the average cost per pound of cotton consumed by Pepperell's mills we find that there were major swings of considerable amplitude. This cost, which had begun to decline from a high of 88.7 cents in 1864–65, continued its downward course during the 1870's, and by 1876–77 reached the 1850 level of 11.71 cents. During the following fourteen years the cost fluctuated up and down from this level. For seven years from 1891–92 onward it dropped, touching a low of 6.63 cents in 1898–99 and rising again in five years to the level of about 11 cents. Unfortunately our series of average costs stops in 1907–08, with the last entry in a volume of semiannual statements of the agent.

Pepperell's average costs per pound of cotton consumed fluctuated in a fashion similar to the average price of average-grade cotton in the South, as Appendix 15 shows. Although there were many causes for diffierences in the two series, such as differences in quality, Pepperell's added costs of getting the cotton into the mills, and the lag between time of purchases and actual consumption, we find the two series remarkably alike. As one would expect, however, Pepperell's figures did not fluctuate so violently as did the composite ones. For the years for which Pepperell's figures are missing we see from the other series that cotton prices rose again during the first World War, but not so much as during the Civil War. A high of 35.4 cents a pound was reached for cotton marketed in the United States in the year 1919–20. The price dropped in the following years, but in 1923–24 it was still more than twice the former normal level.

There were many factors of importance affecting the price of cotton in the United States which we cannot cover. For example, one was the disastrous effect of the boll weevil, which cut production of cotton throughout the South. Others were the effect of the weather on the supply, the effect of business conditions in the United States as well as throughout the world on the demand, and of increasing competition with cotton grown elsewhere. Since cotton comprised the largest cost of Pepperell's manufactured goods, these factors cannot be neglected nor were they by the treasurers, who followed carefully the changes from day to day, and often from minute to minute, as given by the exchanges.

During this period the various charges for getting cotton from the hands of the growers in the South to the mills in the North were reduced. Most important among the causes for this reduction was the practice of shipping the cotton directly from a small center to the mills. Often the whole trip was accomplished in the same freight car. This method cut out the expenses which were incurred when the cotton was handled at the major ports in the South and again in Boston. In the 1870's, as we have seen, Pepperell's treasurer was engaged in building more adequate storage space in Biddeford. Some of the buildings were erected near the railroad tracks, so that the unloading of the cotton was quite simple. In time the treasurer came to store little cotton in Boston, most of it going directly to Biddeford.

As a result of more direct routes for cotton, the treasurer's countinghouse in Boston carried on less work pertaining to handling cotton than previously. The treasurer did not need to attend to all the details of receiving cargoes of bales of cotton, moving, storing, and finally shipping them off to the mills in Maine. But the responsibility for seeing that the cotton arrived safely at its destination was still one of the treasurer's duties.

He insured the cotton with local companies. He paid for the cotton after having received from the South a bill of lading with the draft attached—payable on sight, which in Massachusetts meant after three days.[11] The treasurer, or one of his clerks to whom the job had been delegated, sent on to the cotton inspector in the mills detailed information about the cotton which had been purchased and which was in transit. At the mills, as we have seen, the weights of the bales were checked.

In Boston the treasurer's duties concerning cotton, other than buying, were largely clerical and concerned with adjusting claims to losses. After a while he was able to turn over many of the latter problems to the Cotton Freight Bureau, which was the commercial agency of the Arkwright Club concerned with the transportation of cotton.[12]

Thus we see that the treasurer of the Pepperell Manufacturing Company was still much concerned about cotton for the mills. While many of his duties became lighter during this period, particularly those pertaining to the arrival of cotton in Boston, others grew in importance: a large portion of the responsibility for buying could not be delegated to others; and the daily and hourly market fluctuations had to be followed with much care. On the other hand, the treasurer did have the advantage of much more information than had been available earlier. He was conscious of how important the cost of cotton was to the profits of the company. In the following pages we shall see another important part of his job which also contributed to the success of the company—the handling of the financial problems.

THE TREASURER CONSERVES RESOURCES

During this second period the treasurer had less of a job on his hands in the management of finances than previously, but the keynote to the new situation was not struck during the first two years. Indeed, John A. Blanchard, who took over the duties of treasurer in the middle of the financial year 1870–71, had many problems to solve. Blanchard took drastic action. On the balance sheet for June 30, 1871, we find that he had eliminated from the assets more than $900,000 due from Francis Skinner

& Co., and that he had paid off about $400,000 of the notes outstanding six months earlier. At the same time he reduced the book value of the plant by almost $600,000 and wiped out the various reserve funds, except a few thousand dollars for improving the mills. He went so far as to request new capital. In the spring of 1871 the stockholders, at the behest of the treasurer and directors, voted to increase the capital stock by $200,000, as they had been given authority to do by the State of Maine in 1856. Thus, in less than six months Blanchard had improved the company's financial position considerably, as Appendix 33 shows.

In the following year and a half Blanchard determined many of the policies which succeeding treasurers were to follow. He built up again from profits the fund for enlarging and renovating the mills; he set aside the dividends received on the stock of the Lewiston Bleachery & Dye Works for the ultimate extinction of the investment. Reserves for particular purposes were a fundamental part of the company's accounting in the following decades. Such reserves made the directors more cautious perhaps in their determination of dividends, since they saw smaller figures of net profit and surplus. Blanchard, however, was not able to reduce appreciably the items of cloth on hand and notes receivable. As a result, total assets on June 30, 1872, stood at almost $2,500,000, a level which was maintained fairly consistently in the following twenty-six years. (See Appendix 33.) In his brief period in office, Blanchard accomplished a great deal. Unfortunately he died too soon—in December of 1872.

Blanchard's successor, Edward W. Codman, continued many conservative policies. During his term of office he paid off many notes, so that Pepperell became largely free from debt. He set up other reserve funds, such as a fund made up of insurance premiums which had been returned each year from various mutual insurance companies. Probably he thought of this fund as Pepperell's protection against bad losses by fire which could not be covered completely by insurance policies. While Codman did not revive the old insurance fund on sales—it was not necessary with the shorter period of credit—he did start up again the former guarantee fund against bad debts on goods sold, at the former rate of 1½ per cent of gross sales. Like his predecessor he set aside funds for improving the mills, which were drawn upon as needed. He considerably reduced notes receivable so that Pepperell would be safer if panic threatened unusual losses. Also, he saw that the sales agent maintained reasonable balances, about one-sixth of the annual sales.

As treasurer of Laconia, Codman, like his predecessors in office, had more difficult problems to solve because Laconia for a long time had not been so profitable or in such good financial condition as Pepperell. Laconia's difficulties resulting from Skinner's failure were greater than Pepperell's. As we have noted, Blanchard, in 1871, had written off over $800,000 which Francis Skinner & Co. owed and had paid off about $500,000 of the notes outstanding. At the same time he had felt that the thousand shares of stock outstanding were not worth $1,000 each. The stockholders had been forced to accept a par of $400 and were asked to subscribe to 1,000 new shares at the new par. In the spring of 1873 Codman and his directors asked the stockholders for approval for a further subscription to 500 shares at $400 each. Thus from 1871 to 1875 the stockholders had contributed $600,000 in new capital to Laconia. Whereas Pepperell's stockholders received dividends regularly throughout these years, Laconia's received none in 1875 and 1876 and only $12 a share in February and August of 1877. They may have become impatient at this delay of return on their investment. What other cause there was for dissatisfaction with Codman, we do not know. But in the fall of 1877 he resigned as treasurer from both companies.

In Codman's place came George Dexter, who during his term of office of twenty-four years made a success of both companies. In both he was more conservative than either Blanchard or Codman.

From 1877, the year of his election, to 1899, the year of Pepperell's merger with Laconia, Dexter pursued very conservative policies. In fact, since his balances underestimate Pepperell's strength and his earnings figures do not disclose always the full extent of the profits, the extent of his success cannot be fully measured. It was his policy to keep the plant in Biddeford valued at $1,200,000, although additions of buildings and machinery were increasing its productive capacity considerably. It was also Dexter's policy to state the value of cotton and cloth on hand at less than their cost. Moreover, he set aside annually additions to the various reserve funds, so that the company would be in a strong position. He kept the company as free from debt as possible. In ten of his twenty-one years he had no notes payable at the end of June. In 1892, notes payable were highest, $400,000, because inventories of cotton and balances with the sales agent were high, but within a year notes payable dropped to $10,000. All these policies can be deduced from his balance sheets and letters and reports to the directors. Years later William Amory commented to a government official in reporting data for tax purposes, "You will readily see that the balances submitted to my stockholders have always been ultra conservative and have been so for the last three generations and more." [13]

In the 1899 merger with Laconia, however, Pepperell's strength was to some extent disclosed to the stockholders and to the public. In addition to an extra dividend of $150, Pepperell's stockholders were given seven shares at $100 each in place of one old share of $500. Laconia's stockholders, on the other hand, while they received an extra dividend of $50 before the merger, were given only three and a half shares at $100 each in the new company in place of their former $400 share. Thus Pepperell's stockholders received some of the reserves which had been piling up, not only in dividends but also in stock of the new company, while Laconia's received only the equivalent of their previous amount of stock in dividends and in new stock. At the time of this change in capitalization on May 10, 1899, several of Pepperell's reserve funds were wiped out, but they were soon opened again, as shown by the balance sheet of June 30, 1899, in Appendix 33.

For sixteen years of operation under the Maine charter of 1899, while three treasurers were in office—Dexter, DeNormandie, and Amory—reserve funds were built up from profits, dividends of the Lewiston Bleachery & Dye Works, and returned insurance premiums, but a large amount was also left in the surplus account. We shall see that in this period extra dividends were declared more frequently than earlier. Apparently DeNormandie was not so cautious as Dexter. This would be natural inasmuch as DeNormandie was young and lacked the experience that Dexter had gained during the long period of downward movement of prices in the preceding century. DeNormandie, however, continued many of the conservative policies of his predecessor, as Appendix 33 shows.

Eight years after DeNormandie had resigned as treasurer to become a member of the selling house and Amory had been elected to take his place, we find an organizational change taking place in Pepperell. In the spring of 1915 Amory and the other directors introduced a plan for a shift to a Massachusetts voluntary association or trust. At the same time Amory planned an increase in stock; the stockholders were to be given three new shares for one old. He thought this increase advisable for several reasons, which he stated in letters to stockholders in the following vein:[14]

> This is in reply to your letter of the 1st instant. We have not contemplated a distribution of any cash. As you know, the present company is under-capitalized and has always sold at a high figure,—several times the par. This contemplated move is to have the capital more nearly represent the value of the property and to enable us to pay a lower dividend per share without decreasing any stockholder's return.
>
> At the same time this should relieve the Massachusetts stockholders from some taxation, widen the market and increase the value of the stock.

William Amory also began valuing Pepperell's property at higher levels. He raised the value of the plant in Biddeford, for example, by roughly $1,000,000, and set up separate accounts for investments in land, water power, lumber, and towing property. As previously, the cotton on hand was valued at less than cost; cloth on hand also came to be carried at slightly less than cost.

When the price of cotton soared during the first World War,

the treasurer charged off various amounts from profits to meet a later drop in price. For the six months ending December 31, 1917, Amory charged off $500,000 from profits for this purpose and set it in a separate reserve fund, which shows on the balance sheet. At the end of the following six months' period, he set aside $500,000 as a reserve for cotton and again, at the end of the next six months, he added $500,000 in a similar manner. Walter H. Bradley continued many of Amory's practices. At the end of December, 1919, he reported to the trustees that he had set up $1,000,000 as a reserve for cotton. For the following six months he recommended $2,000,000, but evidently the trustees approved of the addition of only $1,000,000. In this fashion, which had prevailed in the Pepperell Company for many decades, the treasurer in good times set aside reserves for future difficult ones.

The difficult years were not slow in appearing. Three million dollars of the reserves Bradley used in the two fiscal years 1920–21 and 1921–22; in the first to change from a loss to a profit, and in the second to reduce the loss and to add a reserve for machinery. In the following year Bradley set aside $300,000 as additional reserve for cotton, making the total reserve for cotton at that time $800,000, which would be needed when cotton fell to normal levels again.

Although Bradley continued his predecessor's policies of maintaining reserves to meet possible future contingencies, the fact that the government was introducing a more standardized form of accounting in conjunction with its income tax regulations prevented him from stating his balances and earnings as conservatively as formerly. Thus, as we shall see in the following section, Pepperell, after a long record of profitable operation, at last reported some losses.

PROFITS AND DIVIDENDS

Although we have been concerned with the treasurer's policies in using profits after dividends to build up the financial position of the Pepperell Manufacturing Company, we have not discussed the pattern of annual profits and dividends for this period of fifty-four years. Logic appears to demand a reversal of treatment, but I feel that profits came only when there was excellent performance on the part of the executives of the company and their selling house: principally on the part of the treasurer, who purchased cotton and conserved the resources; the mill agent, who produced goods and, with the treasurer, made improvements in the machinery and buildings in Biddeford; and the selling house, which disposed of the goods.

Perchance I am influenced in my order of treatment by the treasurer's methods. Generally he did not know until the day when he made up his semiannual accounts how great the profits might be. As we have seen, at that time he set up values for cotton and cloth on hand to preserve the sound position of the company. Also, he aimed to keep the profit level fairly steady. Both objectives could be attained by taking figures lower than cost and raising or lowering them, as compared with the figures determined six months earlier. From gross profits he set aside additions to reserves—some on a regular and some on an irregular basis. As a result of these practices, profits are significant only over the long run; they mean little in a particular year or in a stretch of a few years.

If we consider separately each of the two parts of this span of fifty-four years, we may gather still more about the treasurer's policies concerning profits. From 1870–71 through 1897–98, profits averaged about $197,000. The low for these years was $123,000 in 1883–84, and the high of $413,000, surprisingly enough, was in the second difficult year of this period, 1871–72. Thus we may say that extremes mean little. Naturally, however, Pepperell's profits tended to be lower in depression years and higher in good ones, as Appendix 36 shows. In the second part of this period, 1898–99 through 1923–24, we find that profits fluctuated much more around their average of $711,000. This fluctuation can be attributed partly to business conditions and partly to government regulation of accounting. As a result of both factors we find a loss in the two years 1921–22 and 1923–24; this had not occurred previously in this middle period. Other low years occurred in earlier depressions, in 1901–02, 1903–04, and 1910–11, when profits were less than $200,000 a year. Extremely good years, according to the figures in Appendix 36, were from 1915–16 through 1919–20, when profits were over $1,000,000 and, once, over $3,800,000.

Certainly from a perusal of these figures one can say that Pepperell was a profitable company from 1870–71 to 1923–24, although competition was keen. During the first twenty-eight years profits averaged annually about 16 cents for each dollar of capital stock. During the following sixteen years, when the capital stock stood at $2,556,000, profits were nearly 13 cents on each dollar. In the last ten, when the capital stock was three times as great, profits averaged nearly 13 cents on each dollar. This record demonstrates that at least one company in the cotton textile industry could make good profits throughout a long period.

For the major part of this period few persons besides the treasurer and directors or trustees knew much about the company's record. To be sure, the treasurer reported orally a statement of condition and earnings at the stockholders' meetings; usually few attended those meetings, although there was an increase in attendance in the difficult years following the first World War.

For most of this period the company did not publish an annual statement. In fact, the treasurer felt that the record, except for dividends, was none of the public's concern. In 1894, when the federal income tax and tariff law was under consideration, George Dexter wrote to the mill agent, "I would burn them [the books] rather than submit to such degredation. If the Income Tax bill passes, we can be forced to show everything and for that reason I trust the Tariff bill will never be passed." [15] Although the tax bill was passed, within a year the Supreme Court found it unconstitutional. Thus the disclosing of Pepperell's figures was postponed for a time.

Dexter's successors, however, had to file reports with both the State and federal governments. As a "foreign" corporation Pepperell was compelled from 1903 through 1914 to file a statement of condition in Massachusetts and to pay a small excise tax. Thereafter, as a Massachusetts voluntary association, Pepperell continued to file a statement but paid no tax.[16] Starting in 1909 the company filed statements of condition as well as of earnings with the federal government, and, as we have noted earlier, paid taxes on income.

After a time the Pepperell Manufacturing Company began to distribute typewritten reports to stockholders who attended the annual meetings or who requested copies.[17] In 1922 a printed sheet containing the annual report was issued, followed in 1923 and 1924 by a two-page printed leaflet. Thus, by the end of this period the treasurer was yielding to public opinion. No longer was Pepperell a secluded company run by Boston men in the tradition of the old-time merchants.

Although the stockholders knew little about their company, they were willing to trust their funds for many years to their treasurer and directors and trustees. We find that, as earlier, many of the stockholders held Pepperell stock for many years; after their deaths their widows, children, or estates continued to keep it. In fact, we discover that almost half the surnames on the dividend record of 1872 appear again forty-three years later on a similar record.

During this period the number and size of holdings increased. Between 1872, when the new subscription to stock was completed, and 1915, after the second split-up of stock, the number of owners increased from 360 to a few more than 1,000. The average size of holding also increased: in 1872 it was about 7 shares with a par value of $500; in 1915 the average was 76 shares, par value $100. But of greater interest was the variation in the size of holding. In 1872, 80 per cent of the stockholders held less than 10 shares and the largest holding was 120 shares. In 1915 about 20 per cent held less than 10 shares; on the other hand, about 90 per cent held less than 210 shares, the investment equivalent to 10 shares in 1872, if we take into account the splits of 1899 and 1915. The largest holding in 1915 was 1,389 shares, and there were four others who held more than 1,000 shares.

There was a growing tendency for this stock to be held by women and estates. Whereas 22.5 per cent of the stockholders were women and 12.5 per cent were trustees, guardians, or executors of estates in 1872, 40 per cent were women and 20 per cent were trustees, guardians, or executors of estates in

1915. At both times a few educational or charitable institutions held stock, about one per cent in the earlier year and about 3 per cent in the later. It thus appears that the majority of stockholders had come to be concerned with the safety and stability of investment.

The treasurer and directors or trustees maintained a suitable dividend record. We see from Table 7 that they declared dividends regularly, year in and year out, from 1871 through 1924, with extra dividends at times.

For the first part of the period (through February, 1899) we find that the company declared semiannual dividends on the $500 stock in amounts which varied from $25 to $40. The average regular dividend was about $31 semiannually, or $62 annually. This amounted to a return of over 12 per cent on the par value of the stock. In addition there were two extra dividends—$200 on May 14, 1887, after the second attempt to consolidate with Laconia had fallen through, and $150 on May 10, 1899, at the time of the merger with Laconia. Thus, during the first twenty-eight years of this period the stockholders fared very well with regular dividends each six months and two extra dividends.

The second part of this period can again be divided into two parts. The first covered the time from the consolidation in the spring of 1899 to the formation of the Massachusetts voluntary association in 1915. During this time the stockholders received $12 annually in regular dividends on their $100 stock, of which they held seven shares in place of one former $500 share. On their previous investment they therefore received regular dividends of $84 a year, which was more than the previous average of $62. In addition the stockholders received five extra dividends during these sixteen years, which amounted in all to $140 a share or, on the equivalent of the one old share, $980. As a result of the number and size of the extra dividends in these years, Pepperell was likened to an oil field in which there were regular paying wells in addition to a few gushers.

In the last ten years of this middle period, dividends were still higher. The stockholders held three shares in place of the one held in the preceding sixteen years and twenty-one in place of one original $500 share. On the new stock in the first year they received $3.00 semiannually, but thereafter $4.00. At the latter rate the dividends amounted to $8.00 a year per share; on the previous investment basis this equaled $24 a year; or, on the still earlier investment basis, $168 a year. Pepperell's stockholders, then, were very fortunate in their regular dividends. In addition they received six extra ones, which totaled $33 a share. On the basis of former holdings this would have amounted to $99 a share or, on the still older basis, $693 a share. No wonder that, during these years also, the reputation of the company for occasional spurts of dividends became widespread!

Pepperell's stockholders had, therefore, sufficient grounds to trust their treasurer, with the assistance of directors or trustees, to carry on their company without interference on their part. They were receiving excellent returns from a company in an old industry. Few other companies in the industry had maintained a record of dividends in each calendar year, as had Pepperell from the time $400 had been paid on each share in 1852. Among the large companies which had been organized before the Civil War there were only three others which to 1924 had an unbroken record of dividends in each calendar year. Significantly, all three were among the companies whose goods were sold by Bliss, Fabyan & Co. They were Androscoggin of Lewiston, incorporated in 1860; Boston Duck Co., of Ware, incorporated in 1845; and Otis Co., also originally of Ware, incorporated in 1840. But none of these maintained such a high rate of dividends as did Pepperell.[18]

Pepperell's stockholders were fortunate also in that, among their number, there was a group of men who were deeply concerned over the decline in the company after the first World War. They wanted Pepperell to continue its profitable record even though conditions in the industry were poor. They proposed a new treasurer for the company—one who already had a record of strengthening cotton manufacturing companies. Accordingly, on November 5, 1924, Walter H. Bradley resigned from office and the trustees elected Russell H. Leonard, who, as we shall see later, completely altered Pepperell's course.

TABLE 7

DIVIDENDS, 1871–1924

Date Payable	Amount	Date Payable	Amount	Date Payable	Amount	Date Payable	Amount
Aug. 1, 1871	$ 25[a]	Feb. 1, 1882	$ 35	Feb. 1, 1892	$ 35	Aug. 1, 1901	$ 6
Feb. 1, 1872	25	Aug. 1, 1882	35	Aug. 1, 1892	35	Feb. 1, 1902	6
Aug. 1, 1872	30	Feb. 1, 1883	35	Feb. 1, 1893	35	Aug. 1, 1902	6
Feb. 1, 1873	30	Aug. 1, 1883	35	Aug. 1, 1893	35	Feb. 2, 1903	6
Aug. 1, 1873	30	Feb. 1, 1884	30	Feb. 1, 1894	30	Feb. 2, 1903	20[b]
Feb. 1, 1874	30	Aug. 1, 1884	30	Aug. 1, 1894	30	Aug. 1, 1903	6
Aug. 1, 1874	30	Feb. 2, 1885	30	Feb. 1, 1895	30	Feb. 1, 1904	6
Feb. 1, 1875	30	Aug. 1, 1885	30	Aug. 1, 1895	35	Aug. 1, 1904	6
Aug. 1, 1875	30	Feb. 1, 1886	30	Feb. 1, 1896	35	Feb. 1, 1905	6
Feb. 1, 1876	30	Aug. 2, 1886	30	Aug. 1, 1896	35	Aug. 1, 1905	6
Aug. 1, 1876	25	Feb. 1, 1887	30	Feb. 1, 1897	35	Aug. 1, 1905	35[b]
Feb. 1, 1877	25	May 14, 1887	200[b]	Aug. 2, 1897	35	Feb. 1, 1906	6
Aug. 1, 1877	25	Aug. 1, 1887	30	Feb. 1, 1898	25	Aug. 1, 1906	6
Feb. 1, 1878	25	Feb. 1, 1888	35	Aug. 1, 1898	35	Nov. 6, 1906	50[b]
Aug. 1, 1878	25	Aug. 1, 1888	35	Feb. 1, 1899	35	Feb. 1, 1907	6
Feb. 1, 1879	25	Feb. 1, 1889	35	May 10, 1899	150[b]	Aug. 1, 1907	6
Aug. 1, 1879	25	Aug. 1, 1889	35	Aug. 1, 1899	6[c]	Feb. 1, 1908	6
Feb. 2, 1880	30	Feb. 1, 1890	35	Feb. 1, 1900	6	Aug. 1, 1908	6
Aug. 2, 1880	30	Aug. 1, 1890	35	Mar. 1, 1900	10[b]	Feb. 1, 1909	6
Feb. 1, 1881	40	Feb. 2, 1891	35	Aug. 1, 1900	6	Aug. 1, 1909	6
Aug. 1, 1881	35	Aug. 1, 1891	35	Feb. 1, 1901	6	Nov. 22, 1909	25[b]

TABLE 7 (continued)

Date Payable	Amount	Date Payable	Amount	Date Payable	Amount	Date Payable	Amount
Feb. 1, 1910	$ 6	Aug. 1, 1914	$ 6	Aug. 1, 1917	$ 4	Aug. 2, 1920	$ 6[b]
Aug. 1, 1910	6	Feb. 1, 1915	6	Feb. 1, 1918	4	Feb. 1, 1921	4
Feb. 1, 1911	6	Aug. 2, 1915	3[d]	Aug. 1, 1918	4	Aug. 1, 1921	4
Aug. 1, 1911	6	Feb. 1, 1916	3	Aug. 1, 1918	6[b]	Feb. 1, 1922	4
Feb. 1, 1912	6	May 15, 1916	10[b]	Feb. 1, 1919	4	Aug. 1, 1922	4
Aug. 1, 1912	6	Aug. 1, 1916	4	Aug. 1, 1919	4	Feb. 1, 1923	4
Feb. 1, 1913	6	Feb. 1, 1917	4	Feb. 2, 1920	4	Aug. 1, 1923	4
Aug. 1, 1913	6	Feb. 1, 1917	6[b]	Feb. 2, 1920	4[b]	Feb. 1, 1924	4
Feb. 2, 1914	6	July 3, 1917	1[b]	Aug. 2, 1920	4	Aug. 1, 1924	4

[a] Par value of the stock until the merger of May 10, 1899, $500 each.

[b] Extra.

[c] Par value of the stock from May 10, 1899, to March 15, 1915, $100. Stockholders of the old company received *seven* shares for *one old $500.*

[d] Par value of the stock in the trust from March 15, 1915, through the remainder of this period, $100. Former stockholders received *three* new for *one* old.

Source: PMC, Directors' records, July 19, 1871, through January 22, 1915; Trustees' records, July 22, 1915, through July 23, 1924.

Part III

REJUVENATION, 1924–1945

CHAPTER XI

REACHING AMERICAN CONSUMERS

In Part II of this book we saw how Pepperell ran into difficulties not long after the first World War. Overcapacity in the industry had been built up during the war. Overproduction had been brought about partly through the use of more than one shift. Northern mills could not compete with southern mills.

Now this difficulty, with variations of course, was becoming a conspicuous pattern in the régime of industrial capitalism. Generally industry reached a halting period—a plateau of reduced speed and even threatened extinction. Overcompetition was the common diagnosis. And then the enemies of private business enterprise eagerly scanned the horizon for the storm of doom that was to sweep down upon big business. The doom came all right, but only to a limited number of companies. The resilient survived and grew in stature, stability, and usefulness to society.

There were two principal means of regeneration open to a sick industry. One was to go to Wall Street or State Street and invite investment bankers to take over the ailing company on behalf of the stockholders. On the whole these investment bankers did a good job, though their public relations were crude. Whilst they helped to save individual concerns from drowning, they came near to the point of destroying private business enterprise. It was the fortune of Pepperell to escape this fate of control and resurrection from the outside.

The actual means of recuperation adopted by Pepperell was reorganization from within; and, through a set of new policies, the company marched to new victories. What those new policies were we shall learn in detail as we follow the story to the end. Just now we are disposed to emphasize a new personnel and a new marketing policy.

What the new marketing problems and methods were to be, will be set forth in this chapter. At this point it is perhaps enough to note that incisive changes were occurring in human affairs to which textile factories would have to adjust themselves. Women became emancipated politically, socially, economically, and physically. With the evident approval of the male, they cast off the burdens of yards and yards of clothes and wore only scanty, short garments of clinging and revealing materials. This psychic change reduced the demand for cotton goods, such as ginghams for dresses and muslins for tucked and ruffled petticoats.[1] On a less romantic level Americans prosaically substituted paper for cotton towels and napkins. As if to make the conspiracy complete, foreigners joined with Americans to rob the over-inflated American cotton textile industry of demand for its products.[2] The Japanese textile industry joined with the emancipation of women and the desire for economy to challenge the American industry as never before. Some of the American textile companies could not meet the difficulties, but Pepperell rose magnificently to the occasion.

Without men, new blood if you will, the threatened doom of the industry could not be met. The top choice for Pepperell was a new treasurer—Russell H. Leonard. His previous success indicated that he could safely be given a free hand both to formulate new policies and to choose his own lieutenants.

DEVELOPING AN EXECUTIVE FORCE

In this third period one of the changes which affected all parts of Pepperell's operation was the increase in the number of executives. Previously, as we have seen, the treasurer had been the only one, except when he was nearing retirement and training his successor. In other large cotton textile companies in New England this same early custom prevailed, although there had been many executives for many years in other industries. In 1924 Pepperell's new treasurer, Russell H. Leonard, realized that, if the company was to develop as he visualized that it should, there must be an expansion in the executive force. Within a few years Leonard acquired a group of men, as well as one woman, to assist him in the transformation of the

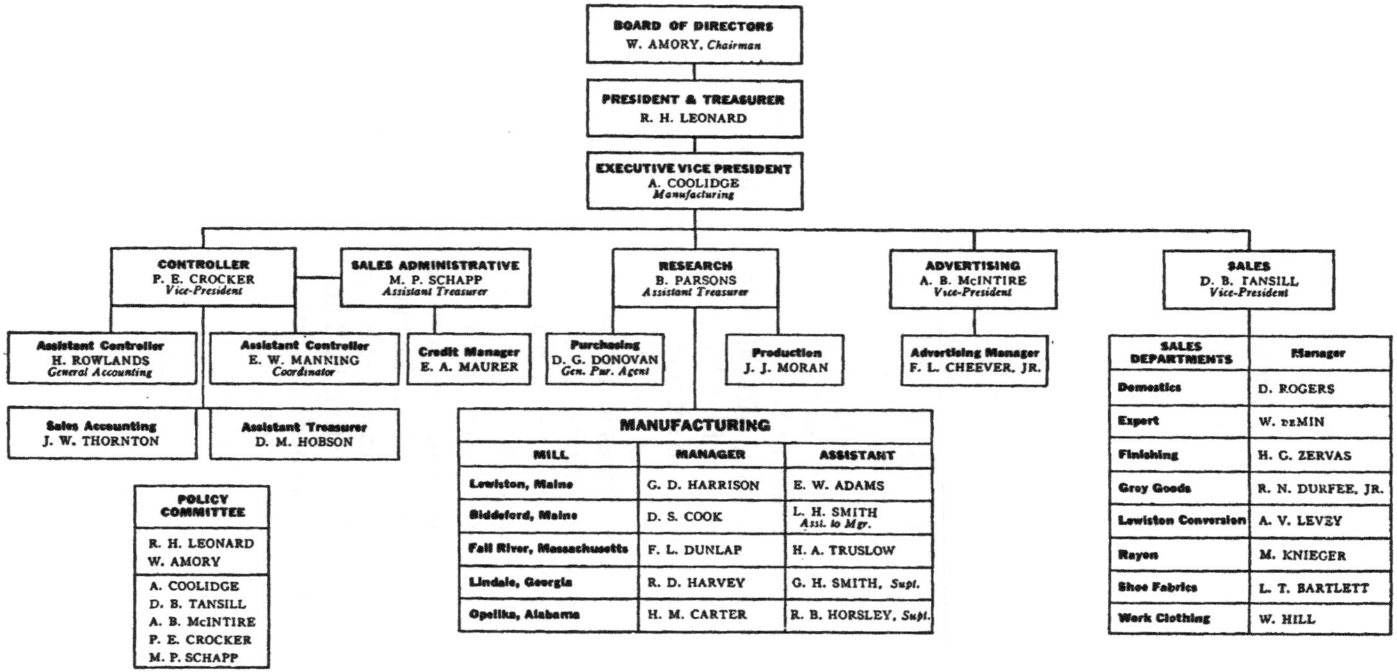

CHART III

Pepperell's Organization Chart, February, 1944

company. (The organization of the company in 1944 can be seen in Chart III.)

The treasurer, however, remained the most important of the executives. As we have already recorded, on November 5, 1924, the trustees of the voluntary association (the Pepperell Manufacturing Company) elected Russell H. Leonard treasurer. At that time he also held a similar position with the Ipswich Mills, a position which he was to retain for about two more years. During these years he had one office with the Pepperell Manufacturing Company on the seventh floor and another with the Ipswich Mills on the sixth floor at 160 State Street, across the street from the old Customs House. Later Pepperell added space on other floors of this building.[3]

Leonard's background and training fitted him peculiarly for his new position. For almost three centuries his ancestors had been engaged in manufacturing in America. At the time of the great Puritan migration to the Massachusetts Bay Colony his ancestor, James Leonard, with his brother Henry, came from Wales to work in the iron foundry at Saugus. After a few years they moved to Taunton to set up a bloomery where bog ore was plentiful. Although Henry and his sons moved elsewhere to set up other iron works, James and many of his descendants stayed in Taunton and its vicinity. Some continued in the iron industry; a few developed from petty to industrial capitalists. Among the latter were Russell H. Leonard's grandfather, Job M. Leonard, and father, Henry B. Leonard, who ran the Mount Hope Iron Works of Somerset until their deaths in the early twentieth century. Russell H. Leonard, not interested in this company, spent two months after his graduation from Harvard College in 1910 in liquidating it. Thus he had the heritage of centuries of business experience but was not hampered in his own efforts by the restrictions of the family's established methods of operation in the iron industry.[4]

Russell H. Leonard chose to cast his lot with the old cotton textile industry of New England, in which he saw a great opportunity for able, aggressive young men not bound by former ways of doing business. At first he served a period of apprenticeship in the industry. For four years he gained experience

RUSSELL H. LEONARD
Chief Executive of the Third Period

WILLIAM AMORY
Presiding Officer of the Third Period

by working as a cotton mill operative, as the secretary to a mill agent, and as a selling agent of cotton yarns. He also increased his knowledge by attending a textile school, by selling commercial paper, and by acting as agent for the United States Tariff Board to collect textile costs both here and in France. After this, Leonard was elected treasurer of the Wampanoag Mills, a cotton textile company of Fall River, not far from his native town of Somerset. During the seven years in which he served this company he increased its earning power by making improvements in the plant, a step which this company, as well as many others in Fall River, needed.[5]

In February of 1922 Leonard resigned this position in Fall River to accept the more difficult one of treasurer of the old Ipswich Mills with plants in Ipswich, Gloucester, Lowell, and Boston, Massachusetts, and in Belmont, New Hampshire. Since the seamless cotton stockings which it produced were being outdated by the full-fashioned hosiery which modern women were demanding, the company needed reorganization. Leonard introduced the latter type as well as rayon undergarments for women. In programs of national advertising he stressed the quality of Ipswich's goods. Thus he was bringing new life into this company when Pepperell's trustees approached him in 1924. They wanted a man who could undertake a job for Pepperell similar to the one that he had performed for Wampanoag and Ipswich. He consented to take on the treasurership of Pepperell, provided that he was given full power to do whatever he considered necessary. Unfortunately for Ipswich, he gave up his position there in 1926.[6]

During this third, and latest, period of the company's history Leonard has been Pepperell's chief executive, as shown in Appendix 10. Throughout the years he has kept the title of treasurer of the Massachusetts voluntary association. In 1926 he became treasurer of the new manufacturing company, with a Massachusetts charter, called at first the Massachusetts Cotton Mills, Inc., and then, in 1927, the Pepperell Manufacturing Company. Of this company we shall learn more in the following chapter. In 1930 Leonard was given the additional title of president of this new company but, although his titles were increased, his duties were not augmented. He was merely adopting the usual American title for the chief executive of a manufacturing company while retaining the old New England one. Later, in 1938, he announced the formation of a policy committee of five of the leading executives, who took over some of his former duties, leaving him with fewer details.[7]

Throughout this period of change Leonard has benefited by advice from older executives in the cotton textile industry. He has sought out William Amory, Pepperell's former treasurer, who kept an office near those of the executives. Since 1921 Amory has served as president of the voluntary association. Since 1927 he has been the presiding officer of the Massachusetts corporation, first with the title of president and then with that of chairman of the board.

Leonard has also had the advice of two other former treasurers of cotton textile companies. At first he kept in close touch with Walter H. Bradley, former treasurer of Pepperell, who for a few months served as vice-president of the voluntary association. After the merger with the Massachusetts Cotton Mills in 1926 Leonard consulted its former treasurer, Edward Lovering, who served as assisting presiding officer of both Pepperell companies. From 1927 until his death in 1941 Lovering was vice-president of the voluntary association and from 1927 to 1930 he was vice-president of the operating company and, thereafter, throughout the rest of his life, vice-chairman of the board.

Chief among Leonard's group of young executives has been Amory Coolidge. After his graduation from Harvard College in 1917, Coolidge served in the Navy, then was a clerk in the Old Colony Trust Co. and later worked for the Amoskeag Manufacturing Co., where various members of his family—Coolidges and Amorys—had held important positions for many years. For a time he was one of Pepperell's clerks in Boston, assisting in cotton buying. Then, early in 1925, Leonard sent him to India, Burma, and Ceylon to investigate possibilities of selling cotton goods. In May of 1925 Coolidge was made Pepperell's assistant treasurer. In 1930 he was also made vice-president of the operating company. By 1940 Coolidge had become executive vice-president of the operating company without giving up his office of assistant treasurer of the voluntary association.[8]

At the same time that Coolidge was made vice-president, two others were similarly recognized. One of them was Donald B. Tansill. Earlier, after attending Columbia University and serving in the first World War, he had been a salesman for Bliss, Fabyan & Co. In 1925 he was selected to head the Pepperell group within the selling house, and in 1927 he was put in charge of Pepperell's independent selling organization, in which capacity he has remained.[9]

The other vice-president in 1930 was Allyn B. McIntire. Earlier he had worked in his father's printing and engraving business, and, for a time, for N. W. Ayer & Son, advertising agency, of Philadelphia. This work was interrupted by service during the first World War. Then, after a short time in New York, he became associated with the advertising firm of Barton, Durstine & Osborn, Inc., as accounting executive. From December, 1924, his relations with Pepperell were close, since Leonard chose that firm as Pepperell's advertising agency. In 1928 McIntire became affiliated with Pepperell, taking over its sales development work, in which was included its advertising.[10]

In 1933 Leonard added a fourth vice-president, Paul E. Crocker, who had been employed by Pepperell for many years. Previously Crocker had been a clerk. In 1925 he was promoted to the position of controller—a position which he has continued to hold.

There have been a number of assistant treasurers—a position which in practice seems to be lower than that of vice-president. For about three years Frederick W. Notman, formerly assistant treasurer of the Massachusetts Cotton Mills, held this position. The other assistant treasurers have continued in office much longer than he. One of them was Morton P. Schapp, who had formerly been employed by Lawrence & Co., selling house for Ipswich, and then by Pepperell in the sales office in New York; he became Pepperell's credit manager. Another assistant treasurer was Brackett Parsons, formerly assistant treasurer of the Ipswich Mills, who developed technical research for Pepperell. Still another was Dorothy M. Hobson, with secretarial, legal, and accounting training and experience, who acted as assistant to the president-treasurer and then to the controller.[11]

In all, these assistant treasurers and vice-presidents of the operating company comprised a group of able, ambitious executives, of quite different natures, but trained in their particular fields. Although some of them lacked broad training, under Leonard's leadership they constructed an effective team; they were young people who, as years passed, became mature in age and experience.

Five of this group of executives have comprised the policy committee—Coolidge, Crocker, and McIntire of Boston, and Tansill and Schapp of New York. Since 1939 they have held meetings at stated times throughout the year and have determined many of the company's policies, though for final review their recommendations have gone to the president-treasurer, who, generally, if the five agreed, would accept them.

Under these top executives a whole structure of assistants and clerks has been built up, in contrast with the maximum of five clerks of the two earlier periods. At one time, during the second World War, there were well over a hundred employees in Boston. In the office in New York there was also an intricate structure, as we shall see later in this chapter.

This whole organization has given rise to questions of the basis for compensation. Should the employees be rewarded in accordance with the degree of success of the company? Many of them contributed directly to the operations, others much less obviously. In the two earlier periods the treasurer's problems had been simple. He himself had received a good salary, never more than $25,000 a year, but an amount which, particularly if he had a fortune, enabled him to live comfortably. Thinking that he knew how much each of his clerks contributed, he rewarded each accordingly. In this third period, when there were many more employees, some plan of compensation for each type of worker became necessary. Basic salaries were determined by competitive conditions. Persons with responsibilities were granted the possibility of a bonus. At first, in 1936, the bonus plan applied only to the top group of vice-presidents and assistant treasurers. In 1938 the president-treasurer joined this group. In place of his recent salary of $100,000 a year, he took a salary of $60,000 with the possibility of a maximum bonus of $40,000. In the following years, before the second World War, a plan was worked out so that everyone in the company earning a salary of $3,000 or more was on a profit-sharing basis. But no one would receive a bonus until final net profits after taxes had reached $800,000; that is, not until stockholders had received a dividend of $8.00 a share. The bonus to salaried workers increased proportionately to profits until $1,800,000 had been earned; after that figure no greater bonus was given, since extremely large profits have been considered the result of abnormal forces outside the executives' control. Those who had a particular responsibility, such as the management of a sales department or of a set of mills, operated under two schemes—profits of their own departments and of the company as a whole. They received rewards according to which method resulted in the larger figure.[12]

During this period employees were given an opportunity to buy shares of stock and thus participate in the success of the company. In 1926 the trustees voted that the treasurer be authorized to purchase 300 shares and to offer them to salaried employees. At first they were allowed to pay for these shares in installments running not more than 18 months, but a few months later the time was changed to a maximum of two years. In 1927 the treasurer was authorized to issue not more than 2,070 shares to the employees, at not less than $100 a share, for cash in installments. Thus the management made it easier for the employees to secure company shares.

By means of these various steps the president-treasurer of the Pepperell Manufacturing Company has created a group of executives who, like him, have been devoted to the company. With them have been associated a number of others, who also have contributed greatly to the company's success. They have brought about many changes in the company's operation—particularly in distribution—as we shall see in the following pages.

ANALYZING THE AMERICAN CONSUMER

Important in Pepperell's new system of distributing goods has been the analysis of the types of goods wanted by the consumer. In the past, as we have seen, the treasurer and selling agent, according to their judgment of the markets for goods, decided the types for each new mill. Thereafter they paid little attention to the needs of the consumers; they produced the same goods year after year, with the unquestioned assumption that people still wanted them. Of course, until the twentieth century there had been little cause for a reconsideration of the consumer's wants, since the old types of goods found ready markets. Before the first World War changes in demand were already becoming apparent, but for a time the war postponed the necessity of an adjustment. After the war, however, problems became acute, with many mills undergoing difficulty in finding a profitable market for their goods. Companies in the North, whose costs were higher than those in the South, had to find profitable types of goods or go out of business.

For the first few years after the first World War, Pepperell tried various measures to improve its position. As we have seen, in 1920 the company secured an advertising agent who placed advertising of sheeting in various magazines. The company also secured a market analyst, who in 1922 and 1923 questioned retailers in ten States in New England and in the Ohio and Mississippi valleys. Some retailers were willing to coöperate in programs of local advertising, window displays, and leaflets. But this attempt to strengthen Pepperell's position was not successful immediately, partly because its sheeting was not distinctive in quality and partly because too few retailers were accustomed to Pepperell's ticket, which had been used on only a portion of its goods.

Fortunately for Pepperell Russell H. Leonard, the new treasurer selected in 1924, throve on difficult situations. He entered enthusiastically into an overhauling of the whole company. In later chapters we shall learn about his changes in the mills, but here we are concerned with one aspect relating to distribution

AMORY COOLIDGE

PAUL E. CROCKER

DONALD B. TANSILL

ALLYN B. McINTYRE

THE FOUR VICE-PRESIDENTS OF THE THIRD PERIOD

DOROTHY M. HOBSON

MORTON P. SCHAPP

BRACKETT PARSONS

THE THREE ASSISTANT TREASURERS OF THE THIRD PERIOD

of the company's products—the analysis of the market to determine what goods to produce and distribute.[13]

In such a study of the market to determine suitable goods Leonard was taking a different approach from that of his predecessor, who had been trying methods of improving the market for the old coarse sheeting. Leonard was eager to produce a new, finer type on which competition would be less keen. He had watched the success of Wamsutta Mills and had taken part in that of the Ipswich Mills. Both of these companies had studied the markets, secured fine-quality products, and promoted them by national advertising, with the aid of the firm of Barrows & Richardson.[14]

Since Barrows & Richardson was not willing to accept the account of one of Wamsutta's competitors, it suggested another agency for Pepperell. This was Barton, Durstine & Osborn, Inc., founded in 1919, which was making a name for itself as a specialist in market analyses and the planning of advertising campaigns. According to advertising awards in the 1920's, it was one of the leading agencies in the country. In December, 1924, a month after Leonard had assumed office, he hired Barton, Durstine & Osborn, Inc., to be Pepperell's advertising agency. With it and its successor agency, Batten, Barton, Durstine & Osborn, Inc., Pepperell continued during the following six crucial years. (Later also for several years Pepperell used the services of this firm, although for two intervals it hired another, H. B. Humphrey Co., and ended this third period with still another, Benton & Bowles, Inc.)[15]

Although in 1924 Leonard believed that Pepperell needed a finer type of goods, a distinctive one which could be promoted easily, he did not stop with such a view. He hired the advertising agency to make an extensive study of the market to determine the advisability of such a move. By questioning wholesalers, retailers, and housewives the agency found that there was room for sheetings with a higher thread count than Pepperell's old carded Red Label, which had 128 threads to the square inch. It advised at first a carded sheet with 144 threads—four more than in some competing sheetings.[16]

This first step, the determination of the advisability of a better sheet for Pepperell, was an important indication of the direction in which Pepperell was to move—away from coarser, cheaper sheetings. To the new sheet was given a distinctive title, Lady Pepperell, that borne by two women in the family for which the company had been named. Close attention was paid to the details of production, finishing, and making up. The sheet was ready for the market in February, 1926. Although competition was severe, this new sheet found a good market, promoted as it was by an ambitious program of advertising as well as by dealer service and by an aggressive salesforce. Later, after further market surveys, Pepperell made two additions to its line of sheets—another carded sheet, called the Pepperell Fine Count, and a fine combed one, named the Pepperell Peeress. Thus, in a short time Pepperell developed a diversified line of sheets to appeal to all income groups in the country, in place of the single coarse one produced for a mass market in 1924.

Convinced of the usefulness of market analysis, Pepperell from time to time has hired companies to make other surveys of the American market for various types of goods, particularly the branded ones, in order to determine how well they would be received and also how best to promote them. After the first few years most of these surveys were less extensive. They were based on questionnaires sent out to a selected list of consumers instead of on interviews with representative people, which made large surveys more expensive but also more reliable. In 1926 Barton, Durstine & Osborn investigated the market for towels. This led to nothing until, in 1937, the agency again studied that market with the result that Pepperell started the production of towels on a small scale. Pepperell used the services of the Curtis Publishing Co. for small surveys of markets for towels in 1936 and of the Gilmore Research Bureau for another survey of sheet and towel markets in 1937. In 1939 Pepperell hired Elmo Roper, often considered the top market analyst, to study the popularity of percale and muslin sheeting in the northeastern quarter of the country. Roper interviewed many people and reported a good market, particularly among the younger women, for a low-priced percale sheeting. As a result, Pepperell increased production of its carded percale sheeting, formerly called Pepperell Fine Count, and renamed it Pepperell Percale.

During the second World War in order to check on Pepperell's reputation and also to determine future trends of purchasing and advertising, the advertising agency, Benton & Bowles, Inc., made several surveys for Pepperell's products by sending out questionnaires to a selected panel of consumers. Benton & Bowles' findings were presented in simple, graphic form. This agency discovered also that consumers rated Pepperell's sheets among the best and that there was a good future market, particularly for the two finer sheets. In addition it investigated the market for work clothing. Thus, by the end of this period Pepperell had improved its position considerably—it had become a favored producer of many types of goods throughout the country.

In addition to hiring the services of research analysts Pepperell has had its own research organization, which has carried on many activities. At first there was a sales development department under the direction of Allyn McIntire. In 1928 the company set up a method of keeping accounting records, with the use of punched cards, in such a way that information about sales, by customers, by areas, and by salesmen, could be obtained easily—a method followed, with a few refinements, ever since. This was a radical departure from the former system of posting daily sales on a sheet and of recording sales to customers in a ledger. In 1930 this department made a detailed study of total sales—by products and by areas for the two fiscal years 1928–29 and 1929–30—and compared Pepperell's performance with a potential buying-power index. But, since outlets in an area might cover a wider territory, this index did not seem a good basis on which to set sales quotas. No other such comprehensive study has been attempted, although one concerning the distribution of sheets was made in 1936.

After 1930 Pepperell's sales development department suffered a setback as did many companies' at that time. Because of the failure of several important statistical organizations to forecast the depression, statistical research in general went under a cloud. For a while Pepperell's sales research continued in Boston under the direction of McIntire. Then it was transferred to the controller. By the middle of 1936 it had been split into three parts: two under the controller in Boston, one called economic research and the other budget control; and the third in New York, under the direction of the vice-president in charge of sales, called sales analysis and market research. The work of these groups dwindled to nothing during the second World War. Thereafter a sales analysis group was started again in New York.

In addition to studies of the domestic market, Pepperell also has made surveys of the foreign market, in which it had played an important part for so long. When Amory Coolidge went to the Orient in 1925 to survey its markets, he found there an opportunity for Pepperell's drills. A few years later Pepperell hired Charles K. Moser, who for a short time left his job as chief of the Far Eastern Section of the United States Bureau of Foreign and Domestic Commerce, to study markets in Japan, China, and India. In 1930 his findings were published in a book entitled *The Cotton Textile Industry of Far Eastern Countries,* in which he warned the industry that these markets would be supplied in the future with products of Asiatic mills, except perhaps for a few fine goods and specialties. In this event Pepperell would either have to eliminate much of its former production of twilled goods or find new markets for them. It found the new markets. Some of the twilled goods were distributed to shoe manufacturers for linings, while others went to the growing abrasive market.[17]

While these studies have assisted in the determination of changes in the production and distribution of various goods, Pepperell has also been able to draw upon other surveys made outside its organization, such as studies made by the government and by various institutions, which were becoming interested in the problems of distribution about this time. In particular the *Distribution of Textiles,* published in 1926, and the *Merchandising of Cotton Textiles,* in 1933, by the Graduate School of Business Administration of Harvard University, threw new light on practices in the industry.[18]

For the discovery of new textiles and new methods of production, Pepperell, like many other textile companies, depended on many sources. On the outside it gained help from textile engineers, textile machine companies, and technical departments of various cotton associations. The company also received help from rayon producers as well as from a chemical company which was a leader in the development of latex, resins, and waxes, which might be used in the Lewiston Bleachery & Dye Works.[19]

From within the company Pepperell also drew new ideas from many people—the heads of sales departments, the salesmen themselves, workers in the mills, and executives, some of the executives even traveling abroad to get information about foreign methods. The company set up no central experimental laboratory, although in each plant there was a testing laboratory. By the end of the period it was the practice to have experiments carried on under the plant superintendent's direction rather than by special operating departments. Thus the superintendent was acquainted with methods under consideration and did not have to be persuaded of the advisability of change. In some cases Pepperell moved too far ahead of consumer demand, as, for example, in the production of a "tapered weave" sheet, in which the central section was much stronger than the edges. Although logically the demand for this sheet should have been great, the company could not develop a good market for it.

During this third, and latest, period of operation, then, Pepperell has changed in this important respect—it has followed closely the needs of the market. As a result of surveys it has adapted its products to appeal to the American consumer. From many sources it has kept informed about established or new types of goods. But this step forward would not in itself have been effective without growth in two other important areas—advertising and selling.

ADVERTISING PEPPERELL'S GOODS

Closely related to the problem of analyzing consumer demand has been that of advertising Pepperell's goods. In fact, as we have already noted, the same organization has carried on both functions. Within the manufacturing company there has been an advertising executive, who has had assistants to carry on the work of sales research, advertising, and dealer service. In the outside advertising agency there has been a staff to plan and carry out advertising programs as well as to make special studies.

Throughout this third period Pepperell's advertising has had a unified approach because a single man has been behind it. Until the spring of 1928 Allyn B. McIntire handled Pepperell's account in the Boston branch of the advertising agency. During those years he dealt with Pepperell's three advertising managers. Since 1928 McIntire has been one of Pepperell's executives, constantly presenting new ideas for advertising. Of sensitive nature, he has been modest about the extent of the contribution made by advertising to the success of the company, although evidence has seemed to demonstrate the worth of advertising. For two years McIntire was in charge of sales development and then became a vice-president in charge of advertising.

The functions of advertising have been divided between Pepperell and its advertising agency. Probably Pepperell assumed more of the load than some other companies, because of McIntire's previous experience in an agency. But McIntire, assisted by F. L. Cheever, Jr., and the agencies jointly worked out programs to keep Pepperell in the public eye.

McIntire directed the publication of the *Pepperell News Sheet,* which was distributed monthly to Pepperell salesmen and to wholesalers, retailers, manufacturers, and other distributors and users of Pepperell's goods. In this publication advance information was given about sales promotion, such as plans for the advertising of sheets and blankets in various national magazines. This service enabled retailers to arrange for tie-ins to get the benefit of the company's advertising. The *News Sheet* also offered suggestions to the retailer through descriptions of displays and layouts of goods for sale. Facts about the company were also included so that all who handled Pepperell's goods could be well informed.

During these years Pepperell was fortunate in having the services of Miss G. A. Erskine, who was in charge of dealer service. She has contributed thousands of ideas about promotions for window-dressing and counter arrangements for the sale of Pepperell's goods and has answered questions from distributors who wrote about their problems. In this way she has supplemented the work of both the advertising agency and the salesforce. During the second World War it was she who scheduled showings of the Pepperell motion picture, *Gift to the General,* which demonstrated ways of taking care of textiles to prolong their usefulness so that most of American production could go for war purposes.

At the same time Pepperell's advertising agencies carried on many supplementary functions.* In Pepperell's first campaign, for example, as we have seen, Barton, Durstine & Osborn, Inc., made a study of the market. It decided on a slightly higher thread count than in competing sheets, so that Pepperell could stress quality rather than price to get sales. For this sheet McIntire selected the name Lady Pepperell, as already noted. He also arranged to have the sheet properly identified by a small cloth tag sewed onto one corner with the proper mark. Formerly, textile companies had been content to paste a paper label on each sheet or bolt of sheeting. The advertising agency also changed the packaging of sheets. Previously it had been the custom to wrap a dozen sheets in a piece of wrapping paper. McIntire designed a special wrapping of an old French design, in which ten different scenes, all related to sheets, were shown. The label for sheets and packages was also distinctive; it was designed to carry out the idea of the wrapping paper. Such was the advertising agency's first preparation of a sheet for advertising and for distribution through new channels.[21]

The Lady Pepperell sheet, in its new type of package, was advertised extensively. At first the former advertising of Pepperell's Red Label Sheeting was continued in seven magazines, and advertisements of Lady Pepperell were inserted in two of

* Here we do not have time to discuss many activities. For a full treatment of an advertising agency I recommend the recent history of N. W. Ayer & Son by Ralph M. Hower.[20]

them, *Vogue* and *Good Housekeeping,* the former to reach a smaller but important group of women in the country and the latter to reach a very large group of women. After four experimental months Lady Pepperell was advertised in the other publications which Pepperell used as media, such as the *Ladies' Home Journal* and *Woman's Home Companion.* These advertisements, as the illustration opposite page 250 shows, had a quality appeal; some carried a picture of a package of sheets, while others showed a luxurious bedroom. Altogether, for the fiscal year ending June, 1926, the total cost of advertising was more than $200,000. The sum spent by Pepperell was greater, according to a trade magazine, than that spent in 1924 by any of the three other manufacturers of sheeting which were advertising; this amount was, however, less than Pepperell's yearly average for the whole period 1925–45, which came to about $300,000. These figures included salaries and other expenses of Pepperell's advertising department, payments for advertising, and commissions to the advertising agency, the last being at the rate of 15 per cent of the gross cost of advertising space. The figures also contained charges by the agency and others for special studies. But these expenditures involved modest sums compared with those spent by advertisers in some other industries.[22]

Since 1926 Lady Pepperell has continued to be advertised in the leading women's magazines. Other media have been used occasionally. A Harvard professor remembers that Pepperell had a billboard advertisement in which there was a slogan, "When you have guests, put Lady Pepperell on the bed." Whether or not these were the precise words, Pepperell's advertisement made an impression which stuck for nearly a score of years. At various times Pepperell has sponsored radio programs, although on the whole such programs have been considered too expensive. When Pepperell added still finer sheets to its line, they too were advertised. Although Pepperell Fine Count has been pushed to some degree, it has been Pepperell Peeress—comparable to Wamsutta's finest—that offered the ultimate in appeal to the quality market. In spite of all efforts to reach a limited group of wealthy women, this sheet has

ADVERTISEMENT OF LADY PEPPERELL SHEETS

seemed to have less acceptance than Wamsutta's, which had a head start of almost a decade.

Variation of product did not rest with the three new sheets. To catch the consumer's attention Pepperell offered sheets in pastel colors and white sheets with colored or Jacquard hems. With colored sheets Pepperell made a success—the first company to do so—although their appeal was limited to a small segment of the market. The colored sheets gave new possibilities for advertising and added to the interest in displays. Other less spectacular innovations were promoted, such as the tapered tape selvage. These promotions kept Pepperell constantly before the public—a necessity in the establishment of a good market, particularly when competitors were using the same methods.

In time other Pepperell products were advertised extensively. For instance, blankets were brought out with distinguishing names. Crib blankets, with new patterns each year, were pushed and found good markets. Some of them were called Baby Pepperell Crib Blankets. In 1929 began the first of the advertisements of garments with a combination of brand names—Pepperell's and the garment maker's. Play suits, for example, were advertised as made by the Reliance Manufacturing Co. from Pepperell fabrics. In 1931 Lord Pepperell shirts, made of Pepperell broadcloth by the McLaughlin Manufacturing Co., were promoted. Numerous other products from time to time have received attention, but never so much as the emphasis placed on the line of sheets.

In 1931 Pepperell simplified its advertising procedure by adopting one trade-mark for all its goods in place of the many for foreign and domestic business which it had developed during the preceding eighty years. Ever since the beginning of operations, Pepperell had stamped the Dragon on drills for China and India. In 1899 it adopted Laconia's Beaver for jeans for the same markets. For the domestic market Pepperell had used many brands of its own as well as those of important purchasers. In the third period Pepperell developed many new trade-marks for its various goods, which were all replaced by the one house-mark, Pepperell Fabrics, with a picture of a dragon, as the illustration at the end of Chapter XIV shows. This single mark made it possible for the consumer, at a glance, to be sure of the maker of the fabric.

During the second World War Pepperell in its advertising stressed the importance of the consumer's doing without necessary textiles so that they could be used by the armed services. By this method the company appealed to patriotism, while at the same time reminding the public of Pepperell's products.

By these programs of advertising, year after year, Pepperell promoted its goods. Since it was earlier in doing this than most cotton textile companies, which had only modest funds to use, it succeeded in winning the approval of a broad market. Its appeals have remained the same—a varied line of sheets.

SELLING PEPPERELL'S GOODS

Early in this third period Pepperell, by deciding to establish its own selling department for its goods, precipitated a movement which affected the prevailing system of distributing through an independent sales agent. Not content with this one radical step, the company took many others, notably that of selling directly to types of customers who previously had been reached through intermediaries.

In the two earlier periods Pepperell's goods, as well as those of many other cotton textile companies in the United States, had been distributed by selling agents. These firms, for a commission, handled the sale of the goods of several manufacturers. Most of the selling was done in the main offices of the agents in New York, although branch offices and traveling salesmen did some of the business. The goods went principally to wholesalers, but also to large manufacturers, large converters, large industrial users, and exporters. This system worked well during the years when the wholesaler was the key to the distribution of goods. But in time other distributors, such as large retailers, chain stores, and mail-order houses, as well as smaller converters and manufacturers of clothing, rebelled and wanted to buy directly from the agents. The selling houses, however, remained loyal to their old customers and refused to deal with the new types of potential buyers. Furthermore, during these years the selling houses were content to sell the same types of goods year after year. These houses were less conscious of the need for change to new goods than the mills which found their profits growing less with keener competition in the industry on the old types of textiles. Thus, for two major reasons, changes in the selling methods were becoming urgent by 1914. The first World War, however, postponed adjustments for a few years.

After the war cotton textile companies altered their arrangements for selling. Many of the stronger ones set up their own sales departments, while the weaker turned to factors who could handle not only the distributing but also the financing of the goods. As a result, many commission houses went out of business, so that by the middle 'forties only a handful of the old type of cotton-textile commission houses remained in existence in New York.[23]

A. Organization of the Selling Department

Pepperell did not make the shift in its merchandising from the selling house to its own sales department abruptly. Early in 1925 Leonard began the organization of a Pepperell Department within the selling house, Bliss, Fabyan & Co., by selecting Donald B. Tansill to represent Pepperell exclusively. At the beginning of the fiscal year 1927–28 he went further and established Pepperell's own sales organization in the agency's headquarters. In January, 1928, the break between the two was completed by the moving of Pepperell's sales organization into offices in the new building at 40 Worth Street—the site of the former Claflin wholesaling business in New York. There, throughout this period, Pepperell has maintained its main sales office on part of the second floor, expanding from 10,000 to 22,000 square feet of space.[24]

With the coöperation of Bliss, Fabyan & Co., Pepperell built up its own original selling organization from members of the former's salesforce. The new Pepperell manager of sales, Donald B. Tansill, was an employee who in a few years had demonstrated his ability as a smooth, suave salesman and a gifted leader of men.

In time, from other selling houses other men came to Pepperell, as, for example, the first credit manager, Leonard Goodwin, and his assistant, Morton P. Schapp. When in 1931 Pepperell acquired the shoe fabrics division of the National Fabric and Finishing Co., another group of salesmen was taken over with it. Altogether during the early years about 60 men sold Pepperell's goods—about 20 from the New York office and about 40 from the other offices scattered throughout the country. During the second World War the force grew smaller, since there was little need for selling effort inasmuch as most of the goods were going to the government and to a few contractors. Some of the salesmen left for the armed service, while others sought temporary jobs in other fields.[25]

Pepperell's main sales office for all goods except shoe fabrics was in New York. There were generally in the New York office various departments for the different types of goods manufactured and purchased, such as sheets, blankets, rayons, fabrics for work clothing, grey goods, wash goods, and goods finished in Lewiston. At one time there was a drapery department also. In addition, there were departments for special functions: one handled the matter of franchise, which covered the special arrangements with clothing manufacturers who used Pepperell's label on their garments. There were also credit, production, and office managers. For a number of years there was a stylist, who assisted in the designing of fabrics.

In 1931 Pepperell and Wellington Sears Co. set up the Manufacturers Textile Export Co., which they owned jointly, for the purpose of handling the export business of many companies. Although business with the Orient had declined, there was still a market for some goods in the Philippines and Cuba. In 1939 Pepperell became the sole owner of the exporting company, which served as its export department while still handling the business of other companies.

For each of Pepperell's sales departments in New York there was a manager, sometimes aided by one or two assistants. In 1941, before the entrance of the United States into the second World War, there were in all fourteen managers and assistants in New York. Not only did they sell goods to customers who came to their offices but they directed sales of their departments throughout the country. In addition to those in the special departments, there were nine general salesmen whose headquarters were also in New York. This represented a reduction to about half the number so employed earlier in this period. While some sold only around New York City, others —whose headquarters were in New York City—covered large territories. In all, the area covered by the men stretched from southern Connecticut along the Atlantic coast to Georgia and southwest to Kentucky. To some were allocated special types of outlets in certain territories, while to others all types of outlets were open.[26]

Starting in 1927 there were general branch sales offices in Boston, Chicago, and San Francisco. For a time, offices were maintained in St. Louis and New Orleans. These were the cities in which Bliss, Fabyan & Co. had had their offices. New ones were opened in Dallas and Atlanta. In 1941 the Boston and Chicago offices each had three salesmen, including the managers. In each of the other three offices there was only one salesman—the manager. Thus it is clear that the salesforce has been concentrated in the eastern half of the country, and particularly in the northeastern quarter.[27]

For a number of years these salesmen were paid a base salary and a commission on sales above a certain quota. In 1928 the commission rate was about one half of one per cent on volume above the quota set for the area. At times there were other special inducements, for instance, a bonus of $1.00 a bale for drills sold to new wholesalers in 1936.[28] But since the men tended to sell the volume lines, this system of commissions was not entirely satisfactory to the company. Before our entry into the second World War a new method of payment was established by which, in place of a commission, the salesmen were given a percentage of profits. This arrangement had the advantage of making the salesmen conscious of the profitable lines, which have not always been the volume ones.

The salesmen's expenses were watched carefully. Each six months estimates for the following period were made out, and monthly actual expenditures compared with the estimates.

Thus the natural tendency of a salesman to be free with money while on the road was somewhat controlled.

In addition to the general salesmen, to make matters more complicated, there were a few specialty men selling rayon goods and Lewiston fabrics. Their offices were in Cincinnati, Cleveland, Minneapolis, and Portland, Oregon. There was one man with an office in Milwaukee who sold both Lewiston fabrics (goods purchased from outsiders and finished in Lewiston) and shoe fabrics. These men were paid entirely on a commission basis.[29] Pepperell's shoe fabrics have generally been handled by special salesmen, many of whom had been selling shoe fabrics long before they became associated with Pepperell.

At this point we must note the connection of Pepperell with the National Fabric and Finishing Co., Inc., which was a composite of older merchandising concerns and which had a bleachery of its own.* From the National Fabric and Finishing Co., Inc., Pepperell took over some converting and some selling but, more important, the manufacture of shoe fabrics. This was in 1931. Pepperell has had few competitors for this shoe fabric business; and, by the end of the third period of its history, it has been estimated, Pepperell was furnishing the shoe manufacturers with about one-third of their total needs. Since these

* The National Fabric and Finishing Co., Inc., was descended in part from the Farnsworth Hoyt Co., of Boston, established in 1856. The connecting link between these two was the Lowell Bleachery, which finished grey goods for northern mills and later for southern mills also. By 1924 the Lowell company had added a bleachery in the South and another in St. Louis. By 1924, also, the Lowell company was experiencing difficult times because of the closing of many of the mills in the North which had been its suppliers. So, in order to survive, the Lowell Bleachery decided to integrate by taking over five merchandising companies which had been its customers. Among these was the Farnsworth Hoyt Co. A new company was started, called the National Fabric and Finishing Co., Inc., to embody the five old companies as well as to hold a subsidiary, the Lowell Bleachery, Inc. But the new parent company's overhead, with the combination of personnel from six companies, was high. Although efforts were made to reduce expenses in order to operate in the black, in 1931 a reorganization became necessary. It gave up the merchandising division; to Pepperell it sold the shoe fabrics and specialty divisions, which had been among the more profitable ones; and in 1934, after ten years of difficulty, the residual organization took as its title the Lowell Bleachery, Inc.[30]

shoe manufacturers were a comparatively small group, about 20 per cent of them producing approximately 80 per cent of the shoes, Pepperell enjoyed a market that could easily be reached.[31]

Pepperell took over from the National Fabric and Finishing Co., in addition to the shoe-fabric inventory on hand, a sales organization under the direction of L. T. Bartlett, who for four years had been a vice-president. Earlier he had run his own business and then for a year had been employed by Bliss, Fabyan & Co. He was thus well fitted to head Pepperell's shoe-fabrics division. This division was set up with its main office in Boston—the old shoe and leather center of the United States. Ten years later (in 1941), under Bartlett, who was still the manager in Boston, there were eleven men selling these goods. There were four with their own offices in Boston, two in Philadelphia and San Francisco, and one each in Cincinnati, St. Louis, and Milwaukee. They combined the sales of Pepperell's fabrics with those of other companies for other parts of the shoes. These men were paid on a commission basis.

Members of Pepperell's general salesforce were welded into a single aggressive organization by several measures. Starting in 1928 Tansill, at his home or at a hotel, held regular Monday evening meetings for the salesforce and others who might be in New York. Thus the men's records were reviewed weekly and plans were made for the following week; they were given little opportunity to take it easy. During the second World War these meetings were discontinued. Throughout that period, as we have already noted, the salesmen received copies of the *Pepperell News Sheet,* which kept them informed not only of events in the advertising and selling departments but of other news about the company. At times, to salesmen away from the office, heads of departments sent bulletins called "Friday night letters." This practice, too, was discontinued for a while, but in 1944 Pepperell resumed bulletins to the salesmen on a monthly basis. By such measures, not used by the former selling house, Pepperell kept its salesforce well informed and aggressive.

At a higher executive level there have also been frequent meetings, concerning sales, devoted to the coördination of sales and production. In fact, they were called "mill meetings." To them went, besides Tansill, representatives of the mills, the production manager in New York, who handled the placing of orders for goods, members of the sales department, and others concerned with the mills' problems. Since 1936, in order to make available a long-time record, minutes of their meetings have been kept. Before the second World War these meetings were quite frequent, particularly for consideration of sheets and blankets. In some years the groups concerned with these lines met once or twice a month. During the war, however, the number of meetings was reduced because the situation had reversed itself: no longer was it a question of how to dispose of the goods, but of how to meet government orders and to have a little left for civilians.

Still other meetings were scheduled for other groups, such as the policy meetings of the chief executives, in which selling problems might be considered among other matters. In all, this third period has been one in which meetings were fostered for various groups in the company. By getting acquainted with one another as well as with operations, the executives hoped to build up a force which would insure Pepperell's success. The extent of this success we shall trace in another chapter.

Here we are concerned with the selling record made by the salesmen. In the year 1937–38 five of the general salesmen sold more than $1,000,000 worth of goods each, while ten others sold between $500,000 and $1,000,000 worth. The reason for these high records lies partly in the inclusion of large manufacturing, chain, and mail-order houses in their territories. For rayons and shoe fabrics, salesmen's records were much lower—these men devoted only part of their time to Pepperell's goods—although one of them did exceed $500,000 principally because of a certain large account.

Expenses for selling per dollar of sales remained about the same for many years, even including the previous period. This comparability existed in spite of an increase from about $180,000 to $720,000 on the average for expenses. For the previous twenty-six years the cost was 2.2 cents; in the last twenty-one years of the third period it was 2.5 cents per dollar of sales.[32]

But actually we are comparing unlike performances, since Pepperell's salesforce did a job of selling quite different from that performed by the selling house. They reached many more customers than in the preceding years and sold many different types of goods. Of course the selling house had also sold a variety of goods. (For all except the plain ones, such as those Pepperell produced, it had charged a commission higher than to Pepperell.) On the whole Pepperell benefited greatly from the assumption of complete control of its selling organization, which it coördinated with other parts of the company.

B. Customers

Pepperell's customers increased in number and in types during this period. This change came about partly through the increase in the types of products which Pepperell had for sale. Most of the goods it manufactured itself, while others it purchased to increase the volume of business. The principal lines among the manufactured goods have been sheetings and blankets from the Biddeford mills; rayon lining and underwear fabrics, cotton marquisettes, and sheetings from the Fall River mills; work-clothing fabrics from the Lindale mills; and drills, jeans, and sheetings from the Opelika mills. (Some of these mills are new-comers and will be presented later.) At times Pepperell has purchased other goods for finishing, such as rayons and shoe linings. Some of the goods have been finished at Lewiston, some in the mills themselves, and some have been sold in the grey. Altogether these fabrics have given Pepperell a wide line to offer its customers.

Pepperell has sought to distribute its goods directly to more *types* of outlets, as Chart IV shows. This policy resulted in many changes in the accounts. Interestingly enough, the *number* of accounts grew until the second World War. The greatest increases took place in Pepperell's first years of self-selling, during which time it also added to its mills. While the estimated number of customers for the year 1923–24 was about 1,300, in 1928–29, which was the second year of the independent sales department, Pepperell had 2,260 different accounts, an increase of nearly 75 per cent. In spite of the depression, the number

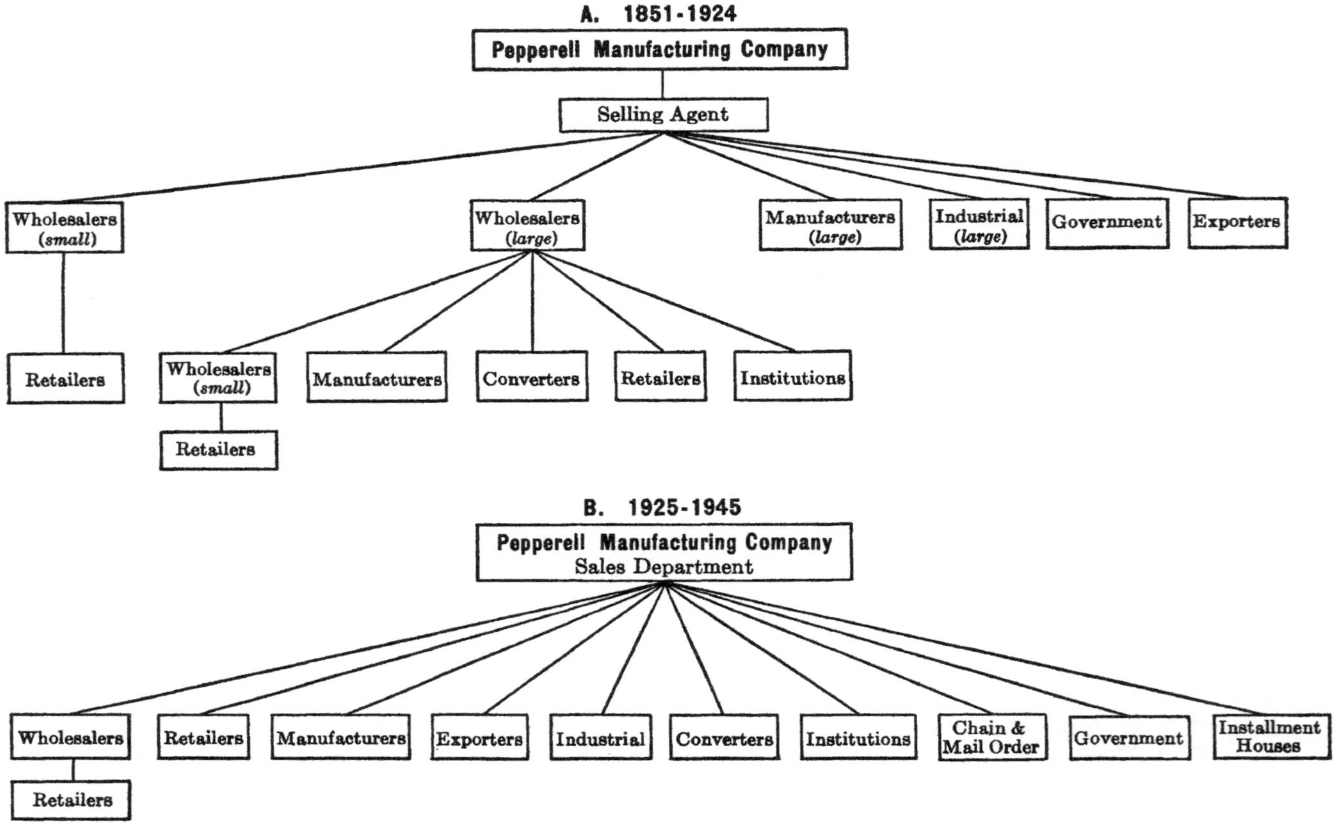

CHART IV

PEPPERELL'S CHANNELS OF DISTRIBUTION, 1851–1945

Source. Ms. P. M. C., Sales Journals, 1851–1867, 1870–1872; Cash Journals, 1906–1908, Ledgers, 1897–1913, Trial Balance Sheets, 1906–1917; Journals, 1924–1927; Area Analysis Control, 1928–1930; Notes, 1931–1932; Sales Analysis, 1932–1945.

grew to 2,570 in 1933. For the next two years it rose to 2,810 and 3,430 respectively, at which level it stayed for the following two years. The next year it increased to 3,560, which was the high point for the period. During the early war years the number of accounts declined to about 1,900 in 1943 and 1944. Thereafter it rose to over 2,000 in 1945.[33]

The number of wholesalers among these accounts has been growing smaller. The decline in wholesaling outlets results partly from a new policy of selling directly to retailers in New England and in large cities generally. In these places Pepperell has wanted to select the particular outlets for goods. Pepperell's policies have also reflected the decline in importance of the dry goods wholesaler throughout the United States.[34] As the country developed there came to be less need for large national or regional wholesalers such as Claflin of New York, who had distributed to smaller wholesalers and retailers. Some of the wholesalers went out of business, while others, like Marshall Field in Chicago, abandoned wholesaling in favor of retailing. While in 1928 Pepperell sold to about 800 wholesalers, ten years later it sold to only 500. Declines in Pepperell's numbers of wholesaler accounts were greatest in the northeastern quarter, in the Pacific and Mountain States, and in the three cotton-growing States east of the Mississippi. Changes after 1938 are difficult to measure because of the upsetting effects of the second World War.

While Pepperell has been selling to fewer and fewer wholesalers, it has been selling to more and more retailers. Whereas in 1924 the selling agency had not sold to any retailers, in 1928 Pepperell sold to 400. Within the following decade the company doubled this number. Increases came first in the industrial East, as one would expect, where population was more concentrated than elsewhere and where results could be watched in the Boston and New York offices. During this decade Pepperell strove for good retail outlets for its sheets and blankets in the principal cities in other parts of the country. As a result, the numbers grew rapidly outside New England. The growth was greatest in the three southern States of Tennessee,

Alabama, and Mississippi, where the number quadrupled. But even so, the number there in 1938 was only half that in New England. Still further possibilities for expanding retail outlets remain to be explored in the postwar period.

Furthermore, the wholesalers lost to the manufacturers, who became the most numerous of all outlets for Pepperell's goods during this period. In the analysis of customer accounts for 1928 all customers besides wholesalers were lumped together and totaled over 1,000. In 1938 the manufacturers alone numbered nearly 1,900. From Pepperell's fabrics they fashioned such garments as overalls and work shirts. They were located principally in the Middle Atlantic States, where the majority of clothing manufacturers were concentrated.[35] Also there were others, called industrial buyers, who used the goods either in the process of manufacture or as a minor part of the finished product, such as backings for abrasives. In 1938 there were comparatively few of these buyers—about 65—some of whom, however, bought in large quantities.

In addition to the wholesalers, retailers, manufacturers, and industrial users, Pepperell sold to other types of customers. In 1938 the institutional customers ranked first in numbers of these other types. Converters came second; in fact, the number of converters of Pepperell's goods was small, when one considers the various types suitable for such outlets. A few chain and mail-order houses, government agencies, and installment-house customers, such as furniture stores which sold bedding with beds, were also on the list. Some of them bought in large quantities.

Unfortunately these accounts do not give the full story concerning the number of customers. Treated as one account were foreign sales (other than Canadian), which were handled by the Manufacturers Textile Export Co. To how many customers this company sold Pepperell's goods the records do not reveal. We do know that this export company dealt with export firms located in New York which bought goods for consumption abroad as well as with firms located in foreign countries. For the last thirteen years of this period we know that annual sales through this export company ranged from over $600,000 to nearly $2,000,000 in value, with the average about $1,000,000. Thus, for this period Pepperell's foreign business was proportionately much less than in the earlier two periods.

Also included as one account were the sales by the shoe fabrics division. For the last fifteen years of this period annual sales of shoe fabrics ranged from not quite $900,000 to over $4,000,000 in value, with the average about $1,500,000. In the fiscal year 1937–38 this division sold to about 550 customers, most of whom were shoe manufacturers.

Unfortunately we cannot compare the totals in volume of goods sold to these various types of outlets, since Pepperell has not computed such totals and many of the early record cards have been destroyed. A study of such data would throw much more light on the importance of each category than does the mere number of outlets, with which we have to be content here. Perhaps, however, other research students in other companies will find material easily available for such a study. We do know that it was Pepperell's practice to sell its sheets and blankets to selected retailers in the important cities throughout the country, as well as to wholesalers who did not compete with these retailers. While Pepperell also disposed of some of its goods to chain stores and mail-order houses, normally this type of customer was not favored, since Pepperell's tickets were not carried by these outlets.

Of Pepperell's many accounts, comparatively few were for large amounts. In 1935–36, a fairly normal year, Pepperell sold about $27,500,000 worth of goods (other than shoe fabrics and for export) to about 3,430 customers, or about $8,000 worth on the average to a customer. Actually, over half the customers bought less than $2,000 worth of goods in this year. To only 98 customers did Pepperell sell goods valued at $50,000 or more, but these 98 bought goods amounting to about $17,000,000. This means that about 3 per cent of Pepperell's general customers purchased about 62 per cent of its goods. Their purchases ranged up to nearly $3,000,000 in value, with the majority, however, in the class from $50,000 to $100,000.

This concentration of sales to large customers was probably similar to that in the preceding periods, except that the relative importance of the types had changed—wholesalers were no longer the most important type of outlet.

For those 98 large customers in 1935–36 we can compile sales by types. We find the following distribution:

TABLE 8

TYPES OF LARGE CUSTOMERS, 1935–36

Types	Number Purchasing $50,000 or More of Goods	Percentage of Sales of Total to Large Customers
Manufacturer	52	52.4
Chain and mail-order	9	18.0
Wholesaler	18	12.6
Government	2	6.9
Retailer	9	3.9
Converter	5	3.5
Industrial	3	2.7

Manufacturers predominated in numbers and amount of purchases among these large customers. They averaged less than the government agencies and the chain and mail-order houses. From these figures we cannot, however, deduce that sales to all customers were in the same proportions, although undoubtedly manufacturers predominated.

During the second World War the pattern of selling changed considerably. Besides contracts with the United States government, Pepperell sought other priority business, so that the majority of its products might go for war purposes. In the year 1942–43, the peak year of government business as well as of total business, Pepperell's sales to large customers rose to over $38,500,000 worth, or over 76 per cent of total sales, exclusive of export and shoe fabrics. The number of large customers grew to 131, making up almost 7 per cent of the total number of customers. The distribution is as follows:

TABLE 9

TYPES OF LARGE CUSTOMERS, 1942–43

Types	Number Purchasing $50,000 or More of Goods	Percentage of Sales of Total to Large Customers
Government	14	41.2
Manufacturer	59	30.1
Industrial	9	10.2
Wholesaler	27	8.5
Chain and mail-order	9	5.9
Converter	3	2.2
Retailer	9	1.7
Institutional	1	0.2

In this abnormal year we find among the large customers still greater concentration of sales to the government, manufacturers, and industrial buyers. While the number of large wholesalers increased 50 per cent, their combined purchases ranked fourth. Numbers of large retailers stayed the same, while their purchases shrank in importance relatively. From our own personal experiences we know that retailers suffered from lack of supplies.

During the war Pepperell sold directly to many government agencies, including the Treasury Department, the Army, the Navy, the Maritime Service, and others. Total value of direct sales for war purposes rose from slightly over $1,000,000 in 1940–41 to a peak of nearly $15,000,000 in 1942–43, when the Armed Forces were being equipped, and declined to less than $8,000,000 for the following fiscal year. The largest sales to any branch of any agency were to the Army's finance officer in Philadelphia. In the year 1942–43 sales to that office reached a peak of over $12,000,000 in value. Thus, in the third major war during its existence Pepperell again assisted in equipping the Armed Forces, this time to a much greater extent than previously, since cotton goods were used for many more purposes.

Government contracts were arranged through the selling organization—through Tansill and the heads of departments. In previous years the department heads had gained experience in dealing with the government, so that they entered these negotiations with knowledge of procedures. Pepperell consciously, according to a policy stated by Leonard, avoided seeking an unfair profit on this business; it sought reasonable prices. But costs were rising, particularly for labor, so that the company could not be sure of the exact costs in the future. As a result, several contracts were renegotiated.

Considering the whole third period, then, we find that Pepperell has secured more customers than ever before. These customers have included a host of small as well as a few large ones. Of the large customers, in normal years the manufacturers came to be predominant; in war years, the government agencies. What the pattern will be in the years following this last period we cannot say now. If the years are prosperous, Pepperell may build up its system of customers, eliminating to a greater degree than in the past those that do not fit into its pattern of promotion.

C. Terms to Customers

During this third period Pepperell has continued many of the past practices of its selling houses. In the same manner terms have been set for the payment of goods by customers. With variations in business conditions, prices and discounts have been changed. In addition the company has established new conditions for dealing with some customers—those using Pepperell's tickets and those including Pepperell's trade-mark on their finished garments.

Terms for payment of goods have remained about the same as in the past. Customarily to distributors of its goods—now wholesalers, retailers, chain stores, and mail-order houses—the company quoted the terms of 3 per cent off if paid in the first 10 days, and as listed if paid at 70 days. To manufacturers the terms were slightly different, depending on the customs of the business. In some instances the terms were net if paid in 10 days; in others, net in 60 days. To those who anticipated payment dates Pepperell allowed interest, a practice which it attempted to stop because the interest rate was higher than that secured at a bank. But plans for this change were checked by freezing of past practices after we had entered the War.[36]

During this period (1924–45) of violent change in business conditions, Pepperell naturally has had to adjust the prices and discounts on its goods a number of times. For sheets, for example, according to the customs of the trade there were one or two new price lists annually from 1924 until 1937 or 1938, after which the policy seems to have been to keep the prices the same and to change only the discounts. For the first part of this period, then, the lists do record changes in prices. For example, according to the eight price lists for Pepperell Peeress, which was introduced in 1930, prices were cut four times, so that from its initial high the price had dropped 33 per cent by 1935. By the spring of 1937 its price had risen to within 12 per cent of its former high—at this level it has remained.

But these prices fail to tell the full story of fluctuations, since they do not disclose the discounts which were also granted. In fairly normal times, as in the late 1920's, it was standard practice to grant discounts of 10, 5, and 2½ per cent on sheets. When business was excellent, discounts were less, as in March, 1937, when on Pepperell Percale the company gave only 7½ per cent. When business grew poorer, discounts mounted: for example, in 1931 for the Red Label type the company granted 10, 5, 5, and 5 per cent to jobbers and large retailers—2½ per cent more than to small retailers. In the sharp decline in business in 1938 the company gave discounts greater than those during the preceding serious depression. It gave 35 per cent for Lady Pepperell and Pepperell Percale, 40 and 2½ per cent for the Red Label, and 45 per cent for Pepperell Peeress. Thus, in a short time, prices after discounts dropped to lows comparable with those in 1931. For a time during the second World War prices and discounts were frozen at existing levels, but when costs of production rose, the government granted increases, which resulted in changes in discounts. For Lady Pepperell, for example, the discount changed from 7.5 per cent as frozen in January, 1942, to 0.3 per cent in June, 1944.

For Pepperell's other goods the history of prices and discounts has differed somewhat. For blankets, for example, we find that constructions and patterns changed so much that it is difficult to find a single type of blanket which was produced throughout. We do find that the Wamba, a part-wool crib blanket, was produced during most of the period. From a high at the beginning of 1929 its price dropped by about 40 per cent in 1933; the price had risen to slightly more than the high of 1929 by late 1941.

Pepperell has made no attempt to compile its own index of prices for all its goods. Instead it has considered the government index of wholesale prices of cotton goods a sufficiently reliable indicator of changes in the prices paid by its customers. Thus we find that the index dropped in 1932 to a low of 54 per cent of the 1926 base. It rose during the following years, so that in 1945 it was more than 20 per cent over that in 1926 and 10 per cent over 1925.[37]

From its licensed manufacturers Pepperell has also received license premiums, since these customers have derived some benefit from Pepperell's advertising. In 1940 the company planned to spend half the premiums, provided that the licensees would meet the amount for advertising and other promotions. By this action both Pepperell and the licensees would benefit. Pepperell has watched these licensed manufacturers much more carefully than the others; their products have had to be a credit to both. Although comparatively few in number among the customers, a large proportion of these licensed manufacturers have been among the large buyers.

The licensing of manufacturers has represented a compromise situation in the growing tendency of vertical integration of textile companies. While others have carried their integration further, Pepperell has been content to prepare only its sheets and blankets in the form used by the ultimate consumer. Problems of styling garments have seemed too difficult and too removed from its operations for Pepperell to undertake. This compromise, with licensees for various types of garments, has worked out well, to the advantage of both; of course there were risks in letting other companies use Pepperell's trade-mark. Pepperell has guarded itself against garments appearing with its trade-mark which might not be to its credit.

During this period Pepperell has worked out elaborate plans for its tickets. Although it has realized the advantages of eliminating all private tickets, it has had to be content to wait until such time as the preference for its goods would be so strong that it could cut out these customers or allow them only the Pepperell tickets. Since originally, long before the beginning of this period, wholesalers had distributed the old Pepperell Red Label sheeting, they have been allowed to continue to use the primary ticket for this grade of sheet. Some of them have been granted a secondary ticket. The other types of customers, when they have not competed with the wholesalers, have been granted primary tickets. On the new grades of sheets, wholesalers and others besides retailers have been granted secondary tickets.[38]

Primary tickets, except for the old carded sheeting, have been given to selected retail outlets. Only one retailer in a city has been so privileged; and, if others have wanted to handle the sheets, they have been given secondary tickets. Thus Pepperell has protected its selected outlets from price-cutting wars, which in the past had been frequent and fierce.[39]

In spite of the increase in credit risk with many more customers, Pepperell has had few customers who did not pay for their goods. In fact, over the period 1928–45, it lost altogether about $150,000 or about .03 of one per cent of sales. This was much less than the .1 of one per cent set up as a reserve on sales in 1927. Losses naturally were greatest during the depression of the early 'thirties. Then in the two years 1930–31 and 1931–32, Pepperell exceeded the rate of reserve, reaching a high of .354 of one per cent of sales in the latter year. In the last three years of this period there were no losses. In 1940 the average experience of the past ten years was used as the rate for reserve, since the government held that the former rate was too high. But there was always the chance of a serious loss which might wipe out the accumulated reserve. This chance was smaller than in the past, when crises affected the financial structure of the country more severely.[40]

In general, during this third period Pepperell has continued past practices with few alterations: it established the practice of charging license fees to the selected manufacturers who used its trade-mark; pushed its own tickets much more than previously when many outlets used their own; and continued to deal with a reliable group of customers who paid their obligations promptly.

D. The Sales Record

As a result of many circumstances, some outside and some within the company, Pepperell's sales have fluctuated, although on the whole they have increased considerably during this period. We may expect great variations in its record in different parts of the country, since there have been different economic conditions, intensities of selling, and types of customers.

If we group Pepperell's fifty sales areas into nine regions, we find that the latter fall into four still larger units. We discover that, in the seventeen years of independent selling, 1928–29 through 1944–45, for which analyses have been prepared, Pepperell made least progress in sales in the unit west of the Mississippi River. There was practically none in the Southwest Central region. In the second half of this period great progress was shown in the Pacific and Mountain regions. There was less in the Northwest Central. Altogether, for this western unit during the first eight years Pepperell's sales increased by about 7 per cent, and in the following nine years by almost 50 per cent. To another unit belong the Northeast Central States, where during the first eight years increases were about 45 per cent, and in the last nine 20 per cent. To a unit by themselves belong Tennessee, Mississippi, and Alabama, where in the first eight years increases were greatest—almost 300 per cent; in the following years increases were slight. To a fourth unit belong the States bordering on or close to the Atlantic Ocean. Here in the first eight years sales increased by about 140 per cent, and in the last nine by another 90 per cent. Of course, the latter figures were swollen by war business, so that, in the Middle Atlantic States alone in the last three years, from 1942–43 to 1944–45, over half of the total sales were made. But even in normal times, this group of Middle Atlantic States was more important than all the other States together.[41]

Total sales during the years of this third period, as Appendix

37 shows, varied considerably. The low point was reached in 1926, with slightly less than $10,000,000 worth sold. Thereafter sales mounted, although with the inevitable decreases in the depression years. In 1937 a new high of $40,000,000 was reached; not until 1942 was this figure reached again, when greater production for the government was under way. It was surpassed in 1943, when value of sales reached a peak of $54,-000,000. There was a slight decline in the following two years, but even so, value of sales for the last year of this period (1945) was over $52,000,000.

Any comparison of Pepperell's sales with indices of business activity means little, since the company throughout this period was changing its productive capacity. The number of spindles in place was adjusted, so that in the four sets of mills in 1945 there were only about 17 per cent more than in Biddeford in 1925. At the same time Pepperell increased the number of hours run per spindle; in 1945 each spindle, on the average, operated two and a half times as many hours as in 1925. Supplementing these two changes there was an increase in efficiency of machinery, so that production in 1945, measured in pounds, was almost 270 per cent greater than in 1925. For these two years there was only a small price change—an increase in 1945 of about 10 per cent over 1925.[42] Therefore, we must look for other factors to explain the increase of 350 per cent in sales. One such factor, as we have already indicated, was the change in types of goods produced in the mills, with which we shall be concerned in the following two chapters.

* * *

During this third period, 1924–45, a rejuvenation took place in the Pepperell Manufacturing Company. It became evident in many ways. Fundamental to this invigoration was the selection of capable management. The trustees proved wise in their choice for treasurer of Russell H. Leonard, who did not belong, as many of his predecessors in office had done, to the class of Boston "blue bloods" which had developed in the nineteenth century. Like the first treasurer, William Dwight, Leonard came from the hinterland, where his family had prospered for many generations. Dwight's family had had mercantile interests; Leonard's, industrial. Although Leonard belonged to a prominent family in a small town, he rubbed elbows with all, a habit which as Pepperell's treasurer he has continued. This is a valuable asset for an executive in the era of national capitalism when the common man is becoming more and more privileged.

By departure from established practices in other respects, Leonard has become known as an able merchandiser as well as administrator. He followed the lead of the Wamsutta and Ipswich Mills in the study, promotion, and production of finer-quality goods. He has not stopped there but, after making other studies, has introduced other goods and carried on research to obtain new products. Thus Pepperell has been able to produce fabrics to appeal to the American consumer, who has been growing more conscious of fine quality and more capricious in his purchases, even of staples such as those sold by Pepperell.

Leonard went further than Wamsutta and Ipswich in one important respect. He set up his own selling organization to carry through the promotions which he planned and to distribute in the manner which he had decided upon. Retailers became important customers for sheets and blankets, with wholesalers retreating to a secondary position. Manufacturers also became valuable customers for some types of goods; in fact, they became the most numerous and probably took a majority of the goods. Since these types of outlets did not take care of all the goods produced, Pepperell sold to chains and mail-order houses and government agencies. But they did not carry the manufacturer's trade-mark and, on this ground as well as on that of lower prices, they were not considered such good customers in the long run. Pepperell wanted to develop a demand for its branded goods throughout the country, so that it would not be squeezed in bad times.

CHAPTER XII

FINE GOODS IN THE NORTH

IN THIS THIRD PERIOD of its history Pepperell made changes in production methods as well as in type of management and in manner of distributing goods. No longer did the company rely upon mills in one locality in New England, but instead diversified risks by maintaining three plants in the North—two sets of mills and a bleachery—and two sets of mills in the South. Production in the North was curtailed while in the South it was increased.

In this chapter we are concerned with production in the North and, in the next, with production in the South. Since conditions were quite different in the two sections, such a division seems natural. Also, we are considering the mills one at a time because their problems were so unlike. But altogether we may gather a knowledge of operations which will provide insight not only into Pepperell but also into much of the industry.

In this chapter we are concerned with operations in four old textile centers in New England—Biddeford and Lewiston in Maine, and Lowell and Fall River in Massachusetts. In all these plants the treasurer made many changes: he cut or eliminated the past scale of operations in three and increased it in only one, the bleachery in Lewiston. This increase seems strange in a period of liquidation of the textile industry in the North, but it can be explained by Pepperell's need for greater integration.

For many years in this period, as we have already seen, Pepperell lived in an atmosphere of industrial gloom. All around it in the North old companies were being liquidated, including the largest of them all, the Amoskeag Manufacturing Co., of Manchester, New Hampshire. Companies in other centers, such as Lowell, Fall River, and New Bedford, were finding it hard to survive; some closed their doors, while a few, after partial liquidation, were put into operation again by different managements. Some moved to the South, where conditions seemed more favorable.

Throughout this period the North declined markedly in importance in the cotton textile industry. Whereas in 1924 the North had 18,000,000 spindles in place—roughly the same number as in the South—in 1945 the North had only 5,000,000, while the South still had 18,000,000. During the second World War the North's position had improved somewhat; it ran its machinery longer hours and thus could compete on more equal terms with the South than previously.[1]

External conditions upset the industry—on the whole for the long-run benefit of the North as well as of the South. The New Deal of Franklin D. Roosevelt set up legislation that provided a floor for minimum wages and a ceiling for length of work-week on a national basis. Thus the mills in the North, long restricted by State laws to a short working day, did not have to continue to contend with the South's long day. Instead of the early sizable spread, the rates of pay became more uniform. State legislation pertaining to restriction of employment of women and children at night continued in force in some States, however, until the second World War when temporarily it was lifted everywhere.

We have noted that for a large part of this period there was a buyer's market for textiles in the United States. Companies had to struggle to dispose of their goods advantageously. By production, and to a slight extent by purchases, Pepperell sought to have a varied line of goods which the advertising and selling departments could push.

SHEETINGS AND BLANKETS IN BIDDEFORD

The treasurer of the Pepperell Manufacturing Company, Russell H. Leonard, made more sweeping changes in the old mills in Biddeford than any of his predecessors had undertaken. While they had added to the productive capacity for the established types of goods, with perhaps a few additional types, Leonard actually cut down capacity, eliminating some of the old products and introducing others. To carry out this change in policy he had the coöperation of able men, many of whom were new to Biddeford. But at times these men found that they had to work out solutions satisfactory to the workers, who were as concerned over the local danger of unemployment as they were over national movements for the establishment of their position. The management, by performing various services for these employees, tried to improve conditions, both for its own long-run benefit and for the immediate and future welfare of the workers. The second World War upset the equilibrium which the management had tried to attain. Many of the workers left for war service, while others sought more remunerative war work, at the very time when the mills needed more workers than before to fill government orders.

At the beginning of this period, as we have already seen, Leonard considered ways of securing a profitable line of goods in Biddeford. He realized that some of the types could be produced more economically in the South, while others were not promising in either section. Also, he saw that to have a more extensive line for selling, additional types of goods should be introduced. As a result of all these factors the volume of production in Biddeford was cut. Instead of a production of 30,000,000 pounds of goods, as in the previous good year (1916), it was less than 25,000,000 annually in this period—in fact, over a period of five years, less than half the former high.[2] At times, in his annual report to the shareholders the treasurer mentioned the advisability of liquidating the mills in Biddeford for more favorable sites elsewhere. This was not done, for apparently the disadvantages of Biddeford have not outweighed its advantages.

In Biddeford there was a return to the former system of concentration on the production of a few lines of goods, a system which had been abandoned to some extent in the middle period, particularly in the Laconia division. Some of the old lines of goods were eliminated, such as shirtings, drills, and jeans, as well as two of the later types, sateens and coutils. As had become common in the cotton textile industry, many of these coarse goods were typically produced in the southern mills. At the end of 1934 the special contracts division, a heritage from the Laconia Company, was discontinued. This division had always been a headache, with its special orders for small amounts, since Pepperell and Laconia were set up fundamentally not for this kind of business but for the mass production of staple goods.

Pepperell continued to produce one of its old lines of goods, wide sheeting; this had been manufactured ever since Mill No. 3 went into operation in 1856. In this period Biddeford made sheetings of several constructions. In 1925 to the muslin sheeting, called Red Label, a finer one called Lady Pepperell was added. In 1942 the production of a combed percale sheeting was started—the Pepperell Peeress—earlier manufactured in the Fall River plant. For two years during the War, however, the company suspended the manufacturing of this line, resuming it in 1944.

In 1928 the mills in the lower (Laconia) division began the production of blankets with machinery moved there from Lowell. For a time some of the former types were continued, such as the domestic cotton, the Asiatic cotton, and the cotton with a small percentage of wool. During this period Biddeford, however, experimented with various types in an attempt to find profitable ones. In 1930 it dropped the all-domestic-cotton blanket and three years later resumed its production. In 1931 it introduced an all-wool blanket, which was eliminated in 1935 and produced again in 1940. In 1936 it introduced a line of blankets of cotton with 25 per cent wool, a much higher wool content than in the earlier mixtures. In 1939 it experimented with two 50 per cent wool blankets, one of which had a triple weave so that the wool was on the outside. But at last, in 1940, the company found a profitable blanket made of 25 per cent wool, 25 per cent cotton, and 50 per cent rayon. Its production was continued throughout the second World War, while the 5 per cent wool grade was eliminated.

These blankets were made for two different groups—adults and babies. For the former the styling of blankets was fairly simple. Generally bed blankets were made in plaids or plain colors. Although Pepperell produced similar styles for cribs,

GILBERT HARRISON

DAVID S. COOK

F. LINCOLN DUNLAP

THREE NORTHERN MANAGERS

AERIAL SURVEY OF MILLS IN BIDDEFORD, ABOUT 1935

greatest attention was paid to Jacquard constructions. While the company had been operating the mills in Lowell, it had introduced designs appropriate for babies. But in Biddeford the company produced a great variety, including designs of animals and children. At the beginning of each calendar year it added new designs while dropping some of the old. Pepperell hired various men as designers, including the noted illustrator and puppet-maker, Tony Sarg. Within this period Pepperell became one of the leading manufacturers of crib blankets.

In 1937, in a small way, the mills in Biddeford began to produce a limited line of towels. These goods were continued throughout the war but were discontinued at its end. The company realized that while towels were a valuable addition to its goods, it needed to produce a much wider line.

These lines of goods were scheduled with greater coöperation among the agent, president-treasurer or vice-presidents, and the selling heads than previously. At the regular so-called mill meetings in New York the various men involved in the production, selling, and general management of the mill talked over problems together. During the second World War, when large orders from the government were taken, records of past performances were compared with schedules to determine how well production was keeping up with orders. Plans for the following months were discussed and solutions to difficult problems sought; thus all three sides—production, general management, and selling—benefited from the exchange of views.

At these meetings knowledge of looms available for each style of goods was fundamental. All the officials had to keep up with changes in machinery in the mills. This was particularly difficult for Biddeford, since many shifts in machinery occurred there. During this period much of the machinery was moved away and some was brought in, though on the average Biddeford lost in equipment. Whereas during the last ten years of the preceding period the Biddeford mills had had almost 300,000 spindles in place, in this period they lost almost 200,000, so that they went back to Pepperell's size in the 1890's or that of Pepperell and Laconia together in the early 1850's.

There were two large exoduses of machinery from Biddeford.

The first was during the years 1924–31, when Pepperell was setting up a new mill in the South, to which much of the Biddeford equipment was moved. The second started in 1935, when the special contracts division, which constituted one whole section of Biddeford's operation, was discontinued. The management moved the best of that machinery to the other divisions in Biddeford, sold what it could, and junked the oldest.

Biddeford replaced some of its old equipment with used machines from other mills. In the first few years the management brought in spinning machinery from the old Lancaster Mills as well as various types from the newly acquired Lowell plant of the Massachusetts Cotton Mills. From the latter came automatic box looms, both cam and dobby, and a few new automatic Jacquard looms, which were suitable for making blankets.

Whenever the executives believed that new machinery was desirable to improve quality, to introduce new fabrics, and to manufacture more cheaply, they purchased it. One of the most significant of these additions was the acquisition in the 1940's of large Barber-Colman spoolers and warpers such as the one in the illustration opposite page 334. Since the tying of threads was automatic, these machines cut down on the work of the operatives. Significant also was the installation of long-draft spinning and roving in the 1930's and super-draft roving in the 1940's, which eliminated the necessity of having as many separate stages as had been required earlier. By 1943, 62 per cent of Biddeford's roving and 85 per cent of its spinning was long-draft, as compared with 40 per cent in the industry.[3]

Since the machinery was allocated to fewer buildings in Biddeford than previously, Pepperell was able to dispose of some property. The Saco-Lowell Machine Shops bought a cotton house in the Pepperell yard and the first mill and its annex in the Laconia yard. Several small buildings near the river were sold to the Cumberland Power Co. Storehouses outside the yards were made available to other interests. Some of Pepperell's remaining space was converted to new uses, for example, the training school and the laboratory for testing. Two new buildings were erected: a dyehouse for blankets in the former Laconia yard and a repair shop not far from the large cotton storehouse. The building in the northwest corner of the Pepperell yard was rebuilt.

Instead of many processes in each large building or group of buildings, the management developed a streamlined flow of work. From the huge cotton storehouse on Pearl Street, for example, the cotton went to buildings on the north side of the Pepperell yard, where it was opened; thence, to the basement of the buildings on the west side for picking and carding. Then it progressed upwards for slubbing, drawing, and spinning. Across the yard the warps were slashed and the yarns woven into sheetings.

On this property in Biddeford taxes had been increasing for many years. In 1935 Leonard protested a tax of $100,000 on a valuation of over $2,500,000. He demanded a reduction—to $50,000 a year. For a year the controversy raged. Meanwhile Leonard secured an option on the Somersworth plant of the Great Falls Manufacturing Co., to which he could move the blanket division. Finally, late in 1936, a compromise was reached.[4] In the following four years, if Pepperell would keep the blanket division in Biddeford, the city would not tax the company for more than $80,000. Evidently this concession was extended for another period, since in 1945 the city granted an abatement so that the tax was about $75,000.

To carry through the changes in the mills in Biddeford the treasurer found it necessary to reorganize the management. From a study which was made in 1925 he found that, from the top down, there was not adequate coöperation among the workers. In the summer of 1925 the former agent left and was replaced by Howard R. Whitehead, a native of the neighboring city of Saco, who had worked in both northern and southern mills.[5] For ten years, while he was carrying through the company's plans for reorganizing the mills, Whitehead had a difficult time in Biddeford. In 1935 he left, and David S. Cook, Pepperell's former agent in Opelika and then its mill manager in New York, took over. Cook was a man to whom workers immediately felt that they could take their problems for help. But this characteristic was somewhat more important in the South than in the North, where labor wanted to deal at arm's length. About Cook we shall hear more in the following chapter.

In order to integrate the two sets of mills, following the selection of a new agent in 1925, there was a rearrangement of the duties of the superintendents. Instead of the earlier plan for a superintendent for each of the two divisions, superintendents by functions were appointed. The man who had been Pepperell's superintendent was made general superintendent of all the mills; Laconia's superintendent was put in charge of carding and spinning, and an outsider (from Fall River) was selected as superintendent of weaving. After a few years, when blanket machinery was moved to Biddeford, there was a further rearrangement of duties. In addition to a general and a mechanical superintendent for all the mills, there was one for white goods and another for colored.

Many changes took place within the other supervisory groups. As overseers retired, others, some quite young but with textile education as well as experience, were selected. These men, with broader training, tended to be more flexible—a quality needed when the customary ways of operating were changing. In 1938, members of the supervisory group formed a Foreman's Club, holding meetings at which informative as well as social programs were instituted for the development of company efficiency and loyalty.

During this period the overseers were relieved of part of their customary duties. In 1925 the agent started a control system of costs by which standards for each department were set up and deviations therefrom computed. In 1930 a time study and production department was set up. As a result of this and other changes many more people, clerical workers as well as others in positions of more responsibility, came to be employed in the office in Biddeford than previously. At various times Pepperell hired outside experts to come in to make time and motion studies, a procedure which had never occurred in either of the two earlier periods. In 1937 a new personnel department took on the function of hiring workers. Gone indeed was the old, independent system where each department was run by an overseer.

Although the overseers could see the prospect of steady employment, many operatives in Biddeford felt less secure. On the one hand, they watched the reduction of the capacity of the mills by the elimination of machinery. Instead of 3,000 workers as in 1925, the mills needed far fewer for a single shift, particularly after 1934. On the other hand, the operatives saw the coming of a second and then of a third shift. But these additions were not so reassuring as larger capacity, since shifts could be cut easily with changes in business. It was in 1930 that Pepperell first added a partial second shift in Biddeford, which, in 1933, after the passage of the National Recovery Act, was augmented. For the remainder of this period there were only a few months in 1938 and 1940 when Pepperell went back to one shift only. In 1936 a partial third shift was started, which was discontinued early in 1938. In the fall of 1938 the sheeting division began to operate on a three-shift basis. A year later the blanket and towel divisions did likewise. Except for a few months in 1940, Pepperell has continued to operate on a three-shift basis, although it was handicapped somewhat during the war years by lack of help. We find that in June of 1944 employment reached a low of 1,600—not enough for even two full shifts, since it was estimated that 1,200 were required for the first, 900 for the second, and 500 workers for the third shift.

Pepperell has had, however, a group of workers, who have remained loyal for many years. Some have felt a particular bond between themselves and the machines which they tended; the weavers, indeed, have regarded as their own the looms to which they have been assigned. According to a tabulation made in 1943 almost 900 workers, or about half the force at that time, had been with the company for at least a decade. Of these there were 21 who had been employed by Pepperell for 50 or more years. On October 23, 1943, Biddeford celebrated an Old Timers' Night with a banquet and dance in the Foreman's Club room, at which pins were presented to all who had been with Pepperell for ten years.[6]

During the first part of this third period women played a minor rôle in the mills. In 1925 only 37 per cent of the employees were women. This percentage rose so that ten years later it was 49, and twenty years later it was 57. But this last figure was abnormal, since it was necessary because of the war to employ women for many jobs which previously had been considered men's.

As in the middle period the majority of the operatives were still of French Canadian stock. There were a few from other countries, English, Greeks, Poles, and Russians, but they made up a small percentage of the whole. By this period many of the operatives, educated in the parochial schools in Biddeford, spoke both French and English.[7] But the past differences of race, language, and religion which had separated many of those in posts of responsibility from others in the mills hindered the development of coöperation among many of the younger generation of workers. This separation tended to prevent many of the ambitious French from seeking responsible positions with the company; instead they turned to the professions and became lawyers, doctors, or priests.

Labor troubles broke out early in this period. In December of 1925, when Whitehead was experimenting with a system of multiple looms, the weavers and loom-fixers, led by union members, walked out because of changes in assignments. In the past they had continued on the same schedules, except when they were promoted to tending more looms for increased wages or when new types of machines replaced the old ones. These workers realized that in the future they would probably have to keep much more continuously at work. Formerly they had had frequent periods of rest if they were efficient, as did many others who watched machines and worked only when threads broke. For a month the mills were closed and then, without a settlement of the difficulty, were reopened. At last, in February, 1926, following negotiations with the secretary of the American Federation of Textile Operatives, an agreement was reached. The union members agreed to return to work and to accept the multiple system of looms. Their leader was not reëmployed.[8] In 1927, apparently as a result of this failure, the loom-fixers' local shifted allegiance to the United Textile Workers of America, affiliated with the American Federation of Labor.[9]

During President Roosevelt's terms of office, unionization of workers increased throughout the country. When a national strike of textile workers was called by the United Textile Workers of America in 1934 for recognition of the union as the official spokesman of textile labor and for a 30-hour week with the same pay as for 40, Pepperell's union members joined the strikers near the end. Shortly thereafter President Roosevelt intervened, asking all of them to return to work while conditions were being investigated. Although the report submitted by the investigating committee, which was headed by ex-Governor Winant of New Hampshire, was hailed by the union as a significant victory, it really was only a strategic retreat.[10] Later the United Textile Workers under a new title, the Textile Workers' Union of America, became affiliated with the Congress of Industrial Organizations instead of the American Federation of Labor. Drives went on throughout New England to increase its membership and to gain recognition as the bargaining agent for all textile mills, under the stimulus of the National Labor Relations Act, which granted the right of self-organization to workers.[11]

In March of 1940 the Textile Workers' Union of America, of the Congress of Industrial Organizations, was designated as the bargaining agent for the mills in Biddeford. As a result a method was established for handling difficulties such as were to arise in the following November about the number of looms assigned to each of 75 battery hands, who had perhaps the most tiresome job of all—working continuously in the noisy, hot, and humid weaving rooms to keep the batteries of bobbins in the looms filled. An arbitration board took up the trouble while the operatives returned to work. A decision was reached during the latter part of January, and work loads were set about 10 per cent lower than the questioned assignment.[12]

For many years another cause for trouble between the workers and the company was frequent cutting of wages. During the depressed period in the industry, which lasted through the 1920's well into the next decade, the operatives took several cuts in rate of pay. Between 1924 and 1932 the agent announced five general cuts in pay, which totaled over 50 per cent. In May of 1933 at last the tide had turned, and he announced a general rise of 12½ per cent.[13]

This first general rise occurred before the federal government, with the assistance of members of the industry, established the code for the cotton textile industry, the first code under the National Industrial Recovery Act. According to its provisions the workers in the North were to receive as much for 40 hours as they had earned formerly for 54, with a minimum wage of 32.5 cents per hour. For a time, following the declaration of the unconstitutionality of the Act, the code continued to be kept by the cotton mills. In 1938 Congress enacted the Fair Labor Standards Act, which set a minimum for wage rates and a maximum for hours. For the year following its passage, maximum hours were to be 44; in the second year, 42; and in the third and thereafter, 40; overtime rates were to be at least time and a half. In 1939 a minimum wage for the cotton textile industry was set at 32.5 cents an hour. Later, in 1941, it was raised to 37.5 cents and, in 1942, to 40 cents an hour.[14]

During the first years of national determination of minimum wages, 1933–45, Pepperell increased its rates several times and cut them only once. The greatest change of all was, of course, when, as a result of the code of 1933, the Biddeford workers on the average had a 52 per cent increase in hourly wages. Four of the ensuing rises were for 10 per cent, one for 7 per cent, and the other two, 5 and 7.5 cents per hour. The cut in 1938 was 12½ per cent.[15] In September, 1941, the mills began to operate overtime, with extra pay to the workers, increasing the first two shifts by 5 hours of work on Saturdays. In 1944 their hours were gradually increased to 48, while the smaller third shift worked only 36 hours a week.[16] Thus, during the latter part of this period the workers were in a much better position financially than before, since they received more pay for shorter hours. As a result of all these changes, total wages paid to workers in Biddeford reached an all-time high in 1943 of over $3,000,000.[17]

Between 1924 and 1945 Pepperell set up more benefits for its workers than ever before. The clinic, which had been established in the earlier period, was expanded. In 1940, for example, its staff comprised two doctors and three nurses.[18] To provide financial aid in case of serious trouble, group insurance was started in 1926, and in 1941 the employees were given the opportunity to join a hospital and surgical insurance plan.[19]

In 1944 Pepperell opened a cafeteria in one of the mill buildings for all who worked in the mills. It provided a variety of good food at nominal prices. The workers have taken advantage of this opportunity to get a balanced, hot meal during their work-day, instead of eating a cold lunch while watching the machines.

In 1937 the company began to increase the workers' knowledge of the company, the executives, and each other by issuing a house organ called the *Pepperell Sheet*. At first it came out irregularly, just for the Biddeford employees, but in time it appeared more frequently (monthly) for all in the northern plants. This publication, typically of 24 pages, has been mailed to the homes of the workers as well as to other people in the communities who might be interested. By pictures and accounts of various activities this newspaper has tried to bring out the human side of life and work. It has carried, for example, special articles about hobbies of many operatives. During the second World War the paper printed letters from boys in the service as well as accounts of the war and of the war uses of Pepperell's products. Since 1943 it has devoted a few pages—on fashions, cooking, and general helpful household hints—which have added to the families' interest. The paper has succeeded to some extent in reaching across the gap between executives and workers, and by specialists in that field the *Pepperell Sheet* has been recognized as one of the outstanding house organs.

In 1938 the company started another worth-while project. It opened classes for those who wished to improve their knowledge of their jobs or to be promoted to more skilled work. The courses were in the following subjects: theoretical carding, practical carding, theoretical spinning, practical spinning, loomfixing, spooling fixing, cotton textile arithmetic, freehand drafting, and textile designing. At first the courses were for men only but, in time, during the war, women also were welcomed. Between 1938 and 1945, 444 employees completed courses. Of them, 55 were promoted to positions as fixers, second hands, and overseers.[20] About the time these courses began, the agent set up a plan of prizes for suggestions. This plan was not particularly successful, although the operatives proposed a few minor changes along the lines of safety and improvements in the machines.

In spite of all the company's efforts, production in Biddeford proved only slightly profitable. There were many handicaps which it took time to remove, such as the special contracts division and an ordinary line of blankets. Profits were earned by these mills in Biddeford despite the depressed state of the textile industry through this period, which lasted until the stimulating years of the second World War, and despite a major depression in industry generally in the early 'thirties together with a minor depression in the later 'thirties. On the other hand, Biddeford's situation has been relieved somewhat by measures which narrowed the spread between costs in the North and South. Its record demonstrates the ability of industrial capitalists to operate successfully, first in an era of financial capitalism and then under national capitalism.

Altogether, evidence is not conclusive as to the wisdom of continuing the operations in Biddeford during the period 1924 through 1945. Only the future may give the final answer. But we do know, as a result of this investigation, that Biddeford by the end of this period was in a much better position than at the beginning. As in its early years the mills were again specializing in a few lines of goods—sheetings and blankets. Productive capacity in Biddeford was also reduced to about the levels of this early period. Changes took place in the personnel and the assignment of duties, particularly those of the supervisors. Gone was the old system, inherited from the petty capitalists, of an independent head for each department. Installed in its place was a modern system of organization.

The status of the operatives was also a new factor as, protected by federal legislation, they organized into a unit which bargained with the management on questions of wage rates, assignment of duties, and other matters affecting both groups. By the end of this period the operatives were securing a wage which was more nearly sufficient for the support of a family. One can only conjecture as to the possible postwar changes.

VARIOUS GOODS IN LOWELL

Late in 1926 the Pepperell Manufacturing Company was strengthened by its consolidation with the Massachusetts Cotton Mills, located in Lowell, a producer of complementary types of goods. Since in this chapter we are concerned with Pepperell's manufacturing in the North, we shall pause briefly to review the history of the Massachusetts Cotton Mills and to consider the details of its merger with Pepperell.*

At first the Massachusetts Cotton Mills made heavy white goods, principally for export, similar to some of those made by Pepperell and Laconia in Biddeford. The goods went largely to China, Africa, and South America. A later president of the company recalled that the explorer Stanley, when he emerged on the Congo River from an expedition into the interior of Africa, recognized as his first sign of civilization a piece of cotton goods, worn by a native, with the company's trade-mark, the flying horse.[22] But by that time, in the late 1880's, the company was feeling the effects of competition of mills in the South. This company was feeling the competition more acutely than Pepperell, since a greater proportion of its goods was among the types first made in the South. Also, Massachusetts had more stringent economic restrictions than Maine. In 1889, when the

* This history of the Massachusetts Cotton Mills can be divided into two periods, the first covering the fifty years from the time of incorporation and organization in 1839 to the end of 1889 and the second of thirty-seven years from 1890 to 1926. During the first period the treasurers were John Amory Lowell and two others, who had previously been employees of the company. Through these years the company prospered about as did other mills in Lowell. From 1842 to 1847 on the original capital of $1,200,000, and from 1847 to 1889 on capital of $1,800,000, the Massachusetts Cotton Mills paid, on the average, 8 per cent annually in dividends; in 1858 it paid none; and in 1862 it paid both a 9 per cent regular dividend and a 20 per cent extra.[21] During these years the stockholders' subscriptions to capital were larger and their returns less, proportionally, than those of Pepperell's stockholders.

treasurer was ready to retire, the directors decided to go outside the company for the new chief executive. They chose Charles L. Lovering, who had demonstrated his ability in another company.

A new epoch in the history of the Massachusetts Cotton Mills started in 1890 with the new treasurer and extended for nearly thirty-seven years, past his death in 1908, through the term of office of his son, Edward. In the first years of this treasurership Lovering tried to make many changes in the old company. While he added to the manufacturing capacity in Lowell, he disposed of property not needed for manufacturing. In 1893 he investigated the possibility of building a mill in the South to which the manufacture of coarser goods could be transferred from Lowell, but the stockholders of the Massachusetts Cotton Mills proved unwilling to subscribe to additional stock for this purpose. Therefore, in 1894 Lovering and others started a new company with a Massachusetts charter, the Massachusetts Mills in Georgia, and obtained subscribers for the necessary $600,000 capital. Approximately a third of the stockholders of the Massachusetts Cotton Mills were among these subscribers, taking about two-thirds of the stock. Two years later the old company took a lease on the new, with the right to purchase it later. Within a dozen years the executives of the new company expanded its property in Lindale, Georgia, from one to three mills, with a total capital of $2,000,000. At the time of Charles L. Lovering's death the Lindale mills had about 90,000 spindles and owned a mill village. Of the history of operations in Lindale we shall hear more in a later chapter. Let it suffice to say here that the property made money. In 1919 the stockholders of the Massachusetts Cotton Mills were willing to subscribe additional capital to acquire this property, the value of which had become apparent to them.[23]

Meanwhile in Lowell the Massachusetts Cotton Mills operated under difficulty, not having built up adequate working capital of its own from profits. In 1910, in order to erect a large storehouse, the stockholders were asked to subscribe to another $1,200,000 of stock, bringing the total for the Lowell company to $3,000,000. The 1919 subscription for acquisition of the

Lindale plant was for $2,000,000 of stock. During these thirty-seven years the stockholders, however, received good dividends except in 1926, when there were none. Dividends ranged from 3 to 14 per cent annually, with 6 per cent in eleven years and 8 per cent in another eleven. The average was about 7 per cent. Thus, throughout this period also, the stockholders of the Massachusetts Cotton Mills subscribed to more stock and received lower dividends than did those of Pepperell.

For the problem of supplying the plant in Lowell with a profitable line of goods, the treasurers of the Massachusetts Cotton Mills found no satisfactory solution. After the coarse white goods had been transferred to the South, the Lowell plant produced bed ticks, jeans, and other goods, dyed in its own plant. When the export business for Lindale's goods declined, these colored goods were transferred to the southern mills, and other types were tried in Lowell. By 1926 Lowell was producing about 300 varieties of goods, including among them blankets, bedspreads, wash fabrics or ginghams, draperies, and work clothing. Practically anything was tried to turn an old dollar into a new one. But costs of production were high in the North, in Massachusetts particularly, where State regulation of labor was more severe than anywhere else and where high local taxes handicapped the manufacturers. For several years the treasurer and directors of the Massachusetts Cotton Mills realized that they were losing almost as much in the North as they were making in the South.

In 1926 Edward Lovering, then treasurer, and the directors faced the fact that a change was necessary if the company's plant in Lowell was to continue in operation. Lovering wished to retire. Through the company's attorney, who was also Pepperell's, the possibility that the two companies might benefit from a merger was brought to the attention of both. The Massachusetts Cotton Mills would gain a capable executive, while Pepperell would add the capacity which Leonard needed to carry through his plans of integration. In the fall of 1926 the directors or trustees of each held several meetings to work out details. Finally, in November the directors of the Massachusetts Cotton Mills sent two circulars to their stockholders, informing them of the proposal and asking for their vote on the merger. Because of the tax situation they were asked, instead of consolidating into one company, to agree to the setting up of a subsidiary, chartered in Massachusetts, and to its transfer to the Pepperell Manufacturing Company—the voluntary association. They agreed to the terms, which included the sale and transfer to the new subsidiary corporation, the Massachusetts Cotton Mills, Inc., of all the assets and property of the old Massachusetts Cotton Mills in return for all the stock of the new one. This new stock was to be sold or transferred to the Pepperell Manufacturing Company in return for 31,250 newly created shares, with the stockholders of the Massachusetts Cotton Mills receiving five Pepperell shares in return for eight of their own old shares.[24]

At the same time, Pepperell's shareholders were sent similar notices. They were also willing to carry through the merger on the terms drawn up, the stock being transferred roughly according to the net quick assets of the two companies and not according to the size of the textile plants. As a result, on December 13, 1926, there were two companies: the Massachusetts voluntary association, the Pepperell Manufacturing Company and its subsidiary with a Massachusetts charter, the Massachusetts Cotton Mills, Inc.

At the end of June, 1927, the organization changed somewhat. Pepperell's shareholders transferred to the Massachusetts Cotton Mills, Inc., all assets and property of the voluntary association, with the exception of 2,500 shares of the corporation's stock which were delivered to the trustees of the association. After this transfer the corporation's name was changed to Pepperell Manufacturing Company. Thus, from July 1, 1927, two companies with the same name have been in existence—a Massachusetts voluntary association, which is merely a holding company, and a Massachusetts corporation, which is an operating company. This confusing state of affairs has persisted, although at times the executives have considered eliminating one or the other of the organizations. So far they have delayed this move because of taxes.[25]

Unfortunately, even with the change in management in 1926, the mills in Lowell proved unprofitable. Although the executives conferred with city and State officials about a reduction in taxes and some abatement was granted, they found no adequate solution.[26] Because of more restrictions and stricter enforcement in such matters as a shorter work-week and building regulations, other costs were also high as compared with those in Maine.[27] In the hope of profits Pepperell hired a stylist to plan new fabrics for the Massachusetts Mills. For a time these mills produced blankets, Peggy cloth, and a few fancies. In the fall of 1927 Pepperell introduced four new lines of blankets in Lowell, but in the summer of 1928 the directors decided that it would be advisable to continue their manufacture only in Biddeford. In September the Lowell mills were closed. In the following years land, buildings, and machinery in Lowell were disposed of. Some of the machinery was transferred to Biddeford and to other company mills. Some of it was bought at private sale by Amoskeag, and the remainder was sold at auction on December 13, 1928. The disposal of the rest of the property took considerable time, not only because of the national depression in the industry but particularly because of the industry's decline in Lowell. By the 1930's several of the other old cotton textile companies, such as the Hamilton, the Tremont & Suffolk, and the Appleton, had disappeared or left Lowell. Only the Merrimack and the Boott remained in the city. The Merrimack had another plant in Huntsville, Alabama, begun in 1899, which by 1930 exceeded the size of the plant in Lowell.[28]

Pepperell thus closed down the Lowell plant of the Massachusetts Cotton Mills, parts of which had been in operation ever since 1840. The plant had grown to a maximum size of over 175,000 spindles and the bleachery and dye house had developed larger capacity than the one in Lewiston. To be sure, part of the Lowell machinery continued in operation in Biddeford, but comparatively few of the operatives in Lowell could find immediate employment in the industry in which they had had experience. In time several small enterprises became tenants in several of the old buildings, which were taken over by the Lowell Industrial Development Co.,[29] but they did not take the place that the Massachusetts Cotton Mills had held in the economy of Lowell.

In efforts to explain why the Lowell textile mills have folded up to such a large extent it has been customary to emphasize high labor costs and high taxes. There is no reason, so far as I can discover, to deny the baneful effect of these two factors. But in fairness to the situation a third factor should be mentioned. The Lowell mills commonly concentrated on the production of staple coarse goods, such as shirtings, jeans, and drills. Since these were the easiest to manufacture, they would naturally be the first to be reproduced in a new region, such as the South, where the processes of textile manufacture were being learned. If the executives of the Lowell mills had put aside financial reserves for alterations and improvements, instead of paying out so much of their earnings in the form of dividends, some adjustments might have been made, so that the mills of Lowell could have shifted to finer work and held their own for a longer period. As it was, Lowell gained the distinction of being the first American city to see its cotton textile industry languish and almost disappear. In this decadence Lowell was to be followed by Fall River and New Bedford, rivals for distinction in the art of killing a golden goose.

FINE COTTONS AND RAYONS IN FALL RIVER

Quite a different experience followed Pepperell's acquisition of a plant in another manufacturing center of Massachusetts. In the autumn of 1929 Pepperell acquired for a modest sum the property of the Granite Mills, located in Fall River. Now, Fall River was more strategically located than Lowell or Biddeford, for it lay in between Boston, the management center, and New York, the marketing center for cotton textiles. True, it had a record of labor unrest far beyond that of either Lowell or Biddeford.

The life of the Granite Mills had been largely under the direction of two treasurers, Charles O. Shove and his son, Charles M. Shove. The company was not established during the first period of expansion in Fall River, which began during the interruption of foreign trade in the first decade of the nineteenth century. Indeed it was set up in the later period, which began about 1858, when the possibility of economical operation by steam made the location in Fall River attractive. The Granite Mills was the second company in the city to be started in this second period; it was incorporated in 1863 and went into operation two years later. Under the Shoves' direction it grew from one to three mills, with over 120,000 spindles. The company prospered to about the same degree as did many others of the same type in Fall River. It paid dividends regularly, at least every year from 1882 to 1923, with the average about 8 per cent. In 1917 the directors declared a stock dividend of 25 per cent, which raised the capital to $1,250,000. The company at first made print cloths—the great specialty of Fall River with its huge print works—and then plain and fancy goods of medium and fine yarns to order.[30]

In 1924 Charles M. Shove decided that it was time for him to retire and for a younger man with experience to take over. But the board of directors did not agree with his plans for choosing a successor. Within the next five years they made life difficult for the four treasurers who did take office and who, given more time and freedom of action, might have saved the company. In 1927 the directors reorganized the capital structure of the company, reducing the old common stock to about a quarter of its former value and adding new preferred. But even with new capital the company did not prosper. In the spring of 1929 it went into receivership, with debts of $750,000 and with current assets of about $20,000 worth of finished goods on hand. At that time the plant was assessed for $1,250,000; two years earlier its value had stood on the financial statement at over $2,000,000. The expectation was that the plant would bring between $500,000 and $750,000.[31]

The strengths and weaknesses of the Granite Mills were shared by many others in Fall River. In fact, the mills in that city were quite unlike the others in the northern centers of New England. Here the chief executives kept their offices right in the mills; they bought cotton from representatives of cotton buyers or brokers; some of them sold the goods directly to distributors, while others transferred them to agents or brokers. By these means they really avoided both Boston and New York. Local men served as the treasurers, while the directors of the forty-four companies in the city and the stockholders were also local people. Fall River was almost an industrial world by itself.

At first Fall River had several advantages over other manufacturing centers—ocean-going vessels could dock there, and the humidity, necessary for spinning medium or fine yarns, was greater. But in time, with changes in transportation rates and the introduction of humidifying systems, these advantages diminished. Nevertheless, the mills had many profitable years in the nineteenth century. Because of this prosperity and because of their isolation from other business centers, the management of Fall River mills did not realize the importance of the changes which were going on outside. For example, they put in few automatic looms while others were adopting them. The administration of these New England mills did not realize until too late the extent of competition from southern mills, several of which in the early twentieth century were turning from coarse to medium-grade goods. They experienced many troubles with the labor force, and restrictions by the State increased their cost of operation. For about four years before the first World War the mills in Fall River went through bad times. Although they had profitable years during the war, afterwards business again slumped, reaching its nadir in 1924. Mill after mill was liquidated. Some were reorganized, while others went out of operation completely. From a peak capacity of 4,000,000 spindles in the early 1920's, the industry in Fall River shrank in twenty years to a quarter of its former size—1,000,000 spindles.[32]

In September, 1929, Pepperell, for back taxes amounting to about $100,000 and for $75,000 in addition, secured the property of the Granite Mills.[33] These three mills, built of the granite for which they had been named, were in good condition and possessed some new machinery. True, during the two preceding years, several changes had taken place; some of the machinery had been removed, leaving only about 60,000

AERIAL SURVEY OF MILLS IN FALL RIVER, ABOUT 1935

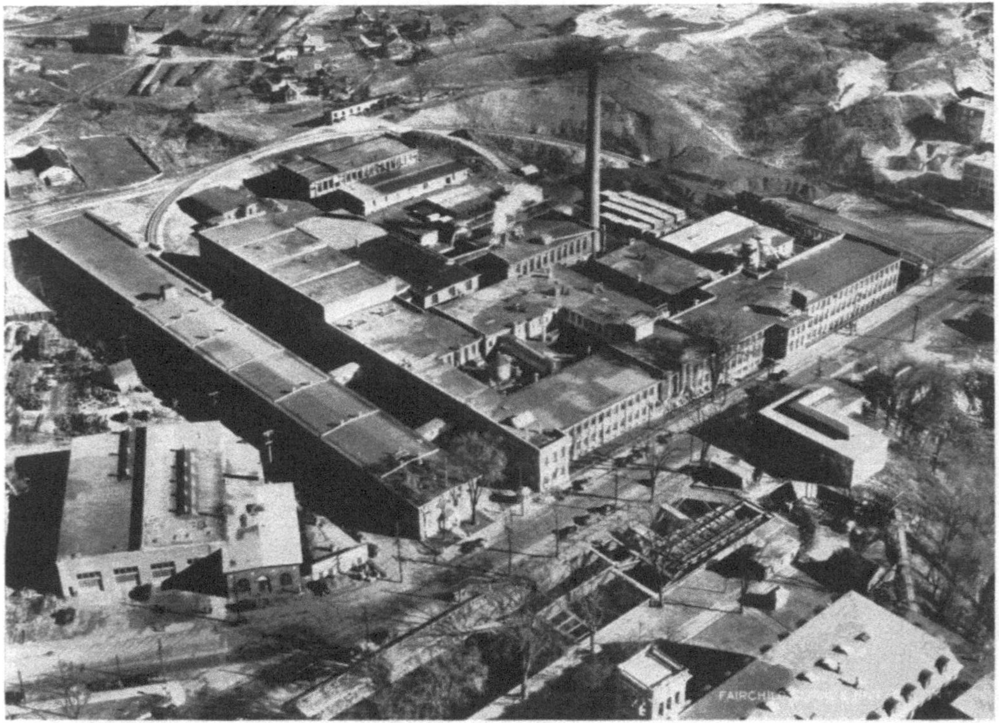

AERIAL SURVEY OF BLEACHERY AT LEWISTON, ABOUT 1935

spindles in two of the three mills. Pepperell immediately disposed of the oldest mill, which was also the smallest and which made the coarser goods. In one mill it kept much of the machinery, with approximately 40,000 spindles for the making of combed cotton goods. Into the other it put, a few years later, machinery for making rayon goods. Together these two mills by 1945 had about 44,000 spindles and 1,550 looms.[34]

In Mill "B," the cotton mill, Pepperell's production increased. Whereas during the first decade under the new ownership its production had not reached 3,000,000 pounds annually, it rose rapidly in the war years to a high of approximately 5,000,000 pounds in 1943. This increase can be accounted for somewhat by a change from the earlier combed sateens, broadcloths, lawns, marquisettes, and sheetings to some coarser goods, such as twills, oxfords, poplins, and shirtings for uniforms. During the war the fine combed sheetings were eliminated. At the same time, this mill introduced rayon marquisettes and Nylon and rayon mosquito netting, the last two of which were used for the protection of the men in the service.

In 1934 Mill "A," formerly a producer of cotton goods, started the manufacture of rayon goods—underwear fabrics and linings. Inasmuch as rayon was purchased in the form of yarn, preparatory and spinning machinery was not necessary for those goods. For a number of years their production, measured in pounds, was slightly lower than that of Mill "B"; during the war it remained less—with a high of nearly 4,000,000 pounds in 1942. Many of its war-time goods were quite light, such as rayon and Nylon parachute cloths.

As agent for these mills in Fall River the president-treasurer of the Pepperell Manufacturing Company placed Leonard Kleeb, Jr., of Swiss birth; Kleeb had gained experience in Fall River and New Bedford as well as in the Ipswich Mills. He continued as Pepperell's agent in Fall River until his death in 1940. Then the assistant agent, F. Lincoln Dunlap, a native of Taunton and a graduate of the textile school in Fall River, took his place. Dunlap was almost as laconic as Calvin Coolidge. Both he and Kleeb were successful in operating the mills in Fall River, although at times their operation was complicated by labor troubles. The mills continued the local practice of securing cotton from local representatives of cotton buyers and added the purchasing of rayon, both under the direction of Amory Coolidge, who was in charge of the procurement of raw materials for all the Pepperell mills.

In these mills in Fall River, in spite of differences in circumstances, Pepperell found that it could apply many of the policies which it had adopted for Biddeford. Here, too, the agents could select able overseers, not only because many overseers were available in the 1930's with the closing of so many mills, but also because of the textile school at Fall River which many operatives and overseers attended to increase their technical knowledge.

From the population of Fall River, at first Kleeb hired about 400 workers for one mill and then, when the second mill went into operation, about as many more. Employment during the twelve years in which both mills were in operation fluctuated only slightly, from a low of about 700 in 1934 to a high of 860 in 1942, when all the looms were operated two shifts of 45 hours each per week.[35]

The composition of the Fall River population differed considerably from that of Biddeford. Instead of a preponderance of one race speaking a foreign tongue, in Fall River there were at least two races speaking two important foreign languages—French and Portuguese. In 1930, for example, almost 30 per cent of the city's population was foreign-born, with about three-quarters from French Canada, England, Portugal, and the Azores. Moreover, about 50 per cent was of foreign or mixed parentage, with about four-fifths of these from French Canada, England, Portugal, the Azores, and Ireland.[36]

The differences in type of labor supply have had important repercussions on the operations of the mills in Fall River. During the early years of the cotton textile industry there, the native population was small. Workers were drawn in from the outside, particularly from England. Some of them followed Samuel Slater's example and came over of their own accord, while others were secured through the efforts of the mills. A few of these workers, as we have noted before, were conscious of their strength. They formed craft unions and, at various times, struck to assert their rights.

From about 1895 on, most of the mills in Fall River have dealt with the workers through unions. They recognized as the representative of labor the Fall River Textile Council, composed of the local craft unions of loom-fixers, knot-tiers, slashers, and weavers belonging to the American Federation of Textile Operatives. The mills also dealt directly with the locals. The mills themselves formed a city-wide organization, the Fall River Cotton Manufacturers' Association. No written agreements with unions existed for many years, only oral ones from time to time. This state of affairs persisted until 1941, when the Congress of Industrial Organizations' Textile Workers Union of America won the bargaining right in one company. Alarmed, the various locals became affiliated with the United Textile Workers of the American Federation of Labor. In 1942, when elections were held in the other mills, there was a close struggle between the two national organizations. In all but two companies, one of which was Pepperell, the Congress of Industrial Organizations won.[37]

In these two companies troubles arose, since members of the locals still wanted to act independently. In 1943 the locals voted to withdraw from the American Federation of Labor and petitioned the National Labor Relations Board for separate representation. Their petitions were dismissed. They struck late in December; the mills were closed for about three weeks until the United Textile Workers of the American Federation of Labor released the locals from their jurisdiction. Then the companies dealt directly with the locals. In May of 1945 another set of elections took place. In Pepperell the independent locals for loom-fixers, slasher tenders, and knot-tiers won the right to be recognized as bargaining agents, while the remaining production and maintenance group, the major part of the plant, voted to be represented by the Textile Workers' Union of America of the Congress of Industrial Organizations.[38]

The employees in Fall River secured increases in rates of pay about commensurate with those in Biddeford. Until the New Deal their hours had been shorter than in Maine—48 a week. Then, as we have seen, federal legislation supplanted State laws in many respects. During the second World War some of the Massachusetts restrictions were lifted temporarily and women could work on the second shift.

For the employees in Fall River, Pepperell provided many of the services which it had extended in Biddeford. In 1939 the mills had, for example, a clinic with an adequate staff and a cafeteria.

During the same year employees began to contribute news for publication in the *Pepperell Sheet,* copies of which were distributed to them. Four years later, a group insurance plan was started.

The Fall River employees also enjoyed a recreation room, where an active social club gave parties at various times throughout the year. As a group they received in 1942 a Minute Man Flag for a high percentage of war-bond purchases. A year later they received still greater recognition for their part in the war—an Army-Navy "E" award for excellence in the production of fabrics for the armed forces.[39] Thus it may be seen that the management, in a comparatively short time, was successful in contributing to the physical and social welfare of the workers as well as in welding them, to some extent, into a working unit.

The workers in these mills in Fall River have been fortunate in that Pepperell has found their operation profitable. While Pepperell kept a few of the former fabrics of the Granite Mills it introduced some new, very successful ones.

BLEACHING, DYEING, AND FINISHING IN LEWISTON

A vital part of Pepperell's own operation in this last period has been the bleaching, dyeing, and finishing of the products made in its various mills. Already, in an earlier chapter, we have discussed Pepperell's ownership of some of the stock of the Lewiston Bleachery & Dye Works of Maine. At the beginning of this period Pepperell's new treasurer found the former arrangement unsatisfactory. He wanted the company to own its own bleaching, dyeing, and finishing plant.

In the spring of 1925, when Pepperell owned only three-eighths of the 3,000 shares of the Lewiston Bleachery & Dye Works, Leonard made it clear to the other owners that he wanted a change. The treasurers of the Lewiston textile companies realized that, if they wanted Pepperell's work to come to Lewiston, they must sell to Pepperell their part in the ownership. In the summer of 1925, Pepperell acquired the rest of the stock for $468,750.[40] The bleachery, however, was not immediately merged into the Pepperell Manufacturing Company; instead, until the end of 1933 it was kept as one of Pepperell's subsidiaries.

A change in the manner of operating the Lewiston Bleachery & Dye Works had occurred about five years prior to its acquisition by Pepperell. In 1920 Gilbert D. Harrison, friendly and democratic, who previously had been superintendent of the Utica Willowvale Bleachery Co., became Lewiston's enterprising agent, and in 1921 its treasurer also. Harrison's period of service was one of progress, but we must divide the honors between him and the new Pepperell executives in Boston who were encouraging him to greater effort. During the five years, 1920 to 1925, the bleachery had been adding to its facilities in spite of unfavorable times. Instead of confining activities to its accustomed bleaching of cotton goods—such as Pepperell sheetings and jeans and the Hill Manufacturing Co.'s muslins and jeans—and to a small amount of dyeing of coutils, jeans, and pocketings, Harrison was beginning to equip the plant for a variety of jobs. During this time he spent about $380,000 on buildings and equipment. He erected a three-story addition to the bleachery building, which had been expanded numerous times before. Later Harrison reported: "It seemed that in the past when a new machine was added, a wart was added to a building to house it." [41] He increased the size of one of the two large storehouses, and built a fine filter plant as well, installed a trolley system for handling cases, and secured new napping and singeing machines, tenter frames, and calenders.[42]

In 1924–25, the last of these five financial years, the Lewiston Bleachery did a variety of work for about 200 different customers, double the number nine years earlier. It did most for the Pepperell Manufacturing Company, about one-third of the total according to the monthly trial balances. For the other owners of stock it did much less work: for the Androscoggin Mills about one-sixth; the Hill Manufacturing Co. one-twelfth; and for the Bates Co. still less. Among the other customers, which included various textile companies, distributors, and converters, the bleachery received from an outsider the greatest amount of business, in fact about the same as from the Hill Manufacturing Co. Thus, the Lewiston Bleachery was making a start towards new business and new customers.[43]

During the following eight years, 1925–33, when the Lewiston Bleachery & Dye Works was one of Pepperell's subsidiaries, even more was expended on buildings and machinery. Most important of all the accessions was a sheet factory, which was added to one of the storehouses. In it the sheetings made by Pepperell and other companies could be made up into sheets and pillow cases. As we remember, in an earlier period an outside company, Ernest Simons, had been doing this work for Pepperell.

Throughout the remaining years of this period, when the Lewiston plant was a department instead of a subsidiary, there was a continuation of expenditures for improvements in the plant. One of the most spectacular was the introduction of huge traveling lifts called "flying fortresses" to carry gigantic rolls of finished sheeting to storage space. By the end of this period, equipment had been installed to carry on work of such special types as Sanforizing, treating flannel for silverware cloth, embossing flannels for casket coverings, converting rayon goods, printing flannels and shoe linings, and adding a Holland finish. During the second World War, when the Lewiston plant did considerable government work, new finishes were added for new uses, such as making goods mildew-proof and water-repellent. In all, Harrison added many operations to keep the plant filled as nearly to capacity as possible all the time.

Harrison bleached, finished, and made into sheets and pillow cases most of the sheetings which Pepperell produced in Biddeford, Fall River, and Opelika. He dyed some of these sheetings pastel colors. He finished the other products of the various Pepperell mills with only a few exceptions: many of the blankets were dyed and finished in Biddeford; some of the goods in Fall River, such as marquisettes and linings, were sold to other converters; and for the work clothing in Lindale the mills themselves dyed the yarns. He continued to do business with outside mills in Maine and to do converting for others. By the end of this period the volume of work done was several times that of 1925. The bleachery, however, still depended on Biddeford for a large share of its business so that its fortunes were tied in with the latter's.

Until the addition of the sheet factory in 1930, the Lewiston Bleachery & Dye Works was almost entirely a man's world. In charge throughout this period, Harrison bore at first the title of agent and then that of general manager. In the plant were several graduates of Bates College, situated in Lewiston. In fact, there was a close relationship between the plant and the college, to their mutual benefit. College boys were given an opportunity for practical work, while the bleachery benefited by their services for short or long periods. Among the men so trained was Edwin W. Adams, who in 1940, after the death of Stephen H. Crowley, was promoted to the position of assistant general manager.

The bleachery had a large number of employees who stayed with it for a long time. In 1943 the management followed the Pepperell policy of recognition of service by giving 426 workers, who had served the company ten or more years, service pins at a special party in the Lewiston Armory. There were nine who had worked over half a century. Altogether about two-fifths of the total number of workers were so honored. This figure is more significant when we consider that the number of employees had about doubled during this period. In 1926 there were only 674, while in 1942 a high of 1,213 was reached.[44]

The population in Lewiston was much like that in Biddeford in that the majority were of French Canadian birth or parentage. There were others from northern as well as a few from southern Europe.[45] Probably the bleachery took in most races. Naturally there were some, of German blood, who had had training in similar businesses in Europe. Workers, on the whole, were less given to expressing their dissatisfaction over working conditions by striking than were those in the cotton textile mills. They were skilled or semiskilled workers, who worked individually or in small groups, with some variety in their work during the day. Their earnings were above those of the cotton textile operative. They came to be represented by the Federation of Dyers, Finishers, Printers, and Bleachers of America, a branch of the Textile Workers' Union of America, C.I.O.[46] As in Biddeford and Fall River, the workers in the Lewiston plant have been offered many services by the company. They have joined with others in the *Pepperell Sheet,* taken out group insurance, and had a clinic and a social club.

In this period Lewiston was recognized as an important part in the operation of the Pepperell Manufacturing Company. Under the company's direction it developed considerably. New equipment made possible many new processes, which contributed to the profitability of Lewiston, both as a finisher and as a converter of goods. But the Lewiston Works still depended on Biddeford for a large share of its business. It is clear that Lewiston's future was closely linked with the cotton mills in Biddeford, particularly when we realize that, after the second World War, the handling of goods of the southern mills was to be directed to a new plant which was being constructed in Opelika. Of the developments in the South, we shall hear more in the following chapter.

* * *

In this third period of Pepperell's history its management stemmed the tide which was sweeping over many mills in New England. The company clung to production in Biddeford, although at times it wondered whether the struggle was worth the effort. In the North, Pepperell added other plants, in Fall River and Lewiston, and abandoned after a short time the one which it had acquired in Lowell. Thus it continued in existence with the risks spread over three plants in the North. In the following chapter we shall see that the company took on two plants in the South to strengthen its structure still further.

During these years Pepperell changed from a producer of coarse white cotton goods to a manufacturer of many types, including cotton, rayon, and woolen, as well as to a finisher and converter of still more types. In Biddeford it continued to make the former type of sheetings, while it added other finer types. It eliminated some, including the famous Dragon drill, the Beaver jean, and special-order goods. It transplanted from Lowell the blanket division of the Massachusetts Cotton Mills, which in time produced blankets of blends of rayon, wool, and cotton. Thus the plant in Biddeford became a combination of the best of two mills—the sheetings of Biddeford and the blankets of Lowell.

In one of the units of the former Granite Mills in Fall River Pepperell continued the manufacture of combed goods, but it changed from the old combination to broadcloths, sheetings, and marquisettes. In the other it introduced the production of rayon goods, chiefly linings and underwear fabrics. It thus combined the old cotton with the rapidly developing rayon industry.

In Lewiston, Pepperell became full instead of part owner of the bleachery. The plant kept on with the former bleaching, while it added other operations, such as dyeing, printing, Sanforizing, mercerizing, coating, and treating in various ways the goods which the mills supplied as well as those which Pepperell purchased as a converter. Thus here too there was a fundamental change in operations.

These various changes in types of goods and operations in the North were accompanied by many other changes. The managements of the plants became more scientific—leaving behind the old-fashioned methods of the petty capitalists which had persisted throughout the two earlier periods. The workers, assisted by the New Deal under Franklin D. Roosevelt, changed also—became more vocal in demanding their rights. They struggled to increase their wages, so that one member of each family might be able to become its full support. So far this struggle has not persisted long enough to determine the final outcome. Perhaps wages of cotton operatives and prices of cotton goods will continue at levels higher than those in the past, with the American consumer becoming accustomed to paying more for his cotton textiles.

During these twenty-one years Pepperell has profited from its mills in the North, but much less so than from those in the South. As we shall see in the following chapter, however, the setting up of a mill in the South has not been a simple task. Perhaps this difficulty will act as a deterring element in the further transfer of the industry to that section of the country.

CHAPTER XIII

COARSE GOODS IN THE SOUTH

IN THE THIRD period of its history the Pepperell Manufacturing Company operated, in addition to its plants in New England, two sets of mills in the South. These mills were acquired in two ways—by consolidating with another northern company, which earlier had expanded in the South, and by building mills. Thus one set of mills bore the imprint of another company's management, while the other bore only Pepperell's.

A short survey of the development of the cotton textile industry in the South may enable us to see these mills in clearer perspective. In the decades before the Civil War, when the North was busy building mills, the South was largely concerned with the production of raw materials, among them cotton, and felt only slightly the urge for the development of manufactures. A few hundred small cotton mills were built, however, giving the South altogether less than 330,000 spindles. During the war some of these mills were destroyed by invading armies, while others, forced to produce as much as possible without adequate maintenance, became unfit for economical operation. Thus, after 1865 the South had almost to start afresh.

For about fifteen years after the Civil War the South was too upset economically as well as politically to start new enterprises. But about 1880 there was a stirring. In 1881 a cotton exposition was held at Atlanta, Georgia, which stimulated not only cotton growing but manufacturing as well. During the next eight years southerners, with the help of local capital, enthusiastically started small companies, particularly in the Carolinas and Georgia. By 1890 there were in the South almost 1,600,000 spindles, about 180 per cent more than there had been a decade earlier. Among these early companies were the

Cannon Manufacturing Co., of North Carolina, and the West Point Manufacturing Co., of Alabama, both incorporated in 1887. In the following decade other southerners as well as northerners, seeing the success of these undertakings, started additional companies and expanded the existing ones, so that again spindles in the South increased by another 180 per cent. Among these companies was the Riverside Cotton Mills, which was established in 1895 in Virginia and which was later to become one of the most important in the industry. In the first decade of the twentieth century, spindles in the South increased 140 per cent; in the second, 45 per cent; and, in the third, 18 per cent. From 1930 on, the industry in the South has maintained a level of about 18,000,000 spindles. Apparently, for a time at least, it has reached a plateau of development.[1]

During the years of rapid expansion in the 1890's, as we have already noted, stockholders of the Massachusetts Cotton Mills turned to building mills in the South. In 1894 they incorporated a southern company and, in the following year, started construction of a mill. In 1896 the Massachusetts Cotton Mills leased this property and the northern company ran the southern, really as a part of itself. In 1919 the Massachusetts Cotton Mills acquired the properties of the subsidiary company, and then in 1926 Pepperell acquired them as a result of its merger with the Massachusetts Cotton Mills. Shortly before Pepperell acquired these mills, it had started its own plant in Alabama on the edge of the city of Opelika.

Among the growing concerns in the South there were developing a few large companies. One was the West Point Manufacturing Co., which had plants along the Chattahoochee River in five separate places. Its mills made coarse goods, such as sheetings, drills, ducks, twills, crashes, and towelings. Although its capital was about the size of Pepperell's before its merger with the Massachusetts Cotton Mills, it had a much smaller number of spindles, about 180,000. Another southern giant was the Cannon Manufacturing Co., which, with capital of $10,-500,000, had mills in two places in North Carolina and one in South Carolina, equipped with a total of about 160,000 spindles. These mills made towelings, crashes, sheetings, and yarns.

Still larger was another, the Riverside & Dan River Cotton Mills, of Virginia, with capital of $13,500,000 and with almost 470,000 spindles, which made a variety of goods, such as chambrays, shirtings, ginghams, checks, plaids, cheviots, and wide sheetings. These three were formidable competitors for other companies which made similar goods, whether in the North or in the South. Scattered through the southern States, particularly near the foothills of the Appalachian Mountains, were many others, smaller, some of which were connected with northern companies and some independent. They added to the interesting mosaic of industrial development in the South. In the following pages we shall examine Pepperell's part in this development.[2]

COARSE WHITE GOODS IN LINDALE, 1896–1926

Before we consider Pepperell's operations in the South, let us, in order to learn something about their character, consider the first thirty years of the older mills, at Lindale, Georgia, when they were run by the Massachusetts Cotton Mills. Since mills in the South differed in so many respects from those in the North, we shall find this early period worth considerable study, in fact much more than it is possible to include here. Lack of adequate records makes impossible a full treatment of operations.

The mills in Lindale, Georgia, which Pepperell acquired in 1926, are located in a region settled, immediately after the Revolution, by pioneers traveling down the valleys between the foothills of the Appalachians. As these settlers encountered opposition from the Indians who were still living in northern Georgia, conflicts broke out, which were ended in 1838 by the removal of the Cherokees to lands west of the Mississippi. Thereafter, settlement of this part of the State proceeded more rapidly and with greater safety. Before the ending of the strife, however, a few people established themselves in the little valley in which we are interested. It was watered by only a small stream called Silver Creek. To be sure, not far away, at the juncture of two navigable rivers, was Rome, which was to become the leading trading center for the northwestern part of the State. Farther away was Atlanta, the business center for the western part of Georgia and the eastern section of Alabama. In 1832, on the banks of Silver Creek a brick mill for grinding flour had been erected, and wheat and cotton were grown near-by. In other small valleys settlement was making considerable progress, until invading armies during the Civil War laid the country waste. Thereafter, life was resumed with the growing of cotton. The crop was handled by firms in Rome, which by this time was connected with the outside world by both boat and railroad. Although a few small cotton mills were started in this section before the 1890's, the locality was still primarily agricultural when the Massachusetts promoters became interested in it.

In 1894, when Charles L. Lovering was looking for a site for the newly created Massachusetts Mills in Georgia, a member of a cotton-buying firm in Rome who had dealt with him suggested places in northwestern Georgia. As a result, twelve locations were investigated carefully. Of these the one called the "Brick Mill" in Floyd County was recommended as the most desirable. Here adequate land was available; in fact, the interested southerners would contribute some land. The land was high enough to be free from floods and convenient to Rome, which was only four miles to the north, and also to Atlanta, which was about seventy miles to the south. Through the property ran two railroads—a very important factor—from which spurs to the mills could be built. Freight rates on coal from East Tennessee, as well as rates on finished goods to New York, were reasonable when compared with those for the other sites. The water supply was adequate for manufacturing purposes, although the water was somewhat hard because of the local limestone. For use in the mills and the village it could be stored in a reservoir on a neighboring hill. Furthermore, cotton of the type needed for coarse goods was grown locally in large quantities, as evidenced by the marketing of 80,000 bales annually in Rome. In the county there was a population of 40,000, from which it seemed reasonable to expect that an adequate supply of operatives could be obtained. Thus the site was good in all

HOMER M. CARTER

R. DONALD HARVEY

TWO SOUTHERN MANAGERS

AERIAL SURVEY OF MILLS AND VILLAGE OF LINDALE, ABOUT 1935

ways but one—the hardness of the water—and, in fact, had a greater number of good points than any of the others.[3]

The northerners decided on the "Brick Mill" site for their mills. For $40,000 they purchased a four-fifths' interest in 200 acres of the local promoting company. They called the property Lindale in place of Boozeville, a name which had been taken from a local family and not from a colloquial expression. Seven years later, in 1902, the northerners acquired 600 acres more and full ownership of the original 200 for $50,000. They also bought the local store, its fixtures, and stock for another $17,000. Thus, within a few years the Massachusetts Mills in Georgia became the sole owner of a sizable holding of property.[4]

Immediately, on the site selected, the northern promoters started the construction of a mill for the manufacture of narrow sheetings, drills, and osnaburgs. They arranged to have the firm of mill engineers, Lockwood, Greene & Co., draw up plans and to have others carry on the construction. The parent or leasing company, the Massachusetts Cotton Mills, purchased many of the materials and provided many services. The Lowell Machine Shops furnished most of the machinery for the first unit, which was equipped with over 30,000 spindles and 1,000 looms. In 1898, only two years after this first mill had gone into production, a second was started for the manufacture of ducks. It was smaller than the first, with 20,000 spindles and 600 looms. For this mill also Lowell furnished much of the machinery. The Draper Co., however, supplied half the looms. Only a few years later (in 1902) a third mill was begun, for the same types of goods as the first, with over 30,000 spindles and 1,300 looms. When it was completed in 1903, the Massachusetts Mills in Georgia had three large mills equipped to produce goods which were unprofitable to manufacture in Lowell but profitable in the South.[5]

An interesting detail in the equipping of these mills was the supplying of Northrup automatic looms by the Draper Co. for the third mill. For the first two the looms had been of the old type. However, before they had worn out, they were replaced. In 1905 practically all in the first mill were replaced by Northrups, and in 1907 a third of those in the second mill. Not until 1915 does it appear that the Northrup became universal. Thus we see that these mills adopted the latest labor-saving looms at about the same time that Pepperell did in Biddeford. They adopted them at about the same time but to a larger extent than the Lowell plant of the Massachusetts Cotton Mills.[6]

Of interest, too, was the fact that for the first fifteen years the looms in Lindale had been not more than 36 inches wide. These were much easier to tend than wider ones. Starting in 1911, looms 46 inches wide were introduced. From the beginning the looms were equipped for two, three, or four harnesses, so that some could make plain goods while others could produce twills.[7]

For many years these three mills continued to manufacture the original types of goods—narrow sheetings, drills, ducks, and osnaburgs—and also others of similar construction—shirtings and flannels. Some of these were sold in the brown and some went to the bleachery of the Massachusetts Cotton Mills in Lowell. In 1917 a dyehouse was started in Lindale, which, when completed, made possible the manufacture of other types of goods, such as denims, stripes, and chambrays. These goods took the place of part of the production of earlier types, which, as we have mentioned before, were becoming unprofitable with the decline in the export trade.[8]

Although records of levels of production in Lindale are not available, total sales of goods for a number of years are at hand. We find, for example, sales of nearly 30,000,000 yards in the year 1901, when two mills were in operation, and of nearly 55,000,000 yards in 1904, when three mills were producing. In the following year sales declined to about 50,000,000 yards. For 1905 to 1925 we have no figures, but we can surmise that sales mounted during the first World War and then declined. For the year 1925 we do know that 36,000,000 yards of Lindale's goods were sold.[9]

While the mills were being constructed in Lindale, facilities for the workers were also being provided. On part of the property, near the mills, the company laid out streets and built houses for the operatives. At first it erected 58 eight-room houses, designed according to northern rather than southern plans in two respects—the houses had two stories and provided for two families. In at least one respect they were southern—they had no basements. According to existing records these houses cost less than $100 a room to build, a reasonable amount indeed. The same style of house was continued for many years in two sections of Lindale, called Old Town and New Town. After the first World War a few one-story, one-family houses were built in another section, called Jamestown; generally they were rented to members of the supervisory group. Altogether, by the end of 1926 there were over 600 living quarters or over 300 houses in Lindale.[10]

In addition to the houses for the operatives, the company provided other buildings. Since Rome was too far away for much of the shopping, local stores were necessary, but the Massachusetts Mills in Georgia did not operate any. Some stores were built in South Lindale, outside the company's property. In Lindale the local promoting company built a store which was run by Daniel W. Barnett. In 1902 this store, as we have already noted, was purchased by the Massachusetts company, which thereafter leased space to Barnett, who had the post office and the exclusive right to sell some goods, such as ice, coal, and wood. The company also leased other space to Brittain Bros., who ran a department store. Later Brittain Bros. bought Barnett out, and the mills took over the supplying of ice, coal, and wood.[11] In both these stores the mill agreed to "honor orders given by the operatives against their time." [12] Thus in Lindale the mills avoided the difficulties of company operation of stores, which became a sore spot in many communities.

For the religious needs of the workers the company contributed to the building and maintenance of churches. There was in Lindale in 1895 only one congregation, the Presbyterian, located in a building which had been erected in 1803 by the Primitive Baptists. Within a few years after the construction of the mills the company assisted in the erection of a Baptist Church on its property and, during the first World War, of a Methodist Church. With these three churches the company made it possible for the workers to develop their religious life in the patterns to which they had been accustomed before coming to Lindale.[13]

The educational needs of the children were considered even earlier than the religious. In the first year of operation of the mill, classes were held in one of the tenements with two teachers in charge. But soon there were too many pupils to be crowded into eight rooms. In 1900 the company started the construction of a schoolhouse, which has been added to from time to time. In 1905, according to existing records, there were 9 teachers for about 400 pupils. During the following years the numbers of both grew but we do not have the number for 1926, the end of Pepperell's second period. Not only did the company furnish the school building but it contributed to the expenses of operating the school. Thus, the children in Lindale have been more fortunate than those in neighboring agricultural communities which depended only on county funds.[14]

Other buildings were added to the village from time to time. Among them were houses for the agent, superintendent, and overseers, as well as an inn for visitors. The company also started a laundry during the first World War. From the beginning the company provided public utilities for the village—running water from faucets located between the houses, and electric lights for the streets. After a few years it installed iceboxes at the end of each street, from which, in summer, families could get ice water to drink. Although streets were built by the company, they were difficult to travel on, particularly during wet weather, because of the deep mud. On the whole, by the end of the first World War the operatives in Lindale had the fundamentals for a decent standard of living.[15]

After the first World War, when the mills in Lindale became actually the property of the Massachusetts Cotton Mills, recreational facilities were developed for the workers. Most important of all was the construction of an auditorium building in honor of those who had died in the service of their country. In it there was space for motion pictures, a swimming-pool, bowling alleys, a pool room, and reading and lunch rooms. Near the mills the company also built a restaurant and a combination of nurses' home and kindergarten. Among other improvements started in 1920 were additional houses in a new section. The total expenditures for these improvements were estimated at $300,000.[16]

Much more interesting than the physical plant in Lindale were the people who were drawn there to work in the mills. They came to form a good working unit largely because of one man, Henry Parish Meikleham, who was agent from 1901 until his death in 1937. Meikleham had the welfare of the workers at heart and started many projects for their benefit. As a result of his solicitous concern for others and because of his winning personality, he was beloved by the operatives, as we shall see demonstrated by their actions in the next period.[17]

Three others preceded Meikleham as agent in Lindale. First among them was Arthur W. Hunking, an engineer from Massachusetts, who stayed for four years and moved on to Huntsville, Alabama, to be in charge of construction of Merrimack's southern mills. For a short time his place was taken by Edward C. Beach, who left in 1900 to take charge of the newly organized Gate City Cotton Mills at East Point, Georgia. Then for a few months, until the treasurer selected a permanent agent, William S. Southworth, agent of the Massachusetts Cotton Mills in Lowell, substituted. Thus, until Meikleham arrived, the mills had not enjoyed the attention of a permanent manufacturing agent.[18]

Captain Harry Meikleham, as he was usually called, proved an excellent man for the job of agent, not only from the workers' but also from the company's point of view. A descendant of the old Virginia families of Jefferson and Randolph and of the New York family of Meikleham, he studied at Columbia as his father and two older brothers had done. But he stayed there for only a short time. In 1891, when he was eighteen years old, he started to gain experience in the cotton industry in the North, perhaps influenced by some of his New England relatives, the Coolidges, who were also descended from Thomas Jefferson. For three years he served as an apprentice in the old Boston Manufacturing Co. For about two years more he worked there, rising to the position of overseer. For another two years he held a similar position with the Stark Mills of Manchester, New Hampshire. Then he went south, to be superintendent of the Aikin Manufacturing Co. of South Carolina for about two years. Thus he had had a variety of experiences when the directors of the Massachusetts Cotton Mills selected him as their agent in Lindale.[19]

There were in Lindale others besides the agents, who had had training in the North. When the first agent, Hunking, was starting up the machinery in the first mill, he had the assistance of a number of men from Lowell—from the Massachusetts Cotton Mills—including the agent, superintendent, overseers, and many other skilled men. Some stayed only a few days at a time, while others remained much longer. One of the latter was C. A. Lester, who acted as weaving overseer for two years. When Hunking left in 1899, some of the overseers in Lindale may have gone back to Lowell or with him to Huntsville. At any rate, we find at this time a number of changes in the supervisory ranks, as there were also in 1900, when the second agent, Beach, left. Probably some of the overseers came to Lindale with Beach and moved on with him to his new company, as was customary in the South. During these years a few overseers were probably drawn from the ranks of other mills in the South. Later, after a number of years of operation, some of the Lindale workers were promoted to supervisory jobs.[20]

In 1899 William Audley Marshall, who since 1895 had been a bookkeeper and then the paymaster, was promoted to the position of superintendent. He was a young man from Alabama, fresh from Alabama Polytechnic Institute, who in Lindale acquired his practical training in cotton manufacturing. Of Scotch descent, he was as careful of saving the company's money as the fourth agent, Meikleham, was of spending it. These two made a good combination, which was broken by the death of Marshall in 1930.[21]

For the first years of operation, then, the Massachusetts Mills in Georgia had the advantage of the direction of men skilled in similar work in Lowell. This was of great importance, since it meant that the new mill could carry on the scheme of operations in the North without any trial and error period.

Since many of these Lowell men were temporary, it meant that a number of southerners were soon given the opportunity of becoming overseers. There were, however, exceptions to this generalization. In 1912 Robert W. Van Tassell came from Lowell to be the mechanical engineer. He stayed in Lindale until his death in 1931. In some departments the overseers stayed for long periods, while in weaving, for instance, there were nine overseers in the first thirty years.[22]

From the neighboring countryside, as the promoters had hoped, came a bountiful supply of workers. Many of them were descendants of early Scotch-Irish settlers who found it difficult to support large families on hilly, stony farms. Some of them flocked in, when they heard of the opportunity of steady employment for a cash wage, glad to leave the old plow handles behind, while others were induced to come by the superintendent, who got numbers of families to join wagon trains to Lindale. Although their ancestors in America had had few advantages, these first workers and their children had great potentialities, which, with more education and better living conditions, are becoming evident today.[23]

Besides these workers from the farms there were a few migrants from other mills in the South. Generally they comprised the more restless element and those perhaps less suited to industrial enterprises. After a time most of these migratory workers moved away from Lindale, but during the first decade of the operation of the mills they contributed a disturbing element to the village. At night, for example, it was considered unsafe for a woman to venture outside her home; occasionally there was shooting down the straight streets. But these were common experiences in southern mill villages during their early years. In time the agent in Lindale was able to eliminate the unruly and keep the law-abiding and industrious workers.[24]

Only those who had a large number of potential workers in the family were welcomed at the mills. This restriction on the company's part was necessary, since the number of houses which it had erected was not adequate if there were only one or two workers to a tenement. In fact, the general rule here as elsewhere in the South was a worker to each room. This meant that there had to be at least four workers in a family. But in the early years there was still greater crowding, with sometimes at least two to a room. These workers included children and adults. In 1903, for example, about a quarter of the workers were under sixteen years of age. In addition, the village was congested by the livestock which the workers had brought along from the farms. These workers, accustomed to living in old houses in the hills and valleys, enjoyed an entirely different experience in new houses in an overcrowded village.[25]

When Meikleham became agent in 1901, he realized that many reforms were necessary to create a quiet and industrious village. He made arrangements for the animals to be kept in a section of the village which was non-residential. Discovering that the men sought relief from the unaccustomed industrial monotony by gambling or by walking the railroad tracks to Rome for liquor, he organized a military company for them; this gave a more wholesome outlet to their energies. In 1903 he had other military companies join in Lindale's ceremonies, which included a barbecue. He arranged to have State dignitaries present, and no doubt this function increased the local pride in the militia. During the first World War Lindale was proud of the alleged fact that it provided four times as many men for the service as any other place of the same size in the United States.[26]

Many other organizations were started for the workers. In 1907, for example, Meikleham organized a band, which came to be recognized as outstanding. Various clubs, some of secret orders, sprang up for the men as well as a few for the women. For the boys a Scout troop was started. By these various measures Meikleham enabled the workers to develop wholesome types of recreation.[27]

In order to have a healthy working force Meikleham found that other measures were also necessary. When there was a smallpox epidemic during his first years as agent, he had the workers lined up and vaccinated. A few years later, when there was a disastrous outbreak of typhoid, he established a pesthouse to which the afflicted were sent. Later he insisted that all employees be inoculated against typhoid annually; those who objected moved away. In 1911 he introduced a village nurse, who because of her unusual attire was called "Leather Britches." She stayed for three years. Another village nurse, Mae Young, was hired in 1918 and stayed until her retirement in 1944. She came to be greatly beloved by the operatives, who realized how much she helped them in their daily lives. In 1921 the company added a clinic, with a nurse in charge. This was continued and expanded, as we shall see, during Pepperell's period of operation.[28]

In still another way Meikleham added to the peace of mind of the operatives. In 1901 he started a burial union to which the operatives could contribute regularly. This took the place of the former passing of the hat when a worker died. The union has continued in operation with increasing benefits. It has been said that no operative has contributed so much as the benefits which his family has received at the time of his death.[29]

While Meikleham was able to promote these various enterprises which contributed to the well-being of the workers, he did not and in fact could not establish immediately the two fundamental benefits—a shorter work-week and higher rates of pay. The South, newer in industrial expansion than the North, lagged behind in these two respects. In 1889 Georgia did pass a law that restricted the number of hours of work to eleven daily or sixty-six weekly for all workers, not just for women and children as was customary in the North. For a full schedule in Lindale the operatives worked 11¾ hours for five days and 7¼ on Saturday. The mills continued to operate on this schedule until 1911, when Georgia limited the hours to 10 daily or 60 weekly. In the sharp depression of 1920–21 the hours of work in Lindale were reduced to 55 weekly, as were those of many other companies in Georgia and Alabama. (This level for full-time work continued until the Roosevelt era.[30]) Thus, during these thirty years the operatives worked much longer hours than workers in the North—particularly those in Lowell and Fall River.

Rates of pay for the operatives in Lindale were lower than in the North, but during these thirty years they increased much more than in the North. By the end of this period, therefore, the southern workers were comparatively much better off. Any discussion of wages in the South must, however, take into consideration the changes in work loads as well as the gradual elimination of children from the ranks. In 1903 about a quarter of Lindale's working force consisted of children under sixteen, as we have already noted. Two years later, children under twelve were not employed. In the following two decades children's services declined in importance as a larger supply of adult workers became available with higher rates of pay.[31]

The children earned little. Some not yet on the payroll went through a period of learning, while others assisted their parents. A typical job was that of sweeper for which the pay was 2 cents an hour in 1898, 3 cents in 1905, and 5 cents in 1910, for a 66-hour week. By March, 1921, this job had apparently been taken over by older employees who were earning much more—24 cents an hour. After some cuts in the postwar depression and after a rise in 1923, a sweeper was earning 19 cents an hour—still as little as any employee in the mill. But by 1921 he was working only 55 hours a week.[32]

For the adults, also, wage rates improved considerably, particularly for those doing unskilled work. The warp spinner, who may be considered typical of the women operatives, earned about 3 cents an hour in 1898, 5½ cents in 1904, and almost 8 cents in 1910. By March, 1921, she was earning 39 cents an hour, but in 1923 only about 20 cents an hour, one cent more than the sweeper.[33]

While women and children held unskilled jobs, men held both unskilled and skilled. Taking the roving man as an example of the unskilled male workers, we find that he earned about 6½ cents an hour in 1898, 7½ in 1904, and 9 1/3 in 1910. In March, 1921, a roving man received 30 cents an hour, and 19 cents, the same as a sweeper, in 1923. Among the skilled men the loom-fixer was the most highly paid of those who worked in the operating departments (that is, excluding the machinists, the carpenters, and in the later years the beamers in the dyehouse), and here we find still smaller increases. In both 1898 and 1904 the fixer was getting $9.00 a week, or about 14 cents an hour. In 1910 his pay went up, the average increase being

83 cents a week, or slightly more than a cent an hour. By March, 1921, he was getting $28.45 a week or about 52 cents an hour, but by January 13, 1923, he was getting $20.96 a week or about 38 cents an hour.[34]

These rates of pay for sample workers in Lindale seem low indeed. They were lower than the rates in Biddeford, but we hesitate to make detailed comparisons because of differences in work loads. According to a government survey, rates of pay in the South a few years before the first World War were over 20 per cent lower than those in the North. During the war the northern operatives received raises first, but the southerners caught up, so that at the end there was about the same differential as before the war. In the postwar years, however, southern rates were cut more drastically than northern, so that the former were about 40 per cent below the latter.[35]

While today we find these rates of pay unbelievably low, we forget how reasonable the operative's cost of living was in the South. Many of his needs were supplied by local products; side meat (salt pork) was 5 cents a pound and frying chickens were 10 cents each in 1898. Some other foods, such as sugar and coffee, were proportionally much higher: sugar sold at sixteen pounds for a dollar, and coffee at eight pounds for a dollar. For a large family a week's supply of food consisting of 100 pounds of flour, a bushel of corn meal, 10 pounds of meat, 10 pounds of lard, 10 pounds of sugar, a dozen eggs, 4 chickens, and 2 pounds of butter, cost $4.73 in 1898 or slightly more than the weekly pay of a roving man. Clothing requirements were simple in the South. A man might wear blue denim overalls and brogans for work, with perhaps a clean pair of overalls on Sunday. Comparatively little fuel was needed to heat the houses. Rents were low. At the beginning an overseer rented a four-room tenement for $1.75 a week. During periods of short schedules of work the rent was cut or eliminated.[36] Altogether the cost of living of the operative in the South was much less than that of the operative in the North, but in both sections the work of more than one person was required to support the family.

The cost of cotton used in the manufacturing of goods was at least double that of wages. During the first part of this period the mills in Lindale used local cotton almost entirely. The treasurer in Boston purchased the bulk of it through the office of Cooper & Brush, which sent orders to the Howell Co., of Rome, to be filled. This arrangement worked out satisfactorily as long as there was an adequate local supply, or until after the first World War when the boll weevil reduced cotton production in northern Georgia. But it was not such an economical method of purchasing as Pepperell instituted later. The charges included brokerage of 50 cents a bale and shipping of $1.50 a bale—about the same as if the cotton had been transferred to the North, while actually it merely had to be transported a few miles to Lindale.[37]

The goods made in Lindale were handled by the Massachusetts Cotton Mills' selling agent, Smith, Hogg & Gardner, and the succeeding partnership, Smith, Hogg & Co. While their terms for handling the goods were similar to those of Bliss, Fabyan & Co. with Pepperell, members of the selling house did not become directors of the textile company and thus have the same opportunities to assist in its direction.[38]

These mills in Lindale proved profitable, as Lovering had prophesied in the 1890's. The trustees authorized dividends to the stockholders, first at the annual rate of 6 per cent and then, from December, 1906, at the rate of 5 per cent. These rates were the same as those paid by the Massachusetts Cotton Mills for the leasing of the mills. From 1896, when the mills went into operation, up to March 1, 1919, when they were sold to the Massachusetts Cotton Mills, the net earnings to the Massachusetts Cotton Mills, after rent and interest on money borrowed, came to almost $4,000,000. Half of these earnings were set aside for a sinking fund with which to retire the stock at the time of its acquisition by the parent company. The other half the Massachusetts Cotton Mills used from time to time to repay money borrowed, to finance additions to the plant in Georgia, and to accumulate a reserve fund. In 1919 there was a reserve fund of $700,000. Thus the stockholders of the Massachusetts Mills in Georgia received a steady return on their investments, while the Massachusetts Cotton Mills took the risks and received the profits after dividends, which were similar to interest in their rate and regularity. In the years in which the southern mills were an integral part of the Lowell company they continued to be profitable. In the four fiscal years from 1923 through 1926, profits before taxes for these mills averaged slightly more than $360,000, with a loss, however, in the fiscal year 1924.[39]

The profitability of these mills in Georgia was the most important factor in bringing about the consolidation of the Massachusetts Cotton Mills with the Pepperell Manufacturing Company at the end of 1926. Under the latter's ownership we shall see that Lindale continued its prosperous record; in fact, it became Pepperell's favorite mill for many reasons. Not the least of these was the coöperative spirit of the workers, who spoke the same language and were potential members of the same society as the management.

CHAMBRAYS IN LINDALE, 1926–1945

When in December of 1926 the Pepperell Manufacturing Company acquired the Massachusetts Cotton Mills, the new owner became vitally concerned with the mills in Lindale. On the whole, Pepperell has continued the policies which proved successful in the past but it has not hesitated to make improvements when they have seemed advisable. Thus, in the second period of operations the mills in Lindale have continued their profitable career at a time when many others, particularly in the North, were finding these years very difficult.

Pepperell carried further the changes in the types of goods which the Massachusetts Cotton Mills had started in 1917. At first it devoted about half of the manufacturing capacity to colored goods, such as denims, stripes, cords, and chambrays for men's work clothing as well as for women's and children's sturdy garments. Before the second World War the colored goods became still more important, with chambrays alone comprising over 70 per cent of the total production. These chambrays could be put to many uses, but the principal one was for men's work shirts.[40]

As colored goods were growing in importance, white goods

were declining. Some of the latter went to Lewiston for bleaching, dyeing, and printing, instead of to Lowell as formerly. In the first dozen years most of these goods were canton flannels and osnaburgs. Occasionally other white goods, such as drills, shirtings, and narrow sheetings, were made. These white goods were suited for many uses: the flannels could be used for parts of work gloves, for polishing cloths, for padding in sport uniforms, and for infants' garments; the osnaburgs, for bagging, in place of burlaps or hessians.

During the second World War, the agent in Lindale spoke of the changes in production as follows:[41]

> The Lindale mill discontinued the manufacture of any fabrics that it did not feel were absolutely necessary to the war program immediately after Pearl Harbor. Two-thirds of the looms here are operating on chambrays for the Navy and herringbone for the Army fatigue uniforms. The other third is producing canton flannel for gun patches, process gloves and bandages, pin checks for Maritime Commission mattress covers; coverts, suitings, and osnaburgs for camouflage.

Pepperell continued to make expenditures for buildings and equipment. Within the first two years Meikleham added to the dyehouse, storehouse, and clothroom building. In 1930 he erected an office building. In 1934, when business was depressed—even in Lindale—he started to add another building for dyeing; when finished, it contained the largest indigo dyeing range then in the world. He also installed a new turbine and improved types of machinery, including long-draft spinning frames and superdraft roving frames as well as Barber-Colman spoolers and warpers. As a result, by 1943 Lindale was running almost entirely long-draft spinning—92 per cent—and 34 per cent long- or super-draft roving. These percentages differed considerably from those for Biddeford, probably because the spinning and roving frames were of various vintages.

During these years the village of Lindale has improved considerably in appearance and comfort. The houses, which formerly had been yellow with green trimmings, were painted white on the outside, while inside they were painted the colors chosen by the tenants. The agent arranged to have the spaces filled in between the supporting pillars beneath the first floor and to have the yards decorated with flowering shrubs. By the end of this period the trees along the streets had grown so that they provided shade and took away the stark appearance of rows of houses. The streets were improved also—paved so that the dreadful days of red mud were no more. During the 1940's Pepperell erected two brick buildings: a modern schoolhouse for the junior high school students, for which it planned later additions so that other classes could be accommodated; and a store, which it has leased to a member of a grocery chain. A sewerage system was put in which, after the war, would make possible modern plumbing in all the houses. In houses which lacked bathrooms, new ones would be built. When these changes are completed, Lindale will be very comfortable indeed.

Henry Parish Meikleham was in charge of Lindale until his death in 1937. He continued throughout his long service the policy of assisting the operatives to improve their circumstances. On more than one occasion the operatives demonstrated their deep appreciation. The first of these was in May, 1932, when, in celebration of his sixtieth birthday, they held a Meikleham Day in which everyone in the village as well as outside guests participated. They contributed to a gift for him, held games, joined in contests, and ate a huge barbecue dinner.[42]

The second demonstration of their loyalty was quite different. In 1934, when the United Textile Workers' Union of America was attempting to organize the cotton workers, outside organizers in flying squadrons tried to appeal to the workers in the southern mill villages. In some cases they received so hostile a reception that bloodshed resulted. Although fighting did not break out in Lindale, for some time the mills were closed in case a large and formidable group should appear. Workers rallied to the protection of the property and to Meikleham, whose life was threatened. For weapons they were equipped only with materials at hand, such as picker sticks. Finally, when Governor Talmage called out the State militia, conditions returned to normal.[43]

In July of 1937 the operatives were grieved to hear of Meikleham's sudden death in New York. Some of them took the trip to Virginia to be present at his burial in the Jefferson family lot. For some time before this, however, they had known that they would continue to have a friendly agent in Lindale. They had grown to trust R. Donald Harvey, who had worked in the mills for a number of years. Harvey, a native of Rome, had been graduated from the Georgia School of Technology in 1920, and then had begun his mill career at Lindale, starting at the bottom to get experience in all departments. After a short time away as superintendent of the Aragon mills, he returned in 1926 to be made assistant superintendent. In 1930, when Marshall was made assistant agent, Harvey became superintendent. In the following year, after Marshall's death, he was appointed assistant agent, a position which he held until his promotion in 1937. Harvey is a good example of the younger southern executive with technical training and a deep fatherly affection for his employees.

During Harvey's years as agent the operatives had another big day—on July 22, 1943, when the Army-Navy "E" was awarded to the mill. A colonel from the Office of the Quartermaster General presented the "E" pennant, which Allyn B. McIntire, from Pepperell's Boston office, accepted. A lieutenant commander of the United States Navy presented the pins, which Roy Penley, one of the operatives with a long service record in Lindale, accepted. There was also an address by the president of the University of Georgia. The baseball field near the mills overflowed with people; in fact the grandstand was not large enough to hold the numbers who attended—over 6,000 in all.[44] This was indeed a precious day which they came to treasure as they did the Meikleham Day of eleven years earlier.

Besides Harvey there were others who secured a technical training before they entered the mills. Some attended the Georgia School of Technology, which was closely related to the mills in the State. These young men, some of whom were children of families which had been employed in the mills, demonstrated the potentialities of the mill operatives when greater opportunities were put within their reach. They therefore had an advantage over many of the overseers in the North, since they understood fully the problems of the workers with no racial or class lines to hinder. They and their wives formed a "smart set," in which there was much entertaining in Lindale as well as in Rome. With the members of this supervisory group the executives from Boston found it easy to talk over problems. During the visits to Lindale they met at the mill as well as more informally at the guest house, Meikleham's former residence, where two of the nurses were hostesses.

This supervisory group as well as the agent took part in the activities of various cotton textile associations, some national, some sectional. Their activities were similar in many respects to those which we have considered earlier in the North. To be sure, there were some differences arising from the diverse situations. In the South, representatives of the mills in several States might talk over problems and approve changes in policies. Such, for example, was the setting of 55 hours as the maximum for a shift late in 1920, and such was the decision to eliminate women and minors from night work, approved in 1931.[45]

Many of the early operatives continued to work in Lindale throughout this second period. Their children and grandchildren have also entered the mills when they were old enough. Over the years the workers have increased in efficiency, in spite of working in noisy, hot, and humid rooms, which were more uncomfortable during a large part of the year than similar rooms in the North. In both sections it was claimed that operatives became accustomed to these conditions. Near the end of this period, however, a start was made in Lindale to air-condition the spinning rooms in one mill as well as the office. When such improvements have been made in the mills, operatives may prefer to stay there rather than in their homes, which during part of the year are uncomfortably hot.

For further evidence of the nature of the working force in

Lindale fortunately we have an elaborate tabulation, made in 1933 before the National Industrial Recovery Act, which reveals the extent of the stability as well as the marital status, sex, and residence of the workers by departments. (It is reproduced in Appendix 24.) As always, questions arise about how typical these figures may be. Because these were set down during the depression, they probably show a heavier proportion of older workers than usual, since there was an attempt to provide work for as many families as possible. The figures, however, are worthy of much study, although we cannot proceed far here. We see, for example, that many departments employed workers for long periods, while others employed them for only a short time. Some of this variation can be explained by the later setting up of some of the departments, as, for example, the dye house in 1917. We find that 135 of the 1,747 employees in 1933 had worked in the mills a quarter-century or more. Of interest, too, is the fact that there were about twice as many men as women in the mills. The preponderance of the former can be explained in part by the company's policy since 1931 of employing no women and minors at night. The extra men may have been drawn from the neighboring countryside or the city of Rome. Lindale still provided the majority, in fact almost three-quarters, of the workers.

The workers' life in Lindale was enriched in many respects during this period. The mill hired men, for example, to work in the mills and to form a professional baseball team, whose success aroused local pride in Lindale. Many clubs for men, women, and children flourished, among them the Sea Scouts for the boys. Barbecues were a favorite entertainment of these clubs, and a legion clubhouse built by the workers on top of one of the hills provided an attractive setting. On Sundays concerts were given by the local band. In 1941 a local newspaper was started. In its columns were reports of social activities by members of the various departments in the mills. This paper thus filled the place of the *Pepperell Sheet* distributed to northern workers.

Educational opportunities improved during this second period. For the children there were increased opportunities for training in the arts, such as singing, writing, and drawing. Near the end of this period, as we have already noted, a new junior high school was built in which there were many modern attractions—a library for regular use, a motion-picture projector, and a victrola with recordings of fine music. But the teachers were still paid poorly, although Pepperell continued to contribute a part of their salaries; during the second World War many of them received less than a new employee in the mills. The teachers were victims of the impoverished condition of much of Georgia, which may continue until large appropriations for education are more general. Several of the junior high school graduates have gone to the neighboring high schools, while some have received still further training. There has been a growing tendency for some of the young people to be dissatisfied with work in the mills. But rather than reduce the training of the more ambitious, Harvey felt that the situation presented a challenge to the mills to make jobs interesting to as many as possible.

For the operatives, textile classes were started. According to Harvey in 1943, these classes have been very successful:[46]

> Several years ago Lindale realized the importance of vocational training classes and fixing schools. These have been conducted in all of the major departments since 1938. These classes, sponsored by the Georgia Department of Vocational Education, have been taught by some of the most capable men in the mills here. This training has been available to all employees on all shifts.
>
> In these schools many men have been trained to take over responsible jobs made vacant by some of the experienced workers who were called into military service. Altogether, fifty-two classes have been sponsored in the entire mill. The total number of students has been 536, of which 64 have been promoted to second hands, third hands, and section men.

There were Bible classes for the men on Sunday morning, at which current problems were discussed by local as well as outside men. These classes compensated for the lack of contact with the outside world. Also, about once a month it was Meikleham's custom to get all the operatives together for a talk, which might include a statement of the company's policies about employment in the future. Some of these meetings, as well as other social activities, were curtailed during the second World War when there was much less free time for all.

Further health measures have been instituted during Pepperell's period of ownership. The clinic has been improved. A village doctor and dentist have been employed part time by the mills. They have checked on new employees and annually on all employees and their children. They have attended to accidents in the mills. The dentist, who came to Lindale in 1931, has had an interesting time. When he arrived he found a lack of interest in dental care. At first he started a program of correction for all the school children up to ten years of age and of examination for all others. This project took eighteen months to carry through. Thereafter he examined all school children and their parents once a year. He found a feeling against teeth cleaning because many believed that it removed the glaze. Some of the employees had teeth in bad condition, with an accumulation of tartar from snuff dipping. Some preferred to let nature take its course until they found it necessary to have their teeth removed and plates put in. But progress has been made.

In 1940 the operatives were given an opportunity to become members of an association for hospital services in Rome, similar to the associations in the large cities in the North. Over 98 per cent of the operatives in Lindale subscribed immediately.[47] They had begun to realize that at times they needed more scientific care than they could get in their homes.

During this period employment in Lindale waxed and waned with the general state of the textile business, although on the whole these operatives were better off than many others. The figures for the end of June of the years 1927 through 1933 show that the mills employed from 1,600 to 1,800 workers, enough for one full shift and a partial second. A full schedule during these years was 55 hours a week for each shift. In 1931, as we have already noted, Pepperell approved of the removal of women and minors from night work. This self-restriction continued until the industrial codes were set up by the New Deal.

From the time the codes were established under the National Industrial Recovery Act, employment in Lindale as well as elsewhere in the South followed a different pattern. In the summer of 1933 hours were limited to 40 for each of two shifts. Even this restricted operation led, however, to greater production than could be disposed of advantageously. By the end of 1933 conditions had become so bad that a cut in hours of 25 per cent was ordered, or a reduction to 60 hours a week for both shifts, a reduction which was put in force at the end of 1933 and in the summer of 1934. Later, under the Fair Labor Standards Act, hours for a shift were limited to 44, then 42, and finally 40 a week. But, during the time when the 40 hours were in force, overtime was necessary in order to fill government contracts. At that time the agent tried to operate with a first shift of 1,500, a second of about 1,000, and a third of about 300. For the years of the New Deal we find that employment was at much higher levels than previously. In two years it reached almost 3,000, while in one, 1938, it dropped to less than 1,000.[48]

But these measurements of the length of the work-week and the number of employees do not reveal the periods when much shorter hours were worked. In the summer of 1934 the agent set up a schedule of two shifts which worked eight hours a day for three days. During this time the operatives were not charged for house rent, electricity, or water.[49] Again, during the recession of 1938, employment fell when the mills were closed for a time.

With the changes in business conditions which influenced the number of operatives, number of shifts, and hours of work, there were, of course, changes in the rates of pay in Lindale. From the time that Pepperell took over the mills in 1926 through the end of the fiscal year 1930, rates of pay remained quite steady. Then, when the debacle arrived and every effort was made to operate profitably, wage rates had to be cut. For the fiscal year 1932, workers in Lindale received less than

$1,000,000, but thereafter conditions improved somewhat. The individual was assured by the national code of 1933 of a minimum of 30 cents an hour, or, if he or she worked 40 hours, $12 a week. This minimum was slightly less than that in the North, which was 32.5 cents an hour or $13 for a 40-hour week. After the Recovery Act had been declared unconstitutional and abolished, rates of pay fluctuated again with business conditions. In 1939, under the Fair Labor Standards Act, minimum rates of pay in the North and in the South were set at 32.5 cents an hour. This minimum was raised to 37.5 cents in 1941, to 40 in 1942, and to 55 in 1945. In spite of this, the average rates of pay in the South have tended to be lower than in the North, since the more skilled were paid proportionally less. During the three years 1943–45 wages paid in Lindale were more than $4,000,000, over four times the amount paid in the depression year 1932.[50]

Of course, all this increase in total pay has not meant a proportional increase for luxuries or savings. As elsewhere, the cost of living had increased. In 1938 it was estimated that the supply of groceries which had sold for $4.73 in 1898 now cost $11.20. During the following years its cost rose higher. But this earlier list of commodities no longer indicated the needs of a family. Their diet has become more varied with the inclusion of fresh fruits and vegetables, which some have purchased while others have grown them in their gardens. Their diet also has included canned fruits and vegetables, some of which again have been purchased while some have been processed in the mill with facilities made available to the workers. Other expenditures probably have increased at a time when throughout the nation there was a heightened desire for radios, furniture, and clothing. In regard to housing the mill workers have been fortunate, since their rents have been low and they have been charged only a small amount for electricity and water. During part of this period, fifty cents a room per week has been the charge for rent. For the single houses in Jamestown (in Lindale) with modern plumbing, the rents have been more, but still less than $20 a month. The worker will ordinarily rent a company tenement in Lindale and be content to pay the low rental. He may locate outside, however, if there is no tenement available in the village, or if he wishes to own a house of his own. All the property in the village of Lindale has continued to be company-owned. Perhaps in the future a modification of this policy may occur, but so far both sides have been content with the present arrangement.

During this second period, to the mills in Lindale the workers have remained loyal—to the agents and to the company which owned the mills. They have realized that the agent had their welfare at heart and have not sought to have others, such as union leaders, come in to represent them.

One major change in operations in Lindale during Pepperell's ownership has been the local purchasing of cotton. We have mentioned that previously the treasurer in Boston purchased the cotton from a broker with a connection in Rome. But in 1927 the assistant treasurer, Amory Coolidge, became dissatisfied with this method, which seemed unnecessarily expensive. If a good cotton buyer could be secured who could purchase cotton right from the cotton fields, the company would benefit. S. H. Smith, a member of an old cotton firm in Rome, which had been successful in its operations ever since 1878 but which he was willing to liquidate, suggested that Pepperell let him carry on its buying. Naturally, he had to prove his ability to act wholly for Pepperell's good. For six years he operated through S. H. Smith & Co. of Rome, set up as subsidiary to Pepperell. Then the company consolidated with Pepperell, and Smith set up a cotton-buying department in the mill yard. He managed his department as though it was completely separate from the mill, hiring and paying his workers. Among them was his son Richard, who was learning classing, an operation which requires years of experience. He also hired crews of Negroes for the heavy work. These Negroes comprised the only large group of this race in the mills. They lived in a different world from the other workers—in a separate section where their children attended a different school.

Smith purchased about half the mills' requirements of cotton from local farmers. In fact he purchased all that the various farmers grew—a method which saved about a dollar a bale.

He weighed the bales and classed the cotton. Those bales which did not come up to specifications were rejected, at a cost which he estimated at about 50 cents a bale. He also bought cotton from Texas for the finer work in the mills. When his purchases exceeded the selling of the finished goods, he hedged; altogether he performed this function for Pepperell very economically. In place of the former brokerage and shipping charges of about $2.00 a bale, he estimated that his costs of operating were about those of brokerage alone.

These savings in the purchase of cotton contributed to the mills' profitability during the years of Pepperell's ownership. Lindale has continued to be a profitable plant, in fact the most profitable of all that Pepperell has operated. Until the second World War, its years of profits were somewhat offset by those of losses—during the great depression of the 'thirties; but during the war, with greater production, total profits have mounted to higher levels than ever before.

Pepperell has thus benefited greatly by the addition of the mills in Lindale, which have continued to enjoy the advantages of the earlier period, such as lines of products, buildings and equipment, supervisory force and operatives. Competition naturally has grown more keen, but the reproduction of a plant of the size and quality of Lindale's is so costly that not many companies would run the risk. In the following pages we shall see how Pepperell set up a mill of its own in this third period of its history.

INDUSTRIAL FABRICS IN OPELIKA, 1925–1945

In this section we are dealing with another southern mill, this one located in Opelika, Alabama. It was built by Pepperell before the Lindale mill was acquired by Pepperell. The reader will do well to compare for similarity and dissimilarity the two ventures into the South. The Opelika mill (first unit) was *built* in 1925, whilst the Lindale property was *acquired* in 1926. Opelika was in Alabama, Lindale in Georgia. They produced different types of fabrics and had somewhat different community facilities. But they were both industrial villages and should be studied as such.

When Leonard, the new treasurer, set out to secure a mill in the South, he turned to Alabama, which was still an agricultural State though it had fair promise of industrial development in the cities of Birmingham and Mobile. Cotton was king of crops in Alabama and cotton was waiting for a mill to process it. Surplus workers might be secured from the farms.[51] Railroads were available for the transportation of the finished products. Power might be secured from an existing electric power company and water from an established municipal water works system.

A desirable site was found on the outskirts of Opelika, a small city near the Georgia boundary, about a hundred miles from the incipient metropolis of Atlanta. A group of citizens were willing to assist Leonard. Provided that Pepperell would construct a mill there, they agreed to convey enough land for a mill and its village and to give other inducements. In fact, they gave over 300 acres, as well as $62,500 in cash, and promised no taxes for five years and a low assessment thereafter. At that particular moment the people of Opelika were probably concerned over their future, since the small yarn mill which had been located there since 1900 was experiencing difficulties. In a short time their deal with Pepperell was completed to the satisfaction of both parties. The land was sufficient for a mill and its village, although not extensive enough for the expansion which was to take place in the next decade. Later Pepperell acquired more land, so that by 1941 it owned about 700 acres.[52]

In April of 1925, on the site selected between the Central Railroad of Georgia and the Western of Alabama, Pepperell began the construction of various buildings, with F. P. Sheldon & Son, of Providence, Rhode Island, as engineers, and with a local company, Batson-Cook & Co., as contractors. This choice of engineers marked a departure for Pepperell, since many of its other buildings, as we have noted, had been erected under the supervision of Lockwood, Greene & Co. The original buildings in Opelika included a large mill. In addition, near the railroad tracks it built an opener room and a warehouse. All were completed within a few months.[53] Such was the first unit at Opelika.

In the following years Pepperell added to its capacity in Opelika. In 1929 and 1930 further major construction took place, with the building of a second unit contiguous to the first and also an office building. In 1939 a combined clinic and doctor's building was erected. Altogether, by 1941 there were 348,260 square feet of floor space, approximately the same space as that in Lindale in 1900, when the first two mills and accompanying buildings there had been completed. Instead of increasing manufacturing capacity from about 57,000 spindles to equal Lindale's 100,000 spindles—a desirable size for operations—Pepperell planned, after the second World War, to expand operations in Opelika by adding only a few thousand more spindles and by erecting a bleachery. By the end of the fiscal year 1945, a start had been made on the latter.

Although Pepperell spared no expense in erecting the buildings in Opelika, great economy was practised in the installations of machinery. On the whole, the first mill in Opelika was supplied with at least two sets of old machinery before any new was purchased. In 1926 it was equipped entirely with old machinery from Biddeford, with the exception of four new breaker pickers. (Some of this machinery was not needed in Biddeford because of reduced operations, while some was being replaced with new machinery.) These machines were arranged in the mill so that weaving was on the first floor, spinning on the second, and carding on the third—much like the original plan in Biddeford. In 1928 and 1929 most of this equipment was discarded at Opelika and more old machinery, from Biddeford, Lowell, and Fall River, was installed. Beginning in 1934 some new machines came to replace the old, at first a few experimentally and then many on a regular basis. The new machines included long-draft spinning from Saco-Lowell, warping and spooling from Barber Colman, and narrow looms from Draper. Even so, by June, 1945, some old machinery still remained. All its roving and spinning frames, however, were the improved long- or super-draft.

As far as the machinery was concerned, the second unit at

BARBER COLMAN SPOOLER, 1943

AERIAL SURVEY OF MILLS AND VILLAGE OF OPELIKA, 1941

Opelika followed a pattern similar to that in the first. Originally equipped in late 1929 and early 1930, it was supplied entirely with used machinery from Biddeford and from the Wampanoag, Merchants, and Granite Mills of Fall River. In the following years some of this was replaced with other old, while some was replaced with improved, types of new machinery. Among the latter were roving frames provided by Whitin, instead of by Saco-Lowell which manufactured some of the machinery used in the first mill. By 1943 all of its roving and spinning was long-draft. At the end of this period the second mill at Opelika still had more old machinery than the first.

In the first unit at Opelika, Pepperell started right in with the manufacture of drills and jeans, such as those formerly made in Biddeford. Although in later years Pepperell has made other goods in the first unit at Opelika, such as twills, ducks, osnaburgs, narrow sheetings, and shoe fabrics, more significantly has it experimented with drills and jeans. As the export trade for finer fabrics dwindled, Opelika built up a reputation for making coarser drills and jeans used by manufacturers of abrasives. These manufacturers required long runs of perfect goods. To this end Opelika bent its best efforts and with outstanding success. During the second World War this skill and experience were to be of considerable importance, for vast quantities of these drills and jeans were required in the use of abrasives for finishing precision parts of vital machinery and military equipment.

For the second unit at Opelika, Leonard planned finer types of fabrics, such as had been produced profitably for many years in the Granite Mills of Fall River. I refer to carded broadcloths and, to a less extent, to suitings and dress goods. Finding success in the field of broadcloths rather difficult in the face of the competition of larger mills, this unit of Opelika turned to wide sheetings, finer even than those previously turned out at Biddeford; and by 1941 these wide sheetings had replaced completely the narrower broadcloths, suitings, and dress goods. During the second World War these wide sheetings were turned out in vast quantities to fill government orders. And yet, as it seems, there is considerable doubt as to whether these goods are the best type for the second unit at Opelika.

Pepperell has spent considerable sums on its village at Opelika as well as on its mills. It erected 100 houses for the white workers in 1925, 50 more in 1926, and 56 more in 1934. The company also has built a few three-room cabins for the Negroes. By 1934 there were 217 houses in the village. Two years later more houses were added. All were comfortable one-story houses, with modern systems of plumbing, costing about $300 a room to build. Houses for the operatives had four rooms, with running water in the kitchens and lavatories. Those for the overseers and second hands had six rooms, with running water in the kitchens and bathrooms. For the agent there was an eight-room house. Rents for these houses have been reasonable. The operatives generally have been charged about 50 cents a room per week. While at first the overseers were not charged rent, in time they came to pay about $14 a month; the agent, as in Biddeford and Lindale, paid no rent. These houses, like those in Lindale, have been attractively painted and landscaped. The roads have been paved. During the second World War there was a need for more housing in Opelika. The company assisted the operatives in building houses, setting aside a whole area for individual sites, departing in this respect from its policies for Lindale.[54]

The company has erected other buildings for the workers' convenience in Opelika, although there was less need for some of them than in Lindale, since the center of Opelika was nearer to the mill than Rome was to Lindale. In 1925 a modern school was erected by Pepperell for the first six grades; this was enlarged so that by 1945 the building contained rooms for nine grades as well as a large auditorium. Here the teachers placed more emphasis on the three "R's" and less on the arts than in Lindale. The teachers were better paid, although the children had to supply their own books and materials.

In 1926 Pepperell erected a union church for the use of both the Baptists and the Methodists. This arrangement worked out satisfactorily for almost twenty years, but by 1945 the two had split, with the Methodists retaining the building and the Baptists meeting in the school auditorium until they could erect their own building. In 1927 the company put up a grocery store, a barber shop, and a theatre. In 1940 it added a guest house, where, as in Lindale, two nurses lived and acted as hostesses for visiting Pepperell executives. In 1942 the company built a new day nursery. Thus, within twenty-one years of its beginning, Pepperell's village in Opelika had many facilities for industrial work and general living.

The cost of the mills, equipment, and village in Opelika was considerable. In June, 1930, after five years of operation, Opelika property was valued at more than $1,800,000. In the following years expenditures increased, particularly for new machinery, as we have seen; at the end of this period (in June, 1945) the machinery was valued at about twice as much as in 1930. Against this a depreciation reserve of nearly $2,000,000 has been set up.

In Opelika, Pepperell provided many of the same services as in Lindale, such as a doctor, and a nurse in the clinic and another in the village. It set up an insurance plan which covered life insurance and sickness, accident, and hospitalization benefits. The Boy Scouts prepared a village paper, the *Dragon,* in which to record news of the workers. In one effort Opelika was more successful than Lindale: a woman was found who was admirably suited for running a day nursery, whereas Lindale had none. She developed a wholesome schedule of play, rest, and meals. The nursery started in 1932 in a four-room cottage. At first enrollment was limited by space and by the unwillingness of some children and parents to comply with the rules. By the third year there was a waiting list for the twenty-four places in the school. In 1942 a new building made possible an enrollment of fifty, with many more on the waiting list. Here children, from two to five years of age, were taken care of during the day. This made possible regular attendance at work on the part of many young mothers at a time when the mills needed every possible worker.

The working force in the mills in Opelika had a combination of the characteristics of those in Lindale in its first and second periods. This mixture was natural, since Opelika, which had started much later, could benefit from the strides made in the industry in the South. No longer was it necessary to draw heavily upon trained men from the North. One example of this change was the selection of the first agent, David Singleton Cook. He was born in Georgia, son of a Methodist minister and brother of a member of the construction firm, Batson-Cook & Co. Before his selection by Pepperell he had taken a course in textile engineering at the Philadelphia Textile School and gained experience in several mills in the South, including the West Point Manufacturing Co. In May, 1925, at the time Pepperell hired him, Cook was only twenty-three years old—young indeed for such a responsible position. He continued as agent in Opelika until November, 1931, when he was transferred to New York to be head of the mill department which, from sketches of sales, prepared plans for mill production. Later, in 1935, he was transferred to Biddeford to be the agent there.

The second agent in Opelika, Homer M. Carter, was also a southerner by birth—a Texan. For four years, until June, 1923, he studied electrical engineering at the Georgia School of Technology and then took a year of post-graduate work in mechanical engineering and commerce. Following this he was employed for short periods by two mills. On July 1, 1925, he was hired by Pepperell to be master mechanic in Opelika. In 1927 he was promoted to the position of superintendent, and in 1931 to that of agent. Through the rest of this period Carter has remained in charge in Opelika, his title changing from agent to manager.

Many of the others in positions of responsibility in the mills in Opelika were recruited from those who had gained their training on the job, as were many of those in Lindale during the first period of operation there. Few as yet in Opelika have acquired a technical knowledge at a textile school, although Opelika is situated very close to Auburn, where in 1929 a new school of textile engineering, as part of the Alabama Polytechnic Institute, was established.

The operatives for the mills in Opelika were drawn from sources similar to those in Lindale. They came from the hilly farms on which they had found it difficult to get much of a living for their large families. They came also from other mills in the South. As yet they have not developed into the unified working force which Lindale has produced. Physical conditions have been similar to those in Lindale, except that so far no air-conditioning equipment has been introduced into the mills.

During this period there was growth in the number of workers, because of the addition of a second mill and the operation of two and three shifts. During the second World War, when enough white workers could not be secured, the agent introduced a few colored employees in one room. Although at first there was resentment at their presence, they were soon accepted; however, they have had their own entrance to the mill and have not mixed with the other workers. In numbers the workers grew from 350 at the end of June, 1926, to over 1,000 during the second World War.

Hours of work changed considerably at Opelika during this period. Until the passage of the National Industrial Recovery Act the schedule for a full work-week called for from 55 to 60 hours. Then 40 hours became the standard, which was maintained with the exceptions as already noted for Lindale, until November, 1940, when 48 hours became necessary. During the first seven years of operation, one shift was normal, except for two years when a partial second was added. From 1933 to November, 1940, two shifts were operated with sometimes a partial third. From the latter part of 1940 through June, 1945, three shifts were attempted although at times the agent could not get the necessary operatives.

Rates of pay fluctuated in Opelika as in Lindale. On the whole, Opelika paid less—explainable in part by different types of goods and in part by the lower standards of living in Alabama. The minima set by the national government were the same. Increases for the more skilled jobs were proportionally less. Whereas a watchman increased his hourly wage from 17 to 52.5 cents an hour between 1929 and 1945, a mechanic increased his from 42.5 to 76.5 cents an hour during the same period. For the majority in the mills, in Opelika as elsewhere, more than one worker has been needed to support a family.

The workers in Opelika had a day of celebration during this period: the occasion was the "E" award, when over 4,000 employees, members of their families, and friends gathered in a grove in the village. They were particularly interested since their former assistant agent, now Col. John P. Baum, was the representative of the Army who presented the award of the pennant, which Donald B. Tansill, vice-president and head of Pepperell's sales department, accepted for the company. Mrs. Hilda Wilks accepted the "E" pins. The governor of Alabama served as master of ceremonies and gave an address.[55] Altogether these ceremonies must have aroused the pride of the workers in their achievements and helped to assuage the feeling of social inferiority which many cotton operatives had.

Opelika was like Lindale in another respect. Cotton was purchased locally by a company cotton buyer; in fact, this arrangement was made before that in Lindale. Like Smith in Lindale, R. D. Williams, Jr., in Opelika had been associated with his father in cotton buying for many years. But in the middle 1920's he was willing to give up his independence and work for Pepperell, since the risks of doing business had become greater. On December 7, 1925, he bought the first bale of cotton for Pepperell. His organization was similar to that in Lindale. About half of the cotton was purchased locally, while the longer staple was compress cotton from the Mississippi delta, secured from Memphis. Williams dealt with various cotton firms, including the largest in the country, Anderson, Clayton & Co. of Texas.

With this system of cotton buying, Opelika was able to operate profitably, on the whole, during the period 1926 through 1945. But the mills had their years of losses—before permanent lines of goods were determined and during the great depression of the 1930's. The extent of the profitability of the new lines during normal times cannot be ascertained since the second World War upset the picture so completely. Whether in the long run Opelika will prove more profitable than Lindale cannot be judged as yet, although during the war Opelika was more successful proportionally.

But Opelika proved Leonard's point that 1924 was not too

late to establish cotton mills in the South. To be sure, he built excellent mills and equipped them at low cost with secondhand machinery, which was plentiful in the North where many mills were being liquidated. In time, when the company found out more about the type of operations which would be most successful and when more money could be spared for Opelika, some new machinery was installed. As in Lindale, the workers were content with the established system of operations in the South. In Opelika the workers have had a deep feeling of loyalty to the company, although perhaps it has not been expressed in so many ways as in Lindale. Workers and supervisors have come from the same source, so that difference in nationality has not been a cause of friction as in the North.

* * *

In this third period Pepperell took part in the industrial development of the South. Unfortunately for the North, this took place at its expense, since capacity in the North was reduced while that in the South was maintained at about the same level. The chief losers in this shift were the mill operatives and the citizens of the mill cities in the North. They lost their jobs directly or indirectly through the increasing poverty of the textile cities. But unfortunately much of the blame fell on their own shoulders, since in many instances they had considered the immediate situation at the expense of the long run. The operatives in the North struck for higher wages at times when the industry was fighting to survive. The government of the cities increased taxes so that operations were more expensive. The States added to the regulations making profitable operation still more difficult. This attitude in the North contrasted with the beckoning hands of workers, cities, and States in the South. No wonder that the latter triumphed in the struggle, although the North had the advantage of mills already built.

In the South, Pepperell had the advantage of acquiring one set of mills already operating and producing profitable lines of goods. Pepperell increased the earning capacity in the lines already laid out. Thus its good fortune cannot be attributed entirely to excellent management, but partly to wisdom in consolidating with a company having such a plant. Pepperell also built a new set of mills—at a considerable cost for buildings but with comparatively little cost for machinery. Types of goods which proved profitable were finally determined for these mills, but previously there had been a period of uncertainty, when profits and losses fluctuated with business conditions. These two sets of mills in the South, however, produced greater profits for Pepperell than the mills in the North. Thus, the South enabled Pepperell to continue its prosperous record.

CHAPTER XIV

SUCCESS DURING TROUBLED TIMES

IN THIS THIRD, and latest, period, Pepperell sought and attained success, while business in the United States was encountering great difficulty. During the late 1920's business operated at high levels, but in the 1930's it was depressed, with only a few short periods of recovery. In fact, until the second World War, profits of corporations were low; whether they were lower than during earlier stretches of years we cannot tell, since figures on profits and losses were not extensively gathered until the first World War. We do know, from income tax returns to the Treasury Department, that from 1926 through 1939 about 500,000 corporations had profits of nearly $50,000,000,000, or about $3,600,000,000 annually. During the first three war years, 1940–42, profits totaled more than those in the earlier fourteen—over $52,000,000,000.[1] Thus business enjoyed a few extremely profitable years in this period, as it had during major wars in Pepperell's past two periods.

For the cotton textile industry, conditions were less favorable than for business in general. For the years 1926–38 we find that a company did not have an even chance for success—total losses were greater than total profits for five separate years and for the thirteen as a whole. When we include the following year (1939), during which there was an improvement in business as a result of the outbreak of the second World War, profits became large enough to change the total from red to black. The total was almost $25,000,000, or approximately $1,800,000 annually for about 900 companies. In the following three war years, profits totaled about $657,000,000, an average of about $219,000,000.[2]

In spite of these troubles in business throughout the country, Pepperell operated profitably. This success came as the result of far greater attention to administration, as well as to advertising, selling, producing, and financing, than ever before. In this chapter we shall be concerned with the company's overall efforts to succeed, as demonstrated in its supervision of production and in its coördination of all parts of the company. We shall also consider the rôle of its shareholders, and, finally, the interest of the general public in the company.

MANAGEMENT OF OPERATIONS

In this third period we find Russell H. Leonard, during his first year of office, departing from custom by appointing an assistant treasurer, Amory Coolidge. The latter took the post, at first assisting in the administration of all functions of the company, including the customary production, purchasing, and finance as well as the newer developments in advertising and selling. But within a few years Coolidge's duties became less general, centering on production and purchasing. To other executives were delegated the responsibility for advertising, selling, and finance. Already we have discussed McIntire's direction of advertising and Tansill's direction of selling. In the following section of this chapter we shall consider Crocker's work in accounting. In this present section let us examine Leonard's and Coolidge's administration, particularly of the mills and of the purchasing of cotton.

In these various duties Coolidge, in turn, was assisted by various others. In Boston he soon had a man in charge of technical research, Brackett Parsons, to whom were given the difficult assignments of trying to make the Lowell mills profitable and of finding successful lines of blankets for Biddeford. Coolidge had another man in charge of general purchasing. In New York he placed a coördinator of production and sales. In each of the five plants there were agents in charge of operations and, in three of them, local representatives who bought cotton. Although several of these men changed jobs during this period, this type of organization, started in 1925, has been maintained throughout the period.[3] (The organization in 1944 is shown in Chart III.)

In the first few years of this third period Leonard took an active part in all phases of administration—the policy-formulation, the management operations, and the control. We have noted, for example, that he took part in the selection of a site for a mill in Alabama. He was also the promoter of other changes in the company's property—the acquisition of stock of the Lewiston Bleachery & Dye Works, the consolidation with the Massachusetts Cotton Mills, the purchase of the plant of the Granite Mills in Fall River, and the selling of the water-power property in Maine. Also, as we have seen, he was concerned with the establishment of new advertising and selling methods, which could not be separated entirely from the manufacturing functions.

At the same time, Leonard lent his assistance to efforts to benefit the textile industry as a whole. In 1926 he was one of the first members of the Cotton Textile Institute, Inc., organized for the general purpose of effecting greater coöperation in the industry as a whole. Immediately the Institute set up a staff for many purposes, including the gathering of statistics, the determination of methods of cost accounting, and the finding of new uses for cotton goods. Also, it formed committees of members, according to types of products, to gather statistics and to study cost accounting. In some of these efforts the Institute was successful, although it did not get the full coöperation of all members of the industry.[4]

In time, as Leonard experienced the fulfillment of his original plans, he withdrew from the management and control of Pepperell and participated only in policy-formulation. In 1939, as we have already noted, he delegated part of the policy-formulation also, first during a period of illness and then as a regular matter, after he had set up a policy committee. But none of the five members of this committee had Leonard's pioneering ability, which he had demonstrated in so many ways in his first years with Pepperell as well as in his earlier business career. By 1945 Leonard was visiting his Boston office at 160 State Street only occasionally. He traveled to New York and to the various plants, spending considerable time in the southern units. Thus he kept aware of what was happening within the company. At first hand he could see how successful his executives' policies proved to be.

During his first decade as an executive, first as assistant treasurer and then as vice-president also, Coolidge's duties in the field of management of the mills were heavy. He coöperated with Leonard in the major changes in plants and directed the arrangement of machinery to produce the various types of goods. In the following decade, 1935–45, he was busy equipping the mills with the latest types of machinery. At the end of this period, as we have noted, Pepperell's mills had the advantage of a larger proportion of new machinery than the cotton textile industry as a whole. Coolidge did not direct these changes entirely from his office in Boston. He went to the mills where he talked with men close to the problems. He was welcomed everywhere, although he was naturally quiet and reserved.

Throughout this period one of Coolidge's principal duties was cotton buying. Earlier he had received training in this work as assistant to Bradley. In 1925 he assumed full responsibility for the buying for the mills in Biddeford. At first he had the assistance of R. A. Fairfield, who had been the cotton classer since 1881. But within a few months Fairfield retired, and his place was filled by William Acton, formerly cotton classer in the Stafford Mills in Fall River. Usually early in the crop season both Coolidge and Acton went south to ascertain the nature of the crop. Later, as a result of this trip, Coolidge would buy cotton from buyers and merchants in Boston, who placed the orders in the favored sections. He soon began the practice of protecting the position of the company in the purchasing of cotton. He compared his position in cotton with that in sales of goods and decided the manner in which to cover his purchases. Thus he reduced the element of risk of loss from falling prices of cotton by hedging, as opposed to the company's former speculative policy. Of course hedging removed the possibility of speculative gains, of which former treasurers had taken advantage. The new policy, however, resulted in greater concentration on production problems.

For the mills other than those in Biddeford, Coolidge did not buy cotton. A local man performed that function, although Coolidge had the responsibility for advising on the position to take in purchases. In each of these groups of mills there was a fundamental reason for individual purchasing. The Fall River plant needed a longer staple of cotton for its combed goods than did the other mills. Also, it had been customary for mills in that city to buy directly from buyers or merchants who knew their peculiar requirements. Pepperell was wise in continuing the past practice. For both the Lindale and Opelika mills there was a local supply of short-staple cotton, which could be used for some of the products. For purchases of this cotton, local mill buyers could do better than those removed from the scene; for the longer-staple cotton from a distance the local mill buyers could do as well as Pepperell's cotton buyer in Boston.

Local representatives carried on the work, again under Coolidge's direction, of purchasing rayon and wool for the mills in Biddeford and Fall River. For various other supplies, which were needed in all the plants, the Boston office still acted as the purchasing center; with the addition of new plants, however, these duties were much greater and demanded the attention of a purchasing agent there.

An entirely new job in this period was that of production manager in New York. The holder of this position coördinated production and sales and thus filled the gap which had existed earlier when an independent sales agent had given orders to the mills for goods. To be sure, formerly the sales agent had considered the efficiency of the mills, but of course he had put first the carrying out of commitments with his customers. In the fourteen years from 1931 to 1945, four of Pepperell's men held this new job. Three of them had had previous training in production, while the fourth and latest had had experience in the billing office in Boston. The production manager was expected to give the mills orders for large amounts of goods, rather than a series of small orders, so that the mills could plan their production advantageously.

In this period Pepperell hired more types of outside experts than previously to carry on various aspects of the work connected with production. From the beginning of its operations,

Pepperell has had outside engineering advice. In this period, however, the company changed from Lockwood, Greene & Co. to F. P. Sheldon Co. of Providence, which not only designed mills but also studied methods of job extension. Already we have mentioned the hiring of efficiency experts for the mills in Biddeford, where time and motion studies of particular jobs were made. The records show that the Barnes Textile Associates of Boston and Ralph E. Loper of Fall River were engaged for this work. Although Pepperell's executives in Boston wished to extend time and motion studies to all the mills, Captain Meikleham, the agent in Lindale for a large part of this period, did not want such aid. In a speech at a meeting of the Textile Operating Executives of Georgia in 1932, Meikleham stated that there had never been an efficiency expert in Lindale. But after his death the new agent, accustomed to modern methods, did not put obstacles in the way of finding more efficient ways of producing.[5]

For the short time in which Pepperell ran the mills in Lowell, it hired a styler in the vain attempt to find different types of goods to produce with the equipment on hand. For the other mills this specialist was not necessary, since those mills were producing standard types of goods which were free from the whims of fashion. Thus Pepperell, for many specialized jobs concerned with manufacturing, has turned to a greater variety of experts than ever before. These experts have made possible further concentration of attention on the part of Pepperell's executives, which became advisable when the company increased its plants and functions.

Individual records of the plants, under Coolidge's direction, have already been discussed. When the total achievement of these plants is studied, we find we have an impressive story. Production of goods increased from slightly over 20,000,000 pounds in 1925 to a high of 83,000,000 pounds in 1942 and 1943. This represents an increase of over 300 per cent, although it was the product of only slightly more spindles, which were run about 240 per cent more hours in 1942 than in 1925. In addition, the company purchased goods, some of which were converted in Lewiston, and then sold them. From 1931 to the second World War, sales of converted goods mounted. But in 1941, although the management continued the purchase of some materials for shoe linings, it decided to give up the purchase of wash goods and to devote its working capital to the expansion of the operation of the mills, which it foresaw would be great during the war.

Total cost of production of these goods naturally increased. For wages to employees in the four sets of mills and the bleachery the company spent over $12,000,000 in each of the years 1943, 1944, and 1945. This is in sharp contrast with the $1,300,000 spent in Biddeford in 1925. Wages rose from about 20 per cent of the sales dollar in 1929 to nearly 24 per cent in 1945. Wages, however, were less important than cost of raw materials, which, as in the past, comprised about half the sales dollar. Whereas in 1929 materials and supplies had constituted slightly less than 50 per cent, for the five years 1939–43 they constituted nearly 60 per cent of the sales dollar.

In this third period Pepperell achieved its expansion in production with much greater attention from the executives than previously. Although Leonard devoted some of his time to these problems, he transferred most of them to Amory Coolidge and his staff. Expansion took place rapidly in the early years of this period, but it was slowed down somewhat by nonavailability of working capital. Of this and of other financial and accounting problems we shall learn more in the following pages.

CONTROLLER'S COÖRDINATION

The treasurer of the Pepperell Manufacturing Company delegated still more of his traditional duties during this third period. To a subordinate, called the controller, he assigned his accounting and financial work. When the company's operations became more complicated, he approved the assumption of new duties by the controller.

Traditionally the treasurer himself had handled all the company's accounting and financial problems with the aid of a few bookkeepers. From the beginning there had been practically no problems in accounting, since Pepperell had adopted the prevailing method for large cotton textile companies in New

England and maintained it substantially without change until 1924. There had been, however, many problems in finance. Pepperell's first treasurer, William Dwight, had difficulty in persuading the established families of New England to subscribe to stock. He also had to struggle to supplement these funds with loans from individuals and banks, associated with him in one way or another. But by his efforts, which were finally successful, as well as by profitable operations during the Civil War, Dwight laid a firm foundation for Pepperell's long life. In the second period the treasurers, with a growing accumulation of fixed and working capital, had the job of conserving funds in prosperous years for the lean ones which were sure to follow. This job they accomplished. The company had operated in the black except in two years, 1922 and 1924, and had declared dividends every year. But in neither of the earlier periods did the treasurers formally try to budget expenses. In their heads they kept rough standards of costs of production, and they tempered operations according to the state of business. Semiannually they prepared a statement of condition and of operations for the trustees. With mills in Biddeford and a small force in the countinghouse in Boston, this system had worked well. But in this third period the diversity of operations made the old system inadequate.

In January of 1925 Leonard made Paul E. Crocker controller of the company. Crocker had been one of Pepperell's bookkeepers, and his promotion signalized a change not only in his own status but also in the status of accounting in Pepperell's organization. Instead of a job performed by a clerk, perched on a high stool, who posted entries in cashbook, journal, and ledger, accounting became a task performed by an executive with a staff of assistants, trained to use office machinery. The system of records for the mills in Biddeford was improved, and modern records were installed at Opelika. In 1927, at the time of the merger with the Massachusetts Cotton Mills and the establishment of Pepperell's own selling department, further improvements were necessary. Tabulating machinery was adopted for handling the voluminous records of sales, payrolls, inventories, and commissions. To the accounting work were added various financial controls. Thus, Pepperell's control system was growing at the same time as that of the profession of controllers in the United States. The formation of the Controllers' Institute of America in 1931 recognized this addition to the business world.[6]

By 1930 the controller's organization had assumed much of the shape which it was to bear throughout this third period. In Boston Crocker had an assistant controller, as well as a man in charge of accounting and insurance. He had another man in charge of billing—the recording of data received from the mills for shipments of goods to customers; earlier this type of work had been performed by the selling house. In New York he had a credit manager, who dealt with the standing of customers and their payments for goods—work also formerly performed by the selling house. In time, as we have seen, a third department developed in Boston, the work of which—budget control and economic research—was merged with other work in Boston before the second World War. As the organization chart in Chapter XI shows, by 1944 Crocker had two assistant controllers in Boston, one in charge of general accounting and the other designated as coördinator. There were two other accounting executives—one in charge of sales accounting and the other with unspecified duties. In the New York office there was a sales administrator, assisted by a credit manager.

In addition to this assistance within the company, Crocker had the aid of outsiders. In three cases the same type of aid was secured as in the past, although the individual firm changed. In 1925, for service of a transfer agent and registrar of shares, Pepperell changed from the Boston Safe Deposit and Trust Co. to the Old Colony Trust Co. For advice on legal as well as on other matters Pepperell turned from Charles H. Tyler of Tyler, Tucker, Eames & Wright to Francis R. Boyd of Loring, Coolidge, Noble & Boyd and later of Gaston, Snow, Hunt, Rice & Boyd. In 1935 Pepperell changed its auditing firm from Amos D. Albee, Son & Co., of Boston to Barrow, Wade & Guthrie & Co., whose main office was in New York.

Crocker, in his rôle as collector of figures and budgeteer of expenses, coördinated all financial functions within the company. From the mills, bleachery, and sales offices, figures flowed into the Boston office. To the many types of information which had been received in the past, pertaining to general accounting, insurance, recording of inventories of cotton, and determination of taxes, new types of data (pertaining to sales of goods and inventories of finished cloth) were now added. All were recorded, generally with more analyses of significant aspects than ever before. From the Boston office to other parts of the company went budgets of expenses as well as reports of operations. The Boston office thus became the nerve center of the whole organization.

Crocker submitted detailed analyses of the position of the company to the president-treasurer for use in his annual reports to the shareholders. For the fiscal year 1944–45, for example, this report covered 81 pages. The data were classified under seven subjects—balance sheet, operating results, general overhead, plant, statistical, sales, and inventories. Some of the tables compared the present with the immediately preceding year, while others, such as employees' wages, covered longer periods. In all, they gave an excellent picture of the company's situation.

Although an analysis of each detailed series of figures in these annual reports would throw much light on the company's operations, here we can touch on only a few summary figures from the consolidated balance sheet and the profit and loss statement. Appendix 34 gives figures for assets and liabilities from 1925 to 1945, which show that the company, then as in the past, was in excellent condition. Funds were adequate for permanent and working capital from shareholders' subscriptions and accumulated surplus, except during the seven years when the company borrowed from the banks. On June 30, 1937 and 1938, the notes payable amounted to $3,500,000. But the company's policy, as in the past, was to be free whenever possible from any conceivable control by bankers. In January of 1936, for example, Crocker pointed out to the salesforce the advisability of selling as much as possible to get funds so that the company might be clear of bank loans by the end of the fiscal year.[7] In this effort the salesmen succeeded. Also, this policy of financial independence accounted for the delay in equipping the mills in Alabama with new machinery. Not until the last five years of this period were funds available for additions in Opelika and in the other mills.

During this period Pepperell was able to maintain high net current assets. In the depression year of 1932, for example, the current assets were over $9,200,000 while current liabilities were only $91,000. This shows a remarkable achievement for a difficult year. By 1945 current assets had expanded to over $22,500,000, while current liabilities were $7,800,000. Thus, while net current assets were higher in the later year, the ratio of current assets to current liabilities was lower.

Each year, for the president-treasurer, Crocker has prepared operating figures which have been summarized in Appendix 37. We find that the company had a much better record than the industry as a whole. Although there were losses in five years of difficulty in the industry, when cotton prices fell precipitously—1925, 1931, 1932, 1935, and 1938—there were profits in the other years, so that the company gained in all $17,000,000 or over $800,000 annually.

To a large extent this fluctuation in returns has been outside the company's control. Ever since the government set up rules for making out income taxes, companies have been forced to follow them, at least for reporting to the government. Until 1925 the government ruled that inventories be valued at cost but thereafter at cost or market whichever was lower; this eased somewhat the fluctuations in value. But the inventory policy was based on the principle of first in, first out, which resulted in great oscillations in profits when prices were changing rapidly. When prices were rising, for example, apparent profits were increased by the inclusion of unrealizable appreciation of value of inventories. On the other hand, when prices were falling, book profits were reduced or wiped out by unrealized inventory losses. This resulted in unfortunate conditions for companies, since they might be unable to keep the unduly high profits in some years to tide themselves over losses in other years. For the government it meant that taxes fluctuated violently—with less coming in during the years when income was most needed. But near the end of this period the government allowed a different method of valuing inventory—on a last-in, first-out basis, often designated as LIFO.[8] At the beginning of the fiscal year 1941–42 Pepperell adopted this method, which promises to make possible a more even record of profits in the future. In fact, profits may assume the regular pattern of the earlier two periods, when treasurers valued inventory as they pleased and set up reserves for future contingencies, instead of following the erratic pattern of 1920 to 1941.

Pepperell's profits have been reduced by unusually heavy taxes. This was particularly true during the very prosperous war years. Its peak of taxes was over $5,000,000 in 1944, which was about five times the maximum during the first World War and about twenty-five times the highest figure immediately after the Civil War.

But altogether, the years 1925–45 have proved successful financially. Through the controller the directors have been able to keep close control over accounting and financing. This control has been made necessary partly by the fact that the profit margin on a yard or pound of goods has been very slight. Of course, many of the acts and reforms instituted by the controller have been actually conceived by the directors and other officers of the company. But it is significant for Pepperell and for business as a whole that an effective coördinating official should occupy a prominent place under the president-treasurer, who himself has been too busy with over-all policies to give much attention to details of control.

SHAREHOLDERS' SATISFACTION

As in the past the shareholders allowed the trustees free rein. Generally not more than fifty attended the annual and special shareholders' meetings in Biddeford—a handful from Pepperell's Boston office with the rest drawn locally, including, indeed, some of the operatives. The latter were interested in the opportunity of seeing the officers as well as in the free luncheon which followed the meeting.

During these twenty-one years the shareholders continued

to vote for the same trustees, until death or old age removed them from the ballot, as Appendix 10 shows. Only one trustee dropped out for business reasons. It had been the practice to include on the board a member of the selling organization, and, in 1926, when Pepperell was in the process of changing from an outside selling house to its own selling department, Philip Y. DeNormandie, a trustee who was also a partner in the selling house, resigned. In DeNormandie's place Russell H. Leonard was elected. The usual occupation of the trustees, who were active in business outside the company, was a combination of legal work and trust management, a combination which became common in the middle period, namely, 1870–1924. There were, however, two trustees who had retired from the position of treasurer of a cotton textile company, William Amory of Pepperell and Edward Lovering of the Massachusetts Cotton Mills. Both of these men contributed advice about management which they had gathered during their years of responsibility. After Lovering's death in 1941, Amory Coolidge was made a trustee. After the death of another trustee, in 1943, E. Kent Swift, the chief executive of the Whitin Machine Works, was suggested. His selection marked a further change from previous policies. He was not a Harvard, but a Williams College, graduate. He was engaged in business not in Boston, but in the industrial village of Whitinsville, a short distance from Worcester, Massachusetts. He represented neither the legal nor the investment field, but the industrial. He had charge of the manufacture of textile machinery. Thus, at the end of this period the composition of Pepperell's board was different from that at the beginning, with greater emphasis on industry than before.

Generally these various trustees, as Appendix 10 shows, were directors of the Pepperell corporation which had the same name as the voluntary association. At first there were three directors drawn from the old Massachusetts Cotton Mills; within a month two of them were replaced by two officers of the Pepperell Manufacturing Company. In 1927 the number of directors was increased to eight—the seven trustees of the voluntary association with the addition of Edward Lovering. The directors individually held one share of stock of the corporation and the association held the remainder. In 1927 the board of directors of the corporation became more important than the trustees of the association. One indication is that the trustees ceased receiving fees for attending meetings, while the directors received $20 for each meeting. Thus, Pepperell's important board of directors was selected in a roundabout fashion by the shareholders of the association.

Although the men on both of these boards have been called upon for advice concerning important matters, they have paid little attention to regular affairs. Ordinarily they have met four times a year—the number of meetings necessary to declare quarterly dividends. In only one year were they called together several times to talk over unusual business, namely, the merger with the Massachusetts Cotton Mills.

During a large part of this third period, from 1924 to 1945, Pepperell's shareholders were of the same type as in the earlier periods. They were Yankees who continued to hold their shares throughout their lives and then passed them on to their children, who in turn might pass them on to their children. In 1924 Pepperell had between 1,600 and 1,700 shareholders for its 76,650 shares. Over a third, or 600, of these shareholders lived near the mills, in Biddeford and Saco. Generally their holdings were small, but a few, such as the local savings banks and an insurance company as well as the heirs of a former agent and superintendent, held large blocks. In all, there were six subscribers in Biddeford and Saco who held 500 or more shares. In these two places the shareholders held slightly more than 20,000 shares. This is a surprising proportion of the total when one considers how small the local capital must have been. It indicates the extent of the local esteem for Pepperell as an investment, an esteem which had been growing and reached its zenith in the last years of the middle period, 1870–1924.

Boston was the business address of the second largest group of shareholders, about 440, many of whom undoubtedly lived in the suburbs. Altogether they held over 37,000 shares, or almost half of the number outstanding. They owned, on the average, larger blocks than the local Maine group. Among them were thirteen who held 500 or more shares. Elsewhere in Maine and Massachusetts there were about 400 holdings aggregating almost 10,000 shares. Outside these two States there were only about 200 owners of stock with 9,000 shares. In fact, there was only one person outside Maine and Massachusetts who held more than 500 shares. All these facts indicate that the ownership of Pepperell shares at the beginning of this period was not only local but was concentrated near the mills or near the counting room.

In 1924 there was a large percentage of small shareholders. About 76 per cent of the total number held less than 50 shares, almost 12 per cent held 50 to 100, and another 12 per cent from 100 to 500 shares. As we have already indicated there were only 10 shareholders, or less than one per cent, who owned 500 or more shares. Of these shareholders, only two held 1,000 or more shares. Thus we see that since the year 1915, when three new shares were given for one old, there had been an increase in the number of the smaller and a whittling down of the larger holders.

At the beginning of this period the proportion of shareholders who were interested chiefly in a regular return on their investment had declined slightly from the peak reached in the previous period. In 1924, however, about 57 per cent of the shareholders were in the two classifications of women and trustees and these two classifications held the majority of the shares. In addition there was a small proportion of institutional holdings included among the miscellaneous classification. Thus it is clear that Pepperell's shares were still considered a good investment for those who wanted income rather than speculative profit. This situation continued throughout the third period of Pepperell's operations, in spite of fluctuations in dividends.

To this group of Pepperell shareholders were added in 1926 the stockholders of the Massachusetts Cotton Mills, who exchanged eight of their shares in that company for five of Pepperell's. Naturally these stockholders fell in classifications somewhat similar to Pepperell's. The majority lived in Massachusetts, where the old set of mills and the counting room were located. In 1926 there were about 1,600 stockholders of the 50,000 shares of $100 par. Of this number, 82 per cent held less than 50 shares, 11 per cent held from 50 to 100, 6 per cent held from 100 to 500, and less than one per cent (in fact only 6 persons) held 500 or more shares. There was therefore a greater scattering of small blocks and a smaller concentration of large holdings than was true of Pepperell. This was to be expected, since the Massachusetts Cotton Mills had not had so successful a record. Among these stockholders, men were a larger percentage of the total than among Pepperell's, although women and trustees were still in the majority. There were also more brokers holding stock than in Pepperell—25, who together held over 1,000 shares.

During the following years changes took place in the ownership of Pepperell's shares. By 1934 Maine's shareholders had declined both in numbers and in relative position; they were second to those in Massachusetts, who represented about half the total number. Third in importance were those in New York. These changes came as the result of reduction in capacity in Biddeford, the opening of a sales office in New York, and Pepperell's admittance to trading on the New York Curb Exchange as an unlisted security on November 23, 1927. From 1934 to 1945 the tendency toward wider holding of shares became more apparent. In 1945 there were 2,750 shareholders. About 36 per cent of them lived in Massachusetts, 16 per cent in New York, and 14 per cent in Maine. The remainder were scattered over 39 States, the District of Columbia, Canada, and England.

Of these shareholders there were many in 1945 with smaller holdings than earlier—about 86 per cent held not more than 50 shares. Nine per cent held between 51 and 100, 5 per cent from 101 to 500, and less than one per cent or only 10 held more than 500 shares. Most of these largest holdings were new, being blocks bought by three of Pepperell's officers and by four brokerage houses.

Among the various types of shareholders there was little change in the relative importance of women and estates. Although the number of men had shrunk slightly, the number of corporations, brokers, and miscellaneous types had increased, with the result that the emphasis on regular returns was about the same. In spite of the depression Pepperell was still a good investment in the eyes of its owners.

Prospective shareholders, as reflected in the prices for shares, have not appreciated Pepperell's value; in fact, they have underrated it as they did the stock of most cotton textile companies in this period. In 1932, as Appendix 38 shows, the prices for shares touched a low of $15.75. In 1945 they reached a high of $231. For eight years the prices were below par—a record quite contrary to that in the previous two periods.

To be sure, Pepperell's shares have never (up to 1947) been listed on any stock exchange. For the first few years of this period they were sold over the counter by brokers in Boston. But in 1927, as we have seen, they were placed among the unlisted shares of the New York Curb Exchange, a move which might have promised better prices with the opportunity for more regular trading. Shareholders seem to have held onto their shares and to have prevented any such popular demand for Pepperell's stock as has existed, for example, in the case of American Telephone and Telegraph Co. shares. In the calendar year 1928 there were sales in only twenty-eight weeks on the Curb. Sales in one week of over 4,000 shares brought the annual total to over 7,000 shares. Four years later, during the depression year of 1932, Pepperell's shares were also traded in irregularly in New York. Sales took place in 31 weeks, 1,300 shares being sold in one week alone. The total for the year was less than 5,000 shares. In the calendar year 1944, when prices were higher, sales took place weekly, ranging from 25 to 500 shares. That year's total was slightly more than 8,000 shares.[9] Thus, basing our conclusion on evidence for three years and on the slight change in numbers of shareholders, we find that there have been comparatively few sales of shares.

In 1945, shortly after the end of this third period, each of Pepperell's shares was split into five shares of $20 par in the hope that there would be more regular trading and a wider distribution so that the shareholders, if they desired, could dispose of their holdings more easily. Immediately, transactions were at new highs in number sold as well as in prices, but by July, 1946, transactions had settled down to smaller fluctuations at a level of about 1,100 shares weekly, with prices ranging from $40 to $51.25 for the new $20 shares. Thus, the new shares changed considerably from the old.[10]

Prices of shares naturally have been influenced by Pepperell's dividend record, which is given in Table 10. Ever since 1852 Pepperell has maintained a record of paying dividends every calendar year, although in one fiscal year, 1932–33, it failed to pay. It has therefore achieved the longest known record of any existing cotton textile company in the United States. In fact, of all the companies whose stock is traded on either the New York Stock Exchange or the Curb Exchange, its record apparently ranks second only to the Pennsylvania Railroad, which is ahead by five years.[11]

In the first six and a half years of this third period Pepperell's shareholders received dividends at the rate of $8.00 annually, first in semiannual and then in quarterly payments. But thereafter the company did not pay regular amounts, particularly in the depression years of the 1930's. In the year 1936–37 it declared dividends of $16 a share, because of federal regulation which penalized the withholding of profits from stockholders. Dividends averaged $7.00 per $100 share. But for shareholders whose inheritance had been kept, as a few had for several generations,[12] these dividends meant an average annual return during this period of about $29.50 per $100 of original investment. This average was slightly more than that of $25.50 for the middle period, but less than that of $38.80 per $100 invested in the first period. For the three periods, dividends for each original subscriber of one share of $500 in 1850 have totaled $11,674.70. This is a much larger return than if a man had lent $500 to a bank in 1850 at the prevailing interest rate of 6 per cent. Total interest payments in 96 years would have been only $2,880 at simple interest and somewhat more at compound. Pepperell's original subscribers have been very fortunate indeed. Later stockholders also benefited, but the degree of their return depended on when they joined the

TABLE 10

DIVIDENDS, 1924–45

Date Payable	Amount per Share[a]	Date Payable	Amount per Share
Feb. 2, 1925	$4.00	Aug. 15, 1936	$3.00
Aug. 1, 1925	4.00	Dec. 15, 1936[f]	5.00
Feb. 1, 1926	4.00	Feb. 15, 1937	3.00
Aug. 2, 1926	4.00	June 28, 1937[f]	5.00
Feb. 1, 1927[b]	4.00	Aug. 16, 1937	3.00
Sept. 1, 1927[c]	4.00	Dec. 5, 1938	1.00
Mar. 1, 1928	4.00	Feb. 15, 1939	2.00
Sept. 1, 1928	4.00	Aug. 15, 1939	2.00
Mar. 1, 1929	4.00	Feb. 15, 1940	3.00
Sept. 3, 1929	4.00	Aug. 15, 1940	3.00
Jan. 2, 1930[d]	2.00	Feb. 15, 1941	3.00
Apr. 1, 1930	2.00	Aug. 15, 1941	4.00
July 1, 1930	2.00	Feb. 16, 1942	4.00
Oct. 1, 1930	2.00	Aug. 15, 1942	4.00
Jan. 2, 1931	2.00	Nov. 16, 1942[g]	2.00
Apr. 1, 1931	2.00	Feb. 15, 1943	2.50
July 1, 1931	1.50	May 15, 1943	2.50
Oct. 1, 1931	1.00	Aug. 16, 1943	2.50
Jan. 2, 1932	1.00	Nov. 15, 1943	2.50
May 16, 1932	1.00	Feb. 15, 1944	2.50
Aug. 15, 1933[e]	3.20	May 15, 1944	2.50
Feb. 15, 1934	3.00	Aug. 15, 1944	2.50
Aug. 15, 1934	3.00	Nov. 15, 1944	2.50
Feb. 15, 1935	3.00	Feb. 15, 1945	2.50
Aug. 15, 1935	1.50	May 15, 1945	2.50
Feb. 15, 1936	1.50		

[a] Par value of shares, $100.

[b] Number of shares increased from 76,680 to 107,930 outstanding on Dec. 13, 1926, by granting 31,250 newly created shares to stockholders of Massachusetts Cotton Mills, Inc., who previously had held 50,000 shares at $100 par of Massachusetts Cotton Mills. By June 30, 1932, 7,900 shares were in the treasury and only 100,000 outstanding. For the remainder of this period, capital outstanding was $10,000,000.

[c] Dividend dates changed from first of February and August to the first of March and September.

[d] Quarterly dividends on the first of January, April, July, and October.

[e] Semiannual dividends in the middle of February and August.

[f] Special.

[g] Quarterly dividends in the middle of February, May, August, and November.

Source: MS. PMC, Trustees' records, 1924–45.

fortunate band. Some of the income from Pepperell stock undoubtedly has furnished capital for other industries and thus helped the expansion of the country. Average returns on such investments were probably much lower than those from Pepperell.

Pepperell's original subscribers and their descendants were also fortunate in their gain in capital and in their mergers with other companies. After their first promise to pay $500 for each share, they have been called upon only once to subscribe further amounts. In 1871 they were given the first opportunity to subscribe to 400 new shares of $500 par, which brought the capital up to $1,200,000. When Pepperell merged with Laconia in 1899, Pepperell's stockholders received seven new shares of $100 par in place of one old one valued at $500. Thus for each original share they now had $700 in the company. Laconia's stockholders had a less fortunate deal, receiving as they did less than the par value of their old stock in the new. In 1915 all Pepperell's stockholders received three new shares in place of one old share of the same par value. Thus the original subscriber's one share increased to a value of $2,100. When Pepperell merged with the Massachusetts Cotton Mills in 1926, the stockholders of the latter received less than the par value of their old holdings for new shares in Pepperell. Pepperell's subscribers have been fortunate in the steps which have increased the company's capital from $1,000,000 in 1857 to $10,000,000 outstanding in the period from 1924 to 1945.

Throughout this third period Pepperell's shareholders have received annual printed reports from the treasurer, who has included a discussion of the company's problems as well as the usual balance sheet and income statement. Thus the shareholders have had facts on which to base their judgment of the merit of their officers, directors, and trustees.

Pepperell's shareholders have had good reasons for their complacency with the management of their company. They have been well rewarded in dividends and in increases in capital value. During this third period, however, many of the local Maine shareholders have been lost, undoubtedly because of the cuts in capacity in the Biddeford mills and the inclusion of mills in other locations. But new shareholders scattered throughout the country have come into the company, so that in 1945 the company had an almost national rather than merely a local coverage. Although the industry has become very speculative, Pepperell's shareholders have considered their holdings not in that light but as good, conservative investments.

THE PUBLIC'S INTEREST

During this period of shift from financial to national capitalism many companies have recognized the wisdom of informing the general public about their activities. They have realized that, if they pursued their past policies of keeping much of their business to themselves, they would be more vulnerable to attack than if they disseminated widely a knowledge of their operations. A few large companies have not yet moved far enough in this direction and have caused business in general still to be regarded with suspicion.

From the beginning of his régime in 1924, Leonard took steps to inform the public about Pepperell, although he appointed no separate public relations executive. His efforts have been rather to inform the groups associated with the company in one way or another, the idea being that their knowledge would spread to wider and wider circles. In his first year in office Leonard started the practice of preparing for the shareholders an annual report, which would give them a good picture of what was taking place in their company. This report included a discussion of the company's problems and some interesting pictures as well as the usual balance sheet, income statement, auditor's report, and list of officers and trustees. In the following years he added material on advertising and sales, appealing to the shareholders somewhat as consumers. These annual reports reached circles outside the shareholder group. Parts were reproduced in the employees' and customers' magazines as well as in newspapers and trade magazines. The financial analysis was included in financial year books. By these means knowledge of Pepperell's operations and financial condition became available to anyone who might be interested. Near the end of this period the excellence of these annual reports was recognized. In 1945 the *Financial World* awarded Pepperell the second prize, and in 1946 the first prize, for an outstanding annual report of the preceding year in the cotton textile industry.

Although Pepperell began the publication of employee magazines primarily for the purpose of improving morale among the employees, these house organs have served to increase the public's knowledge of the company. Since 1937, under the direction of the advertising department, the company has issued the *Pepperell Sheet* for employees in the three northern plants. For those in the southern plants it has assisted in the publication of a newspaper and a small news sheet. In these papers there has been information concerning all aspects of the business but particularly production, including news about the individuals in the mills. The company has also prepared other information for employees, such as special booklets during the second World War in which the employees' contribution to the war effort was stressed. These employee publications have reached audiences beyond the mills—people in the local communities. Indirectly perhaps they have assisted in building up better relations between labor and management generally.

Another company publication, created to assist in selling the goods, has also increased public knowledge about Pepperell. In 1926 the advertising department began the preparation of the *Pepperell News Sheet,* distributing it to the salesforce as well as to retailers, wholesalers, manufacturers, and other purchasers of Pepperell's goods. Persons in these outlets have reached and have influenced many others. It is easy to see that a sales clerk in a department store may pass along to potential consumers information about the company's goods. Thus through this *News Sheet,* directly and indirectly, Pepperell has reached a large number of persons throughout the country.

By its advertising campaigns Pepperell has not only intensified the effect of information which may have been given about the company by local stores, but also made sure that a large proportion of the population in the United States has heard about Pepperell and its goods. Although early campaigns were directed chiefly at women, some of the later ones have been

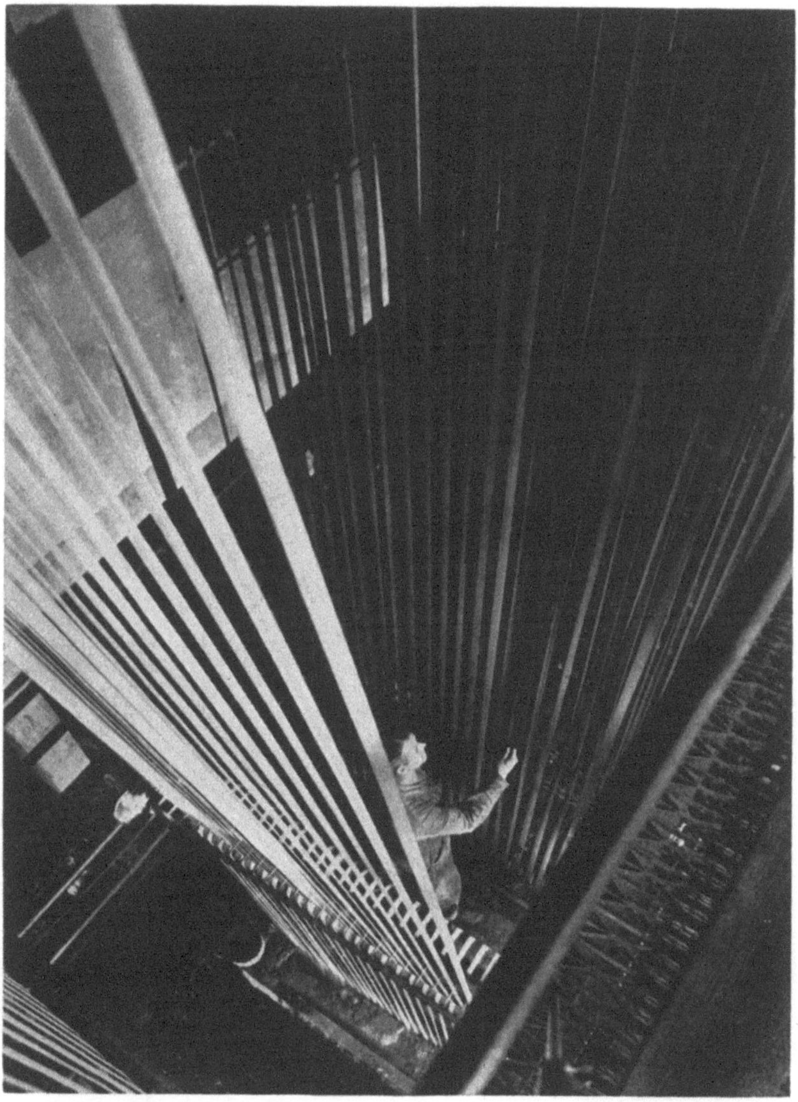

INDIGO DYEING RANGE IN LINDALE, 1945

DISPLAYING THE "E" AWARD IN LINDALE, 1943

aimed at both men and women through magazines read by both.

In other ways Pepperell has spread information about itself. In the middle period we found that the company was responsible for a history, *A Romance of Pepperell,* which caught the attention of the public, particularly business men and students of business. In the third period the company sponsored a study of the foreign market for American textiles called *The Cotton Textile Industry of Far Eastern Countries.* It also assisted in the publication of a story of the company, *The Men and Times of Pepperell,* written by Dane Yorke, librarian in Biddeford.[13] Most recently the company has coöperated in this present volume, which is an independent attempt to review Pepperell's history. Various executives, moreover, have written articles or given speeches which have been published in trade magazines and newspapers. These have filtered through the cotton textile industry to many people associated with it in one way or another. Also, general interest in Pepperell has become so apparent that newspapers carry practically any available bit of news about the company.

Public knowledge of Pepperell has thus grown in two decades. At the end of the first World War few outside the mills and the counting room knew about the company even though they were enjoying its products. Now, after the second World War, a large proportion of the people of this country know about Pepperell.

* * *

In this third period Pepperell has succeeded, while many others have limped along or fallen by the wayside. There seems, however, to be no magic formula that others can apply; rather, Pepperell's good fortune appears to be a combination of several advantages. Certainly one of them has been its wise choice of executives and Leonard's welding of them into an effective team. Not least conspicuous of the policies of Leonard is the free play which he gives to the executives immediately under him. He lets them burn their fingers so that they may learn their own lessons and learn them well.

In this period Pepperell has been alert to timely action in making needed changes. It established a policy of advertising a quality product much earlier than most textile companies did. It was one of the leaders in establishing its own selling department. Although lagging in the development of mills in the South, the company dared to build a set of mills there as well as to acquire another set which had been running profitably for about thirty years. It went against the tide in entering Fall River. In addition it was willing to reduce capacity in Biddeford when costs proved higher there than elsewhere. The natural procedure would have been to continue running the old machinery as long as there was any return on the investment. The company was bold enough to demand the ownership of the bleachery to which it had been sending many of its goods. In all, these were startling efforts which have not escaped public notice.

But all these bold policies would not have been successful without careful control of operations. In Boston the company has had three men in charge of important aspects—advertising, production, and expenses. In New York it has had another in charge of selling. All four have worked together for the success of their company.

As in the past the executives have been fortunate in having a free hand to carry out their policies. Neither the boards of trustees and directors nor the shareholders have interfered. They have been satisfied with the quality of the management as evidenced by its reports and dividends. Although this state might have proved dangerous, instead it has worked to increase the executives' initiative and responsibility.

Through the efforts of many executives the company has been successful in building up good public relations. Although some of these efforts have been conspicuous, others have merely depended on the day-to-day actions of all connected with the company.

Arbitrarily, I have closed the history of the Pepperell Manufacturing Company at the end of its fiscal year 1944–45, which occurred about the same time as the ending of the second World

War and with the passing of a century since the original charter was secured. But this third period has not yet run its full course, since no fundamental change in its management has occurred.

PEPPERELL FABRICS ®

CHAPTER XV

EPILOGUE

In 1945 the Pepperell Manufacturing Company completed nearly a century of successful operation—an unusual record in the cotton textile industry in America. The reasons for Pepperell's long record of success are many. In fact, only after a study of its operations during three periods, the first from 1850 to 1870, the second from 1870 to 1924, and the third from 1924 to 1945, can we gather what the most important factors were. We find explanations in the four principal fields of operation—procurement, production, sales, and finance. Underlying all these, however, were the character and ability of its executives.

Undoubtedly Pepperell has been blessed with many executives who have been extremely well fitted to their jobs and their times. Three of them in particular have contributed greatly to Pepperell's success. At the beginning, when it was wise to have a treasurer with excellent financial resources, William Dwight served Pepperell for sixteen years. In the middle period, when it was advisable to have a treasurer who combined conservatism in methods of handling the company's resources with boldness in purchasing cotton, the directors chose George Dexter, who continued in office from 1877 to 1901. In the third period, when it was imperative to break away from the established ways of carrying on a cotton textile company, particularly in merchandising, the trustees sought out Russell H. Leonard, who by 1945 had served Pepperell for twenty-one years. These three men are the ones who have been principally responsible for Pepperell's success. For shorter times six other treasurers have carried on the work of the company, but the extent of their contributions is not so easily seen as in the case of the three who served longer.

During the first two periods the treasurer was the only executive of the company, except when an assistant treasurer was appointed to be trained as successor. In the third period this situation changed decidedly. Leonard introduced a number of executives—vice-presidents and assistant treasurers—to whom he delegated much responsibility. These men developed their specific departments so that the treasurer's office in Boston could no longer be called a countinghouse. It housed, instead, a group of departmental executive offices, filled with numbers of employees in various capacities. In this respect, in the third period the character of the company changed materially from that which had prevailed in the two previous periods.

Throughout the company's history the treasurer has been concerned with the procurement of the most important material for the mills—cotton. William Dwight combined purchasing from merchants in the South and North with dealing with his son's firms, which purchased in the South for a number of years and then carried on business in the North. Pepperell thus benefited from the preference given it. In the second period the treasurers developed a system of giving orders in Boston to brokers or merchants, through whom Pepperell could get cotton economically. The treasurers did not hedge their purchases but, in constant touch with the market, took risks which resulted in profits. In the third period Pepperell secured cotton in several ways. The president-treasurer turned over the responsibility for cotton purchasing to a vice-president, who directed purchasing for all mills but personally bought only for the mills in Biddeford. In the South the buyers obtained cotton from neighboring fields, where they could secure cotton more economically than from a distance. In this period the company hedged its purchases, in order to concentrate further on problems of production. In all three periods Pepperell has taken full advantage of existing opportunities for purchasing cotton.

In its production of goods Pepperell has operated wisely. It has pursued a policy of securing excellent machinery at favorable times and prices. It has also been moderate in expansion, refraining for many years from building when mills in the South were challenging those in the North. The purchase of other plants has been advantageous. In 1899 it merged with its sister company, the Laconia Company. In the third period capacity was reduced in Biddeford and increased elsewhere by the building of mills in the South, by the merging with the Massachusetts Cotton Mills which had a southern plant, and by the purchase of mills in Fall River and the dye works in Lewiston. By 1945 the company had a capacity of slightly more than 300,000 spindles. This was only a few thousand more than in 1924, but they were distributed in diverse locations where operating conditions were favorable.

Pepperell has sought to make an excellent line of goods. At first it produced shirtings, drills, and jeans, which few other mills made. Soon it added wide sheetings, which had recently been introduced in the industry. These lines were continued throughout the second period, although shirtings declined in importance. It added sateens, used for undergarments, which comparatively few mills at the time were producing. But, during the latter part of this middle period, many mills elsewhere started to produce all these goods, and in the South they were made much more cheaply than in the North. By 1924, Pepperell needed to change its lines of goods or to produce them in the South where costs were lower. In the third period Pepperell adopted both alternatives. In Biddeford the old type of sheeting continued with the addition of a finer weave. The company began to manufacture blankets, some entirely of cotton and some a mixture of cotton, rayon, and wool. The elimination of the other types of goods in Biddeford and the transfer of production of twilled goods to one mill in Opelika followed. In Fall River finer goods, combed sheetings, marquisettes, and rayon lining and underwear fabrics comprised the line. Lindale continued the production of fabrics for work and play clothing. In Opelika, in the second mill, combed sheetings were produced. Thus altogether, in the third period Pepperell produced a diversified line of staple goods for house furnishings, work and play clothing, undergarments and linings, and fabrics for industrial uses.

Pepperell has chosen able men to direct the operation of these mills. At the beginning, it selected an agent who was assisted by a group of overseers. In the second period, it had the services for many years of an agent, who supervised the operations of both Pepperell and Laconia, and also of a superintendent, who attended to the details of Pepperell's operation. The overseers continued to be the bosses of their rooms. But in the third period, the pattern for production changed considerably. From the early industrial system, with its vestiges of both petty and mercantile capitalist systems, it changed to a system of industrial capitalism. Scientific management was introduced. The agents, superintendents, and overseers were assigned specialized duties. But efforts were successfully made to gain their full coöperation as well as that of the employees.

Throughout its history Pepperell has had a group of industrious employees. During the first period, they were largely Yankee girls. But in the second period, French Canadians came to constitute the majority, and this predominance of French workers in Biddeford has continued in the third period. In the old textile center of Fall River there was a different mixture, with French Canadians and Portuguese leading. In Lewiston the employees were similar to those in Biddeford. In the two plants in the South, Pepperell has drawn from the local supply of labor—from the farms which for generations had been tilled by Scotch-Irish stock. When given an opportunity for cash wages and the possibility of improved living conditions, these southerners have been eager to grasp both. Moreover, they have proved coöperative. They have provided a reservoir from which the supervisory group has been secured. On the whole, Pepperell has been fortunate in its employees; they have been industrious and coöperative, thus contributing to the company's success and their own well-being.

Throughout its history Pepperell has sought aggressive selling of its goods. For the first two periods it employed outside agencies for this function. It chose houses of established merit which were expanding and which would push the sales of Pepperell's goods. But in its experience with both selling houses a second generation proved less able than the first, and in time changes became necessary. At the beginning of the third period Pepperell's new treasurer saw the need for a complete change in distribution. He wanted to direct the selling himself. He also wanted to try the use of analyses of the market and advertising that would reach the consumers—functions which the old selling houses had not been accustomed to perform. Fortunately for Pepperell its treasurer instigated these changes in advance of many other companies, thus gaining a head start in the mad rush to become well known to consumers in the United States. Having its own selling department Pepperell changed from the former method of distributing chiefly to few types of outlets—wholesalers, manufacturers, and exporters—to a more telling method of distributing to a wide variety of outlets—wholesalers, retailers, manufacturers, converters, institutions, chains and mail-order houses, government agencies, and exporters. In fact, it distributed to outlets which provided a means of reaching a wider group of consumers throughout the United States and in some foreign countries. Thus on the selling side Pepperell has been progressive, particularly in the third period.

Throughout its first three periods of existence Pepperell has been independent financially. At the beginning, its treasurer had to struggle to get funds with which to operate in the manner which he thought desirable. But he succeeded. In the following two periods, the treasurers have generally had ample funds with which to carry out any changes which they deemed advisable. In the first period, they were able to combine generous dividends with additions to reserve funds. In the second period, the treasurers, still paying generous dividends, conserved their resources so that the company was able to ride out the depressions with hardly any visible decline. But towards the end of this period, the company experienced increasing difficulty in maintaining a continuous record of profits. In the third period, Pepperell operated with years of profits and losses, although the average was still very high.

Throughout the whole period, Pepperell has had a contented group of stockholders. They have given the treasurer and directors or trustees the power to carry out the policies which they have thought right. This viewpoint was the result initially of successful operation and it has been continued when a majority of the stockholders became interested in good returns rather than in speculative risks. In their own passive way the stockholders have therefore contributed to the strength of the company.

In all four fields of operation, then, Pepperell has been managed with skill. As a result its record is outstanding not only for the textile industry but for the whole industrial pattern of America. Indeed, we see in Pepperell an excellent example of a middle-sized company which, with a simple organization, has steadily gone forward. To no outside forces, such as the tariff, can we attach the principal causes for its success. The explanation lies in the series of adjustments, worked out by the executives, to take advantage of changing conditions. In other words, the explanation lies in business administration.

In the pages of this history we have caught glimpses of petty capitalists and have seen the mercantile capitalists give up the ghost in favor of a new system. On the whole, the Pepperell history is the story of a part of that new system—industrial capitalism. This story is all the richer in view of the fact that the competitive phase of that system did not end in disaster but was transformed into financial industrial capitalism (or financial industrialism), in which the lessons of a free competitive régime were fully learned. Efficiency in production and distribution was studied by the executives and mastered, with the result that financial success was assured. As we might infer, then, there was no need to go to Wall Street or State Street for guidance or financial rescue. Indeed, in this story there is no chapter devoted to financial capitalism, or the control by investment bankers. When at some future time the threads of Pepperell's history are again taken up and woven into a new story, there will doubtless be a chapter entitled "Pepperell in the Régime of National Capitalism." Though that phase of growth had some feeble beginnings before 1945, our terminal date, it was largely confined to labor and taxes. The fiber of Pepperell is tough and pliable and we may watch with eager expectation the future adjustments of the company, as social pressures and political necessities challenge its executives.

APPENDICES

APPENDIX 1

NOTICE OF MEETING TO ORGANIZE THE COMPANY, APRIL 9, 1850

NOTICE is hereby given by the undersigned, a majority of the persons named in the Act of Incorporation, that the first meeting of The Pepperell Manufacturing Company, will be holden on Tuesday the ninth day of April A.D. 1850, at the Counting Room of the Saco Water Power Company in Biddeford Maine, at one o'clock P.M. of that day, to organize under the Act of Incorporation of said Pepperell Manufacturing Company passed February 16th 1844:—to make by-laws, choose a Clerk, Treasurer, Directors and such other officers as may be necessary and convenient, and to transact such other business as may be deemed for the interest of the Corporation.

Biddeford
March 12th 1850.

(signed) Saml Batchelder
Josiah Calef
John Anderson
C. S. Daveis

[This notice published in "The Union" and "The Maine Democrat," two public newspapers printed in Saco in the said County of York, under dates of March 22nd, 1850, and of March 26th, respectively.]

Source: MS. PMC, Stockholders' records, 1850–99, p. 1.

APPENDIX 2

CHARTER

FEBRUARY 16, 1844

State of Maine

In the Year of Our Lord one thousand eight hundred and forty four.—

An Act to incorporate the Pepperell Manufacturing Company.—

Be it enacted by the Senate and House of Representatives in Legislature assembled, as follows:—

Section 1. Josiah Calef, Samuel Batchelder, Rufus Nichols, Jonathan King, John Anderson, Parker McCobb, Charles S. Daveis, and their associates and successors are constituted and made a body politic and corporate, by the name of the Pepperell Manufacturing Company, with all the powers and privileges, and subject to all the duties and liabilities provided in the laws of this State, concerning manufacturing corporations:—and are authorized to purchase and hold real and personal estate, not exceeding in value, at any one time, the sum of one million of dollars, and the same may improve, lease, sell and convey, as other proprietors of real and personal estate may lawfully do. And said Company are authorized to carry on, at Saco Falls, in Saco or Biddeford, the manufacture of cotton, and such other materials as may be necessarily or conveniently connected therewith, and may erect and construct such machinery, mills and other buildings as may be useful for that purpose.—

Section 2. The treasurer of said Company shall give notice semiannually in the months of January and July, in some newspaper printed in the County of York, and in case no newspaper is printed therein, then in some newspaper in adjoining county, of the amount of all the assessments, voted by the Company, and actually paid in, and the net amount of the then existing capital stock, the amount of all debts due from said corporation, and also the amount of the capital stock invested in real estate, buildings, machinery and other fixtures.—If any such treasurer shall neglect or refuse to give notice, or shall knowingly publish a false statement, he shall be fined not exceeding two thousand dollars, or be imprisoned not exceeding one year, on indictment and conviction thereof. [p. 2]

Section 3. The said Company are hereby expressly prohibited from contracting debts exceeding at any one time, the amount of the capital stock invested in real estate, buildings, machinery, and other fixtures within the State of Maine, but in no case to exceed one half the amount of the capital stock paid in and remaining undivided:—in which case, the stockholders shall not be liable individually, for the debts of said company.—But if the debts of said company shall at any one time exceed the limitation aforesaid, then the said corporators and their successors shall, at once, become liable individually for such debts.—And it is further required that no person shall be chosen a director or treasurer of said Company unless he be a stockholder therein.—

In the House of Representatives. February 16, 1844. This bill having had three several readings passed to be enacted.—David Dunn Speaker.

Seal of State.—

In Senate, February 16, 1844. This Bill having had two several readings, passed to be enacted. John W. Dana President.

February 16, 1844. Approved.
H. I. Anderson

State of Maine. Secretary's Office.

Augusta, February 16, 1844.

I hereby certify that the foregoing is a true copy of the original deposited in this office, and that in conformity to a law of the United States, passed May 26, 1790, I have caused the Seal of the State to be hereunto affixed.—Philip C. Johnson Secretary of State.—[p. 3]

Source: MS. PMC, Stockholders' records, 1850–99, pp. 2–3.

APPENDIX 3

BY-LAWS, APRIL 9, 1850

ARTICLE 1ST

The officers of this Corporation shall be a Treasurer, Clerk, and nine Directors, one of whom shall be President.

ARTICLE 2ND

There shall be a stated meeting of the Stockholders of [p. 4] The Pepperell Manufacturing Company on the fourth Thursday of July, annually, at such time of that day, and at such place in Saco or Biddeford, in the County of York, and State of Maine, as the Board of Directors shall determine. At the first meeting of the Company for organization, and thence afterwards at said annual meetings, nine Directors, a Clerk and Treasurer, shall be elected by ballot.—A President shall be chosen by the Directors from their number, who shall preside at all meetings of the Directors and of the Corporation. —In case of his absence or inability, a President pro-tempore shall be elected.—The said officers, chosen at the first meeting, shall hold their offices until the next annual meeting, and until others shall be chosen and qualified in their stead.

ARTICLE 3D

All meetings of the stockholders shall be called by written notice to each, deposited in the Post Office, addressed to each person, appearing by the books of the Corporation to be a Stockholder therein, or by an advertisement, signed by the President or Clerk of the Corporation, and published in one or more newspapers printed in said County of York; and in one or more newspapers printed in Boston, in the County of Suffolk, in the State of Massachusetts; such notices to be deposited in the Post Office, or published as aforesaid, at least five days before the day appointed for the meeting.—Special meetings of the Stockholders shall be called in like manner, whenever the Directors shall vote the same to be expedient, and also whenever three or more stockholders, owning not less than one hundred shares, shall, in writing, require the President or Clerk to call such meeting.—The Directors shall determine the time and place of every meeting of the Stockholders for which different provision is not made; and all meetings of the Board of Directors shall be held at such time and place as they shall designate; and shall be called by the President, Treasurer or any one of the Directors, whenever the President or any three of the Directors shall require the same.—Notices of the time and place of every meeting of the Directors shall be given to each of them in writing, deposited in the Post Office. [p. 5]

ARTICLE 4TH

At the meetings of the Corporation all votes shall be given by the Stockholders in person, or by proxy.—Every member shall be entitled to one vote for each share held by him; provided that no one shall be entitled to any vote for any shares beyond one fourth the whole number of shares in the stock of the Corporation.—Authority to act as proxy shall be in writing, signed by the proprietor, and the same or a notarial copy thereof, shall be delivered to the Clerk and remain on his files.

ARTICLE 5TH

The President, Directors, and every officer chosen or appointed by them, or by the Stockholders, shall hold their respective offices until the next annual meeting, and until others shall be chosen and qualified in their stead, excepting in cases of resignation, (which shall always be made in writing,) or death, or removal from office by the Stockholders, excepting that every Director shall cease to be a Director when he ceases to be a Stockholder. No less than a majority of the Directors shall constitute a quorum for the transaction of business; and in all cases in which power is given, or shall be given, to the Directors to do or authorize any act, the same may be done or authorized by a majority of the Board present at their meeting; provided that a quorum be present.—The Directors shall fill any vacancy that may happen in their Board without unnecessary delay, provided it be done by the consent of a majority of all the Directors remaining in office; and until such vacancy be supplied, all the powers and authority conferred on the whole Board of Directors shall be held and enjoyed by such remaining Directors, or a quorum of them, which shall be constituted by a majority of such remaining Directors.

ARTICLE 6TH

The Directors shall choose and appoint all such officers and agents as they may deem needful in the [p. 6] management of the affairs of the Company, excepting those herein required to be elected by the Stockholders, each of whom shall be removable at their pleasure; and the Directors shall assign their respective duties, and fix their compensation.—In case a vacancy happens in any of the offices of the Corporation, chosen by the Stockholders, the Directors shall have power to fill the same, until the next annual meeting.

ARTICLE 7TH

It shall be the duty of the Directors to superintend and direct the business of the Corporation, in all its departments.—To this end they shall have power to purchase and sell, or cause to be purchased and sold, such real estate and personal property, and to erect such buildings and machinery as they may think proper.—They may authorize the Treasurer to hire such sums of money, not exceeding the amount allowed by the Charter, and the Laws of Maine as they may deem necessary for the use of the Corporation.—They shall superintend the conduct of the different officers and agents chosen or appointed by them, and in general shall possess and exercise all powers, whenever needful, in the transaction of the business, and in the management of the concerns of the Corporation.

ARTICLE 8TH

The Clerk shall be sworn to the faithful discharge of his duties by a Justice of the Peace, immediately after his election, and his oath shall be entered with the signature of the magistrate in the Records of the Corporation.—The Clerk shall attend all meetings of the Stockholders, and shall keep Records of their doings, and of all transfers of Stock in the transfer book.—In his absence, a Clerk *pro tempore* shall be elected by the Stockholders, who shall be sworn in like manner, and shall do all things while he remains in office, required of the Clerk of the Corporation. [p. 7]

ARTICLE 9TH

The Treasurer shall give a bond to the Corporation, with sureties to the satisfaction of the Directors, in the penal sum of not less than Eight Thousand Dollars, for the faithful discharge of his trust.—He shall have an office in Boston, accessible to all persons having business with the Corporation, or any of its officers or agents.—He shall keep the Common Seal, and all deeds, promissory notes, and valuable papers of the Corporation.—He shall collect all assessments and moneys, that may be due to the Corporation, and disburse the same pursuant to the contracts of the Corporation, or the order of the Board of Directors.—He shall surrender notes and other promissory papers on payment thereof, and discharge such mortgages and surrender such security as may have been given concerning the same. He shall keep a regular set of books concerning the accounts of the Corporation, and of all its funds that may pass through his hands.—He shall lay before the Directors, whenever thereto requested, a written statement of all notes, drafts, promises, and contracts, made, signed, endorsed, accepted, or surrendered by him since his last previous statement thereof:—an abstract of all moneys paid and received; a statement of all property bought and sold, and such other matters as he or the Board of Directors may deem important.—He shall make a complete settlement of the accounts and books, at least annually, and as much oftener as the Board of Directors shall require.—He shall render an account of his doings to the Stockholders at their annual meeting.—He shall notify the Stockholders of all assessments.—He shall issue certificates of stock in the manner and form prescribed by the By-laws; receive receipts therefor, and keep a Stock Book, wherein he shall register the names of the Stockholders, and the number of Shares held by each.

ARTICLE 10TH

The Corporation shall have a Common Seal, bearing the words "Pepperell Manufacturing Company." [p. 8]

ARTICLE 11TH

The salaries of the Treasurer, Agents, and all other persons employed on account of the Corporation, shall be determined by the Directors.

ARTICLE 12TH

The Capital Stock of the Corporation shall be divided into Shares of Five Hundred Dollars each, which shall be numbered in progressive order, beginning at number one.—The holders of Shares in the Capital Stock shall be entitled to Certificates thereof, signed by the President and Treasurer, and authenticated by the Common Seal.—And the Certificates and Transfers shall be in such form conformable to law, as the Directors may prescribe.

ARTICLE 13TH

If the proprietor of any share shall neglect or refuse to pay any sum assessed thereon, for the space of thirty days after the time appointed for the payment thereof, the Treasurer of the Corporation may sell, by public auction, a sufficient number of the Shares of such delinquent proprietor to pay all assessments then due from him, with all lawful charges and expenses, and every such sale shall be conducted and completed pursuant to the requirements of the laws of said State of Maine.

ARTICLE 14TH

The Treasurer shall have power to cause insurance to be made on the property of the Corporation for such sum or sums as the Directors may deem advisable.

ARTICLE 15TH

No alteration shall be made in these By-laws without the assent thereto, by a vote of a majority in interest of the Stockholders, at a legal meeting of the Corporation; and the proposition to alter the By-laws shall be mentioned in the notices calling said meeting, but the nature of the proposed alteration need not be therein stated. [p. 9]

Source: MS. PMC, Stockholders' records, 1850–99, pp. 4–9.

APPENDIX 4

LIST OF ORIGINAL SUBSCRIBERS

Whereas the Directors of the Saco Water Power Company propose to sell and convey to the Pepperell Manufacturing Company, for the Sum of *Five hundred thousand dollars;* certain property Situated in Biddeford, in the State of Maine; being with some modifications, the property described in the votes passed at the last annual meeting, of the Saco Water Power Company.

We the Subscribers hereby agree with the Pepperell Manufacturing Company to take the number of shares set against our respective names in the Stock of the Pepperell Manufacturing Company; a corporation created by the laws of the State of Maine, of which the capital Stock *One Million of dollars,* is divided, into Two thousand Shares, of Five hundred dollars Each; Provided these our Subscriptions shall not be binding, until Two thousand shares in said Pepperell Manufacturing Company are subscribed; and we hereby agree with said Pepperell Manufacturing Company, to pay instalments on the shares by us subscribed to the Extent of Sixty per cent thereof in our Notes, at *Four, Eight, Twelve, Sixteen, and Twenty, Months,* bearing interest from date of said sale; and the balance whenever said Directors may deem Expedient to call for the payment of the Same.

Boston June 22d 1850

Names	*Number of Shares*
Thomas Wigglesworth	Twenty shares
Amos A. Lawrence	Twenty shares
I. Ingersoll Bowditch	Twenty shares
Ozias Goodwin	Twenty shares
Saml. Batchelder	Thirty shares
Thos. Wigglesworth Jr.	Twenty shares
L. G. Wigglesworth by Thos. Wigglesworth Jr.	Five shares
Saml. P. P. Fay	Ten shares
John Anderson by W. Dwight by letter	Eight shares
Danl. Treadwell	Ten shares
S. S. Littlehale	Ten shares

Names	*Number of Shares*
Nathan Rice	Four shares
Chas. H. Brown	Fifteen shares
John Clark	Forty-seven shares
Eben Francis	Fifteen shares
Isaac Parker	Four shares
J. J. Dixwell	Twenty shares
Geo. B. Dixwell by J. J. Dixwell	Twenty shares
J. J. Dixwell self & J. J. B. trustees	Five shares
James Longley	Twelve shares
Parker Wilder & Co.	Fifty-five shares
J. B. Thornton by W. D.	Twenty-four shares
Abbott Lawrence by J. L. Atty	Forty shares
J. H. Wolcott	Ten shares
Thomas Wigglesworth by Ed Wigglesworth	Five shares
Edward Wigglesworth	Five shares
E. A. Bourne	Seven shares
Josiah Calef	Two shares
William Savage	Nineteen shares
Edw. D. Peters	Ten shares
Edward S. Rand of Newburyport	Nine shares
H. M. Hayes	Twenty-nine shares
Haliburton Fales	Six shares
S. B. Fales by Haliburton Fales	Six shares
Susan Maria Fales by Haliburton Fales	Six shares
L A C A Dunlap by Haliburton Fales	Eight shares
Edward Clark by Letter	Fifteen shares
Isaac Kendall	Five shares
William P. Haines by W. D.	Six shares
A. E. Hildreth	Ten shares
F. Howes	Three shares
F. Howes, Executor	Two shares
John D. McCrate	Three shares
Geo. Putnam by Ebenr. Francis	Four shares
Enoch Chase	Two shares
Oliver B. Morris by W. D.	Two shares
Josiah Stickney	Ten shares
John Hurd	Five shares
Thos. Bartlett by Thos. B. Hall	Two shares
John Ware	Ten shares
John Williams	Six shares
Benj. Thaxter	Six shares
Sam. Swett	Twenty-three shares
Jno. B. Swett by Sam. Swett	Nine shares
Benj. Wheatland	Four shares
John Hathaway	Ten shares

Names	*Number of Shares*
Dwight Boyden	Ten shares
John F. Anderson	Three shares by letter
Samuel J. Anderson	Two shares by letter
Theodore Matchett	Fourteen shares
Wm. Thomas	Ten shares
Benjamin Loring	Fifty shares
John Hooper	Nineteen shares
Calvin W. Clark by order	Twelve shares
Benj. Humphrey	Twenty shares
Thomas Lamb	Ten shares
James Arnold by M. P. Wilder	Two shares
Wm. P. Perkins	Ten shares
William Parsons	Ten shares
Isaac Parker (Boston)	Four shares
J. W. Edmands	Twenty shares
Thomas Dwight	Thirty shares
C. Bradbury & Trustee transferred	Twenty-four shares
Israel Whitney	Twelve shares
R. K. Hough Jr.	Five shares
Augs. Aspinwall	Ten shares
Thos. B. Curtis by Thos. Brown	Three shares
A. Heard	Thirty shares
Thaddeus Nichols	Twelve shares
Estate Josh. Blake by T. Nichols, Trustee	Thirteen shares
Richard Fletcher	Ten shares
S. Hooper	Eighty shares
William P. Hooper	Two shares
Otis Holmes	Four shares
Edward Austin	Five shares
Stephen Fairbanks	Ten shares
Samuel W. Swett	Three shares
Samuel W. Swett Trustee	Two shares
Elizabeth B. Swett by S. S. Swett Atty	Four shares
William B. Swett by S. W. Swett Atty	Four shares
Sam Goddard	Eleven shares
N. H. Emmons	Ten shares
Geo. Howe	Sixteen shares
Franklin King (Kg Dexter) J. B.	Five shares
Milton Slocomb	Twenty shares
Amos Chase	Two shares by letter
Sarah C. Emery	Three shares by letter
Daniel Cleaves	Four shares by letter
Rob Waterston, by J. T. Weld	Thirteen shares
William Dwight	Seven hundred & sixty-four shares

Supplementary List from William Dwight's Subscription up to July 20, 1850

Names	*Number of Shares*
John Albree	12 shares
Holmes Ammidown	5 shares
N. W. Bowditch	10 shares
P. W. Freeman	3 shares
George H. Gray	5 shares
Dudley Hall	5 shares
Mary Hedge	1 share
H. M. Holbrook	10 shares
Samuel Johnson	20 shares
C. J. Morrill	5 shares
Lyman Nichols	8 shares
Padelford & Fay	10 shares
J. M. Pierce	4 shares
William P. Pierce	4 shares
Joshua Sears	10 shares
Nathanial Snow	2 shares
Joshua Tucker	2 shares
George W. Wales	2 shares
Washington Williams	1 share

Source: MS. PMC, List of subscribers, 1850–51.

APPENDIX 5

REPORT OF COMMITTEE ON CONSOLIDATION WITH LACONIA CO.

NOVEMBER 25, 1878

1st The Pepperell Co is to obtain permission to increase its capital to \$2,000,000—by the issue of 1600 shares, par \$500—with the right to hold real estate to the amount of \$2,000,000 & such personal property as may be needed for the transaction of its business.

2d The Pepperell Co offers to buy all the property of the Laconia Co for \$1,000,000 paying cash for it, but also gives to the stockholders of the Laconia Co the right to subscribe to the new Pepperell 1600 shares at a premium of 40%—or \$700 a share. The result would be a capital of \$2,000,000—165,000 spindles & cash means of say from \$900,000 to \$1,000,000.

Laconia stockholders would get either the market price, \$400 per share in cash, or right to take an interest in the new Company at a little less than the present market price of the Pepperell stock. The advantages accruing to this Company would be the certainty that in the future the same harmony of action which has for some years characterized the working of the two companies, would be secured beyond peradventure.

That the Laconia Co in its present good condition and with its present means is no longer open to the objections which might, at one time, have been urged against it—but is now able to manufacture very nearly as cheaply as the Pepperell and will form a valuable addition to it.

That the necessity exists, if we would keep certain lines of goods popular and at the head of the market for their class, to make a large quantity—larger perhaps than we may find it convenient to manufacture in one mill, and by having at our command the enlarged capacity of the Laconia we can retain our place in the market.

That controlling both our own trade marks and those of the Laconia will enable us to produce a style of goods best suited to the organization of the mill, either in the Pepperell or Laconia, as may prove most economical.

That owning the Water Power in common it is necessary for each company to be run without inconvenience to the other, and should either company ever insist on what are its own peculiar rights, as existing under the old contracts with the Saco Water Power Co—one company or the other could be seriously inconvenienced and subjected to considerable loss of product and to increased expense in running its machinery.

If the proposed plan is carried out the new Company will add to the quick capital already existing in the two companies the sum of $120,000—thus giving ample means, and allowing for the completion of the proposed renovation of the Pepperell, without crippling our active capital.

The capital proposed—$2,000,000, will be a moderate one for the number of spindles you will have in the enlarged Pepperell—165,000—when the plans proposed some years ago are carried out.

If we do not bring the two concerns together while we can, and anything in the future arises to disturb the present harmony—we think the stockholders of the Pepperell will greatly regret not having taken the Laconia when they could get it at a reasonable price—That the price is a reasonable one the number and condition of the spindles and the cost at which the mill produces goods sufficiently prove—

The two companies are today practically one concern: the same President; very nearly the same board of Directors; the same Agent at the Mill; the same Selling Agents and the same Treasurer.

The advantages of this close intimacy and harmony are very apparent:—why not make such connection permanent while we have the opportunity?

[Signed] Wm. B. Howes, George Dexter, A. E. Hildreth — Committee of Directors Pepperell Manuf. Co.

Source: MS. PMC, Directors' records, Nov. 25, 1878.

APPENDIX 6

LETTERS TO A STOCKHOLDER ABOUT CONSOLIDATION, NOV. 27 AND DEC. 13, 1886

Boston Nov. 27th, 86.

Roscoe L. Bowers Esq.

My dear Sir

Yrs 24th was received—I asked Mr. Howe to see & explain to you our reasons for believing the union of the two companies desirable.

The Pepperell directors thought some increase of product in their yard was likely to be needed before many years, & had plans made for a new mill—but it seemed to us if we could spend our money in rearranging the Laconia & get an increase of product there, it would be better & work for the advantage of both corporations, if put together. The Laconia has done very well, but it would not do so well if the Pepperell had 30% more spindles; and if we rearrange the Laconia & use its water power that mill can probably manufacture more cheaply than it does now—but we do not want to spend our accumulations on such changes & be left with a very small quick capital.

The reason the Laconia is taken at the present ratio of value to the Pepperell is that the name and reputation of the latter is much higher than that of the former and must be considered in any attempt at union—Simply taking the number of spindles & the quick capital, I quite agree with you that the Laconia should be worth more than 440—But it does not sell for more & it has not paid on the average of the past 12 years more than the proportion of 7^{2} [½] to 3.

We think the regularity of the dividend is better assured to the new stock than to the old—Of course, with 10 hours & other adverse legislations, we may make less money in the future than in the past—but if the two corporations, separately, can do as well as most manufacturing establishments I believe—together—they can do better.

The joint ownership of the water & the necessity of harmony you know about—as things are running now it's of little consequence—but if either mill thought they would act independently of the other there would be serious loss to the weaker—

You ask for the standing of the two companies at the last annual meeting. The Pepperell had $1,179,350—quick and the Lac 442,738—Dividends of Pepp 75 c 86 have averaged 12% Laconia 5¾. If the consolidated company pays 8%, or $24 on 3 shares, it is the same as 6% on the old Lac par—and as the united quick capitals—after rearranging the Laconia—would be enough for our wants—if we made as much in the next 12 years as we have in the past, we could pay more than 8%—We have now received replies from say 1600 shares of Pepp & 1800 shares of Laconia & including your stock there is say 5% of it not assenting in the Pepp & 3% of it in the Laconia—only 9 stockholders in both companies not having given their consent—

I think there are more Pepp stockholders, without Laconia, that think the valuation of their stock is too low than there are Laconia, without Pepperell, who say its their stock that suffers; and I am inclined to believe we have put them in on as nearly a fair basis, as it is possible to arrive at.

I am in hopes that you will see the mutual benefit which is likely to result from the Union & withdraw your opposition.

Yrs very truly
[signed] George Dexter

Source: MS. PMC, Treasurer's letter book, 1884–87, pp. 395–397.

Boston Dec. 13th, 86.

R. L. Bowers Esq.

My dear Sir

I have just received yrs—I think you do not sufficiently recognize the fact that the Pepperell name & good will is worth a great deal—Many of the Pepperell stockholders think more than we have reckoned it at in our relative prices of the two companies—What opposition we have met with here has been from the Pepperell side—of Laconia stockholders, we lack but 12 shares of having 90% of the whole assenting. I can readily imagine that the new stock—after it be issued will bring 175 —a share or the equivalent of 525 for a present share of Laconia & while you may be right that the Laconia alone would do better in the next few years than she would do under the present proposed union—I think for a steady permanent pull the stockholders will find as good & more steady dividends & not so fluctuating a stock as they now have—It is quite true we have a good quick capital—we also have to spend some money & might at any time have to reduce our quick.

The next time I am in Biddeford I will try to find time to see you. I hear so often that the Pepperell are getting the worst of the trade that I am inclined to believe the Directors struck about right on their relative values.

Presumably I am indifferent about the success of the Union—except I dont like to have so much work thrown away & what over ¾ of the stockholders of any corporations want, I think ought to be done.

Yrs very truly
[signed] George Dexter

Dec. 13 Laconia consenting 2238 shares
Pepperell " 1916 "

Source: MS. PMC, Treasurer's letter book, 1884–87, pp. 407–408.

APPENDIX 7

A. CIRCULAR LETTER, MAY 1, 1899

Boston May 1, 1899

To the Stockholders of the Pepperell Mf Co & of the Laconia Co.

Your directors are of the opinion that it is of great importance to permanently secure the harmony which at present exists between the two companies in the operation of their large plants situated on the same water power in Biddeford Maine: to make it possible in the future to develop the unused power at the various falls on the river, now owned in common by the two companies & to save in the expenses by being able to run the mills more conveniently.

In order to obtain these results your directors propose a Union of the two companies and beg to lay before you the following plan.

A new company has been formed with a capital of $2,556,000—divided into shares of $100. each. If the stockholders vote to carry out the union of the two companies, Consolidated Manufacturing Company will use the name of Pepperell Manufacturing Company.

The Pepperell Mf Co is to receive a cash dividend from undivided profits of $150. a share and is then to sell to the new company its entire property and good will and receive in stock 7 shares of the new stock for 1 share of the old stock.

The Laconia Company is to receive a cash dividend from undivided profits of $50- a share and is then to sell to the new company its entire property and good will and receive in stock 3½ shares of new stock for 1 share of the old stock.

For the purpose of ascertaining whether the stockholders wish to carry out the plan as described special meetings will be held in Biddeford on Wednesday the 10th day of May, legal notices of which are herewith sent which will be voted in accordance with the wishes of the stockholders. If the proxy is returned without an objection in writing it will be voted in favor of the Union. Any proxy returned, signed, in the enclosed envelope and received will have a revenue stamp affixed to it here & will be voted in accordance with the orders of the stockholder.

James Longley President Thomas Wigglesworth George F. Fabyan Charles P. Bowditch Henry S. Grew Francis S. Welch George Dexter Treasurer	Directors of the Pepperell Mf Company and of the Laconia Company

Source: MS. PMC, Directors' records, Apr. 7, 1899.

AGREEMENT

PEPPERELL MANUFACTURING COMPANY

AGREEMENT made this tenth day of May, 1899, between Pepperell Manufacturing Company, a corporation organized under a special act of the State of Maine, hereinafter called the seller, and Consolidated Manufacturing Company, a corporation organized under the general law of the State of Maine, hereinafter called the buyer.

Whereas Pepperell Manufacturing Company and Laconia Company are corporations so located and existing that their business can be carried on more economically if carried on by one corporation;

Whereas the directors and stockholders of both Pepperell Manufacturing Company and Laconia Company have voted to sell all the real and personal property, franchises, good will, and trade-marks of each (less a dividend to be declared and paid prior to the consummation of such sale of $150 per share of Pepperell Manufacturing Company, amounting in the aggregate to $360,000, and $50 per share of Laconia Company, amounting in the aggregate to $125,-000), to Consolidated Manufacturing Company, and to receive therefor shares of the stock of Consolidated Manufacturing Company; to divide such shares of stock among their shareholders and to determine their separate corporate existences.—

NOW THEREFORE, IN CONSIDERATION OF THE PREMISES, THIS AGREEMENT WITNESSETH:—

First. The seller agrees to sell to the buyer and the buyer agrees to buy of the seller all the real and personal property, franchises, good will, and trade-marks of the seller, (less a dividend of $150 per share as aforesaid) for 16,800 shares of the capital stock of the buyer of the par value of $1,680,000, the total authorized capital stock of the buyer being $2,556,000, divided into 25,560 shares of the par value of $100 each.

Second. The seller agrees to convey such real and personal property franchises, good will, and trade-marks to the buyer upon the receipt of such shares of the capital stock of the buyer of the par value of $1,680,000, and the buyer agrees to deliver to the seller therefor such shares. The sale to be made as of the date hereof.

IN WITNESS WHEREOF the buyer and seller have hereto set their respective corporate hands and seals the day and year first above written.

Source: MS. PMC, Stockholders' records, May 10, 1899, pp. 131–132.

B. NOTICE OF STOCKHOLDERS' MEETING, MAY 10, 1899

To the Stockholders of the Pepperell Manufacturing Company:

A meeting of the stockholders of Pepperell Manufacturing Company will be held at the office of the Company at Biddeford, Maine, at one o'clock in the afternoon, on Wednesday the 10th day of May, 1899, for the following purposes:—

1. To see if the stockholders will vote to enter into an agreement with Consolidated Manufacturing Company, a corporation organized under the general law of the State of Maine with an authorized capital stock of $2,556,000, divided into 25,560 shares of the par value of $100 each, for the sale to such Consolidated Manufacturing Company of all the real and personal property, franchises, good will, and trade-marks of Pepperell Manufacturing Company, (less a dividend, to be declared and paid prior to the consummation of such sale, of $150 per share, amounting in the aggregate to $360,000,) for 16,800 shares of the capital stock of such Consolidated Manufacturing Company of the par value of $1,680,000, in accordance with the terms of a proposed contract, a copy of which is hereto attached and marked "A."

2. To see if the stockholders will vote to authorize the President and Treasurer of Pepperell Manufacturing Company to, in its name, make, execute, acknowledge, and deliver such last mentioned contract, and to make, execute, acknowledge, and deliver all deeds, assignments, and other instruments, and do all acts necessary to carry out such last mentioned contract.

3. To see if the stockholders will vote to distribute such 16,800 shares of the capital stock of such Consolidated Manufacturing Company, of the par value of $1,680,000, among the stockholders of Pepperell Manufacturing Company, giving to stockholders of Pepperell

Manufacturing Company for each share of the stock of Pepperell Manufacturing Company seven shares of the stock of the Consolidated Manufacturing Company.

4. To see if the stockholders will vote that such distribution of such 16,800 shares of the stock of Consolidated Manufacturing Company among the stockholders of Pepperell Manufacturing Company is a final distribution of the assets of Pepperell Manufacturing Company.

5. To see if the stockholders will vote to dissolve Pepperell Manufacturing Company and authorize its President and Treasurer to take the necessary legal steps to procure such dissolution.

BURTON H. WINSLOW
Clerk Pepperell Manufacturing Company.

APPENDIX 8

OFFICERS AND DIRECTORS, 1850–1870

Office	*Officers*	*Term*
Treasurer	William Dwight	1850–66
	William P. Haines	1866–71
President	John Clark	1850–51[a]
	Samuel Hooper	1851–53, 1855–66
	J. J. Dixwell	1853–55
	William Dwight	1866–70
Clerk	William P. Haines	1850–51, 1856–66
	Jabez Smith	1851–56[a]
	Ferguson Haines	1866–71

Directors	*Term*	*Harvard Class*	*Occupation*
Samuel Batchelder	1850–58		Treasurer of Portsmouth Steam Mills.
William Dwight	1850–70	1825	Treasurer of 3 Biddeford companies.
Thomas Dwight	1850–50, 1859–66	1827	Lawyer.
Charles H. Brown	1850–50[b]		Wharfinger; president of Atlas Bank.
Edward Austin	1850–59		Merchant in foreign trade.
Samuel Hooper	1850–70		Merchant in foreign trade.
Marshall P. Wilder	1850–50		Member of Parker, Wilder & Co.
G. W. Hallett	1850–50[b]		Merchant.
John Clark	1850–51[a]	1816	Treasurer of Great Falls Mfg. Co.
William Parsons	1850–70		Merchant.
J. J. Dixwell	1850–70		Merchant; president of Mass. Bank.
Francis Skinner	1851–65[a]		Member of Francis Skinner & Co.
Thomas Wigglesworth, Jr.	1858–1900	1833	Merchant in foreign trade.

[a] Died in office.

[b] Did not attend a single meeting.

Directors	*Term*	*Class*	*Occupation*
Josiah Bardwell	1865–70		Member of Francis Skinner & Co.
William P. Haines	1866–71	°	Treasurer of 2 Biddeford companies.

° Graduate of Dartmouth College, Class of 1831.

Source: MS. PMC, Stockholders' records, 1850–1900; Directors' records, 1850–1900. *Harvard Quinquennial Directory, 1636–1920. General Catalogue of Dartmouth College, 1769–1925.* Allan Forbes, *Rich Men of Massachusetts*, 1852. B. W. Dwight, *Descendants of John Dwight of Dedham, Massachusetts. New England Union Mercantile Directory, 1849.*

APPENDIX 9

OFFICERS, DIRECTORS, AND TRUSTEES, 1870–1924

Office	*Officers*	*Term*
Treasurer	John A. Blanchard	1871–72[a]
	Edward W. Codman	1873–77
	George Dexter	1877–1901
	Philip Y. DeNormandie	1901–07
	William Amory	1907–19
	Walter H. Bradley	1919–24
President	William Parsons	1870–70
	John A. Blanchard	1870–71
	Lyman Nichols	1871–78[a]
	Thomas Wigglesworth, Jr.	1878–91
	Charles P. Bowditch	1891–98
	James Longley	1898–1916[a]
	Charles P. Bowditch	1916–21[a]
	William Amory	1921–
Clerk	Ferguson Haines	1866–71
	C. F. Page	1871–78
	William P. Haines	1878–79[a]
	Moses W. Webber	1879–80
	Burton H. Winslow	1880–1915
Secretary	William Amory	1915–20
	Matthew W. Colquhoun	1920–27

Comment: William P. Haines, who resigned in January, 1871, omitted from list of treasurers for this period. He has been considered as belonging to the first period.

[a] Died while in office.

Directors and Trustees	*Years in Office*	*Harvard College Class*	*Occupation*
Thomas Wigglesworth, Jr.	1858–1900	1833	Merchant; then investor of personal fortune.
John A. Blanchard	1870–72[a]	—	Previously partner in Blanchard & Blodgett and Blanchard, Converse & Co., dry goods wholesalers.
Lyman Nichols	1870–78[a]	—	Earlier, dry goods jobber & importer; president Boston National Bank, Boston, and Clinton & Fitchburg R. R.
A. E. Hildreth	1870–82	—	Employee of J. M. Osgood, auctioneer; president, Cambridge Gas Co.
Charles L. Young	1870–73	—	Partner, Young & Emmons, merchants.
Henry Sigourney	1871–74[a]	1851	Merchant.
James Longley	1871–1916[a]	—	Partner, Robinson & Longley, 1865–70; vice-president Boston Safe Deposit & Trust Co.; director of several companies.
George F. Fabyan	1872–1907[a]	—	Partner, Bliss, Fabyan & Co.; treasurer of several textile companies.
Edward W. Codman	1873–78	1854	Earlier, partner of father's wine company; treasurer of Pepperell and Laconia, 1873–77.
John A. Blanchard, Jr.	1874–85[a]	1864	Partner, export company until 1871; in cotton for year; retired from business at end of 1872.
George Dexter	1878–1910[a]	1855	In export trade; cotton buyer prior to treasurer of Pepperell and Laconia, 1877–1901.
William B. Howes	1878–79[a]	1838	Earlier, attorney or counsellor of law (1849).
Charles P. Bowditch	1879–1921[a]	1863	Trustee of estates; archaeological student; director of many companies.

[a] Died while in office.

Directors and Trustees	*Years in Office*	*Harvard College Class*	*Occupation*
Henry S. Grew	1882–1910[a]	—	Vice-president of Suffolk Savings Bank; director of several companies.
William P. Walley	1885–91[a]	1864	Lawyer.
Francis C. Welch	1892–1919	—	Lawyer; director of many companies; president of State Street Exchange, Boston Pier, and Commercial Wharf.
George Wigglesworth	1900–16	1874	Lawyer; treasurer of M. I. T.; director of many companies.
Philip Y. DeNormandie	1907–26	1891	Treasurer of Pepperell, 1901–07; then partner in Bliss, Fabyan & Co.
William Amory	1910–	1891	Treasurer of Pepperell, 1907–19; retired.
Philip Dexter	1910–33	1889	Lawyer; director of many companies.
Robert Saltonstall	1916–17	1892	In cotton for a time.
Thomas P. Beal	1916–23[a]	1869	President of Second National Bank since 1888.
Edward W. Grew	1918–45[a]	1889	Partner, Meredith & Grew, real estate.
Henry Wheeler	1917–40	1878	Lawyer, partner in Hutchins & Wheeler.
E. Sohier Welch	1910–	1909	Lawyer.
Neal Rantoul	1921–	1892	Member of F. S. Moseley & Co., broker; director of several companies.

Comment: Names of directors who resigned in the fall of 1870 have been omitted. In 1915 the former directors became trustees. Walter H. Bradley, treasurer from 1919 to 1924, was never a trustee.

[a] Died while in office.

Source: MS. PMC, Directors' and trustees' records, 1858–1924; Harvard College, Class Books; Harvard University, *Quinquennial Catalogue; Boston Directory*, 1850–1920; *N. E. Union Mercantile Directory, 1849; Who's Who in New England, 1909.*

APPENDIX 10

OFFICERS, TRUSTEES, AND DIRECTORS, 1924–1945

A. Voluntary Association

Office	*Officers*	*Term*
President	William Amory	1921–
Vice-President	Walter H. Bradley	1924–25
	Edward Lovering	1927–41[a]
	Amory Coolidge	1944–
Treasurer	Russell H. Leonard	1924–
Assistant Treasurer	Amory Coolidge	1925–
	Frederick W. Notman	1928–30
	Brackett Parsons	1932–
Secretary	Matthew W. Colquhoun	1924–27
	Paul E. Crocker	1927–
Assistant Secretary	Dorothy M. Hobson	1943–47[a]

Trustees	*Term*	*Harvard Class*	*Occupation*
William Amory	1910–	1891	Retired; former treasurer of Pepperell.
Philip Y. DeNormandie	1907–26	1891	Member of Bliss, Fabyan & Co.
Philip Dexter	1910–33	1889	Attorney at law.
Henry Wheeler	1917–40	1878[b]	Attorney; member of Hutchins & Wheeler.
Edward W. Grew	1918–45[a]	1889[c]	Member of Meredith & Grew, Inc., real estate.
Neal Rantoul	1921–	1892	Member of F. S. Moseley & Co., brokers.
E. Sohier Welch	1910–	1909[d]	Attorney at law and trustee.
Russell H. Leonard	1926–	1910	Pepperell executive.
Edward Lovering	1933–41[a]	[e]	Retired; former treasurer of Massachusetts Cotton Mills.

[a] Died while in office.

[b] Graduate also of Law School of Harvard University.

[c] Attended Law School of Harvard University.

[d] Graduate also of Law School of Boston University.

[e] Attended Harvard College.

Trustees	Term	Harvard Class	Occupation
William Dexter	1940–43[a]	1919[b]	Attorney; member of Choate, Hall & Stewart.
Amory Coolidge	1941–	1917	Pepperell executive.
E. Kent Swift	1943–	[f]	President, treasurer, and general manager of Whitin Machine Works.

B. Massachusetts Corporation, 1926–1945[g]

Office	Officers	Term
President	Edward Lovering	1926–27
	William Amory	1927–30
	Russell H. Leonard	1930–
Vice-President	Edward Lovering	1927–30
	Amory Coolidge	1930–
	Donald B. Tansill	1930–
	Allyn B. McIntire	1930–
	Paul E. Crocker	1933–
Chairman	William Amory	1930–
Vice-Chairman	Edward Lovering	1930–41[a]
Treasurer	Russell H. Leonard	1926–
Assistant Treasurer	Amory Coolidge	1926–
	Frederick W. Notman	1928–32
	Brackett Parsons	1932–
	Dorothy M. Hobson	1933–47[a]
	Morton P. Schapp	1938–46
Clerk	Frederick W. Notman	1926–27
	Paul E. Crocker	1927–40
Secretary	Paul E. Crocker	1940–
Assistant Secretary	Dorothy M. Hobson	1940–47[a]

Directors	Term
Edward Lovering	1926–41[a]
Frederick W. Notman	1926–26[h]
John M. Foster	1926–26[i]
Russell H. Leonard	1926–
Amory Coolidge	1926–26, 1940–

[a] Died while in office.

[b] Graduate also of Law School of Harvard University.

[f] Graduate of Williams College in 1900.

[g] From December, 1926, through June, 1927, title was Massachusetts Cotton Mills, Inc.

[h] Former clerk of the Massachusetts Cotton Mills.

[i] Attorney at law, graduate of Harvard College in 1911 and of Law School.

Directors	*Term*
William Amory	1927–
Edward W. Grew	1927–45[a]
Philip Dexter	1927–31
E. Sohier Welch	1927–
Henry Wheeler	1927–40
Neal Rantoul	1927–
William Dexter	1939–43[a]
E. Kent Swift	1943–

[a] Died while in office.

Source: MS. PMC, Trustees' records, 1924–45.
MS. MCM, Inc., Directors' records, 1926–27.
MS. PMC, Directors' records, 1927–45.
Harvard Alumni Directory, 1937.
Boston Directory of Directors, 1926, 1940.
Who's Who in New England, vol. 3, 1938.

APPENDIX 11

A. COTTON BUYERS BY LOCATION, 1850–1861

	Years	*Number in bales*
Memphis, Tennessee		
David Park & Co.	1851–52	1,249
R. E. Orne & Co.	1852–54	2,755
O. B. Parker	1852–54	2,625
J. Bardwell	1854–55	2,448
J. Bardwell & Co.	1855–57	9,005
Dwight, Gill & Co.	1857–61	13,712
Total		31,794
Mobile, Alabama		
Dexter & Abbot	1851, 1852, 1854	900
A. Brown & Son	1852	170
J. Bardwell	1854	2,684
Dwight & Co.	1855	271
J. Bardwell & Co.	1855–57	5,977
D. A. Dwight & Co.	1857–61	7,900
Total		17,902
Columbus, Georgia		
Hall & Deblois	1851, 1853, 1855	4,450
Hall & Dexter	1855–59	8,433
Jos. Hanserd	1859–61	2,510
Total		15,393
Savannah, Georgia		
Padelford, Fay & Co.	1851–53, 1855	7,593
Cohen & Fosdick	1853	183
Octavus Cohen & Co.	1855–59, 1860–61	5,365
Total		13,141

	Years	Number in bales
Boston, Massachusetts		
By treasurer	1850–60	4,877
By D. A. Dwight	1860–61	5,895
Total		10,772
New Orleans, Louisiana		
W. C. Hichborn	1850–52	4,215
J. G. Robinson	1852	501
Dwight & Co.	1855–56	586
D. A. Dwight & Co.	1856–59, 1860–61	3,523
Total		8,825
New York, New York		
By treasurer and others through brokers	1852–60	7,448
Apalachicola, Florida		
N. J. Deblois	1854	500
Nourse & Brooks	1859–61	2,826
Total		3,326
Shreveport, Louisiana		
J. Bardwell	1855	2,469
Galveston, Texas		
A. H. Ladd	1854	300
Biddeford, Maine		
Laconia Co.	1851	20
Not placed		
Chas. Wilkins & Co.	1853	25

Source: MS. PMC.
List of cotton invoices, 1850.
List of cotton invoices, 1865–74.
Notes and bills receivable and payable, 1850–71.
Cotton invoices and miscellaneous cotton papers, 1850–65.
Bills of lading for cotton, 1850–60, 1864; cotton cash vouchers, 1851–66.
Letters to treasurer about purchase of cotton, Laconia and Pepperell, 1844–66.

B. COTTON BUYERS BY LOCATION, 1862–1870

	Years	*Amount in bales*
Boston, Massachusetts		
D. A. Dwight & Co.	1863–June, 1866[a]	26,071
D. A. Dwight & Co.	July, 1866–June, 1870[a]	14,060
F. Skinner & Co.	1862	5
A. Emerson & Co.	1864	196 est.
Total		40,332
New York, New York		
D. A. Dwight & Co.	1862–June, 1866[a]	3,222
D. A. Dwight & Co.	July, 1866–June, 1870[a]	9,979
Total		13,201
Mobile, Alabama		
A. J. Ingersoll	1865, 1867	300
Not placed	1866–70	5,122
Total		5,422
Memphis, Tennessee		
N. C. Robbins	1862–64	1,585
Geo. M. Gill	1865	667
Gill & Simpson	1865–66	450
Gill & Maury	1869	101
E. L. Dorr & Co.	1869	52
Not placed	1866–70	1,253
Total		4,108
New Orleans, Louisiana		
W. H. Boynton & Co.	1863–64	1,051
Nourse & Brooks	1866–68	303
D. A. Dwight & Co.	1864–65	250
E. L. Dorr & Co.	1870	50
Not placed	1864–70	1,556
Total		3,210

[a] It is assumed that all the cotton was bought in Boston by this company during the period as well as that in New York with the exceptions noted. Evidence missing for the purchases through others. Notes receivable indicate sizable amounts paid to these companies.

	Years	Amount in bales
Columbus, Georgia		
Epping, Hanserd & Co.	1866, 1869–70	549
Not placed	1866–70	2,125
Total		2,674
Galveston, Texas		
Jos. H. Metcalf	1870	188
Not placed	1867–70	1,379
Total		1,567
Charleston, South Carolina		
Not placed	1868–70	1,418
Augusta, Georgia		
Jos. H. Metcalf	1865	863
Not placed	1866–67	504
Total		1,367
Savannah, Georgia		
Not placed	1866–70	1,349
Eufalfa, Alabama		
H. P. Adams	1865, 1870	100
Not placed	1869–70	913
Total		1,013
Macon, Georgia		
R. B. Watson	1870	298
Not placed	1869–70	350
Total		648
St. Louis, Missouri		
N. C. Robbins	1862	78
Biddeford & Saco, Maine		
Laconia Co.	1867	30
York Co.	1863	4
Thomas R. Lane	1863	1
Total		35

B. COTTON BUYERS BY LOCATION, 1862–1870 (continued)

	Years	*Amount in bales*
Portland, Maine		
J. Wescott & Son	1867	25
Providence, Rhode Island		
Not placed	1868	104
Liverpool, England		
J. L. Bowes & Bro.	1864	390

Comment: Totals of these figures are larger than those for consumption by mills since some of this cotton was lost in transit, burned, or sold.

Source: MS. PMC.
List of cotton invoices, 1850–65; 1865–74.
Notes and bills receivable and payable, 1850–71.
Cotton invoices and miscellaneous cotton papers, 1850–65.
Bills of lading for cotton, 1850–60, 1864; and cotton cash vouchers, 1851–66.
Letters to treasurer about purchase of cotton, Laconia and Pepperell, 1844–66.

APPENDIX 12

PURCHASES, CONSUMPTION, STOCK ON HAND, AND AVERAGE COST OF COTTON, 1850–1870

Twelve Months Ending	Purchases (In bales)	Consumption (In bales)	Stock on Hand at End of Period (In bales)	Average Cost per Pound (In cents)[a]
June 28, 1851	1,923	766	1,157	14.7
June 26, 1852	7,979	6,160	2,976	10.1
June 25, 1853	9,068	8,465	3,579	10.3
June 24, 1854	6,798	7,269	3,108	10.9
June 23, 1855	6,865	6,925	3,048	10.3
June 21, 1856	10,010	8,256	4,802	10.0
June 20, 1857	9,217	10,485	3,534	11.5
June 19, 1858	12,262	8,364[b]	6,632	12.9
June 18, 1859	11,312	11,068	6,876	12.8
June 16, 1860	9,262	11,252[b]	4,881	12.7
June 15, 1861	14,102	12,969[b]	6,010	12.4
June 14, 1862	1,112	4,492[b]	1,723	12.7
June 13, 1863	7,616	7,670[b]	1,319	41.0[c]
June 25, 1864	11,554	11,697	1,176	65.8
June 24, 1865	7,491	8,074	593	88.7
June 23, 1866	11,500	9,484	2,609	48.7
June 29, 1867	9,087	10,529[b]	1,148	37.9
June 27, 1868	10,446	10,433	1,162	23.2
June 29, 1869	12,281	11,343[b]	2,099	25.7
June 25, 1870	8,574	9,749	924	25.4

[a] Average cost for the twelve months found by averaging the two six-months' costs.

[b] In 1858, 800 bales stored at Biddeford sold by the treasurer. In 1860, 5 bales lost by fire or in shipment. In 1861, 4 bales lost by fire or in shipment. In 1862, 900 bales sold and 7 lost by fire or in shipment. In 1863, 350 bales sold. In 1867, 19 bales lost by fire or in shipment. In 1869, 1 bale lost in fire or in shipment.

[c] Average cost lowered by entering 12.7 cents for the 350 bales sold, at average cost of previous year.

Comment: By the end of June, 1851, two mills were in operation. The third mill was in operation by June 21, 1856.

Source: Compiled from records in the Pepperell manuscripts. List of cotton invoices, 1850–56, 1865–74; Semiannual statements of agent, 1851–65, 1866–75; and Semiannual statements of treasurer, 1851–65.

APPENDIX 13

PRODUCTION, CONSUMPTION, AND PRICE OF COTTON IN THE UNITED STATES 1850–1870

Year	Production (In running bales)	Consumption (In running bales)	Average Price (Per Pound) Upland Cotton (Cents)
1850	2,454,442	422,626	12.1
1851	3,126,310	617,468	9.5
1852	3,416,214	736,468	11.0
1853	3,074,979	663,204	11.0
1854	2,982,634	641,391	10.4
1855	3,665,557	731,484	10.3
1856	3,093,737	761,614	13.5
1857	3,257,339	550,708	12.2
1858	4,018,914	867,489	22.1[a]
1859	5,387,052[b]	845,410	11.0
1860	3,849,469	841,975	13.0
1861	4,500,000	369,226	31.3
1862	1,600,000	287,397	67.2
1863	450,000	219,540	101.5
1864	300,000	344,278	83.4
1865	2,269,316	614,540	43.2
1866	2,097,254	715,258	31.6
1867	2,519,554	844,044	24.9
1868	2,366,467	860,481	29.0
1869	3,011,996[b]	796,616	24.0
1870	4,352,317	1,026,583	17.0

[a] Obviously a typographical mistake for 12.1 cents.

[b] Equivalent 400-pound bales. Bales in this period averaged about 445 bales. Weights gradually increasing.

Comment: "Production statistics relate, when possible, to the year of growth, but when figures for the growth year are wanting, those for a commercial crop, which represent the trade movement, have been taken." Statistics of production, 1850–70, compiled from Publications of Department of Agriculture.

Prices of upland cotton from 1850–70 taken from reports of the Department of Agriculture.

The statistics of consumption for 1850–70 compiled from publications of the Department of Agriculture. The statistics relate to the 12 months during which the crop of the specified year was chiefly marketed, and not to the calendar year specified.

Source: U. S. Department of Commerce, Bureau of the Census, *Bulletin 167*, 1930, pp. 57–58.

APPENDIX 14

FREIGHT RATES FOR COTTON, 1851–1852

Date	From New Orleans to Liverpool[a]	From New Orleans to Boston[b]	From Savannah to Boston[c]	From Mobile to Boston[d]	From Apalachicola to Boston[e]
1851					
Sept.	3/8 to —	. . . .	. . . .	1/2	. . . .
Oct.	7/16 to —	$2; 9/16; 5/8	5/16	. . . .	. . . .
Nov.	1/2 to —	5/8; 1/2	3/8	. . . .	. . . .
Dec.	3/8 to 7/16	1/2	3/8	1/2	1/2
1852					
Jan.	13/32 to 7/16	1/2	3/8	1/2; 9/16	. . . .
Feb.	3/8 to 13/32	1/2	3/8	1/2	1/2
Mar.	5/16 to 3/8	1/2	. . . .	9/16	. . . .
Apr.	9/16 to —	5/8	5/16	. . . .	. . . .
May.	1/4 to 5/16	1/2–5/8	. . . .	. . . .	. . . .
June.	5/16 to 3/8	. . . .	. . . .	. . . .	. . . .
July.	5/16 to	. . . .	. . . .	. . . .	. . . .
Aug.	5/16 to 3/8	$1.25	. . . .	. . . .	. . . .

[a] Rates in fractions of a pence per pound. The low for March was given as 15/16 and assumed a mistake. MS. PMC, Letters to treasurer about the purchase of cotton, New Orleans Prices-Current, *Commercial Intelligencer and Merchant's Transcript*, Sept. 1, 1852.

[b] Rates in fractions of a cent per pound with the exception of the first and last, which are in dollars per bale. In addition, there was a primage charge of 5% of the freight charge. Rates from MS. PMC, from bills of lading, and letters to treasurer about the purchase of cotton.

[c] Rates in fractions of a cent per pound from bills of lading and letters to the treasurer, MS. PMC.

[d] Rates in fraction of a cent per pound from MS. PMC, bill of lading, and letters to the treasurer about the purchase of cotton.

[e] Rates in fraction of a cent per pound with the addition of a primage charge of 5%. Rates from bills of lading, MS. PMC.

APPENDIX 15

PURCHASES, CONSUMPTION, STOCK ON HAND, AND AVERAGE COST OF COTTON OF THE PEPPERELL MANUFACTURING COMPANY AND AVERAGE PRICE IN THE SOUTH 1871–1924

	Pepperell Manufacturing Company				South
Twelve Months Ending	Purchases (In bales)[a]	Consumption (In bales)[b]	Stock on Hand at End of Period (In bales)[c]	Average Cost per Pound (In cents)[d]	Average Price per Pound (In cents)[e]
June 24, 1871	13,050	10,500	3,474	17.36	17.0
June 29, 1872	9,795	11,135	2,134	19.03	20.5
June 28, 1873	11,601	11,642	2,093	20.10	18.2
June 27, 1874	12,908	12,145	2,856	18.01	17.0
June 26, 1875	10,451	10,526	2,781	16.70	15.0
June 24, 1876	13,096	13,919	1,958	13.93	13.0
June 30, 1877	15,389	13,552	3,795	11.71	11.7
June 29, 1878	16,468	16,142	4,121	11.42	11.3

[a] Purchases of cotton which were ultimately used in the mills. Losses by fire, such as that of 1880–1881, when 1,933 bales were destroyed, were not included, as well as losses in transit and sale of cotton which had been stored.

[b] Consumption of cotton by the mills during the twelve months.

[c] Stock on hand at end of period does not include that in process of manufacture.

[d] Average cost of cotton consumed for the twelve months found by averaging the two six-months' costs. This figure is not exact for much of the period, since from June 26, 1880, on, cost of cotton on hand was carried at figures which varied considerably from cost of cotton consumed.

[e] These prices are for the marketing year, which includes the winter and spring following the growing. Thus these prices are placed one year later than those of the Bureau of the Census. Various figures are combined into this series. For 1911 on, they are prices per pound for upland cotton received by growers; for 1903 through 1910, they are the prices of average grade marketed in New Orleans before April 1; for 1891 through 1902, average price of middling on the New Orleans Cotton Exchange; earlier still, from reports of Department of Agriculture.

PEPPERELL MANUFACTURING COMPANY SOUTH (continued)

Twelve Months Ending	Purchases (In bales)[a]	Consumption (In bales)[b]	Stock on Hand at End of Period (In bales)[c]	Average Cost per Pound (In cents)[d]	Average Price per Pound (In cents)[e]
June 28, 1879	17,563	16,429	5,255	10.64	10.8
June 26, 1880	18,712	18,573	5,394	12.00	12.0
June 25, 1881	19,332	17,689	7,037	12.13	11.3
June 24, 1882	22,365	20,980	8,422	12.13	12.2
June 30, 1883	21,515	21,471	8,466	11.50	10.6
June 28, 1884	19,326	21,025	6,767	11.20	10.6
June 27, 1885	20,781	21,063	6,485	10.90	10.5
June 26, 1886	23,454	23,036	6,903	10.30	9.4
June 25, 1887	24,721	23,080	8,544	10.25	10.3
June 30, 1888	23,404	24,220	7,728	10.10	10.3
June 29, 1889	24,615	24,130	8,213	10.50	10.7
June 28, 1890	25,720	24,468	9,465	10.85	11.5
June 27, 1891	25,049	26,140	8,374	10.70	8.6
June 25, 1892	31,774	26,100	14,048	9.25	7.3
July 1, 1893	20,609	25,880	8,777	9.19	8.4
June 30, 1894	27,358	26,520	9,615	8.43	7.5
June 29, 1895	32,585	27,506	14,694	7.18	5.9
June 27, 1896	23,540	27,452	10,782	7.98	8.2
June 26, 1897	24,068	26,352	8,498	8.13	7.3
July 2, 1898	30,304	24,833	13,969	7.00	5.6
PEPPERELL DIVISION					SOUTH
July 1, 1899	26,430	29,698	10,701	6.63	4.9
June 30, 1900	29,285	29,625	10,361	7.75	7.6
June 29, 1901	23,720	25,016	9,065	9.00	9.3
June 28, 1902	29,945	29,166	9,844	9.00	8.1
June 27, 1903	27,696	28,997	8,543	9.38	8.2
June 25, 1904	23,865½	24,680½	7,728	10.88	12.2
July 1, 1905	32,697	28,291	12,134	11.63	8.7
June 30, 1906	28,789	30,429	10,494	10.88	10.9
June 29, 1907	29,296	29,747	10,043	10.25	10.0
June 27, 1908	24,333	26,246	8,130	12.00	11.5
June 30, 1909	33,917	[f]	[f]	[f]	9.2
July 2, 1910	21,818	[f]	[f]	[f]	14.3

[f] Not available.

LACONIA DIVISION

Twelve Months Ending	Purchases (In bales)[a]	Consumption (In bales)[b]	Stock on Hand at End of Period (In bales)[c]	Average Price per Pound (In cents)[e]
July 1, 1899			8,906	
June 30, 1900	25,767	25,250	9,423	
June 29, 1901	19,837	22,250	7,010	
June 28, 1902	23,925	27,568	8,367	
June 27, 1903	25,841	26,044	8,164	
June 25, 1904	23,953	24,681	7,436	
July 1, 1905	31,137[g]	26,573	12,000[g]	
June 30, 1906	25,389[g]	27,876	9,513	
June 29, 1907	25,270	25,356	9,427	
June 27, 1908	22,375	23,481	8,321	
June 30, 1909	28,254	23,805	12,770	
July 2, 1910	19,424	24,929	7,265	
BOTH DIVISIONS				SOUTH
June 1911	37,329			14.0
June 1912	59,498			9.6
June 1913	60,004			11.5
June 1914	62,285			12.5
June 1915	70,006			7.3
July 1, 1916	68,620		22,751	11.2
June 30, 1917	63,386	62,298	23,839	17.3
June 29, 1918	60,871	61,228	23,482	27.1
June 1919	42,598			28.8
June 30, 1920	58,457			35.4
June 30, 1921	40,761			15.8
June 30, 1922	48,611			16.9
June 30, 1923	57,930			22.9
June 30, 1924	39,794			28.7

[g] Estimated.

Source: MS. PMC, Agent's semiannual statements, 1866–1908; Claim books of Pepperell Division, 1909–25; Goods manufactured and invoiced weekly, cotton account, 1916–18; List of cotton invoices of Laconia Division, 1899–1912; Claim book, 1907–08; Estimate for Laconia's stock on hand on June 30, 1905, made so that its level was about the same as that for the Pepperell Division. Other missing figures computed, using stock on hand, purchases, consumption. U. S. Bureau of the Census, *Bulletin 167*, *Cotton Production and Distribution*, season of 1929–30, pp. 57–58.

APPENDIX 16

THE PLAN FOR MACHINERY IN 1850

Place	Mill No. 1	Mill No. 2
Picker House		
Calvert Openers................	4	4
Pickers of 3 beaters.............	7	7
Attic Story of Mill		
Breaker Cards..................	84	84
Lap Winders...................	2	2
Fifth Story of Mill		
Finisher Cards.................	84	84
Railway Heads.................	24	24
Drawing Frames...............	12	12
Speeders of 24 spindles..........	12	12
Extensors......................	16 of 60 spindles	28 of 36 spindles
Fourth Story of Mill		
Warp Frames of 128 spindles.....	60 [7,680 spindles]	70 [8,960 spindles]
Filling Frames of 128 spindles....	30 [3,840 spindles]	20 [3,456 spindles]
Third Story of Mill		
Warpers.......................	20	24
Dressing Frames................	16	16
Second Story of Mill		
Looms.........................	228	312
First Story (Basement) of Mill		
Looms.........................	168	144
Filling Frames of 128 spindles....	27 [3,456 spindles]	27 [3 456 spindles]

Source: MS. PMC, Plan for Machinery, 1850.

APPENDIX 17

NUMBER OF SPINDLES IN BIDDEFORD, 1870–1924

A. PEPPERELL MANUFACTURING COMPANY AND LACONIA COMPANY, 1870–1899

Year	Pepperell Manufacturing Company	Laconia Co.	Both Companies
1870	71,000	57,696	128,696
1875	80,000	65,000	145,000
1880	85,000	75,000	160,000
1885	97,696	77,748	175,444
1890	105,000	78,876	183,876
1895	110,000	90,000	200,000
1899	113,000	93,000	206,000

B. PEPPERELL MANUFACTURING COMPANY, 1899–1924

Year	Pepperell Division	Laconia Division	Both Divisions
1899	113,000	93,000	206,000
1905	120,672	101,072	221,744
1910	136,608	102,608	239,216
1915	136,608	154,992	291,600
1920	136,608	154,992	291,600
1924	136,672	154,992	291,664

Source: Pepperell Manufacturing Company: 1870, *Dockham's United States Cotton, Woolen, Silk & Linen Manufacturers' Report and Directory*, 1870–71, p. 48; 1875, 1874–75, p. 32; 1880, MS. PMC, Agent's letter book, 1880, p. 273; 1885, Agent's general letter book, 1883–85, p. 753; 1890, Treasurer's report, Jan. 24, 1890; 1895, Agent's general letter book, 1894–96, p. 476; 1899, Treasurer's letter book, 1897–1901, p. 300; 1905, Clarence Gove's Notebook—figures for 1903 for Pepperell and for 1901 for Laconia; 1910, Clarence Gove's Notebook; 1915, Treasurer's letter book, 1920–21, p. 519; 1920, *loc. cit.;* 1924, Production records weekly, 1922–25.

Laconia Co.: 1870, MS. LC, Treasurer's ledger balances, Dec. 31, 1870. 1875, *Dockham's Report*, 1874–75, p. 32; 1880, MS. PMC, Agent's general letter book, 1880–81, p. 38; 1885, *ibid.*, 1881–84, p. 844, figure for 1884; 1890, *ibid.*, 1890–92, p. 104; 1895, Assistant treasurer's letter book, 1915–20, p. 291, figure for 1894; 1899, Treasurer's letter book, 1920–21, p. 300.

APPENDIX 18

MACHINERY IN 1893

Picking and Carding Rooms

25 Kitson openers
25 Kitson intermediates
29 Kitson finishers
8 Kitson lappers
2 Kitson thread extractors
1 Calvert willow
66 Saco Water Power breaker cards
198 Saco Water Power finisher cards
38 Saco Water Power railway heads
231 Platt cards
1 Hetherington card
161 Pettee cards
Mason drawing frames for 410 deliveries
Hetherington drawing frames for 124 deliveries
2 Lowell doublers
1 Saco Water Power doubler
32 Saco Water Power slubbers
36 Saco Water Power intermediates
105 Saco Water Power fly frames

Spinning Rooms

432 Saco Water Power Ring Frames [77,104 spindles]
42 Saco Water Power Mule Frames [35,520 spindles]

Warping, Spooling, Size and Dressing Rooms

39 Saco Water Power spoolers
22 Hopedale warpers
10 Lewiston warpers
2 Hopedale banding machines
5 Lowell slashers
7 Howard & Bullock slashers with Lowell cylinder
10 Size kettles

Weaving Rooms

686 – 30″ Colvin looms
425 – 36″ " "
223 – 39″ " "
85 – 40″ " "
150 – 48″ " "
48 – 60″ " "
456 – 30″ looms with Colvin pick and lathe
308 – 40″ Lowell looms
22 – 105″ Saco Water Power looms
72 – 67″ Lewiston looms
67 – 77″ " "
197 – 86″ " "
66 – 105″ " "
8 – 110″ " "
1 – 40″ Whitin loom
40 – 67″ " looms
124 – 77″ " "
124 – 86″ " "
100 – 96″ " "

Cloth Rooms

2 – 36″ Eliott cloth folders
2 – 40″ Eliott cloth folders
1 – Lowell stamping machine
5 – Lowell hydraulic presses
2 – Opening and measuring machines for wide cloth
4 – 40″ Curtis & Marble shearers
1 – 96″ Curtis & Marble calender
4 – 40″ Dinsmore stitching machines
1 – 96″ Dinsmore stitching machine

Comment: Name of machine may be that of maker of frame and not necessarily that of the important parts, as, for example, spinning frames.

Source: MS. PMC, Machines and operatives, 1893–1903; Sectional elevations & memo of machinery, 1886–96; Contracts for machinery, 1888–1904; Agent's letter books, 1887–88.

APPENDIX 19

AGENT'S CONSTRUCTION ACCOUNT[a]
1874–1918

Year ending June 30	Construction	Year ending June 30	Construction
1874	$41,125.16	1900	$65,869.35
1875	250,285.94	1901	19,853.65
1876	112,481.46	1902	87,006.07
1877	33,498.17	1903	212,922.07
1878	52,509.31	1904	90,870.15
1879	97,558.52	1905	93,805.23
1880	125,717.86	1906	117,410.00
1881	294,935.20	1907	349,511.65
1882	171,159.69	1908	123,411.78
1883	99,840.72	1909	347,445.78
1884	95,636.37	1910	791,256.87
1885	69,787.10	1911	346,648.67
1886	62,219.10	1912	412,283.16
1887	32,764.31	1913	628,885.63
1888	202,520.74	1914	198,621.14
1889	122,474.39	1915	112,178.13
1890	45,059.05	1916	256,185.80
1891	186,472.27	1917	247,701.04
1892	170,550.02	1918	82,390.31
1893	140,026.59		
1894	54,094.50		
1895	123,656.36		
1896	64,496.88		
1897	14,039.58		
1898	31,392.71		
1899	46,002.83		

[a] Construction includes both building and machinery. For the fiscal year 1899, figure includes construction of the Pepperell Manufacturing Company until time of consolidation and of the Pepperell Division. For the following years, figures include construction for both divisions.

Source: MS. PMC, Agent's semiannual statements; Construction account; 1875–94, Agent's monthly account with treasurer; Construction, 1891–1919.

APPENDIX 20

NUMBER OF WORKERS HIRED, 1850–1854

Month	1850	1851	1852	1853	1854
Jan.		137	123	59	59
Feb.		91	104	58	43
Mar.		53	141	101	92
Apr.		61	117	91	102
May		115	147	90	123
June		151	104	80	83
July		140	113	61	56
Aug.		101	116	78	71
Sept.		134	134	76	85
Oct.		130	73	54	61[a]
Nov.		114	56	68	[b]
Dec.	46	135	67	50	[b]
Total	46	1,362	1,295	866	775

[a] Figures through Oct. 18 only.
[b] No signatures given.

Source: MS. PMC, Contract book, 1850–54.

APPENDIX 21

NUMBER OF EMPLOYEES IN EACH MILL
1850–1855

Four Weeks Ending	Mill No. 1	Mill No. 2	Total
1850			
Dec. 28	34	3[a]	37
1851			
Jan. 11[b]	73	5	78
Feb. 8	203	[c]	203
Mar. 8	267	12	279
Apr. 5	263	21	284
May 3	262	32	294
May 31	309	78	387
June 28	339	153	492
July 26	332	224	556
Aug. 23	323	256	579
Sept. 20	301	270	571
Oct. 18	308	306	614
Nov. 15	323	383	706
Dec. 13	316	404	720
1852			
Jan. 10	350	403	753
Feb. 7	351	434	785
Mar. 6	361	458	819
Apr. 3	402	480	882
May 1	398	487	885
May 29	419	518	937
June 26	426	501	927
July 24	452	481	933

[a] First period for Mill No. 2, Dec. 2–Jan. 11. Of those listed, three were hired before Dec. 28.

[b] Two-weeks' period.

[c] No payroll given for Mill No. 2 for this period.

NUMBER OF EMPLOYEES IN EACH MILL (continued)
1850–1855

Four Weeks Ending	Mill No. 1	Mill No. 2	Total
Aug. 21	429	465	894
Sept. 18	417	503	902
Oct. 16	396	514	910
Nov. 13	397	462	859
Dec. 11	390	467	857
1853			
Jan. 8	390	460	850
Feb. 5	379	463	842
Mar. 5	400	451	851
Apr. 2	408	505	913
Apr. 30	411	503	914
May 28	420	496	916
June 25	426	483	909
July 23	390	453	843
Aug. 20	367	443	810
Sept. 17	400	425	825
Oct. 15	393	398	791
Nov. 12	405	395	800
Dec. 10	376	414	790
1854			
Jan. 7	380	417	797
Feb. 14	381	407	788
Mar. 4	396	415	811
Apr. 1	407	439	846
Apr. 29	439	464	903
May 27	456	492	948
June 24	446	463	909
July 22	429	429	858
Aug. 19	389	391	780
Sept. 16	356	406	762
Oct. 14	390	411	801
Nov. 11	371	440	811
Dec. 9	396	444	840

NUMBER OF EMPLOYEES IN EACH MILL (continued)
1850–1855

Four Weeks Ending	Mill No. 1	Mill No. 2	Total
1855			
Jan. 6	402	475	877
Feb. 3	391	434	825
Mar. 3	381	461	842
Mar. 31	408	473	881
Apr. 28	413	475	888
May 26	413	471	884
June 23	442	491	933
July 21	441	499	940
Aug. 18	419	468	887
Sept. 15	420	459	879
Oct. 13	421	470	891
Nov. 10	419	471	890
Dec. 8	401	467	868

Source: MS. PMC, Payrolls, 1850–55.

APPENDIX 22

CONTRACT FOR LABOR, 1850–1854

PEPPERELL COMPANY

BIDDEFORD, ME.

Whereas, by an Act of the Legislature of the State of Maine, approved August 10th, 1848, it was among other things enacted *that in all Contracts for Labor, ten hours of actual labor should be a legal day's work:—and that no person should be required or holden to perform more than ten hours labor in any one day except in pursuance of an Express Contract requiring a greater length of time;—and that said Act should take effect and be in force on and after the twentieth day of April, eighteen hundred and forty-nine:—*

Now, therefore, We the undersigned, in Consideration of our Wages, and for the purpose of making such express contract for a greater length of time, severally PROMISE and AGREE, to and with the Pepperell Company, that while we remain in the employ of said Company, we will severally work as many hours each day, and for each and every day's work, as the Mills were usually run, at corresponding seasons of the year, prior to the twentieth day of April, A. D. 1849: And that while in said employ, we will faithfully observe and keep the Rules and Regulations published, or that may from time to time be published for the observance of those in the employ of said Company.

The undersigned severally acknowledge each to have received a copy of the foregoing Memorandum of Contract, embodied in the General Regulations of said Company.

Source: MS. PMC, Contract book, 1850–54, contract pasted inside front cover.

APPENDIX 23

AVERAGE RATES OF WEEKLY EARNINGS FOR SELECTED TYPES OF WORKERS, 1852–1870

Year[a]	Warp Spinners—Girls Mill No. 1		Weavers—Girls Mill No. 2		Carding Room Men pickers Mill No. 1	Weaving Room Men Mill No. 2
	By job	By week	By job	By week		
1852	$2.76	$3.23	$3.31	$2.14	$4.04[b]	$6.63
1853	3.06	3.25	3.46	2.79	3.75[b]	6.48
1854	3.30	3.42	3.62	2.96	4.21[b]	6.48
1855	3.06	3.48	3.84	2.70	4.77[b]	6.72
1856	3.12	3.06	3.72	2.82	4.42[b]	6.48
1857	3.18	3.54	3.42	2.64	4.67[b]	6.48
1858	2.82	2.52	2.34		3.75[b]	5.52
1859	3.20		3.06		3.98[b]	6.28
1860	3.24		3.06		4.68	6.78
1861	3.12		3.38		4.86	6.84
1862	2.56		3.03		4.52	6.80
1863	2.46		[c]		4.50	[c]
1864	2.95		3.67		5.85	7.43
1865	4.00		4.40		6.90	9.67
1866	4.60		5.30		8.70	10.50
1867	4.80		5.60		8.83	10.80
1868	4.20		4.74		8.76	10.80
1869	4.38		5.28		8.82	12.00[b]
1870	4.68		5.22		8.82	10.14

[a] Second payroll period in the year used to avoid the Christmas holiday, from 1852 through 1864. From 1865 through 1870, the first was used since it did not include Christmas.

[b] Not calculated in the analysis. Computed from figures given.

[c] Mill not in operation throughout this period.

Source: MS. PMC, Monthly statements of mill expense, 1851–70; Analysis of payroll, 1852–59; Payrolls, Mill No. 1, 1850–59.

APPENDIX 24

LENGTH OF EMPLOYMENT BY DEPARTMENTS, LINDALE DIVISION, 1933

Years of Work	Card.	Spin.	Weave	Dress.	Spool. Warp.	Dye House	Cloth Room	Shop	Cotton Yard	Cloth Yard Shipping	Village	Nap.	Farm Garden	Off.	Total
0–1	51	61	47	1	22	6	13	6	4	4	7	0	3	0	225
1–2	24	38	38	2	18	7	10	5	4	1	7	0	4	3	161
2–3	33	33	39	7	14	11	10	5	2	3	3	0	0	1	161
3–4	33	26	29	7	8	7	5	2	3	2	3	1	1	1	128
4–5	16	29	34	7	6	2	4	2	0	1	1	1	0	0	103
5–6	13	27	23	1	10	2	10	2	1	0	1	0	2	0	92
6–7	12	20	18	4	11	2	5	2	4	0	1	1	0	0	80
7–8	14	11	26	2	13	5	5	1	2	0	1	0	0	2	82
8–9	10	10	20	4	5	10	6	6	0	1	0	1	0	1	74
9–10	8	4	7	4	4	0	9	8	1	0	0	0	0	1	46
10–11	8	9	17	2	7	4	3	3	2	1	2	0	0	1	59
11–12	9	7	8	3	3	3	1	2	1	1	0	1	1	0	40
12–13	7	16	10	1	1	1	3	3	1	1	0	0	0	0	44
13–14	2	6	7	0	2	1	1	3	1	2	0	0	0	0	25
14–15	3	6	9	3	2	1	2	0	2	0	0	0	1	0	29
15–16	7	13	12	0	4	0	4	3	2	1	0	0	0	0	46
16–17	4	4	8	4	1	0	2	1	2	0	0	0	0	0	26
17–18	3	2	9	0	3	0	1	0	0	0	0	2	0	0	20
18–19	3	7	10	2	0	0	1	4	0	0	0	1	0	0	28
19–20	1	4	10	1	1	1	1	1	1	1	0	0	0	0	22
20–21	7	6	19	4	2	1	1	2	1	0	2	0	0	0	45
21–22	3	2	6	2	3	1	0	1	0	1	0	0	0	0	19
22–23	3	4	9	2	0	0	1	1	0	1	0	0	0	0	21
23–24	1	6	9	0	1	3	0	2	0	0	0	0	0	1	23
24–25	3	2	4	1	1	0	0	2	0	0	0	0	0	0	13
25–26	6	7	6	0	3	0	1	2	0	0	0	2	0	0	27
26–27	3	4	8	0	1	0	0	1	1	0	0	0	0	0	18

Years of Work	Card.	Spin.	Weave	Dress.	Spool. Warp.	Dye House	Cloth Room	Shop	Cotton Yard	Cloth Yard Shipping	Village	Nap.	Farm Garden	Off.	Total
27–28	3	2	6	2	0	0	0	1	3	0	0	0	0	0	17
28–29	0	3	7	1	0	0	2	1	0	0	0	0	0	1	15
29–30	2	0	6	2	0	0	0	0	2	0	0	0	0	1	13
30–31	2	1	6	0	0	0	0	1	0	0	0	0	0	0	10
31–32	1	1	5	0	0	0	0	3	0	0	0	0	0	1	11
32–33	2	1	3	1	0	0	0	1	0	0	0	0	0	0	8
33–34	1	4	1	1	0	0	0	1	0	0	0	0	0	1	9
34–35	0	1	1	0	1	0	0	0	0	0	2	0	0	2	7
Total	297	377	477	71	146	68	101	78	40	21	30	10	12	17	1,747

	Card.	Spin.	Weave	Dress.	Spool. Warp.	Dye House	Cloth Room	Shop	Cotton Yard	Cloth Yard Shipping	Village	Nap.	Farm Garden	Off.	Total
Average Yrs.	7.3	7.5	10.2	11.2	6.9	6.5	6.9	12.3	10.5	7.4	5.3	13.4	4.0	15.5	8.6
Total married	198	183	330	51	90	54	58	63	26	12	19	9	9	8	1,110
Single	99	191	150	20	58	14	43	15	14	8	12	1	3	9	637
Males	219	189	378	58	23	59	61	78	40	18	31	10	12	13	1,189
Females	78	185	102	13	125	9	40	0	0	2	0	0	0	4	558
Residence															
Lindale	231	293	356	55	98	52	67	63	28	7	4	4	1	16	1,275
Boozeville	29	25	20	7	18	0	8	3	0	0	0	1	1	1	113
Country	26	28	79	8	27	14	22	7	8	11	23	4	9	0	226
Rome	11	28	25	1	5	2	4	5	4	2	4	1	1	0	93

Source: MS. PMC, Lindale Division, Memoranda.

APPENDIX 25

ANNUAL PRODUCTION OF GOODS BY TYPES, MILL NO. 1, 1851–1870

(In thousands of yards)

Twelve Months Ending		Shirtings				Flannels		Jeans		Drills		Sheetings		
	N	O	R	E	Other	F	J	BJ	PJ	30″	33″	77″	86″	Total
June 28, 1851		282	39	427										748
June 26, 1852		1,087	677	1,166		426	141							3,497
June 25, 1853		1,107	935	871		896	887							4,696
June 24, 1854	41	1,445	1,171	842		459	575							4,533
June 23, 1855	316	1,322	1,600	1,206		19								4,463
June 21, 1856	409	971	1,594	1,272		400								4,646
June 20, 1857	514	1,486	1,245	695		226	189							4,355
June 19, 1858	567	1,171	478	359	101	135	427							3,238
June 18, 1859	621	1,561	1,364	384			513							4,443
June 16, 1860	773	1,326	977	480			722							4,278
June 15, 1861	773	1,321	975	664			755							4,488
June 14, 1862	363	753	803	683		160	336	351		201				3,650
June 13, 1863	448	523	503	76	24			235		437				2,246
June 25, 1864	749	1,105	733	180	153		93	414		40	231			3,698
June 24, 1865	523	691	378	262			298	107		123	206			2,588
June 23, 1866	783	1,208	900	511			569							3,971
June 29, 1867	448	842	1,424	905			733							4,352
June 27, 1868	627	1,077	1,270	560			722							4,256
June 26, 1869	402	1,151	1,427	218			969		36			23	3	4,229
June 25, 1870	668	363	1,414	419			573					117	99	3,653
Totals	9,025	20,792	19,907	12,180	278	2,721	8,502	1,107	36	801	437	140	102	76,028

ANNUAL PRODUCTION OF GOODS BY TYPES, MILL NO. 2, 1851–1870
(In thousands of yards)

Twelve Months Ending	Drills						Shirtings			Flannels	Ptg. Cloth	Jeans			Duck				Total
	D	H°D	AD	WD	DD	3 yd.	G	N	Other	F	P	J	BJ	PD	8 oz.	10 oz.	12 oz.	Other	Total
June 28, 1851....	7																		7
June 26, 1852....	3,678																		3,678
June 25, 1853....	5,642																	186	5,828
June 24, 1854....	3,049						407		897		879							80	5,312
June 23, 1855....	1,835						2,049			97	344	1,006							5,331
June 21, 1856....	2,766						838			401		1,275							5,280
June 20, 1857....	2,564	404					1,017			162		985							5,132
June 19, 1858....	3,271	393					425					405							4,494
June 18, 1859....	4,811											793							5,604
June 16, 1860....	5,549											305							5,854
June 15, 1861....	5,859											335							6,194
June 14, 1862....	569																	228	797
June 13, 1863....	655	311						17	40			13	43		125	338	109		1,651
June 25, 1864....	2,299	36	136	401						45			65	61	289	81	14		3,427
June 24, 1865....	826			379		598									68	80	321	59	2,331
June 23, 1866....	1,955			491	314			183				390			703				4,036
June 29, 1867....	1,945			1,431			632	390				668							5,066
June 27, 1868....	3,450			438			122	259				712							4,981
June 26, 1869....	4,170			419				232				351							5,172
June 25, 1870....	2,524			474								1,281							4,279
Totals........	57,424	1,144	136	4,033	314	598	5,490	1,081	937	705	1,223	8,519	108	61	1,185	499	444	553	84,454

ANNUAL PRODUCTION OF GOODS BY TYPES, MILL NO. 3, 1856–1870
(In thousands of yards)

Twelve Months Ending	Shirtings			Jeans		Drills					Sheetings							Total
	R	E	Other	J	BJ	D	H^aD	H^bD	H^cD	55″	48″	58″	67″	77″	86″	96″	105″	
June 21, 1856.....	298	314												36	45	45	43	781
June 20, 1857.....	1,994	1,053	83									61	80	123	141	183	86	3,804
June 19, 1858.....	1,581	784		440								68		87	114	98	42	3,214
June 18, 1859.....	2,048	1,085		888								102		132	203	176	87	4,721
June 16, 1860.....	2,084	997		1,022								72		185	192	206	86	4,844
June 15, 1861.....	1,626	1,199		894		575						107		196	174	281	58	5,110
June 14, 1862.....	935	619		314		60						111		65	67	48		2,219
June 13, 1863.....	1,065	354	177	297	482	1,100	70	12	19		234	147		64	57	72		4,150
June 25, 1864.....	1,605	780		761	153	38	47		38	64	23	159		97	156	281		4,202
June 24, 1865.....	1,152	702		660	5					103		119		123	135	209		3,208
June 23, 1866.....	1,796	789		895								234		182	158	204	42	4,300
June 29, 1867.....	1,969	925		979								228	24	158	175	267	46	4,771
June 27, 1868.....	1,935	894		955								193	37	161	242	174	12	4,603
June 26, 1869.....	955	467		1,789		607						178	50	121	185	293		4,645
June 25, 1870.....	1,732	711		1,258								160	99	120	221	277	32	4,610
Totals..........	22,775	11,673	260	11,152	640	2,380	117	12	57	167	257	1,939	290	1,850	2,265	2,814	534	59,182

Source: MS. PMC, Agent's semiannual statements, 1851–75.

APPENDIX 26

YARDS PRODUCED BY TYPE, 1871–1911[a]

Twelve Months Ending in June	Shirtings	Sheetings	Drills	Jeans	Sateens	Other Twills, Constitutions, Coutils	Total
1871	6,879,635	1,202,537	3,830,623	790,766	125,469	......	12,829,030
1876	5,523,877	2,013,339	3,415,942	1,984,679	3,452,530	155,702	16,546,069
1881	4,850,569	2,455,487	9,225,729	3,302,729	2,282,590	61,777	22,178,881
1886	5,688,431	3,201,994	12,700,885	3,671,147	3,458,429	1,400	28,722,286
1891	7,074,824	4,692,750	13,336,664	5,109,719	2,109,291	23,545	32,346,793
1896	6,657,433	6,288,922	12,870,542	7,426,499	704,470	99,074	34,046,940
1901	5,388,553	6,368,561	13,125,719	6,490,572	1,267,840	54,733	32,695,978
1906	1,216,722	7,832,874	15,544,813	10,765,518	1,411,487	20,878	36,792,292
1911	1,156,549	8,314,379	9,317,058	8,015,162	1,273,141	1,790,418	29,866,707

[a] Figures for Pepperell Manufacturing Co. 1871–96, and for Pepperell Division 1901–11. Figures after 1911 not available since distribution of goods given in pounds, not in yards.

Source: MS. PMC, Agent's semiannual statements, 1866–1908; Manufacture and disposal, 1910–12.

APPENDIX 27

PRODUCTION, 1871–1924

Fiscal Year Ending In June	Production (In Yards)	Fiscal Year Ending In June	Production (In yards)
1871	12,829,030	1900[a]	66,589,126
1872	14,040,692	1901	60,746,244
1873	14,187,920	1902	70,533,791
1874	15,000,513	1903	67,988,702
1875	12,977,171	1904	57,969,858
1876	16,546,077	1905	69,872,762
1877	16,643,834	1906	74,446,072
1878	20,120,913	1907	68,872,904
1879	19,924,511	1908	61,071,360
1880	22,782,018	1909	61,890,174
1881	22,178,881	1910	64,987,133
1882	26,338,365	1911	61,146,290
1883	27,690,418	1912	66,322,923
1884	27,976,691	1913	70,107,547
1885	26,419,697	1914	73,072,397
1886	28,722,286	1915	73,122,996
1887	29,498,771	1916	75,021,460
1888	29,909,140	1917	70,715,557
1889	30,738,950	1918	70,395,144
1890	30,676,528	1919	47,385,483
1891	32,346,793	1920	72,311,047
1892	33,021,620	1921	57,153,572
1893	32,929,311	1922	47,808,042
1894	32,427,094	1923	56,861,712
1895	33,710,345	1924	45,454,437
1896	34,046,940		
1897	33,687,676		
1898	31,570,057		
1899[b]	36,653,205		

[a] Figures for both divisions of the Pepperell Manufacturing Company from 1900 through 1924.

[b] Figures for Pepperell Manufacturing Company to May, 1899, and Pepperell Division, May–June, 1899.

Source: MS. PMC, Agent's semiannual statements, 1866–1908; Treasurer's reports to directors or trustees, 1880–1924.

APPENDIX 28

PARKS, WRIGHT & CO. AND SUBSEQUENT PARTNERSHIPS AND CORPORATION, 1831–1940

A. Partners, 1831–1927

1. Parks, Wright & Co., 1831–47
    - Luther Parks, 1831–47
    - John S. Wright, 1831–47
    - Ephraim P. Whitman, 1831–47
2. Wright & Whitman, 1847–63
    - John S. Wright, 1847–63
    - Ephraim P. Whitman, 1847–61[a]
    - John H. Wright, 1861–63
    - George L. Whitman, 1861–63
3. J. S. & E. Wright & Co., 1863–74
    - John S. Wright, 1863–74[b]
    - Eben Wright, 1863–74
    - John R. Wright, 1863–74
    - Cornelius N. Bliss, 1868–74
    - George F. Fabyan, 1868–74
4. Wright, Bliss & Fabyan, 1874–82
    - Eben Wright, 1874–81[b]
    - John H. Wright, 1874–79[b]
    - Cornelius N. Bliss, 1874–82
    - George F. Fabyan, 1874–82
    - Orlando H. Alford, 1880–82
5. Bliss, Fabyan & Co., 1882–1927
    - Senior Partners
        - Cornelius N. Bliss, 1882–1911[b]
        - George F. Fabyan, 1882–1907[b]
        - Orlando H. Alford, 1882–1908[b]
        - Peder Olsen, 1882–1907[b]
        - Jacob Edwards, 1882–90[a]

[a] Retired from the partnership.
[b] Died while in office.

George Fabyan, 1907[c]–27
Edwin H. Baker, 1898–1909[a]
Cornelius N. Bliss, Jr., 1911[c]–27
Francis W. Fabyan, 1909[c]–27
Philip Y. DeNormandie, 1907–27

Junior Partners
George Fabyan, 1898–1907[c]
Cornelius N. Bliss, Jr., 1901–11[c]
Francis W. Fabyan, 1901–09[c]
Eustis L. Hopkins, 1917–27
Edward B. Field, 1918–27
William B. Markell, 1919–27
S. Robert Glassford, 1919–27

B. Directors and Officers, 1927–1940

Bliss, Fabyan & Co., Inc., 1927–40[d]
- George Fabyan, director, 1927–31[e]
- Cornelius N. Bliss, Jr., director, 1927–36; chairman of board, 1927–32
- Francis W. Fabyan, director, 1927–31[e]
- Philip Y. DeNormandie, director, 1936–39; treasurer, 1927–30[e]
- Eustis L. Hopkins, director, 1927–40; vice-president, 1927–32; chairman of board, 1932–40
- Edward B. Field, director, 1927–31[e]
- William B. Markell, director, 1927–31[e]
- S. Robert Glassford, director, 1927–40; president, 1927–40
- Malcolm Black, director, 1933–40; secretary & treasurer, 1932–40[e]
- H. Davis Halliwell, director, 1933–40; vice-president, 1933–40
- R. D. Vanderbilt, director, 1932–40; vice-president, 1931–40
- G. Edward Buxton, director, 1932–40
- Thomas D. Mackay, director, 1937–40; vice-president, 1936–39
- T. Holt Haywood, vice-president, 1936–39
- S. L. Lewis, Jr., vice-president, 1938–39

[a] Retired from the partnership.

[c] Date not certain; assume promoted when vacancy occurred.

[d] Incorporated July 1, 1927; during 1931 to 1933 in process of reorganization; discontinued business Feb. 1, 1940.

[e] Date not certain.

Source: *Boston Daily Advertiser,* May 23, 1831. Notice of formation of co-partnership on May 18, 1831; July 5, 1847. Notice of change in co-partnership on July 1, 1847; July 13, 1874, last of advertisements of J. S. & E. Wright & Co. found, and on Aug. 19, 1874, first of Wright, Bliss & Fabyan; May 1, 1861, notice of change in partners on Apr. 1.

Boston Daily Advertiser, June 12 and 13, 1908, notice of death of Orlando H. Alford in Brookline, June 11, 1908, aged 66; Dec. 29, 1879, notice of death of Dr. John Harvey Wright, U.S.N. in 65th year.

Boston Directory, 1828–32, 1865–1927. Many dates not determined exactly since directory came out in the spring of the year and gave conditions as of that time. Some dates of death of partners were however given exactly, as that of John H. Wright, Dec. 26, 1879, George F. Fabyan, Jan. 18, 1907, and Peder Olsen, June 17, 1907.

Directory of Directors in the City of Boston & Vicinity, 1906–40.

New York Directory, 1909–10.

Directory of Directors in the City of New York, 1904–40.

Commerce & Finance, vol. 16, no. 48 (Nov. 20, 1927), p. 2492, historical sketch; vol. 17, no. 19 (May 9, 1928), p. 1058.

Southern Textile Bulletin, May 19, 1932, p. 11.

Textile World, Feb., 1940, p. 160, account of discontinuance of business.

N. E. Cotton Manufacturers' Association, Catalogue of Members, 1866–1917, in *Transactions.*

N. E. Historic & Genealogical Register, vol. 30, pp. 117–118 for the life of John S. Wright (1788–1874); vol. 34, pp. 417–418, for life of John H. Wright (1815–79); vol. 36, pp. 91–92, for life of Eben Wright (1819–81).

Lamb's Textile Industries of the United States, vol. 1, p. 349, account of life of Orlando H. Alford; vol. 2, pp. 79-81, account of life of Cornelius N. Bliss; vol. 1, pp. 347–348, life of George F. Fabyan.

Interview with S. Robert Glassford, Oct. 26, 1944.

APPENDIX 29

PARKS, WRIGHT & CO. AND SUBSEQUENT PARTNERSHIPS AND CORPORATION

Accounts of Manufacturing Companies, 1831–1940

1. Parks, Wright & Co. 1831[a]
    Commission business in American goods and wool.
2. Wright & Whitman, 1849[b]
    Boston Duck Co., Palmer, Mass.
    Columbian Manufacturing Co., New Ipswich, N. H.
    Cordis Co., Millbury, Mass.
    Otis Co., Ware, Mass.
    Palmer Co., Palmer, Mass.
    Thorndike Co., Palmer, Mass.
3. J. S. & E. Wright & Co.
    A. 1870[c]
    Boston Duck Co., Palmer, Mass.
    Columbian Manufacturing Co., Mason, N. H.
    Cordis Mills, Millbury, Mass.
    Lowell Hosiery Co., Lowell, Mass.
    Otis Co., Ware, Mass. (includes Palmer Co., Palmer, Mass.)
    Thorndike Co., Palmer, Mass.
    Warren Cotton Mills, West Warren, Mass.
    B. 1873[d]
    Androscoggin Mills, Lewiston, Me.
    Bates Manufacturing Co., Lewiston, Me.
    Boston Duck Co., Palmer, Mass.
    Columbian Manufacturing Co., Mason & New Ipswich, N. H.
    Continental Mills, Lewiston, Me.

[a] Boston *Daily Advertiser,* May 23, 1831.

[b] *New England Mercantile Union Directory,* 1849, compiled.

[c] *Dockham's Directory of Cotton, Woollen, Silk & Linen Manufacturers,* 1870–71.

[d] MS. PMC, Photostat of Price List, J. S. & E. Wright & Co., May 3, 1873.

Cordis Mills, Millbury, Mass.
Franklin Co., Lewiston, Me.
Laconia Co., Biddeford, Me.
Lowell Hosiery Co., Lowell, Mass.
Oriental Print Works, Apponaug, R. I.
Otis Co., Ware and Palmer, Mass.
Pepperell Manufacturing Co., Biddeford, Me.
Putnam Manufacturing Co., Putnam, Conn.
Sutton Hosiery Mills.
Thorndike Co., Palmer, Mass.
Warren Cotton Mills, West Warren, Mass.

4. Bliss, Fabyan & Co.

A. 1884[e]

American Printing Co., Fall River, Mass.
Androscoggin Mills, Lewiston, Me.
Annisquam Mills, Rockport, Mass.
Bates Manufacturing Co., Lewiston, Me.
Boston Duck Co., Palmer, Mass.
Columbian Manufacturing Co., New Ipswich & Greenville, N. H.
Cordis Mills, Millbury, Mass.
Laconia Co., Biddeford, Me.
Lowell Hosiery Co., Lowell, Mass.
Oriental Print Works, Warwick & Apponaug, R. I.
Otis Co., Palmer & Ware, Mass.
Pepperell Manufacturing Co., Biddeford, Me.
Thorndike Co., Palmer, Mass.
Victoria Mills, Newburyport, Mass.
Warren Cotton Mills, Warren, Mass.

B. 1899[f]

American Printing Co., Fall River, Mass.
Bates Mfg. Co., Lewiston, Me.
Boston Duck Co., Palmer, Mass.
Columbian Mfg. Co., Greenville, N. H.
Cordis Mills, Millbury, Mass.
Edwards Mfg. Co., Augusta, Me.
Laconia Co., Biddeford, Me.

[e] Commercial Agency Reports, New York, *Mill Reports,* Mar., 1884, compiled.

[f] *Davison's Textile Blue Book,* 1899–1900, compiled.

Lowell Hosiery Co., Lowell, Mass.
Otis Co., Ware & Three Rivers, Mass.
Pepperell Mfg. Co., Biddeford, Me.
Thorndike Co., Thorndike, Mass., and West Warren, Mass. (includes Warren Cotton Mills).

C. 1912[g]

Androscoggin Mills, Lewiston, Me.
Bates Mfg. Co., Lewiston, Me.
Boston Duck Co., Palmer, Mass.
Columbian Mfg. Co., Greenville, N. H.
Cordis Mills, Millbury, Mass.
Edwards Mfg. Co., Augusta, Me.
Otis Co. (includes mills formerly of Palmer Co.), Three Rivers, Palmer, Ware, Mass.
Pepperell Mfg. Co. (includes mills of Laconia Co.), Biddeford, Me.
Thorndike Co. (includes mills of Warren Cotton Mills), Thorndike & West Warren, Mass.

5. Bliss, Fabyan & Co., Inc.

A. 1927[h]

Adora Hosiery Mills.
Androscoggin Mills, Lewiston, Me.
American Cellulose & Chemical Mfg. Co., Ltd.
Bates Mfg. Co., Lewiston, Me.
Edwards Mfg. Co., Augusta, Me.
Kingston Knitting Co., Boston, Mass.
Otis Co. (includes mills formerly of Boston Duck Co., Columbian Mfg. Co., and Palmer Co.) Ware, Palmer, Mass., Mason Village, N. H.
Pepperell Mfg. Co. (includes mills formerly of Laconia Co.) Biddeford, Me.
Henry Taubel & Son.
Thorndike Co. (includes mills formerly of Cordis, Warren, and Morgan Cos.) Palmer, Warren, Mass.

B. 1936[i]

Alabama Mills, Birmingham, Ala.
Androscoggin Mills, Lewiston, Me.

[g] *Ibid.*, 1912–13, compiled.
[h] *Ibid.*, 1927, p. 1039.
[i] *Ibid.*, 1936, p. 763.

Brown Mfg. Co., Concord, N. C.
Cornelius Cotton Mills, Cornelius, N. C.
Eagle & Phenix Mills, Columbus, Ga.
Glencoe Mills, Inc., Burlington, N. C.
Highland Park Mfg. Co., Charlotte, N. C.
L. Banks Holt Mfg. Co., Graham, N. C.
Lebanon Woolen Mills, Lebanon, Tenn.
Miltonia Mills, Milton Mills, N. H.
Mount Alto Bedspread Co., Calhoun, Ga.
Owens Mfg. Co., Tullahoma, Tenn.
Wennonah Cotton Mills, Lexington, N. C.
Amana Society, Inc., Amana, Iowa.
Bates Mfg. Co., Lewiston, Me.
Edwards Mfg. Co., Augusta, Me.
Glen Raven Silk Mills, Glen Raven, N. C.
Hill Mfg. Co., Lewiston, Me.
Kuenzel Mills Co., New Bremen, Ohio.
Morgan Cotton Mills, Laurel Hill, N. C.
Otis Co., Ware, Mass.
Profile Cotton Mills, Jacksonville, Ala.
York Mfg. Co., Saco, Me.

APPENDIX 30

PRICES CHARGED FOR PRINCIPAL TYPES OF GOODS IN THE BROWN
1852–1870

(In cents per yard)

Jan. of the year	Shirting N's – 30″ Low	N's – 30″ High	O's – 33″ Low	O's – 33″ High	R's – 36″ Low	R's – 36″ High	E's – 39″ Low	E's – 39″ High	Jeans Low	Jeans High	Drills Low	Drills High	Ducks Low	Ducks High	Flannels Low	Flannels High	Sheetings 57″ Low	57″ High	77″ Low	77″ High	86″ Low	86″ High	96″ Low	105″ Low
1852[a]	....	....	6.25	6.50	6.75	7.00	7.50	....	....	....	7.00	7.25	....	....	10.00	....	....	....	....	....	....	....	....	....
1853	....	....	7.00	7.25	7.50	7.75	8.00	8.25	8.50	9.00	7.63	8.00	....	....	10.00	....	....	....	....	....	....	....	....	...
1854	....	....	8.00	8.25	8.75	....	9.00	9.25	8.50	....	7.75	....	11.50	....	10.25	10.25	....	....	....	....	....	....	....	....
1855	7.00	7.50	8.00	8.25	8.50	8.75	9.00	9.25	8.50	9.00	7.75	8.00	....	....	....	....	....	....	....	....	....	....	....	....
1856	7.00	7.25	7.50	8.00	8.00	8.50	8.50	9.00	8.75	9.00	8.00	....	....	....	10.50	....	....	....	....	....	....	....	....	....
1857	7.50	....	7.50	8.00	8.00	8.50	8.50	9.00	9.00	....	8.50	8.75	....	....	....	....	....	....	23.00	....	26.00	....	28.00	31.00
1858	7.00	....	7.75	....	8.13	8.25	8.25	8.75	9.00	....	8.75	9.25	....	....	....	....	13.50	14.00	17.00	17.50	21.00	....	27.00	....
1859	7.50	....	8.00	8.25	8.75	....	9.00	9.75	9.00	....	8.63	8.75	....	....	....	....	15.00	....	19.00	....	22.00	23.00	24.00	26.00
1860	7.75	....	8.50	....	9.00	....	9.50	....	9.00	9.25	8.75	9.00	....	....	....	....	15.00	....	23.00	....	25.00	27.00	29.00	32.00
1861	7.25	....	8.00	8.75	8.00	9.25	9.25	9.75	9.00	....	9.00	....	....	....	....	....	16.00	....	24.00	....	27.00	....	29.00	....
1862	11.00	....	12.50	13.00	13.00	14.00	15.00	....	15.00	....	13.00	18.50	30.00	37.00	....	....	23.00	....	29.00	....	....	....	....	....
1863	20.00	23.50	21.50	28.00	22.00	27.50	....	....	28.00	30.00	....	....	40.00	48.00	....	....	45.00	52.00	....	....	....	....	....	....
1864	26.50	28.50	30.00	....	32.75	33.00	35.00	35.50	36.00	38.50	38.50	41.00	62.00	....	....	....	60.00	61.00	82.50	87.50	87.50	95.00	....	....
1865	39.00	....	42.50	....	44.00	47.00	....	....	41.00	49.00	60.00	....	88.00	198.00	....	....	90.00	....	100.00	112.00	115.00	....	....	....
1866	23.00	27.00	24.50	29.00	27.50	31.00	28.50	32.00	32.50	....	30.00	33.00	....	....	....	....	50.00	....	85.00	90.00	100.00	105.00	115.00	....
1867	14.50	15.00	16.50	17.00	18.50	19.00	20.50	21.00	21.50	22.00	21.00	22.50	....	....	....	....	35.00	36.00	48.00	53.00	58.00	63.00	70.00	....
1868[b]	10.00	10.50	11.00	11.50	12.50	....	13.00	13.50	10.00	15.00	14.00	17.50	....	....	....	....	22.50	....	30.00	32.50	37.50	40.00	42.50	....
1869	11.50	....	12.50	....	13.50	....	14.50	....	....	....	17.00	....	....	....	....	....	32.50	....	45.00	....	50.00	....	55.00	....
1870	12.50	....	13.00	....	14.00	....	15.00	....	....	....	17.00	....	....	....	....	....	....	....	40.00	....	45.00	....	....	....

[a] Prices for shirtings O's and E's in April of 1851 were 6¾ to 7½ and 8 to 8½ cents per yard, respectively.
[b] Figures for Dec. 31, 1867, used, since figures for 1868 are missing.

PRICES CHARGED FOR PRINCIPAL TYPES OF GOODS, BLEACHED AND DYED
1852–1870
(In cents per yard)

Jan. of the year	Jeans				Drills							Sheetings[a]									
	Bleached		Dyed Corset Colors		Bleached		Dyed Corset Colors	Dyed Blue		Flannels Bleached		6/4		8/4		9/4		10/4		11/4	
	Low	High	Low	High	Low	High	Low	Low	High	Low	High	Low	High	Low	High	Low	High	Low	High	Low	High
1852	....	....	....	....	7.00	7.50	8.00	8.50	....	....	....	....	....	....	....	....	....	....	....	....	....
1853	9.00	9.25	9.50	9.75	8.25	8.50	....	....	....	....	....	....	....	....	....	....	....	....	....	....	....
1854	9.00	....	....	....	8.00	....	....	....	....	10.75	....	....	....	....	....	....	....	....	....	....	....
1855	9.00	9.50	9.50	....	7.75	8.00	....	9.25	....	....	....	....	....	....	....	....	....	....	....	....	....
1856	9.00	9.25	9.50	10.00	8.25	8.50	....	....	....	11.00	....	....	....	....	....	....	....	....	....	....	....
1857	9.50	9.75	10.00	....	....	....	....	10.50	....	11.00	11.50	....	....	....	....	29.00	....	31.00	....	34.00	....
1858	9.25	9.50	9.50	....	....	....	....	10.00	10.25	....	....	14.50	....	19.00	....	22.50	24.50	23.00	27.00	27.00	27.50
1859	9.00	9.50	9.00	10.00	9.00	....	....	10.50	....	....	....	15.50	....	21.00	....	23.50	....	25.00	27.00	27.50	28.00
1860	9.25	10.00	9.75	10.00	9.25	....	....	....	....	....	....	16.00	....	24.00	....	28.00	....	28.00	32.00	33.00	35.00
1861	9.00	9.75	9.50	10.00	....	....	....	....	....	....	....	17.00	....	25.00	....	29.00	....	32.00	....	35.00	....
1862	15.00	....	14.00	15.00	....	....	....	....	....	....	....	21.00	26.00	32.00	....	36.00	....	....	....	44.00	....
1863	31.50	....	25.00	....	....	....	....	....	....	....	....	....	....	....	....	65.00	....	43.75	65.00	....	....
1864	....	....	....	....	....	....	....	....	....	....	....	....	....	....	....	....	....	....	....	....	....
1865	....	....	....	....	....	....	....	....	....	....	....	67.50	....	82.50	....	95.00	....	80.00	107.50	....	....
1866	33.50	....	....	....	....	....	....	....	....	....	....	50.00	....	85.00	....	100.00	102.50	112.50	115.00	....	....
1867	21.50	22.00	21.50	22.50	....	....	....	....	....	....	....	37.50	38.00	50.00	....	60.00	65.00	72.50	75.00	....	....
1868[b]	14.00	14.50	14.00	15.00	....	....	....	....	....	....	....	22.50	25.00	30.00	32.50	35.00	45.00	40.00	45.00	47.50	55.00
1869	....	....	....	....	....	....	....	....	....	....	....	30.00	....	42.50	....	47.50	....	60.00	....	....	....
1870	....	....	....	....	....	....	....	....	....	....	....	32.50	....	40.00	....	45.00	....	50.00	....	....	....

[a] These are the same five types as in the brown, reduced in width about 5%.

Source: MS. PMC, Sales sheet, Apr.–June, 1851; Sales books, 1851–67 ;*Commercial & Financial Chronicle*, Jan. 2, 1869, p. 24, and Jan. 4, 1870, p. 27.

APPENDIX 31

EXPORTS, 1852–1868

Twelve Months Ending in June	Number of Merchants	Total Amount Exported	Total Amount Exported as Percentage of Total Gross Sales
1852	26	$183,959.44	33.7
1853	18	273,595.76	33.8
1854	7	87,595.76	11.3
1855	2	10,403.78	1.4
1856	8	58,602.95	7.0
1857	10	94,480.31	9.0
1858	14	278,659.71	22.6
1859	26	304,846.31	22.2
1860	24	425,751.14	29.1
1861	21	581,520.41	42.6
1862	3	17,584.00	2.3
1863	—	—	—
1864	—	—	—
1865	—	—	—
1866	1	15,000.00	0.4
1867	7	360,888.97	12.2
1868[a]	8	132,471.39	12.6

[a] Figures for first six months only.

Source: MS. PMC, Sales books, 1851–67, compilation by merchants. Appendix 35 for Gross Sales, 1852–67.

APPENDIX 32

TREASURER'S SEMIANNUAL LEDGER BALANCES, DECEMBER 31, 1851–JUNE 30, 1870

A. Assets

At the end of six months	Total Buildings & Equipment[a]	Balance of Account with Mill Agent[b]	Cloth on Hand[c]	Sales Agent's Balances[d]	Notes Receivable[e]	Cotton in Hands of the Treasurer[f]	Cotton Agents' Balances[g]	Suspense Account[h]	Misc. Prepayments[i]	Cash[j]	Total Assets[k]
Dec. 31, 1851	$538,211.48	$60,186.59	$38,086.76	$46,057.28	$111,378.78	$24,234.93	$ 8.98	$ 68.81	$13,912.88	$14,210.05	$ 846,356.54
June 30, 1852	538,211.48	231,519.27	5,734.60	190,863.83	146,214.64	0.00	22,844.40	660.07	23,056.03	56,038.01	1,215,142.33
Dec. 31, 1852	538,211.48	143,613.98	16,567.09	144,488.05	154,481.96	253,917.48	20,185.79	2,505.19	20,085.61	57,536.35	1,351,592.98
June 30, 1853	538,211.48	307,776.46	51,944.21	123,563.55	242,157.53	0.00	0.50	1,858.39	29,983.57	23,813.99	1,319,309.68
Dec. 31, 1853	538,211.48	164,736.89	26,081.80	261,768.62	197,964.80	135,808.38	5,100.00	5,942.94	13,410.63	9,799.36	1,358,824.90
June 30, 1854	538,211.48	330,203.03	58,419.16	99,909.85	267,338.92	0.00	6,869.83	12,449.89	10,737.72	10,662.03	1,334,801.91
Dec. 31, 1854	538,211.48	288,835.60	82,124.49	107,424.30	260,678.22	0.00	38,261.69	20,221.78	8,606.78	580.90	1,344,945.24
June 30, 1855	538,211.48	491,089.15	52,180.70	205,412.93	93,126.59	10,842.81	97,701.22	19,538.86	16,239.08	9,500.29	1,533,843.11
Dec. 31, 1855	538,211.48	661,738.40	79,750.05	240,728.80	113,832.96	259,117.58	115,471.91	14,869.47	22,454.15	4,684.92	2,050,859.72
June 30, 1856	538,211.48	1,015,448.70	118,461.70	225,560.00	97,477.86	0.00	107,921.46	16,719.98	30,280.25	7,401.66	2,157,483.09
Dec. 31, 1856	538,211.48	866,412.93	63,711.30	350,582.69	171,141.03	567,735.60	71,468.17	14,548.10	29,458.90	32,963.47	2,706,233.67
June 30, 1857	538,211.48	1,075,823.19	271,838.14	113,864.90	150,657.60	21,104.87	0.00	44,355.69	41,254.80	26,336.93	2,283,447.60
Dec. 31, 1857	538,211.48	869,897.48	54,042.11	35,637.14	380,338.02	20,691.40	40,744.16	41,832.70	21,820.82	11,677.91	2,014,893.22
June 30, 1858	538,211.48	1,279,796.45	19,299.28	53,767.55	32,761.40	285.84	0.00	21,235.34	36,485.60	12,504.06	1,994,347.00
Dec. 31, 1858	538,211.48	953,057.45	25,959.41	113,748.79	63,255.65	479,148.23	90,430.59	41,653.73	21,019.88	2,649.05	2,329,134.26
June 30, 1859	538,211.48	1,336,510.67	12,530.34	130,064.92	117,307.98	6,011.33	0.00	38,580.29	3,882.38	4,122.53	2,187,221.92
Dec. 31, 1859	538,211.48	1,042,212.00	25,437.59	99,398.12	293,642.69	149,637.53	27,207.75	40,089.38	1,254.88	4,461.36	2,221,552.78
June 30, 1860	538,211.48	1,185,692.16	4,069.71	261,338.68	329,897.75	1,639.99	0.00	40,301.82	3,754.82	41,741.77	2,406,648.18
Dec. 31, 1860	538,211.48	1,493,707.58	38,797.85	231,009.87	273,492.75	2,231.29	500.00	39,075.13	1,279.82	654.24	2,618,960.01

[a] From Dec., 1851, through June, 1862, the figures include only those set up at the beginning for the first two mills. Starting in Dec., 1862, the costs of the third mill as well as of various changes in Biddeford were included in this account.

[b] Includes expenditures for construction, cotton on hand, and miscellaneous other assets.

[c] Cloth in hands of the selling agent, the bleacheries, and the mi lagent.

[d] Sales agent's balances are differences between sales made and cash and notes turned over to the treasurer.

[e] Notes Receivable are those in the hands of the treasurer, which have not been discounted.

[f] Cotton in hands of the treasurer and cotton suspense account of June 30, 1855, June 30, 1857, June 30, 1859, Dec. 31, 1860, and June 30, 1861.

[g] Includes prepayments for cotton.

[h] Suspense accounts are those not settled; comprise sales largely. Claflin, Melden & Co. had a balance in Dec., 1861, of $3,723.80; in June, 1862, of $8,661.23; and in Dec., 1862, of $11,958.16.

[i] Included payments for insurance, burlaps, waste, and various others.

[j] Cash in hands of the treasurer.

[k] Total assets as given in the treasurer's balances with three exceptions. In June, 1861, total assets added up to $170 less than total liabilities, so I added this amount to cash. In Dec., 1851, and Dec., 1857, the loss was put by the treasurer on the liability side, but I have transferred it to the asset side.

TREASURER'S SEMIANNUAL LEDGER BALANCES, DECEMBER 31, 1851–JUNE 30, 1870 (continued)

A. ASSETS

At the end of six months	Total Buildings & Equipment[a]	Balance of Account with Mill Agent[b]	Cloth on Hand[c]	Sales Agent's Balances[d]	Notes Receivable[e]	Cotton in Hands of the Treasurer[f]	Cotton Agents' Balances[g]	Suspense Account[h]	Misc. Pre-payments[i]	Cash[j]	Total Assets[k]
June 30, 1861	538,211.48	1,286,140.24	65,672.88	109,353.51	405,682.69	51,249.55	822.92	118,759.99	3,754.82	18,862.23	2,598,510.31
Dec. 31, 1861	538,211.48	1,209,109.37	76,317.01	189,368.68	275,351.28	0.00	0.00	171,673.32	4,079.93	69,567.88	2,533,678.95
June 30, 1862	538,211.48	998,138.70	149,812.60	157,458.21	129,704.35	0.00	0.00	138,692.81	2,475.00	188,862.65	2,303,355.80
Dec. 31, 1862	1,382,856.10	176,521.76	24,722.64	441,103.95	121,413.74	0.00	97,040.77	143,888.05	0.00	294,151.38	2,681,698.39
June 30, 1863	1,382,856.10	469,277.23	18,671.34	615,055.43	21,651.10	0.00	125,500.00	124,892.31	2,771.94	5,772.41	2,766,447.86
Dec. 31, 1863	1,382,856.10	468,011.36	370.40	807,850.02	29,756.10	59,780.10	12,032.24	82,765.07	0.00	175,309.14	3,018,730.53
June 30, 1864	1,382,856.10	644,851.68	104,893.02	1,186,544.76	73,823.14	0.00	0.00	79,821.85	18,247.02	38,050.82	3,529,088.89
Dec. 31, 1864	1,184,803.74	902,303.03	57,839.19	1,543,760.92	167,531.63	28,248.56	50,000.00	0.00	27,215.70	192,317.37	4,154,020.14
June 30, 1865	1,184,803.74	440,362.02	5,752.97	1,349,527.76	103,421.49	0.00	1,365.87	0.00	22,117.95	37,896.24	3,145,248.04
Dec. 31, 1865	l	1,257,531.40	5,941.02	l	l	l	l	l	l	l	l
June 30, 1866	l	754,267.93	334,366.85	l	l	l	l	l	l	l	l
Dec. 31, 1866	l	659,964.62	155,733.06	l	l	l	l	l	l	l	l
June 30, 1867	l	372,729.23	333,351.19	l	l	l	l	l	l	l	l
Dec. 31, 1867	l	285,800.99	291,903.46	l	l	l	l	l	l	l	l
June 30, 1868	l	239,223.58	l	l	l	l	l	l	l	l	l
Dec. 31, 1868	l	l	l	l	l	l	l	l	l	l	l
June 30, 1869	l	457,758.11	l	l	l	l	l	l	l	l	l
Dec. 31, 1869	l	288,519.78	l	l [m]	l	l	l	l	l	l	l
June 30, 1870	l	297,371.94	l	l [n]	l	l	l	l	l	l	l

[l] Figures not available.
[m] Balance in cash due from F. Skinner & Co. on Jan. 1, 1870, $424,000.
[n] Liabilities of F. Skinner & Co. to Pepperell on Sept. 21, 1870, $706,564.23.

Source: MS. PMC, Treasurer's semiannual statements, 1851–65; Agent's semiannual statements, 1851–75; Sales book, 1865–67; Directors' records, Jan. 1 and Feb. 11, 1870. *Daily Evening Traveller*, Boston, Mass., Sept. 21, 1870.

B. Liabilities

At the end of six months	Capital & Surplus: Capital Stock[a]	Capital & Surplus: Insurance & Guarantee Fund for Sales[b]	Capital & Surplus: Repair & Reserve Fund for Buildings[c]	Capital & Surplus: Profit [& Loss][d]	Capital & Surplus: Total Capital & Surplus[e]	Current Liabilities: Notes Payable[f]	Current Liabilities: Accounts Payable[g]	Current Liabilities: Total Current Liabilities[h]	Total Liabilities[i]
Dec. 31, 1851.....	$ 536,265	$ 0.00	$ 0.00	$ 1,546.98[j]	$ 534,718.02	$ 191,348.96	$120,289.56	$ 311,638.52	$ 846,356.54
June 30, 1852.....	786,375	7,785.75	0.00	66,137.35	860,298.10	329,753.76	25,090.47	354,844.23	1,215,142.33
Dec. 31, 1852.....	798,228	15,453.42	34,137.35	0.00	847,818.77	394,623.95	109,150.26	503,774.21	1,351,592.98
June 30, 1853.....	800,000	23,949.23	80,264.24	84,207.56	988,421.03	295,912.09	34,976.56	330,888.65	1,319,309.68
Dec. 31, 1853.....	800,000	32,338.59	132,471.80	59,125.01	1,023,935.40	303,524.19	31,365.31	334,889.50	1,358,824.90
June 30, 1854.....	800,000	39,415.83	159,596.81	70,175.96	1,069,188.60	230,311.94	35,301.37	265,613.31	1,334,801.91
Dec. 31, 1854.....	800,000	45,773.35	197,772.77	46,527.56	1,090,073.68	229,411.92	25,459.64	254,871.56	1,344,945.24
June 30, 1855.....	800,000	53,787.93	212,772.77	68,699.64	1,135,260.34	359,483.10	39,099.67	398,582.77	1,533,843.11
Dec. 31, 1855.....	800,000	59,383.18	249,472.41	64,121.70	1,172,977.29	820,379.09	57,503.34	877,882.43	2,050,859.72
June 30, 1856.....	800,000	68,850.51	281,594.11	71,156.12	1,221,600.74	814,126.31	121,756.04	935,882.35	2,157,483.09
Dec. 31, 1856.....	994,000	76,540.58	320,753.23	75,735.77	1,467,029.58	1,161,309.72	77,894.37	1,239,204.09	2,706,233.67
June 30, 1857.....	1,000,000	85,361.10	356,486.00	48,499.51	1,490,346.61	739,788.68	53,312.31	793,100.99	2,283,447.60
Dec. 31, 1857.....	1,000,000	75,222.52	360,985.51	28,355.62[j]	1,407,852.41	557,582.78	49,458.03	607,040.81	2,014,893.22
June 30, 1858.....	1,000,000	52,356.99	312,194.97	70,241.45	1,434,793.41	514,131.78	45,421.81	559,553.59	1,994,347.00
Dec. 31, 1858.....	1,000,000	64,509.92	342,436.42	70,515.12	1,477,461.46	813,067.30	38,605.50	851,672.80	2,329,134.26
June 30, 1859.....	1,000,000	54,473.76	400,326.64	93,730.59	1,548,530.99	611,000.29	27,690.64	638,690.93	2,187,221.92
Dec. 31, 1859.....	1,000,000	67,105.48	444,057.23	102,010.70	1,613,173.41	581,732.50	26,646.87	608,379.37	2,221,552.78
June 30, 1860.....	1,000,000	83,494.57	496,067.93	172,466.75	1,752,029.25	619,904.14	34,714.79	654,618.93	2,406,648.18
Dec. 31, 1860.....	1,000,000	97,722.29	608,534.68	139,171.60	1,845,428.57	703,398.90	70,132.54	773,531.44	2,618,960.01
June 30, 1861.....	1,000,000	109,368.28	687,706.28	108,212.82	1,905,287.38	655,717.78	37,505.15	693,222.93	2,598,510.31

[a] Capital Stock of 2,000 shares on which $500 was to be paid in by Aug. 2, 1856.
[b] Built up by annual deductions from sales and decreased by being drawn on to meet losses in payments for goods. Drop on Dec. 31, 1864, and June 30, 1865, not explained in other records.
[c] Built up from profits.
[d] Profit and Loss before dividends. Twice there were losses—Dec. 31, 1851, and Dec. 31, 1857.
[e] Computed from four preceding series of figures.
[f] Comprises "permanent" loans, demand loans, and short-term loans. Proportions of each not determined from other records.
[g] Comprises the miscellaneous small payments, with the exception of Dec. 31, 1851, when $104,668.70 was payable to the Saco Water Power Co.; Dec. 31, 1852, when $78,126.89 was payable for cloth; and June 30, 1856, when $60,260.50 was payable for cotton.
[h] The sum of Notes and Accounts Payable.
[i] The sum of Capital & Surplus and Current Liabilities.
[j] Loss.

TREASURER'S SEMIANNUAL LEDGER BALANCES, DECEMBER 31, 1851–JUNE 30, 1870 (continued)

B. Liabilities

At the end of six months	Capital & Surplus: Capital Stock[a]	Capital & Surplus: Insurance & Guarantee Fund Sales[b]	Capital & Surplus: Repair & Reserve Fund for Buildings[c]	Capital & Surplus: Profit [& Loss][d]	Capital & Surplus: Total Capital & Surplus[e]	Current Liabilities: Notes Payable[f]	Current Liabilities: Accounts Payable[g]	Current Liabilities: Total Current Liabilities[h]	Total Liabilities[i]
Dec. 31, 1861.....	1,000,000	93,754.44	735,919.10	100,565.78	1,930,239.32	576,278.59	27,161.04	603,439.63	2,533,678.95
June 30, 1862.....	1,000,000	83,118.33	785,723.63	257,668.04	2,126,510.00	163,342.08	13,503.72	176,845.80	2,303,355.80
Dec. 31, 1862.....	1,000,000	108,594.48	974,152.92	585,814.51	2,668,561.91	0.00	13,136.48	13,136.48	2,681,698.39
June 30, 1863.....	1,000,000	135,272.28	864,299.86	257,251.91	2,256,824.05	495,000.00	14,623.81	509,623.81	2,766,447.86
Dec. 31, 1863.....	1,000,000	131,383.65	921,551.77	238,260.75	2,291,196.17	682,000.00	45,534.36	727,534.36	3,018,730.53
June 30, 1864.....	1,000,000	184,743.81	962,923.09	450,207.31	2,597,874.21	885,688.23	45,526.45	931,214.68	3,529,088.89
Dec. 31, 1864.....	1.000,000	20,169.98	995,000.00	170,496.07	2,185,666.05	1,873,859.32	94,494.87	1,968,354.09	4,154,020.14
June 30, 1865.....	1,000,000	21,008.68	1,000,000.00	7,057.15	2,028,165.83	1,061,283.50	55,898.71	1,117,182.21	3,145,248.04
Dec. 31, 1865.....	1,000,000	k	k	537,500.75	k	k	k	k	k
June 30, 1866.....	1,000,000	k	k	188,386.14	k	k	k	k	k
Dec. 31, 1866.....	1,000,000	k	k	159,605.85	k	k	k	k	k
June 30, 1867.....	1,000,000	k	k	79,658.70	k	k	k	k	k
Dec. 31, 1867.....	1,000,000	k	k	7,190.47	k	k	k	k	k
June 30, 1868.....	1,000,000	k	k	222,359.54	k	k	k	k	k
Dec. 31, 1868.....	1,000,000	k	k	166,636.46	k	k	k	k	k
June 30, 1869.....	1,000 000	k	k	140,582.67	k	k	k	k	k
Dec. 31, 1869.....	1,000.000	k	k	98,910.27	k	k	k	k	k
June 30, 1870.....	1,000,000			106,542.40	k	k	k	k	k

[k] Figures not available.

Source: MS. PMC, Treasurer's semiannual statements, 1851–65; Directors' records, 1865–70.

APPENDIX 33

LEDGER BALANCES, 1871–1924

A. Assets[a]

1. 1871–1898

At the End of June	Plant	Cotton in Process & on Hand	Mill Agent's General Supplies	Sales Agent's Balance	Cloth on Hand	Notes Receivable	Insurance Notes	Miscellaneous[b]	Cash	Total
1871.......	$ 989,641	$316,179.79	$31,942.84	$238,220.56	$ 57,602.96	$ 18,384.00	$ 0.00	$ 19,397.64	$ 85,441.87	$1,756,810.66
1872.......	1,200,000	282,185.84	29,076.57	344,269.50	144,615.46	303,517.84	7,943.59	37,500.00	138,922.69	2,488,031.49
1873.......	1,200,000	300,292.85	26,904.08	284,700.15	232,512.94	181,261.84	1,773.00	42,915.38	182,663.52	2,453,023.76
1874.......	1,200,000	321,983.18	41,029.31	343,537.66	251,823.35	2,250.03	10,400.00	132,947.01	169,399.94	2,473,370.48
1875.......	1,200,000	296,658.38	43,268.31	246,050.02	210,057.18	988.71	9,934.39	57,500.00	139,688.06	2,204,145.05
1876.......	1,200,000	174,000.00[c]	29,085.64[c]	342,450.47	140,996.77	11,884.96	14,678.21	59,013.73	87,490.40	2,059,600.18
1877.......	1,200,000	282,810.00	28,685.36	310,990.42	149,767.14	1,535.77	19,951.27	76,260.25	92,874.43	2,162,874.64
1878.......	1,200,000	282,689.47	34,441.74	310,118.63	99,905.36	822.83	19,198.39	6,000.00	180,797.90	2,133,974.32
1879.......	1,200,000	312,339.53	25,750.98	363,249.86	64,460.83	62,571.53	8,000.00	4,142.50	22,265.34	2,062,780.57
1880.......	1,200,000	349,826.62	31,072.58	397,204.42	139,727.00	82,000.00	8,900.00	7,355.10	12,220.76	2,228,306.48
1881.......	1,200,000	433,960.45	21,041.38	406,044.35	22,271.50	55,000.00	12,890.00	18,475.17	36,826.82	2,206,509.67
1882.......	1,200,000	517,432.41	31,528.92	290,313.32	35,748.20	170,000.00	9,263.32	2,500.00	18,562.87	2,275,349.04
1883.......	1,200,000	448,238.06	31,932.83	367,295.23	24,018.70	260,000.00	11,025.00	0	24,664.47	2,367,174.29
1884.......	1,200,000	338,841.93	26,270.80	314,734.23	188,711.00	253,500.00	12,029.52	0	59,634.71	2,393,722.19
1885.......	1,200,000	347,044.22	18,927.35	457,452.64	43,850.23	255,575.34	9,788.84	0	120,971.35	2,453,609.97
1886.......	1,200,000	339,776.39	13,563.30	507,147.29	45,939.49	265,000.00	10,387.98	0	123,661.62	2,505,476.07
1887.......	1,200,000	367,913.21	22,112.18	534,263.08	25,476.69	30,000.00	10,379.67	0	2,127.47	2,192,272.30
1888.......	1,200,000	367,363.61	22,734.94	460,751.42	22,870.29	70,000.00	10,227.00	0	84,762.34	2,238,709.60
1889.......	1,200,000	399,753.03	25,968.17	469,253.25	24,328.85	160,000.00	10,798.09	0	80,640.74	2,370,742.13
1890.......	1,200,000	461,879.78	31,704.04	561,195.72	23,947.25	225,000.00	10,955 47	0	24,691.74	2,539,374.00
1891.......	1,200,000	389,127.98	25,717.45	568,097.07	39,419.65	170,000.00	12,688.31	10,000.00	121,200.73	2,536,251.19
1892.......	1,200,000	517,686.26	18,334.66	734,837.57	19,887.91	0	9,952.07	0	79,828.67	2,580,527.14
1893.......	1,200,000	276,422.01	19,690.34	593,601.82	65,565.57	0	12,923.32	0	23,069.36	2,191,272.42
1894.......	1,200,000	306,363.94	22,252.81	720,752.10	60,469.11	0	12,513.73	0	44,965.34	2,367,317.03
1895.......	1,200,000	390,789.42	18,401.13	694,102.14	28,343.00	30,000.00	13,574.26	0	135,584.99	2,510,794.94
1896.......	1,200,000	369,579.97	15,293.18	523,783.67	138,954.90	0	13,255.21	0	225,792.59	2,486,659.52
1897.......	1,200,000	281,825.23	14,754.12	651,344.77	99,962.31	125,000.00	12,808.83	0	149,254.02	2,534,949.28
1898.......	1,200,000	391,258.34	25,614.05	535,830.38	48,395.71	105,000.00	11,779.60	0	456,058.07	2,773,936.15

[a] Figures for Dec. 30, 1870, which are of interest, are as follows: Plant, $1,569,728.78; Cotton in Process and on Hand, $172,972.99; Mill Agent's General Supplies, $43,693.08; Sales Agent's Balances, $295,530.82; Cloth on Hand, $209,854.02; Notes Receivable, $109,539.81; F. Skinner & Co. and J. Bardwell & Co., charges payable, $922,554.74; Miscellaneous, $903.27; Cash, $132,426.97; and total, $3,457,204.48.

[b] From June, 1872, through Dec. 1887, Miscellaneous includes investment in Lewiston Bleachery & Dye Works, which was stated at $37,500 except in Dec., 1872, when it was $34,875. This includes also cotton advances, loans to Laconia Co., advances for machinery, and occasional interest.

[c] Estimated from total for both cotton in process and on hand and general supplies of $203,085.64.

Source: MS. PMC, Trial Balances, 1871–98.

LEDGER BALANCES, 1871–1924 (continued)

A. Assets

2. 1899–1914[a]

At the End of June	Plant	Mill Agent's Balance[b]	Sales Agent's Balance	Cloth on Hand	Notes Receivable	Insurance Notes	Miscellaneous[c]	Cash	Total
1899	$2,556,000	$372,261.41	$1,168,868.23	$117,337.86	$34,000.00	$ 0.	$ 0	$ 463,554.67	$4,712,022.17
1900	2,555,000	316,831.68	857,001.33	294,886.26	30,500.00	21,522.60	1,000	862,915.76	4,939,647.63
1901	2,555,000	371,799.94	1,488,092.68	154,609.68	21,500.00	21,778.81	1,000	528,876.35	5,142,657.46
1902	2,555,000	317,964.64	744,468.77	434,910.19	9,000.00	21,664.79	1,000	1,228,812.24	5,312,820.63
1903	2,555,000	149,199.60	1,026,704.96	46,627.20	3,500.00	22,500.73	1,000	1,266,186.33	5,070,718.82
1904	2,555,000	266,851.15	767,299.72	227,762.62	0	23,419.15	1,000	1,196,777.89	5,038,110.53
1905	2,555,000	195,073.51	1,098,804.86	60,384.85	0	23,396.80	1,000	1,737,426.69	5,671,086.71
1906	2,555,000	179,646.16	1,071,925.49	71,146.54	0	23,621.91	1,000	1,540,617.85	5,442,957.95
1907	2,055,000	397,246.11	1,035,045.94	329,719.12	0	24,456.90	1,000	608,338.40	4,450,806.47
1908	2,055,000	224,591.22	1,140,864.33	384,646.87	0	25,677.70	1,000	830,619.92	4,662,400.04
1909	2,055,000	581,146.99	1,184,056.92	27,545.72	0	28,234.25	85,375	1,654,506.95	5,615,865.83
1910	2,055,000	261,454.42	876,501.99	626,699.37	0	29,783.25	94,005	1,043,169.80	4,986,613.83
1911	2,055,000	314,815.67	1,172,485.45	393,960.35	0	30,020.78	98,785	998,983.23	5,064,050.48
1912	2,055,000	315,194.18	1,173,687.20	412,255.55	0	31,710.50	104,505	1,317,563.96	5,409,916.39
1913	2,055,000	489,328.43	1,272,842.42	388,088.46	0	37,711.77	11,002	993,976.57	5,247,949.65
1914	2,055,000	551,752.10	1,313,506.19	586,781.90	0	0.	31,002	776,587.88	5,314,630.07

[a] For both the Pepperell and Laconia divisions.
[b] Includes both cotton and general supplies.
[c] Includes $1,000 of the company's stock; $84,375 of the Lewiston Bleachery & Dye Works' stock, 1909–12, which is stated at $1.00 in 1913 and 1914; Atlantic Insurance Co.'s scrip, 1910–12, which is stated at $1.00 in 1913 and 1914; and stock in Clark Power Co. for 1912–14.

Source: MS. PMC, Trial Balances, 1899–1914.

3. 1915–1924[a]

At the End of June	Plant	Mill Agent's Balances	Sales Agent's Balances	Cloth on Hand	Notes Receivable	Land, Water, Lumber & Towing Property[b]	Stock & Scrip[c]	Liberty Loan	Cash	Total
1915	$3,000,000	$1,424,680.56	$1,078,598.31	$ 812,735.66	$25,000.00	$400,000.00	$246,000	$ 0	$1,355,513.11	$ 8,342,527.64
1916	3,000,000	1,909,697.76	1,287,445.26	362,717.67	26,000.00	275,000.00	246,000	0	1,532,563.55	8,639,424.24
1917	3,000,000	3,007,131.07	2,079,362.51	74,930.17	1.00	301,834.24	212,500	250,000.00	721,195.38	9,646,954.37
1918	3,000,000	3,887,246.98	3,124,067.02	10,000.00	1.00	286,480.93	212,500	900,860.01	922,033.67	12,343,189.61
1919[d]	3,000,000	4,026,947.08	2,428,557.45	433,334.81	1.00	275,200.00	212,500	2,668,187.51	200,416.92	13,245,144.77
1920	3,000,000	2,643,837.15	4,329,615.69	1,298,772.47	1.00	308,475.00	212,501	1,523,912.00	625,585.57	13,942,699.88
1921[d]	3,000,000	1,359,439.22	1,860,829.30	3,156,645.86	1.00	344,568.57	212,501	1,523,912.00	370,473.11	11,828,370.06
1922[d]	3,000,000	2,892,488.72	2,202,462.03	2,768,390.22	1.00	349,332.89	212,501	1,510,834.00	100,463.40	12,936,473.26
1923[d]	3,000,000	3,380,330.65	3,338,050.25	1,430,099.04	1.00	358,583.05	212,501	500,156.26	1,801,960.32	14,021,681.57
1924[d]	3,000,000	2,681,881.79	2,001,992.33	3,121,873.02	1.00	378,466.96	212,501	0	2,189,893.97	13,586,610.07

[a] For both the Pepperell and Laconia Divisions of the newly created Massachusetts voluntary trust of the same name as the former Maine corporation.
[b] Property which had formerly been carried at nominal figures.
[c] Stock and Scrip which had formerly been carried at nominal figures.
[d] Figures taken from typewritten, printed, and published reports which differed slightly from those made out by treasurer for trustees.

Source: MS. PMC, Trial Balances, 1915–24; PMC, Annual reports for 1919, 1921, 1922, 1924.

LEDGER BALANCES, 1871–1924 (continued)

B. LIABILITIES

1. 1871–1898

At the End of June	Capital and Surplus: Capital Stock	Guarantee on Sales	Enlargement & Renovating	Dividends Lewiston B. & D.W.	Returned Ins. Premiums	Depreciation Reserve	Profit & Loss	Current Liabilities: Notes Payable	Bills Payable	Suspense Account	Interest & Discount on Notes	Total
1871...	$1,075,800	$ 0	$ 6,558.48	$ 0	$ 0	$ 0	$ 50,000.00	$613,042.02	$ 11,410.16	$ 0	$ 0	$1,756,810.66
1872...	1,200,000	0	126,704.32	1,312.50	0	0	535,287.32	606,599.67	6,268.11	0	11,859.57	2,488,031.49
1873...	1,200,000	0	106,938.10	4,500.00	0	0	784,501.81	345,527.21	6,984.19	0	4,572.45	2,453,023.76
1874...	1,200,000	0	95,812.94	10,125.00	4,196.96	0	880,961.58	212,426.21	55,717.11	10,923.10	3,207.58	2,473,370.48
1875...	1,200,000	0	100,000.00	17,625.00	9,057.92	0	631,206.28	187,500.00	53,068.98	2,820.00	2,866.87	2,204,145.05
1876...	1,200,000	10,000.00	21,584.41	25,125.00	17,366.21	0	614,339.51	149,000.00	13,075.23	6,750.00	2,359.82	2,059,600.18
1877...	1,200,000	30,441.01	23,736.21	32,625.00	25,767.39	0	641,041.48	185,000.00	11,309.12	11,900.00	1,054.43	2,162,874.64
1878...	1,200,000	44,339.87	56,226.90	2,625.00	32,001.61	0	650,090.75	100,000.00	22,353.19	25,448.10	888.90	2,133,974.32
1879...	1,200,000	56,406.40	47,000.00	6,375.00	57,763.54	0	659,295.18	0	22,807.62	13,132.83	0	2,062,780.57
1880...	1,200,000	81,735.05	71,282.14	21,375.00	70,812.85	0	720,803.11	25,000.00	37,298.33	0	0	2,228,306.48
1881...	1,200,000	114,718.35	0	28,875.00	80,815.77	0	707,049.97	28,900.00	44,330.58	1,820.00	0	2,206,509.67
1882...	1,200,000	149,995.67	0	34,875.00	101,010.74	0	698,470.31	45,000.00	43,136.70	0	2,860.62	2,275,349.04
1883...	1,200,000	186,004.68	91,353.30	40,500.00	114,320.74	0	693,470.31	0	41,525.26	0	0	2,367,174.29
1884...	1,200,000	216,335.79	94,936.11	48,000.00	128,510.87	0	661,275.86	0	42,532.31	1,760.00	371.25	2,393,722.19
1885...	1,200,000	246,193.66	100,624.58	55,500.00	142,342.50	0	653,928.63	0	53,025.26	1,995.34	0	2,453,609.97
1886...	1,200,000	277,751.68	100,624.58	64,875.00	160,328.46	0	647,771.09	0	54,125.26	0	0	2,505,476.07
1887...	1,200,000	307,175.24	150,624.58	74,250.00	176,060.21	0	182,037.01	50,000.00	52,125.26	0	0	2,192,272.30
1888...	1,200,000	342,670.69	150,624.58	81,750.00	189,570.41	0	217,568.66	0	56,525.26	0	0	2,238,709.60
1889...	1,200,000	377,977.69	150,624.58	98,625.00	203,990.47	0	283,519.13	1,400.00	54,605.26	0	0	2,370,742.13
1890...	1,200,000	407,040.70	150,624.58	106,125.00	218,623.04	0	392,742.66	0	56,025.26	8,192.76	0	2,539,374.00
1891...	1,200,000	444,313.17	150,624.58	113,625.00	231,056.99	0	322,391.19	1,000.00	71,120.26	2,120.00	0	2,536,251.19
1892...	1,200,000	186,027.10	50,000.00	139,875.00	249,905.32	0	276,349.62	400,000.00	78,370.10	0	0	2,580,527.14
1893...	1,200,000	220,247.45	0	147,375.00	265,876.66	0	276,899.78	10,000.00	70,873.53	0	0	2,191,272.42
1894...	1,200,000	236,766.21	0	154,875.00	280,554.70	0	298,822.58	125,000.00	71,298.54	0	0	2,367,317.03
1895...	1,200,000	262,232.62	50,000.00	162,375.00	298,281.41	0	396,907.59	0	129,917.55	11,080.77	0	2,510,794.94
1896...	1,200,000	294,844.38	50,000.00	169,875.00	309,194.06	0	373,313.79	1,500.00	87,873.53	58.76	0	2,486,659.52
1897...	1,200,000	326,642.14	50,035.77	177,375.00	328,276.99	0	367,053.09	0	85,507.53	58.76	0	2,534,949.28
1898...	1,200,000	360,014.40	50,028.32	184,875.00	347,203.46	125,000	386,777.45	0	118,470.73	58.76	1,508.03	2,773,936.15

Source: MS. PMC, Trial Balances, 1871–98.

2. 1899–1914

At end of June	Capital and Surplus: Capital Stock	Guarantee on Sales	Dividends Lewiston B. & D. W.	Returned Ins. Premiums	Depreciation Reserve	Profit and Loss	Current Liabilities: PMC, Div. Unpaid	Bills Payable	Suspense Account	Interest	Accident Liability	Total
1899....	$2,556,000	$ 34,060.81	$ 7,500.00	$ 2,861.78	$ 100,000.00	$1,861,301.15	$ 0	$131,551.08	$18,747.35	$ 0	$ 0	$4,712,022.17
1900....	2,556,000	101,464.30	22,500.00	45,342.33	300,000.00	1,768,313.76	220	128,233.73	17,573.51	0	0	4,939,647.63
1901....	2,556,000	166,455.67	31,875.00	88,597.13	500,000.00	1,666,243.39	340	115,408.08	16,304.26	1,433.93	0	5,142,657.46
1902....	2,556,000	234,548.56	39,375.00	134,212.91	650,000.00	1,547,037.06	460	124,945.56	16,241.54	0	10,000.00	5,312,820.63
1903....	2,556,000	316,076.23	46,875.00	173,927.14	750,000.00	1,032,054.61	780	163,857.62	16,005.54	5,142.68	10,000.00	5,070,718.82
1904....	2,556,000	385,474.51	56,250.00	210,282.08	750,000.00	928,120.07	900	131,077.45	10,006.42	0	10,000.00	5,038,110.53
1905....	2,556,000	478,139.71	67,500.00	266,852.52	900,000.00	1,218,945.82	1,020	170,596.47	300.00	1,732.19	10,000.00	5,671,086.71
1906....	2,556,000	191,727.95	11,250.00	42,434.16	1,100,000.00	1,275,012.25	470	255,763.59	300.00	0	10,000.00	5,442,957.95
1907....	2,556,000	180.250.18	22,500.00	83,794.55	900,000.00	578,931.15	1,090	117,940.59	300.00	0	10,000.00	4,450,806.47
1908....	2,556,000	259,974.32	33,750.00	126,540.64	900,000.00	653,761.49	1,210	120,940.59	300.00	0	9,923.00	4,662,400.04
1909....	2,556,000	358,240.13	50,625.00	172,160.74	1,000,000.00	1,215,246.85	1,330	252,607.59	300.00	0	9,355.52	5,615,865.83
1910....	2,556,000	442,418.07	70,312.50	222,534.07	1,000,000.00	552,523.08	1,700	120,940.59	8,930.00	0	11,255.52	4,986,613.83
1911....	2,556,000	537,646.01	104,062.50	273,283.55	1,000,000.00	445,374.51	1,820	119,153.91	13,710.00	0	13,000.00	5,064,050.48
1912....	2,556,000	629,377.13	120,937.50	322,320.69	1,000,000.00	477,990.95	1,940	272,019.12	16,730.00	0	12,601.00	5,409,916.39
1913....	2,556,000	730,147.46	132,187.50	374,658.07	1,000,000.00	327,975.50	2,060	112,019.12	301.00	0	12,601.00	5,247,949.65
1914....	2,556,000	833,249.09	132,187.50	386,029.36	171,062.02	1,110,640.98	2,180	112,019.12	301.00	0	10,961.00	5,314,630.07

Source: MS. PMC, Trial Balances, 1899–1914.

LEDGER BALANCES, 1871–1924 (continued)

B. Liabilities

3. 1915–1924

At the End of June	Capital and Surplus								Current Liabilities			
	Capital Stock	Guarantee	Reserve for Machinery	Depreciation	Dividends Lewiston B. & D. W.	Re-serve for Cotton	Reserve for Taxes	Profit and Loss	Unpaid Divi-dends	Notes Payable	Bills Payable	Total
1915...	$7,668,000	$112,785.28	$ 0	$ 112,591.81	$ 5,625.00	$ 0	$ 0	$ 434,024.01	$ 0	$ 0	$ 9,501.54	$ 8,342,527.64
1916...	7,668,000	56,166 40	0	184,415.01	16,875.00	0	0	654,466.29	0	0	59,501.54	8,639,424.24
1917...	7,668,000	107,453.87	0	264,713.97	33,750.00	0	450,000.00	1,105,663.92	1,488.00	0	15,884.61	9,646,954.37
1918...	7,668,000	192,504.17	0	510,323.66	50,625.00	500,000	953,288.55	2.173,884.23	2,064.00	292,500	0	12,343,189.61
1919...	7,668,000	258,033.67	0	694,809.79	67,500.00	500,000	0	3,410,753.59	2,736.00	640,000	3,311.72	13,245,144.77
1920...	7,668,000	372,798.80	0	936,353.24	150,000.00	500,000	0	4,312,235.84	3,312.00	0	0	13,942,699.88
1921...	7,668,000	425,398.87	0	841,057.76	189,375.00	500,000	0	2,200,554.43	3,984.00	0	0	11,828,370.06
1922...	7,668,000	476,667.08	1,196,464.06	1,002,891.18	211,875.00	500,000	0	1,677,845.94	2,730.00	200,000	0	12,936,473.26
1923...	7,668,000	551.134.20	1,224,646.01	1,318,811.59	223,125.00	800,000	200,000.00	2,035,964.77	0	0	0	14,021,681.57
1924...	7,668,000	600,811.30	1,172,075.90	1,642,122.63	252,375.00	800,000	0	1,451,225.24	0	0	0	13,586,610.07

Source: MS. PMC, Trial Balances, 1915–24.
PMC, Annual reports for 1919, 1921–24.

APPENDIX 34

ASSETS AND LIABILITIES, 1925–1945

A. Assets

Year Ending June 30	Plant and Equipment[a]	Depreciation Reserve[b] (deduct)	Net Plant & Equipment[c]	Cash	Accounts Receivable[d]	Inventories[e]	Notes Receivable[f]	Government Securities	Investments[g]	Prepaid & Sundry Items[h]	Postwar Refund on Excess Profits Tax	Total Assets
1925	$ 3,603,140.94	$1,879,787.47	$1,723,353.47	$2,873,933.65	$2,297,475.88	$ 3,860,603.63	$	$	$212,502.00	$	$	$10,967,868.63
1926	4,318,655.29	1,990,970.74	2,327,684.55	2,419,472.04	1,411,037.31	4,121,752.40	....	....	691,252.00	....	....	10,971,198.30
1927	8,656,258.39	2,317,809.32	6,338,449.07	346,229.90	3,563,859.77	8,710,567.29	....	....	718,348.03	....	....	19,677,454.06
1928	9,059,706.89	2,797,006.99	6,262,699.90	562,562.98	3,072,223.76	8,357,373.33	60,332.52	....	746,130.81	43,019.69	....	19,104,342.99
1929	10,125,309.41	3,163,590.57	6,961,718.84	1,190,839.27	2,368,045.86	8,101,296.85	32,301.69	....	696,252.00	169,009.49	....	19,519,464.00
1930	12,965,724.53	4,095,634.93	8,870,089.60	420,052.73	2,614,644.94	7,390,678.96	119,147.36	....	....	234,247.26	....	19,648,860.85
1931	12,528,956.07	4,702,506.59	7,826,449.48	1,605,014.63	2,539,318.57	7,551,733.35	....	....	....	281,026.64	....	19,803,542.67
1932	13,029,247.60	5,197,264.78	7,831,982.82	2,187,528.69	1,642,555.62	5,252,461.47	125,000.00	....	89,307.65	228,866.77	....	17,357,703.02
1933	13,331,171.89	5,732,273.98	7,598,897.91	1,035,483.92	2,320,915.89	7,055,618.86	....	....	174,779.68	225,950.83	....	18,411,647.09
1934	14,059,257.23	6,316,048.65	7,743,208.58	690,560.81	2,671,370.12	10,739,544.70	....	....	99,329.68	276,837.94	....	22,220,851.83
1935	14,629,944.16	6,778,455.24	7,851,488.92	575,009.32	3,085,600.50	9,644,876.14	....	....	99,409.68	306,916.43	....	21,563,300.99
1936	15,398,009.04	7,231,533.31	8,166,475.73	1,194,425.13	3,092,100.85	7,467,445.53	....	....	99,409.68	260,552.91	....	20,280,409.83
1937	16,298,101.56	7,689,680.54	8,608,421.02	1,287,692.51	4,133,329.05	10,788,771.14	....	....	99,527.36	398,570.28	....	25,316,311.36
1938	16,659,595.14	8,140,458.12	8,519,137.02	673,570.30	2,477,511.95	9,691,224.61	....	....	99,527.36	393,534.56	....	21,854,505.80
1939	16,772,239.59	8,507,725.91	8,264,513.68	646,573.84	2,886,583.69	7,408,239.28	....	....	99,527.36	327,959.37	....	19,633,397.22
1940	17,088,726.51	8,930,490.96	8,158,235.55	588,586.28	2,915,420.86	8,525,304.55	....	....	99,527.36	210,225.55	....	20,497,300.15
1941	17,255,068.90	8,935,123.20	8,319,945.70	868,066.04	4,660,808.54	9,018,809.60	....	....	99,527.36	383,685.64	....	23,350,842.88
1942	17,363,439.66	8,743,583.90	8,619,855.76	1,959,876.47	5,617,439.68	10,340,064.30	....	....	99,527.36	430,088.36	....	27,066,851.93
1943	17,197,637.13	8,928,759.34	8,268,877.79	2,618,039.82	2,949,475.19	9,123,737.30	....	6,000,000.00	99,527.36	313,162.71	367,000.00	29,739,820.17
1944	16,410,333.60	8,505,622.70	7,904,710.90	2,155,796.91	3,724,975.99	9,479,206.36	....	6,500,000.00	99,527.36	454,065.28	826,059.22	31,144,342.02
1945	16,831,470.90	8,777,040.83	8,054,430.07	4,173,437.92	2,006,972.06	8,826,942.33	....	7,500,000.00	99,527.36	332,297.85	1,261,086.94	32,254,694.53

[a] Value of plant and equipment rose with increase in plants. In 1925 there were only the old plant in Biddeford and one new mill in Opelika which was in process of construction. In 1927 the account included the two plants of the former Massachusetts Cotton Mills—the mills in Lowell and in Lindale. By 1929 the mills in Lowell were being liquidated. By 1930 one of the mills in Fall River of the former Granite Mills was in operation. In this year also, the plant in Lewiston was included in this account, instead of an investment. By 1930 also, a second unit in Opelika was operating. By 1934 a second unit in Fall River went into operation. Increases in the following years came largely through increases in equipment.

[b] Rate of depreciation reserve, 1925 through 1928, at the rate of $1.00 per spindle in place in the northern mills and at $1.25 in the southern, which did not allow for time of operation. In 1929, and thereafter, maximum depreciation set at $1.00 in North and $1.50 in South.

[c] Equals Plant and Equipment minus Depreciation Reserve.

[d] For goods sold.

[e] Inventories of cotton, cotton in process, cloth on hand, and miscellaneous supplies. From 1925 through 1941, inventories priced at cost or market, whichever lower, for raw material, stock in process and finished goods, and at cost as regards supplies. In 1942, method substituted of pricing at last in, first out.

[f] Anticipation tax notes in Biddeford.

[g] Investments, 1925–29, in subsidiaries, including the Lewiston Bleachery & Dye Works. In 1930 the consolidated statement included statement of latter. Since net assets were greater than value of investment, surplus increased. From 1932 to 1945, investments in Pepperell stock at cost.

[h] Includes insurance premiums as well as other prepayments and sundry assets.

Source: MS. PMC, Treasurer's reports, 1925–28; MS. PMC, Controller's reports, 1929–45; Comments from PMC, Annual reports, 1925–45

ASSETS AND LIABILITIES, 1925–1945 (continued)

B. Liabilities

Year Ending June 30	Capital Stock[a]	Capital Stock in Treasury[b]	Capital Stock Outstanding (Net)[c]	Surplus[d]	Notes Payable[e]	Bills & Accounts Payable & Accruals[f]	Tax Reserves (Federal)[g]	Contingency Reserves[h]	Total Liabilities
1925	$ 7,668,000.00	$	$ 7,668,000.00	$ 3,299,868.63	$	$	$	$	$10,967,868.63
1926	7,668,000.00	....	7,668,000.00	3,303,198.30	....	....	....	....	10,971,198.30
1927	10,793,000.00	....	10,793,000.00	8,053,029.96	535,000.00	296,424.10	....	....	19,677,454.06
1928	10,793,000.00	....	10,793,000.00	8,216,808.00	....	94,534.99	....	....	19,104,342.99
1929	10,793,000.00	....	10,793,000.00	8,467,888.52	....	258,575.48	....	....	19,519,464.00
1930	10,793,000.00	202,200.00	10,590,800.00	8,735,750.74	....	322,310.11	....	....	19,648,860.85
1931	10,793,000.00	765,900.00	10,027,100.00	8,764,125.40	....	262,317.27	....	750,000.00	19,803,542.67
1932	10,790,000.00	790,000.00	10,000,000.00	7,266,761.24	....	90,941.78	....	....	17,357,703.02
1933	10,790,000.00	790,000.00	10,000,000.00	8,191,091.83	....	96,055.26	124,500.00	....	18,411,647.09
1934	10,790,000.00	790,000.00	10,000,000.00	9,195,957.54	2,000,000.00	649,894.30	375,000.00	....	22,220,851.84
1935	10,790,000.00	790,000.00	10,000,000.00	8,193,315.36	2,500,000.00	815,098.79	54,886.84	....	21,563,300.99
1936	10,790,000.00	790,000.00	10,000,000.00	9,022,991.29	....	598,516.66	658,901.88	....	20,280,409.83
1937	10,790,000.00	790,000.00	10,000,000.00	9,571,530.57	3,500,000.00	1,082,290.00	948,402.81	214,087.98	25,316,311.36
1938	10,790,000.00	790,000.00	10,000,000.00	7,483,680.23	3,500,000.00	516,337.88	134,880.55	219,607.14	21,854,505.80
1939	10,790,000.00	790,000.00	10,000,000.00	8,065,936.25	250,000.00	768,321.15	329,532.68	219,607.14	19,633,397.22
1940	10,790,000.00	790,000.00	10,000,000.00	8,921,369.86	500,000.00	634,958.25	440,972.04	....	20,497,300.15
1941	10,790,000.00	790,000.00	10,000,000.00	10,206,550.94	....	1,480,578.54	1,163,713.40	500,000.00	23,350,842.88
1942	10,790,000.00	790,000.00	10,000,000.00	11,393,880.45	....	1,746,298.92	3,426,672.56	500,000.00	27,066,851.93
1943	10,790,000.00	790,000.00	10,000,000.00	12,169,107.89	....	1,982,289.47	5,088,422.81	500,000.00	29,739,820.17
1944	10,790,000.00	790,000.00	10,000,000.00	13,062,583 95	....	1,316,119.63	6,265,638.44	500,000.00	31,144,342.02
1945	10,790,000.00	790,000.00	10,000,000.00	14,405,516.95	....	1,541,002.35	6,308,175.23	....	32,254,694.53

[a] In 1925 and 1926, 76,668 shares of stock at $100 par outstanding of the voluntary association. This was increased in 1927 by the issuance of 31,250 shares to the stockholders of Massachusetts Cotton Mills and 2,070 shares to be disposed of later as trustees determined. At times in later years, some of stock outstanding was purchased so that capital stock outstanding (net) would total only $10,000,000.

[b] See note a.

[c] See note a.

[d] Capital and earned surplus. Figure for 1927 reflects increase brought about by merger with the Massachusetts Cotton Mills.

[e] Borrowings caused largely by increases in sales, which made necessary more working capital.

[f] Includes dividends payable of $215,800 in 1930 and of $150,363 in 1931; of processing taxes payable of $305,288.40 in 1934 and of $364,110.94 in 1935.

[g] Reserves largely for federal income tax. Great increases in reserves during second World War because of higher rates of income and of excess profits tax.

[h] In 1931, figure of $500,000 established, part of reserve set aside in earlier period against shrinkage in inventories, which had been deducted annually from value of inventories. In 1931, $250,000 added was part of proceeds of sale of power properties. In 1932, reserve applied to adjustment in inventories. In 1940, reserve transferred to surplus and again in 1945. Reserve of $500,000 set up in December, 1940.

Source: MS. PMC, Controller's reports, 1929–45; Treasurer's reports, 1925–28; and Annual reports for reserves and bills and accounts payable and accruals for 1937 from 1938 report and also comments, 1925–45.

APPENDIX 35

A. EXPENSES OF MANUFACTURE, 1851–1870

Twelve Months Ending	Cotton Expense	Mill Expense No. 1	Mill Expense No. 2	Mill Expense No. 3	General Expense	Total Expense
June 28, 1851	$ 32,935.94	$ 12,563.59[a]	$ 92.29[a]	....	$ 4,403.53	$ 49,995.35
June 26, 1852	248,756.44	56,015.62	47,855.48	....	46,526.52	399,154.06
June 25, 1853	382,757.37	70,310.78	70,632.82	....	76,694.29	600,395.26
June 24, 1854	354,794.30	68,141.69	64,989.86	....	80,997.98	568,923.83
June 23, 1855	320,063.37	67,722.43	68,377.11	....	87,049.54	543,212.45
June 21, 1856	365,052.47	72,290.74	70,772.85	$ 23,085.12[b]	110,522.86	641,724.04
June 20, 1857	545,087.35	68,868.38	69,587.83	83,879.09	143,889.18	911,311.83
June 19, 1858	502,598.40	43,966.19	54,230.08	55,898.89	115,551.75	772,245.31
June 18, 1859	688,715.86	61,785.32	70,041.05	81,705.00	128,228.78	1,030,476.01
June 16, 1860	669,742.11	60,256.82	72,987.46	84,417.58	124,922.21	1,012,326.18
June 15, 1861	732,167.48	61,406.33	74,685.25	87,756.06	131,861.62	1,087,876.74
June 14, 1862	293,410.96	42,806.11	17,798.61	32,166.58	83,185.36	469,367.62
June 13, 1863	1,296,747.84	34,422.67	36,601.74	60,186.58	113,416.46	1,541,375.29
June 25, 1864	2,904,091.62	57,314.39	65,984.53	89,782.49	157,851.18	3,275,024.21
June 24, 1865	2,813,750.28	57,950.03	74,404.04	86,194.19	176,085.67	3,208,384.21
June 23, 1866	2,041,055.49	90,498.77	99,685.53	128,210.24	226,780.93	2,586,230.96
June 29, 1867	1,806,563.07	102,508.33	117,955.45	145,942.86	224,119.66	2,397,089.37
June 27, 1868	1,121,559.15	92,789.87	107,204.56	130,437.20	207,548.42	1,659,539.20
June 26, 1869	1,305,514.16	88,798.83	104,430.22	129,428.36	218,375.10	1,846,546.67
June 25, 1870	1,116,633.04	86,233.15	94,581.13	125,799.60	203,579.23	1,626,826.15

[a] Only part of payroll since Dec. 2, 1850, allocated to mill expense.
[b] Includes operations since Sept. 3, 1855, only.

Source: MS. PMC, Agent's semiannual statements, 1851–75.

B. GROSS SALES, SUNDRY CHARGES ON SALES, AND NET SALES, 1851–1870

Twelve Months Ending in June	Gross Sales[a]	Commissions and Charges by F. Skinner & Co.[b]	Bleaching & Dyeing Bills[c]	Insurance Paid by Treasurer	Incidental Expense Account of Treasurer[d]	Interest Account of Treasurer[e]	Guarantee and Insurance Funds on Sales[f]	Misc. Charges, Wharfage, Taxes, etc.[g]	Total Sundry Charges[h]	Net Sales[i]
1851	$ 26,188.98	$ 856.42				0			$ 856.42	$ 25,332.56
1852	546,546.27	14,016.04				$39,786.52			53,802.56	492,732.71
1853	808,556.11	19,709.62	10,085.32	3,044.27	5,003.38	36,780.64	16,163.48	1,249.30	92,036.01	716,520.10
1854	775,103.38	17,893.56	5,930.07	4,868.34	6,103.89	32,509.52	15,466.60	581.55	83,353.53	691,749.85
1855	747,670.47	21,825.15	7,114.97	4,383.36	5,129.18	29,343.91	14,936.21	259.58	82,992.36	664,678.11
1856	834,942.69	22,821.04	17,892.98	4,295.23	5,581.63	56,869.52	16,702.41	400.06	124,643.87	710,298.82
1857	1,048,337.96	30,825.51	28,863.14	8,617.09	6,469.40	75,243.74	20,978.38	565.40	171,562.66	876,775.30
1858	1,233,049.29	32,378.47	20,546.59	7,967.00	7,727.72	73,260.97	24,681.60	285.15	166,847.50	1,066,201.79
1859	1,373,912.54	35,024.75	36,011.17	6,857.12	7,236.87	59,922.72	27,483.60	652.51	173,188.74	1,200,723.80
1860	1,465,042.86	34,308.36	23,528.69	5,102.50	7,398.59	70,655.81	29,341.42	668.99	171,004.36	1,294,038.50
1861	1,467,454.95	37,631.44	31,876.27	5,355.00	6,910.08	82,793.65	29,354.37	426.66	194,347.47	1,273,107.48
1862	757,045.26	21,608.32	10,420.44	5,000.00	7,378.81	27,062.53	15,075.30	403.18	86,948.58	670,096.68

[a] Before sundry charges. Includes sales at the mill (1853–55, 1866–70), incidental income, and sales by agent. For 1851, sales for three months; these figures from the treasurer's cloth account vary slightly from those in other accounts.
[b] Includes various charges besides commissions, which were 1½% of gross sales from 1854 to 1870.
[c] Paid by the treasurer.
[d] Includes treasurer's salary, clerks' salaries, office rent, expenses of stockholders' meetings, etc.
[e] Covers interest on loans and discounts of notes.
[f] Set aside each year to provide against losses from bad accounts. At first, guarantee fund was 1½% of gross sales and insurance fund ½%.
[g] Largely wharfage from 1852 through 1862. In 1863, 1864, 1866, 1867, and 1868, only U. S. revenue tax. In 1864, City of Biddeford Special Tax of $20,686.66 and U. S. revenue tax.
[h] Total of preceding charges.
[i] Equals gross sales minus total sundry charges.

Twelve Months Ending in June	Gross Sales[a]	Commissions and Charges by F. Skinner & Co.[b]	Bleaching & Dyeing Bills[c]	Insurance Paid by Treasurer	Incidental Expense Account of Treasurer[d]	Interest Account of Treasurer[e]	Guarantee and Insurance Funds on Sales[f]	Misc. Charges, Wharfage, Taxes, etc.[g]	Tota Sundry Charges[h]	Net Sales[i]
1863	2,613,369.75	55,176.55	5,165.10	5,930.88	6,848.99	267.44	52,268.65	38,768.20	164,425.81[j]	2,448,943.94[k]
1864	4,237,811.32	88,659.67	17,865.13	5,854.44	7,244.17	37,921.68	84,748.94	120,361.43	362,655.46	3,875,155.86
1865	3,945,176.59	84,330.17	32,361.97	6,164.50	7,328.04	113,921.94	0.00	191,838.91	435,945.53[j]	3,509,231.06
1866	3,579,975.27				226,119.78[l]			201,228.68[m]	427,348.46	3,152,626.81[k]
1867	2,963,021.62				123,189.28[n]			145,155.57[o]	268,344.85	2,694,676.77
1868	2,304,624.31				114,840.00[p]			82,468.86[q]	197,308.86	2,107,315.45
1869	2,015,629.00				100,781.00[r]			0.00	100,781.00	1,914,848.00
1870	1,648,710.00				82,436.00[r]			0.00	82,436.00	1,566,274.00

[j] Corrected. Used total of individual charges.
[k] Corrected so that charges and net sales equaled gross sales.
[l] Total for charges other than taxes. Sundry charges not classified as in previous years. Includes charges and commissions, freight, and "To bring to cash" for June, 1865, through May, 1866, from miscellaneous volume where sales figures were one month ahead of those in Sales Book.
[m] Taxes paid on sales, June, 1865, through May, 1866.
[n] In 1866–67, charges of $63,093.80 include "To bring to Cash" for 12 months and charges and freight for two months which were $13,980.06, or 2.5% of sales. Estimate for these charges for year made at rate of 2.5% of gross sales.
[o] Taxes paid for June, 1866, through May, 1867.
[p] In 1867–68, the charge "To bring to Cash" given for 9 months, $42,521.37. Estimate for the year made at the same percentage, 2.4% of gross sales. Charges and freight estimated at 2.5% of gross sales, or $57,615.61.
[q] Taxes given for 9 months only of year, June through Feb.
[r] Estimates at 5% of gross sales.

Source: MS. PMC, Sales sheet, Apr.–June, 1851, Sales books, 1851–67; Treasurer's semiannual statements, 1851–65; Miscellaneous book, which gives monthly gross sales, charges, sales before tax, and tax, 1862–68; Estimates for 1869 and 1870, using Pepperell's production and Laconia Company's production and gross sales.

C. EXPENSES, TOTAL NET SALES, PROFITS, AND DIVIDENDS
1851–1870

Twelve Months ending in June	Goods on hand at beginning of year[a]	Expense of Manufacturing Goods[b]	Total Mfg. Expense of Goods Sold[c]	Total Net Sales[d]	Profits[e]	Dividends Payable[f]
1851	$ 0.	$ 49,995.35	$ 24,864.72	$ 25,332.56	$ 467.84	$ 0
1852	25,130.63	399,154.06	418,550.09	492,963.08	74,412.99	0
1853	5,734.60	600,395.26	554,185.65	716,520.10	162,334.45	64,000
1854	51,944.21	568,923.83	562,448.88	691,749.85	129,300.97	64,000
1855	58,419.16	543,212.45	549,450.91	664,678.11	115,227.20	64,000
1856	52,180.70	641,724.04	575,443.04	710,720.86	135,277.82	64,000
1857	118,461.70	911,311.83	757,935.39	877,204.73	119,269.34	72,000
1858	271,838.14	772,245.31	1,024,784.17	1,066,670.00	41,885.83	40,000
1859	19,299.28	1,030,476.01	1,037,244.95	1,201,490.66	164,245.71	80,000
1860	12,530.34	1,012,326.18	1,020,786.81	1,295,264.26	274,477.45	100,000
1861	4,069.71	1,087,876.74	1,026,273.57	1,273,657.99	247,384.42	120,000
1862	65,672.88	469,367.62	385,227.90	670,660.58	285,432.68	120,000
1863	149,812.60	1,541,375.29	1,672,516.55	2,448,655.65	776,139.10	760,000
1864	18,671.34	3,275,024.21	3,188,802.53	3,877,270.59	688,468.06	400,000
1865	104,893.02	3,208,384.21	3,338,757.39	3,515,836.79	177,079.40	400,000
1866	[g]	2,586,230.96	[g]	3,152,626.81	725,886.00	400,000

Twelve Months ending in June	Goods on hand at beginning of year[a]	Expense of Manufacturing Goods[b]	Total Mfg. Expense of Goods Sold[c]	Total Net Sales[d]	Profits[e]	Dividends Payable[f]
1867	[g]	2,397,089.37	[g]	2,694,676.77	239,264.00	270,000
1868	[g]	1,659,539.20	[g]	2,107,315.45	229,550.00	150,000
1869	[g]	1,846,546.67	[g]	1,914,848.00	307,219.00	200,000
1870	[g]	1,626,826.15	[g]	1,566,274.00	205,452.00	200,000

[a] Goods on hand at the beginning of the fiscal year in hands of selling agent, mill agent, and bleacheries.

[b] Cost of manufacturing goods during twelve months.

[c] Equals goods on hand at beginning, plus expense of manufacturing minus goods on hand at beginning of next year.

[d] Equals net sales by selling agent (gross minus sundry charges) plus sales at mill in years, 1852, 1856–65. Thus this column does not always agree with net sales in previous table.

[e] Equals total net sales minus total manufacturing expense of goods sold.

[f] Within fiscal year.

[g] Not available.

Source: Goods on hand at beginning of year from MS. PMC, Treasurer's semiannual statements, 1851–65; not available after 1865.

Expense of Manufacture from section A of this appendix.

Total net sales from section B of this appendix, plus sales at mill from MS. PMC, Treasurer's semiannual statements, 1851–65.

Profits from MS. PMC, Treasurer's semiannual statements, 1851–65; and from Controller's memo on profits, 1866–70.

Dividends Payable, calculated from number of shares outstanding and amounts of dividends declared by directors.

APPENDIX 36

EXPENSES, SALES, PROFITS, AND DIVIDENDS, 1871–1924

A. Manufacturing and Sundry Expenses on Sales

1. 1871–1898

	Manufacturing			Sundry Expenses									
Fiscal Year Ending June 30	Goods on Hand at Beginning[a]	Goods Manufactured[b]	Cost of Bleaching[c]	Commissions to Selling Agent[d]	Charges by Selling Agent[e]	Freight Charges[f]	Interest Charges[g]	Guarantee Account[h]	Incidental Expense[i]	Insurance on Mills[j]	Renovating Account[k]	Miscellaneous[l]	Total Expense[m]
1871....	$296,298.65	$1,289,145.38	$29,981.67	$53,650.76	....	....	$39,556.38	....	$ 9,995.46	$ 5,284.82	....	$ 5,409.24	$1,671,719.40
1872....	57,602.96	1,482,968.25	64,374.53	64,230.67	....	....	32,360.52	....	10,318.69	5,101.89	....	....	1,572,342.05
1873....	144,615.46	1,602,374.88	69,148.36	60,211.61	....	....	24,574.27	....	9,145.59	6,000.00	....	....	1,683,557.23
1874....	232,512.94	1,538,453.83	60,738.50	41,843.09	$12,308.39	....	13,105.47	....	9,310.07	9,047.72	....	....	1,665,496.66
1875....	251,823.35	1,258,992.91	56,382.87	19,941.35	24,019.08	....	6,453.42	....	12,065.26	11,774.00	....	....	1,431,395.06
1876....	210,057.18	1,384,622.76	64,346.53	22,800.67	26,981.29	....	13,908.41	$23,030.82	8,833.10	10,096.73	$ 10,000.00	....	1,633,680.72
1877....	140,996.77	1,154,329.00	57,258.91	18,900.42	23,561.91	....	13,845.89	22,229.83	9,467.41	10,986.00	50,000.00	....	1,351,809.00
1878....	149,767.14	1,334,500.34	61,172.91	22,307.78	27,527.59	....	14,365.67	26,703.62	8,438.74	11,000.00	85,000.00	....	1,640,878.43
1879....	99,905.36	1,238,308.65	52,421.81	20,785.33	28,118.86	....	7,904.16	24,997.41	8,145.37	12,185.14	88,331.62	....	1,516,642.88
1880....	64,460.83	1,523,909.20	59,773.18	27,520.28	18,080.26	....	6,440.36	29,518.33	10,078.87	12,442.51	150,000.00	....	1,762,496.82
1881....	139,727.00	1,493,680.25	49,009.42	27,054.28	28,320.71	....	8,815.21	32,334.16	10,000.30	17,374.98	216,152.28	....	2,000,197.09
1882....	22,271.50	1,783,135.93	58,465.71	28,868.66	14,655.43	$14,690.00	13,487.44	34,657.09	9,940.19	23,461.37	175,159.69	....	2,143,044.81
1883....	35,748.20	1,862,133.63	56,209.41	30,269.38	19,206.36	7,027.83	3,599.41	36,400.00	10,503.29	17,615.16	99,840.72	....	2,154,534.69
1884....	24,018.70	1,788,346.70	67,552.09	25,542.78	21,119.63	5,381.79	7,150.88	30,555.71	13,358.38	20,884.39	99,219.18	....	1,912,832.23
1885....	190,298.00	1,612,032.75	73,659.73	27,128.99	19,553.55	13,705.85	2,451.42	32,590.88	12,936.06	20,536.97	75,475.57	....	2,036,519.54
1886....	43,850.23	1,698,891.38	64,530.72	25,921.53	13,445.80	13,383.99	2,745.31	31,129.23	13,011.19	16,532.87	62,219.10	....	1,939,721.86
1887....	45,939.49	1,738,734.77	60,335.53	27,313.99	15,872.82	15,742.55	744.10	32,811.69	14,201.01	20,670.45	82,764.31	....	2,029,654.02
1888....	25,476.69	1,765,603.29	52,896.88	29,483.38	13,902.17	17,031.98	18,402.54	35,433.18	15,093.53	18,680.54	202,520.74	....	2,171,654.63
1889....	22,870.29	1,882,115.62	60,847.20	30,457.25	12,454.82	16,471.82	16,265.30	36,649.65	14,939.95	18,501.92	122,474.39	....	2,209,719.36
1890....	24,328.85	1,947,174.42	66,143.62	30,919.80	13,717.02	16,033.77	13,876.22	37,203.75	14,667.30	19,431.02	45,059.05	....	2,204,607.57
1891....	23,947.25	2,053,012.70	75,203.04	31,677.26	15,580.52	17,848.74	5,486.14	38,092.15	15,299.23	20,977.41	22,484.98	....	2,280,189.77
1892....	39,419.65	1,881,623.60	72,748.34	32,744.94	13,454.95	16,894.63	18,804.91	41,535.58	15,279.45	20,986.72	220,550.02	....	2,354,154.88

	Manufacturing			Sundry Expenses									
Fiscal Year Ending June 30	Goods on Hand at Beginning[a]	Goods Manufactured[b]	Cost of Bleaching[c]	Commissions to Selling Agent[d]	Charges by Selling Agent[e]	Freight Charges[f]	Interest Charges[g]	Guarantee Account[h]	Incidental Expense[i]	Insurance on Mills[j]	Renovating Account[k]	Miscellaneous[l]	Total Expense[m]
1893....	19,887.91	1,860,344.95	75,671.72	28,863.38	14,979.56	19,988.46	30,066.04	34,511.33	15,849.71	19,249.81	90,026.59	....	2,143,873.89
1894....	65,565.57	1,758,625.92	64,217.13	27,472.11	16,600.99	17,479.16	15,152.56	32,967.16	16,524.26	19,637.66	54,094.50	....	2,027,867.91
1895....	60,469.11	1,626,406.26	75,964.96	29,009.56	17,730.01	22,105.91	16,723.11	34,811.49	17,923.68	19,412.02	173,656.36	7,000.00	2,072,869.47
1896....	28,343.00	1,790,835.95	86,576.86	29,028.86	13,587.66	19,698.39	8,811.05	31,721.86	18,128.68	20,394.68	64,567.36	....	1,972,739.45
1897....	138,954.90	1,716,674.00	64,560.00	32,027.07	13,503.23	20,253.35	5,431.45	32,027.07	17,612.69	20,468.01	14,039.58	....	1,975,589.04
1898....	99,962.31	1,459,876.51	65,000.56	30,385.90	12,928.45	21,424.26	....	30,385.90	16,197.53	20,227.00	31,385.26	125,000.00	1,864,377.97

[a] Goods on hand at beginning of fiscal year as valued by the treasurer.
[b] Goods manufactured within the year include actual mill expense and general expense as reported by the mill agent and cost of cotton used as computed by the treasurer.
[c] Includes cost of dyeing and finishing. Until June, 1874, included by treasurer among sundry charges, but thereafter among the manufacturing costs.
[d] Includes general and freight charges through Dec., 1873. Rate for commission, according to contract, Oct. 10, 1870, with J. S. & E. Wright & Co. was 1¼%. Starting January 1, 1896, rate was 1½%.
[e] Include freight through June, 1881, and for six months ending June, 1883, and Dec., 1883.
[f] Freight charges on goods sold. See note e.
[g] Include interest on borrowed money and discounts on prepayments.
[h] Account set aside from profits at the rate of 1½% of gross sales to meet possible losses from bad debts. Part of fund not so used set aside as a reserve for future contingencies.
[i] Includes the treasurer's salary, Pepperell's share of the countinghouse expense, and miscellaneous other expenses.
[j] Amounts paid to insurance companies from which refunds were obtained which were added to reserves.
[k] Funds set aside for improvements, parts of which might be spent within the current year with the remainder kept as a reserve.
[l] In 1871 this comprised $2,871.74 for U. S. tax and $2,537.50 for endorsing notes by treasurer pro tempore and others.
[m] Total expense equals the sum of all columns for the current year minus the first column, for the beginning of the next year.

Source: MS. PMC, Statements of Operation, 1871–98.

EXPENSES, SALES, PROFITS, AND DIVIDENDS, 1871–1924 (continued)

A. Manufacturing and Sundry Expenses on Sales
2. 1899–1924

Fiscal Year Ending June 30	Manufacturing: Goods on Hand at Beginning[a]	Manufacturing: Goods Manu-factured[b]	Manufacturing: Cost of Bleaching & Coloring	Sundry Expenses: Commis-sions to Selling Agent[c]	Sundry Expenses: Charges by Selling Agent	Sundry Expenses: Freight Charges	Sundry Expenses: Interest Charges[d]	Sundry Expenses: Guarantee Account	Sundry Expenses: Incidental Expense[e]	Sundry Expenses: Insurance on Mills[f]	Sundry Expenses: Renovating Account[g]	Sundry Expenses: Depreci-ation[h]	Sundry Expenses: Miscel-laneous[i]	Sundry Expenses: Total Expenses[j]
1899[k]..	$ 48,395.71	$ 2,436,249.13	$101,793.62	$ 50,409.36	$ 21,429.87	$34,611.84	$ 1,508.05	$ 46,913.85	$ 23,190.27	$30,085.77	$ 77,411.29	$100,000.00	....	$ 3,031,674.74
1900...	117,337.86	3,507,090.46	148,681.14	71,868.05	27,219.25	42,567.74	8,363.51	66,879.59	35,614.98	41,536.00	65,869.35	200,000.00	....	4,038,141.67
1901...	294,886.26	3,453,999.64	133,050.83	70,316.29	19,192.03	33,368.80	....	65,622.86	34,904.69	43,885.50	19,770.75	200,000.00	....	4,214,387.97
1902...	154,609.68	3,976,287.22	141,317.24	73,266.41	29,918.94	47,212.36	888.29	68,150.73	27,543.70	45,350.60	87,006.07	150,000.00	....	4,366,641.05
1903...	434,910.19	4,037,613.98	141,495.36	88,073.05	35,446.65	49,886.10	....	81,836.18	25,929.32	44,259.61	212,922.07	100,000.00	....	5,205,745.31
1904...	46,627.20	4,116,983.12	134,501.48	74,892.91	25,699.19	37,592.43	....	69,435.82	26,542.35	46,096.32	90,870.15	....	....	4,441,478.35
1905...	227,762.62	4,722,427.10	127,163.37	99,949.91	32,421.32	46,431.17	....	92,640.20	27,957.16	42,912.22	93,805.23	150,000.00	....	5,603,085.45
1906...	60,384.85	4,681,981.49	133,478.85	98,790.34	34,064.87	45,062.25	....	91,717.89	28,667.57	46,211.83	237,410.99	200,000.00	....	5,586,624.39
1907...	71,146.54	4,405,400.84	145,797.72	95,194.13	27,291.48	35,218.58	13,854.15	88,522.23	31,216.82	47,528.23	349,511.65	500,000.00	....	5,480,963.25
1908...	329,719.12	4,438,503.63	147,429.51	85,838.47	25,230.04	25,521.96	813.63	79,724.14	29,592.49	49,464.75	123,411.78	....	....	4,950,602.65
1909...	384,646.87	4,258,154.85	164,058.17	105,508.64	32,909.20	38,514.75	....	98,327.41	26,729.79	48,574.42	467,445.78	100,000.00	....	5,697,324.16
1910...	27,545.72	4,844,096.05	188,356.59	91,741.02	29,667.95	33,706.69	3,909.64	85,277.08	45,544.41	54,874.61	671,256.87	....	$ 2,500.00	5,451,777.26
1911...	626,699.37	5,047,344.41	174,771.83	102,521.96	37,817.89	32,834.09	11,752.93	95,266.88	27,608.88	57,125.24	346,648.67	....	....	6,166,431.80
1912...	393,960.35	4,775,262.23	182,480.90	100,268.54	33,197.00	40,594.47	8,355.20	93,144.89	32,171.57	53,452.42	572,283.16	....	....	5,872,915.18
1913...	412,255.55	5,439,984.88	170,331.57	108,898.55	36,397.85	38,594.76	628.80	100,770.33	41,088.71	60,836.50	468,885.63	....	....	6,490,584.37
1914...	388,088.46	6,094,534.25	191,679.57	112,191.11	38,023.05	35,510.80	2,635.56	103,822.19	34,398.98	55,400.71	196,621.14	....	....	6,666,123.92
1915...	586,781.90	4,966,710.11	257,444.40	96,071.35	39,423.52	31,167.97	5,945.06	147,478.09	49,813.52	14,245.95	60,769.94	164,000.00	....	5,607,116.15
1916...	812,735.66	5,508,316.00	301,573.34	136,358.81	39,766.32	49,528.30	....	43,967.07	69,699.40	23,941.82	....	328,000.00	70,789.22	7,021,958.27
1917...	362,717.67	7,294,931.28	387,632.17	176,442.44	46,913.02	48,332.33	6,189.64	53,989.89	86,427.60	35,547.01	....	328,000.00	462,314.54	9,214,507.42
1918...	74,930.17	11,706,767.38	434,722.68	272,052.06	53,238.35	40,444.55	36,065.83	83,137.15	75,357.38	28,829.74	....	328,000.00	1,563,707.75	14,687,253.04

Fiscal Year Ending June 30	Manufacturing: Goods on Hand at Beginning[a]	Manufacturing: Goods Manufactured[b]	Manufacturing: Cost of Bleaching & Coloring	Sundry Expenses: Commissions to Selling Agent[c]	Sundry Expenses: Charges by Selling Agent	Sundry Expenses: Freight Charges	Sundry Expenses: Interest Charges[d]	Sundry Expenses: Guarantee Account	Sundry Expenses: Incidental Expense[e]	Sundry Expenses: Insurance on Mills[f]	Sundry Expenses: Renovating Account[g]	Sundry Expenses: Depreciation[h]	Sundry Expenses: Miscellaneous[i]	Sundry Expenses: Total Expenses[j]
1919...	10,000.00	10,014,573.64	386,369.98	212,059.96	59,790.56	10,948.46	....	65,199.66	103,754.50	18,449.51	....	328,000.00	19,473.11	10,795,284.57
1920...	433,334.81	18,279,515.92	628,910.10	375,625.39	111,825.17	10,695.78	....	114,997.25	119,014.71	61,709.86	....	328,000.00	9,657.67	19,174,514.19
1921...	1,298,772.47	10,057,900.56	746,243.93	170,734.46	106,699.71	28,337.03	....	52,708.53	125,589.89	4,954.53	....	328,000.00	13,370.36	9,776,665.61
1922...	3,156,645.86	8,656,437.35	698,400.53	166,381.36	70,413.82	24,637.18	....	51,504.53	102,228.82	18,678.27	....	328,000.00	18,355.86	10,523,293.36
1923...	2,768,390.22	11,609,962.90	848,854.27	266,272.59	97,420.81	13,000.94	17,731.52	81,409.80	170,405.89	11,768.28	....	370,597.00	516,526.32	15,342,241.50
1924...	1,430,099.04	11,218,065.28	819,808.62	182,991.59	91,937.42	6,912.67	....	55,828.94	173,878.77	6,372.41	....	370,597.00	24,778.26	11,259,396.98

[a] Goods on hand at beginning of fiscal year as valued by the treasurer. For the beginning of 1925, goods on hand amounted to $3,121,873.02.

[b] Goods manufactured within the year include actual mill expense and general expense as reported by the mill agent and cost of cotton used as computed by the treasurer. In 1915, treasurer added to cost of manufacturing $250,000 to write off trade-marks. In 1918, treasurer added $500,000 as a reserve for cotton; in 1919, $500,000; and in 1920, $2,000,000.

[c] Commissions to selling agent: for Pepperell at 1⅓%, while for Laconia 1¾%.

[d] Interest on borrowed money. Guarantee account set aside from profits at rate of 1½% of gross sales. For six months ending June, 1915, treasurer charged off $94,754.49 in addition to regular charge for notes of H. B. Claflin Co. Starting Dec. 31, 1915, guarantee was charged at ½%.

[e] Includes salary of treasurer and countinghouse expense as well as legal, advertising, etc., expenses.

[f] Premiums paid, 1899–1914; in 1915 and thereafter, premiums paid minus dividends received from insurance companies.

[g] Funds set aside from profits, 1899 through Dec., 1914. Thereafter funds set aside for depreciation.

[h] Funds set aside regularly.

[i] Miscellaneous—in 1910 and in following years as shown liability insurance payments with in addition in 1916, $62,864.82 for loss by fire; 1917, $450,000 reserve for federal taxes; 1918, $1,050,000 reserve for taxes and $500,000 for cotton; 1923, $200,000 reserve for federal taxes and $300,000 reserve for cotton.

[j] Equals sum of all columns for current year minus the first column, for beginning of following year.

[k] Figures for year 1899 include those for Laconia Division (and Laconia Company) for the last six months. To Pepperell's goods on hand in 1899 should be added Laconia's of $177,013.84 on Dec. 31, 1898.

Source: MS. PMC, Statements of Operations, 1899–1924; PMC, Annual reports for 1919, 1921–24.

EXPENSES, SALES, PROFITS, AND DIVIDENDS, 1871–1924 (continued)

B. SALES, PROFITS, AND DIVIDENDS
1. 1871–1898

Fiscal Year Ending June 30	Goods Sold at Mill[a]	Goods Sold by Selling Agent[b]	Total Sales[c]	Profit[d]	Dividends Payable[e]
1871	$ 2,233.90	$1,826,110.13	$1,828,344.03	$156,624.63	$100,000
1872	2,909.16	1,982,722.50	1,985,631.66	413,289.61	110,000
1873	4,221.71	2,080,786.76	2,085,008.47	401,451.24	144,000
1874	3,828.98	1,929,768.77	1,933,597.75	268,101.09	144,000
1875	15,441.96	1,566,752.97	1,582,194.93	150,799.87	144,000
1876	7,511.36	1,776,462.31	1,783,973.67	150,292.95	144,000
1877	7,048.45	1,481,990.15	1,489,038.60	137,229.60	120,000
1878	5,466.03	1,764,461.67	1,769,927.70	129,049.27	120,000
1879	1,796.26	1,640,591.85	1,642,388.11	125,745.23	120,000
1880	8,354.15	1,947,650.60	1,956,004.75	193,507.93	132,000
1881	4,334.25	2,153,609.50	2,157,943.75	157,746.66	168,000
1882	6,230.91	2,298,433.82	2,304,664.73	161,619.92	168,000
1883	2,380.14	2,411,507.85	2,413,887.99	259,353.30	168,000
1884	692.08	2,035,545.70	2,036,237.78	123,405.55	156,000
1885	4,338.18	2,168,834.13	2,173,172.31	136,652.77	144,000
1886	389.86	2,075,276.59	2,075,666.45	135,944.59	144,000
1887	472.96	2,187,446.98	2,187,919.94	158,265.92	624,000
1888	373.23	2,362,813.05	2,363,186.28	191,531.65	156,000
1889	359.54	2,443,310.29	2,443,669.83	233,950.47	168,000
1890	360.30	2,480,251.11	2,480,611.41	276,003.84	168,000
1891	340.87	2,539,477.35	2,539,818.22	259,628.45	168,000
1892	3,651.25	2,619,724.69	2,623,375.94	269,221.06	768,000
1893	9,582.66	2,300,756.48	2,310,339.14	166,465.25	168,000
1894	336.01	2,197,811.67	2,198,147.68	170,279.77	156,000
1895	320.01	2,310,766.33	2,311,086.34	238,216.87	144,000
1896	283.51	2,114,790.34	2,115,073.85	142,334.40	168,000
1897	270.87	2,135,139.51	2,135,410.38	159,821.34	168,000
1898	390.43	2,025,726.90	2,026,117.33	161,739.36	144,000

[a] Goods sold at mill include sales there, goods used, as well as yarn and batting sold occasionally.

[b] Goods on which commission was charged.

[c] Sum of the first two columns. Income from dividends on stock of Lewiston Bleachery & Dye Works and returned premiums on insurance policies not considered; they were added to special reserve funds.

[d] Total sales minus total expense in section A.1. of this appendix.

[e] Dividends payable to stockholders. Regular ones payable the first of Aug. and Feb. In 1871, number of shares 1,000, which was increased to 1,200 during the year. First dividends paid on new shares, Feb., 1872.

Source: MS. PMC, Statements of operation, 1871–98; Directors' records, 1870–98; dividends, 1860–99.

EXPENSES, SALES, PROFITS, AND DIVIDENDS, 1871–1924

B. SALES, PROFITS, AND DIVIDENDS (continued)
2. 1899–1924

Fiscal Year Ending June 30	Goods Sold at Mill[a]	Goods Sold by Selling Agent[b]	Total Sales[c]	Profit[d]	Dividends Payable[e]
1899	$ 9,985.37	$3,194,257.74	$3,204,243.11	$172,568.37	$528,000
1900	46,486.73	4,458,639.55	4,505,126.28	466,984.61	562,320
1901	41,675.53	4,374,857.35	4,416,532.88	202,144.91	306,720
1902	33,830.46	4,527,946.86	4,561,777.23	195,136.17	306,720
1903	50,725.32	5,455,746.14	5,506,471.46	300,726.15	817,920
1904	489.89	4,628,880.43	4,629,370.32	187,891.97	306,720
1905	16,063.98	6,175,840.68	6,191,904.66	588,819.21	306,720
1906	446.86	6,114,527.04	6,114,973.90	528,349.51	1,206,320
1907	42,305.88	5,901,483.27	5,943,789.15	462,825.90	1,584,720
1908	649.23	5,314,699.86	5,315,349.09	364,746.44	306,000
1909	2,782.34	6,554,860.54	6,557,642.88	860,318.72	306,000
1910	27,249.34	5,685,139.03	5,712,388.37	260,611.11	945,720
1911	10,935.03	6,351,126.20	6,362,061.23	195,629.43	306,000
1912	962.37	6,209,659.84	6,210,622.21	337,707.03	306,000
1913	1,080.77	6,718,021.63	6,719,102.40	228,518.03	306,000
1914	1,514.48	6,921,479.37	6,922,993.85	256,869.93	306,000
1915	89,291.42	5,919,011.88	6,008,303.30	401,187.15	306,000
1916	117,675.39	8,336,742.71	8,454,418.10	1,432,459.83	1,226,880
1917	2,978.06	10,797,980.21	10,800,958.27	1,586,450.85	1,073,520
1918	9,524.42	16,627,430.07	16,636,954.49	1,949,701.45	690,120
1919	3,664.31	13,039,932.34	13,043,596.65	2,248,312.08	613,440
1920	11,766.55	22,999,443.55	23,011,210.10	3,836,695.91	1,073,520
1921	7,120.94	10,541,452.33	10,548,573.27	771,907.66	820,160
1922	4,706.73	10,306,422.65	10,311,129.38	212,163.98[f]	613,440
1923	5,827.96	16,281,962.31	16,287,790.27	945,548.77	613,440
1924	4,734.17	11,165,786.91	11,170,521.08	88,875.90[f]	613,440

[a] Includes sales at mill, goods used, as well as sales of yarn.
[b] Goods on which commission was charged.
[c] Sum of the first two columns. Income from dividends of Lewiston Bleachery & Dye Works and returned premiums on insurance policies until 1915 not considered; they were added to special reserve funds.
[d] Total sales minus total expenses in section A.2. of this appendix.
[e] Dividends payable to stockholders. Regular ones payable the first of Aug. and Feb. In 1899, 25,660 shares; in 1915, 76,680.
[f] Loss.

Source: MS. PMC, Statements of operation, 1899–1924; Directors' records, 1898–1915; Trustees' records, 1915–24; Annual reports for 1919, 1921–24.

APPENDIX 37

PROFIT AND LOSS STATEMENT, 1925–1945

Year Ending June 30	Total Net Billings[a]	Total Cost of Production[b]	Net General Overhead[c]	Federal Taxes	Transfer to Reserves	Net Earnings[d]	Dividends Paid
1925	$11,575,550	$12,116,005	$ 407,393	$ 3,863	$535,792[e]	$ 415,919[f]	$ 613,440
1926	9,836,369	8,961,789	399,165	141,115[e]		616,530	613,440
1927	15,352,722	13,563,942	808,715			980,065	738,200
1928	19,803,313	17,563,366	1,101,384	11,585	100,000	1,026,978	863,200
1929	16,762,107	14,810,345	747,571	89,910		1,114,281	863,200
1930	18,246,089	17,129,301	802,582	4,204	350,000[e]	660,002	1,079,000
1931	17,128,803	16,640,636	1,070,608			582,441[f]	757,000
1932	14,919,142	15,895,976	972,724		750,000[e]	1,199,558[f]	296,404
1933	17,745,636	15,785,026	1,036,280			924,330	
1934	28,606,879	25,634,379	967,679	397,135		1,607,685	602,819
1935	28,986,092	28,921,611	1,002,544		500,000[e]	438,063[f]	583,374
1936	29,640,764	27,019,017	1,701,517	201,151[e]		1,121,359	291,684
1937	39,941,251	34,935,341	2,268,269	633,526		2,104,115	1,555,576
1938	26,415,096	26,328,241	1,931,943		222,630[e]	1,796,169[f]	291,681
1939	28,490,548	25,767,980	1,676,135	175,000		871,433	291,681
1940	29,343,709	26,184,562	1,737,646	299,996		1,121,505	485,135
1941	38,639,270	33,527,541	1,759,785	983,400	500,000	1,868,544	583,362
1942	48,224,968	41,183,550	1,726,272	3,350,000		1,965,146	777,816
1943	53,466,275	45,627,419	1,575,827	4,300,000		1,963,029	1,069,497
1944	51,358,317	42,915,650	1,501,922	5,075,000		1,865,745	972,270
1945	52,069,875	43,704,447	1,630,225	4,920,000	500,000[e]	2,315,203	972,270

[a] Total Net Billings equals billings less intercompany sales.

[b] Total cost of production of goods sold includes cotton, labor, general expense of mill, depreciation, freight charges, State, city, and security taxes.

[c] Total of general administrative, advertising, selling, and sundry charges minus sundry credits.

[d] Net Earnings before dividends.

[e] Credit.

[f] Deficit.

Source: MS. PMC, Treasurer's report, 1925–28; Controller's report, 1929–45.

APPENDIX 38

HIGH AND LOW PRICES FOR STOCK[a]
1853–1945

Year	High	Low	Year	High	Low	Year	High	Low
1853	$ 540	$ 525	1884	$1,085	$ 980	1914	$305⅜	$290
1854	525	450	1885	1,182½	1,000	1915	346⅛	305
1855	550	450	1886	1,150	1,060	1916	194½	120¾
1856	625	520	1887	1,205	1,052½	1917	204	188
1857	575	400	1888	1,202½	1,080	1918	206	190
1858	620	425	1889	1,315	1,202½	1919	210	188
1859	620	570	1890	1,377½	1,340	1920	220	200
1860	805	615	1891	1,370	1,325	1921	202	178
1861	710	610	1892	1,365	1,200	1922	180	164⅜
1862	1,350	670	1893	1,540	1,255	1923	167½	134
1863	1,250	1,050	1894	1,337½	1,250	1924	142½	108
1864	1,238	1,080	1895	1,532½	1,252½	1925	142	107
1865	1,260	950	1896	1,500	1,205	1926	141	110⅛
1866	1,378	1,060	1897	1,355	1,275	1927	106	98
1867	1,200	880	1898	1,325	1,100	1928	114	84
1868	1,033	902	1899	1,475	1,325	1929	113½	85
1869	995	797½	1899	264	225	1930	105	78
1870	978	597½	1900	280	255	1931	79	28
1871	700	550	1901	260	240	1932	41	15¾
1872	757½	700	1902	260	255	1933	83½	26⅛
1873	778	712	1903	260	250	1934	101	69
1874	820	737½	1904	260	240	1935	89½	52¾
1875	763	720	1905	275	240	1936	149¾	55
1876	755	700	1906	302½	260	1937	151	58½
1877	775	712½	1907	320	290	1938	86	54¾
1878	800	700	1908	294	276¼	1939	94¾	58
1879	865	722½	1909	332	294	1940	91¾	53
1880	975	865	1910	315	292	1941	98	79
1881	1,253	975	1911	300	261	1942	101	81
1882	1,220	1,120	1912	290½	280	1943	125	104
1883	1,148	1,085	1913	309	290⅜	1944	158½	125
						1945	231	151½

[a] Par value of stock $500 from 1853 to 1899, with the exception of the years until 1857, when only $400 paid in. In 1899, former stockholders given seven new shares of $100 par in place of one former $500. In 1915, stockholders given three new for one old of the same par.

Source: Figures for 1853–97 from Joseph G. Martin, *A Century of Finance;* 1898–1907 from material furnished by William B. Dana Co.; 1908–26 from Mr. Crocker's notebook; 1926–45 from *Moody's Industrials,* 1936, p. a112, 1944, p. a49, 1945, p. 581, 1946, p. 913. Transactions until 1927 were over the counter in Boston, while those thereafter were as recorded by the New York Curb Exchange.

NOTES AND REFERENCES

CHAPTER I

Material for the chapters in the first period has been obtained largely from manuscript records of the Pepperell Manufacturing Company which have been deposited in Baker Library at the Graduate School of Business Administration of Harvard University. A few volumes are still in the company's hands, such as records of meetings of stockholders and directors not only of the Pepperell Manufacturing Company but also of the companies which have merged with Pepperell, particularly the Laconia Co., Saco Water Power Co., and the Massachusetts Cotton Mills. On the whole, for this and the second period, Pepperell's records in the manuscript collection in Baker Library are very comprehensive, though the records of the companies with which Pepperell merged are not so complete. In all, there are more than 1,000 volumes and over 70 boxes of unbound material. For the third period, company records in Baker Library are very few. I have had to find additional material in the various offices and plants of the company. In the references in the following pages I have abbreviated the company names, as PMC for Pepperell Manufacturing Company, SWPC for Saco Water Power Co., and LC for Laconia Co.

For the first chapter I have drawn largely from the stockholders' records, the directors' records, and lists of dividends, as well as from directors' records of the Saco Water Power Co. Only in cases of quotation or of possible uncertainty of source have I given a definite reference for my statements. As a result, the sources given below are largely the publications which have been consulted.

1. U. S. Census Office, 7th Census, 1850, Census Reports, *Abstract* (Washington, 1853), pp. 154–155.

2. George Folsom, *History of Saco and Biddeford* (Saco, 1830), pp. 205, 210, 266–267; James Montgomery, *A Practical Detail of the Cotton Manufacture of the United States of America* (Glasgow, 1840), p. 199.

3. *Dictionary of American Biography* (N. Y., 1928–36), vol. 14, pp. 456–457.

4. *Loc. cit.*

5. *Loc. cit.;* Folsom, *op. cit.,* p. 305.

6. *Ibid.,* p. 306.

7. *Loc. cit.;* Montgomery, *op. cit.,* pp. 200–201.

8. MS. SWPC [Saco Water Power Co.], Charter, Mar. 22, 1837; circular, 1839; letter, Jan. 1, 1844; Annual Report, July 15, 1847.

9. MS. SWPC, Report, Mar. 8, 1847; addition to Charter, Mar. 24, 1847; assessments.

10. MS. SWPC, Directors' records, Sept. 25, 1847.

11. *Ibid.*, July 20, 1850.

12. MS. PMC [Pepperell Manufacturing Company], Stockholders' records, Apr. 18, 1871.

13. *Ibid.*, July 24, 1851.

14. Abner Forbes, *Rich Men of Massachusetts* (Boston, 1852), pp. 26, 324.

15. *New England Union Mercantile Directory,* 1849.

16. B. W. Dwight, *Descendants of John Dwight of Dedham* (N. Y., 1874), pp. 896, 901.

CHAPTER II

For material for Chapter II, I have drawn heavily upon published works, as the following notes indicate. I have, however, consulted the manuscript collections, in Baker Library, of Almy, Brown & Slater and of the Boston Manufacturing Co., in which there is still much information which has not been utilized by students. An example is the material available on the original equipping of the mills of the Boston Manufacturing Co., which throws a slightly different light on the subject from the view which is usually held.

1. Edward Baines, *History of the Cotton Manufactures in Great Britain* (London, 1835), pp. 25–26, 32, 77–79.

2. U. S. Secretary of the Treasury, *Letter from the Secretary of the Treasury, transmitting tables and notes on the Cultivation, Manufacture, and Foreign Trade of Cotton* (Washington, 1836), p. 108.

3. Frank W. Taussig, *State Papers and Speeches on the Tariff* (Cambridge, 1892), pp. 62–71; Frank W. Taussig, *Tariff History of the United States,* 8th edition (N. Y., 1931), for an account of the tariff and in particular the details pertaining to the cotton textile industry.

4. George S. White, *Memoir of Samuel Slater, the Father of American Manufactures* (Philadelphia, 1836), pp. 37, 57, 84.

5. *Ibid.*, pp. 48–49; William R. Bagnall, *The Textile Industries of the United States, 1636–1810* (Cambridge, 1893), vol. 1, pp. 122–126; Samuel Batchelder, *Introduction and Early Progress of the Cotton Manufacture in the United States* (Boston, 1863), pp. 33–34.

6. White, *op. cit.*, pp. 40–41, 76; Paul Joseph Mantoux, *The Industrial Revolution in the Eighteenth Century,* revised edition, translated by Marjorie Vernon (N. Y., 1927), pp. 228–238; MS. Almy, Brown & Slater, vol. 1, p. 213.

7. Bagnall, *op. cit.*, pp. 240–242, 185–186; Perry Walton, *The Story of Textiles* (Boston, 1912), p. 182; Mantoux, *op. cit.*, pp. 241–243; White, *op. cit.*, p. 248.

8. Bagnall, *op. cit.*, pp. 209, 277, 368.

9. Albert Gallatin, *Report from the Secretary of the Treasury, on the Subject of Manufactures* (Washington, 1810), Appendix B; *Niles' Weekly Register* (Nov. 18, 1815), vol. 9, p. 190.

10. MS. Almy, Brown & Slater, vol. 1; Bagnall, *op. cit.*, pp. 369, 444–446; Gallatin, *op. cit.*, p. 9; White, *op. cit.*, pp. 75, 126, 127, 189; Caroline Ware,

The Early New England Cotton Manufacture (Boston, 1931), p. 245; N. S. B. Gras and Henrietta M. Larson, *Casebook in American Business History* (N. Y., 1939), p. 225; Batchelder, *op. cit.*, pp. 33–34.

11. Gallatin, *op. cit.*, p. 11; Bagnall, *op. cit.*, p. 547.

12. MS. Boston Manufacturing Co., Stockholders' records, vol. 1.

13. *Ibid.*, vols. 2, 10, 25, 26, 192; Nathan Appleton, *Introduction to the Power Loom and the Origin of Lowell* (Lowell, 1858), p. 9; Greville and Dorothy Bathe, *Jacob Perkins* (Philadelphia, 1943), pp. 44–45.

14. *Ibid.*, p. 21; MS. Boston Manufacturing Co., vols. 2, 25, 186, 187.

15. Boston Manufacturing Co., Report, 1901; Appleton, *op. cit.*, pp. 15–16.

16. MS. Boston Manufacturing Co., vols. 25, 34.

17. Appleton, *op. cit.*, pp. 11–12; MS. Boston Manufacturing Co., vol. 2.

18. Joseph G. Martin, *Twenty-One Years in the Boston Stock Market, 1835–56* (Boston, 1856); George Waldo Browne, *The Amoskeag Manufacturing Co. of Manchester, New Hampshire; a History* (Manchester ?, 1915), pp. 29–52; U. S. *Executive Documents*, 1st session, 22d Congress (Washington, 1833), vol. 2, pp. 48–49, 464.

19. U. S. 7th Census, 1850, Reports, *Abstract* (1853), p. 154.

20. *Ibid.*; *N. E. Union Mercantile Directory, 1849;* J. G. Martin, *Twenty-One Years;* Amos A. Lawrence, *The Conditions and Prospects of American Cotton Manufactures in 1849–1850* (N. Y.?, 1849); *Hunt's Merchants' Magazine* (1848), vol. 18, p. 593; (1850), vol. 22, p. 684; (1859), vol. 41, p. 439; *Farm & Mechanic,* July 13, 1848.

21. J. G. Martin, *Twenty-One Years.*

22. C. Ware, *New England Cotton Manufacture,* pp. 138–160, 178–197.

23. Appleton, *op. cit.*, pp. 15–16; Lawrence, *op. cit.*, p. 28; U. S. Dept. of Commerce, Bureau of the Census, Bulletin No. 167, *Cotton Production and Distribution* (Washington, 1930), pp. 57–59.

24. Reference in Victor Clark's notes to Michel Chevalier, Chap. xiii; Harriet H. Robinson, *Loom and Spindle* (N. Y., 1898), p. 82; Charles Dickens, *American Notes,* vol. 1, pp. 159-160.

25. Robinson, *op. cit.*, p. 195.

CHAPTER III

This chapter dealing with Pepperell's purchasing of cotton was based on various types of manuscript records of the company. These included cotton letters from the buyers to the treasurer, which included prices-current for the period 1850 to 1866 and cotton invoices listed by the agent in Biddeford, the first volume for 1850 to 1865 and the second for 1865 to 1874. I got additional information from other types of records, such as cotton acceptances, bills of lading, cotton cash vouchers, insurance policies, and various bills for charges. Altogether this material was adequate for the period 1850 to 1865 and quite inadequate for 1865 to 1870. Usually I have not made any reference to these records except when a direct quotation or definite statement was selected from them. Additional sources of information follow at this point.

1. Matthew B. Hammond, *The Cotton Industry* (N. Y., 1897), pt. 1, pp. 68–74.

2. MS. PMC, Sundry letters, Oct. 15, 1852, Sept. 22, and Oct. 15, 1859.

3. MS. PMC, Treasurer's letter book, 1850–53, letter of Jan. 29, 1852.

4. Hunt's *Merchants' Magazine* (1851), vol. 25, p. 659; Hammond, *op. cit.*, pp. 289–290; Bradstreet Co., *A Journal of Trade, Finance and Public Economy* (1886), vol. 13, p. 227.

5. MS. PMC, Cotton letters, letter from Bardwell, Oct. 21, 1852.

6. Boston Board of Trade, *Fifth Annual Report,* 1859, p. 166.

7. MS. PMC, Treasurer's letter book, 1850–53, letter of Aug. 23, 1851.

8. *Ibid.,* letter of Oct. 18, 1851.

9. *Ibid.,* letter of Dec. 31, 1851.

10. *Ibid.,* letter of Jan. 9, 1852.

11. R. Arthur Arnold, *The History of the Cotton Famine* (London, 1864), p. 165.

12. MS. PMC, Treasurer's semiannual statements, June 30, 1862, and Dec. 31, 1863; miscellaneous report in papers used at directors' and stockholders' meetings.

13. MS. PMC, Agent's listing of cotton invoices, 1865–74, invoices of 1867.

14. *Ibid.,* 1850–65, for Jan., 1854.

15. MS. PMC, Cotton letters, 1850–66, New Orleans prices-current, Sept. 1, 1852.

CHAPTER IV

For this chapter on the operation of the mills in Biddeford there is a wealth of information in the stockholders' and directors' records; in letters exchanged between treasurer and agent, between selling house and mill agent, and between treasurer or mill agent and others; in business records kept by the mill agent—cashbooks, bill books, contract book, payrolls, lists of cotton invoices, and semiannual statements; and also in the semiannual statements of the treasurer. Unfortunately, for the last six years of the period most of the correspondence and the semiannual statements of the treasurer are missing. Following are the sources which are not evident from the reading of the text.

1. *Union and Journal* (Biddeford, Maine), July 4, 1879; Gideon Tibbetts Ridlon, *Saco Valley Settlements and Families* (Portland, 1895), p. 705; *General Catalogue of Dartmouth College,* 1759–1925; MS. PMC, Bill book, 1862–66.

2. MS. SWPC, Votes at annual meeting, Aug. 11, 1849; Report of the directors, Oct. 31, 1855, p. 21; Montgomery, *Cotton Manufacture,* p. 166.

3. MS. SWPC, Votes at annual meeting, Aug. 11, 1849.

4. MS. SWPC, Rents, 1851–70, 1865–68.

5. MS. SWPC, Directors' records, Jan. 25 and Mar. 8, 1847, Dec. 9, 1853, Jan. 3 and Mar. 10, 1854; MS. LC [Laconia Company], Directors' records, Jan. 28, Mar. 9 and Apr. 3, 1854; MS. PMC, Directors' records, Mar. 11, 1854.

6. MS. SWPC, Report of committee, Dec. 5 and 13, 1862; MS. PMC, Direc-

tors' records, Dec. 10 and 20, 1862, Sept. 20, 26, and 29, Nov. 8, and Dec. 12, 1866.

7. MS. SWPC, Report to the directors, Apr. 25, 1850; *The Union* (Saco, Maine), Nov. 2, 1859.

8. MS. SWPC, Report to the directors, Apr. 25, 1850.

9. MS. PMC, Directors' records, Feb. 14, 1854; letter to treasurer from agent, May 13, 1862; semiannual statements of the treasurer, 1851–65.

10. MS. PMC, Directors' records, July 29, 1868.

11. MS. SWPC, Memorandum, Oct. 17, 1848; report, Apr. 25, 1850.

12. Montgomery, *op. cit.*, digest of pp. 25–111.

13. MS. SWPC, Memorandum, Oct. 17, 1848; blotter, 1849–51, p. 68; report, Apr. 25, 1850; MS. PMC, Directors' records, May 9, 1851.

14. MS. SWPC, Letters to treasurer from S. J. Wethrell, Oct. 22, 1850–Apr. 15, 1851; report of treasurer, July 24, 1851; MS. PMC, Vouchers, 1852, No. 30; J. D. Van Slyck, *Representatives of New England—Manufacturers* (Boston, 1879), pp. 186, 504–505.

15. MS. PMC, Letter book, 1850–53, letter, Apr. 14, 1851; sundry letters, May 2, Sept. 12, and Oct. 13, 1851; vouchers, 1851, 1852.

16. MS. PMC, Plans for machinery, 1851; agent's cash books, 1850–53; letter of treasurer to agent, Apr. 21, 1853.

17. MS. PMC, Letter of agent to treasurer, Apr. 4, 1853; directors' records, Feb. 14, 1854.

18. MS. PMC, Agent's copy letter book, letters, Feb. 22, 1854; letters of agent to treasurer, Mar. 6, Oct. 31, Dec. 20, 1854, Mar. 28, and Apr. 3, 1856; bill books, 1854–57; vouchers, 1855-56; cash book, 1850-56; orders, 1854–67.

19. MS. PMC, Sundry letters, Apr. 23, 1862.

20. MS. PMC, Semiannual statements of treasurer, 1851–65.

21. MS. PMC, Letter to agent from treasurer, Nov. 21, 1857.

22. Norman Ware, *The Industrial Worker, 1840–1860* (Boston, 1924), pp. 116–117; Susan M. Kingsbury, *Labor Laws and Their Enforcement* (N. Y., 1911), p. 55; MS. LC, Letters to treasurer from agent, Aug. 2 to Oct. 29, 1850; Robinson, *Loom and Spindle,* p. 63.

23. C. Ware, *New England Cotton Manufacture,* p. 227.

24. MS. PMC, Letter of agent to treasurer, Sept. 29, 1853.

25. MS. PMC, Payrolls, 1850–71; U. S. Census Office, 10th Census, 1880, *Census Reports* (Washington, 1886), vol. 20, p. 348; Boston Board of Trade, *Annual Report,* Merchants' Exchange, 1858, p. 53, and 1863, p. 97.

26. MS. PMC, Payrolls, 1850–70; U. S. Census Office, 9th Census, 1870, *Census Reports* (Washington, 1872), vol. 3, p. 478.

27. MS. PMC, Contract book, 1850–54; payrolls, 1852, 1869; U. S. Census Office, 7th Census, 1850, *Census Reports* (Washington, 1853), pp. 9, 61; U. S. Census Office, 9th Census, 1870, *Census Reports* (Washington, 1872), vol. 1, pp. 1, 162, 358, 414.

28. N. Ware, *Industrial Worker,* pp. 144–147; Montgomery, *op. cit.*, pp. 173–174; Hunt's *Merchants' Magazine,* Dec. 1853, p. 763; *Union and Journal,* Apr. 28, 1867; Kingsbury, *op. cit.*, pp. 109, 111.

29. MS. PMC, Unbound papers of boarding houses, 1857.

30. U. S. 10th Census, 1880, *Reports* (1886), vol. 20, p. 349.

31. MS. PMC, Copy letter book of agent, letter, Feb. 23, 1852; bill book, 1851–52; letter to treasurer from agent, Apr. 29, 1854; MS. LC, Sundry letters to treasurer, Feb. 27 and Mar. 1, 1860.

32. U. S. 10th Census, 1880, *Reports* (1886), vol. 20, p. 439.

33. Edgar W. Martin, *The Standard of Living in 1860* (Chicago, 1942), p. 395.

34. MS. PMC, Semiannual statements of the treasurer, 1851–65; sales journals, 1851–67; letters to agent from selling agent, Jan. 13, 1857; letters to agent from treasurer, Jan. 7 and Apr. 9, 1857.

35. MS. PMC, Computed from total expense of manufacturing and number of yards; see Appendices 25 and 35 of this volume.

36. MS. PMC, Semiannual statements of the treasurer, 1851–65.

37. *Ibid.;* Letter of treasurer to agent, May 22, 1857.

38. MS. PMC, Bleachery bills, 1851–66.

39. MS. PMC, Copy letter book of agent, 1850–55.

40. MS. PMC, Insurance policies, 1845–66; letter of agent to treasurer, Dec. 26, 1854.

41. *Union and Journal,* 1866–69; MS. PMC, Cash books, 1850–57.

42. MS. PMC, Bill book, 1850–51; semiannual statements of the treasurer, 1851–65.

CHAPTER V

Material on the selling of Pepperell's goods is limited. Since there is little information in the directors' records and the correspondence between various persons connected with Pepperell, I have had to rely largely on the sales journals which cover the period 1851 through 1867; on the treasurer's volumes of notes receivable and payable, 1850 to 1871; on reports of sales of product by Francis Skinner & Co., 1851 through 1864; and on notes receivable handed over to the treasurer by Francis Skinner & Co., 1851 through 1857. Again, where the source is not clear from the text, I have given it below.

1. Acton, Massachusetts, *Vital Records to 1850,* pp. 102, 222, 297; Rev. James Fletcher, *Acton in History* (1890), Biographies, p. 1; Forbes, *Rich Men of Mass.,* p. 139; *Boston Tax List,* 1821; *Boston Directory,* 1822–32; *Daily Advertiser* (Boston, Mass.), advertisement, Jan. 1, 1831; *American Advertising Directory for the Year,* 1831, 1832; Middlesex County Court, Cambridge, Mass., Probate Records, Estate of Abraham Skinner.

2. Mason A. Green, *Springfield Memoirs* (1876), p. 615; Middlesex County Court, Probate Records, Will of Francis Skinner; *Sketches and Business Directory of Boston,* 1860–61, p. 159; *Boston Directory,* 1833–70.

3. *Boston Directory,* 1818–70; Boston *Evening Transcript,* Nov. 24, 1905, p. 1; *Quinquennial Catalogue of Harvard University, 1636–1920,* p. 247; Middlesex Court, Will of Francis Skinner; MS. PMC, Directors' records, June 15, 1877; letter to agent from selling agent, July 29, 1857; Forbes, *op. cit.,* pp. 35, 43.

4. *N. Y. Directory,* 1845–70.

5. MS. PMC, Letters to agent from selling agent, 1857–66; William Hurd Hillyer, *James Talcott, Merchant, and His Times* (N. Y., 1937). This book gives an account of another commission house in New York; on methods of selling in Pepperell's first period, the chapter "Franklin Street Days," pp. 100–123, is of interest.

6. Boston Board of Trade, *Report of the Committee,* 1858, p. 5.

7. *Ibid.,* p. 4.

8. *American Advertising Directory,* 1832, pp. 30–31; *Sketches and Business Directory of Boston,* 1860–61, p. 309; *Daily Evening Traveller* (Boston, Mass.), Sept. 21, 1870.

9. Middlesex Court, Will of Francis Skinner; Suffolk County Court, Boston, Mass., Probate Records, Henry K. Horton.

10. Will of Francis Skinner; MS. PMC, Reports of sales, 1865.

11. [William Sturgis] *Report of Mr. Sturgis's Committee to Twenty-Eight Manufacturing Companies* (Boston, 1852).

12. MS. LC, Letter to treasurer from A. & A. Lawrence & Co., Oct. 1, 1851; directors' records, Mar. 8, 1853; sales journals, 1846–61.

13. *Report of Mr. Sturgis's Committee,* p. 4.

14. MS. PMC, Certificates of stock, 1852–70.

15. MS. PMC, Notes payable and receivable, 1850–71.

16. MS. Dane, Dana & Co., vol. 6, 1852.

17. MS. PMC, Letters to the treasurer from agent, 1855–66; notes payable and receivable, 1850–71.

18. MS. PMC, Letter to agent from selling agent, Dec. 20, 1857.

19. MS. PMC, Letters to agent from selling agent, 1855–66.

20. The analysis of customers in this and following paragraphs is based on a study of customers given in Pepperell's sales journals, 1851–67, accompanied by information secured from many business directories.

21. The analysis of customers in this and other paragraphs is based on a study of customers given in Laconia's sales journals, 1846–61, accompanied by information secured from many business directories.

22. MS. Dane, Dana & Co., vols. 4–5.

23. *Ibid.,* vol. 4, letter, Oct. 24, 1853.

24. Massachusetts Historical Society (Boston) *Proceedings,* vol. 46, p. 216.

25. Middlesex Court, Will of Francis Skinner.

26. Suffolk Court, Probate Records, Henry K. Horton.

27. Boston *Daily Evening Transcript,* Sept. 12 and 22, 1870; Baltimore *American & Commercial Advertiser,* Dec. 31, 1869, and Jan. 3, 1870; *Commercial & Financial Chronicle,* Oct. 16, 1869, pp. 505–506, Oct. 23, 1869, pp. 538–539.

28. MS. PMC, Directors' records, Jan. 27, Feb. 11, and Aug. 16, 1870; *Boston Directory,* 1870.

29. Boston *Daily Evening Transcript,* Sept. 12 and 21, 1870; Boston *Daily Advertiser,* Sept. 14, 1870; Boston *Daily Evening Traveller,* Sept. 21–22, and 24, 1870; MS. PMC, Directors' records, Oct. 31, 1870, Nov. 25, 1878.

30. MS. PMC, Letters to agent from treasurer, Sept. 18 and Nov. 21, 1857.

31. MS. PMC, Letter to treasurer from selling agent, Jan. 26, 1862; *Horace B. Claflin, 1811–1885* (N. Y.), pp. 9–10.

CHAPTER VI

Material for Chapter VI was fairly adequate for 1850 through 1865 and quite inadequate for 1865–70. I have drawn largely from the treasurer's volumes of notes payable and receivable, mentioned in Chapter V; from the treasurer's semiannual statements for 1851 to 1865; from receipts for dividends, 1860 through 1871; from minutes of meetings of the directors and stockholders, 1850 through 1870. As in the preceding chapters, where the source for a statement is not evident I am giving it below.

1. William R. Scott, *The Constitution and Finance of English, Scottish and Irish Joint-Stock Companies to 1720* (Cambridge, England, 1910–12).

2. MS. PMC, Cash voucher, Oct. 26, 1850, Apr. 14 and 25 and Nov. 1, 1855, and Aug. 1, 1865; cotton letter from J. B. Toulmin & Son, Mobile, Dec. 27, 1853; directors' records, 1850–70.

3. MS. PMC, Cash vouchers, 1851–65.

4. MS. PMC, Cash vouchers, 1852–65; Directors' records, Sept. 20, 1866; *Boston Directory,* 1867–70; *Boston Stock Exchange,* 1893 [pages not numbered].

5. MS. PMC, Cash voucher, July 22, 1856, which gives compensation for 1853–55.

6. MS. PMC, Receipts for assessments, 1850–57.

7. The authorization to increase the capital stock to $1,200,000 was not mentioned in the stockholders' records until May 3, 1871.

8. Material for this section of the chapter drawn largely from the treasurer's five volumes of notes payable and receivable, 1850–71.

9. MS. PMC, Semiannual statements of the treasurer, 1851–65; letter to agent from treasurer, Sept. 25, 1857.

10. Material for this section of the chapter drawn from the treasurer's five volumes of notes payable and receivable, 1850–71; sales notes receivable handed over to treasurer from selling agent, 1851–57.

11. Forbes, *Rich Men of Mass.,* p. 29.

12. J. G. Martin, *Twenty-One Years;* Joseph G. Martin, *Boston Stock Market, Eighty-Eight Years, 1798–1886* (Boston, 1886); Joseph G. Martin, *A Century of Finance, 1798–1898* (Boston, 1898).

13. MS. PMC, Letter to the treasurer from the selling agent, Sept. 23, 1857.

14. Massachusetts, *Supplement to the General Statutes,* vol. 1, 1860–72, 2d ed., William A. Richardson & George R. Sanger, Published by the Commonwealth, 1873, pp. 436, 539.

15. MS. PMC, Cotton cash vouchers, 1851–66; notes payable and receivable, 1850–71.

16. *Ibid.*

17. *Ibid.*

CHAPTER VII

For the middle period of this history the records deposited by the Pepperell Manufacturing Company in Baker Library are most abundant. Of great value is the series of letters exchanged daily by Pepperell's treasurer and mill agent. Of less value are the general letters sent by the treasurer's and mill agent's offices to various companies. In addition there are sets of records similar to those for the earlier period, which give details of operations. In this period the treasurer began the recording of the facts which he reported semiannually to the directors or trustees. (These are of interest; they have been kept by the company in its offices.) For descriptions of property in Biddeford, plans drawn up by the Boston Manufacturers' Mutual Fire Insurance Co. are of great assistance. I have also been able to draw to some extent from the manuscript collections of the companies with which Pepperell merged. Besides, I have talked with a number of people who were connected with Pepperell in this period, including two treasurers, Philip Y. DeNormandie and William Amory. Altogether, material for this period has been the most satisfactory with which to work. Letters give intimate pictures of what was happening and interpret the records given in figures. As in earlier chapters, when the source of the evidence is not clear, it is given below.

1. *Boston Directory,* 1830–70.
2. *Ibid.,* 1855–73; Boston *Evening Transcript,* Dec. 22, 1904.
3. MS. PMC, Treasurer's letter book, 1883–84.
4. Material about George Dexter gathered from the following sources: Mary Caroline Crawford, *Massachusetts Famous Families* (Boston, 1930), vol. 2, pp. 143–162; Orrando Perry Dexter, *Dexter Genealogy, 1642–1904* (N. Y., 1904), pp. 115–116; Harvard College, Class of 1855, *Second Annual Report, 1880* (Cambridge, 1880); Boston *Evening Transcript,* July 5 and 6, 1910; *Boston Directory,* 1863–77; *New York Directory,* 1862–78.
5. Harvard College, Class of 1891, *Twenty-Fifth Anniversary Report* (Cambridge, 1916), pp. 85–86.
6. *Ibid.,* p. 5; Browne, *Amoskeag Manufacturing Company,* p. 232.
7. Harvard College, Class of 1905, *Second Annual Report* (Cambridge, 1911), pp. 40–41; *Third Annual Report* (Cambridge, 1915), p. 41; *Fourth Annual Report* (Cambridge, 1920), pp. 37–39; *Sixth Annual Report* (Cambridge, 1930), p. 73.
8. MS. PMC, Treasurer's letter books, 1880–1921; Arkwright Club, *By-Laws & List of Officers and Members, 1920; Journal of Commerce & Commercial Bulletin,* Oct. 18, 1939.
9. Taussig, *Tariff History,* pp. 192–193, 235–236, 432–436, 465–467.
10. James H. Lamb, *Textile Industries of the United States,* edited by E. Everton Foster (Boston, 1916), vol. 2, p. 112.
11. *Ibid.,* vol. 1, p. 405; clipping from Biddeford *Daily Journal,* Jan., 1910.
12. *Ibid.*
13. MS. PMC, M. W. Colquhoun's Scrap book, clipping, Oct. 30, 1915.

14. MS. PMC, Treasurer's report to the directors, Jan. 20, 1886, and Jan. 18, 1900.

15. New England Cotton Manufacturers' Association, *Transactions,* no. 9, pp. 8–9, no. 10, pp. 47–52.

16. *Ibid.,* no. 50, pp. 11–46, article by William F. Draper, "The History of Spindles."

17. MS. PMC, Contract book for machinery, 1888–1904, pp. 34, 60, 61, 63.

18. MS. PMC, Mill agent's general letter book, 1907–09, p. 714.

19. *Davison's Textile Blue Book,* 1899–1900; U. S. Census Office, 12th Census, 1900, *Census Reports* (Washington, 1902), vol. 9, pp. 54–55.

20. U. S. Census Office, 15th Census, 1930, *Census Reports, Manufactures* (Washington, 1933), vol. 2, p. 247.

21. MS. PMC, Trustees' records, Oct. 18, 1918; Annual Report, 1931, pp. 4–5.

22. MS. SWPC, Treasurer's reports, 1883–1915; Annual Report, July 20, 1848; MS. PMC, Trustees' records, 1918–21.

23. Georgia Drew Merrill, *History of Androscoggin County, Maine* (Boston, 1891), p. 391.

CHAPTER VIII

Material for Chapter VIII has been drawn largely from series of letter books, payrolls, directors' and trustees' records, the treasurer's reports to the directors or trustees, and the treasurer's semiannual balances and income statements. While most of these records are now deposited at Baker Library, the valuable series of payrolls from 1886 to the present is still in the office in Biddeford. I have supplemented written information by talks with several persons in Biddeford. Where the source of facts and opinions is not evident, I have given it below.

1. Material about men in the mills found in correspondence about the time of change in position.

2. MS. PMC, Agent's letter book, 1880–82, p. 160.

3. National Association of Cotton Manufacturers, *Transactions,* no. 88–92.

4. James G. Garland, *Garland Genealogy* (Biddeford, 1897), pp. 175–176; *Biddeford Weekly Journal,* Jan. 26, 1906.

5. Material about overseers compiled from payroll books and letter books.

6. MS. PMC, Mill agent's general letter book, 1891–92, p. 401.

7. Maine, Bureau of Industrial and Labor Statistics, *Seventh Annual Report* (Augusta, 1893), p. 189.

8. Maine, Department of Labor and Industry, *Excerpt from Third Biennial Report, 1915-16* (Waterville, 1917), pp. 71, 189.

9. *Ibid.,* p. 22.

10. Maine, Secretary of State, *Statistics of Industries and Finances of Maine, Third Report* (Augusta, 1884), p. 145; MS. PMC, Agent's letter book, 1909–10, Dec. 17 and 23, 1909; MS. PMC, Assistant treasurer's letter book, 1915–20, p. 262.

11. MS. PMC, Clarence Gove's little notebook.

12. Maine, Secretary of State, *Statistics of Industries and Finances of Maine, Second Report* (Augusta, 1883), p. 121.

13. Herbert J. Lahne, *The Cotton Mill Worker* (N. Y., 1944), pp. 175–188.

14. MS. PMC, Wage rates, 1893–1907, gives a schedule of machinery, duties, number of operatives, and rates of pay.

15. MS. PMC, Treasurer's letter book, 1880–81, pp. 77–78.

16. *Ibid.*, 1897–1901, p. 119.

CHAPTER IX

Material for Chapter IX was the most limited of all. In the manuscript collection in Baker Library there were a sales journal for 1870–71, eight sales ledgers for 1897–1913, seven cash journals for 1906–19, and eleven trial balance volumes for 1906–17. In addition I have secured price lists and an auction catalogue from Robert Vanderbilt, who was connected with Bliss, Fabyan & Co. for many years. I have talked with two other members of the selling house, S. Robert Glassford and Philip Y. DeNormandie, both of whom have died recently. Mr. Glassford prepared for me a memorandum on selling, which has proved extremely valuable in ascertaining the former methods of selling by a commission house. From these sources, as well as from letter books and a few publications, I have pieced together the account given in this chapter. Where the source is not evident in the text, I have given it below.

1. *New England Historic & Genealogical Register,* vol. 30, pp. 117–118.

2. Lamb, *Textile Industries,* vol. 2, pp. 79–81.

3. *Dockham's United States Cotton, Woollen, Silk & Linen Manufacturers' Report & Directory,* 1870–71; Commercial Agency Reports, *Mill Reports,* N. Y., Mar., 1884; *Davison's Textile Blue Book,* 1924.

4. Boston, Board of Trade, *Nineteenth Annual Report,* Jan. 8, 1873; Lamb, *op. cit.,* vol. 1, p. 348; Bankers Service Company, *Directory of Directors in the City of Boston and Vicinity,* 1910–40.

5. *Textile World,* Feb., 1940, p. 160; Business Directories of New York, Philadelphia, Boston, and Baltimore, 1869; MS. PMC, Photostat of price list of J. S. & E. Wright & Co., 1873.

6. *Chicago Directory,* 1903; *Commerce & Finance,* vol. 48 (Nov. 20, 1927), p. 2492.

7. *N. E. Hist. & Gen. Register,* vol. 34, pp. 417–418.

8. MS. PMC, Reports and questionnaires, 1922–23.

9. New York *Times,* June 26, 1914.

10. MS. PMC, Treasurer's letter book, 1881–83, p. 426.

11. Memorandum written by S. Robert Glassford after conference, Oct. 26, 1944, about the customary methods of selling, with names of important purchasers; this memo is used as basis of this and much of five following paragraphs.

12. MS. PMC, Treasurer's letter book, 1917–19, p. 257.

13. *Ibid.*, 1897–1901, p. 651.

14. MS. PMC, Photostat of price list of auction catalogue, May 23, 1876; treasurer's letter book, 1881–83, pp. 500–501, 1883–84, p. 211, 1893–97, pp. 198, 206, 222; treasurer's report to directors, Jan. 22, 1895.

CHAPTER X

For material in Chapter X, I have drawn upon the statements of balances and income; records of meetings of stockholders, directors, and trustees; semi-annual reports of the treasurer to the board of directors and trustees; and the treasurer's letters to the mill agent and others. For the discussion of cotton purchasing I have used, in addition, the mill agent's listing of cotton invoices, cotton-purchasing sheets, and cotton orders. Unfortunately they do not give full information about cotton purchases for the entire period. Sources, not evident in the text, are given below.

1. MS. PMC, Directors' records, July 24, 1882, and July 23, 1912.

2. *Ibid.*, Feb. 5, 1880 (increase to $6,000 a year voted, so assumed earlier salary $5,000); MS. LC, Directors' records, Feb. 5, 1880 (increase to $4,000 a year voted, so assumed earlier salary $3,000).

3. Hammond, *Cotton Industry*, pt. 1, p. 327.

4. Bradstreet's *Journal*, vol. 13, pp. 226–227; Boston *Journal of Commerce*, vol. 28, no. 1 (Apr. 17, 1886), p. 4; Hammond, *op. cit.*, p. 294.

5. Bradstreet's *Journal*, vol. 13, p. 227.

6. MS. PMC, Treasurer's letter book, 1893–97, p. 508.

7. *Loc. cit.*

8. MS. PMC, Treasurer's letter book, 1920–21, p. 191.

9. Hammond, *op. cit.*, pt. 1, p. 302.

10. *New York Cotton Exchange, 1871–1923,* pp. 31–42.

11. Bradstreet's *Journal*, vol. 13, pp. 226–227.

12. Arkwright Club, *By-Laws & List of Officers,* Boston, 1920, p. 18.

13. MS. PMC, Treasurer's letter book, 1914–17, pp. 249–250.

14. *Ibid.*, p. 226.

15. *Ibid.*, 1893–97, p. 363.

16. MS. PMC, Statement of condition, 1903–14, with copies of State laws which applied to Pepperell.

17. MS. PMC, Treasurer's letter book, 1920–21, p. 689.

18. J. G. Martin, *A Century of Finance*, pp. 128–133, 136; *Moody's Industrials,* 1924.

CHAPTER XI

For the chapters in this third period, material has been secured from many sources. Many officials and employees in the offices and plants of the Pepperell Manufacturing Company have generously contributed invaluable information. Generally I have not referred to them. In the company's possession is most of the manuscript material, which is not available to the public without the company's authorization. The material used for Chapter XI includes records of meetings of stockholders, directors, and trustees; personnel records; minutes of department meetings, 1936 to 1945; organization charts; and sales records. The company has published information about itself, including annual reports for the whole period: the *Pepperell News Sheet,* a monthly paper, started in 1926, for the salesforce and customers; and the *Pepperell Sheet,* started in 1937, for the employees in the northern plants. In addition, news about Pepperell has appeared in many trade papers.

1. U. S. Bureau of the Census, *Statistical Abstract of the United States, 1944–1945* (Washington, 1945), pp. 848–849.

2. *25 years: Assn. of Cotton Textile Merchants of N. Y.,* pp. 18–19.

3. Ipswich Mills, Annual Report, 1926 and 1927.

4. J. H. Beers & Co., *Representative Men and Old Families of Southeastern Massachusetts* (Chicago, 1912), pp. 686, 1264–1266; Harvard College, Class of 1910, *Third Report, 1915* (Cambridge, 1917), p. 184.

5. *Ibid., Twenty-Fifth Anniversary Report, 1935* (Cambridge, 1935), pp. 440–441; *Textile World,* vol. 61 (Feb. 11, 1922), p. 1038; Sanford & Kelley, *Fall River, Mass., Statistics Relating to Its Cotton Manufacturing Corporations for the years 1917, 1919–1922, 1924* (New Bedford, Mass., 1918, 1920–23, 1925); Thomas Russell Smith, *The Cotton Textile Industry of Fall River, Massachusetts* (N. Y., 1944), pp. 100–105.

6. Harvard, 1910, *Twenty-Fifth Anniversary Report,* pp. 440–441; *Textile World,* vol. 61 (Feb. 11, 1922), p. 1038; Ipswich Mills, Annual Report, 1926 and 1927; reports and accounts, 1928.

7. MS. PMC, Directors' records, May 3, 1938; *Pepperell Sheet,* vol. 2, no. 5 (Nov.–Dec., 1938).

8. Harvard, 1917, *Triennial Report, 1920* (Cambridge, 1921), p. 263; *Decennial Report, 1927* (Cambridge, 1927), p. 43; *Vicennial Report, 1937* (Cambridge, 1937), p. 25.

9. MS. PMC, Treasurer's report [in Feb., 1925].

10. *Ibid.*

11. Ipswich Mills, Annual Report, 1926 and 1927; *Commerce & Finance,* vol. 16 (Nov. 9, 1927), p. 2343.

12. MS. PMC, Directors' records, Dec. 2, 1936, Feb. 4, May 3, and Aug. 4, 1938; conference with Mr. Crocker, Sept., 1946.

13. *Textile World,* vol. 70 (Dec. 4, 1926), pp. 3335–3336.

14. *Printers' Ink,* Jan. 13, 1921, p. 68; Apr. 7, 1921, p. 18; Sept. 15, 1921, pp. 165–166; and Apr. 23, 1925, pp. 4, 6, 170, 173–174.

15. *Textile World,* vol. 70 (Dec. 4, 1926), pp. 3335–3336; *Printers' Ink,* Sept. 27, 1928, pp. 57–58; Ralph M. Hower, *The History of an Advertising Agency: N. W. Ayer & Son at Work* (Cambridge, 1939), pp. 339–343, 401; MS. PMC, Department minutes, May 6, 1940.

16. *Textile World,* vol. 70 (Dec. 4, 1926), pp. 3335–3336; *Sales Management,* Jan. 5, 1929, pp. 18–19.

17. *Commerce & Finance,* vol. 17 (May 9, 1928), p. 1055.

18. Harvard University, Bureau of Business Research, *Distribution of Textiles* (Cambridge, 1926); Melvin T. Copeland and Edmund P. Learned, *Merchandising of Cotton Textiles* (Boston, 1933).

19. MS. PMC, Changes in machinery, draft of letter, Sept. 30, 1943.

20. Cambridge, 1939. A new edition is now going through the press.

21. *Textile World,* vol. 70 (Dec. 4, 1926), pp. 3335–3336.

22. *Ibid.,* vol. 67 (Feb. 6, 1925), pp. 834–835; vol. 70 (Dec. 4, 1926), pp. 3335–3336; *Commerce & Finance,* vol. 17 (May 9, 1928), p. 1055; MS. PMC, Controller's report, 1929–45; PMC, Annual Report, 1926.

23. *25 Years: Assn. of Cotton Textile Merchants of N. Y.,* pp. 5–12, 60–61.

24. *Textile World,* vol. 78 (Dec. 20, 1930), p. 2918; *Commerce & Finance,* vol. 17 (Jan. 4, 1928), p. 44; PMC, Annual Report, 1926–28.

25. *Commerce & Finance,* vol. 16 (Mar. 9, 1927), p. 2343; PMC, Annual Report, 1931; MS. PMC, Dept. minutes, Jan. 19, 1942.

26. MS. PMC, Bulletin 555, July 17, 1941; sales by salesmen, 1938.

27. MS. PMC, Bulletin 555.

28. *Ibid.,* Dept. minutes, Apr. 13, 1936.

29. *Ibid.,* Bulletin 555.

30. Lowell Bleachery, Inc., Annual Report, 1934, and letter to stockholders, Oct. 1, 1924. E. S. Emerson & Co., Report on Lowell Bleachery, 1919. National Fabric and Finishing Co., Inc., Annual Report, 1927–30; interim report, Aug. 31, 1931; letters to stockholders, 1925–26; balance sheet, Sept. 30, 1926.

31. *Pepperell Sheet,* vol. 11, no. 2 (Feb., 1947).

32. MS. PMC, Controller's report, 1929–45.

33. MS. PMC, Sales analysis controls, 1928–30; sales analysis reports, 1932–45. These two sets of reports provide material for much of this section.

34. U. S. Bureau of the Census, *Census of Business, Wholesale Trade, 1939* (Washington, 1942), pp. 92–145.

35. *Idem, Census of Manufacturers, 1939* (Washington, 1942), vol. 2, pt. 1, pp. 396–508.

36. Prices from MS. PMC, Sales journals, 1925–27; price lists, 1926–46.

37. *Statistical Abstract, 1931,* p. 355, *1933,* p. 281, *1942,* p. 373, *1944–45,* p. 418; U. S. Bureau of Foreign and Domestic Commerce, *Survey of Current Business,* Jan., 1946, p. S–4, and Nov., 1946, p. S–4.

38. MS. PMC, Dept. minutes, Apr. 27, 1938.

39. *Ibid.,* Dec. 15, 1936, Apr. 27, 1938, and Nov. 14, 1944.

40. MS. PMC, Controller's report, 1929–45.

41. MS. PMC, Sales analysis controls, 1928–30, with notes for 1930–32; sales analysis reports, 1932–45.

42. *Statistical Abstract, 1931,* p. 335; *1933,* p. 281; *1942,* p. 273; *1944–45,* p. 418. *Survey of Current Business,* Jan., 1946, p. S–4, and Nov., 1946, p. S–4.

CHAPTER XII

For material on the operation of the mills in the North I have drawn heavily upon conversations with various people and from impressions gained from visits to the mills. As in the chapter immediately preceding, I have used the controller's reports, departmental minutes, annual reports, the *Pepperell News Sheet,* and the *Pepperell Sheet.* In addition, I have gained much valuable information from a compilation of changes in machinery and production in the mills, 1925–43, which was lent me by Mr. Parsons. For details the notebook of the former paymaster in Biddeford, Mr. Clarence Gove, has been of assistance. Where the source of material is not evident from the text, I have given it below.

1. *Statistical Abstract, 1926,* pp. 797–798 and *1944–45,* pp. 848–849; *Assn. of Cotton Textile Merchants of N. Y.: Ten Years;* spindles in the North in 1945 estimated about the same as in 1944.

2. MS. PMC, Treasurer's reports, Jan. 1 and July 1, 1916; controller's reports, 1929–45.

3. U. S. Dept. of Labor, Bureau of Labor Statistics, *Effects of Mechanical Changes in the Cotton Textile Industry, 1910–36,* pp. 4–5, 12, 17.

4. Biddeford *Journal,* Nov. 27, 1936; Portland *News,* Dec. 16, 1936.

5. *Textile World,* vol. 67 (May 23, 1925), p. 3411; vol. 67 (June 6, 1925), p. 3704.

6. *Pepperell Sheet,* vol. 7, no. 12 (Dec., 1943).

7. U. S. Census Office, *Census Reports, 15th, 1930,* vol. 3, pt. 1, pp. 1029, 1031; *16th, 1940,* vol. 2, pt. 3, pp. 477, 496.

8. *Commerce & Finance,* vol. 15 (Dec. 9, 1925), pp. 2388, 2409; and the following in vol. 16 (1926): Jan. 6, p. 41, Jan. 13, p. 61, Feb. 3, p. 305, Feb. 10, p. 353, Feb. 17, p. 397.

9. Lahne, *Cotton Mill Worker,* p. 211.

10. *Ibid.,* p. 231.

11. U. S. National Labor Relations Board, *Annual Report,* June 30, 1936.

12. Letter from office manager, James F. Smith, Dec. 31, 1946; Clarence Gove's notebook.

13. *Ibid.*

14. Lahne, *op. cit.,* p. 141.

15. Clarence Gove's notebook; letter from James F. Smith, Dec. 31, 1946.

16. *Ibid.*

17. MS. PMC, Controller's report, 1929–45.

18. PMC, *Pictorial Trip through the Pepperell Clinics,* included with Annual Report of 1940.

19. *Pepperell Sheet,* vol. 2, no. 5 (Nov.–Dec., 1938); vol. 5, no. 5 (May, 1941).

20. Letter from James F. Smith, Dec. 31, 1946. *Pepperell Sheet,* vol. 2, nos. 4 and 5 (Sept.–Oct. and Nov.–Dec., 1938); vol. 6, nos. 1 and 9 (Jan. and Sept., 1942); vol. 8, no. 12 (Dec., 1944).

21. MS. MCM (Massachusetts Cotton Mills), Directors' records, 1839–89. These records provide the source for much of the material in this section.

22. MS. MCM, President Loring's comments, Nov. 30, 1926.

23. MS. MCM, Directors' records, 1890–1919; dividends, 1887–1900; MM in

Ga. (Massachusetts Mills in Georgia), Dividends, no. 1; Boston Mfrs.' Mutual Fire Insurance Company's *Survey of Lowell Industrial Development Company*, Aug. 16, 1933; *Davison's Textile Blue Book*, 1908–09.

24. MCM, Corporation records, Circular no. 30, 1926, Dec. 14, 1926.

25. MS. PMC, Trustees' records, Apr. 14, 1927; directors' records, May 14, 1941; letters in trustees' records, 1927 and 1936.

26. *Commerce & Finance*, vol. 16 (Feb. 23, 1927), p. 437; vol. 16 (Nov. 9, 1927), p. 2341.

27. U. S. Dept. of Labor, Women's Bureau, *Bulletin*, no. 66 (1929), pp. 38–42.

28. *Davison's Blue Book*, 1899–1936; *Textile World*, Mar., 1899, p. 103, and Apr., 1899, p. 103.

29. Boston Mfrs.' Mutual Fire Ins. Co.'s *Survey*, Aug. 16, 1933.

30. Smith, *Cotton Textile Industry of Fall River;* F. M. Peck and H. H. Earl, *Fall River and Its Industries* (N. Y., 1877), pp. 123–125; J. G. Martin, *A Century of Finance; Moody's Industrials;* Sanford & Kelley, *Fall River, Mass., Statistics, 1924–29.*

31. *Ibid.; Commercial & Financial Chronicle*, vol. 128 (Apr. 27, 1929), p. 2818; Sanford & Kelley, *Fall River, Mass., Statistics 1924–29.*

32. Smith, *Cotton Textile Industry of Fall River.*

33. MS. PMC, Letter to Thomas B. Bassett, Aug. 30, 1929; *Commercial & Financial Chronicle*, vol. 129 (Oct. 5, 1929), p. 2236.

34. MS. PMC, Controller's report, 1929–45; Boston Mfrs.' Mutual Fire Ins. Co.'s *Survey*, June 13, 1934; Sanford & Kelley, *Fall River, Mass., Statistics, 1923–29;* Peck and Earl, *op. cit.*, p. 123.

35. MS. PMC, Controller's report, 1929–45; PMC, *Presentations of Awards*, 1943.

36. U. S. Census Office, *Reports, 15th, 1930*, vol. 3, pt. 1, pp. 1098–1099, 1100–1101.

37. U. S. Labor Relations Board, *Decisions and Orders*, vol. 39, pp. 910–919; vol. 41, pp. 18–19; vol. 42, pp. 518–524; vol. 43, pp. 692–694; vol. 58, pp. 1307–1315; vol. 61, pp. 858–866.

38. *Ibid.*

39. PMC, *Presentations of Awards.*

40. PMC, Annual Report, 1925–34; MS. PMC, Directors' records, Dec. 27, 1933; *Commerce & Finance*, vol. 14 (Aug. 5, 1925), p. 1527.

41. MS. PMC, Changes in Machinery, 1925–43.

42. *Davison's Blue Book*, 1917, 1918–19; MS. LB & DW (Lewiston Bleachery & Dye Works), Directors' records, Dec. 21, 1921–May 28, 1925; statements, May 31, 1922–May 30, 1925; expenditures and receipts, Nov. 30, 1921–May 30, 1925; Boston Mfrs.' Mutual Fire Ins. Co.'s *Survey*, July 7, 1931.

43. MS. LB & DW, Trial balances, 1914–25.

44. PMC, Lewiston Division, *Program*, Dec. 17, 1943; MS. PMC, Controller's report, 1930–45.

45. U. S. Census Office, *Reports, 15th, 1930*, vol. 3, pt. 1, pp. 1029, 1031.

46. U. S. Labor Relations Board, Boston, Mass., information from file.

CHAPTER XIII

For Pepperell's operation of the two sets of mills in the South I have drawn upon the same sources as those for Chapter XII. For the history of the mills in Lindale before Pepperell's acquisition I have gathered material from manuscript records in Baker Library and in Pepperell's offices and from various publications concerning mills in the South. Since I have used a variety of sources for the years 1896 to 1926, I have generally acknowledged them below.

1. *Statistical Abstract, 1942,* p. 941; *Davison's Blue Book,* 1888, 1898–99.
2. *Ibid.,* 1924.
3. MS. MM in Ga., Memorandum on Sites by A. W. Hunking, Feb. 4, 1895.
4. *Ibid.;* MS. MM in Ga., Copy of letter, Feb. 21, 1895, with notation of acceptance; copy of agreement, Mar. 15, 1902; cashbook, no. 1, May 28, 1895.
5. *Ibid.;* MS. PMC, Lindale Division, Brief history of Lindale by C. H. Edmondson, Oct. 4, 1944.
6. MS. MM in Ga., Cashbook, no. 1 and no. 2; MS. MCM, Journal D; MS. PMC, History of Lindale.
7. MS. MM in Ga., Cashbook, no. 1 and no. 2.
8. *Ibid.,* Journal A; MS. PMC, History of Lindale.
9. MS. MCM, Letter, Dec. 10, 1926; South. Div., Journal, 1897–1904; ledger, 1902–06.
10. MS. MM in Ga., Offer by V. H. Hedden & Sons, June 14, 1895; MS. MM in Ga., Cashbook, no. 1 and no. 2; MS. PMC, History of Lindale; estimate of number of houses in 1926 from airplane view of about 1935 and the sources listed.
11. MS. MM in Ga., Letters, May 23, Sept. 10, Sept. 24, Nov. 25, 1902; lease for 3 years between Daniel W. Barnett and Lindale Co., May 27, 1895; copy of letter, Feb. 21, 1895; copy of decree of Floyd Superior Court, Jan. 14, 1903; *Lindale Newspaper,* Nov., 1939, in which is news from *Georgia Free Lance* of 1905; MS. MCM, Southern Mill, Cashbook.
12. MS. MM in Ga., Letter, Sept. 10, 1902, to Messrs. Brittain Bros.; substance of one paragraph in copy of letter, Feb. 21, 1895.
13. *Ibid.,* Land granted the Baptist Church, Aug. 2, 1904; deed, June 25, 1904; Journal A; M. L. Jackson, *Lindale* (July, 1932).
14. MS. MM in Ga., Letter from School Commissioner, Mar. 14, 1898; payments for teachers, 1896–97, 1899.
15. *Lindale Newspaper,* Nov., 1939; MS. PMC, Lindale Division, Sketch of Lindale, 1938; Battey, *A History of Rome and Floyd County, 1922,* vol. 1, p. 355.
16. *Lindale Newspaper,* Nov., 1939; MS. PMC, Sketch of Lindale, 1938.
17. *Ibid.,* Supervisory Force in Lindale, 1895–1945.
18. MS. MM in Ga., Cashbook; Supervisory Force in Lindale, 1895–1945; Nat. Assn. of Cotton Mfrs., *Transactions,* vols. 67, 69, 71.
19. Columbia University, *Alumni Register,* 1754–1931 (N. Y., 1932), p. 593; Robert Isham Randolph, *The Randolphs of Virginia* (Chicago?, 1936?), 2114a–

2114a14, note 2114a; *Southern Textile Bulletin,* Speech by Meikleham, Mar. 24, 1932, pp. 16, 17, 23, 24; Jackson, *op. cit.*

20. MS. MCM, Cashbooks, H–J; MS. PMC, Supervisory Force in Lindale, 1895–1945.

21. *Ibid.*

22. Jackson, *op. cit.*

23. *Southern Textile Bulletin,* Recollections of employee in neighboring mill, Mar. 5, 1931, p. 34a; Jackson, *op. cit.*

24. Holland, Thompson, *From the Cotton Field to the Cotton Mill* (N. Y., 1906), pp. 96–117, 162–181; T. M. Young, *The American Cotton Industry* (N. Y., 1903), pp. 54–55, 63, 75–76, 91.

25. MS. PMC, Sketch of Lindale, 1938.

26. *Ibid.;* PMC, *Lindale Goes to War* (1943), p. 37.

27. MS. PMC, *Sketch of Lindale,* 1938; PMC, *Lindale Goes to War,* p. 37.

28. Jackson, *op. cit.;* MS. PMC, *Sketch of Lindale,* 1938.

29. Jackson, *op. cit.;* data from C. H. Edmondson, Mar., 1945.

30. Georgia, *Acts and Resolutions of the General Assembly,* 1899, no. 599; MS. MM in Ga., Time book, 1903–04; MS. MM in Ga., Wage rates, 1898–1910; Georgia, *Acts,* 1911, no. 279; *Commercial & Financial Chronicle,* vol. 111 (Dec. 11, 1920), p. 2337; vol. 111 (Dec. 25, 1920), p. 2533; *Textile World,* vol. 59 (Feb. 21, 1921), p. 1279.

31. *Lindale Newspaper,* Nov., 1939.

32. MS. MM in Ga., Wage rates, 1898–1923.

33. *Ibid.*

34. *Ibid.*

35. U. S. Bureau of Labor Statistics, *Monthly Labor Review,* vol. 40 (May, 1935), pp. 1174–1175.

36. MS. PMC, Sketch of Lindale, 1938; *Southern Textile Bulletin,* vol. 40 (Mar. 5, 1931), p. 15.

37. MS. MCM, Southern Division, Ledger, 1902–13.

38. MS. MCM, Directors' records, pp. 295–296; *Boston Directory,* 1886, 1896, 1906, 1916, 1917.

39. MS. MM in Ga., Trustees' records, 1899–1919; MS. MCM, Indenture, Feb. 24, 1919; MS. MCM, Directors' records, 1899–1916, pp. 346–347, 357–359, 367a–368, 388; MCM, *Treasurer's Report,* profit and loss for the year ending Jan. 2, 1926; MS. MCM, Reports, 1923–26, now in possession of E. Manning.

40. Sources for material in this section include the controller's reports; the compilation of changes in machinery; annual reports; sketches of the history of Lindale, already referred to; list of the supervisory force, 1895–1945; and the *Lindale Bulletin,* 1941–45. My visit to Lindale in March, 1945, aided in the gathering of material and in dispelling the view, held by some, that the condition of workers in the South was poor.

41. PMC, *Presentation Ceremonies.*

42. Jackson, *op. cit.*

43. *Southern Textile Bulletin,* 1934: June 28, p. 10; July 17, p. 18; Aug. 9, pp. 14–15; Sept. 6, p. 5; Sept. 20, pp. 6, 14; and Oct. 25, pp. 24, 52, 54.

44. PMC, *Presentation Ceremonies.*

45. *Southern Textile Bulletin,* Mar. 12, 1931, pp. 12–13, 23–25.

46. PMC, *Presentation Ceremonies.*

47. *Lindale Bulletin,* vol. 1, no. 18 (1941).

48. *Textile Bulletin,* Dec. 7, 1933, p. 11, June 7, 1934, p. 14, Sept. 27, 1934, p. 4; MS. PMC, Controller's report, 1929–45; schedules of workers from superintendent, Mar., 1945.

49. *Textile Bulletin,* June 7, 1934, p. 16, and Aug. 9, 1934, p. 17.

50. MS. PMC, Controller's report, 1929–45; Lahne, *Cotton Mill Worker,* p. 165; New York *Times,* Feb. 28, 1945, p. 1.

51. Alabama University, Bureau of Business Research, *Alabama County Statistical Abstracts,* 1943, pp. 2, 183–185.

52. MS. PMC, Trustees' records, Jan. 23 and Oct. 20, 1925. PMC, Annual Report, 1925, pp. 2–3. *Textile World,* vol. 67 (Jan. 24, 1925), p. 477; vol. 67 (Mar. 21, 1925), p. 1985; and vol. 69 (Feb. 6, 1926), pp. 1097, 1099.

53. PMC, Annual Report, 1925, pp. 2–3. *Textile World,* vol. 67 (Mar. 21, 1925), p. 1985; vol. 67 (Apr. 5, 1925), p. 2331; vol. 67 (Apr. 11, 1925), p. 2567; vol. 69 (Feb. 6, 1926), pp. 1097, 1099.

54. *Ibid.,* pp. 1097, 1099; *Southern Textile Bulletin,* Aug. 30, 1934, p. 26.

55. PMC, *Presentation Awards.*

CHAPTER XIV

For Chapter XIV I have drawn upon the same types of records as in the preceding chapters. Here I have depended to a great extent upon the minutes of meetings of stockholders, trustees, and directors, the treasurer's and controller's reports, the records of holdings of stockholders, and the annual reports. Where the source of information is not evident from the text, I have given it below.

1. U. S. Treasury Department, Bureau of Internal Revenue, *Statistics of Income,* 1926–42.

2. *Ibid.*

3. MS. PMC, Organization charts, 1927–44.

4. Cotton Textile Institute, Inc., *Annual Report,* 1927–32, 1942–43. *Commerce & Finance,* vol. 15 (Oct. 27, 1926), p. 2205; vol. 16 (May 18, 1927), pp. 8–9.

5. *Southern Textile Bulletin,* Mar. 24, 1932, pp. 16–17, 23–24.

6. Controllers Institute of America, Inc., *Year Book,* 1932, pp. 6, 45.

7. MS. PMC, Dept. minutes, Jan. 3, 1936.

8. John H. MacDonald, *Controllership, Its Functions and Technique* (N. Y., 1940), pp. 75–84.

9. *Commercial & Financial Chronicle,* vols. 126–127 (1928); vols. 134–135 (1932); vols. 158–159 (1944).

10. *Ibid.,* vols. 160–161 (1945); vols. 162–163 (1946); vol. 164 (1947).

11. *Business Week,* Feb. 3, 1945, p. 56.

12. One example has been traced through the years, that of Lyman Nichols and his heirs.

13. Dane Yorke, *The Men and Times of Pepperell* (Boston, 1945).

INDEX

Bei Fragen zur Produktsicherheit wenden Sie sich bitte an:
If you have any questions regarding product safety,
please contact:

Walter de Gruyter GmbH
Genthiner Straße 13
10785 Berlin
productsafety@degruyterbrill.com